Chasing Criminal Money

Challenges and Perspectives on Asset Recovery in the EU

Edited by
Katalin Ligeti and Michele Simonato

• HART •
PUBLISHING
OXFORD AND PORTLAND, OREGON
2017

Hart Publishing
An imprint of Bloomsbury Publishing Plc

Hart Publishing Ltd
Kemp House
Chawley Park
Cumnor Hill
Oxford OX2 9PH
UK

Bloomsbury Publishing Plc
50 Bedford Square
London
WC1B 3DP
UK

www.hartpub.co.uk
www.bloomsbury.com

Published in North America (US and Canada) by
Hart Publishing
c/o International Specialized Book Services
920 NE 58th Avenue, Suite 300
Portland, OR 97213-3786
USA

www.isbs.com

HART PUBLISHING, the Hart/Stag logo, BLOOMSBURY and the Diana logo are trademarks of Bloomsbury Publishing Plc

First published 2017

British Library Cataloguing-in-Publication Data

A catalogue record for this book is available from the British Library.

ISBN: HB: 978-1-50991-207-0
ePDF: 978-1-50991-205-6
ePub: 978-1-50991-206-3

Library of Congress Cataloging-in-Publication Data

Names: Ligeti, Katalin, editor. | Simonato, Michele

Title: Chasing criminal money / Katalin Ligeti and Michele Simonato.

Description: Oxford ; Portland : Hart Publishing, 2017. | Series: Hart studies in European criminal law ; volume 3 | Includes bibliographical references and index.

Identifiers: LCCN 2016053061 (print) | LCCN 2016055292 (ebook) | ISBN 9781509912070 (hardback : alk. paper) | ISBN 9781509912063 (Epub)

Subjects: LCSH: Reparation (Criminal justice) | Forfeiture.

Classification: LCC K5534 .C48 2017 (print) | LCC K5534 (ebook) | DDC 347.4/077—dc23

LC record available at https://lccn.loc.gov/2016053061

Typeset by Compuscript Ltd, Shannon
Printed and bound in Great Britain by Lightning Source UK Ltd

To find out more about our authors and books visit www.hartpublishing.co.uk. Here you will find extracts, author information, details of forthcoming events and the option to sign up for our newsletters.

FOREWORD

JOHN AE VERVAELE*

Chasing criminal assets does not sound like a traditional tool of criminal justice. In reality, though, it has become one of its main tools and objectives when dealing with organised crime and serious offences. In the past decades, many criminal law jurisdictions have put into place asset recovery laws and strategies, and many have done so to comply with obligations under international law, be it global or regional. Asset recovery laws and strategies are far from being technical issues reserved for a specialised audience. They are not only about how to follow the criminal money and eventually get it; they have a lot to do with the general objectives of criminal justice systems and the trade-off between effectiveness and human rights.

Asset recovery laws include provisions on freezing, seizure, confiscation (forfeiture) and asset sharing, and affect substantive criminal law, criminal procedure and mutual legal assistance. This already shows that asset recovery is not restricted to post-conviction execution. Quite the opposite, the hard core can be found in the pre-trial setting, where it guarantees that the assets can be identified, do not flee or simply evaporate. The link with criminal suspicion required for coercive freezing and seizure is just one of the debates. Can freezing and seizure measures be taken in a proactive, anticipative phase, for instance in the administrative enforcement setting? Or can preventive confiscation be imposed as an administrative measure? What is the extent of the freezing and seizure? Can it include all property, unless the licit origin is proven by the suspect? Do we need special financial investigation techniques in the criminal procedure and do the same procedural guarantees apply? Even if we focus on the final decision of confiscation of proceeds of crime, there is a growing tendency to unlink it from the criminal conviction. The new vocabulary is a real expression of the changing concepts: preventive confiscation, extended confiscation, non-conviction based confiscation, *in rem* confiscation.

This book contains updated and elaborated scientific contributions on the issues that were addressed, from many perspectives, both in terms of expertise and national background, at an international conference in Luxembourg in June 2015. A range of questions concerning the objectives and scope of national and

* Professor in economic and European criminal Law, Utrecht School of Law (the Netherlands); Professor in European criminal law at the College of Europe, Bruges (Belgium); President of the International Association of Criminal Law (AIDP-IACL).

supranational strategies targeting criminal money are addressed. The book chapters are grouped into two parts. The first part deals with the core aspects of asset recovery, ie the powers granted to law enforcement authorities to gain possession over tainted property and the dilemmas that these powers create. The second part then turns to distinct features that make up the complexity of asset recovery. It highlights not only several national practices of model potential, but also a broad range of overarching challenges, such as the role of financial investigation units, the difficulties linked to virtual currencies and the social use of recovered assets. The contributions look in detail at different phases of asset recovery, allowing the reader to journey throughout this 'complex legal process'. They also show how different legal realities try to address legal questions related to the balance between efficiency and human rights protection.

The European Union defines the scope and the approach of the entire volume; likewise, the contribution to the improvement of its legal framework is the intended objective. Nevertheless, the book does not overlook the broader global picture, in which asset recovery has a high priority. Since it is only around a decade since this term was officially adopted in an international law instrument, its infancy calls for conceptual clarification and development of common understandings of the crucial underlying questions related to the objectives and functions of the criminal justice systems. As it stands the constitutional and human rights courts have not been able to deliver this common understanding from the point of view of fundamental and human rights protection.

Both European and non-European lawyers, from the academia and from practice, will find in this book information and inspiration. In every continent, many countries are elaborating and discussing reforms of their legal systems in order to ensure an increased effectiveness of the efforts against criminal wealth. The coherence of these reforms is even more important in a globalised context. For this reason, this volume can only be welcomed as one of the first—and certainly not the last—attempts to identify and define the shape of such a complex enforcement mechanism.

CONTENTS

LIST OF CONTRIBUTORS

Peter Alldridge, Drapers' Professor of Law, Queen Mary, University of London (UK)

Isidoro Blanco Cordero, Professor at the University of Alicante (Spain)

Johan Boucht, Professor at the University of Oslo (Norway)

Stefan Cassella, Consultant—former federal prosecutor (US)

Jacek Czarnecki, Graduate student at the University of Oxford—attorney in Warsaw (Poland)

Andrea Di Nicola, Assistant Professor of Criminology at the Faculty of Law of the University of Trento (Italy)

Michael Fernandez-Bertier, PhD candidate at the Université catholique de Louvain (Belgium)

Elizabeta Ivičević Karas, Associate Professor at the University of Zagreb (Croatia)

Radha Ivory, Lecturer at University of Queensland (Australia)

Colin King, Senior Lecturer at the University of Sussex (UK)

Katalin Ligeti, Professor of European and International Criminal Law at the University of Luxembourg (Luxembourg)

Francesco Mazzacuva, Postdoctoral researcher at the University of Parma (Italy)

Frank Meyer, Chair of Criminal Law and Procedure including International Criminal Law, University of Zurich (Switzerland)

Michele Panzavolta, Associate Professor at KU Leuven (Belgium)

Marc Penna, Belgian Financial Intelligence Processing Unit (Belgium)

Michele Simonato, Postdoctoral researcher at the Utrecht University (the Netherlands)

Sunčana Roksandić Vidlička, Assistant Professor at the University of Zagreb (Croatia)

Dirk Van Daele, Professor at the Institute of Criminal Law and the Leuven Institute of Criminology of the Faculty of Law, KU Leuven (Belgium)

Laura Vande Reyde, Research assistant at the Leuven Institute of Criminology of the Faculty of Law, KU Leuven (Belgium)

John AE Vervaele, Professor in economic and European criminal law, Utrecht School of Law (the Netherlands); Professor in European criminal law at the College of Europe, Bruges (Belgium); President of the International Association of Criminal Law (AIDP-IACL)

Barbara Vettori, Assistant Professor of Criminology at the Faculty of Political and Social Sciences, Catholic University of Milan (Italy)

CHASING CRIMINAL MONEY

The fight against dirty money is not a new topic, nor a recent problem. It has existed within international and national agendas since the 1980s. Nonetheless, the evolving complexity of criminal skills and networks; the increasingly global dimension of crime; the financial crisis; and the alleged unsatisfactory results of the efforts hitherto undertaken cause us to re-pose and re-discuss some questions. This book addresses several issues concerning the reasons, objectives and scope of national and supranational strategies targeting criminal money, as well as the concrete modalities to overcome its obstacles. The main objective is to explore where the EU stands and where it ought to go, providing useful input for policy-makers and further research. Nevertheless, the problems are not limited to the EU area, and assets—particularly money—cross EU borders much more easily than people do. The reflections developed in the chapters, therefore, aim at going beyond these EU borders. The book is divided into two parts. The first one focuses on the core of asset recovery policies, namely confiscation or forfeiture laws, and explores in particular some issues concerning the respect of fundamental rights. The second part addresses other problematic aspects related to the asset recovery process, such as the return of assets to victim countries, the cross-border investigations on dirty money, and the social use of confiscated assets.

Volume 3 in the series Hart Studies in European Criminal Law

Hart Studies in European Criminal Law

Series Editors: Professor Katalin Ligeti, University of Luxembourg; Professor Valsamis Mitsilegas, Queen Mary University of London; Professor Anne Weyembergh, Brussels Free University

Since the Lisbon Treaty, European criminal law has become an increasingly important field of research and debate. Working with the European Criminal Law Academic Network (ECLAN), the series will publish works of the highest intellectual rigour and cutting edge scholarship which will be required reading for all European criminal lawyers.

The series is happy to consider both edited and single authored titles. The series defines 'European' and 'criminal law' in the broadest sense, so books on European criminal law, justice and policy will be considered. The series also welcomes books which offer different methodological approaches.

Volume 1: *EU Criminal Law after Lisbon: Rights, Trust and the Transformation of Justice in Europe* by Valsamis Mitsilegas
Volume 2: *Challenges in the Field of Economic and Financial Crime in Europe and the US* by Vanessa Franssen and Katalin Ligeti
Volume 3: *Chasing Criminal Money: Challenges and Perspectives On Asset Recovery in the EU* Edited by Katalin Ligeti and Michele Simonato

Asset Recovery in the EU: Towards a Comprehensive Enforcement Model beyond Confiscation? An Introduction

KATALIN LIGETI* AND MICHELE SIMONATO**

Background

The fight against dirty money is not a recent problem for practitioners or policy makers. Nor is it a new topic in academic literature. It has existed within international and national agendas for at least three decades, ever since the 'age of proceeds'[1] started to impose a new approach on profit-driven crime. Compared to the 1980s, raising awareness of its importance seems less of an urgent issue now, and it is difficult to find a single country, or scholar, stating that it is not worth removing criminal money from the economy.

The fact that recovering money has become an indisputable objective may be due to the multiple intertwined rationales for asset recovery. The punitive dimension is perhaps the most evident. Depriving criminals of their profit means hitting them 'where it hurts most', in the sense that for many criminals it might be worse to lose everything than to spend a certain period of time in jail and then enjoy the obtained profit once released.[2] On the other hand, the idea that 'crime does

* Professor of European and International Criminal Law at the University of Luxembourg.

** Post-doctoral researcher at the Utrecht Centre for Regulation and Enforcement in Europe (RENFORCE), Utrecht University.

[1] See M Gallant, *Money Laundering and the Proceeds of Crime: Economic Crime and Civil Remedies* (Cheltenhamw, Edward Elgar, 2005) 1. See also, among others, G Stessens, *Money Laundering: A New International Law Enforcement Model* (Cambridge, Cambridge University Press, 2000) 4; P Alldridge, *Money Laundering Law* (Oxford, Hart Publishing, 2003) 89; JAE Vervaele, 'Economic Crimes and Money Laundering: A New Paradigm for the Criminal Justice System?' in B Unger and D van der Linde (eds), *Research Handbook on Money Laundering* (Cheltenham, Edward Elgar, 2013) 379, 383; PC Van Duyne, MS Groenhuijsen, AAP Schudelaro, 'Balancing Financial Threats and Legal Interests in Money-Laundering Policy' (2005) 43 *Crime, Law & Social Change* 117; B Vettori, *Tough on Criminal Wealth* (Dordrecht, Springer, 2006) 1.

[2] Criticism to such an assumption has been expressed, for example, by H Nelen, 'Hit Them Where It Hurts Most?' (2004) 41 *Crime, Law & Social Change* 517.

not pay' is also a moral imperative and a corollary of the general principle that no one should benefit from his/her wrongdoing (*commodum ex injuria sua non habere debet*). One might therefore note a retributive approach behind the quest for greater asset recovery irrespective of the label of the confiscatory measures in different national systems: in other words, criminals deserve to lose every single economic advantage derived from their unlawful behaviour.

A strong response to crime profit can also be understood in light of its preventive function. On the one hand, removing crime proceeds from the offenders prevents them from using such proceeds to finance other criminal activities (special prevention). On the other hand, it could also have an impact on other potential perpetrators, who would be discouraged from committing profit-driven crimes if aware that such potential profit is likely to be traced and confiscated (general prevention).

What is more, asset recovery can have an important strategic function in the fight against organised crime and terrorism. Leaders of criminal organisations are rarely directly involved in the commission of predicate offences; therefore criminal proceedings and individual sanctions against perpetrators often fail to reach the top of the organisation. Here asset recovery can ensure that the illicit proceeds are removed and recovered from the criminal organisation and can thereby contribute to dismantling the organisation.[3]

Another important reason behind asset recovery is its potential benefit to the state. Confiscated assets can be used for the compensation of victims, but they can also be used for the development of the legitimate economy or for furthering other public policies. It is self-evident how this last justification of asset recovery gains relevance in the context of a global financial crisis.

This general well-established consensus on the goals of asset recovery is in stark contrast to the unsatisfactory results of the efforts undertaken heretofore. This invites the requestioning and rediscussing of several aspects of asset recovery, especially in light of the evolving complexity of criminal skills and networks, and the increasingly global dimension of crime. This book therefore addresses a range of questions concerning the objectives and scope of national and supranational strategies targeting criminal money, as well as the concrete modalities to overcome the obstacles to the fight against it. It publishes the papers presented at the international conference 'Chasing Criminal Money in the EU: New Tools and Practices?', which took place in Luxembourg on 15 and 16 June 2015.

The main objective of the book is to explore where the EU stands on criminal asset recovery and where it ought to go, providing useful input for policy makers

[3] See M Kilchling, 'Finance-Oriented Strategies of Organized Crime Control' in L Paoli (ed), *The Oxford Handbook of Organized Crime* (New York, Oxford University Press, 2014) 655; E Savona, 'The Businesses of Italian Mafias' (2015) 21(2) *European Journal on Criminal Policy and Research* 217; P Faraldo Cabana, 'Improving the Recovery of Assets Resulting from Organised Crime' (2014) 22 *European Journal of Crime, Criminal Law and Criminal Justice* 13; L Campbell, *Organised Crime and the Law* (Oxford, Hart Publishing, 2013) 201.

and further research. The primary focus on the EU relates to the EU's potential to be at the forefront of criminal asset recovery in the international context. Nevertheless, the problems discussed in this book are not limited to the EU legal system. Assets, especially money, cross the EU's external borders much more easily than do people. The reflections developed in the different chapters, therefore, go beyond the EU legal framework.

I. The EU Concept of Asset Recovery: A Terminological Clarification

'Asset recovery' is one of the main tools of the fight against criminal money. It can be observed and analysed from several perspectives, since it is a concept with a broader scope than the mere confiscation of criminal property and comprises several aspects. Due to its wide scope and the lack of clear legal definitions, it is worth clarifying the meaning of the relevant terms in the EU debate. On the theoretical level, one may note a certain incongruity between the concept of asset recovery as developed in public international law, namely by UN Conventions,[4] and the notion used by EU legislation. According to the UN—as illustrated also in Chapter 8—asset recovery is confined specifically to corruption offences in a transnational context. Recovering stolen assets essentially means to return to the country of origin the money that corrupt governments have stolen from populations and then placed or invested abroad, thereby concealing such funds from law enforcement authorities.[5] In contrast, the ambition of the EU is to deal with asset recovery in a broader and more comprehensive way, in order to make it a sort of 'enforcement model' for the fight against illegal proceeds deriving from any profit-driven crime (ie beyond corruption). Furthermore, its scope is not limited to the transnational context: although it is undeniable that policies on asset recovery aim at making cross-border co-operation smoother, they have a strong impact on national legal systems and necessarily apply even in purely domestic cases.

As in the EU law discourse, in this book 'asset recovery' is understood as a multiphase process to be launched every time a criminal offence has generated a financial gain, wherever the money is located. Such a process relies on confiscation or forfeiture laws, but is initiated before and goes beyond confiscation: it starts with the financial investigations aimed at tracing the proceeds of crime, and includes

[4] In particular, the UN Convention against Corruption of 31 October 2003 (UNCAC).

[5] See D Claman, 'The Promise and Limitations of Asset Recovery under the UNCAC' in M Pieth (ed), *Recovering Stolen Assets* (Bern, Peter Lang, 2008) 333; C Monteith and P Gomes Pereira, 'Asset Recovery' in N Boister and RJ Currie (eds), *Routledge Handbook of Transnational Criminal Law* (Abingdon Routledge, 2015) 137; R Ivory, *Corruption, Asset Recovery, and the Protection of Property in Public International Law. The Human Rights of Bad Guys* (Cambridge, Cambridge University Press, 2014) 22.

the freezing of assets;[6] their management; the confiscation—or forfeiture—of crime proceeds and instrumentalities; and finally their disposal.

In this sense, asset recovery has emancipated itself both from legislation on corruption and anti-money laundering (AML) policies,[7] which provide for the criminalisation of money laundering (enforcement pillar) and the establishment of a detection apparatus (prevention pillar).[8] Although there is a close relationship and an apparent overlap between the two concepts (confiscation laws are considered a crucial aspect of the 'enforcement pillar' of any AML regime), asset recovery includes other aspects that traditionally do not fall within the ambit of AML strategies. Here we are referring to those phases, such as asset management, repatriation and disposal of assets, that are not normally addressed by AML instruments. Furthermore, the asset recovery process in principle may tackle assets that have not yet been 'laundered'. In other words, asset recovery is a general enforcement tool concerning any asset and any crime, which usually relies upon AML laws especially as regards the modalities to trace and confiscate dirty money.

II. The EU Legal Framework on Asset Recovery, Between Co-operation and Harmonisation

Besides the actions undertaken by the United Nations[9] and the Council of Europe,[10] in the last years the EU has adopted several instruments covering certain aspects of 'asset recovery'.[11] Starting in 1998, this topic has been addressed by the EU legislature on many occasions, focusing in particular on the facilitation of

[6] Many countries distinguish between freezing and seizure: the former refers to money held in bank accounts and real estate, while the latter usually refers to all other assets, including cash. However, the EU legal framework—namely Framework Decision 2003/577/JHA on the execution in the European Union of orders freezing property or evidence [2003] OJ L196/45—refers only to freezing orders, covering both money in bank accounts and other assets.

[7] Money laundering can be considered 'one of the most insidious channels enabling legitimate activities to be contaminated by illicit activities and an indispensable transition process, without which the purchasing power acquired through crime would remain merely potential, usable within illegal circles but incapable of translating into real economic power' (European Parliament Resolution of 25 October 2011, Organised Crime in the European Union).

[8] See P Reuter and EM Truman, *Chasing Dirty Money. The Fight against Money Laundering* (Washington, DC, Institute for International Economics, 2004) 46.

[9] See the UN Convention against Illicit Traffic in Narcotic Drugs and Psychotropic Substances of 20 December 1988; the UN Convention against Transnational Organized Crime of 12 December 2000; and UNCAC.

[10] See the Convention on Laundering, Search, Seizure and Confiscation of the Proceeds from Crime of 8 November 1990; and the Convention on Laundering, Search, Seizure and Confiscation of the Proceeds from Crime and on the Financing of Terrorism of 16 May 2005.

[11] See MJ Borgers, 'Confiscation of the Proceeds of Crime: The European Union Framework' in C King and C Walker (eds), *Dirty Assets. Emerging Issues in the Regulation of Criminal and Terrorist Assets* (Farnham, Ashgate, 2014) 27.

co-operation between national authorities, the principle of mutual recognition and the harmonisation of national laws.

A. The Attempt to Approximate National Legislation: A Far-Reaching Objective?

The EU legislator soon realised that different traditions of EU legal systems give rise to an extremely fragmented setting on asset recovery, much more so than in other areas of criminal law. For example, while, in this book, we use the terms 'confiscation' and 'forfeiture' synonymously to indicate any judicial decision depriving persons of their assets, it is important to stress that these concepts encompass a great variety of legal instruments and approaches.

Although the traditional 'basic' form of confiscation is normally conceived as a judicial order concerning property related to a specific crime for which the owner has been convicted, there are many other types of confiscation, going beyond the direct proceeds of a crime ('extended confiscation'), not requiring a final conviction ('non-conviction-based confiscation'), targeting property of equivalent value to the proceeds of crime ('value confiscation') or not belonging to the convicted person ('third party confiscation'). In some countries, confiscation orders might also be issued outside criminal proceedings, in a distinct and autonomous set of proceedings (eg the civil forfeiture in UK and Ireland). And every EU country has different rules and peculiarities as regards each type of confiscation measure.

Therefore, the EU has been striving for almost two decades to harmonise the existing concepts. The primary reason for this attempt is the relationship between co-operation and diversity: the existing dissimilarities seem to hinder international co-operation, because it is difficult for requested countries to execute foreign confiscation orders if such orders are based on schemes that are completely at odds with their own national approach. A separate, but equally important, reason is linked to the policy objective to broaden the scope and enhance the efficiency of national asset recovery procedures, ie to ensure that each Member State reinforces its engagement in the fight against criminal wealth.[12] This is done primarily by encouraging Member States to provide for new forms of confiscation, different from the traditional concept of removal of property after the final conviction in criminal proceedings.

For example, one of the main attempts to harmonise forfeiture schemes concerns 'extended confiscation' regimes (ie the possibility to also confiscate, following conviction, assets belonging to the perpetrator that are not strictly related to the specific crime for which he/she was convicted). Framework Decision

[12] On the function of harmonisation in general, see especially A Weyembergh, 'The Functions of Approximation of Penal Legislation within the European Union' (2005) 12 *Maastricht Journal of European and Comparative Law* 149.

2005/212/JHA[13] sought to introduce such a concept in relation to all Member States. However, the Framework Decision had little success, partly due to its own normative technique: it provided for three different criteria as regards the assessment of assets other than those strictly related to the conviction,[14] leaving Member States the choice of whether to transpose only one criterion (and which one), two or even all of them. As a result, some Member States follow one method to define the scope of extended confiscation and some follow the other two methods, whilst other Member States have chosen not to transpose any of them. The EU Commission itself[15] identified the lack of clarity of some provisions and the lack of coherence between existing provisions as two crucial causes of the unsatisfactory scenario.[16]

The problem was compounded by the inconsistency with another instrument built upon the principle of mutual recognition, namely Framework Decision 2006/783/JHA on the mutual recognition of confiscation orders,[17] which rendered the lack of harmonisation (sought by the 2005 Framework Decision) a legitimate obstacle to co-operation. Indeed, the grounds for refusal stipulated in the 2006 Framework Decision allow the executing authority to refuse the execution of orders relating to 'extended confiscation' if the issuing Member State has adopted a different option(s) of the 2005 Framework Decision than the executing Member State and if the assets concerned cannot be confiscated following the option adopted by the executing Member State. This ultimately runs counter to

[13] Framework Decision 2005/212/JHA of 24 February 2005 on Confiscation of Crime-Related Proceeds, Instrumentalities and Property [2005] OJ L68/49.

[14] Framework Decision 2005/212/JHA, Art 3, para 2: 'Each Member State shall take the necessary measures to enable confiscation under this Article at least: *(a)* where a national court based on specific facts is fully convinced that the property in question has been derived from criminal activities of the convicted person during a period prior to conviction for the offence referred to in paragraph 1 which is deemed reasonable by the court in the circumstances of the particular case, or, alternatively, *(b)* where a national court based on specific facts is fully convinced that the property in question has been derived from similar criminal activities of the convicted person during a period prior to conviction for the offence referred to in paragraph 1 which is deemed reasonable by the court in the circumstances of the particular case, or, alternatively, *(c)* where it is established that the value of the property is disproportionate to the lawful income of the convicted person and a national court based on specific facts is fully convinced that the property in question has been derived from the criminal activity of that convicted person'.

[15] See 'Report on Framework Decision 2005/212/JHA' COM (2007) 805; 'Report on Framework Decision 2003/577/JHA' COM (2008) 885; 'Report on Framework Decision 2006/783/JHA' COM (2010) 428; 'Report on Decision 2007/845/JHA' COM (2011) 176; Communication to the European Parliament and the Council, 'Proceeds of Organised Crime. Ensuring that "Crime Does Not Pay"' COM (2008) 766.

[16] An external study mandated by the EU Commission, 'Assessing the Effectiveness of EU Member States' Practices in the Identification, Tracing, Freezing and Confiscation of Criminal Assets' (2009), pointed out some of the obstacles to effective confiscations, such as the fragmented approach to confiscation measures, difficulties related to asset management, lack of adequate resources and specialisation of involved authorities.

[17] Framework Decision 2006/783/JHA of 6 October 2006 on the application of the principle of mutual recognition to confiscation orders [2006] OJ L328/59.

the essence of mutual recognition, whereby foreign orders should be executed even if based on different national rules.[18]

Against this background, instead of merely updating the mutual recognition instruments, the EU Commission decided to present a new legislative proposal that led to the adoption of Directive 2014/42/EU, which partially repeals the 2005 Framework Decision but does not touch upon the co-operation instruments.[19] The new Directive—which must be implemented by every Member State (except the UK and Denmark) by Autumn 2016—represents a benchmark for future reflections on some key aspects of asset recovery. As to extended confiscation, the Directive overcomes the three options provided by the 2005 Framework Decision with a single provision:

> Member States shall adopt the necessary measures to enable the confiscation, either in whole or in part, of property belonging to a person convicted of a criminal offence which is liable to give rise, directly or indirectly, to economic benefit, where a court, on the basis of the circumstances of the case, including the specific facts and available evidence, such as that the value of the property is disproportionate to the lawful income of the convicted person, is satisfied that the property in question is derived from criminal conduct.[20]

However, this provision offers little guidance to the Member States as to its interpretation, and many aspects remain to be explored and discussed. For example, what does it mean that the examining court must be 'satisfied' of the criminal nature of an asset? Where is the limit to consider property derived from previous, unproven, criminal conduct? Is there a way to distinguish tainted assets from legitimate property?

Another crucial area where the EU is trying to approximate the different national approaches to forfeiture measures in the EU is non-conviction-based confiscation (ie measures against property independent from previous criminal convictions).[21] The text of the Directive 2014/42/EU is quite limited on this aspect, too:

> Where confiscation … is not possible, at least where such impossibility is the result of illness or absconding of the suspected or accused person, Member States shall take the necessary measures to enable the confiscation of instrumentalities and proceeds in cases where criminal proceedings have been initiated regarding a criminal offence which is liable to give rise, directly or indirectly, to economic benefit, and such proceedings could have led to a criminal conviction if the suspected or accused person had been able to stand trial.[22]

[18] In general, see especially A Klip, *European Criminal Law*, 3rd edn (Cambridge, Intersentia, 2016) 400; V Mitsilegas, *EU Criminal Law* (Oxford, Hart Publishing, 2009) 115. As regards confiscation orders, see also M Simonato, 'Extended Confiscation of Criminal Assets: Limits and Pitfalls of Minimum Harmonisation in the EU' (2016) 41(5) *European Law Review* 723.

[19] Directive 2014/42/EU of 3 April 2014 on the freezing and confiscation of instrumentalities and proceeds of crime in the European Union [2014] OJ L127/39. It is worth mentioning that, despite the initial ambitions of the EU Commission, the Directive ultimately has limited scope, due both to inner limits of the legal basis provided by the Treaties and to policy considerations.

[20] Directive 2014/42/EU, Art 5, para 1.

[21] See JP Rui, 'Introduction' in JP Rui and U Sieber (eds), *Non-Conviction-Based Confiscation in Europe* (Berlin, Duncker, 2015) 1.

[22] Directive 2014/42/EU, Art 4, para 2.

One might even argue that there is no real obligation for Member States in this regard, nor elaboration of a new model of confiscation,[23] since the Directive suggests employing confiscation without conviction in very limited cases (illness or absconding of the suspect). Furthermore, in one recital it further narrows down the potential impact of this provision on national legal systems, by stating that 'the existence of proceedings in absentia in Member States would be sufficient to comply with this obligation'.[24]

In any case, such non-conviction-based confiscation does not appear to be similar to the existing concept on non-criminal forfeiture typical of some jurisdictions, such as the UK and Ireland,[25] where autonomous non-criminal proceedings are conducted on assets of an illicit nature. It appears to be even more distant from some models developed outside the EU, such as the civil asset forfeiture in US law.[26] On the other side of the Atlantic, the non-criminal alternative to taking over the property of dirty assets is an extremely powerful tool in the hands of law enforcement authorities, at both the federal level and the state level. In particular, prosecutors are granted the possibility to choose between pursuing the conviction of the defendant and disregarding issues relating to the proof of the criminal liability of the offender to focus instead on the assets only. Ever since modern civil assets forfeiture statutes were introduced,[27] the amount of assets recovered has steadily increased,[28] so that today the debate is rather about limiting the incisiveness of those statutes.[29]

From our perspective, it is interesting to observe how parallel enforcement mechanisms can coexist and be used for similar purposes.[30] It might even surprise a European lawyer to read that civil asset forfeiture is plainly considered by the US Supreme Court—in order to decide on the applicability of the 'excessive fine' clause of the Eight Amendment (what we would call 'proportionality')—as a tool which may pursue to some extent not only remedial, but also punitive purposes.[31] Yet it is not considered as a criminal measure. For this reason, the entire range of

[23] See M Simonato, 'Directive 2014/42/EU and Non-conviction Based Confiscation: A Step Forward on Asset Recovery?' (2015) 6(2) *New Journal of European Criminal Law* 213.

[24] Directive 2014/42/EU, Recital 15.

[25] See I Smith, 'Civil Asset Recovery—The English Experience' in Rui and Sieber (n 21) 31; C King, 'Civil Forfeiture in Ireland: Two Decades of the Proceeds of Crime Act and the Criminal Assets Bureau', this volume, Chapter 3.

[26] SD Cassella, *Asset Forfeiture Law in the United States*, 2nd edn (New York, Juris, 2012) 29; T Barnet, 'Legal Fiction and Forfeiture: An Historical Analysis of the Civil Asset Forfeiture Reform Act' (2001) 40 *Duquesne Law Review* 77; LW Levy, *A License to Steal. The Forfeiture of Property* (Chapel Hill, University of North Carolina Press, 1996).

[27] Cassella (ibid) 37.

[28] According to the statistics published on the website of the Department of Justice (www.justice.gov/afp/reports-0), the value of forfeited assets in 2014 was above $4 billion, compared with $93 million in 1986.

[29] See DM Carpenter et al, *Policing for Profit. The Abuse of Civil Asset Forfeiture* (Arlington, Institute for Justice, 2015).

[30] See MM Cheh, 'Civil Remedies to Control Crime: Legal Issues and Constitutional Challenges' (1998) 9 *Crime Prevention Studies* 45.

[31] See especially *Austin v US*, 509 US 602 (1993). See Cassella (n 26) 60.

constitutional rights provided for defendants in criminal proceedings is not recognised as pertaining to property owners subject to civil asset forfeiture. Nonetheless, they are increasingly granted some fair trial rights, such as the right to a jury and the right to cross-examine witnesses. The level of protection, however, is still very much debated and criticised even after recent reforms.[32]

While in the US there is consolidated experience on non-criminal confiscation, in continental Europe the success of this form of confiscation is much more limited and its development raises many questions that remain unanswered by the EU legal framework.[33] The EU legislator at least seems to be willing to address them in the near future, by exploring, for example, whether it is necessary and feasible to put forward a more far-reaching model of non-conviction-based forfeiture.[34]

The resistance is strong, though. Many Member States do not seem ready to include such a powerful tool in their legal system. In the name of the protection of 'legal traditions', it is seen as outrageous—or at least dangerous—to deprive someone of his or her right to property before he or she is proven guilty.[35] From a more pragmatic perspective, national enforcement authorities may not find enough incentives to chase only the money if criminals are not or cannot be pursued with criminal sanctions.[36]

Indeed, the traditional distinction between criminal and non-criminal sanctions is definitely challenged when measures traditionally elaborated within the criminal law realm (confiscation measures) are applied in another context, without the full application of the safeguards offered by criminal justice. Nevertheless, in any jurisdiction—both national and supranational—the borders of criminal law are increasingly blurred, and it cannot be denied that in many areas administrative and private law sanctions have a punitive dimension, too.[37] Analysing such

[32] See also D Pimentel, 'Forfeiture Revisited: Bringing Principle to Practice in Federal Court' (2010) 13 *Nevada Law Journal* 1, 32; B Skorup, 'Ensuring Eight Amendment Protection from Excessive Fines in Civil Asset Forfeiture Cases' (2012) 22 *Civil Rights Law Journal* 427. Although not adopted, it is worth mentioning that in January 2015 the Fifth Amendment Integrity Restoration Act was introduced in the House of Representatives (HR 540) proposing new rules, inter alia, on the burden on proof, the presumption of innocence and the disposal of forfeited assets.

[33] See, eg, J Vogel, 'The Legal Construction that Property Can Do Harm—Reflections on the Rationality and Legitimacy of "Civil" Foerfeiture' in Rui and Sieber (n 21) 225.

[34] See the Statement by the European Parliament and the Council on an analysis to be carried out by the Commission, 31 March 2014, 7329/1/14.

[35] See J Boucht, 'Civil Asset Forfeiture and the Presumption of Innocence under Article 6(2) ECHR' (2014) 5 *New Journal of European Criminal Law* 221; AH Ochnio, 'Implementation of the New EU Directive on Confiscation in Poland: The Challenge of Overcoming the Negative Historical Experiences of Confiscation Orders' (2016) 24 *European Journal of Crime, Criminal Law and Criminal Justice* 19.

[36] See, eg, F Verbruggen, 'Proceeds-Oriented Criminal Justice in Belgium: Backbone or Wishbone of a Modern Approach to Organised Crime?' (1997) 5(3) *European Journal of Crime, Criminal Law and Criminal Justice* 314, 337.

[37] See A Weyembergh and N Joncheray, 'Punitive Administrative Sanctions and Procedural Safeguards: A Blurred Picture that Needs to be Addressed' (2016) 7(2) *New Journal of European Criminal Law* 190; A Weyembergh, 'Introduction' in F Galli and A Weyembergh (eds), *Do Labels Still Matter? Blurring Boundaries between Administrative and Criminal Law* (Brussels, IEE, 2014) 9; C Harding, 'The Interplay of Criminal and Administrative Law in the Context of Market Regulation: The Case of

trends and the rationale behind different approaches is therefore helpful in elucidating the factors determining certain policy choices and their consequences.

However, it is not an easy challenge to understand what is truly non-criminal or what ought to be criminal (ie when private or administrative law does not suffice and criminal law becomes necessary), or what kinds of safeguard should also be provided in a non-criminal law context ending with a strong sanction. Questions concerning the development of non-conviction-based confiscation measures touch upon a myriad of dilemmas regarding the function of confiscation, the scope of certain fundamental rights and the limits of enforcement powers.[38] For this reason, the EU might not be in a position to find a common answer for all its Member States, and might eventually decide to focus only on the improvement of the horizontal co-operation mechanisms based on mutual recognition.[39] This seems to be the direction chosen by the EU Commission, and according to the recent action plan on terrorism a new proposal will be presented by the end of 2016.[40] By presenting a new proposal based on mutual recognition, the objective of the EU legislator will be limited to the transnational context, by ensuring that every national decision on assets—whatever the model upon which it is based—can be enforced throughout the whole European territory.

B. The International Dimension of Criminal Gains and the Quest for more Efficient Co-operation during the Investigations

It is well known that assets related to a crime are increasingly located in jurisdictions other than the one where the offence was committed or where the criminal proceedings are being conducted. This may be due to the inherent transnational nature of the crime, such as in the case of smuggling offences, or to the fact that perpetrators transfer abroad the assets gained from the commission of a crime. In order to have a chance of recovering such assets, national law enforcement authorities conduct financial investigations to identify what property may be subject to confiscation and where such property is located.

Normally, financial investigations aimed at tracing forfeitable assets are carried out together with criminal investigations, since the same investigations are also useful in finding evidence of criminal activities linked to financial transactions that can be used to prove the defendant's liability. For this reason, some authors

Serious Competition Infringements' in V Mitsilegas, P Alldridge and L Cheliotis (eds), *Globalisation, Criminal Law and Criminal Justice: Theoretical, Comparative and Transnational Perspectives* (Oxford, Hart Publishing, 2015) 199.

[38] See JP Rui and U Sieber, 'NCBC in Europe—Bringing the Picture Together' in Rui and Sieber (n 21) 245.

[39] See the Statement by the European Parliament and the Council on mutual recognition, 31 March 2014, 7329/1/14.

[40] See the Communication from the Commission to the European Parliament and the Council on an Action Plan for strengthening the fight against terrorist financing, 2 February 2016, COM(2016)

use the concept of 'integrated investigations'.[41] Nevertheless, in some countries and in certain circumstances (in particular, when the forfeiture is issued outside the framework of criminal proceedings), financial investigations can be autonomous and independent from criminal investigations.[42]

Every investigative technique developed at the national level encounters obstacles when assets are located beyond national borders. Such difficulties are faced both in the identification (or tracing) and in the preservation (or freezing) of criminal money, ie the situation where an authority needs to make sure that the target of the financial investigations is not used, transferred or further concealed before the final decision on confiscation.[43]

One may assume that these difficulties are less pertinent in the EU, since it is the objective of the EU to become a single area where the co-operation between law enforcement authorities is smoother than in a purely international context. To this end, the EU has undertaken a number of initiatives in the last decade to improve the co-operation between different national authorities. In addition to the abovementioned 2006 Framework Decision on the mutual recognition of confiscation orders, co-operation in the pre-confiscation phase has been addressed. Particular focus was on the exchange of information between Member States, on the one hand, and the enforcement of coercive investigative measures abroad, on the other.

As a first step, the EU has centred its efforts on making the already existing international mechanisms swifter and more effective in practice. An example is Council Decision 2007/84/JHA concerning the cooperation between Asset Recovery Offices (AROs).[44] This decision is intended to complete the CARIN network,[45] obliging every Member State to set up one central authority as an ARO and providing

50 final. See also the Discussion Paper of the Conference on Strengthening the Mutual Recognition of Freezing and Confiscation Orders (Brussels, 20 June 2016), available at http://ec.europa.eu/justice/criminal/files/discussion-cr-event-20160620_en.pdf.

[41] See, eg, R Golobinek, *Financial Investigations and Confiscations of Proceeds of Crime: Training Manual for Law Enforcement and Judiciary* (Strasbourg, Council of Europe, 2006).

[42] See, eg, MS Groenhuijsen and T Kooijmans, 'Financial Investigation and Confiscation Orders in a Broader Perspective: Developments in Dutch Criminal Law' in G Antonopoulos et al (eds), *Usual and Unusual Organising Criminals in Europe and Beyond: Profitable Crimes, from Underworld to Upper World—Liber Amicorum Petrus van Duyne* (Apeldoorn, Maklu, 2011) 55.

[43] See MJ Borgers and JA Moors, 'Targeting the Proceeds of Crime: Bottlenecks in International Cooperation' (2007) 15 *European Journal of Crime, Criminal Law and Criminal Justice* 1.

[44] Council Decision 2007/845/JHA of 6 December 2007 concerning cooperation between Asset Recovery Offices of the Member States in the field of tracing and identification of proceeds from, or other property related to, crime [2007] OJ L332/103. The objective is to ensure close co-operation and direct communication between national authorities involved in the tracing of illicit proceeds and other property that may become liable to confiscation (see Recital 3). For this purpose, each ARO established in one Member State is able to send a specific and detailed request for information to its counterpart in another Member State. The rules for this co-operation are those set forth in Framework Decision 2006/960/JHA of 18 December 2006 on simplifying the exchange of information and intelligence between law enforcement authorities of the Member States of the European Union [2006] OJ L386/89.

[45] The Camden Assets Recovery Inter-Agency Network (CARIN), established at the Hague on 22–23 September 2004, constitutes a global network of practitioners and experts from 53 jurisdictions and nine international organisations that has the intention of enhancing mutual knowledge on methods and techniques in the area of cross-border identification, freezing, seizure and confiscation of the proceeds of, and other property related to, crime. CARIN's permanent secretariat is hosted at Europol.

a legal basis for the exchange of information between the AROs of all the Member States.

As to the second aspect, the coercive measures to be enforced abroad could consist of investigative measures having a particular impact on the fundamental rights of interested persons, or decisions to provisionally deprive the owners of the right to dispose of the asset. The EU introduced the principle of mutual recognition (according to which a foreign decision should be automatically recognised and executed as if it were issued by a national authority) with regard to judicial decisions on the freezing of assets. On the basis of Framework Decision 2003/577/JHA, a competent national authority in the executing Member State should recognise a 'freezing order' (ie any measure taken by another judicial authority in the issuing Member State in order to provisionally prevent the destruction, transformation, movement, transfer or disposal of property) 'without any further formality'. It should hence 'take the necessary measures for its immediate execution in the same way as for a freezing order made by an authority of the executing State'.[46] The 2003 Framework Decision, following the structure and model of the Framework Decision on the European Arrest Warrant, applies not only to freezing orders issued in view of the subsequent confiscation of property, but also to freezing orders issued to secure evidence (ie regardless of any possibility or intention to proceed with the confiscation).

The EU has also recently applied the mutual recognition principle to a general instrument covering almost all investigative measures, including the interception of telecommunications and the monitoring of bank accounts. The European Investigation Order consists of a decision issued by a Member State 'to have one or several specific investigative measure(s) carried out in another Member State' or 'for obtaining evidence that is already in the possession of the competent authorities of the executing State'.[47] Directive 2014/41/EU therefore covers and replaces the part of the 2003 Framework Decision concerning freezing orders issued to secure evidence. On the other hand, the Framework Decision will remain in force as regards freezing orders issued for the purpose of subsequent confiscation of property, ie issued with the objective of preventing the dissipation of assets that need to be recovered.

These efforts of the EU legislator, however, have yet to meet the envisaged objectives. The co-operation does not seem to be as swift and effective as it should be, and some barriers to asset recovery are still present within the EU borders. For example, in its report on the implementation of the 2003 Framework Decision on freezing orders, the EU Commission acknowledged an overall failure.[48] Only a few Member States implemented that instrument within the prescribed

[46] Framework Decision 2003/577/JHA, Art 5.

[47] Art 1 of the Directive 2014/41/EU of 3 April 2014 regarding the European Investigation Order in criminal matters [2014] OJ L130/1.

[48] COM (2008) 885 final, 22 December 2008.

deadline.[49] Furthermore, even the implementation in those good performing countries presented several shortcomings, in particular as regards the optional grounds for refusal, which were often written into domestic law as mandatory, contrary to the intention of the Framework Decision.[50]

Once again, one may observe how the key issues are often identified in the interplay between different rules. The obstacles arising with international co-operation during investigations, indeed, seem to be due, inter alia, to differences in procedural frameworks, the different standards required in order to apply to coercive measures and the different natures of the authorities involved in financial investigations.[51] The success of asset recovery, in particular as regards tracing of assets, does not depend only on the conduct of the traditional actors of criminal procedure, but is increasingly determined by the information gathered—and exchanged—by non-judicial[52] and even non-public actors.[53]

C. Conclusion: What is the Way Forward?

One may clearly understand the message coming from the EU legislator: it is necessary to boost the asset recovery process throughout the Union in order to better fight profit-driven crime and to increase the level of security of EU citizens. What

[49] As at April 2016, two Member States have still not implemented the Framework Decision.

[50] It is worth mentioning that some years after the 2003 Framework Decision of the freezing order, the principle of mutual recognition has also been applied to confiscation orders. In this case, Framework Decision 2006/783/JHA on the application of the principle of mutual recognition to confiscation orders was intended to provide the legal basis for a new method of co-operation, replacing the traditional mutual legal assistance with rules under which a Member State recognises and executes in its territory a confiscation order issued by a competent court of another Member State. Like other mutual recognition instruments, that Framework Decision also provides for possible grounds for 'non-recognition'. The rationale for non-recognition in some cases is the protection of fundamental rights of interested persons, in others to allow the executing authority not to accept an order issued according to rules (of the issuing Member State) that are at odds with its own legal system. It is important to note that the report from the Commission on the implementation of the 2006 Framework Decision, COM (2010) 428 final, 23 August 2010, defined the implementation as unsatisfactory. Only 13 Member States had transposed the Framework Decision into their national systems (as at April 2016, four Member State still have not implemented the Framework Decision at all). Moreover, most of the 13 complying Member States added additional grounds for refusal.

[51] See M Simonato and M Lassalle, 'A Fragmented Approach on Asset Recovery and Financial Investigations: A Threat to Effective International Judicial Cooperation?' in Z Đurđević and E Ivičević Karas (eds), *European Criminal Procedure Law in Service of Protection of European Union Financial Interests: State of Play and Challenges* (Zagreb, Croatian Association of European Criminal Law, 2016) 132. For an overview of different investigative measures and rules in Europe, see K Ligeti (ed), *Toward a Prosecutor for the European Union*, vol 1 (Oxford, Hart Publishing, 2013).

[52] See the contribution of M Penna, 'The "Pre-investigative" Role of Financial Intelligence Units in Recovering Assets', this volume, Chapter 12.

[53] See M Bergström, 'Money Laundering' in V Mitsilegas, M Bergström and T Konstadinides (eds), *Research Handbook on EU Criminal Law* (Cheltenham, Edward Elgar, 2016) 335, 352; M van den Broek and H Addink, 'Prevention of Money Laundering and Terrorist Financing from a Good Governance Perspective' in B Unger and D van der Linde, *Research Handbook on Money Laundering* (Cheltenham, Edward Elgar, 2013) 368.

is more difficult to analyse is the implementation of such a policy. The EU legal framework on asset recovery is far from being a consolidated and rational code. Supranational instruments are sometimes incoherent, and are often incomplete. In many cases they contain vague or ineffective provisions.

Furthermore, the implementation of the EU policy is complicated by the interaction with policy at the national level. In some cases, the same EU policy is embraced by Member States that have assimilated in their legal systems the idea that the response to crime cannot be limited to the prosecution of the offenders but must also include the pursuit of their illicit gain. In other cases, it is hampered by national approaches that tend to disregard the potential of asset recovery and, besides having inadequate laws, do not provide their enforcement authorities with sufficient resources, training and capacity.

The diverging answers to the crucial questions concerning confiscatory powers and their limits therefore represent an obstacle to the EU ambition, and in particular to the development of EU-wide models of asset recovery. Among the strategies the EU has developed to overcome this obstacle, the improvement of co-operation mechanisms and the strengthening of mutual recognition seem by far the most pragmatic. Yet they still have several pitfalls, which make it difficult to assess how far the EU is from completing the project of building an area of 'freedom, security and justice', where national borders should not represent an obstacle in the recovery of criminal assets and, in particular, where the enforcement of a national decision beyond national borders should be much easier than in a purely international context.

However, if the problem lies not only in the difficult co-operation between national authorities, but also in national policies conflicting with the objectives set by the EU, it is doubtful whether the improvement of mutual recognition instruments would suffice to effectively enforce the message conveyed by the EU. In this regard, even if it is more problematic, the quest for common models through the harmonisation of national systems is more ambitious, and certainly more inspiring from a theoretical perspective. Finding a synthesis between diverging solutions to the same problem—provided that it is perceived as the same common problem—engages scholars in endless efforts. Besides the dilemmas related to the nature of confiscation measures, many questions remain open as regards the other phases of the asset recovery process, without which confiscation measures would be ultimately ineffective.

For example, if—as posited earlier—one of the rationales of asset recovery is the potential benefit for society as a whole, should the EU undertake any initiative that considers criminal money as an asset that could be beneficial for the whole European society? Confiscated assets, indeed, are not necessarily destroyed, but 'can be reinjected into legal, clean, transparent and virtuous economic circuits'.[54] Nevertheless, only a few countries have specific laws or programmes on this final

[54] European Parliament, 'Report on Organised Crime in the European Union' 2010/2309(INI), 6 October 2011, §10.

stage of asset recovery, and, despite increasing awareness of the opportunities that asset recovery can provide,[55] co-ordinated policies have not been launched at supranational level yet.[56]

This is just one example of the perspectives that need to be considered when looking at the way forward. The chapters contained in this volume will shed light on other aspects of the asset recovery process, and on the challenges that the EU must overcome.

III. Objective and Structure of the Book

This book aims at addressing the issues outlined above to the largest possible extent. The chapters are grouped into two parts. The first part deals with the core aspects of asset recovery, ie the powers granted to law enforcement authorities to gain possession over tainted property and the dilemmas that these powers create. The second part then considers the distinct features that make up the complexity of asset recovery. It highlights not only several national practices of model potential, but also a broad range of overarching challenges, such as the role of financial investigation units (FIUs), the difficulties linked to virtual currencies and the social use of recovered assets.

A. Part I: Confiscation Laws and their Boundaries

The first part of the book focuses on the central phase of asset recovery and looks into confiscation—or forfeiture—laws. These determine the substantive scope of asset recovery, ie what assets law enforcement authorities can target, and the extent to which law enforcement authorities may impinge on individual rights of interested persons. Although there is ample discussion in scholarly writing and jurisprudence on which assets ought to be considered 'dirty', some fundamental issues are still ambiguous today. It is debated, in particular, whether confiscation orders should be extended or if, in some cases, the traditional safeguards provided by criminal law and procedure should be done away with; in other words, should the fight against criminal money be detached from the fight against criminals?

[55] See Basel Institute of Governance, 'The Need for New EU Legislation Allowing the Assets Confiscated from Criminal Organisations to be Used for Civil Society and in Particular for Social Purposes', study requested by the EU Parliament's Committee on Civil Liberties (Justice and Home Affairs, 2012).

[56] The 2011 EU Parliament Resolution on organised crime highlighted 'the urgent need for European legislation on the re-use of crime proceeds for social purposes'. Art 10, para 3 of Directive 2014/42/EU just states that 'Member States shall consider taking measures allowing confiscated property to be used for public interest or social purposes'.

The case law of the European Court of Human Rights (ECtHR) does not provide for general guidelines as to the balance between the expansion of confiscatory powers and the protection of fundamental rights. Contrary to national constitutional courts, the jurisdiction of the ECtHR does not know the abstract review of a legal provision as such, but, rather, looks at that provision in the context of a concrete case. The case law, therefore, hardly gives comprehensive conceptual answers.

In the area of confiscation, the 'classic' question is about the definition of the concept of a criminal penalty: under what conditions a measure—irrespective of its legal nature under national law—may qualify as a criminal penalty for the purposes of the application of the rights laid down in the European Convention on Human Rights. For instance, if confiscation is not considered a criminal penalty, but rather an administrative or civil sanction, should certain safeguards characteristic of criminal procedure nevertheless apply? Can the presumption of innocence have any relevance in a non-criminal setting?

These and other questions are addressed in the first part of the book. The various chapters will explore the nature of confiscation. Regardless of its labelling under national law, what features should lead one to consider confiscation as a criminal penalty? Is the extent of the interference with private property decisive, or is the violation of fair trial rights? Or the inner and ultimate purpose of confiscation? Can a criminal penalty be distinguished from other, non-criminal, measures on the basis of its function?

In Chapter 1, Panzavolta adopts a comparative approach to provide an overview of the trends observable in several jurisdictions as regards confiscation measures. He deals with 'confiscation without conviction' from both an EU law and a human rights perspective, and explores whether forfeiture models that do not provide for the assessment of individual criminal liability are acceptable in light of the European fundamental rights framework. Starting from the criteria of criminal punishment—namely the goal of a measure and its impact on the position of the individual—he argues that non-conviction-based confiscation measures may be more acceptable than other solutions, such as the extension of criminalisation in relation to the possession of illegitimate assets. He aims to demonstrate that it is possible to keep non-conviction-based forfeiture schemes outside the realm of criminal law, and that there is margin to develop non-criminal models not violating fundamental rights, provided that they encounter clear limits (including those deriving from the proportionality principle) and that factual presumptions are used only to a limited extent.

An overview across several jurisdictions is also offered by Fernandez-Bertier. Differently to the previous contribution, Chapter 2 provides a historical analysis of what the author defines as 'asset deprivation measures' and aims to identify common patterns in the development of asset recovery policies in both common law and civil law systems. He looks into the birth and evolution of such policies, from the 'general confiscation' of ancient times to the targeting of the proceeds of crime in modern criminal law. This historical account helps to assess the rationale and justification of national confiscation regimes in a differentiated way.

In Chapter 3, King focuses on one national system that several years ago adopted a far-reaching model of non-conviction-based forfeiture. Observing the Irish system, particularly its evolution over two decades, and the debate sparked in Ireland offers a paradigmatic example of the challenge to find the right balance between efficiency and individual safeguards. King has the merit to show at the same time the advantages and the weaknesses, or the critical aspects, of the Irish model. What emerges from the chapter is not a radical critique of civil asset forfeiture, but rather a rigorous analysis of the requirements that must be met in order to comply with due process standards.

A somewhat stronger criticism of non-criminal forfeiture measures is expounded by Mazzacuva, who, in Chapter 4, offers an analysis of the Italian system of preventive confiscation. The determination of its real nature, beyond the labels adopted by the Italian legislator, has been considered problematic ever since its adoption a number of decades ago. Contrary to some common law systems, Italian preventive confiscation is not designed as an *in rem* measure; nevertheless, it is far from being a traditional *in personam* criminal confiscation and, due to its efficiency in tackling criminal organisations' assets, it is often considered as an effective example of non-conviction-based confiscation that should be adopted in other Member States. However, the issues linked to its real nature—and consequently to the applicable safeguards—has generated contradictory national case law. Recently, the Italian Supreme Court has denied the punitive character of preventive confiscation. The author therefore scrutinises the reasoning of this landmark judgment, arguing that it is far from watertight. Although the object of the analysis is the Italian system, the arguments developed in this chapter—namely those related to the functions of confiscation and to the strict interpretation of criminal law safeguards—clearly apply beyond the Italian context.

The understanding of goals and functions of confiscation measures is further explored in Chapter 5, where Boucht shifts the focus to the concept of extended confiscation (ie, as said earlier, a conviction-based confiscation that also targets assets unrelated to the specific conviction). Extended confiscation is traditionally considered a measure *in personam*, but one having a broad scope and including other tainted assets linked to the punished person. Is it, however, really possible to assess the property's nature without judging the (further) liability of the convicted owner? The author pinpoints the problematic aspects of such a mechanism and scrutinises whether and to what extent criminal measures can be expanded without impinging on fundamental rights, and whether it is therefore feasible to loosen the borders of such measures. In his conclusion, he critically assesses the tendency to adopt extended confiscation. In Boucht's opinion, compared to civil forfeiture schemes, there are elements of extended confiscation that are inherently more difficult to reconcile with fundamental criminal law principles.

In Chapter 6, Blanco continues with a study of the limits of measures affecting the right to property and looks into the impact of confiscation on third parties. The aim of ensuring that the crime does not pay has led to an expansion of the scope of application of confiscation provisions to third parties. Confiscation laws may, therefore, operate to the detriment of innocent third persons whose property could be subject to confiscation because it was either used in the commission of, or derived from, a crime. Blanco rightly concludes that this trend poses significant challenges to the right to property, and national provisions must be formulated in such a way as to represent the principle of proportionality.

B. Part II: Asset Recovery as a Multi-faceted Process

As mentioned earlier, the recovery of criminal assets does not just consist of the forfeiture of proceeds and instrumentalities of crime, but relies on a complex interplay between several actors in various phases. The second part of the book therefore adopts a broader perspective and observes asset recovery in context by addressing several aspects concerning the rationale of policies against tainted money ('Why is it necessary to enhance them?'), the assessment of undertaken efforts ('What is not working?') and the future perspective of the fight against criminal money ('How could it work better?'). The aim of this part is to combine a broader policy view with closer observation of the challenges posed by international co-operation, which are of fundamental importance to understanding the complexity of asset recovery.

After decades of global efforts addressing criminal proceeds, it is worth looking back to determine whether national and supranational legislatures need merely update the weapons used in this fight, or rather change their approach in depth. In other words, on what fronts should the EU focus in order to obtain satisfactory results?

To this end, in Chapter, 7 Alldridge explores the functions and justifications of AML laws in relation to the recovery of assets. Taking the example of the recent case of HSBC, the author demonstrates the problematic relationship between tax offences and AML policies. Although dealing in particular with the English approach—namely with the proposed legislation to criminalise offshore tax evasion—the arguments developed in this contribution have a broader scope. They highlight the risks stemming from the extreme expansion of criminal law, and in general the risks linked to interplay between tax evasion and criminal justice.

In Chapter 8, Ivory adopts a comprehensive view on asset recovery challenges, embracing public international law and global governance, international relations and the rule of law. Why is it still difficult to return to victim countries the assets stolen by corrupt governments and transferred abroad? The reader may appreciate the complexity of the issues at stake, which are clustered by the author in four intertwined dimensions—barriers to recovery, human rights, effectiveness and rationality. The author does not aim to identify solutions to such challenges. Nevertheless, she offers a remarkable contribution to disentangling all the elements composing such a complex picture.

Dealing with the return of assets to victim countries, Meyer focuses on Switzerland and, by analysing the recent reforms of Swiss law, he illustrates whether and to what extent the Swiss approach can represent an example for other jurisdictions. Chapter 9, therefore, provides an overview of the reasons and features of the legislative developments, and points out at the same time the challenge linked to its practical implementation. In this way, the author offers an outlook on what the new Swiss system may realistically achieve—a question that, given the significance of Switzerland as a financial centre, may gain relevance in the international discourse on asset recovery.

Ivičević Karas and Roksandić Vidlička bring to the book another crucial perspective to fully understand the importance of policies against dirty money. Chapter 10 studies the role of asset recovery in 'transitional' societies. Focusing on the Croatian system, the authors describe the difficulties in recovering the proceeds of economic crimes committed during the country's transformation process—in particular, the difficulty in obtaining a conviction of the perpetrators due to the approach of the Croatian Constitutional Court. The authors analyse the legal reforms adopted in Croatia and the solutions—both legislative and judicial—that could help to overcome the obstacles to prosecuting perpetrators of crimes typical of 'transitional justice' and to recovering their unlawful gains. They conclude their analysis by assessing whether the direction taken by the Croatian legal system may represent a benchmark for other countries re-emerging from difficult internal situations.

In addition, Chapter 10 illustrates that the success of any reform depends on the concrete implementation of the new instruments by all relevant and responsible bodies. Despite its crucial position in the asset recovery process, indeed, any forfeiture measure alone will not be effective if the other phases are overlooked.

In Chapter 11 and Chapter 12, Cassella and Penna, respectively, address some aspects of the first phase of asset recovery, ie the identification of criminal assets, in particular once they cross national borders. Accordingly, they study questions related to the types of financial investigations needed to trace criminal assets, the nature of the authorities in charge of these financial investigations and the persisting obstacles to reaching assets moved across borders.

Cassella provides an overview of the US system, focusing on the approach taken by federal authorities towards assets located in other jurisdictions. He explains how it is not possible to provide for a single catch-all solution for every situation, and thereby argues in favour of the importance of having a panoply of available options in order to ensure the effectiveness of the recovery efforts. Criminal and civil measures have long coexisted in the US system; one or the other route is chosen by the prosecution following the assessment of which one is best suited to reach the goal. The author notes advantages and pitfalls of the different options, clarifying their potential for cross-border asset recovery.

Penna, on the other hand, underlines the importance of non-judicial actors in the detection of illicit financial flows for the purpose of the recovery of dirty money. Providing some insight into the functioning and the results of the Belgian FIU, Chapter 12 also lists the advantages of and limits to the co-operation between FIUs and other actors, exposing the challenges arising with the EU multi-level system relying on the interaction between authorities of different status and powers.

The chapter written by Czarneski completes the picture of investigation by exploring the challenges of tracing criminal money in the case of virtual currencies. It is difficult to enforce AML and counter-terrorist financing laws on Bitcoin and other digital currencies or to confiscate proceeds of crime effectively if the assets are in digital currencies. Chapter 13 analyses how AML and counter-terrorist financing laws can be applied to cryptocurrencies and argues in favour of extending the EU legislative framework in that respect. Czarneski acknowledges at the same time that the current regulatory tools might prove inadequate for future digital technologies and invites a more general reflection on how to identify, trace and remove criminal gains in the digital environment.

The chapters of the second part of the book favour an integrated approach to asset recovery and clearly argue that the success of efforts to recover assets depend on co-ordinated and comprehensive strategies. In this context, it is decisive that the recovery of dirty assets is not only detrimental to criminals, but also beneficial for the community.

The final chapters therefore focus on two main questions: who should be the owner of the confiscated assets? What should be done with recovered assets? The chapters shed light on these less-discussed aspects of asset recovery by analysing trends and weaknesses in existing practices. At the same time, they explore possibilities and parameters for new EU policies, setting the co-ordinates for a debate that will engage scholars, policy makers and practitioners working in different fields in the coming years. For example, while the UN framework on corruption offences clearly provides for the return of confiscated assets to the victim country,[57] the EU legal framework on other profit-driven offences does not always clarify which jurisdiction should keep the confiscated assets (in other words, who is the legitimate owner of the dirty money). Practice and agreements of 'asset sharing' may represent an incentive to execute complex requests of mutual assistance and to increase the co-operation with countries outside the EU.

Van Daele and Vande Reyde study the concept, rationale and limits of the international legal framework on asset sharing. Chapter 14 explains the current possibilities for sharing confiscated assets in the EU, as well as the room for manoeuvre within and the margin for improvement of the current system. In order to conduct their analysis, the authors focus on the arrangements between two neighbouring Member States—Belgium and the Netherlands—and show how such practices may help overcome the bottlenecks of international co-operation in asset recovery.

In the concluding chapter, Vettori and Di Nicola present and discuss the results of their research on asset disposal and related practices in the EU Member States.

[57] See Art 51 UNCAC.

They thus evaluate the existing models by pointing out best practices, as well as major problems. They recall certain national experiences of 'social re-use', outlining their potential and peculiarities. From such a thorough analysis, they derive conclusions about the adoption of similar programmes in other jurisdictions and the possible development of a supranational EU model. Although stressing the importance of co-ordinated policies, the conclusions also highlight the necessity of taking into consideration the specific circumstances existing at the national level. In other words, the success of an EU model of social re-use relies on some degree of flexibility.

Part I

Forfeiture and Fundamental Rights: Open Questions in the Twenty-First Century

1

Confiscation and the Concept of Punishment: Can There be a Confiscation Without a Conviction?

MICHELE PANZAVOLTA*

Introduction

On 3 April 2014, the European Union formally adopted Directive 2014/41/EU on the freezing and confiscation of instrumentalities and proceeds of crime in the European Union.[1] The goal of the Directive is to establish minimum rules to approximate the Member States' freezing and confiscation regimes, thus facilitating mutual trust and effective cross-border co-operation.[2]

After setting out the definitions and the scope of its application, the Directive addresses four different measures which are the object of harmonisation at the European level: confiscation (Article 4), extended confiscation (Article 5), confiscation from a third party (Article 6) and freezing (Article 7).[3]

When comparing the text of the Directive with the original proposal, a difference immediately shows. The proposal contemplated a fifth measure, labelled 'non-conviction-based confiscation', which was dropped during the negotiation. Article 5 of the proposal provided for an obligation on Member States to take the necessary measures to enable them to confiscate proceeds and instrumentalities without a criminal conviction, following proceedings which could, if the

* Professor of Criminal Law at KU Leuven (Belgium). Guest professor at the University of Hasselt (Belgium).

[1] Directive 2014/42/EU of the European Parliament and of the Council of 3 April 2014 on the freezing and confiscation of instrumentalities and proceeds of crime in the European Union (2014) OJ L127/39.

[2] See Recital 5 of Directive 2014/42/EU.

[3] For an analysis of the Directive, see M Simonato, 'Directive 2014/42/EU and Non-Conviction Based Confiscation: A Step Forward on Asset Recovery?' (2015) *New Journal of European Criminal Law* 213.

suspected or accused person had been able to stand trial, have led to a criminal conviction where: (i) the death or permanent illness of the suspected or accused person prevents any further prosecution; or (ii) the illness or flight from prosecution or sentencing of the suspected or accused person prevents effective prosecution within a reasonable time and poses the serious risk that it could be barred by statutory limitations.[4]

True, it must be acknowledged that the content of Article 5 of the proposal has largely been transfused into the current text of Article 4. Article 4, paragraph 2 in fact provides for cases of confiscation in cases where conviction of the offender is impossible due to illness or flight (ie if the suspect/defendant absconded).[5] Yet the fact remains that the European drafters did not want to use the label 'confiscation without conviction'. It seems this is not just a mere problem of symbols (or communication). As was observed in the literature, 'the attempts to widen the legal scope of non-conviction-based confiscation have been highly controversial', because the concept is 'unknown … in many EU Member States that follow a so-called civil law system, but also because it is deemed to be a possible source of violation of human rights'.[6] Therefore, the question arises: what is the problem with confiscation without conviction? What did the European drafters fear? Can there be a confiscation without conviction? Or, to put in other terms, what is the relationship between confiscation and conviction?

This chapter will try to provide an answer to these questions by mixing the general EU law perspective with a human rights perspective and a comparative perspective. First, it will offer a brief overview of the state of affairs on confiscation, together with some brief historical remarks. Then it will tackle the question raised: is it acceptable to have a confiscation without conviction? The question will be discussed as to how it concerns (i) measures of confiscation without conviction passed within criminal proceedings and consequent safeguards and (ii) measures of confiscation adopted outside of criminal proceedings and/or without safeguards of criminal proceedings. The aim of the chapter is thus to identify whether confiscation without conviction is a measure which can be accepted in modern human-rights-compliant criminal justice systems and, if so, what features it could have.

[4] Commission, 'Proposal for a Directive of the European Parliament and of the Council on the freezing and confiscation of proceeds of crime in the European Union', COM (2012) 85.

[5] Art 4, para 2 provides: 'Where confiscation on the basis of paragraph 1 is not possible, at least where such impossibility is the result of illness or absconding of the suspected or accused person, Member States shall take the necessary measures to enable the confiscation of instrumentalities and proceeds in cases where criminal proceedings have been initiated regarding a criminal offence which is liable to give rise, directly or indirectly, to economic benefit, and such proceedings could have led to a criminal conviction if the suspected or accused person had been able to stand trial.'

[6] R Esser, 'A Civil Asset Recovery Model. The German Perspective and Human Rights' in JP Rui and U Sieber (eds), *Non-Conviction-Based Confiscation in Europe* (Berlin, Duncker & Humblot, 2015) 71.

It should be noted that the terms 'confiscation' and 'asset forfeiture' are used synonymously herein, to indicate the deprivation of a defendant of a title to property, which is hence transferred to the state.[7] The reader should also be warned from the beginning that the chapter takes a stance which views the idea of confiscation without conviction (and not merely for reasons of necessity) favourably, but only as long as certain conditions are in place.

I. A Look Backwards

In his famous *Dei delitti e delle pene*, Cesare Beccaria struck a very severe judgment on confiscation, which at that time was coupled with the banishment of the convicted, following the famous maxim 'qui confisque le corps confisque le biens'. He wrote:

> The confiscation of effects, added to banishment is a greater punishment than banishment alone; there ought then to be some cases, in which, according to the crime, either the whole fortune should be confiscated, or part only, or none at all. The whole should be forfeited, when the law which ordains banishment declares, at the same time, that all connections or relations between the society and the criminal are annihilated. In this case the citizen dies; the man only remains, and, with respect to a political body, the death of the citizen should have the same consequences with the death of the man. It seems to follow then, that in this case, the effects of the criminal should devolve to his lawful heirs. But it is not on account of this refinement that I disapprove of confiscations. If some have insisted, that they were a restraint to vengeance and the violence of particulars, they have not reflected, that, though punishments be productive of good, they are not, on that account, more just; to be just, they must be necessary.
>
> Even an useful injustice can never be allowed by a legislator, who means to guard against watchful tyranny, which, under the flattering pretext of momentary advantages, would establish permanent principles of destruction, and, to procure the ease of a few in a high station, would draw tears from thousands of the poor. The law which ordains confiscations sets a price on the head of the subject, with the guilty punishes the innocent, and, by reducing them to indigence and despair, tempts them to become criminal. Can there be a more melancholy spectacle than a whole family overwhelmed with infamy and misery from the crime of their chief? A crime, which, if it had been possible, they were restrained from preventing, by that submission which the laws themselves have ordained.[8]

[7] This is not the case in other countries. In the UK, for instance, forfeiture of assets is distinct from the confiscation: while the former takes away the proprietary right of the individual on some property, the latter is an order for payment of a specified sum of money (see DJ Dickson, 'Towards More Effective Asset Recovery in Member States—the UK Example' (2009) 10 *ERA Forum* 435, 436).

[8] C Beccaria, *An Essay on Crimes and Punishments*, trans ED Ingraham (Philadelphia, Philip H Nicklin, 1819) 87.

The bitter criticism of Beccaria is mirrored by the comments of Voltaire to the text:

> it is a received maxim of the bar, that, he who forfeits life, forfeits his effects—a maxim in greatest rigor in countries where custom holds the place of principle. Thus, as we already have remarked the children of those who voluntarily terminate their wretched days are doomed to perish with hunger, as if they were the children of a murderer. So that, in every case, an entire family is punished for the crimes of an individual.[9]

These words remind us how harsh a measure a confiscation penalty can be. But is confiscation today the same confiscation of which Beccaria and Voltaire gave so critical an account? Is our present confiscation the same as the one portrayed by the ancient regime idea 'qui confisque les corps confisque le biens'? Is it still true that the degradation of a convicted person entails the loss of citizenship rights and thus the forfeiture of the right to property? The answer is clearly in the negative.

Much has changed since those times. Beccaria's words of condemnation concerned the so-called *confiscation générale*, a measure whereby all property of the convicted is forfeited by the state. That was the rule 150 years ago. *Confiscation générale* dates back to the times of the ancient regime.[10] In France, it was first abolished in 1790. It was then reintroduced, abolished again and once more reintroduced, but with specific limits. In today's society, the confiscatory measures which normally apply concern the forfeiture of specific items of property. We are therefore mostly confronted with forms of *confiscation special.* In some countries, *confiscation générale* is explicitly forbidden, sometimes even at the constitutional level, as is the case in Belgium.[11] In other countries, such as France, the *confiscation générale* remains, but only for extremely serious cases.[12]

II. Different Forms of Confiscation

In more recent times, we observe a new phenomenon: the development of different forms of confiscation. From a legal point of view, confiscation appears as a multifaceted concept, with different shapes and classifications.

The first significant variance is whether confiscation is treated as a principal penalty or just as an ancillary one. In some cases, confiscation is seen as a principal

[9] ibid 224.

[10] For a historical account of confiscation in the *ancien régime*, see A Monti, 'Illegitimate Appropriation or Just Punishment? The Confiscation of Property in Ancien Régime Criminal Law and Doctrine' in L Luigi, M Barbot and L Mocarelli (eds), *Property Rights and Their Violations. Expropriations and Confiscations, 16th–20th/La propriété violée. Expropriations et confiscations, XVIe-XXe siècles* (Peter Lang, Bern, 2012) 15.

[11] Art 17 of the Consitution reads: 'La peine de la confiscation des biens ne peut être établie' (in the Dutch text 'De straf van verbeurdverklaring der goederen kan niet worden ingevoerd').

[12] The measure is still foreseen by the *Code pénal* (Art 37 and following) mostly for crimes of significant gravity, such as crimes against humanity, trafficking in human beings, terrorism, major

(or main) criminal penalty. Sometimes it is used in substitution of a prison penalty (as can happen in France). In the majority of cases, confiscation is a secondary/complementary criminal penalty, that is, a penalty which adds to/complements a main criminal penalty.[13] Confiscation can also take place outside of the realm of criminal law. It can be a preventative (or security) measure[14] or, following a similar but slightly different logic, an administrative[15] or even a civil measure. And sometimes the criminal, preventative, administrative and civil forms can intertwine with each other (as, for instance, in civil asset recovery).

The fragmentation has increased in recent years, in conjunction with the expansion of the importance of confiscation in the fight against crime. The policy idea that 'crime should not pay' has multiplied the cases and forms of confiscation.[16]

There are cases where confiscation has been passed after conviction, referring to assets used for or derived from the crime in question. However, there are also cases of extended confiscation (after conviction), where the forfeiture extends to property owned by the offender that is not directly linked to any crime.[17] Here, the proceedings can be coupled with the underlying criminal proceedings or can be detached/disconnected from proceedings on individual liability (as can be the case in England[18] or the Netherlands),[19] and they are often based on the use of

drug offences and criminal association. However, it is also foreseen for money laundering and forgery of money. In some cases it is mandatory (eg crimes against humanity), in others it is left to judicial discretion. The measure has survived a challenge in front of the Constitutional Court, which upheld it: see Constitutional Court, 26 November 2010. For a general overview, see A Beziz-Ayache, 'Confiscation' in Y Mayaud (ed), *Dalloz Répertoire de Droit Pénal et de Procédure Pénale*, II (Paris, Dalloz, 2012).

[13] This is the case, for instance, for Belgium (Art 7 and Art 7-*bis* of the criminal code): see D Bernard, B Dejemeppe and C Guillaine, 'La confiscation pénale: une peine finalmente pas si accessoire' in P Jadoulet, JF Germain and C Guillain (eds), *Questions spéciales en droit pénal* (Brussels, Larcier, 2011) 55; and Italy (Art 240 of the criminal code): see M Panzavolta and R Flor, 'A Necessary Evil? The Italian "Non-Criminal System" of Asset Forfeiture' in Rui and Sieber (n 6) 111.

[14] This is the case, for instance, for Belgium with regard to the confiscation of tickets of unallowed lotteries (Art 303 Criminal Code) or the confiscation of prohibited weapons (Art 8, section 2 Law 8 June 2006); see R Verstraeten and F Verbruggen, *Strafrecht en Strafprocesrecht* (Antwerp, Maklu, 2014) particularly fn 258.

[15] This is the case, for instance, for the Italian *confisca di prevenzione*; on this, see Panzavolta and Flor (n 13) 111.

[16] On the policy approach that crime should not pay, see P Alldridge, 'Theory: Justifications for Forfeiture, Confiscation and Criminalisation' in *Money Laundering Law: Forfeiture, Confiscation, Civil Recovery, Criminal Laundering and Taxation of the Proceeds of Crime* (London, Hart Publishing, 2003) 45; M Levi, 'Taking the Profit Out of Crime: The UK Experience' (1997) *European Journal of Crime, Criminal Law and Criminal Justice* 228; M Kilchling, 'Tracing, Seizing and Confiscating Proceeds from Corruption (and other Illegal Conduct) Within or Outside the Criminal Justice System' (2001) *European Journal of Crime, Criminal Law and Criminal Justice* 264; from a Dutch perspective, see H Nelen, 'Hit Them Where it Hurts the Most' (2004) 41 *Crime, Law and Social Change* 517.

[17] See J Boucht, 'Extended Confiscation and the Proposed Directive on freezing and Confiscation of Criminal Proceeds in the EU: On Striking a Balance between Efficiency, Fairness and Legal Certainty' (2013) 21 *European Journal of Crime, Criminal Law and Criminal Justice* 127.

[18] In the context of financial investigations, see T Howse, 'England' in K Ligeti (ed), *Toward a Prosecutor for the European Union, Volume 1: A Comparative Analysis* (Oxford, Hart Publishing, 2013) 133, 138.

[19] See Arts 36e and following of the Criminal Code.

presumption and lower standards of proofs. There are also cases of value confiscation and third party confiscation. Value confiscation refers to the forfeiture of other assets in replacement of the assets that ought to have been confiscated but could not be taken away (could not be found). Third party confiscation identifies the confiscation of assets which are not in the property of the authors of a crime (perpetrators or accomplices), whether convicted/suspected, but which are the property of other people (to whom the assets were transferred, or who purchased them).[20] Besides confiscatory measures, there also are freezing measures, which often differ only through being temporary. Freezing measures can also be imposed at the international level, in the context of what are called 'smart sanctions' (eg the *Kadi* case).[21]

There are forms of confiscation which are labelled as civil confiscation (civil asset recovery) or confiscation by independent orders (independent from a previous conviction), which are both forms of confiscation without a previous conviction.[22] In common law countries, civil asset forfeiture schemes are strongly developed. However, forms of confiscation aside from a conviction for a criminal offence are also known in civil law countries within the continent: in Germany, for instance, there is the so-called *Selbständige Anordnung* (Article 76 Strafgesetzbuch, StGB);[23] and in Italy there is a form of non-conviction-based confiscation called

[20] See I Blanco Cordero, 'Modern Forms of Confiscation and Protection of Third Parties', this volume, Chapter 6.

[21] Mr Kadi was identified as being an individual associated with Usama bin Laden and the Al-Qaeda network, and was listed on the Sanctions Committee Consolidated List. His name was added to the list in Annex I to Council Regulation (EC) No 467/2001 of 6 March 2001 by Commission Regulation (EC) No 2062/2001 of 19 October 2001. He was subsequently listed in Annex I to Council Regulation (EC) No 881/2002 of 27 May 2002. Mr Kadi brought before the General Court an action seeking the annulment of the Regulations in so far as they concerned him. The General Court dismissed the action (GCEU, 21 September 2005, Case T-315/01 *Kadi v Council and Commission* [2005] ECR II-3649). The case was then taken to the Court of justice of the European Union, which reversed the previous decision (CJEU, 3 September 2008, Joined Cases C-402/05 P and C-415/05 P *Kadi and Al Barakaat International Foundation v Council and Commission* [2008] ECR I-6351). The Court annulled Regulation No 881/2002 in so far as it concerned Mr Kadi by holding that it did not provide for sufficient communications of the reasons and did not offer an opportunity for the person concerned to be heard, in breach of the principle of EU law of the effectiveness of judicial review. In consequence of the ruling, Mr Kadi was then provided with a statement of reasons concerning the insertion of his name in the list and was given an opportunity to provide any relevant information he wished. Mr Kadi went on to challenge again the freezing measures. The General Court annulled the contested Regulation (GCEU, 30 September 2010, Case T-85/09 *Yassin Abdullah Kadi v European Commission* [2010] ECR II-05177) for breaching the right of the defence, the right to effective judicial protection and the principle of proportionality in the interference with private property. The subsequent appeal was dismissed by the Court of Justice (CJEU, 18 July 2013, Cases C-584/10 P, C-593/10 P and C-595/10 P *European Commission and United Kingdom of Great Britain and Northern Ireland v Kadi*). For similar cases, see GCEU, 12 December 2006, Case T-228/02 *Organisation des Modjahedines du peuple d'Iran v Council* and GCEU, 23 October 2008, Case T-256/07 *People's Mojahedin Organization of Iran v Council.*

[22] For a clear and precise overview, see JP Rui, 'Introduction' in Rui and Sieber (n 6) 1.

[23] Esser (n 6) 75.

confisca di prevenzione (preventative confiscation, an anti-mafia measure contained in the so-called Anti-mafia Code).[24] In some cases, they represent the answer to the difficulty of confiscating certain assets through criminal trials. In other countries, such schemes are a policy choice—sometimes rooted in old legal doctrines and traditions—which represents an alternative, parallel option to a criminal trial. Confiscation without conviction can take place within a civil track (as in the common law civil asset forfeiture),[25] within an administrative track (as in the Italian *confisca di prevenzione*) or even within the criminal track.

The picture of confiscation is therefore very fragmented, which makes it difficult to deal with confiscation as a whole. Even when looking only at confiscation within the criminal realm, the difficulty of dealing with a multifaceted concept remains. A clear example is the relationship between confiscation and *ne bis in idem*. Clearly, an asset cannot be confiscated twice in connection with the same crime. But does the imposition of a final confiscatory measure prevent the authorities from adjudicating upon the same crime (*rectius*, criminal facts)? The answer can vary depending on whether confiscation is a principal penalty or a complementary or ancillary one. And the question can become even more perplexing when posed in relation to transborder contexts. *Non bis in idem* figures as a reason for non-recognition in instruments of mutual recognition, including Framework Decision 2006/783 on the mutual recognition of confiscation orders. Imagine a person who has been convicted in one country for an offence that carries a prison sentence, but without any confiscation of assets. Can confiscation alone be imposed by another country which then seeks co-operation for its enforcement? Now imagine a confiscatory measure being imposed on certain criminal assets, but with no conviction of individuals. Can the individuals later be tried or punished by another country which then issues a European arrest warrant for the purpose of enforcing a pre-trial custody order or a prison sentence?

III. Confiscation: Is a Unitary Vision Possible?

In light of the diverse and multifarious nature of confiscation, one could be inclined to reject all attempts of generalisation and reach the conclusion that every form of confiscation must be viewed separately. A similar approach is partly correct, in that each form of confiscation certainly presents autonomous features.

[24] Panzavolta and Flor (n 13) 111; F Mazzacuva, 'The Problematic Nature of Asset Recovery Measures: Recent Developments of the Italian Preventive Confiscation', this volume, Chapter 5.

[25] In the vast bulk of literature, see particularly: for the United States, the works of SD Cassella, particularly *Asset Forfeiture Law in the United States: A Treatise on Forfeiture Law*, 2nd edn (New York, Juris, 2013); and in England, I Smith, T Owen and A Bodnar, *Asset Recovery: Criminal Confiscation and Civil Recovery* (Oxford, Looseleaf, 2014).

From a descriptive point of view (describing the law as it is), it can be the right approach to take. But the approach remains silent as to the features that confiscation must have. In all cases, confiscation entails a deprivation of property/rights from an individual: should the legislature be bound by constraints, rules or principles when imposing confiscation? The answer to this question requires one to consider confiscation as much as possible in a unitary way.

The first unitary remark is that confiscation is a measure against the right to property.[26] All forms of confiscation consist of the deprivation of property rights with regard to some items or objects. In this respect, confiscation must comply with the provision concerning the protection of the right to property. Such provisions can be found in constitutional charts and in supranational human rights instruments. In Europe, it is natural to think of Article 1 of the First Protocol to the European Convention on Human Rights (ECHR).[27] Nevertheless, the rules concerning the protection of property are quite permissive if compared, for instance, with the rules concerning the right to liberty. The existence of a legal basis (that is sufficiently clear and precise) and of some form of public interest tend to suffice if the medsure is not grossly disproportionate to its aim. Such an approach leaves the determination of whether the intervention is necessary to the states, and their discretion is almost unlimited.[28] With regard to confiscation of criminal assets, it would normally be considered legitimate from the perspective of the right to property if the measure is provided for by the law (since it is not too difficult to justify the existence of a public interest).[29] It is quite exceptional for the European Court of Human Rights (ECtHR) to find a violation with regard to the breach of the right to property.[30]

For the Court, confiscation is a legitimate restriction of property rights, particularly when concerning objects connected to criminal activities. As the Court observed in *Rummi v Estonia*,

> confiscation in criminal proceedings is in line with the general interest of the community, because the forfeiture of money or assets obtained through illegal activities or paid

[26] For an in-depth analysis of this point, see JP Rui and U Sieber, 'NCBC in Europe: Bringing the Picture Together' in Rui and Sieber (n 6) 263; Esser (n 6) 96.

[27] But also Art 17 of the Charter of Fundamental Rights of the European Union. See also Section XI below. For an example of an assessment of a lack of proportionality in the restriction of the right to property carried out by the Courts of the European Union, see CJEU, 3 December 2009, Joined Cases C-399/06 P and C-403/06 P *Faraj Hassan*; GCEU, 30 September 2010, Case T-85/09 *Yassin Abdullah Kadi v European Commission*, §§192–95.

[28] S Trechsel, *Human Rights in Criminal Proceedings* (Oxford, Oxford University Press, 2006) 561.

[29] The Strasbourg Court openly recognises 'l'ampleur de la marge d'appréciation dont disposait l'État défendeur': *Aboufadda v France* App No 28457/10 (ECtHR, 14 November 2014), §34.

[30] One such exception is the case *Sud Fondi Srl et autres v Italy* App No 75909/01 (ECtHR, 20 January 2009). For another case see *Grifhorst v France* App No 28336/02 (ECtHR, 26 February 2009). For a recent case of conviction due to the lack of a fair balance between right to property and general interest in the assessment of national courts, see *Paullet v the United Kingdom* App No 6219/08 (ECtHR, 13 May 2014), concerning the forfeiture of gains after a conviction (for dishonestly obtaining a pecuniary advantage, false identity and driving without insurance).

> for with the proceeds of crime is a necessary and effective means of combating criminal activities. Confiscation in this context is therefore in keeping with the goals of the Council of Europe Convention on Laundering, Search, Seizure and Confiscation of the Proceeds from Crime, which requires State Parties to introduce confiscation of instrumentalities and the proceeds of crime in respect of serious offences. Thus, a confiscation order in respect of criminally acquired property operates in the general interest as a deterrent to those considering engaging in criminal activities, and also guarantees that crime does not pay.[31]

When looking only at the rules concerning the right to property, it is clear that confiscation is legitimate even outside the realm of criminal law.[32] Hence, it could be said that confiscation without conviction is not prohibited. The same conclusion holds true if confiscation is looked at from the perspective of the right to privacy, under Article 8 ECHR. The forfeiting of assets could in some cases represent a breach of personal life, which requires a legal basis, a legitimate aim and an assessment of proportionality.[33] The grid of Article 8, however, makes it possible that an interference with privacy be adopted outside the realm of criminal law, with no connection to the conviction of the person. A measure interfering with privacy can have the prevention of disorder as one of its aims, regardless of any connection with criminal proceedings.[34]

IV. Is Confiscation a Penalty?

Besides the rules protecting the right to property (and, to a minor extent, the right to privacy), are there any other parameters/standards with which confiscation must comply? Are there rules which preclude that confiscation be imposed without an accompanying conviction for an offence?

The answer to these questions requires tackling the largely debated issue of the nature of confiscation. Is confiscation a penalty? The problem at stake can be

[31] *Rummi v Estonia* App No 63362/09 (ECtHR, 15 January 2015). See also *Denisova and Moiseyeva v Russia* App No 16903/03 (ECtHR, 1 April 2010); *Phillips v the United Kingdom* App No 41087/98 (ECtHR, 5 July 2001).

[32] At times, the Strasbourg Court observed that there is some slight difference between the two situations (confiscation within the criminal realm and confiscation outside the criminal realm) with regard to the assessment of proportionality. For instance, in *Tas v Belgique* App No 44614/06 (ECtHR, 12 May 2009) the Court held: 'Contrairement aux cas dont la Cour a eu à connaître dans les affaires Agosi c. Royaume-Uni, Air Canada c. Royaume-Uni, et Welch c. Royaume-Uni, où la confiscation avait été décidée en vertu de la compétence discrétionnaire de la douane, la confiscation litigieuse en l'espèce se situait dans le cadre du droit pénal. Or, dans le cadre d'une confiscation à titre de sanction, il faut que le propriétaire du bien confisqué puisse invoquer son innocence, sans quoi le juste équilibre entre la protection du droit au respect des biens et les exigences de l'intérêt général n'est pas respecté.'

[33] The assessment of proportionality within the framework of Art 8 is more stringent than in the context of Art 1 Protocol 1 ECHR (see, among others, *Aboufadda v France* (n 29) §44).

[34] Trechsel (n 28) 540.

simply described: if confiscation must be viewed as a penalty for criminal behaviour, it follows that it should then comply with the many principles concerning the application of criminal penalties, starting from a stricter legality principle. Furthermore, the principle of legality becomes applicable, as well as a strong proportionality principle and the safeguards of criminal justice, which include the presumption of innocence with its corollaries (including the rule of conviction only beyond reasonable doubt) and strong participation rights. On the contrary, if confiscation cannot be considered a penalty, then the principle of legality is less stringent, the principle of proportionality of the measure becomes less strict and the safeguards which are applicable need not be those that are applicable in criminal matters, but can be those of the civil/administrative realm of the law. This means that the decision can be based on a balance of probabilities and presumptions can be used,[35] that defence rights are of lesser importance and the like.

The answer to the nature of confiscation depends on many factors. First, it depends on the formal classification, whether criminal or not (according to national categories, although they are not absolute). It also depends on the concept of penalty/punishment (see Section V) and, connected to this, the forfeited objects (what it is that will be taken; see Section VI).

Traditionally, confiscation was considered to be a penalty. It was often taken to be a secondary consequence of the conviction of a person. A convicted person would lose his status as a citizen and consequently the right to property (*qui confisque les corps, confisque les biens*). It is certainly the case that a form of *confiscation générale* would constitute a penalty (regardless of whether it can be considered legitimate and compatible with the principles of humanity and proportionality of punishments). But now that a confiscation of the entire property of a person is in principle precluded, can it still be said that confiscation is a penalty? The question is whether the modern forms of confiscation (*confiscation spéciale*) constitute a penalty.

If we look at the legislation of the European Union, we find conflicting hints on this point. Article 1 of the Framework Decision 2005/214 (on the mutual recognition of financial penalties) provides that '[a] financial penalty shall not include: …—orders for the confiscation of instrumentalities or proceeds of crime'. On the other hand, Article 2c of the Framework Decision 2006/783 (on the mutual recognition of confiscation orders) states that a confiscation order 'shall mean a final penalty or measure imposed by a court following proceedings in relation to a criminal offence or offences, resulting in the definitive deprivation of property'. In the first provision, it would appear that confiscation does not fall in the concept of penalty, while, in the second, it appears that confiscation can constitute a penalty (although it could also be a 'measure').

[35] Although we know from *Salabiaku v France* App No 10519/83 (ECtHR, 7 October 1988) §28 that some presumptions are allowed even in the realm of criminal law.

These arguments need not be overemphasised. For instance, it could be said that Framework Decision 2005/214 simply aimed to exclude confiscation orders from its scope, but had no intention to take a stance on the nature of confiscation. With regard to Framework Decision 2006/783, it could be said that the instrument takes into account all possible qualifications present at the national level, without implying that confiscation orders possess a peculiar (criminal or non-criminal) nature. Nevertheless, these two provisions are a clear sign of the difficulties that can be encountered when answering the question of the nature of confiscation at the supranational/theoretical level.

A look at the case law of the ECtHR does not help solve the issue. On some occasions, confiscation was treated as a penalty, thus requiring the higher standards of legality provided for by Article 7 ECHR. This was the Court's position in decisions such as *Welch v United Kingdom* (concerning a case of extended confiscation after conviction on the basis of a retroactive application of the 1986 Drugs Trafficking Offences Act),[36] *Sud Fondi srl v Italy*[37] and *Varvara v Italy* (both concerning cases of confiscation of unlawful constructions imposed after criminal proceedings but in connection with an acquittal).[38] In *Geerings v the Netherlands*, the Court found that the imposition of an order of extended confiscation for offences for which the defendant had already been acquitted constituted a violation of the presumption of innocence.[39]

But it is also possible to identify a different strand of case law, where confiscation does not require the application of the safeguards foreseen within the criminal realm and consequently is not viewed as a criminal penalty (and a fortiori does not constitute a separate criminal charge). This was the case in decisions such as *Butler v UK* (concerning a civil forfeiture order issued on the basis of the Drug Trafficking Act without criminal proceedings ever being started)[40] and *Rummi v Estonia* (where the confiscation order of what looked to be the objects—or profits—of the offence was passed after proceedings were closed due to the death of the defendant).[41] The reasoning developed in *Walsh v UK* (concerning a restraint order obtained by the Assets Recovery Agency with a view to recovering the proceeds of unlawful conduct within the meaning of the Proceeds of Crime Act 2002) was in a similar vein. The measure was challenged in front of the Strasbourg Court for breach of the safeguards of Article 6, including the presumption of innocence. The Court rejected the claim and emphasised that the aim of the

[36] *Welch v UK* App No 17440/90 (ECtHR, 9 February 1995) §27.

[37] *Sud Fondi* (n 30) §§111–18 (Italy was convicted for the lack of clarity and foreseeability of the law).

[38] *Varvara v Italy* App No 17475/09 (ECtHR, 29 October 2013).

[39] *Geerings v The Netherlands* App No 30810/0 (ECtHR, 31 March 2007), according to which a previous acquittal does not justify any following orders of confiscation of assets.

[40] *Butler v UK* App No 41661/98 (ECtHR, 27 June 2002).

[41] *Rummi v Estonia* App No 63362/09 (ECtHR, 15 January 2015).

measure was not punitive or deterrent, but rather intended to recover assets which did not lawfully belong to the applicant.[42]

It is difficult to reconstruct a coherent picture out of the previous decisions. As I have already argued, if confiscation orders are formally labelled as criminal measures, the Court will take them to fall within the notion of criminal punishment, although they may not constitute a separate criminal charge from the trial in which the defendant was found liable.[43] However, the same is not true when the national qualification is administrative. In the latter case, the Court seems to adopt a case-by-case approach, which leaves the interpreters with some uncertainty as to what precisely the outcome of the Court's judgment could be. However, the number of cases in which the Court considered an administrative confiscation to be in essence equivalent to a criminal penalty remains significantly smaller than the number of cases in which the opposite was held. When looking at these cases, it appears that, as a rule, administrative confiscation is treated as a non-criminal measure, which means that it need not require all the safeguards typical of criminal law.

In the large majority of cases, confiscation outside of criminal proceedings was considered to fall outside the realm of criminal law and was thus scrutinised under the lens of the less stringent safeguards applicable outside of that realm. The archetype of such an approach is the ECtHR case law on the Italian *confisca di prevenzione*. The *confisca di prevenzione* is a hybrid measure which falls somewhere between criminal and administrative law. Formally administrative, it was devised mostly with a view to circumventing the difficulties of tackling organised crime by means of ordinary criminal proceedings. In essence, the public authorities can forfeit the assets of dangerous persons, whose dangerousness derives from the fact that they are suspected of being connected to mafia associations or of being involved in other serious offences.[44] In a series of cases, the Strasbourg Court consistently held that the *confisca di prevenzione* could not be considered as a form of adjudication upon a criminal charge and that Article 6 could therefore find application only in its civil tenet.[45] The same conclusion can also be inferred by the case *Dassa Foundation v Liechtenstein*, where the Court equated the confiscation of criminal assets to a civil measure against unjust enrichment.[46]

[42] *Walsh v UK* App No 43384/05 (ECtHR, 21 November 2006).

[43] *Phillips v UK* App No 41087/98 (ECtHR, 5 July 2001) §§34–35.

[44] For a more precise and elaborate account of such measures see Panzavolta and Flor (n 13).

[45] *Raimondo v Italy* App No 12954/87 (ECtHR, 22 February 1994); *Arcuri v Italy* App No 52024/99 (ECtHR, 5 July 2001); *Riela v Italy* App No 52439/99 (ECtHR, 4 September 2001); *Licata v Italy* App No 32221/02 (ECtHR, 27 May 2004); ECtHR, *Leone v Italy* App No 30506/07 (ECtHR, 2 February 2010).

[46] *Dassa Foundation and others v Liechtenstein* App No 696/05 (ECtHR, 23 December 2004), which compares the civil forfeiture orders of Liechtenstein to unjustified enrichment. However, it appears difficult to make such a comparison, because unjustified enrichment is a civil restitution measure,

V. Identifying Criminal Punishment

Beyond the not always consistent patterns of precedents of the Strasbourg Court, one question arises. When should the safeguards of criminal law accompany the confiscation of assets and when should it instead be possible to forfeit assets without those safeguards? The issue inevitably requires the identification of what exactly defines punishment.

When talking of the standards for the identification of a penalty, the ECtHR's well-known *Engel* criteria remain undoubtedly the point of departure.[47] They have certainly proved useful on many occasions.[48] They have largely been employed by the ECtHR and, more recently, by the Court of Justice of the European Union (CJEU) in the context of *ne bis in idem* cases, to establish whether, and in under what circumstances, an administrative decision or penalty could be considered a prior criminal penalty for the application of the principle.[49] The *Engel*

which is based on some loss of earning of another private individual. It seems awkward to view civil forfeiture orders as a form of restitution of the unjust enrichment to the state, unless moving from the premise that the state is the natural owner of all properties which do not lawfully belong to individuals.

[47] *Engel and others v the Netherlands* App No 5100/71 (ECtHR, 8 June 1976) §82. The Court was confronted with the issue of whether a disciplinary measure could nonetheless count as criminal. In response, the Court developed a threefold test: 'it is first necessary to know whether the provision(s) defining the offence charged belong, according to the legal system of the respondent State, to criminal law, disciplinary law or both concurrently. This however provides no more than a starting point. The indications so afforded have only a formal and relative value and must be examined in the light of the common denominator of the respective legislation of the various Contracting States.' The Court went on: 'The very nature of the offence is a factor of greater import. When a serviceman finds himself accused of an act or omission allegedly contravening a legal rule governing the operation of the armed forces, the State may in principle employ against him disciplinary law rather than criminal law. In this respect, the Court expresses its agreement with the Government.' Lastly, the Court said: 'However, supervision by the Court does not stop there. Such supervision would generally prove to be illusory if it did not also take into consideration the degree of severity of the penalty that the person concerned risks incurring. In a society subscribing to the rule of law, there belong to the "criminal" sphere deprivations of liberty liable to be imposed as a punishment, except those which by their nature, duration or manner of execution cannot be appreciably detrimental. The seriousness of what is at stake, the traditions of the Contracting States and the importance attached by the Convention to respect for the physical liberty of the person all require that this should be so.'

[48] *Öztürk v Germany* App No 8944/79 (ECtHR, 21 February 1984) §50 ('The first matter to be ascertained is whether or not the text defining the offence in issue belongs, according to the legal system of the respondent State, to criminal law; next, the nature of the offence and, finally, the nature and degree of severity of the penalty that the person concerned risked incurring must be examined, having regard to the object and purpose of Article 6 (art. 6), to the ordinary meaning of the terms of that Article (art. 6) and to the laws of the Contracting States'). See also *AP, MP and TP v Switzerland* App No 71/1996/690/882 (ECtHR, 29 August 1997) §39; *Campbell and Fell v UK* App No 7819/77 (ECtHR, 28 June 1984) §§68–69.

[49] See also CJEU, 5 June 2012, Case C-489/10 *Łukasz Marcin Bonda*, §37 ('According to that case-law, three criteria are relevant in this respect. The first criterion is the legal classification of the offence under national law, the second is the very nature of the offence, and the third is the nature and degree of severity of the penalty that the person concerned is liable to incur'). More recently, CJEU, 26 February 2013, Case C-617/10, *Åklagaren v Hans Åkerberg Fransson* ('Next, three criteria are relevant for the purpose of assessing whether tax penalties are criminal in nature. The first criterion is the legal

criteria have often helped solve challenging legal conundrums.[50] Nevertheless, it can hardly be denied that those criteria are vague and fluid themselves. They also do not offer a clear answer with regard to the issue of confiscation.

The *Engel* criteria are used to identify what falls within the concept of 'criminal charge'. First, the formal national classification is relevant (whether criminal or not). Next, the nature of offence is to be taken into account. Lastly, the degree of severity of the penalty is of importance. It has already been argued that if the national classification labels the measure as a criminal one, it cannot evade the safeguards foreseen within criminal law. However, the other two criteria lack some precision. Moreover, it remains unclear whether they ought to be pondered together, or whether one criterion alone could be relevant in determining the criminal nature of the charge/punishment. The Strasbourg Court has in some cases endorsed the latter position, but that does not solve all potential difficulties.[51]

For instance, it appears that the severity of the penalty can in some cases be a sufficient basis alone.[52] If a very oppressing penalty is imposed on an individual, it can hardly be denied that its application must be accompanied by the strong safeguards of criminal law. Imagine a prison penalty being imposed for whatever reason: could it ever be argued that the penalty imposed had no criminal character, or that it could be imposed without complying with a strict legality principle and with the other safeguards which characterise criminal proceedings? A similar reasoning would open a dangerous breach in the system of protection of safeguards within criminal law. Some penalties are criminal punishment in themselves, regardless of any other accompanying factor. In this respect, a truly afflictive measure deserves to be viewed as a criminal penalty simply on this basis.

However, the problem arises as to when a penalty can be considered truly (or significantly) afflictive. Intrinsic elements of penalties are the pain, discomfort, vexation and nuisance that they create. But the problem then arises as to the precise kind of impact on the individual which identifies a penalty. For instance, would a shaming effect be sufficient to describe a measure as punishment? Is there a way to measure shame so that it could constitute a sufficiently precise standard of legal regulation? There is a significant body of literature on shaming sanctions.[53] It would appear that, while the category can represent a useful tool from a criminological standpoint, it is less suited for use as a normative legal term, at least unless the shaming effect is not precisely typified through clear and binding standards.

classification of the offence under national law, the second is the very nature of the offence, and the third is the nature and degree of severity of the penalty that the person concerned is liable to incur').

[50] See Trechsel (n 28) 17.

[51] *Lauko v Slovakia* App No 26138/95 (ECtHR, 2 September 1988) §57; *Lutz v Germany* App No 9912/82 (ECtHR, 25 August 1987) §55.

[52] Unlike the conclusion upheld by the ECtHR in *Welch* (n 36) §32, according to which 'the severity of the order is not in itself decisive'.

[53] J Whitman, 'What is Wrong with Inflicting Shame Sanctions?' (1998) 107(4) *The Yale Law Journal* 1055; J Whitman, *Harsh Justice* (Oxford, Oxford University Press, 2005).

With regard to the parameter of 'afflictiveness', many would probably agree that a custodial penalty has an afflictive nature. There is no doubt that prison sentences constitute an afflictive sentence. In general, it could be said that all measures which directly impinge on the personal liberty or the corporal integrity of a person are as such afflictive, in that they reach a degree of severity that warrants the application of all safeguards of criminal law (regardless of the internal national label). But is this the case for financial/economic penalties? What does afflictive mean with regard to the impact on an individual's right to property? Is any adverse consequence on a person's property a punishment? If the answer to this last question were in the positive, such an approach would stretch the concept of punishment too far, making it almost impossible to distinguish a civil financial consequence from a criminal penalty.

With regard to patrimonial consequences, it is clear that the severity of the penalty is not adequate enough to constitute a good landmark, because the same negative consequences could be endured outside of criminal law. A measure which has adverse financial consequences to a person cannot be considered as criminal, administrative or civil simply on the basis of the parameter of severity.[54] A distinction between criminal and non-criminal patrimonial measures requires a look at further elements than severity alone.

In the *Engel* formula, the only remaining factor is the nature of the offence. But what do European courts (the ECtHR and CJEU) mean when they talk about the second parameter, the 'nature of the offence'? It is clear that the formula should not be intended as 'nature of the proceedings'.[55] But beyond this clarification, what does the formula really mean? For instance, if we use the division between criminal offences and regulatory offences, with the second being the regulation of behaviours which are not *mala in se* (notwithstanding that the division between *mala in se* and *mala quia prohibita* is all but sharp itself), should we come to the conclusion that it is prohibited for a lawmaker to turn a traditional criminal offence (such as murder or theft or robbery or fraud) into an administrative breach? This would seem too narrow an application of the formula, because the largest field of application of the *Engel* case law deals precisely with regulatory offences. And quite certainly the Court did not intend to let all regulatory offences be dealt with outside of criminal law.[56] What the Court might intend with 'nature of the offence' is that certain types of breach ought to belong to criminal law, either because they are comparable to other similar breaches criminalised within national law (internal comparison) or because they are treated as an offence in all other states to the extent that they inherently carry the stigma typically attached to

[54] From this perspective, the same conclusion was upheld by the ECtHR in *Welch* (n 36) §32.

[55] See the criticism on this point by Trechsel (n 28) 19.

[56] Eg the cases *Öztürk* (n 48) and *Benedoun v France* App No 12547/86 (ECtHR, 24 February 1994) (where the Court excluded that a regulatory offence in the field of tax law could be considered criminal).

criminal law (external comparison).[57] However, even after this refinement based on the comparative approach, the formula still remains vague.

It is no surprise that in some cases the Strasbourg Court tried to move beyond the tripartite *Engel* test and to look at other variables. Such an attempt was made in *Welch v United Kingdom*. In this case, the Court discussed the parameter of the 'nature of the offence' as if it meant 'the connection with a criminal offence' and found that the confiscation order had been issued in connection with drug offences.[58] The Court then looked at the severity of the offence and found that the criterion could not be conclusive. It thus considered that, beyond the severity of the measure, regard had to be had to further factors: (i) the existence of ('sweeping') statutory presumptions in the making of a confiscation order; (ii) the fact that the order was not limited to actual enrichment or profit, but to all proceeds of crime; (iii) the possibility for the judge to exercise discretion; and (iv) the fact that a confiscation order could be converted into a prison sentence.[59] The other standards used by the Court are certainly useful for better identifying the existence of a criminal punishment but nevertheless seem insufficient. Even in some civil or administrative punishment, the judge can exercise discretion or rely on statutory presumptions. Furthermore, the possibility of converting a confiscation order into a prison sentence seems to show that *Welch* was a case where the parameter of the severity of the sentence could be considered decisive in itself.

The problem thus remains: what differentiates a criminal punishment from other forms of punishment when the penalty is in itself not so severe (to constitute a deprivation or restriction of personal liberty) as to make it a criminal penalty? Does the goal of a measure matter? Some confiscatory measures are aimed at preventing crime, others at repressing crimes. Some are backward looking, while others are forward looking. The preventive/repressive divide is emphasised, for instance, in the ECtHR decision in *Butler*.[60]

The dichotomy between prevention and repression carries a danger, in that it intersects the sensitive areas of the theory of punishment and its rationales. It is

[57] The idea that the court should resort here to comparative analysis is defended by Trechsel (n 28) 20.

[58] The reasoning partly betrayed the logic of the criterion, because the fact that a confiscation order is imposed in connection with an offence does not necessarily mean that the confiscation order is imposed because the individual committed an offence. To put it in clearer terms, the fact that confiscation is applied in connection with an offence does not necessarily mean that it is passed as a form of reaction/punishment for the individual committing an offence. The point could be clarified by drawing a parallel with civil orders to restore damages: a judicial decision ordering the restoration of damages caused by a crime is certainly taken in connection with a crime, but is not the 'criminal' punishment for the offence.

[59] *Welch* (n 36) §33.

[60] In *Butler* (n 40), the Court observes that, in its opinion, 'the forfeiture order was a preventive measure and cannot be compared to a criminal sanction, since it was designed to take out of circulation money which was presumed to be bound up with the intentional trade in illicit drugs. It follows that the proceedings which led to the making of the order did not involve "the determination … of a criminal charge".'

already difficult to agree on a uniform and comprehensive theory of punishment at the national level. It is even more so at European level, and for this reason it might be that the ECtHR 'gives national authorities a generous discretion to draw the line between punitive and preventive measures'.[61] Furthermore, the divide between prevention and repression is not at all clear, in theory or in practice. All penalties have elements of prevention in themselves. Prevention can consist in measures de facto equivalent to penalties (eg imprisonment or confinement in an institution). In a large set of cases, it is difficult to clearly discern whether the goal of the legislature was more a preventative or a repressive one. And even if the intention of Parliament were clear, a measure that aims at prevention could always have elements of repression and vice versa.[62]

Some argue that the confusion between prevention and repression is a reason for much concern, because 'punishment and prevention are fundamentally different'. Hence they advocate that the two functions should be segregated into two systems.[63] Yet it would be hard to wholly separate the two functions. This is not just because there is a 'continuum' that goes from 'predicted danger to consummated harm'.[64] The point is that in modern societies punishment also entails prevention, and the machinery of repressive criminal justice naturally incorporates some preventative ends. On the other hand, prevention can be framed autonomously, but only as long as it does not take the form of afflictive measures which are substantially equivalent to a punishment. Confiscation is the perfect example: in many cases, it is intended by the lawmaker as a form of prevention (it is often called a security measure, whether inside or outside the realm of criminal law), but it can just as well represent a punishment or a penalty, as was seen above. It is for these reasons that the watershed cannot be found in the aim of the measure, whether punitive or preventative.

Some scholars distinguish between punishment and penalties in that the former has an expressive quality—of communicating censorship—that penalties lack, but this point of view has been rightly criticised because it is difficult to pinpoint the communicative aspect of penalties (when does a person feel censored?).[65] Following a different perspective, it is argued that the distinction should look at the aim of the measure: 'punishment aims at the suffering of wrongdoers to deter others', but 'penalties are not aimed at making the offender suffer'; 'they are aimed at

[61] Rui and Sieber, 'NCBC in Europe' (n 26) 262.

[62] In *Lauko* (n 51) § 58, the Court found that the legal provision under scrutiny had a criminal nature due to 'the deterrent and punitive purpose of the penalty imposed' on the applicant and in the Court's reasoning the two elements of deterrence (prevention) and punishment (repression) seem intertwined and inextricable.

[63] P Robinson, 'Punishing Dangerousness: Cloaking Preventive Detention as Criminal Justice' (2001) 114(5) *Harvard Law Review* 1429, 1432 and 1455.

[64] A Dershowitz, 'The Law of Dangerousness: Some Fictions about Predictions' (1970) 23 *Journal of Legal Education* 24, 26.

[65] V Tadros, 'Criminalization and Regulation' in A Duff, L Farmer, SE Marshall, M Renzo and V Tadros (eds), *The Boundaries of the Criminal Law* (Oxford, Oxford University Press, 2010) 163.

redistributing wealth'.[66] But here again—just like with the prevention/repression divide—we run into the problem that it is difficult to speculate on the aims of the lawmaker, and nothing excludes that the lawmaker could pursue both prevention and repression with a single measure.

The view that is taken here is that a criminal penalty is something that targets individuals for their actions. Criminal law should punish actions (or failures to act), but not a mere status or situation. A crime must consist in a conduct—that is, in a form of action (or failure to act). Whether criminal law intends to prevent some harm from happening, deter somebody from doing harm or impose a just desert on somebody who caused harm, its aim should be to target a conduct (or the conduct of failing to act). This criterion turns out to be very useful with regard to confiscation. Some confiscatory measures are imposed only with a view to removing property which could in itself be dangerous, either because it is inherently dangerous or because it is a product (or by-product) of criminal activity. Other confiscatory measures are imposed in connection with an individual wrongdoing. The latter type is a criminal form of confiscation, whereas the former type is not.

In conclusion, when a measure (a confiscation order in our case) is applied for reasons that are independent of the action of a specific individual, it cannot be considered a criminal penalty unless the degree of severity of the measure is so serious that it naturally falls within the realm of criminal law (as happens in cases concerning deprivation/restriction of personal liberty). If a measure, which is not significantly afflictive, does not target an individual conduct (whether commission or omission), then it can legitimately be considered a non-criminal measure (unless the lawmaker has explicitly chosen the criminal label). On the contrary, if a measure targets an individual action and is a response to such action, then it can be viewed as a form of criminal punishment (regardless of the label used by the lawmaker). In short, a criminal penalty must target an action. In a 'non-criminal penalty', the action of the individual is irrelevant.

Some might contend that the suggested criterion does not escape the criticism previously raised against the other theories—in other words, everything depends upon the aim and intention of the lawmaker, which is always difficult to divine. In response to such objection, it can be said that what counts is not the aim of the lawmaker but the objective function of the measure, which can be ascertained with very simple reasoning: is confiscation related or not to the action of a specific individual? Does it depend on the identification of a specific person? If we mentally eliminate the action of specific (identified or identifiable) individuals, would it still be possible (and logically conceivable) to confiscate the property?

[66] ibid.

VI. Confiscation and its Objects

In order to make the reasoning clearer, it is necessary to look more closely at the objects of confiscation.[67]

Having made the distinction between measures which target dangerous property and measures which target individual's actions, it becomes essential to reflect upon the different objects which can be forfeited by a confiscation order. There is dangerous property, which can be confiscated regardless of a connection with an offence. This is the case, for instance, with per se dangerous items (such as weapons, explosives and drugs). Here, it can be said that the element of punishment is absent because the property is taken away for reasons related to the control of public order, irrespective of the behaviour of an individual or of the need to stigmatise, prevent or repress a conduct.

The question of whether confiscation constitutes punishment therefore seems to be directly relevant only for non-inherently dangerous items (and money is certainly an important and frequent example). When the forfeited property is related to an offence, we can distinguish whether it constitutes the *corpus delicti*, the means of committing the crime (*instrumentum delicti*), the result of the crime (*productum delicti*) or the profits of the crime. With regard to profits, it is often debated whether confiscation should be limited to the net gains effectively made by the criminals (the net principle or, following the popular german expression, *nettoprinzip*) or whether it should cover all revenues (*bruttoprinzip* or gross principle).

It could be said that all the above items are dangerous, although here the dangerousness is not an intrinsic feature of the forfeited object but rather the result of its being connected to a criminal activity. Items connected to an offence (such as the means of the crime, or the products or profits of the crime) could be considered dangerous because they are somehow connected to unlawful activities, and hence potentially capable of furthering criminal activity, or disrupting or distorting public order and the legal economy. Nevertheless, such an approach could be criticised as it overemphasises the concept of dangerousness related to the crime. Here the discussion could be between proponents of two different approaches: the idea that whatever comes into contact with the crime is dangerous; and a more moderate view that only some items which show a specific and intrinsic link with the crime are dangerous. For instance, the forfeiture of a laptop could be viewed as the removal of a dangerous item only if the laptop were an essential element in the commission of the crime (as, for instance, in crimes against information systems, computer-related crimes or content-related crimes), but not if the laptop were merely used to exchange an email with an accomplice.

[67] For an analysis of the different fucntions of confiscation in relation to its objects, see J Vogel, 'The Legal Construction That Property Can Do Harm' in Rui and Sieber (n 6) 233, distinguishing between contraband, proceeds and instrumentalities.

A similar debate could concern the adoption of the gross principle or of the net principle when calculating the profits of a crime. Several authors believe that the use of a gross principle shows elements of punitiveness of the confiscatory measure.[68] It would seem that, while the taking away of net revenues is the effect of removing the economic distortion created by the crime, the forfeiting of all revenues following a gross principle goes a step further. Here too, however, the discussion remains open as to what part of the criminal profits could be considered dangerous with regard to harming the public order or distorting the economy.

VII. Confiscation Without Conviction

In the reflections above, the conclusion was reached that when confiscation targets objects or items regardless of an individual action, it cannot be considered to amount to a criminal penalty. The measure shall still require a reason of general interest for the forfeiture of the goods, but need not respect all safeguards of criminal law. In these cases, the confiscatory measure need not be preceded by a formal conviction for a criminal offence.

As previously mentioned, forms of non-conviction-based confiscation are present in a number of countries. This does not per se mean that such forms are legitimate. It is, however, a sign that the position claiming that confiscation is always a criminal penalty could hardly be defended even from a purely comparative perspective.

Forms of extended confiscation are even more popular. In extended confiscation, a convicted person is deprived of assets in connection with offences other than the one for which he has been convicted. Some might argue that extended confiscation is not a form of non-conviction-based confiscation because it requires a prior conviction. This is true formally, but in substance the assets forfeited with an extended order bear no direct relationship with the allegations for which the defendant has been found guilty. Property is forfeited here on the basis of the fact that the convicted person is dangerous or that he holds property which, though not linked with the crime, can (often presumptively) be linked with a more general criminal lifestyle.[69] The degree of such presumptions can vary significantly. Sometimes the presumption is formally not allowed, in that the judge must be convinced on the basis of existing evidence that a link between the property and a criminal activity exists; but the judge need not identify the crimes in

[68] Rui and Sieber, 'NCBC in Europe' (n 26) 263.

[69] As Boucht (n 17) 129 observes, 'this is normally achieved by removing the causation requirement between the criminal offence and the proceeds, and by watering down some of the traditional criminal procedural safeguards, for instance by reversing the burden of proof or lowering the standard of proof (or both)'.

detail.[70] In some cases, it is required that the prosecutor show that the property is connected with other (sometimes similar) offences perpetrated by the convicted person (offences for which no conviction has been passed), and the use of presumptions is tolerated.[71] In other cases, the link with other offences (other than the one for which a conviction was passed) is much milder: the law forfeits all exceeding income for which the convicted cannot prove a lawful acquisition.[72] When the link with the crime tends to vanish, the forfeiture of assets can no longer be justified on the basis of a derivation of property from the crime for which a conviction has been passed. Extended confiscation in this regard seems to constitute a form of punishment, at least in all those instances where there is no need to prove a link with the crime. In this respect, extended confiscation is a perfect example of measuring the relationship between crime, conviction and forfeiture.

It could be argued that extended confiscation is only passed at the end of proceedings characterised by all the safeguards of criminal law. Once more, the remark would not be entirely appropriate, because what matters is that the safeguards are applied with regard to an individual confronted with a specific allegation (offence). If property is forfeited at the end of the trial but for its connection with a crime for which no conviction was passed, it is true that the individual enjoyed the safeguards of criminal law, but with regard to an offence for which no confiscation was imposed; and on the other hand, the individual did not enjoy those safeguards with regard to the responsibility for the crime for which forfeiture was in the end adopted.

If further gains are forfeited, ie gains that bear no direct relation with the criminal conduct for which a conviction was passed, then the forfeiture of these further gains is in essence a form of financial penalty imposed on the defendant for the committed offence (more or less like a fine) with a view to punishing him or (most likely) to deterring him from crimes.

Even some forms of third party confiscation are non-conviction-based. When the innocent third party suffers a deprivation of assets, it endures a negative consequence without having been convicted. Therefore, the remark that the measure follows a conviction is not pertinent because it is the conviction of a person other than the one who bears the sacrifice. Here, however, it all depends on the reason behind the confiscation: if the confiscation is intended to remove dangerous or criminal property, the case is not problematic; if, however, the forfeiture of third parties' rights is the consequence of an extended confiscation, the situation falls under the situation above.

[70] Esser (n 6) 74.

[71] This is the case, for instance, for the Netherlands in Art 36e of the Criminal Code, which allows the judge to forfeit the illegally acquired gains.

[72] This is the case, for instance, of the Italian system, where the forfeiture is extended to all property for which the convicted person cannot give evidence of a legal title of acquisition (Art 12-*sexies* Decree Law 36 of 1992).

VIII. The Legitimate Scope of Confiscation of Conviction

It follows from the previous remarks that confiscation can be considered as a non-criminal measure when it targets assets and not actions (and unless the lawmaker has explicitly qualified it as a form of criminal penalty/measure). Its object must therefore be assets which are inherently (per se) dangerous or that are connected to a crime and for this reason deserve to be removed.

The link of property with the crime is particularly important, because this constitutes the *in rem* element, ie the element which ensures that what is targeted is the property, not the person (*actio in rem* and not *action contra personam*). In this respect, confiscation can be passed without conviction when it aims at removing the illegal proceeds of crime (such as means, gains and consequences of the crime). Is it comparable to unjust enrichment? A similar comparison was made in the *Dassa Foundations v Liechtenstein* case,[73] and less emphatically in *Walsh v UK*.[74] The parallel should not be overemphasised. In unjust enrichment, the aim of the measure is to restore the initial distribution of wealth. Confiscation is instead oriented more towards the protection of public order and the legal economy, and it pursues goals which go beyond the removal of unwarranted/unjustifiable profits. It would appear that confiscation can be more properly described either as a public order measure or, when talking about criminal profits, an 'economic measure', an instrument to protect the free market.[75]

When the above conditions are met, the removal of gains and other dangerous or criminal property should in principle be non-discretionary (*an* and *quantum*). The only cases in which confiscation could be lifted concern: (i) situations where the recovery of property would be too expensive, if the non-forfeiture does not significantly affect public order; or (ii) situations where the goods have meanwhile been acquired by bona fide third parties, as long as no disruption of public order would follow.

Besides these two orders of exceptions, there would seem to be no strong reason to confer further discretion on the authorities. As the Strasbourg Court noted in *Welch*, discretion seems logically connected more with the infliction of punishment than with a public order/economic measure aimed at removing unlawful and/or dangerous items.

[73] *Dassa Foundation and others v Liechtenstein* App No 696/05 (ECtHR, 23 December 2004).

[74] *Walsh* (n 42).

[75] For a similar, though not entirely equivalent, approach, see Vogel (n 67) 232 (finding the rationale behind confiscation in an economic analysis of criminal law).

IX. Countering Objections

Three objections can be raised against the idea of confiscation targeting property and thus not requiring an accompanying conviction.

The first objection is that assets cannot be considered guilty. Only people can in fact be guilty. In other words, the derivation of assets from a crime can be established only if all the features of the crime have been uncovered, including the subjective profile of the offender. After all, what if money is connected with a crime which was committed in the exercise of self-defence or in the presence of an excuse?

The counter objection here could well be that nothing prevents defences or excuses being considered in the (separate) proceedings for confiscation, just as a discussion on defences or excuses may take place in civil litigation concerning the restoration of a tort which also constituted an offence. But it is important here to reaffirm that, although the litigation can take into account specific individual circumstances, the forfeiture of criminal property does not per se require the attribution of guilt to a specific individual. It is sufficient that a crime, for which no defence is present, is identified without necessarily having to discuss the profile of the attribution of guilt.

The second objection is connected to the first one and concerns the impossibility for persons to challenge the confiscation order without asserting their own innocence concerning the crime. In essence, the argument here is that the only effective defence for a person could be to assert that they did not commit the offence. This would in essence represent a reversal of the burden of proof, which would breach the presumption of innocence. This argument fails to consider that it remains possible for a person to show and prove the legitimate acquisition of property. In any case, nothing precludes the lawmaker from excluding the use of potentially self-incriminating material in parallel/subsequent criminal trials.

One aspect in particular should be considered here: the use of presumptions is not infrequent in confiscation cases. A common presumption is that property in the possession of a person which is not proportionate to the income of that person is considered to be of criminal origin unless the holder can prove that it was lawfully acquired. In essence, such presumptions reduce the burden of proof upon the prosecution and shift most of the evidentiary burden onto the holder of the assets. In such cases, a defence based on the person's innocence would not be successful: the defendant needs to offer proof of a lawful purchase of the assets in question. However, as was argued above, and shall later be clarified, the use of too wide-ranging presumptions must be avoided in confiscation without conviction, because it would otherwise break the link between property and crime.

In this respect, one further aspect deserves reflection: if a person is required to prove the lawful acquisition of an item after a significant amount of time, the proof of the acquisition might be difficult. For example, it is difficult to give evidence of a lawful acquisition of an item which was acquired 20 or more years before.

The third objection concerns the risk of hardship for the innocent person (and the guilty). However, it should be possible to arrange for 'humanitarian' solutions, next to the provisions which allow the confiscation of assets. In Germany, for instance, the code of criminal procedure (§73c Strafprozeßordnung, StPO) provides for an exception to the rules on confiscation (including extended confiscation) if it would constitute an undue hardship for the concerned person ('soweit er fur den Betroffenen eine unbillige Harte ware'). The expression is general and refers to hardship for the person affected—an expression which is broader than just hardship for the defendant. Furthermore, it should be considered that the protection of bona fide third parties should in principle be granted. If the measure is an economic measure aimed at avoiding distortion of the market, it should be said that when certain goods have reached innocent third parties, the protection of such parties should prevail.

X. A Minor Evil?

The discussion on whether a measure of confiscation without conviction would be compliant with our grid of fundamental rights also needs to consider one further factor: the risk of allowing other, more dangerous, legislative trends.

In some countries, new crimes have been introduced which punish the possession of properties linked to crime or criminal activity. A perfect example of such a trend is the provision of Article 321-6 of the French Criminal Code,[76] which punishes the possession of property disproportionate to the person's income if the person does not offer justification for it and if the person entertains relations with convicted criminals.[77]

Offences of this sort represent an attempt to introduce a mechanism which is de facto equivalent to what could be pursued with a confiscatory measure, but go a step further. They criminalise people for their presumptive danger. What is punished is a status (the fact of being in possession) more than a behaviour. The conduct of the offence is simply the failure to give adequate evidence of one's innocence. The reversal of the burden of proof here becomes the basis for the conviction. The person has in essence to show her innocence, and there is no doubt about the stigma which accompanies a conviction. Similar offences go against

[76] The article provides: '1. Le fait de ne pas pouvoir justifier de ressources correspondant à son train de vie ou de ne pas pouvoir justifier de l'origine d'un bien détenu, tout en étant en relations habituelles avec une ou plusieurs personnes qui soit se livrent à la commission de crimes ou de délits punis d'au moins cinq ans d'emprisonnement et procurant à celles-ci un profit direct ou indirect, soit sont les victimes d'une de ces infractions, est puni d'une peine de trois ans d'emprisonnement et de 75 000 euros d'amende. 2. Est puni des mêmes peines le fait de faciliter la justification de ressources fictives pour des personnes se livrant à la commission de crimes ou de délits punis d'au moins cinq ans d'emprisonnement et procurant à celles-ci un profit direct ou indirect.'

[77] *Aboufadda* (n 29).

several basic principles of criminal law, from the legality principle to the presumption of innocence. They even breach the harm principle, because mere possession without justification cannot be considered harmful. It might be dangerous, but it is certainly not per se harmful.[78]

Just like confiscation, these offences are based on a presumption of dangerousness, which is grounded on some symptomatic traces. Unlike confiscation, these offences target the person and not the property. In that respect, they are more aggressive than confiscation and pose greater risks to individual liberties. Nonetheless, they could survive judicial scrutiny thanks to the deferential approach of courts when scrutinising the shape and content of criminal offences. The French provision of Article 321-6 came under the attention of the Strasbourg Court in a case concerning suspicious funds coming from drug trafficking. The applicants owned property which was disproportionate to the income. The authorities believed that it was the fruit of the drug trafficking activity of their son. The defendants could not give sufficient evidence of a legitimate acquisition. They were convicted and the family house was confiscated. The Court found no breach of the ECHR with regard to Article 1 of Protocol 1 or Article 8.[79] On both points, the Court found that the legal basis was present, and that the measure was proportionate to the legitimate aim pursued. It remains to be seen whether in a future case the provision could survive a challenge brought under Article 7 ECHR. In light of the arguments set out above, the answer should be in the negative, but, as mentioned, the degree of discretion which national lawmakers enjoy in front of the ECtHR (and the majority of national constitutional courts) might allow such an offence to survive judicial scrutiny even under that parameter.

The risk of opposing confiscation without conviction is that it may induce the lawmakers to introduce more of these sorts of crimes. In this respect, confiscation can be viewed as a 'minor evil' compared to the higher risks to liberties and safeguards which accompany the choice of criminalisation.[80]

However, this does not mean that, as a worse punishment option, confiscation without conviction should be allowed without limits. If it is possible to introduce forms of confiscation without conviction, it does not follow that all sorts of confiscation without conviction are possible. Certain limits must be set out and respected.

[78] It is also for this reason that any attempt to ground the confiscation of illegal assets on the principle of harm should be viewed with scepticism.

[79] *Aboufadda* (n 29).

[80] The opposite view is taken by M Fazekas and E Nanopoulos, 'The Effectiveness of EU Law: Insight from the EU Legal Framework on Asset Confiscation' (2016) 24 *Journal of Crime, Criminal Law and Criminal Justice* 39, 50, when raising doubts on the viability of a uniform European regime of confiscation.

XI. Limits

It stems from the above considerations that confiscation without conviction should be permitted only when there is a link between some property and the crime. The crime (or type of crime) with which a link is established should be determined with some precision. A general reference to a criminal lifestyle, based on rumours or very weak circumstantial evidence, would not suffice. It must be required that the derivation of the property from the crime be established on the basis of evidence which is sufficiently cogent.

The use of presumptions can be allowed, but if such presumptions go as far as to erode the causal link between the property and the crime, then the measure turns into a punitive one, because it is the dangerousness of the individual that justifies the forfeiture and no longer the dangerousness of some property.[81] For instance, the assumption that 'all property passing through the offender's hands over a six-year period is the fruit of drug trafficking unless he can prove otherwise'[82] would seem too far reaching in that it breaches a direct connection between the property and the crime. In this respect, the use of assumptions based on the possession of disproportionate wealth (compared to income) is per se insufficient unless it is accompanied by further, stronger evidence (which could also be circumstantial, but still requires the establishment of a link with a criminal activity). In essence, it can be said that the stronger the presumption and the weaker the link with crime, the more relevant becomes the subjective link between property and a dangerous individual (which turns the measure from a public order/economic measure into a punishment, with the liability for some undefined forms of criminal behaviour remaining implicit in the adoption of the measure). And some parts of the Italian anti-mafia legislation seem in this respect slightly too far reaching.[83]

Secondly, forfeiture must be limited to objects which are directly related to crime. This does not exclude the confiscation of objects which are obtained as a transformation of gains/profits of the crime, as long as this transformation can clearly be traced. The reasoning requires that close attention be paid to value confiscation. When value confiscation is applied simply on the basis that the profits of crime are not found in a person's possession, the underlying judgment is that the person is considered to be the beneficiary of the crime, hence she holds a responsibility for the crime. When value confiscation is applied beyond cases where there are traces of an individual action to hide or transform criminal property, it would seem to carry an intrinsic punitive element.

[81] This could be expressed with the words used in *Welch* (n 35), that no 'sweeping statutory presumptions' should be tolerated.

[82] As was the case in *Welch* (n 36) § 33.

[83] See my position in Panzavolta and Flor (n 13) 157.

Finally, it is important in any case that proportionality be respected, following the rules spelled out by Article 1 Protocol 1 ECHR[84] and by Article 52 of the Charter of Fundamental Rights of the European Union in relation to Article 17 of the same Charter (and not directly Article 49 of the Charter of Fundamental Rights of the European Union, CFR, which refers to the proportionality principle with regard to criminal penalties).

Conclusions

With the above arguments, the chapter has tried to shed some light on confiscation and its nature. The difficulty of looking at confiscation is that it is a many-sided concept. The attempt to reach a unitary vision is always fraught with difficulty because it frequently happens that the aspects which capture the attention of some are not the same as those that are the focus of others. Being mindful of this difficulty entails that any general remark must be made with great caution and attention.

The picture of confiscation is highly diverse from country to country also in light of the different accompanying qualifications. The EU instruments attempts no harmonisation of categories, hence the present fragmented situation is likely to remain unchanged for the future, unless an attempt to streamline the nature of confiscation is undertaken by the national lawmakers. The points which deserve attention in this regard are whether confiscation constitutes punishment or not and, if so, whether it is a principal penalty or a secondary one.

In light of the given arguments, it seems plausible to argue that not all forms of confiscation need be viewed as a form of criminal penalty. It is possible, in fact, to draw a distinction between forms of confiscation which target the property for its dangerous nature or for it being related to a crime and forms of confiscation which target an action. Confiscation does not constitute a penalty and therefore does not require a prior conviction if it targets dangerous or criminal property. On the contrary, a prior criminal conviction (or at least an assessment of guilt carried out in accordance with the safeguards of criminal law) is needed if the confiscation order targets the conduct of a person, if it is a reaction to what a specific person has done (or has failed to do).

Given this premise, it would seem appropriate to move all 'non-punishment' cases of confiscation outside of criminal law. In several cases, the confiscation of dangerous and criminal property (means and profits of crime directly related to the offence) in fact still retains a criminal label at the national level, with the consequence that stronger safeguards apply. It seems that greater efficiency could be

[84] See particularly the principles spelled out in *Paullet* (n 30).

achieved here without endangering human rights by taking these forms of confiscation into the civil or administrative realm, similarly to what happens in the civil asset forfeiture schemes of common law.

The next challenges for non-conviction-based confiscation, then, concern a greater effort of clarification and, in some cases, harmonisation with regard to specific points: the identification (and mutual recognition) of competent authorities involved in the recovery of criminal assets; the powers to be given to these authorities in order for them to investigate and trace the criminal assets when acting outside of criminal proceedings; and the reduction of the gap between national procedures and standards of judgments. In essence, the challenge is to ensure a body of common rules for non-conviction-based-confiscation in order to ensure sufficient trust between countries.

2

The History of Confiscation Laws: From the Book of Exodus to the War on White-Collar Crime

MICHAËL FERNANDEZ-BERTIER*

Introduction

Over the past decades, the legal literature has highlighted the correlation between unlawful conduct and money. The importance of the financial element of crime has been increasingly acknowledged. As a result, criminal policies focusing on the deprivation of ill-gotten gains have surfaced throughout the world[1] and have been constantly evolving.[2] To comprehend the progressive emergence of criminal policies focused on property, where criminal asset recovery strategies stand today and where they are orienting themselves, it is important to first fully understand their origins and how they have been cemented into our modern laws to become an integral part of the very fabric of criminal law and criminal procedure.

This chapter therefore aims to identify some general trends of the evolution of legal mechanisms by which governments confiscate[3] property associated with criminal conduct, from the Bible's Exodus to the twenty-first-century war on white-collar crime. First, the chapter provides for a general yet succinct analysis of the ancient confiscation laws which flourished from ancient times to the early twentieth century and can be considered to be the ancestors of the modern apparatuses (Section I). The focus is then switched to modern confiscation laws,

* PhD Candidate, Université catholique de Louvain (Belgium); Lecturer at Solvay Brussels School of Economics and Management; Member of the Brussels and New York Bars.

[1] MM Gallant, *Money Laundering and the Proceeds of Crime. Economic Crime and Civil Remedies* (Cheltenham, Edward Elgar Publishing, 2005) Preface, vi.

[2] SD Cassella, *Asset Forfeiture Law in the United States*, 2nd edn (New York, Juris Publishing, 2012) Preface, iv.

[3] Or 'forfeit', as referred to in certain common law systems—the notions of 'confiscation' and 'forfeiture' both being used as synonyms in this contribution for simplification purposes. Their strict interchangeability can, however, be challenged (eg when comparing the UK and US terminology).

ie the rebirth and revolution of asset deprivation tools from the second part of the twentieth century onwards as an entirely new crime fight strategy—under the policy slogan 'crime should not pay' (Section II).

As far as the scope *ratione loci* is concerned, this discussion gives a general description of the evolution of confiscation instruments that have developed throughout the Western world. Whereas the literature has traditionally outlined the history of either common law or (to a lesser extent) civil law traditions, the stance taken here is to study the parallel (and sometimes overlapping) evolution of confiscation laws in both legal families with a view to highlighting their possible interactions. With the progressive establishment of the nation states, a closer look is then taken at the specific national legislations that have been the primary influence on chasing criminal property in recent history—namely, those of the USA, the UK and Italy.[4] The focus is put on the horizontal legal transplanting of confiscation laws.[5] Very limited attention is given to vertical transplants since relevant inter/supranational instruments within the field of asset recovery (such as the United Nations (UN), the Financial Action Task Force (FATF), the Council of Europe (CoE) and the European Union (EU)) are discussed in other chapters of this book.

Concerning the scope *ratione materiae* of this contribution, it essentially focuses on the 'confiscation' of assets (which embraces the notion of 'forfeiture' when applicable),[6] ie the permanent deprivation of (illicit) property, which entails the transfer of their ownership to the state.[7] Confiscation can be 'general' (or of 'estate') or 'special' in nature. The former, which was extensively used in the past, entails the deprivation of the entire estate of an individual after his conviction. In contrast, special confiscation, which prevails today, targets assets which are specifically related to crime; it is not, however, automatically connected to a prior conviction. As regards the nature of the assets subject to special confiscation, the following developments primarily contemplate two forms of property: the instrumentalities of crime (ie property used for the commission of an offence) and the proceeds of crime (ie any economic advantages derived from an offence).[8] A third

[4] The USA and Italy are considered to be pioneers in elaborating modern confiscation laws and have done so contemporaneously; as for the UK—besides the fact that England originally exported its common law system to the USA, hence thoroughly influenced that latter's confiscation tradition—it possesses one of the most comprehensive asset recovery legislative frameworks in the world and it is located at the convergence of two legal traditions (ie a common law tradition jurisdiction within the European—and civil law—Union).

[5] 'Legal transplants' may be defined as the 'borrowing and transmissibility of rules from one society or system to another'. A Watson, *Legal Transplants: An Approach to Comparative Law* (Edinburgh, Scottish Academic Press, 1974) 19.

[6] eg in the USA and the UK.

[7] There has been a noticeable lack of interest in the literature as to the question of the temporary deprivation of alleged criminally related property. Only recently did political (and hence legislative) authorities realise the fundamental need for 'freezing' or 'seizing' (alleged) criminally related property at a very early stage of proceedings with a view to its subsequent permanent deprivation.

[8] The proposed terminology emanates from both common law jurisdictions and supranational instruments. Yet civil law systems employ a different and more diverse classification than exposed, such as the 'object', 'instruments', 'product' and 'profits' of the offence.

type of confiscable property that is seldom cited, contraband (ie unlawful goods per se that cannot be possessed or produced), is not discussed given its limited interest as far as historical developments are concerned.[9]

I. Ancient Confiscation Laws: From Confiscation of Estate to Confiscation of the Instrumentalities of Crime

The concept of depriving the assets of an individual where associated with crime is as old as the hills. From ancient times to the early twentieth century, the birth and evolution of the concept of confiscation within the Western world was steadily the object of two parallel streams: (i) the legal tradition from which the mechanisms emerged; (ii) and the procedural nature of the measures utilised. This dual movement is noteworthy, given the considerable influence it had (and still has today; see below, Section II) on the birth and evolution of the confiscation of dirty assets.

(i) After a brief history of common domination of the Roman rule in the first centuries AD, Britain and continental Europe's legal cultures progressively and increasingly diverged.[10] This schism's apex resulted, around the twelfth century, in the contemporaneous development and subsequent consolidation of the civil law[11] and common law divide.[12] Hence, confiscation mechanisms flourished across the occidental culture within two distinct legal system traditions. This dichotomy influenced considerably how they emerged and expanded through the ages and jurisdictions.

(ii) Early history showed the development of two particular judicial procedures of recovering criminally related property, ie *in personam* ('against the person') and *in rem* ('against the thing') proceedings. The *in personam* procedure ordinarily relied on the prior conviction of an individual, whereas the latter was originally based on the legal fiction that the property itself was guilty of an offence. *In rem* confiscation could thus be sought outside of criminal proceedings and without any consideration as to the culpability or prosecution of its owner. Whereas *in personam* deprivation spread concurrently in both civil and common law systems

[9] The two exceptions to this affirmation are the US Prohibition era fight against bootlegging (contraband alcohol) and the increased international fight against drug trafficking (contraband substances).

[10] Especially under the Anglo-Saxon dynasty, which lasted from the 6th to the 11th century.

[11] Also referred to as 'continental' or 'Romano-Germanic' law. The notion of 'civil law' derives from *ius civile*, ie the law applicable to Roman citizens. The civil/continental law roots come from the compilation of Roman law by Justinian in the 6th century AD.

[12] Whereas it first emerged after the Norman Conquest of the 11th century, then coexisted with other systems of law, 'common law' triumphed in England in the 17th century. See also TFT Plucknett, *A Concise History of the Common Law* (Indianapolis, Liberty Fund, 2010).

(A), the *in rem* conception of confiscation was exclusively endemic to common law jurisdictions (B).[13]

A. The Birth of *In Personam* Confiscation of Estate in Civil/Common Law Jurisdictions

In personam criminal confiscation is the most widespread device developed historically. It found its roots in ancient times, flourished under Roman rule and pursued its evolution separately in both common law and civil law traditions. The conviction-based instrument first emerged in the form of confiscation of estate. It mostly remained so until the nineteenth century despite its harsh character and the various criticisms it suffered—inter alia, estate confiscation implied that the family and heirs of the guilty defendant had also to forfeit their rights to the property. It was then replaced by special criminal confiscation, which has since prevailed.

Conviction-based deprivation can be traced as far back as to ancient Greece,[14] where criminal law provided for economic sanctions such as fines and confiscation. However, confiscation was considered to be more severe than fines, and was thus only used on rare occasions.[15] Under Roman law, not only was confiscation often expressly enacted, but it was also the tacit consequence of every death penalty.[16] The punishment was present in the Cornelian Law of the first century BC, which instituted that assassins and poisoners shall be sentenced to exile and the confiscation of all their property.[17] It was subsequently reaffirmed in, among others, Paul's *Sentences*,[18] then enshrined in Justinian's *Digest*, which imposed the deprivation of all property of the condemned as a punishment for specific offences.[19] The codification of the Roman law by Emperor Justinian in the sixth century AD (including the *Digest*) became the legal basis for sentencing on the European continent, and remained so throughout the Middle Ages and modern times.[20] Partial and total confiscation doctrines of Roman law were thus revived and largely implemented

[13] ie Britain and the USA. The situation has changed in the recent past since some civil law jurisdictions have been implementing non-conviction-based forms of confiscation (see Section II below).

[14] That is, around the 5th and 4th centuries BC.

[15] G Hallevy, *The Right to Be Punished. Modern Doctrinal Sentencing* (Heidelberg, Springer, 2013) 5. The author refers to SC Todd, *The Shape of Athenian Law* (1995) 143.

[16] G Drage, *The Criminal Code of the German Empire*, 2nd edn (Clark, NJ, Lawbook Exchange, 2007) 87.

[17] As mentioned in Justinian's *Digest* (*Dig*) 48.8.3.5 (6th century). For an English translation of the *Digest*, see SP Scott, *The Civil Law Including the Twelve Tables, the Institutes of Gaius, the Rules of Ulpian, the Opinions of Paulus, the Enactments*, 6th edn (Clark, NJ, The Lawbook Exchange, 2006).

[18] In combination to exile for homicide. *Pauli Sententiae* 5.23.1, which dates back to the 3rd century AD.

[19] Among which falsification and forgery. See *Dig* 48.10.1.13. See also *Dig* 48.20.1. Sometimes the confiscation of (at least) a third of the property would be established. See, eg, *Dig* 48.7.1.

[20] Hallevy, *The Right to Be Punished* 6.

by judges until the beginning of the eighteenth century,[21] since general confiscation was the punishment for more than 400 crimes across Europe.[22] It can also be argued that the policy slogan 'crime should not pay' emerged from Roman law, for the *Digest* affirmed that 'no one can improve his condition by his own wrong'.[23] Looking to England, forfeiture laws originated during the Anglo-Saxon period, which started in the sixth century and prevailed until the eleventh.[24] Yet it is through the consolidation of the common law that criminal confiscation of estate became deep rooted in Britain, via the fifteenth-century acts of 'attainder'.[25] Attainder, the oldest and best known[26] form of confiscation of early English law, was a punishment for counts of treason and felonies. It was likened to the judicial declaration of civil death,[27] for it led the convicted person to forfeit all his lands and personal property to the Crown.[28] The success and recourse to estate confiscation was (at least partially) due to the large revenue it generated for the Crown.[29] But as the feudal system evolved, the application of general confiscation narrowed.[30]

With the advent of the modern era, civil law countries reaffirmed the use of confiscation as a criminal penalty. This revival, however, led to the progressive disappearance of confiscation of estate during the Age of Enlightenment,[31] for its abolition was considered at least as crucial as the restriction of the death penalty.[32] Some of the most important thinkers of the time stood up against the measure.

[21] C Calisse, *A History of Italian Law*, vol 1 (Washington, Beardbooks, 1928) 408; A Monti, 'Illegitimate Appropriation or Just Punishment? The Confiscation of Property in *Ancient Régime* Criminal Law and Doctrine' in L Lorenzetti, M Barbot and L Mocarelli (eds), *Property Rights and their Violations. Expropriations and Confiscations, 16th-20th Centuries* (Bern, Peter Lang, 2012) 4.

[22] 'From homicide to forgery of coins, to apostasy'. Monti (ibid) 5, referring to G Claro, *Volumen alias liber quintus, Venetiis, apud Ioannem Antonium ab Antoniis* (1570) § *Finalis*, q 78.

[23] 'Nemo ex suo delicto meliorem suam condicionem facere potest'. Ulpiano, *Dig*. 50.17.134.1.

[24] Until the Norman Conquest of Britain in 1066. A D'Amato and SB Presser, 'Anglo-Saxon Law' in *The Guide to American Law: Everyone's Legal Encyclopedia* (Eagen, MN, West Group, 1983) vol 1, 251, available at anthonydamato.law.northwestern.edu.

[25] Attainder for treason or felony implied three principal consequences for the person: confiscation of all good and chattels, lands and tenements to the king; corruption of blood; and extinction of civil rights. GJ Chin, 'The New Civil Death: Rethinking Punishment in the Era of Mass Conviction' (2012) 160 *University of Pennsylvania Law Review* 1789, 1794 (quoting the New York Court of Appeal in *Avery v Everett*, 18 NE 148, 150 (NY 1888)); JR Lander, 'Attainder and Forfeiture' (1961) 4(2) *The Historical Journal* 119.

[26] JR Maxeiner, 'Bane of American Forfeiture Law—Banished at Last?' (1977) 62 *Cornell Law Review* 768, 770.

[27] C Doyle, *Crime and Forfeiture* (Congressional Research Service, 2015) 2.

[28] WJ Hughes and EH O'Connell Jr, 'In Personam (Criminal) Forfeiture and Federal Drug Felonies: An Expansion of a Harsh English Tradition into a Modern Era' (1984) 11(4) *Pepperdine Law Review* 613, 619, referring to JJ Finkelstein, 'The Goring Ox: Some Historical Perspectives on Deodands, Forfeitures, Wrongful Death and the Western Notion of Sovereignty' (1973) 46 *Temple Law Quarterly* 169, 183.

[29] Maxeiner (n 26) 773.

[30] Hughes and O'Connell (n 28) 619.

[31] ie during the 18th century—with some exceptions, such as in France.

[32] M Pieth, 'Financing of Terrorism: Following the Money' in M Pieth (ed), *Financing Terrorism* (Dordrecht, Kluwer Academic Publishers, 2012) 117.

For example, Beccaria considered general confiscation to be 'one of the baleful and authorised injustices carried out and approved for centuries, even by educated men and in free republics'.[33] The underlying idea was that punishments had to impact solely on those guilty of the offence (not their family or heirs) and be proportionate to it.[34] Hence, following the birth and extension of doctrinal debates as regards its legitimacy and atrocity, and starting from the second part of the eighteenth century, confiscation of estate was gradually repealed by enlightened despots such as Leopold II of Tuscany in his reform of criminal law.[35] Special (or partial) confiscation of criminal assets—ie the deprivation of the instrumentalities, contraband and other objects specifically related to the crime—started to replace general confiscation.[36] The concept of confiscating the proceeds of crime only appeared in the course of the twentieth century. Similarly to what happened in civil law, general confiscation survived only briefly in the modern era in common law jurisdictions—principally because of the harsh consequences of attainder on innocent descendants.[37] The US Constitution banned it in late eighteenth century,[38] whereas the First US Congress simply prohibited the use of *in personam* confiscation of estate as a punishment for federal crimes,[39] leading to the almost complete disappearance of criminal confiscation for the next couple of centuries.[40] Britain abolished the use of general confiscation in the last third of the nineteenth century.[41] Like the USA, the UK reinstated the use of special criminal confiscation of contraband, instrumentalities and the proceeds of crime during the second half of the twentieth century—mainly as a new means to tackle efficiently the illicit gains derived from the drug trade (and organised crime) and then all forms of acquisitive crime (see Section II below).

[33] Beccaria was already of the opinion that punishments should impact only the convicted person since criminal liability was personal. Monti (n 21) 1.

[34] Monti (n 21) 2, 14; nonetheless, 'confiscation of the estate seemed to never completely disappear. It has been outlined that is would return, when liberal political system were in crisis' (16).

[35] *Edict of the Grand Duke of Tuscany, for the Reform of Criminal Law in His Dominions* (Tuscany, W Eyred, 1789) 22.

[36] eg the French Penal Code of 1810 (which established penalties of both special and general confiscation, arts 7 and 11); the Belgian Penal Code of 1867 (which instituted special confiscation at Art 43—while general confiscation was banished by Art 12 of the Constitution of 1831); the German Imperial Penal Code of 1871 (which also provided for special confiscation. Drage (n 16) 87.

[37] ie 'corruption of blood'. Maxeiner (n 26) 774, 779.

[38] ie in 1787 (to the exception of the offence of treason). *United States v Martino*, 681 F2d 952, 962 (5th Circ 1982); Hughes and O'Connell (n 28) 614.

[39] Congress did so only a few years after the Constitutional ban. See Act of April 30, 1790, Ch 9, § 24, 1 Stat 117 ('no conviction or judgment … shall work corruption of blood, or any forfeiture of estate'). See also Hughes and O'Connell (n 28) 619.

[40] MR Ford, 'Criminal Forfeiture and the Sixth Amendment's Right to Jury Trial Post-Booker' (2007) 101 *Northwestern University Law Review* 1371, 1403. According to Maxeiner (n 26) 779, some confiscations continued to be ordered within criminal proceedings, and in personam.

[41] It was abolished in Britain in 1870 (and finally repealed for outlawry in 1938). RT Naylor, 'Follow-the-Money Methods in Crime Control Policy', study prepared for the Nathanson Centre for the Study of Organized Crime and Corruption, York University, Toronto, December 1999, available at www.ncjrs.gov/nathanson/washout.html.

In brief, criminal confiscation laws originally emerged both in common and civil law traditions in the form of general confiscation. They progressively vanished starting from the eighteenth century to be replaced by the prevailing form of deprivation we see today: special conviction-based confiscation of illicit property.

B. The Birth of *In Rem* Confiscation in Common Law Jurisdictions

It has been argued that the very first historical model of confiscation of criminally related property—and the birth of *in rem* confiscation—emerged in biblical times:[42] the book of Exodus provided for the (confiscation and) sacrifice of the ox that had gored a man, with no need for the prior conviction of its owner.[43] Yet some have debated whether said concept of deprivation was in any real sense a confiscation.[44]

The genuine genesis of non-conviction-based deprivation of assets that were used to commit a wrongdoing (ie instrumentalities of crime) can rather be traced back to medieval English law. After the conquest of Britain by the Normans and the emergence of the common law around the twelfth century, the institution of the deodand instrument developed somewhat in correlation to the biblical tradition.[45] The confiscation of the deodand, ie the object that accidently caused the death of a person,[46] is said to have given rise to the (ancient) legal fiction of the 'guilty property' and to the *in rem* theory.[47] The deodand mechanism was largely used during medieval times, but was abolished in England in the middle of the nineteenth century.[48] Despite its existence in Britain, no similar *in rem* device existed in Roman law or modern civil law during the same period. Its adoption and use in the USA seems equally inexistent.[49]

[42] *United States v 785 St Nicholas Ave* 983 F2d 396, 401 (1993). See also BT Johnson, 'Restoring Civility—The Civil Asset Forfeiture Reform Act of 2000: Baby Steps Towards a More Civilized Forfeiture Regime' (2001) 35 *Indian Law Review* 1045, 1047; M Van den Berg, 'Proposing a Transactional Approach to Civil Forfeiture Reform' (2015) 163 *University of Pennsylvania Law Review* 867, 873; D Pimentel, 'Forfeitures Revisited: Bringing Principle to Practice in Federal Court' (Fall 2012) 13 *Nevada Law Journal* 1, 8.

[43] Exodus 21:28, 'if an ox gores a man or a woman, that they die: then the ox shall be surely stoned, and his flesh shall not be eaten; but the owner of the ox shall be quit'.

[44] Since the ox was not 'regarded as the instrument by which its owner had killed the man'. Finkelstein (n 28) 185.

[45] Deodand derives from *deo dandum*, ie 'to be given to God'; its construction can be traced back to the 13th century. Finkelstein (n 28) 170 ff; OW Holmes Jr, *The Common Law* (Boston, The Law Book Exchange, 1881) 24.

[46] eg the ox, the knife, the cart, the sword. Holmes (ibid) 25.

[47] *Calero-Toledo v Pearson Yacht Co* 416 US 663, 680–83 (1974); Maxeiner (n 26) 770. Yet Maxeiner opines that 'reliance upon deodand as a general forfeiture principle of early English law is probably misplaced' (772).

[48] Deodands Act of 1846, 9 & 10 Victoria, ch 62.

[49] Calero-Toledo v Pearson Yacht Co 416 US 663, 682–83.

Notwithstanding the above, the modern form of non-conviction-based confiscation such as is implemented in contemporary common law jurisdictions is generally seen as a heritage of the British Navigation Acts of the mid-seventieth century. Said Acts allowed for the confiscation of an entire ship whose owner or master had violated customs or revenue laws.[50] The deprivation was ordered through the filing of a civil claim 'against the thing', ie *in rem*. Said procedure replaced the impractical prosecution of the individual responsible for the wrongdoing, given their absence due to being overseas.[51] In 1789, the First US Congress used the British Acts as a model to introduce a confiscation mechanism of the vessel for the collection of custom duties with no need of prior criminal conviction of any individual.[52] Various offences—among which were those related to the slave trade and piracy—led later on to the *in rem* confiscation of ships under federal law.[53] Despite multiple constitutional challenges against the mechanism, the US Supreme Court upheld its validity.[54] The following century resulted in a limited expansion and even application of the *in rem* instrument within both the USA and UK jurisdictions.[55]

The most remarkable evolution of *in rem* deprivation took place from the last third of the twentieth century onwards: starting with the response to the growth of criminal organisations and drug trade. The non-conviction-based mechanism, which the UK only implemented in the early twenty-first century, was and still is mostly a monopoly of common law jurisdictions (see Section II below).

Put briefly, ancient *in rem* confiscation laws emerged in common law systems exclusively in the form of special confiscation. The mechanism was transformed in the twentieth century into modern forms of non-conviction-based devices that are currently spreading across the Western world.

II. Modern Confiscation Laws: The Birth and Exponential Development of Confiscation of the Proceeds of Crime

Between the early nineteenth century (in civil law jurisdictions) and the late twentieth century (in common law systems), and following the progressive

[50] The liability apparently extended to employees as well. Maxeiner (n 26) 774.

[51] *Austin v United States* 509 US 602 (1993), 615–16. Guilt was therefore not required and the *in rem* legal fiction created.

[52] Act of July 31, 1789, ch 5, §§ 12, 36, 1 Stat 29, 39, 47 (repealed); *The Palmyra* 25 US 1, 14–15 (1827).

[53] See, eg, the Act of 3 March 1819; Cassella (n 2) 29; Hughes and O'Connell (n 28) 618.

[54] *The Palmyra* (n 52). See also *United States v Brig Malek Adhel* 43 US 210 (1844).

[55] An exception was made for the increased confiscation of vehicles used for bootlegging, ie for transporting contraband liquor during the American Prohibition era of the 1920s–30s. M Williams, J Holcomb, T Kovandzic and S Bullock, 'Policing for Profit. The Abuse of Civil Asset Forfeiture' (Arlington, Institute for Justice, March 2010) 10.

ban of general confiscation across jurisdictions (see Section I.A above), special criminal confiscation of assets was reinstalled as part of the sentence of convicted offenders.[56] At that time, the deprivation was mainly ordered against the contraband and instrumentalities of an unlawful conduct.[57] The concept of confiscating the proceeds of the convicted person's illicit activities was virtually nonexistent until the late twentieth century,[58] ie until the impetus of the US Congress and the birth of 'the age of the proceeds'.[59]

The last third of the twentieth century hence incurred a dramatic change in focus when it came to targeting criminal property: for the first time, legislators allowed for the confiscation of proceeds of crime as a means to tackle more efficiently the scourge of organised crime and the drug trade.[60] At that time, criminals could enjoy the fruits of their illicit activities when released from prison, for no device existed to target said property. Over time, however, and in light of the alleged efficacy of targeting criminal proceeds, the instrument was progressively extended to almost all forms of acquisitive crime. Today, depriving wrongdoers from their unlawful profits is a major crime-control strategy worldwide. The following developments hence mostly focus on the recent concept of confiscation of the proceeds of crime and the exponential development of modern laws pursuing efficacy and efficiency purposes. Less attention is devoted below to the divides between (i) common law and civil law and (ii) *in rem* and *in personam*.

(i) When it comes to the distinction between common law and civil law, one can observe a slow but progressive harmonisation of the two traditions within the last decades through the use of legal transplants (mostly in the form of reinforced influence of the former on civil law systems).[61] Although the dichotomy is still relevant today, the strict common/civil law distinction appears to be less clear-cut than hitherto, and might be gradually fading away: a moderate but progressive intermingling of legal traditions is taking place based on the confluence of global criminal policies targeting dirty assets and the political discourse that 'crime should not pay'.

(ii) On the other hand, the use of *in rem–in personam* terminology has been declining recently. This may, in part, be because the idea that property could be considered guilty of an offence 'sounds strange to the modern ear'.[62] The legal

[56] Conviction-based confiscation is traditionally qualified either as a 'penalty' or as a 'security measure'.

[57] Accordingly, Cassella (n 2) 900.

[58] One exception might consist in the Italian Penal Code (Art 240), which had already established in its 1931 version the possibility of confiscating the 'profit' of crime following conviction of a defendant.

[59] Gallant (n 1) 1.

[60] In parallel with the recovery of instrumentalities, which is still intensively used—especially when it comes to money and other property directed to commit crime.

[61] On the recent Americanisation of civil law countries, see M Siems, *Comparative Law (Law in Context)* (Cambridge, Cambridge University Press, 2015) 203.

[62] Cassella (n 2) 31.

fiction is outdated.[63] It has given way to more modern concepts of *in rem* confiscation that allow the government to assume title to criminally tainted property.[64] Hence, distinguishing between non-conviction-based (mostly civil/administrative) and conviction-based (criminal) instruments seems more suitable today than the former dichotomy—though they embrace similar, albeit not identical, realities.

A. The 1970–80s War on Drugs and War on Organised Crime: The Rebirth of Confiscation Laws and the Focus on the Proceeds of Crime

It is traditionally recognised that the cornerstone of the emergence of criminal policies devoted to depriving criminals from their illicit proceeds lies in the American impetus of the early 1970s and its subsequent influence on the rest of the Western world.

After having banished estate deprivation in the late eighteenth century (see Section I.A above), the concept of criminal confiscation remained virtually nonexistent in American law for a couple of centuries. In 1970, for the first time, the US Congress considered confiscation as an anti-crime initiative.[65] It revived conviction-based confiscation as a new approach to tackling both organised crime[66] and the drug trade.[67] The modern deprivation instrument and new criminal sanction rapidly became an established feature of federal law enforcement.[68] Hence, in 1970, within the scope of an all-out 'war on organized crime',[69] Congress decided to use confiscation as a way to tackle the inefficiency of traditional forms of punishment against the organised crime industry[70] through focusing on the criminal enterprise's source of economic power itself, ie the lifeblood of

[63] The fiction was 'about as irrational and unjust a proposition as a sober mind can concoct'. Finkelstein (n 28) 257.

[64] Cassella (n 2) 34.

[65] HJ Garretson, 'Federal Criminal Forfeiture: A Royal Pain in the Assets' (2008) 18 *Review of Law and Social Justice* 45, 46.

[66] For developments regarding the concept and history of organised crime in the USA—especially during the 1960s–80s, see TS Bynum (ed), *Organized Crime in America: Concepts and Controversies* (New York, Criminal Justice Press, 1987); L Paoli and C Fijnaut (eds), *Organized Crime in Europe. Concepts, Patterns and Control Policies in the European Union and Beyond* (Dordrecht, Springer, 2004) 24.

[67] Most criminal organisations were involved in drug trafficking because of the large profits derived from such activities. Hence, the 'war on drugs' and the 'war on organized crime' were already correlated to some degree in the 1970s.

[68] Ford (n 40) 1373.

[69] Which was declared by President Nixon on 11 February 1969. JR Nash, *The Great Pictorial History of World Crime*, vol 2 (Lanham, Rowman & Littlefield, 2004) 355.

[70] In criminal organisations, new people stepped forward immediately to replace convicted felons—with little or no impact on the enterprise itself. The focus on confiscation was aimed at attacking the foundations of the organisation directly: 'as long as the property of organized crime remains, new leaders will step forward to take the place of those we jail'. S Rep No 91-617 (1969) 78–79.

crime.[71] The discussions resulted in the adoption of the Organized Crime Control Act of 1970 (OCCA) and the very first disposition for the criminal confiscation of illicit proceeds.[72] Simultaneously to the reinforcement of the fight against criminal organisations, Congress decided to toughen its stance on the drug trade. Hence, less than a fortnight after the adoption of OCCA, the Comprehensive Drug Abuse Prevention and Control Act of 1970 was enacted[73] and the Nixon administration's 'war on drugs' began.[74] The adoptions of the two pieces of legislation were revolutionary in the USA not only because they targeted proceeds of crime for the first time,[75] but also because they imposed confiscation as a criminal punishment directly on an individual (and not *in rem*).[76] Following that first impulse, confiscation laws expanded dramatically within the context of drug fight in the late 1970s and 1980s.[77] For example, within the context of the Reagan administration's enhanced 'war on drugs' and 'war on organized crime',[78] both criminal and civil (ie non-conviction-based) confiscation devices were made applicable concurrently.[79] The American model has undoubtedly had a significant influence on the rest of the world with regard to the development of both conviction-based and non-conviction-based instruments.

A decade later, in the early 1980s, the American impetus had led to the development of legislation devoted to the deprivation of proceeds of crime in a limited number of European jurisdictions, such as Italy and the UK.[80]

In the twentieth century, Italy was facing similar societal and economic scourges as the USA, namely a deep-rooted presence of organised crime and drug

[71] ibid 79. The belief was that confiscation of the illicit proceeds of crime would 'strike at the profits of organized crime and wipe out its hold on legitimate organizations'. L LW Levy, *A License to Steal: The Forfeiture of Property* (Chapel Hill, University of North Carolina Press, 1996) 76.

[72] The Organized Crime Control Act of 1970, Pub L 91-452, 84 Stat 922 (15 October 1970). See Title IX of OCCA, ie the Racketeer Influenced and Corrupt Organizations Act, 18 USC, § 1963.

[73] The Comprehensive Drug Abuse Prevention and Control Act of 1970, Pub L No 91-513, 84 Stat 1236 (27 October 1970), s 511 (contraband and instrumentalities) and s 408(a)(2) (proceeds).

[74] See the 1973 declaration of the President of an 'all-out, global war on the drug menace'. R Nixon, 'Message to the Congress Transmitting Reorganization Plan 2 of 1973 Establishing the Drug Enforcement Administration', 28 March 1973, available at www.presidency.ucsb.edu.

[75] Yet in a limited way. 'The idea of forfeiting the proceeds of crime was entirely new'. Cassella (n 2) 33.

[76] Garretson (n 68) 46.

[77] ie through the 1978 and 1986 reforms of the Drug Abuse Act: the Psychotropic Substances Act of 1978, Pub L 95-633, 92 Stat 3778 (10 November 1978); The Anti-Drug Abuse Act of 1986, Pub L 99-570, 100 Stat 3207 (27 October 1986).

[78] See the 1982 and 1986 declarations of President Reagan. Ronald Reagan, 'Remarks Announcing Federal Initiatives Against Drug Trafficking and Organized Crime', 14 October 1982, available at www.presidency.ucsb.edu; 'Declaring War on Organized Crime', *New York Times*, 12 January 1986.

[79] eg Act of 12 October 1984, Pub L No 98-473, s 306(b). Accordingly, see *United States v Schmalfeldt*, 657 F Supp 385, 395 (WD Mich 1987).

[80] To understand the reasons underlying the export of the American war on drugs, see J Gerber and EL Jensen (eds), *American Style. The Internationalization of Failed Policy and its Alternatives* (New York, Garland Publishing, 2001) 7.

trafficking.[81] It was hence quite (re)active in developing legislation that had the same purposes as the American-magnified 'wars'—besides the already long existing provision allowing for the criminal confiscation of the profit of crime.[82] Profit-oriented anti-crime strategies directed towards criminal confiscation appeared in Italy in the 1970s.[83] In 1982, the legislator passed the Rognoni-La Torre Act following the death of two renowned officials.[84] The law, which marked a turning point in the asset recovery strategy, established a mandatory conviction-based confiscation of the assets (proceeds and instrumentalities) related to the crime of mafia association.[85] More importantly, it also implemented a non-conviction-based[86] and, to some extent, extended preventive form of confiscation targeting the assets of mafia-type organisations (*confisca di prevenzione*), which still remains a singular and much debated legal instrument.[87] Both procedures were adopted to target the proceeds (and instrumentalities) of organised crime. In the light of the above, one might suggest that a correlation may have existed between the American impetus and the development in Italy of legal devices targeting the proceeds of organised crime (and the drug trade).[88]

[81] The presence of Italian mafia families in the USA and the interactions existing between their members there and in Italy have often been presented and described by the historical and legal literature. See eg EU Savona, 'Mafia Money-Laundering versus Italian Legislation' (1993) 1, 3 *European Journal on Criminal Policy and Research* 31.

[82] ie Art 240 of the Italian Penal Code of 1930, which provides for the facultative criminal confiscation of the instrumentalities and (direct) profits of unlawful conducts. The notion is, however, interpreted as akin to the term 'proceeds', ie any economic advantage (direct or indirect) derived from crime. S Davide, 'La confisca del profitto' (doctoral thesis, Università degli Studi di Milano-Bicocca, 2010) 43, referring to legislative work of 1930: ministero della Giustizia, *Relazione ministeriale sul progetto di codice penale*, I, 280.

[83] See M Panzavolta and R Flor, 'A Necessary Evil? The Italian "Non-criminal System" of Asset Forfeiture' in JP Rui and U Sieber (eds), *Non-conviction-Based Confiscation in Europe. Possibilities and Limitations on Rules Enabling Confiscation without a Criminal Conviction* (Berlin, Max Planck Institute, 2015) 117.

[84] Law of 13 September 1982, No 646. The adoption of the act followed the murders by the mafia of Parliament Member La Torre (who had presented in 1980 a draft bill aimed at tackling the unlawful profits of criminal organisations) and of General Alberto Dalla Chiesa, in April and September 1982 respectively. The act was adopted in 'great haste' a few days after the assassination of the general, who had been sent to Sicily to fight the mafia. B Vettori, *Tough on Criminal Wealth: Exploring the Practice of Proceeds from Crime Confiscation in the EU* (Dordrecht, Springer, 2007) 7; L Paoli, 'Seizure and Confiscation Measures in Italy: An Evaluation of their Effectiveness and Constitutionality' (1997) 5(3) *European Journal of Crime, Criminal Law and Criminal Justice* 256.

[85] Art 416*bis* of the Italian Penal Code as introduced by the Rognoni-La Torre Law of 1982.

[86] Some have argued that civil confiscation 'has been entrenched for more than fifty years in Italy'. S Panović-Đurić (ed), *Impact Study on Civil Forfeiture* (Belgrade, Council of Europe, 2013) 16. This contribution nonetheless pinpoints the early 1980s as the date of birth of the mechanism within the Republic.

[87] Section II.B(iii) below. For a thorough discussion of the Italian preventive confiscation mechanism, see D Piva, 'Anti-mafia Forfeiture in the Italian System' in C King and C Walker (eds), *Dirty Assets. Emerging Issues in the Regulation of Criminal and Terrorist Assets* (Surrey, Ashgate, 2014) 71. See also F Mazzacuva, 'The Problematic Nature of Asset Recovery Measures: Recent Developments of the Italian Preventive Confiscation', this volume, Chapter 4.

[88] On the influence of the US legislations on Italy see, eg, ML Cesoni, *Les dispositifs de lutte contre les organisations criminelles* (Gent, Academia Press, 2005) 11.

When it comes to the UK, the political drive towards targeting criminal assets was also developed in response to the increase in drug trafficking in and outside Britain.[89] Yet, unlike the USA (and Italy), the new profit-oriented strategy was not a part of a 'strategic attack' against organised crime—though it became so later on.[90] The historical turning point happened in 1981, when the House of Lords denounced the fact that the proceeds of crime could not be retrieved in criminal cases according to the law in vigour:[91] despite the (timid and narrow) reintroduction of criminal confiscation through the Misuse of Drugs Act of 1971, no order allowed for the deprivation of the illicit proceeds of offenders generally.[92] Hence, several acts targeting the post-conviction criminal confiscation of proceeds were adopted[93] from 1986, starting with the Drug Trafficking Offences Act.[94] Although the deprivation order initially solely targeted the unlawful gains derived from drug trade, similarly to the American impulse, subsequent legislation quickly expanded its applicability to all acquisitive indictable offences[95] and then specifically to terrorism.[96] While direct evidence of such affirmation is difficult to find, it has also been argued that the chasing the money approach developed in the UK has followed the US legislation and practice.[97]

In short, most confiscation mechanisms targeting criminal proceeds have spread globally following the impetus of the USA, and its (alleged) influence on a limited number of domestic orders (ie Italy and the UK) and then on international and supranational instruments (respectively adopted by the UN, FATF and CoE). Additionally, the Italian experience, coupled with the UK and Irish examples, seems to have nurtured the EU's attention with a view to implementing new strategies and legal instruments oriented towards asset recovery.[98]

[89] D Feldman, 'A Survey of English Forfeiture Law' in S Food (ed), *Illicit Drugs and Organized Crime: Issues for a Unified Europe* (Chicago, Office of International Criminal Justice, 1991) 25.

[90] For developments regarding the concept of organised crime in the UK, see L Campbell, *Organised Crime and the Law, A Comparative Analysis* (Hart Publishing, London, 2013).

[91] In *R v Cuthbertson and Others* (1981) AC 470. Critics emerged because confiscation of the criminal proceeds was not possible since the funds were not 'instrumentalities of crime' covered by the law. M Levi, 'Taking the Profit Out of Crime: The UK Experience' (1997) 5 *European Journal of Crime, Criminal Law and Criminal Justice* 228, 229.

[92] Feldman (n 92) 26.

[93] Pursuant to the recommendation of the Hodgson Committee. D Hodgson, *Profits of Crime and their Recovery: The Report of a Committee Chaired by Sir Derek Hodgson* (London, Ashgate, 1984).

[94] The Act was designed 'to make provision for the recovery of the proceeds of drug trafficking'. Drug Trafficking Offences Act of 1986, ch 32. It also criminalised money laundering in the UK, which testifies to the complementary roles of confiscation and money laundering to target the financial element of crime.

[95] Criminal Justice Act 1988, s 71(9)(c). The use of such confiscation orders nonetheless remained underused. P Alldridge, *Money Laundering Law. Forfeiture, Confiscation, Civil Recovery, Criminal Laundering and Taxation of the proceeds of Crime* (Oxford, Hart Publishing, 2003) 80.

[96] Prevention of Terrorism (Temporary Provisions) Act 1989, s 13. T Millington and MS Williams, *The Proceeds of Crime*, 4th edn (Oxford, Oxford University Press, 2013) 2.

[97] P Bean, 'American Influence on British Drug Policy' in Gerber and Jensen (n 83) 80, 91. See also N Dorn, K Murji and N South, *Traffickers. Drug Markets and Law Enforcement* (London, Routledge, 1992) 73.

[98] This assertion is not further discussed in this contribution for brevity.

B. The 1990s–2010s War on Acquisitive Crime: The Consolidation and Multiplication of Confiscation Laws

Once the first confiscation laws targeting the proceeds of crime were adopted, law enforcement authorities and legislators around the Western world quickly understood the potential benefits of such instruments. On the other hand, they also quickly realised the limits of the existing mechanisms for traditional conviction-based confiscation, which proved not to be very effective in terms of actual recovery of criminal proceeds. Within that context, most jurisdictions started to broaden their existing confiscation laws or adopt new ones. Starting in the 1990s, three tendencies emerged: (i) the extension of confiscation mechanisms to all sorts of acquisitive crime (instead of focusing solely on the drug trade and organised crime); (ii) the adoption of 'extended' forms of conviction-based confiscation; and (iii) the adoption (or expansion) of non-conviction-based confiscation. The two last innovative forms/trends of asset recovery tools were developed for supposedly enhanced efficacy/efficiency when compared to the traditional criminal confiscation mechanism. Said devices have been increasingly replicated throughout the Western world. It is suggested they will be of critical influence within the next decade with regard to profit-oriented anti-crime strategies. It must finally be noted that the last decades have also witnessed a limited development of non-judicial forms of confiscation of (alleged) criminal assets.[99]

(i) The Expansion of Confiscation Laws to All Acquisitive Crimes

The final decade before the millennium undoubtedly marked a shift in the use of anti-crime strategies focused on asset deprivation. Yet the legal and prosecutorial culture towards depriving criminal proceeds was certainly not as strong across all the Occident at that time.

Within that context, the USA set the tone for future proponents of increased enforcement of confiscation: in the 1990s, the mechanism 'came into prominence as a law enforcement tool in the United States'; it became an essential weapon at the disposal of prosecuting authorities.[100] Whereas at the beginning of the decade the US Department of Justice was mostly using confiscation in drug cases, it broadened its use at the end of the 1990s to a tremendous range of serious offences.[101] In parallel to the American dynamic, national legislators, politicians and practitioners of the Western world became aware of the usefulness of targeting criminal assets to combat crime. Thus they reinforced and expanded their legal dispositions accordingly. The UK was no exception to the rule. Although initially confiscation specifically targeted the drug trade, further asset deprivation

[99] eg the US administrative forfeiture.
[100] Cassella (n 2) 28.
[101] Cassella (n 2).

laws quickly arose to cover all serious offences[102] due to the political dissatisfaction resulting from the infrequent use of confiscation orders.[103] For its part, Italy has traditionally been considered as being at the forefront of the asset recovery policies in the EU as regards both its legal framework and its culture of implementation. The 1990s therefore saw the focus of Italian law enforcement authorities on targeting criminal property steadily increase both in numbers and value of deprivation orders.[104]

At the supranational level, it must be highlighted that the UN, FATF, CoE and even the EU all contributed to the expansion and reinforcement of seizure and confiscation instruments to tackle at least serious and organised crime, and sometimes any and every type of (lucrative) offence.[105]

(ii) The Consolidation of Extended Conviction-Based Confiscation Laws

Besides the generalisation of the use of asset deprivation laws to fight criminal behaviours, the 1990s witnessed the consolidation of another essential device of the asset recovery strategy (after its limited emergence in the 1980s within the scope of the war on drugs, see below) 'extended' criminal (ie *in personam*) confiscation. Extended confiscation is generally understood as the deprivation of the 'unjustified assets' of a felon after his criminal conviction.[106] The term 'extended' relates to property other than directly connected to the crime the person was convicted for. Said confiscation habitually relies on (rebuttable) presumptions of illegality of the property of the defendant, such as a disproportion between his legal income and his property.[107] The mechanism generally applies to serious forms of acquisitive crime.

Interestingly enough, the US legal system is not traditionally associated per se with the emergence and growth of extended criminal confiscation mechanisms, although it appears to have possessed comparable provisions within the unique scope of drug-related offences from as early as 1984.[108] 'Extended' confiscation

[102] See, eg, the Criminal Justice Act 1988, s 71(9)(c), which expanded confiscation to many sorts of non-drug-related offences. See also the Criminal Justice (International Co-operation) Act 1990; the Criminal Justice Act 1993; the Drug Trafficking Act 1994; the Proceeds of Crime Act 1995.

[103] Alldridge (n 98) 78; Gallant (n 1) 109.

[104] See Center for the Study of Democracy, 'Antimafia: The Italian Experience in Fighting Organised Crime', Policy Brief No 31 (October 2011) 4, Figure 2, available at www.csd.bg; Paoli (n 87) 258.

[105] Such developments are not considered any further here as the discussion focuses on horizontal legal transplants of confiscation laws.

[106] G Turone, 'Legal Frameworks and Investigative Tools for Combating Organized Transnational Crime in the Italian Experience' (2007) *UNAFEI 134th International Training Course Visiting Experts' Papers* 48, 58.

[107] See J Boucht, 'Extended Confiscation: Criminal Assets or Criminal Owners?', this volume, Chapter 5.

[108] Federal provisions allowed the use of rebuttable presumptions for the criminal confiscation of 'any property' of a person convicted for drug-related offences provided that the property was acquired in a specific time-frame and that it had no other likely source than drug offences. 21 USC 853(d) as amended by Pub L 98-473, Title II, §§ 303, 2301(d)–(f), 12 October 1984, 98 Stat 2044, 2192, 2193. See

is rather generally connected to European Member States, such as the UK and Italy (whose legislation is considered to be exemplary), within the scope of fighting organised crime and the drug trade. It then spread through further legal orders during the 1990s–2000s to target serious and organised crime generally.[109] A form of extended (hence presumption-based) confiscation appeared in the UK in the Drug Trafficking Offences Act of 1986 through the rebuttable assumption, amongst others, that all the property the defendant had acquired within a six-year time-frame prior to the commencement of the criminal proceedings or he had held since his conviction was of illicit origin. The mechanism was then expanded to defendants convicted of a wide variety of serious or lucrative non-drug-related offences through the passing of the Proceeds of Crime Act (POCA) 1995.[110] The extended confiscation regime still in vigour today is contained in the Proceeds of Crime Act 2002.[111] In Italy, extended conviction-based deprivation appeared in 1992–94 as a direct result of the conviction of defendants for mafia-type crimes.[112] Pursuant to the legal provisions, the convicted person's property was (and still is today) presumed to be criminally related on the basis of a disproportion between the defendant's assets and his legal income: absent convincing allegations of the lawful acquisition of the property by the defendant, confiscation of the unjustified assets shall be ordered. The statutory assumptions established in both legislations made it possible to confiscate the assets of convicted offenders unless they prove they had been acquired legitimately.[113]

Extended conviction-based confiscation is becoming an established feature of European legal systems since Directive 2014/42/EU[114] has imposed such a

also J Gurulé, *Complex Criminal Litigation: Prosecuting Drug Enterprises and Organized Crime*, 3rd edn (New York, Juris Publishing, 2013) 335–38. Further, it has been argued that RICO provisions (as part of OCCA 1970) have been used in practice to target property that was not and exceeded profits of crime. TG Reed, 'American Forfeiture Law: Property Owners Meet the Prosecutor' (1992) *Cato Policy Analysis No 179*, available at www.cato.org.

[109] Appearing, for example, in Ireland in 1996 and in Belgium in 2002.

[110] Which amended the Criminal Justice Act 1988: Alldridge (n 98) 81.

[111] The 1995 provisions constituted the progenitors of the Proceeds of Crime Act 2002 extended confiscation model. Alldridge (n 98) 81. The regime in vigour is the result of the consolidation of both the 1988 and 1994 Acts in POCA 2002. R Monty, 'Tracing and Confiscating Illicit Proceeds: The Perspective of the Defence' (2011) 11(4) *Era Forum* 545, 553.

[112] The new form of confiscation was implemented in Art 12*quinquies* of Act No 356 of 1992, though this was declared unconstitutional for it conflicted with the presumption of innocence (*Corte Costituzionale*, Sentenza 17 February 1994, No 48): according to Panzavolta, the unconstitutional provision constituted 'an offense of possession of assets incompatible with a person's income'. The deprivation of unjustified assets was reinstalled in Art 12*sexies* through the adoption of Law Decree 399 of 1994, converted into Act 501 of 1994. Paoli (n 87) 257; Panzavolta and Flor (n 86) 117.

[113] Levi (n 94) 228; Alldridge (n 98) 145.

[114] Art 5 of Directive 2014/42/EU of the European Parliament and of the Council of 3 April 2014 on the freezing and confiscation of instrumentalities and proceeds of crime in the European Union (2014) OJ L127/39. The device was first tentatively established in Council Framework Decision 2005/212/JHA of 24 February 2005 on confiscation of crime-related proceeds, instrumentalities and property (2005) OJ L68/49. Yet, the instrument resulted unsuccessful for being unclear and unevenly transposed in domestic legal orders.

harmonised mechanism on the EU Member States. The Directive, the efficacy of which will have to be evaluated in the future, is the only supranational instrument to have expressly called for the implementation of such a form of deprivation in national legal orders.

(iii) The Expansion of Non-conviction-Based Confiscation

Since the 1990s, the efficacy and alleged virtues of non-conviction-based (or *in rem*) confiscation has been a topic of increased interest to legislators worldwide—and accordingly much debated.

Not surprisingly, the impetus of this discussion results from the revolution of the American confiscation regime in the 1970s and 1980s. At that time, the US Congress decided to revive confiscation, particularly through the deprivation of the proceeds of crime and via both criminal and civil proceedings.[115] The enactment of the contemporary non-conviction-based confiscation statutes pursued the same goal as the Navigation ones, ie to grant authorities the power to target property where the case made it too difficult to prosecute the author of illegal activities.[116] It should be noted that at that time, and contrary to civil law systems, it was commonly accepted in the USA that confiscation was a civil sanction imposed on the guilty property rather than a criminal one imposed on its owner.[117] The reform allowed for the confiscation of criminal property through proceedings separated from the guilt of an individual under the term 'civil forfeiture'. At the end of the 1980s, non-conviction-based confiscation was sought quite actively and aggressively in drug cases by the US Department of Justice.[118] By the 1990s, the USA had not only greatly expanded the scope of criminal confiscation, but also expanded the authority of civil confiscation to most federal crimes.[119] The US tradition is thus considered to have substantially influenced other common law jurisdictions towards the adoption of new forms of non-conviction-based deprivation of criminal assets.[120] For example, Ireland and the UK[121] successively implemented a civil (*in rem*) form of confiscation of illicit property in their national legal orders through the adoption of their respective

[115] Hence, in addition to establishing a criminal and *in personam* form of deprivation, the Congress reinforced the war against acquisitive crime by authorising a concurrent *in rem* procedure for the confiscation of said proceeds.

[116] The direct lineage between both instruments is undisputed: until 2006, the civil confiscation procedure (applicable to any and every criminal activity) relied on the admiralty and maritime rules discussed here. That year, the Supreme Court finally got rid of a '200-year dependence' on said statutes. Cassella (n 2) Preface, vii.

[117] Maxeiner (n 26) 768.

[118] Pimentel (n 42) 13.

[119] Cassella (n 2) 34.

[120] Gallant (n 1) 109. See also Campbell (n 93) 203m commenting on the influence of the 'historical tradition of forfeiture and the contemporary American approach'.

[121] But not only. South Africa and Australia are among the Commonwealth nations that followed the same evolution.

Proceeds of Crime Acts of 1996 and 2002. A more singular, yet well-known, form of non-conviction-based recovery of criminal property lies in the Italian (hence civil-law-based) preventive confiscation of 1982. The latter device is noteworthy because it is non-conviction-based and it rests (at least in part) on the use of presumptions with a view to confiscating a person's unjustified assets (similarly to extended conviction-based-confiscation). To some extent, one could further argue it (mostly) qualifies as an *actio in personam*.[122] It has been in vigour for over three decades although its popularity grew during the 1990s.[123] As of today, such civil/administrative proceedings devoted to the deprivation of criminal assets are being increasingly debated. Absent any successful fundamental rights challenge, non-conviction-based devices are predicted to expand increasingly within the next decade across the Western world (and civil law jurisdictions) given the avowed limits of criminal—hence conviction-based—confiscation.[124]

Although supranational institutions have generally remained silent as regards the necessity of implementing such mechanisms,[125] the EU implemented (to a very limited extent) its first harmonised non-conviction-based device through the adoption of the 2014/42/UE Directive.[126] However, the *in personam* instrument does not resemble the common law form of 'civil forfeiture' in any way and is already subject to criticism.[127]

[122] Contrary to the habitual parallelism that exists between non-conviction-based and *in rem* confiscation. Yet, the mechanism is seemingly a hybrid one 'that leans very much towards an *actio in rem*, albeit still requiring a connection with an individual'. Panzavolta and Flor (n 86) 124.

[123] Center for the Study of Democracy (n 107) 4, Figure 2.

[124] Such as the mechanisms adopted in Romania (2007), Bulgaria (2012), Slovenia (2012) and the Slovak Republic (2011) (and to some extent Estonia). Eurojust, 'Report on Non-conviction-Based Confiscation', General Case 751/NMSK—2012 (April 2013).

[125] This is due to the persisting sensitivity of the topic. The United Nations Convention against Corruption of 2003 was the first to suggest to member states that they should allow the confiscation of property without a criminal conviction 'when the offender cannot be prosecuted by reason of death, flight or absence or in other appropriate cases' (Art 54(c)). The FATF followed the same approach in 2003 by encouraging countries to adopt non-conviction-based confiscation when consistent with their domestic law: R3 of the 2003 40 Recommendations; R4 of the 2012 revised version.

[126] Art 4, para 2 of Directive 2014/42/EU (n 116). The EU has nonetheless already suggested that discussions be undertaken and a feasibility study issued concerning the adoption, at Union level, of more advanced non-conviction-based confiscation devices than those established by the Directive. eg See, eg, the Joint Declaration of the Council and Parliament, Proposal for a Directive of the European Parliament and of the Council on the freezing and confiscation of proceeds of crime in the European Union [first reading]—Approval of the final compromise text, 28 November 2013, 16861/13 ADD 1; Communication from the Commission to the European Parliament, the Council, the European Economic and Social Committee and the Committee of the Regions, The European Agenda on Security, 28 April 2015, COM (2015) 185 final, 17.

[127] For a thorough critical analysis of the mechanism, see M Fernandez-Bertier, 'The Confiscation and Recovery of Criminal Property: A European State of the Art' (2016) 18 *ERA Forum* 1; M Simonato, 'Directive 2014/42/EU and Non-conviction-Based Confiscation: A Step Forward on Asset Recovery?' (2015) 6(2) *New Journal of European Criminal Law* 213; F Alagna, 'Non-conviction Based Confiscation: Why the EU Directive is a Missed Opportunity' (2015) 21(4) *European Journal on Criminal Policy and Research* 447; JP Rui and U Sieber, 'Non-Conviction-Based Confiscation in Europe. Bringing the Picture Together' in Rui and Sieber (eds), *Non-conviction-Based Confiscation in Europe: Possibilities and Limitations on Rules Enabling Confiscation Without a Criminal Conviction* (Berlin, Duncker & Humblot/Freiburg, Max-Planck-Institut für ausländisches und internationales Strafrecht, 2015) 245.

C. The 2000s War on Terror: The Redefinition of the Scope and Remit of Confiscation Laws

Just as Presidents Nixon and Reagan declared a 'war on drugs' and a 'war on organized crime' in the 1970–80s, leading to the birth and expansion of the age of proceeds, President Bush was the first to expressly declare a 'war on terror' on 20 September 2001[128] as a means to further expand governance through crime control.[129] The Al-Qaeda terrorist attacks on US soil marked a paradigm shift in the search for criminal money.[130] In brief, the war on terror led to three global and simultaneous evolutions as regards targeting assets beyond the call for criminalising the act of terrorism financing:[131] the expansion of the remit of confiscable assets; the partial rebirth of general confiscation; and the birth of far-reaching asset-freezing regimes.

First, targeting terrorist property has led to the redefinition of the paradigm of dirty assets: terrorism per se is not an acquisitive form of crime but, rather, is driven by ideological/political purposes.[132] Money represents a 'means to an end rather than an end in itself'.[133] Hence, whereas confiscation strategies used to focus mostly on the proceeds of crime—where the monies derive from—they now reinsist on the need to target the instrumentalities of crime—where the assets are directed to.[134] Said otherwise, the notion of 'terrorist property' theoretically covers all the assets that are likely to be used for the purpose of terrorism, ie any and all property traceable in any way to crime.[135]

Secondly, the legislative frenzy that followed the 9/11 attacks might have contributed to a partial rebirth of confiscation of estate—although this evolution seems to be limited to a number of jurisdictions and is not a true novelty in itself.[136] For example, the US Patriot Act[137] established that once a person is

[128] President Bush's address to a Joint Session of Congress and the Nation, *Washington Post*, 20 September 2001.

[129] J Simon, *Governing through Crime: How the War on Crime Transformed American Democracy and Created a Culture of Fear* (New York, Oxford University Press, 2007) 10, 260.

[130] Gallant (n 1) 1.

[131] Which was imposed, among others, by Resolution 1373 of the Security Council of the UN, S/RES/1373 (2001) of 28 September 2001 (1.b).

[132] See Alldridge (n 98) 216.

[133] RE Bell, 'The Confiscation, Forfeiture and Disruption of Terrorist Finances' (2003) 7(2) *Journal of Money Laundering Control* 105.

[134] See Gallant (n 1) 3.

[135] See Alldridge (n 98) 216; Gallant (n 1) 3.

[136] Civil law jurisdictions had already established similar provisions within the fight against criminal organisations, such as the confiscation of all the property at the disposal of a criminal organisation. Yet, some national courts have mitigated the harshness of said provisions. See generally ML Cesoni (ed), *La lutte contre le blanchiment en droit belge, suisse, français, italien et international. Incrimination et confiscation, prévention, entraide judiciaire* (Brussels, Bruylant, 2013).

[137] Uniting and Strengthening America by Providing Appropriate Tools Required to Intercept and Obstruct Terrorism Act, Pub L 107-56, 115 Stat 272 (26 October 2001), s 806, which amends 18 USC § 981(a)(1)—see Section II.G below.

engaged in terrorism, the government can confiscate all his assets whether they are connected to terrorism or not.[138] Because no nexus is required between the crime and the scope of the property ultimately confiscated, it can be stated that all property is genuinely 'lost on the basis of ownership'.[139] Further, the terrorist confiscation order can be obtained through either conviction-based (*in personam*) or non-conviction-based (*in rem*) proceedings.[140] In the end, any property can be confiscated even if it was 'not used in committing the crime and was not obtained by the financial proceeds of the crime'.[141]

Lastly, and more symptomatically, the international terrorist attacks gave birth to a critical mechanism which allows for the temporary—hence (said to be) preventive—deprivation of all the financial assets of a person suspected to be related to terrorism. The 'targeted financial sanctions regimes'[142] as a new form of crime control instrument to counter terrorism and its financing were invented by the Security Council of the United Nations.[143] They mostly focus on property, but also include travel bans. The preventive sanctions apply where an individual or organisation is suspected of being involved in committing or facilitating terrorist activities, hence is registered on a blacklist. When so listed, all of the person's funds, financial and other economic resources are frozen[144] indefinitely. However, it cannot strictly be likened to a form of 'freezing of estate'. The regimes established at the UN level[145] have since been replicated at the supranational—eg the EU—[146] level and therefore find application at the national level.[147] Within this context, some individuals have been deprived of their assets for about a decade on the basis of mere suspicions—what one could liken to a covert act of confiscation or even to a 'criminal law in disguise' despite the purported preventive and administrative nature of the measures.[148]

[138] SD Cassella, 'Forfeiture of Terrorist Assets under the USA Patriot Act of 2001' (2002) 34(1) *Law and Policy in International Business* 7; Cassella (n 2) 4; Doyle (n 27) 4.

[139] DB Cohen and JW Wells (eds), *American National Security and Civil Liberties in an Era of Terrorism* (New York, Palgrave Macmillan, 2004) 44.

[140] The dispositions (ss 106 and 806 of the Patriot Act) 'are silent about giving an exemption to the terrorist's heirs'. ibid.

[141] CW Michaels, *No Greater Threat: America after September 11 and the Rise of a National Security State*, 2nd edn (New York, Agora Publishing, 2005) 92.

[142] FATF, 'International Best Practices: Targeted Financial Sanction Related to Terrorism and Terrorist Financing (Recommendation 6)', June 2013, 3.

[143] ie Resolutions S/RES/1267 (1999) of 15 October 1999 (4.b) and S/RES/1373 (2001) of 28 September 2001 (1.c).

[144] Except for humanitarian exemptions—which will not be discussed in this chapter.

[145] ie the 1267 (1999) and 1373 (2001) asset freezing mechanisms.

[146] Through the adoption of successive Common Positions and Regulations by the Council of the European Union. See C Eckes, *EU Counter-Terrorist Policies and Fundamental Rights* (Oxford, Oxford University Press, 2009) 12; C Eckes, 'EU Counter-Terrorist Sanctions: The Questionable Success Story of Criminal Law in Disguise' in C King and C Walker (n 90) 317.

[147] Through the decisions of national authorities to enforce supra/international sanctions or to autonomously investigate and list persons suspected to be related to terrorism.

[148] Eckes, 'EU Counter-Terrorist Sanctions' (n 146) 317, 347. For a critical discussion of the controversial terrorist asset freezing regimes, see inter alia R Pijnen, 'Terrorism Lists and Freezing of Assets: Getting Behind Appearances' (2011) 4 *Eucrim* 167; Eckes, 'EU Counter-Terrorist Sanctions', 317;

It should be noted that other international instruments have insisted on the necessity to deprive individuals temporarily or permanently of funds used/allocated for the purpose of committing or derived from terrorism (financing) offences.[149]

D. The 2000–10s War on White-Collar Crime: The (Over)extensive Interpretation of Confiscation Laws

The 'war' on crime metaphors used by Presidents Nixon, Reagan and Bush have allowed for a major reorientation (not to say transformation) of governance through the culture of control,[150] through, among others, profit-oriented anti-crime strategies. One may thus wonder whether in the next decade we will witness a declaration of 'war on white-collar crime'[151] and the development of even more far-reaching asset recovery policies: it is argued that, by tackling white-collar crime, the US Congress has once again changed the landscape of forfeiture.[152] This statement may certainly be used to explain the expansion of the culture of confiscation around the world,[153] since Western governments have recently increased their willingness to prosecute white-collar offences. This war started in the USA in the early 2000s,[154] and has accelerated rapidly in the past years. Following the outbreak of the global economic crisis in 2008, the investigation and prosecution of economic and financial crime increased substantially not only in the USA but throughout the international community (with more or less success)—giving a new dimension to the investigation and prosecution of major international financial and banking institutions.

One might argue that the year 2008 represents a new turning point in chasing criminal money strategies, with the launch by national law enforcement authorities of a new witch hunt against the economic and financial sector—and their correlative crimes. There is a certain coherence to the fact that confiscation has been used more extensively and aggressively than ever lately against such forms

F Galli, 'The Freezing of Terrorists' Assets: Preventive Purposes with a Punitive Effect' in F Galli and A Weyembergh (eds), *Do Labels Still Matter? Blurring Boundaries between Administrative and Criminal law. The Influence of the EU* (Brussels, Editions de l'Université de Bruxelles, 2014) 42.

[149] eg the UN International Convention for the Suppression of the Financing of Terrorism of 1999, 9 December 1999, New York, Art 8; the FATF IX Special Recommendations of 2001, Special Recommendation 3 (amended in February 2008 then merged in 2012 with the 40 Recommendations to fight money laundering: R4 of the 2012 revised version).

[150] Simon (n 129) 260.

[151] Although authors have already made use of such a term of art decades ago: N Abrams, 'Assessing the Federal Government's "War on White-Collar Crime"' (1980) 53 *Temple Law Review* 984.

[152] AW Dery, 'Overview of Asset Forfeiture' (2012) *Business Law Today* 1.

[153] Accordingly, see N Ryder, 'To Confiscate or not to Confiscate? A Comparative Analysis of the Confiscation of the Proceeds of Crime Legislation in the United States of America and the United Kingdom' (2013) 8 *Journal of Business Law* 767.

[154] See, eg, the prosecutions deriving from the WorldCom, Enron and Tyco scandals.

of unlawful behaviour: white-collar crime is the most illustrative form of acquisitive crime and involves the largest amounts of illicit money. Hence, jaw-dropping figures relating to confiscation orders have derived from high-profile cases and have resulted in confiscation figures of billions of dollars, such as in the *BNP Paribas*[155] and *Madoff* cases.[156] What must be highlighted from these decisions is the draconian interpretation that prevails as regards the confiscable amount: far from the concept of net profits or even gross proceeds, it is the money that has 'flowed' unlawfully, ie every dollar that has been channelled in violation of the law, that is ultimately and potentially confiscable by the government.

Lately, prosecutors in the Western world have decided to be tougher than ever on white-collar (corporate) offenders. The greatest amounts of property confiscated by the US federal government relate to white-collar crime offences,[157] which seems only logical given the tremendous sums of money that globally flow every day through corporate and financial entities and professionals. One could then argue that corporate crime defendants are becoming the new cash cow of governments through the profitable crime control instrument of confiscation, the best days of which are yet to come.

Conclusion

Asset recovery laws have ancient roots. They emerged in the classical age in the form of confiscation of estate, which was ordered against convicted offenders. Such a harsh punishment vanished with the advent of the modern era. In parallel, asset deprivation developed and stabilised through the centuries in the form of

[155] eg The BNP Paribas criminal confiscation of over $8.8 billion was imposed on 1 May 2015 following the bank's violation of economic embargos with Sudan, Iran and Cuba. *United States v BNP Paribas SA*, 14 Cr 460 (SDNY 2015). It is quite symbolic as it constituted the 'largest financial penalty ever imposed in a criminal case'. The money confiscated from BNP Paribas was the money it had 'knowingly and willfully moved … through the US financial system on behalf of sanctioned entities', ie potentially all the assets traceable to the offence. It is noteworthy that the additional criminal fine amounted to 'only' $140 million, which testifies to the potential extensive and harsh character of confiscation orders today. USDOJ, 'BNP Paribas Agrees to Plead Guilty and to Pay $8.9 Billion for Illegally Processing Financial Transactions for Countries Subject to US Economic Sanctions', 30 June 2014; USDOJ, 'BNP Paribas Sentenced for Conspiring to Violate the International Emergency Economic Power Act and the Trading with the Enemy Act', 1 May 2015, both available at www.justice.gov.

[156] An unrealistic (and hence unrecoverable) preliminary order of confiscation of $170.8 billion was pronounced by the New York Court against Bernard Madoff in 2009 as a result of his infamous Ponzi scheme. The preliminary deprivation order consisted in the sum of money that 'flowed into his business as a result of his fraudulent scheme'. *United States v Bernard L Madoff*, 09 Cr 213 (DC 2009) 2–3, 43.

[157] Absent complete figures from other jurisdictions. 'According to most recent statistics, half of all federal forfeiture cases involve white collar crime. This development is crucial to understanding the importance of asset forfeiture in contemporary criminal prosecutions'. Dery (n 152) 1.

special confiscation as a means to target the instrumentalities of crime and contraband. Yet the true (r)evolution (or rebirth) of asset deprivation can be traced back to the 1970s and the emergence of criminal policies focused on the proceeds of crime, the rationale being that crime should not pay. Although they first targeted the drug trade and organised crime, confiscation laws progressively expanded to cover any and every type of acquisitive crime—with a reinforced focus on terrorist assets following the 9/11 attacks and white-collar wrongdoing pursuant to the global financial crisis.

More than ever, confiscation (coupled with the prevention and repression of money laundering) seems to be the strategic weapon of choice against acquisitive crime, not only for serious offences but also for petty ones. Yet many countries and supranational institutions point out the lack of actual use of confiscation and the lack of enforcement of deprivation orders. A shift in prosecutorial culture, led by the USA, nonetheless appears to be operating to a greater or lesser extent throughout the Western world with a view to enhancing the attention of law enforcement authorities towards the need for depriving criminals of their dirty assets. Similarly, a recent increase in awareness can be observed regarding the need to seize and freeze (alleged) criminal property, ie there is a new focus on temporary deprivation devices. Targeting assets given the recent developments in and the rise of the war on white-collar crime—especially in times of budgetary constraints—it is fair to say that criminal policies focused on property have their best days ahead. After all, 'crime should not pay' is a motto that has been repeated in many (supra) national debating chambers over the last couple of decades. Hence, confiscation shall undoubtedly be an issue in virtually all proceedings which entail profitable unlawful activities.

3

Civil Forfeiture in Ireland: Two Decades of the Proceeds of Crime Act and the Criminal Assets Bureau

COLIN KING*

Introduction

Two decades have passed since Ireland adopted civil forfeiture to tackle serious/organised crime: a move that represented a radical change in criminal justice strategies and came at great cost to individual rights. Civil forfeiture allows for property to be seized by, and forfeited to, the State even in the absence of criminal conviction against the person in possession of that property. There are thus significant concerns in relation to due process and property rights. The purpose of this chapter is to explore the law and policy of civil forfeiture in Ireland, drawing upon the extensive case law and commentary over the course of the past two decades. The Irish model of civil forfeiture is regularly used as an exemplar of best practice in other jurisdictions[1]—both common law and civil law—as well as at the EU level.[2] There is thus great merit in examining the Irish model in some depth.

* Senior Lecturer at the University of Sussex, UK. I would like to thank John Child, Jen Hendry and the editors for their helpful comments on an earlier draft.

[1] eg Booz Allen Hamilton, 'Comparative Evaluation of Unexplained Wealth Orders', prepared for the US Department of Justice (Washington DC, National Institute of Justice, 2011). In Vettori's assessment of the 'law in practice' across different EU Member States, civil forfeiture in Ireland was rated as: 93/100 (investigative phase), 95/100 (judicial phase), and 100/100 (disposal phase). B Vettori, *Tough on Criminal Wealth: Exploring the Practice of Proceeds from Crime Confiscation in the EU* (Dordrecht, Springer, 2006) 78.

[2] eg G Mitchell, 'Thematic Paper on Organised Crime. Asset Confiscation as an Instrument to Deprive Criminal Organisations of the Proceeds of their Activities' (Special Committee on Organised Crime, Corruption and Money Laundering, September 2012). For arguments in favour of an EU civil forfeiture regime, see F Alagna, 'Non-conviction Based Confiscation: Why the EU Directive is a Missed Opportunity' (2015) 21(4) *European Journal on Criminal Policy and Research* 447.

Irish authorities regularly proclaim their successes, and emphasise how civil forfeiture adheres to human rights norms. Others disagree—quite strongly. This chapter offers a review of the state of the art. Before looking at the relevant legislation, the first section of the chapter explores the context behind the adoption of civil forfeiture, namely concern surrounding serious/organised crime and the associated, highly charged, political discourse. Civil forfeiture is not a new tool, however; rather, a similar type of legislation had previously been enacted in the anti-terrorism realm, and this experience was influential in designing the Proceeds of Crime Act 1996 (POCA).

After setting out this background, the chapter moves on to consider the legislative framework adopted in both POCA and the Criminal Assets Bureau Act 1996, as well as the subsequent wave of legal challenges that inevitably followed. Challenges to the legislation, on the grounds of constitutional arguments, were ultimately unsuccessful. This leads on to the next section, namely a critique of: due process concerns, circumventing criminal procedural safeguards, the supposed 'civil' nature of civil forfeiture process, the failure of the Irish courts to operate as a check against legislative excess, interference with property rights and the powers afforded to the Criminal Assets Bureau (CAB), as well as its limited accountability.

Finally, the chapter issues a call to arms to other disciplines: much of the extant research on civil forfeiture is from law or criminology scholars. There is a need for greater insight from, or in collaboration with, other disciplines (including economics, business management, psychology, sociology) to consider issues such as effectiveness, the use of civil forfeiture in the corporate realm and procedural fairness.

I. Background

A. The Politics of Law and Order

Over the course of the past two decades, the Irish State has been active in its efforts to tackle organised criminal activities. This proactive approach can be seen by, inter alia, a more restrictive approach to bail; expanded police powers relating to arrest, detention and questioning; the establishment of an ad hoc witness protection programme; increased use of the non-jury Special Criminal Court; expanded surveillance powers; and new criminal law offences, including an offence of participating in organised crime type activities.[3] One of the most significant changes—and

[3] For discussion of such measures, see L Campbell, *Organised Crime and the Law: A Comparative Analysis* (Oxford, Hart, 2013).

the focus of this chapter—is the adoption of civil forfeiture, accompanied by the establishment of the multi-agency CAB.[4] This section examines political discourse in the build up to the passing of POCA and the Criminal Assets Bureau Act 1996.[5]

In the wake of the murders of a member of An Garda Síochána (Irish police) and an investigative journalist,[6] political discourse was highly charged: as O'Donnell and O'Sullivan point out, these murders 'generated the conditions where a harsh response to perceived lawlessness became acceptable'.[7] Politicians widely spoke of 'professional thugs',[8] 'home grown Mafia'[9] and 'drug barons'.[10] Politicians were widely critical of perceived inadequacies in the conventional criminal process; and it was widely claimed that 'godfathers of crime'[11] were able to avoid arrest and conviction by virtue of operating at a remove from the coalface of criminal activity. A new criminal justice strategy—whereby the focus would be on the financial incentive of crime—came to the fore: under POCA it would now be possible for the State to seize 'criminal' assets even in the absence of criminal conviction. The enactment of this radical new procedure—civil forfeiture—was accompanied by the creation of a new multi-agency body tasked with implementing the focus on criminal money, the CAB. The rationale underpinning this shift in emphasis towards criminal money is clear:

> The conventional criminal justice system is simply not equipped to bring the so-called crime bosses to justice since they can rarely be directly linked with the execution of a crime. They can, however, be linked with the enormous profits generated by their crimes.[12]

Similarly, in an oft-quoted passage, Deputy O'Donnell stated:

> We have given the courts power to seize the assets of those convicted of certain crimes and to restrain the assets of those facing certain criminal charges, but given the difficulties experienced in getting convictions, or even gathering evidence, a new power is needed to restain [*sic*] the use of assets outside the context of criminal proceedings. To date we have dealt only with assets which are the fruits of past crimes. What we need to

[4] The multi-agency nature of the Bureau is reflected in its composition, ie it brings together police, taxation, and revenue officials.

[5] Much of this discourse reflects the 'indices of change' identified by Garland: D Garland, *The Culture of Control: Crime and Social Order in Contemporary Society* (Oxford, Oxford University Press, 2001).

[6] Detective Garda Jerry McCabe was murdered by members of a terrorist group during an armed robbery on 6 June 1996 and Veronica Guerin was murdered by a criminal gang on 26 June 1996.

[7] I O'Donnell and E O'Sullivan, 'The Politics of Intolerance—Irish Style' (2003) 43(1) *British Journal of Criminology* 41, 48.

[8] Seanad Éireann, Criminal Assets Bureau Bill, 1996, Second Stage, 9 October 1996, vol 148, col 1547, per Senator Mulcahy.

[9] Dail Éireann, Private Members' Business—Organised Crime (Restraint and Disposal of Illicit Assets) Bill, 1996, Second Stage, 2 July 1996, vol 467, col 2442, per Deputy Shatter.

[10] ibid, vol 467, col 2486, per Deputy Gregory.

[11] Dail Éireann, Private Members' Business—Measures Against Crime: Motion, 2 July 1996, vol 467, col 2396, per Deputy Harney.

[12] Dail Éireann, Organised Crime Bill (n 9), vol 467, col 2463, per Deputy Byrne.

> do now is prevent assets being used as the seeds of future crimes. To put it another way, if we cannot arrest the criminals, why not confiscate their assets?[13]

Against this backdrop, and in a remarkably short space of time, the Proceeds of Crime Bill passed through all parliamentary stages, and was signed into law on 4 August 1996.[14]

B. Anti-Terrorism Influence

It is often suggested that the Irish civil forfeiture provisions were directly influenced by similar measures in the United States. It is true that the US RICO legislation was highlighted by some politicians during the passage of the Proceeds of Crime Bill. For example, Deputy Willie O'Dea stated:

> The notion that assets can be frozen, or that they can be frozen without anybody being convicted, is not new. Such legislation has been in operation in the United States for more than a decade. ... the United States now has legislation which allows for the forfeiture of assets which are suspected of being the proceeds of crime, even when a prosecution never ultimately takes place.[15]

He continued:

> The United States ... has infinitely more draconian legislation on the seizure and forfeiture of assets and this has consistently withstood constitutional challenge. The director of the forfeiture office of the United State's Department of Justice was recently quoted as describing the asset seizure legislation in the United States as, 'the most valuable and powerful we have against organised crime'.[16]

Such comments notwithstanding, a more influential framework was found much closer to home—in anti-terrorism legislation permitting the seizure of funds allegedly belonging to the Irish Republican Army (IRA).

The Offences Against the State (Amendment) Act 1985 (OAS(A)A 1985) was introduced, on a temporary basis,[17] to enable forfeiture of property held by an unlawful organisation. Under section 2 of this legislation, where the Minister for Justice was of the opinion that money held in a bank was the property of an unlawful organisation, he could freeze that money and require it to be paid into the High Court. If proceedings were not brought for the return of this money within a

[13] Dail Éireann, Organised Crime Bill (n 9), vol 467, col 2435, per Deputy O'Donnell.

[14] This was only five weeks after the death of Veronica Guerin on 26 June 1996. For further discussion of the backdrop to this legislation, see C King, 'Hitting Back at Organised Crime: The Adoption of Civil Forfeiture in Ireland' in C King and C Walker, *Dirty Assets: Emerging Issues in the Regulation of Criminal and Terrorist Assets* (Farnham, Ashgate, 2014) 141; J Meade, 'Organised Crime, Moral Panic and Law Reform: The Irish Adoption of Civil Forfeiture' (2000) 10(1) *Irish Criminal Law Journal* 11.

[15] Dail Éireann, Organised Crime Bill (n 9), vol 467, col 2473, per Deputy O'Dea.

[16] Dail Éireann, Organised Crime Bill (n 9), vol 467, col 2474, per Deputy O'Dea.

[17] The OAS(A)A 1985 had a limited lifespan (three months), unless extended by the government. The legislation was only used on one occasion and was then allowed to lapse.

six-month period, the Minister could apply *ex parte* to the High Court for an order directing that the money be paid to the Exchequer. The OAS(A)A 1985 was signed into law on 19 February 1985 and the next day was used to freeze money (IR£1.75 million) held in a bank account in Navan, County Meath. This legislation was unsuccessfully challenged in *Clancy v Ireland*.[18] In a rather brief judgment, Barrington J held that, while the legislation provides for freezing, and paying into the High Court, of money without notice to the account holder, it

> does not confiscate his property or deprive him of a fair hearing. He is entitled to claim the funds in the High Court and he is entitled to a fair hearing there though, admittedly, the onus of proof is on him to establish his title. In the event of a mistake having been made there is provision for the payment of compensation.[19]

Barrington J went on to find that 'the Act of 1985 amounts to a permissible delimitation of property rights in the interests of the common good'.[20] The OAS(A)A 1985, then, provided a 'clear and direct precedent' for the civil forfeiture provisions under POCA.[21]

II. Legislative Framework

A. Outline of the Proceeds of Crime Act

The primary legislation governing civil forfeiture in Ireland is the Proceeds of Crime Acts 1996–2005 (POCA).[22] At the outset, it is worth briefly distinguishing civil forfeiture from post-conviction confiscation.[23] Post-conviction confiscation is dependent upon successful prosecution and conviction. As such, all of the enhanced procedural protections of the criminal process apply, including, inter alia, the presumption of innocence and the heightened criminal standard of proof beyond reasonable doubt. At the confiscation hearing (ie when the criminal proceedings are concluded), the civil standard of proof applies.[24] Contrariwise,

18 [1988] IR 326. The decision in *Clancy* was considered by the Supreme Court in *Murphy v GM; Gilligan v CAB* [2001] 4 IR 113, 144–45.

19 *Clancy v Ireland* [1988] IR 326, 335.

20 ibid 336.

21 Dail Éireann, Organised Crime Bill (n 9), vol 467, col 2409, per Deputy O'Donoghue.

22 The 1996 Act was amended by the Proceeds of Crime (Amendment) Act 2005, which specifies that the two Acts are together to be known as the Proceeds of Crime Acts 1996–2005. In this vein, whereas until 2005 'POCA' was used to refer to the 1996 Act, since then 'POCA' has been used to refer to the Act, as amended.

23 Criminal Justice Act, 1994. For a discussion, see M Ashe and P Reid, *Money Laundering: Risks, Liabilities and Compliance* (Dublin, FirstLaw, 2007).

24 eg Criminal Justice Act 1994, s 4(6).

with civil forfeiture under POCA, property may be seized even in the absence of criminal conviction: civil forfeiture is said to operate *in rem* (against the property), rather than *in personam* (against the individual). What follows is a brief overview of POCA. The long title to the Act provides that it is:

> An Act to enable the High Court, as respects the proceeds of crime, to make orders for the preservation and, where appropriate, the disposal of the property concerned and to provide for related matters.

'Proceeds of crime' is defined as 'any property obtained or received at any time (whether before or after the passing of this Act) by or as a result of or in connection with criminal conduct'.[25] 'Criminal conduct' is defined as

> any conduct:
>
> (a) which constitutes an offence or more than one offence, or
> (b) which occurs outside the State and which would constitute an offence or more than one offence –
>
> i. if it occurred within the State,
> ii. if it constituted an offence under the law of the state or territory concerned, and
> iii. if, at the time when an application is being made for an interim or interlocutory order, any property obtained or received at any time (whether before or after the passing of this Act) by or as a result of or in connection with the conduct is situated within the State.[26]

Significantly, in proceedings under the Act, it is not necessary for an application to relate particular proceeds to a particular crime.[27]

Section 2 of POCA makes provision for an interim order—a pre-trial restraint order.[28] The application for an interim order can be brought by a senior police officer, an authorised officer of the Revenue Commissioners or the CAB. If granted, this order prohibits disposal of, or otherwise dealing with, or diminishing the value of specified property.[29] Applications for an interim order are usually brought on an *ex parte* basis, the rationale being to ensure that assets cannot be dissipated or removed from the jurisdiction pending a full *inter partes* hearing.[30] An interim order can only be granted where the court is satisfied that a person is in possession or control of specified property that constitutes, or was acquired with, proceeds

[25] POCA, s 1(1), as substituted by POC(A)A, s 3.
[26] POCA, s 1(1), as inserted by POC(A)A, s 3.
[27] *FMcK v AF; FMcK v EH* [2005] IESC 6.
[28] Proceedings shall be held otherwise than in public: POCA, s 8(3).
[29] POCA, s 2(1), as amended by POC(A)A, s 4.
[30] While the risk of dissipation may be one consideration, such a risk is not a formal requirement under the Act: *FMcK v DC* [2006] IEHC 185. Jurisprudence relating to Mareva and Anton Pillar orders in the commercial field applies to *ex parte* applications under the Proceeds of Crime Act, thus there is an obligation of full disclosure on the part of the applicant: ibid. For an example of where a s 2 order was lifted for lack of full disclosure, see *CAB v Base Garage Supplies Ltd* [2013] IEHC 302.

of crime and is of a certain minimum value (€13,000).[31] The civil standard of proof applies[32] and belief evidence is admissible.[33] The court may also direct the respondent to file an affidavit specifying the property that he is in possession or control of, or his income and sources of income for a specified period (not exceeding ten years up to the date of application of the order), or both.[34] Documentary evidence is also admissible.[35] An interim order lasts for 21 days and then lapses unless an application for an interlocutory order is brought during that period.[36]

Section 3 of POCA provides for an interlocutory order; whilst this is described as an 'interlocutory order', the section 3 hearing is to be regarded as the trial of the action.[37] An application for an interlocutory order can be brought by a senior police officer, an authorised officer of the Revenue Commissioners or the CAB. Where it appears to the court that a person is in possession or control of specified property that constitutes, or was acquired with, proceeds of crime and is of a certain minimum value (€13,000), the court shall grant an interlocutory order. Where an interlocutory order is granted, that order prohibits disposal of, or otherwise dealing with or diminishing the value of, specified property.[38] Here, again, the civil standard of proof applies[39] and belief evidence is admissible.[40] The court may also direct the respondent to file an affidavit specifying the property that he is in possession or control of, or his income and sources of income for a specified period (not exceeding ten years up to the date of application of the order), or both.[41] Documentary evidence is also admissible.[42] The legislation explicitly

[31] POCA, s 2(1).

[32] POCA, s 8(2).

[33] POCA, s 8(1). To briefly explain: the legislation permits a senior police officer or revenue official to state his/her 'belief' that a person is in possession or control of specified property that constitutes or stems from proceeds of crime and that the value of that property is not less than €13,000. If the court is satisfied that there are reasonable grounds for that belief, then it shall be admitted as evidence.

[34] POCA, s 9(1), as renumbered by POC(A)A, s 11. Such an affidavit is not admissible in criminal proceedings against that person or spouse, except where such proceedings relate to perjury arising from statements in the affidavit: POCA, s 9(2), as inserted by POC(A), s 11.

[35] POCA, s 16A, as inserted by POC(A)A, s 12.

[36] POCA, s 2(5). This does not require that the application be actually moved in court within the 21-day period: *FMcK v AF; FMcK v EH* (n 27).

[37] *FJMcK v AF and JF* [2002] 1 IR 242; *FJMcK v FC, PL, and MAC; FJMcK v MJG, T Ltd, and E Ltd* [2001] 4 IR 521.

[38] POCA, s 3(1). Post-2005, there is provision for a consent disposal order to be granted at this stage where all parties agree to such an order, in which case s 4A applies: POCA, s 3(1A), as inserted by POC(A)A, s 5. By virtue of POCA, s 8(3), a hearing under section 3 may be held in camera: see *CAB v MacAviation Ltd* [2010] IEHC 121.

[39] POCA, s 8(2).

[40] POCA, s 8(1). In *McK v D* [2004] 2 IR 470, McCracken J set out a step-by-step approach to be followed in proceedings under POCA. The application of this seven-step approach can be seen in, eg, *CAB v W* [2010] IEHC 166. *cf PB v AF* [2012] IEHC 428, where the court declined to admit belief evidence under s 8(1).

[41] POCA, s 9(1), as renumbered by POC(A)A, s 11. Such an affidavit is not admissible in criminal proceedings against that person or spouse, except where such proceedings relate to perjury arising from statements in the affidavit: POCA, s 9(2), as inserted by POC(A)A, s 11.

[42] POCA, s 16A, as inserted by POC(A)A, s 12.

provides a safeguard that 'the Court shall not make the order if it is satisfied that there would be a serious risk of injustice'.[43] A further safeguard is that, at any time when an interlocutory order is in force, the respondent or any other person claiming ownership of any of the property concerned can apply to the court to have the order varied or discharged.[44] Subject to being discharged, an interlocutory order normally continues until (i) the determination of an application for a disposal order in relation to the property concerned, (ii) the expiration of the ordinary time for bringing an appeal from that determination or (iii) if an appeal is brought, the determination or abandonment of that appeal or any further appeal, or the expiration of the ordinary time for bringing any further appeal.[45]

Before moving on, it is worth briefly mentioning situations concerning expenses incurred by a respondent. At any time while an interim or interlocutory order is in force, an application can be made to the Court to enable the discharge of reasonable living and other necessary expenses (including legal expenses in relation to proceedings under POCA) or to enable the carrying on of a business, trade, profession or other occupation to which the property concerned relates.[46]

At any point when an interim order or an interlocutory order is in force, the court may appoint a receiver to take possession of any property to which the order relates. Subject to the court's directions, the receiver will manage, keep possession of, dispose of or otherwise deal with any property over which he is appointed.[47] In practice, where a receiver is to be appointed, the Bureau Legal Officer will be appointed to this role.

Section 4 provides for a disposal order: after an interlocutory order has been in force for seven years, the court, on application, may grant a disposal order directing that the property be transferred (subject to any terms and conditions specified by the court) to the Minister for Finance or to such other person as the court may determine.[48] While it would appear that the court has a discretion under section 4(1), section 4(2) explicitly states that the court

[43] POCA, s 3(1). There are different perspectives on this safeguard: for example, Ashe and Reid describe it as 'an important safeguard', whereas O'Higgins is more critical, describing it as 'a vague and intangible yardstick'. See M Ashe and P Reid, 'Ireland: The Celtic Tiger Bites—The Attack on the Proceeds of Crime' (2001) 4(3) *Journal of Money Laundering Control* 253, 259; M O'Higgins, 'The Proceeds of Crime Act 1996' (1996) *Bar Review* 12, 12. For an example of where it was argued (unsuccessfully) that the making of a s 3 order would result in a serious risk of injustice, see *CAB v O'Brien* [2010] IEHC 12.

[44] POCA, s 3(3). In practice, this opens the possibility for victims of crime to apply to court to have their rights recognised. For an in-depth consideration of an application under s 3(3), see *Murphy v Gilligan* [2011] IEHC 62. The Supreme Court declined to reopen this issue in *Murphy v Gilligan* [2014] IESC 43. *cf CAB v Kelly* [2012] IEHC 595.

[45] POCA, s 3(5).

[46] POCA, s 6(1), as amended by POC(A)A, s 8. See, eg, *MFM v MB* [1998] IEHC 174.

[47] POCA, s 7(1). The appointment of a receiver was unsuccessfully challenged in *Murphy v GM; Gilligan v CAB* (n 18) 125.

[48] POCA, s 4(1). The hearing under s 4(1) may be adjourned for up to 2 years: POCA, s 4(7). A hearing under s 4 may be held in camera: POCA, s 8(3). For an example of s 4 in practice, see *Murphy v Gilligan* [2011] IEHC 464.

> *shall* make a disposal order ... unless it is shown to its satisfaction that that particular property does not constitute, directly or indirectly, proceeds of crime and was not acquired, in whole or in part, with or in connection with property that, directly or indirectly, constitutes proceeds of crime.[49]

The civil standard of proof continues to apply at this stage.[50] The effect of a disposal order is to deprive the respondent of his rights (if any) in the property concerned and, upon the order being made, the property shall stand transferred to the Minister for Finance or other specified person.[51] Similar to section 3, here, too, there is a safeguard in that the court shall not grant a disposal order if it is satisfied that there would be a serious risk of injustice.[52] Since 2005, there has been provision for a disposal order to be granted before the seven-year period has elapsed where an application is made with the consent of all the parties concerned. The effect of such a consent disposal order is the same as an order under section 4.[53]

Two final points are worth mentioning: first, section 11(7) of the Statute of Limitations does not apply in relation to proceedings under the Act.[54] Secondly, compensation provisions in relation to interim, interlocutory and disposal orders are set out in section 16.[55]

A new section 16B was inserted by the Proceeds of Crime (Amendment) Act 2005, making provision for a corrupt enrichment order. A person is corruptly enriched if he 'derives a pecuniary or other advantage or benefit as a result of or in connection with corrupt conduct, wherever the conduct occurred'.[56] Where the court is satisfied that a defendant has been corruptly enriched, the court may grant a corrupt enrichment order directing the defendant to pay to the Minister for Finance, or such other person as specified by the court, an amount equivalent to the amount by which it determines that the defendant has been so enriched.[57] The standard of proof under this section is that applicable to civil proceedings.[58] Belief evidence is admissible.[59] The court may also direct the defendant to file

[49] POCA, s 4(2). Emphasis added.

[50] POCA, s 8(2).

[51] POCA, s 4(4). The Minister may sell or otherwise dispose of any such property. Any money realised under this section shall be paid into or disposed of for the benefit of the Exchequer: POCA, s 4(5). Contrast this with the Asset Recovery Incentivisation Scheme (ARIS)in the UK.

[52] POCA, s 4(8). For consideration in the context of the 'family home' see *CAB v Kelly* [2012] IESC 64.

[53] POCA, s 4A, as inserted by POC(A)A, s 7.

[54] POC(A)A, s 10.

[55] POCA, s 16.

[56] POCA, s 16B(1)(a), as inserted by POC(A)A, s 12. 'Corrupt conduct' is defined as 'any conduct which at the time it occurred was an offence under the Prevention of Corruption Acts 1889 to 2001, the Official Secrets Act 1963 or the Ethics in Public Office Act 1995': POCA, s 16B(1)(b), as inserted by POC(A)A, s 12.

[57] POCA, s 16B(2), as inserted by POC(A)A, s 12.

[58] POCA, s 16B(8), as inserted by POC(A)A, s 12.

[59] POCA, s 16B(5), as inserted by POC(A)A, s 12.

an affidavit specifying the property owned by him or his income and sources of income, or both.[60] Unlike the affidavit that can be required in proceedings under sections 2 (interim order) and 3 (interlocutory order), there is no time restriction here. An *ex parte* application can be brought to the court for an order prohibiting the defendant, or any other person having notice of the order, from disposing of, otherwise dealing with or diminishing the value of the property during a specified period.[61]

B. The Criminal Assets Bureau

The agency tasked with implementing POCA is the CAB.[62] Indeed, the establishment of such a specialised agency was described as 'a necessary adjunct to [the] assets' freezing Bill and is somewhat consequential to it'.[63] The CAB is established as a body corporate with perpetual succession, an official seal, the power to sue and be sued in its corporate name, and the power to acquire, hold and dispose of land, or an interest in land or any other property.[64] The CAB is headed by a senior police officer (the Chief Bureau Officer)[65] and adopts a multi-agency approach, with officials from An Garda Síochána (police), the Revenue Commissioners (taxation) and the Department of Social Protection (social welfare).[66] A bureau officer retains the powers and duties vested in him by virtue of his position as a Garda, a member of the Revenue Commissioners or an officer of the Minister for Social Protection.[67] There are many benefits to this multi-agency approach, including pooling of professional expertise, improved management of resources and decreased duration of investigations.[68] As Lemieux says, in the context of transnational police cooperation: 'In theory the coordination of resources should

[60] POCA, s 16B(6)(a), as inserted by POC(A)A, s 12. Such an affidavit is not admissible in criminal proceedings against that person or spouse, except where such proceedings relate to perjury arising from statements in the affidavit: POCA, s 16B(6)(b), as inserted by POC(A)A, s 12.

[61] POCA, s 16B(4), as inserted by POC(A)A, s 12.

[62] While much of the discussion on CAB relates to civil forfeiture powers, and these powers are the focus of this chapter, it is important to realise that CAB does have significant taxation and social welfare powers too.

[63] Dáil Éireann, Criminal Assets Bureau Bill, 1996, Second Stage, 25 July 1996, vol 468, col 1031, per Deputy McCreevy.

[64] CABA, s 3(2). The objectives and functions of the Bureau are set out in CABA, ss 4 and 5.

[65] CABA, s 7.

[66] CABA, s 8.

[67] CABA, s 8(2) and (8). The rationale behind this was explained during the passage of the CAB Bill in the following terms: 'each of the three agencies will bring their own powers and expertise to the bureau and, by means of section 8 of the Bill, will exercise these powers in a mutually supportive and concerned manner.' Dáil Éireann, Criminal Assets Bureau Bill (n 63), vol 468, cols 1025 and 1026, per Minister Quinn.

[68] A useful analogy here can be found in international police cooperation against transnational drug trafficking: F Lemieux, 'Tackling Transnational Drug Trafficking Effectively: Assessing the Outcomes of the Drug Enforcement Administration's International Cooperation Initiatives' in F Lemieux, *International Police Cooperation: Emerging Issues, Theory and Practice* (Devon, Willan Publishing, 2010) 260.

allow police forces to surpass their individual capacities by improving the efficiency of operations and reducing the cost of managing investigations.'[69]

The multi-agency approach facilitates greater cooperation and collaboration between officials from different agencies,[70] the sharing of powers and duties,[71] greater admissibility of evidence[72] and the sharing of information.[73] The Criminal Assets Bureau Act also makes provision for a bureau officer to be 'accompanied or assisted in the exercise of [his or her] powers or duties by such other persons (including bureau officers) as [he or she] considers necessary'.[74] The Criminal Assets Bureau Act contains a number of provisions in relation to investigatory powers, including provision for anonymity of non-Garda bureau officers.[75] The Act makes provision for a search warrant to be issued by a District Court judge, where there are reasonable grounds for suspecting that evidence of or relating to assets or proceeds deriving from criminal conduct, or to their identity or whereabouts, is to be found in a particular place.[76] In situations of urgency where it is impracticable to apply to a District Court judge, a senior police officer (ie not below the rank of superintendent) may issue such a warrant.[77] Post-2005, there is provision for an 'Order to make material available',[78] a 'tipping-off' offence in relation to such an order,[79] and an order in relation to obtaining information regarding any property held in trust.[80] There is now provision for non-Garda bureau officers, accompanied by a Garda bureau officer, to attend at and participate in questioning a person detained pursuant to section 4 of the Criminal Justice Act 1984 or section 2 of the Criminal Justice (Drug Trafficking) Act 1996.[81]

A number of offences are also set out in the Criminal Assets Bureau Act. It is an offence to publish or cause to be published the fact that a person is, or was, a bureau officer or member of staff at the bureau, or is a member of the family of such a person, or the address of any such person.[82] It is an offence to delay,

[69] ibid 266. Lemieux does acknowledge that 'there are few rigorous, empirical evaluations of the performance of multi-jurisdictional teams' (ibid 266). The same point can equally be made in relation to the lack of rigorous, empirical evaluation of the multi-agency Criminal Assets Bureau. It is to be hoped that criminologists or policing scholars will take up this challenge and carry out empirical review of CAB.

[70] CABA, s 8(5).

[71] CABA, s 8(6)(c).

[72] CABA, s 8(6)(d).

[73] CABA, s 8(5) and (7). In *CAB v Craft* [2001] 1 IR 121, 133 O'Sullivan J stated: 'The members of the Criminal Assets Bureau are entitled to exchange information amongst themselves and clearly they would be in dereliction of duty if they failed to do this in an appropriate case.'

[74] CABA, s 8(6)(a).

[75] CABA, s 10.

[76] CABA, s 14(1), as substituted by Criminal Justice Act 2006, s 190.

[77] CABA, s 14(2) and (3).

[78] CABA, s 14A, as inserted by POC(A)A, s 18.

[79] CABA, s 14B, as inserted by POC(A)A, s 18.

[80] CABA, s 14C, as inserted by POC(A)A, s 18.

[81] CABA, s 8(6A), as inserted by Criminal Justice Act 2007, s 58.

[82] CABA, s 11(1).

obstruct, impede, interfere with or resist either a bureau officer in the exercise or performance of his powers or duties or a member of staff of the bureau who is accompanying or assisting such a bureau officer.[83] It is an offence to utter or send threats to, or in any way intimidate or menace, a bureau officer or member of staff of the bureau, or the family or either such person.[84] It is an offence to assault or attempt to assault a bureau officer, a member of staff of the bureau or a family member of either such person.[85] Where a Garda bureau officer has reasonable cause to suspect that a person is committing, or has committed, an offence under section 12, 13 or 15 of the Criminal Assets Bureau Act, or an offence under section 94 of the Finance Act 1983, that officer may arrest that person without warrant or require the person to give his or her name and address.[86] Where a person is charged with an offence under either section 13 or 15 of the Criminal Assets Bureau Act, no further proceedings (other than remanding in custody or on bail) shall be taken except by, or with the consent of, the Director of Public Prosecutions.[87]

C. Legal Challenges

Unsurprisingly, a number of legal challenges ensued, but the Irish courts have consistently upheld the constitutionality of POCA. The leading decision is the joined case of *Murphy v GM, PB, PC Ltd, GH and Gilligan v CAB*.[88] In that case, the Supreme Court upheld the constitutionality of the Act and also dismissed a number of challenges on non-constitutional points. The arguments advanced are worth further attention: it was argued that POCA essentially formed part of the criminal law, not the civil law, and that persons affected by this legislation were deprived of traditional criminal law safeguards.[89] Furthermore, it was alleged that: the Act permitted oppressive delays; the maxim *audi alteram partem* was violated; the privilege against self-incrimination was contravened; the Act was over-broad and vague; the Act violated the guarantee of private property; there was an impermissible interference with the judicial function; the Act purported to allow, or at least recognise, the possibility of an appeal from the Supreme Court to a non-specified court or authority; and, finally, the Act had retrospective effect (contrary to Article 15.5) and extraterritorial effect (contrary to Articles 29.3 and 29.8).

[83] CABA, s 12(1).
[84] CABA, s 13(1).
[85] CABA, s 15(1).
[86] CABA, s 16(1).
[87] CABA, s 17.
[88] Above n 18. This case was an appeal from separate High Court decisions in *Gilligan v CAB* [1998] 3 IR 185 and *Murphy v GM, PB, PC Ltd* [1999] IEHC 5.
[89] The specific safeguards mentioned were the presumption of innocence, the standard of proof, trial by jury and the rule against double jeopardy.

These arguments were dismissed by the Supreme Court. The court first noted that the legislation enjoys a presumption of constitutionality,[90] and then addressed each of the above arguments in turn. In relation to the criminal nature of the proceedings, the court began by stating:

> It is almost beyond argument that, if the procedures under ss 2, 3 and 4 of the Act of 1996 constituted in substance, albeit not in form, the trial of persons on criminal charges, they would be invalid having regard to the provisions of the Constitution. The virtual absence of the presumption of innocence, the provision that the standard of proof is to be on the balance of probabilities and the admissibility of hearsay evidence taken together are inconsistent with the requirement in Article 38.1 of the Constitution that: 'No person shall be tried in any criminal charge save in due course of law.' It is also clear that, if these procedures constitute the trial of a person on a criminal charge, which, depending on the value of the property, might or might not constitute a minor offence, the absence of any provision for a trial by jury of such a charge in the Act would clearly be in violation of Article 38.5 of the Constitution.[91]

The key question for the court, then, was whether the procedures under POCA are criminal in nature. After reviewing a number of authorities,[92] the court stated that the indicia of crime are 'conspicuously absent in the present case'[93] and continued:

> in proceedings under ss. 3 and 4 of the Act of 1996, there is no provision for the arrest or detention of any person, for the admission of persons to bail, for the imprisonment of a person in default of payment of a penalty, for a form of criminal trial initiated by summons or indictment, for the recording of a conviction in any form or for the entering of a *nolle prosequi* at any stage.[94]

The court further rejected the contention that the presence of *mens rea* is a prerequisite to an order under either section 3 or 4: such 'orders can be made even though it has not been shown to the satisfaction of the court that there was *mens rea* on the part of the person in possession or control of the property'.[95] The court went on to say that forfeiture of property that represents the proceeds of crime 'is not a punishment and its operation does not require criminal procedures'.[96]

The argument that the Act permitted oppressive delays was swiftly dismissed by the court, since

[90] See *McDonald v Bord na gCon (no 2)* [1965] IR 217; *East Donegal Co-Operative Livestock Mart Ltd v Attorney General* [1970] IR 317.

[91] *Murphy v GM; Gilligan v CAB* (n 18) 135.

[92] Including *Attorney General v Southern Industrial Trust Ltd* (1957) 94 ILTR 161; *Melling v O'Mathghamhna* [1962] IR 1; *Clancy* (n 19); *McLoughlin v Tuite* [1989] IR 82; and *O'Keeffe v Ferris* [1993] 3 IR 165 (HC), [1997] 3 IR 463 (SC). The court also referred to the US decision in *United States v Ursery* (1996) 518 US 267.

[93] *Murphy v GM; Gilligan v CAB* (n 18) 147.

[94] *Murphy v GM; Gilligan v CAB* (n 18) 147.

[95] *Murphy v GM; Gilligan v CAB* (n 18) 148. See also *Murphy v Gilligan* (n 44) para 8 *et seq.*

[96] *Murphy v GM; Gilligan v CAB* (n 18) 153.

> the procedure under the Act is perfectly capable of being operated in such a manner as to ensure that no unreasonable delay elapses between the making of the interim order and the interlocutory order: that indeed is clearly what the Act envisaged.[97]

In relation to the seven-year period between the making of an interlocutory order and a disposal order, the contention that such delay is unduly oppressive was rejected as it 'rests on the misconception' that the application for a disposal order equates to the trial of the action. A person affected by an interlocutory order under section 3 can apply, at any point when such an order is in force, to have that order varied or discharged.[98]

The court also swiftly dealt with the complaint regarding the maxim *audi alteram partem*. After reiterating that

> it is to be presumed that the Oireachtas intended that procedures provided for under the Act would be conducted in accordance with the principles of constitutional justice and that any departure from those principles will be restrained or corrected by the courts[99]

it was said:

> the court is satisfied that in any case brought under the procedures laid down by the Act, the affidavits grounding the interim and interlocutory application of necessity will indicate to the respondents the nature of the case being made on behalf of the applicant. Nor is the provision for the admission of hearsay of itself unconstitutional: it was a matter for the court hearing the application to decide what weight should be given to such evidence. The court is satisfied that there is no substance in these grounds of challenge to the constitutionality of the legislation.[100]

The next ground for challenge was that there was no equality of arms, given that the applicant could rely on opinion evidence whereas the respondent could not. Again, the court swiftly rejected this argument:

> the respondents to an application under s 2 or s 3 will normally be the persons in possession or control of the property and should be in a position to give evidence to the court as to its provenance without calling in aid opinion evidence.[101]

[97] *Murphy v GM; Gilligan v CAB* (n 18) 154.

[98] *Murphy v GM; Gilligan v CAB* (n 18) 154. This reasoning was applied in *Murphy v Gilligan* (n 44) para 12 *et seq*. It was said: 'Insofar as the first-named respondent's contention in relation to delay is based upon a claim that the 1996 Act mandates a seven year delay prior to a disposal application being brought and that the present proceedings have lasted for nearly seven more years and such delay is excessive, the court is satisfied that the first-named respondent cannot rely upon this contention as it was open to him at any time since the making of the s 3 order, including during the seven year period provided for in s 4, to bring an application under s 3(3). It is the first-named respondent himself who chose not to commence such an application until 2009 and in those circumstances the legal authorities relied upon by the first-named respondent in relation to delay in criminal trials have no application. In criminal trials it is for the prosecution to bring matters before the court whilst in s 3(3) applications it is for persons, such as the first-named respondent, who are affected by s 3 orders to commence such applications. If they delay in commencing such applications they cannot seek to rely on such delay' (para 14).

[99] *Murphy v GM; Gilligan v CAB* (n 18) 154.

[100] *Murphy v GM; Gilligan v CAB* (n 18) 155.

[101] *Murphy v GM; Gilligan v CAB* (n 18) 155.

The argument that the Act contravenes the privilege against self-incrimination was also dismissed:

> Parties to civil proceedings, whatever their nature, may find themselves in a position where they are reluctant to adduce evidence beneficial to them because it might also expose them to the risk of a criminal prosecution. That factual position, however, cannot be equated to a statutory provision obliging a person to give evidence, even in circumstances where his or her evidence might be incriminating. Similarly, the fact that a person can be required to file an affidavit specifying his or her property and income cannot, on any view, be equated to a statutory provision requiring a person to adduce evidence which may incriminate him or her. The court is satisfied that these grounds of challenge are also without foundation.[102]

The next argument dealt with by the court related to whether the Act was overly broad and vague, specifically as regards the term 'proceeds of crime' and the court's power not to grant an order where there is 'a serious risk of injustice'. In relation to the former, it was said that

> in every case before an order can be made, the court must be satisfied on the balance of probabilities that on the evidence adduced to it in that particular case the property in respect of which the freezing order is sought was the proceeds of crime.[103]

In relation to the latter, it was said that, while this power

> is undoubtedly wide in its scope, that can only be in ease of the individuals whose rights may be affected and the court, in applying these provisions, will be obliged to act in accordance with the requirements of constitutional justice.[104]

As such, this challenge was also rejected.

Neither did the court dwell on the argument that the Act violated the guarantee of property rights under the Constitution. The court adopted the decision of Barrington J in *Clancy v Ireland*, concerning the Offences Against the State (Amendment) Act 1985, where it was held that that legislation was 'a permissible delimitation of property rights in the interests of the common good'.[105] The challenge to POCA was also rejected on this ground.

The next argument to be rejected was the challenge on the ground of interference with judicial function in that the legislation requires the High Court to make an order in certain circumstances: 'it is perfectly permissible for the legislature to provide that, where certain conditions are met, the making of an order of a particular nature by a court may be mandatory rather than discretionary'.[106]

The court also rejected the challenge to the legislation based on the grounds of retrospective effect and extraterritorial effect:

[102] *Murphy v GM; Gilligan v CAB* (n 18) 156.
[103] *Murphy v GM; Gilligan v CAB* (n 18) 156.
[104] *Murphy v GM; Gilligan v CAB* (n 18) 156.
[105] *Clancy* (n 19) 336.
[106] *Murphy v GM; Gilligan v CAB* (n 18) 156.

> The Act does not offend in any way the prohibition in Article 15.5 against declaring acts to be infringements of the law which were not so at the date of their commission. The fact that it enables the court to make orders in respect of property constituting the proceeds of crimes committed before the coming into force of the legislation is not in any sense a contravention of that prohibition.[107]

The court continued:

> Nor was the fact that the legislation may be operated so as to require the compliance of citizens within the jurisdiction with orders of the court directing the transfer of property in their possession or control to a receiver appointed by the court in circumstances where the property is in another jurisdiction constitute in any way a breach of the principles of international law which the State accepts under Article 29 of the Constitution.[108]

Another argument advanced was that the Act impermissibly authorised and/or recognised the possibility of an appeal from the Supreme Court to a non-specified court or authority. Again, this argument was rejected:

> The court is satisfied that the words 'or if any further appeal' in s 2(5)(c) are, at worst, surplusage and, in accordance with well established principles of statutory construction, can be disregarded where the result would otherwise be unconstitutional or would, as in this case, produce an absurd or anomalous result.[109]

Finally, the court declined to consider whether POCA conflicted with the European Convention on Human Rights, on the ground that the Convention was not then part of domestic law. The Supreme Court, accordingly, upheld the constitutionality of POCA. It will be argued in the next section, however, that the courts erred in this regard.

III. A Critique of the Irish Model

While welcomed by some,[110] civil forfeiture has been heavily criticised by others as undermining due process. Lea, for example, describes the non-conviction based

[107] *Murphy v GM; Gilligan v CAB* (n 18) 157. See also *Murphy v Gilligan* (n 44) para 6.2.

[108] *Murphy v GM; Gilligan v CAB* (n 18) 157.

[109] *Murphy v GM; Gilligan v CAB* (n 18) 157.

[110] eg SD Cassella, 'Civil Asset Recovery: The American Experience' (2013) *EUCrim: The European Criminal Law Association's Forum* 98; F Cassidy, 'Targeting the Proceeds of Crime: An Irish Perspective' in T. Greenberg et al, *Stolen Asset Recovery: A Good Practices Guide for Non-Conviction Based Asset Forfeiture* (London, World Bank) 153; J Simser, 'Perspectives on Civil Forfeiture' in S Young, *Civil Forfeiture of Criminal Property: Legal Measures for Targeting the Proceeds of Crime* (Cheltenham, Edward Elgar, 2009) 13; A Kennedy, 'Justifying the Civil Recovery of Criminal Proceeds' (2004) *Journal of Financial Crime* 8.

approach to seizing assets as 'a frontal assault on due process',[111] while Gallant notes that 'the chronic critique of asset recovery is that the takings do not, for the most part, comply with procedural and substantive rights. Regulation manages to secure title to tainted assets at the expense of the rule of law.'[112] Gray argues that, despite the 'civil' label, civil forfeiture is in fact criminal in nature and due process protections should apply.[113] In the Irish context, Campbell argues that CAB and POCA 'indicate a realignment of the approach adopted by the agents of the State in the fight against organised crime, and demonstrate a preference for the needs of the State over the individual's right to due process'.[114] In my own previous work, I have been critical of the use of civil processes to avoid enhanced procedural protections of the criminal process,[115] arguing that civil forfeiture undermines due process rights[116] and is a step 'too far'.[117]

The use of the civil process—essentially as a less burdensome alternative to the criminal process—gives rise to concern, not least that it allows the State to circumvent enhanced procedural protections that apply in the criminal process.[118] There are good reasons to insist upon such procedural protections in criminal proceedings: indeed, the relationship between the State and the individual, the imbalance between the State's and a defendant's resources, the potential consequences of a guilty verdict, avoiding wrongful convictions and respecting individual dignity and autonomy can all be cited as relevant justifications.[119]

My argument is that civil forfeiture, albeit purporting to be civil, ought to properly be regarded as being of a criminal nature and, therefore, should attract criminal procedural safeguards. For example, in criminal proceedings, the applicable standard of proof is proof beyond reasonable doubt. In contrast, under POCA, section 8(2) provides that the applicable standard of proof is the civil standard,

[111] J Lea, 'Hitting Criminals Where It Hurts: Organised Crime and the Erosion of Due Process' (2004) 35 *Cambria Law Review* 81, 83.

[112] M Michelle Gallant, 'Money Laundering Consequences: Recovering Wealth, Piercing Secrecy, Disrupting Tax Havens and Distorting International Law' (2014) 17(3) *Journal of Money Laundering Control* 296, 299.

[113] A Gray, 'Forfeiture Provisions and the Criminal/Civil Divide' (2012) 15 *New Criminal Law Review* 32; A Gray, 'The Compatibility of Unexplained Wealth Provisions and "Civil" Forfeiture Regimes with Kable' (2012) 12 *Queensland UT Law and Justice Journal* 18.

[114] L Campbell, 'Theorising Asset Forfeiture in Ireland' (2007) 71 *Journal of Criminal Law* 441, 455.

[115] C King, 'Using Civil Processes in Pursuit of Criminal Law Objectives: A Case Study of Non-conviction Based Asset Forfeiture' (2012) 16(4) *International Journal of Evidence and Proof* 337.

[116] C King, 'Civil Forfeiture and Article 6 of the ECHR: Due Process Implications for England and Wales and Ireland' (2014) 34(3) *Legal Studies* 371.

[117] J Hendry and C King, 'How Far Is Too Far? Theorising Non-conviction-Based Asset Forfeiture' (2015) 11(4) *International Journal of Law in Context* 398.

[118] See, eg AX Fellmeth, 'Civil and Criminal Sanctions in the Constitution and Courts' (2005) 94(1) *Georgetown Law Journal* 1.

[119] See, eg A Ashworth, 'Four Threats to the Presumption of Innocence' (2006) *International Journal of Evidence and Proof* 241; R Lippke, 'Justifying the Proof Structure of Criminal Trials' (2013) *International Journal of Evidence and Proof* 323.

namely the balance of probabilities. This lower standard of proof allows for criminal allegations to be tested against the civil standard of proof. As Gallant reinforces, 'it is significantly easier to prove matters of fact and law to the civil standard of a balance of probabilities than it is to prove the same beyond a reasonable doubt'.[120]

There are also concerns relating to the presumption of innocence: for example, a person might be acquitted in criminal proceedings but subsequently confronted with civil forfeiture proceedings based on the very same allegations and evidence. Of course, a 'not guilty' verdict does not establish actual innocence—it merely establishes that the prosecution case did not establish guilt beyond reasonable doubt—but to allow civil forfeiture proceedings in such a circumstance effectively undermines that acquittal. In other words, 'In essence, a person is being "punished" for his wrongdoing, albeit in civil proceedings, having been found "guilty", in the eyes of both the State and his fellow citizens, of the offence for which he had been previously acquitted'.[121]

The circumvention of criminal procedural protections can be seen in *McK v SG*.[122] There, the defendant had been suspected of involvement in an armed hijacking of a truck; however, he was never charged in connection with that offence. During the police investigation, a sum of money had been seized from the defendant's home. The defendant successfully applied to the District Court for an order, under the Police Property Act 1897, directing that the money be returned to him. Subsequent to that order, proceedings were initiated under POCA, based on opinion evidence from Chief Superintendent McK and testimony from Garda O'K, who was a member of the team investigating the armed hijacking. In granting an order under section 3 of POCA, White J stated:

> from a consideration of the evidence of Chief Superintendent McK. and the evidence of Garda O'K. I am satisfied that the Plaintiff has made out a prima facie case that the monies in question constitute directly or indirectly the proceeds of crime.

He went on to say:

> I accept that the Defendant was never prosecuted in any respect in relation to the armed hijacking. Nevertheless this fact alone does not persuade me that the monies are not directly or indirectly the proceeds of crime, on the contrary, in all the circumstances of the case, I am more than satisfied, on the balance of probabilities that they are.

This case clearly demonstrates how POCA can operate to undermine criminal procedural protections.

[120] MM Gallant, *Money Laundering and the Proceeds of Crime: Economic Crime and Civil Remedies* (Cheltenham, Edward Elgar, 2005) 19.

[121] MM Gallant and C King, 'The Seizure of Illicit Assets: Patterns of Civil Forfeiture in Canada and Ireland' (2013) 42 *Common Law World Review* 91, 97. See also RT Naylor, 'Wash-out: A Critique of Follow-the-Money Methods in Crime Control Policy' (1999) *Crime, Law and Social Change* 1, 41.

[122] [2006] IEHC 447.

Much of the due process criticisms levied against POCA stem from its purported civil nature. Yet, despite it being 'unquestionably draconian',[123] the Irish courts, as we have seen above, have upheld the constitutionality of POCA. The Irish courts, however, are more concerned with form rather than substance: as I have argued elsewhere, 'we must look beyond the face of the legislation to consider whether the provisions of the Act are, de facto, concerned with criminal, as opposed to civil, matters'.[124]

While the legislature did intend to create a civil process, the argument advanced here is that civil forfeiture should instead be deemed a criminal process. It is lamentable that the Irish courts have failed to stand up to the legislature in this respect. The approach of the Irish courts, in granting judicial imprimatur to civil forfeiture, has been subjected to criticism. For example, Campbell points out that

> the courts have held, using somewhat circular logic, that a procedure is not a criminal process if it does not involve characteristics such as arrest or detention. However, it appears that it is the avoidance of these aspects at the stage of enactment which facilitates the depiction of forfeiture as civil. For example, while the lack of detention under the Proceeds of Crime Acts may be cited as evidence that the proceedings are not criminal, the initial classification of the process as civil in nature by the legislature has resulted in the fact that an individual may not be detained.[125]

A punitive purpose underpins civil forfeiture—as illustrated in the political debates discussed above in Section I.[126] Retribution[127] and deterrence[128] clearly weighed on the minds of politicians. And, of course, civil forfeiture proceedings can result in stigma.[129] While the Irish courts have suggested that civil forfeiture

[123] *Murphy v GM; Gilligan v CAB* (n 18) 136, per Keane CJ. In *FJMcK v FC, PL, and MAC; FJMcK v MJG, T Ltd, and E Ltd* [2001] 4 IR 521, 524 Keane CJ recognised that procedures under POCA are 'of an unusual nature and they are of course, self evidently, and it is not using excessive language to say, of a draconian nature'.

[124] King (n 115) 345.

[125] L Campbell, 'The Recovery of "Criminal" Assets in New Zealand, Ireland and England: Fighting Organised and Serious Crime in the Civil Realm' (2010) 41 *Victoria University of Wellington Law Review* 15, 23.

[126] See J Meade, 'Organised Crime, Moral Panic and Law Reform: The Irish Adoption of Civil Forfeiture' (2000) 10(1) *Irish Criminal Law Journal* 11.

[127] eg 'The killing of Veronica Guerin was a calculated attack on the freedom of each and every person in this country. It was an act designed to silence not alone the late Veronica Guerin but everybody who might follow in her footsteps. It was an act of unspeakable evil which was carried out for a specific and defined purpose. Veronica Guerin was killed because she investigated and wrote about organised crime. She had become a threat to criminals and to their continued enjoyment of illegally acquired assets. She was killed so that criminals could hold on to the proceeds of crime. Are we as a community … prepared to tolerate the continued unhindered existence in our midst of people who have accumulated vast and unexplained wealth? If we are, I suggest Veronica Guerin died in vain'. Dail Éireann, Organised Crime Bill (n 9), vol 467, cols 2405–06, per Deputy O'Donoghue.

[128] eg 'What we need to do now is prevent assets being used as the seeds of future crimes. To put it another way, if we cannot arrest the criminals, why not confiscate their assets?' Dail Éireann, Organised Crime Bill (n 9), vol 467, col 2435, per Deputy O'Donnell.

[129] eg 'Cab Gets Order to Seize 146 000 € as Proceeds of Crime from Sligo Family', *Irish Times*, 15 December 2011; 'Alleged Criminal Must Forfeit House and Car,' *Irish Times*, 4 February 2014.

serves reparative purposes,[130] it is posited here that such proceedings primarily serve criminal law purposes and that the courts ought to have intervened to insist that criminal procedural safeguards apply in civil forfeiture proceedings.

Another area that has attracted criticism is the impact on property rights. Even before POCA was enacted in 1996, concern had been raised as to the constitutionality of seizing property in the absence of criminal conviction: it was thought that such a procedure might constitute an 'unjust attack' on property rights guaranteed by the Constitution.[131] When civil forfeiture was challenged before the courts, however, such criticisms were rejected.[132] It was found that civil forfeiture does not constitute an 'unjust attack' on property rights. Emphasis was also placed on balancing rights to property against the public interest. For example:

> While the provisions of the Act may, indeed, affect the property rights of a respondent it does not appear to this court that they constitute an 'unjust attack' under Article 40.3.2, given the fact that the State must in the first place show to the satisfaction of the court that the property in question is the proceeds of crime and that thus, prima facie, the respondent has no good title to it, and also given the balancing provisions built into ss.3 and 4 [of the Act].
>
> This court would also accept that the exigencies of the common good would certainly include measures designed to prevent the accumulation and use of assets which directly or indirectly derive from criminal activities. The right to private ownership cannot hold a place so high in the hierarchy of rights that it protects the position of assets illegally acquired and held.[133]

The courts have also said:

> The issue in the present case does not raise a challenge to a valid constitutional right of property. It concerns the right of the State to take, or the right of a citizen to resist the State in taking, property which is proved on the balance of probabilities to represent the proceeds of crime. In general such a forfeiture is not a punishment and its operation does not require criminal procedures. Application of such legislation must be sensitive to the actual property and other rights of citizens but in principle and subject, no doubt, to special problems which may arise in particular cases, a person in possession of the proceeds of crime can have no constitutional grievance if deprived of their use.[134]

Again, however, we are confronted with the absence of important criminal procedural safeguards: the State is depriving a person of property on the basis that that property constitutes proceeds of crime, yet the *civil* standard of proof applies. Most people, I venture, would agree with the idea that crime should not pay; of course

[130] *Gilligan* (n 88) 217–18.

[131] Law Reform Commission, 'Report on the Confiscation of the Proceeds of Crime' LRC 35-1991 (Dublin, Law Reform Commission, 1991) 51.

[132] The courts, in considering POCA, were influenced by the decision in *Clancy* (n 19).

[133] *Gilligan* (n 88) 237, per McGuinness J.

[134] *Murphy v GM; Gilligan v CAB* (n 18) 153, per Keane CJ.

a person who has benefited from criminal conduct should be denied the benefit of that conduct. Yet, any such deprivation of property ought to require the higher criminal standard of proof. To say, as the Supreme Court does, that civil forfeiture under POCA 'is not a punishment' misrepresents the reality of the situation.

The next issue to consider is the agency tasked with implementing civil forfeiture—the CAB.[135] That the CAB is essentially a policing agency, with extensive powers, adds significant concern. CAB officers retain the powers and duties that they have by virtue of their position as a Garda, a member of the Revenue Commissioners or an officer of the Minister for Social Protection, as the case may be. There is provision for a bureau officer to be 'accompanied or assisted in the exercise of [his or her] powers or duties by such other persons (including bureau officers) as [he or she] considers necessary'.[136] This is stated very broadly and would appear to include assistance by non-bureau officers. Presumably, this provision was included to enable assistance from technical experts (eg computer specialists), but the broad wording of this provision does not confine assistance to such persons. Moreover, there is no requirement as to background or training necessary before a person can accompany or assist a bureau officer.

Another concern relates to the sharing of powers: 'A bureau officer who assists another bureau officer under [section 8(6)(a)] shall have and be conferred with the powers and duties of the first-mentioned bureau officer for the purposes of that assistance only.'[137] This opens the possibility[138] of non-police officers being bestowed with policing powers where they are assisting a Garda bureau officer. As Harfield points out (in relation to the UK Serious Organised Crime Agency):[139] 'In adopting the position that police powers are no longer exclusively for police officers to execute, the Government has altered radically the relationship of the citizen to the use of police powers and the accountability inherent there.'[140]

A final concern to emphasise in relation to the CAB is its limited accountability. While an Annual Report is to be prepared,[141] these reports are inadequate in terms of being an effective accountability mechanism. Not only is the detail rather limited,[142] but also the national Parliament simply plays a passive role in receiving

[135] For a critique of the Bureau and its powers, see C King, 'Follow the Money Trail: "Civil" Forfeiture of "Criminal" Assets in Ireland' in P van Duyne et al (eds), *Human Dimensions in Organised Crime, Money Laundering, and Corruption* (Nijmegen, Wolf Legal, 2013).

[136] CABA, s 8(6)(a).

[137] CABA, s 8(6)(c).

[138] In practice, it appears that policing powers have only been exercised by Garda bureau officers to date. I thank Frank Cassidy for this point.

[139] The Serious Organised Crime Agency (SOCA) has since been replaced by the National Crime Agency, but the point equally applies to that new agency.

[140] C Harfield, 'SOCA: A Paradigm Shift in British Policing' (2006) 46(4) *British Journal of Criminology* 743, 751.

[141] CABA, s 21.

[142] Though this may be somewhat understandable: 'For operational effectiveness and statutory confidentiality reasons the Bureau is required to keep specific details of many of its actions confidential': Criminal Assets Bureau, *Annual Report 2005* (Dublin, Stationery Office, 2006) 7.

these reports.[143] As has been pointed out elsewhere (in relation to the UK Serious Organised Crime Agency): 'In the absence of proper public accountability, scrutiny—whether this is through research, parliamentary committee or through openness to public debate—becomes even more important.'[144]

Conclusion

The Proceeds of Crime Acts and the Criminal Assets Bureau Act have now been on the statute book for two decades, and have received a great deal of praise during that time. For example, in 2010 the Department of Justice and Law Reform published a White Paper on Crime discussion document in which civil forfeiture powers and the multi-agency Criminal Assets Bureau were commended as a 'very effective tool'.[145] That document went on to say:

> The Bureau has been successful over the years in seizing the proceeds of criminal activity in an effective and visible manner. It represents a new form of policing designed to disrupt and disable the capacity of targeted individuals to participate in further criminal activity.[146]

The Minister for Justice, Equality and Law Reform has lauded the work of the Bureau as follows:

> The Criminal Assets Bureau has been at the forefront of the fight against organised crime, including drug trafficking, in this jurisdiction since its inception in 1996. The significant successes that the Bureau continues to achieve by its operations demonstrates the effectiveness of its approach in pursuing illegally gotten gains.[147]

A note of caution must be sounded, however, and this chapter has identified a number of areas that give rise to concern, not least the use of civil processes to avoid criminal procedural protections. Notwithstanding extensive criticism in this regard, the Irish courts have upheld the constitutionality of civil forfeiture, thereby giving judicial imprimatur to this hugely controversial power.

Given that civil forfeiture is here to stay, the purpose of this chapter has been to set out the 'state of the art'—specifically, how the legislation and case law have

[143] For greater discussion of accountability, see M den Boer, 'Towards an Accountability Regime for an Emerging European Policing Governance' (2002) 12(4) *Policing and Society* 275.

[144] B Bowling and C Murphy, 'Serious Organised Crime under New Labour' (2007) *Criminal Justice Matters* 32, 33.

[145] Department of Justice and Law Reform, *Organised and White Collar Crime* (White Paper on Crime, Discussion Document No 3, October 2010) 6.

[146] ibid 6.

[147] Dail Éireann, Written Answers—Criminal Assets Bureau, vol 661, 24 September 2008, per Minister Ahern.

developed over the past two decades. The focus is very much on legal developments; indeed, much of the extant literature on civil forfeiture has examined this topic from a legal and/or criminological standpoint. Yet there is a great deal of scope for other disciplines to contribute to debates about civil forfeiture and add fresh perspectives. For example, it would be interesting to explore the use of civil forfeiture to combat corporate wrongdoing, especially in light of difficulties in prosecuting such behaviour, and ask whether it is appropriate (or desirable) to use such a tool instead of conventional criminal processes. Another potential issue to explore relates to procedural fairness, and the experiences of those confronted by civil forfeiture actions. So, too, would it be interesting to examine the 'new' form of policing, the structures, and accountability mechanisms of the CAB. A further idea would be to consider the question of impact or effectiveness: while there has been some such work in respect of anti-money laundering or counter-terrorist financing powers,[148] there is a notable lack of such research in relation to asset recovery. It is hoped that this chapter will spark interest from other disciplines to bring their skill set to examine civil forfeiture measures.

Postscript

Subsequent to the writing of this chapter, the Oireachtas passed the Proceeds of Crime (Amendment) Act 2016 on 27 July 2016—in response to a number of shootings in Dublin.[149] This legislation makes provision for administrative seizure and detention, ie a bureau officer can now seize and detain property with a value of at least €5,000 for an initial period of up to 24 hours. The Chief Bureau Officer of CAB may authorise detention for a further period not exceeding 21 days. There is provision for a person to apply to the Court to have the authorisation varied or revoked, and there is provision for compensation to be paid to a person who suffers loss as a result of property being detained.[150] Significantly, the 2016 Act reduces the monetary threshold before property can be subject to an order under POCA—from €13,000 to €5,000.[151]

[148] eg B Unger et al, *The Economic and Legal Effectiveness of the European Union's Anti-money Laundering Policy* (Cheltenham, Edward Elgar, 2014); M Levi, 'Combating the Financing of Terrorism: A History and Assessment of the Control of "Threat Finance"' (2010) 50 *British Journal of Criminology* 650.

[149] See, generally, Seanad Éireann, Proceeds of Crime (Amendment) Bill 2016: Second Stage, 5 July 2016. *cf* C Lally, 'Gardaí Believe Gangland Killing Linked to the Kinahan-Hutch Feud', *Irish Times*, 2 July 2016.

[150] POCA, s 1A, as inserted by POC(A)A 2016, s 3.

[151] POC(A)A 2016, ss 4–6, amending POCA, ss 2, 3 and 8.

4

The Problematic Nature of Asset Recovery Measures: Recent Developments of the Italian Preventive Confiscation

FRANCESCO MAZZACUVA*

Introduction

It is always difficult to define what a penalty is and when a sanction should be considered as criminal in nature. In order to assess the nature of a measure and to determine which safeguards should apply, the European Court of Human Rights (ECtHR) goes beyond the label—ie the formal definition adopted by national legislators—and looks at its concrete purposes. In this regard, the ECtHR distinguishes three possible purposes: reparation, punishment and prevention. In particular, the antithetical relationship between punishment and prevention is motivated by distinguishing, on the one hand, prevention narrowly aimed at preventing an individual from committing an offence and, on the other hand, prevention in a broader sense which may also include punitive elements.[1]

* Postdoctoral researcher at the University of Parma.

[1] See especially the leading cases *Engel and o v The Netherlands* App Nos 5100/71, 5101/71, 5102/71, 5354/72 and 5370/72 (ECtHR, 8 June 1976) §80; *Öztürk v Germany* App No 8544/79 (ECtHR, 21 February 1984) §50; *Welch v United Kingdom* App No 17440/90 (ECtHR, 9 February 1995) §30; *Jussila v Finland* App No 73053/01 (ECtHR, 23 November 2006) §35. On this topic, see especially Groupe de recherche droits de l'homme et logiques juridiques, 'La "matière pénale" au sens de la Convention européenne des droits de l'homme, flou du droit penal' [1987] *Revue de science criminelle et droit pénal comparé* 819. See also F Mazzacuva, 'La materia penale e il "doppio binario" della Corte europea: le garanzie al di là delle apparenze' [2013] *Rivista italiana di diritto e procedura penale* 1908, in which it is noted how the dichotomy between the different meanings of prevention, which can be seen in the Court of Strasbourg case law, can be reinterpreted by distinguishing, first of all, prevention where adverse consequences are inflicted as a necessity or on purpose (in this case, the safeguards connected to the culpability principle should be applied) from another sense of prevention where that consequences represent basically a by-product in the struggle to tackle social dangerousness.

The same, more or less, occurs at national level. The Italian Constitutional Court started to follow the same approach of the ECtHR[2] in order to assess whether a certain measure, even if defined otherwise by the legislator, is criminal in nature and thereby triggers all the constitutional safeguards provided with regard to criminal charges and penalties.

It is even more difficult to assess whether confiscation falls within that category. As it is usually observed by courts and scholars, confiscation is a legal tool whose nature and functions change according to its prerequisites and objects.[3] Among the various forms of confiscation, the one concerning the proceeds of criminal activities has undergone important developments, both in Italian and European law. This evolution has sparked a lively debate on its real nature, and to the principles to be followed in its application.

Such a debate is particularly relevant in Italy, where incisive measures have been introduced in order to tackle criminal organisations and their profit. Shedding light on the Italian approach, therefore, can be of relevance for the EU legal framework. In particular, it is worth outlining the latest developments in the field of 'preventive confiscation', since two decisions of the Supreme Court (Corte di cassazione) have recently addressed the issue of its nature. Firstly, the Fifth Section of the Supreme Court ruled that this type of confiscation is punitive in nature. Two years later, however, the Court *en banc* (Sezioni Unite) promptly overruled this new interpretation and reaffirmed the mere preventive nature of the measure.

The purpose of this chapter is to examine the arguments used by the Supreme Court to justify such a qualification, as well as to present some critical remarks on that approach. In particular, these remarks will take into consideration the supranational perspective, and will address the real nature of this form of confiscation and the principles that may be endangered by its extensive application.

[2] See the important Judgment No 196 of 2010, in which the Constitutional Court has ruled that, in order to apply the principle of non-retroactivity (Art 25 of the Italian Constitution), we must distinguish between punishment and strictly intended prevention. To this end, the Court notes security measures, but, ambiguously, is silent on preventive measures.

[3] This is nowadays a common opinion among scholars, but is reflected in Decision No 29 of 1961 of the Italian Constitutional Court, according to which confiscation can have a different juridical nature in the various provisions which regulate it. Its core is always the forfeiture of assets, but this forfeiture can be ordered for various reasons and to various ends. Consequently, it is sometimes, in nature and function, a punishment or a security measure, or else a civil measure or even an administrative one. One must then consider confiscation not in an abstract and generic sense, but in its concrete manifestation in each provision.

I. 'Preventive Confiscation' in Italy

Confiscation, in Italy like elsewhere, is a multi-form concept.[4] There are, indeed, many types of confiscation. There is a general provision in the Criminal Code (adopted in 1930 and still in force today) and there are other types of confiscation provided by 'special' laws, in particular with respect to organised crime. Among these special types, it is worth stressing the relevance of the extended confiscation[5] and the so-called 'preventive confiscation'. The latter is the Italian measure that has most influenced the EU debate on non-conviction-based confiscation. For some aspects, it may be considered as a non-criminal confiscation *tout court*, in the sense that not only can it be ordered without any previous conviction, but also it does not depend on the initiation of criminal proceedings against property owners at all.

The preventive confiscation was introduced in the anti-mafia legislation of 1982.[6] Its regime has since been amended several times. The most important amendments were introduced in 2008 and 2009, and in 2011 the whole legal framework was consolidated in the so-called 'Anti-mafia Code' (Decree No 159 of 2011).

This kind of measure is characterised by the fact that it does not require a criminal conviction but three different kinds of prerequisites: (i) a suspicion that the individual belongs to a criminal organisation (or, since 2008, that he has committed certain crimes not necessarily connected with organised crime);[7] (ii) an assessment of his 'social dangerousness' (*pericolosità sociale*), meaning his likelihood to commit further crimes;[8] and (iii) a disproportion between the assets owned and

[4] See V Manes, 'Nullum crimen sine confiscatione' [2015] *Rivista italiana di diritto e procedura penale* 1261; A Alessandri, 'Confisca nel diritto penale' in *Digesto delle discipline penalistiche*, III (Torino, Utet, 1989) 42.

[5] Art 12-*sexies* of Law Decree No 306 of 1992.

[6] On the development of 'anti-mafia' legislation, see M Panzavolta and R Flor, 'A Necessary Evil? The Italian "Non-Criminal System" of Asset Forfeiture' in JP Rui and U Sieber (eds), *Non-Conviction-Based Confiscation in Europe* (Berlin, Dunker & Humblot, 2015) 111, 118.

[7] For instance, Art 1 of the Anti-mafia Code provides that the preventive measures can be applied, among others, to: (i) whoever is deemed, based on factual elements, to be habitually involved in crime; (ii) whoever is deemed, based on factual elements related to the conduct and the standard of life, to be living off the proceeds of crime; and (iii) whoever is deemed, based on factual elements related to the demeanour, to be usually involved in the commission of crimes against the physical or moral integrity of minors, or against public health, security or peace. Moreover, Art 4 of the same code provides for further cases in which the suspicion of an offence (not connected to organised crime) may lead to the application of the preventive confiscation.

[8] Required by Arts 2 and 6 of the Anti-mafia Code. See Art 203 of the Penal Code, which makes reference to the criteria provided for by Art 133, such as the reasons for the crime, the personality of the accused, his court records, his behaviour before and after the commission of the offence and his life conditions.

his income, which creates a presumption that those assets are obtained illegally.[9] When these requirements are satisfied, the public prosecutor asks the court to order the confiscation of the disproportionate assets.

It should be noted that the assessment of dangerousness has never be too relevant in the application of the measures, since it is often assumed on the basis of the other two requirements. In fact, the courts tend to take into consideration the criminal history of the accused rather than the likelihood of committing new crimes.

Moreover, according to the important amendment introduced in 2008, it is not even necessary to verify that the individual needs to be 'dangerous' at the time when the measure is imposed.[10] This means that preventive confiscation can be imposed if the individual is no longer dangerous (eg if he is no longer engaged in criminal activities), or even if he is deceased. Indeed, this modification of the preventive confiscation's prerequisites was adopted following the courts' interpretation, whereby it was possible to confiscate assets from the suspect's heirs even if they were not suspected of having engaged in any criminal activity.[11]

Two other relevant amendments were also introduced by the legislator in 2008: the extension of preventive confiscation to individuals suspected of having committed several crimes not connected to the mafia phenomenon; and the possibility to confiscate assets of equivalent value in case it turns out to be impossible to trace the assets whose origin is (probably) illegal.[12]

Such a regime raises the question of whether this kind of confiscation is really 'preventive' in nature. More generally, the real nature of a confiscation measure has been debated since 1930, when the comprehensive provision introduced in the Criminal Code[13] defined it as a 'security measure' (*misura di sicurezza*). Therefore, confiscation was grouped together with other legal tools with the main goal of tackling 'social dangerousness'. Such a legislative choice has always been severely criticised in the literature since confiscation measures are usually applied without actually verifying if either the property involved or its owner is actually 'dangerous'.[14]

[9] For an analytical overview on these requirements, among others, see Panzavolta and Flor (n 6) 124.

[10] In particular, this solution was adopted by Law Decree No 92 of 2008, converted as Law No 125 of 2008, as well as by Law No 94 of 2009, which amended para 6-*bis* of Art 2-*bis* of Law No 575 of 1965. This solution is confirmed today by Art 18, para 1 of the Anti-mafia Code. The requirement of actual dangerousness is still present in case personal preventive measures (such as 'special supervision') must also be imposed.

[11] This solution was affirmed by the Supreme Court *en banc* in the Corte di cassazione Judgment No 18, 3 July 1996.

[12] See para 10 of Art 2-*ter* of Law No 575 of 1965 introduced by Law Decree No 92 of 2008 and the amended version of Art 12-*sexies* of Law Decree No 306 of 1992. This solution is today confirmed by Art 25 of the Anti-mafia Code.

[13] Art 240 of the Italian Criminal Code.

[14] See especially Alessandri (n 4); G Grasso, 'Commento all'articolo 240' in M Romano, G Grasso and T Padovani (eds), *Commentario sistematico del codice penale* III (Milan, Giuffré, 2011) 521.

This criticism did not, however, gain momentum in jurisprudence, except with regard to 'value confiscation'.[15] In that case, the Supreme Court held that it cannot be considered as a mere security measure, but as a punitive sanction that triggers the application of all the criminal law safeguards, including the principle of non-retroactivity.[16] It is interesting to note, however, that more recently national courts have justified the wide application of value confiscation due to its 'compensatory' function.[17] Such an approach is usually unknown in the realm of criminal law, and more inherent with the realms of torts and contracts.

As said, the debate on the nature of confiscation has focused particularly on preventive confiscation. Indeed, the above-outlined legal framework conflicts to some extent with the traditional principles of criminal law, whereby a punitive measure can be imposed only after proving guilt beyond reasonable doubt, according to the procedural rules that ensure a fair trial of the suspect. Nevertheless, preventive confiscation has always been justified on the grounds that this measure is not a penalty *stricto sensu*, since it has only a preventive purpose. Consequently, since it is not considered as a criminal penalty, national courts have ruled in favour of its retroactive application, in the sense that such a measure could be applied also to facts committed before the entry into force of the law widening the scope of preventive confiscation.

However, if one considers the above-mentioned prerequisites, as well as the various modifications that the legislation has undergone over time, especially in the last ten years, one can question the labelling of this type of confiscation as 'preventive'. And recently the Supreme Court has had the opportunity to return to this subject.

II. The Recent Decisions of the Italian Supreme Court

The amendments to the regulation of preventive confiscation introduced in the last years convinced the Fifth Section of the Corte di cassazione (in the *Occhipinti*

[15] This is notably the form of confiscation which allows the recovery of assets whose value corresponds to the proceeds of crime, if confiscation of the latter is not possible.

[16] This solution has been adopted for different types of value confiscation, starting in 2009: see Corte di cassazione, 24 September 2009, No 39173; Corte di cassazione, 24 September 2009, No 39172; Corte di cassazione, 29 January 2009, No 11912; Corte di cassazione, 28 July 2009, No 33409.

[17] In particular, courts have ruled for the collective responsibility of co-authors of the crime with respect to confiscated assets; for the possibility of subtracting from the total the amount that has already been paid to the revenue service in case of tax-related crimes; for the possibility of subtracting the costs that companies incurred to realise the criminal conduct (the so-called *Nettoprinzip*); and for the possibility of imposing the measure with respect to third parties (both individuals and legal persons) who have benefited from the crime (even where they were not criminally liable but were 'in bad faith'). Recently, another Sezioni Unite judgment affirmed that confiscation and value confiscation of proceeds of crimes can be applied even if the offence is time-barred because the measure does not have a real punitive purpose (see Corte di cassazione, Sezioni Unite, 26 June 2015, No 31617).

decision of 2013) to deny for the first time that confiscation was preventive in nature, opting instead for qualifying it as punitive.[18] More precisely, the Court had to decide whether confiscation could be applied to an individual on probation, who, by definition, was thus not dangerous. The Court first recognised that the law now expressly permits confiscation in case the individual is on probation. However, since this amendment deprived confiscation of a truly preventive purpose, the Court ruled that the measure, in its post-amendment version, could not be applied retroactively and, since the illicit activity was carried out before 2008, it could not be applied in this case.

Two years later, the Sezioni Unite was called upon to answer a similar legal question. The case concerned two women who were suspected of burglary and owned a relevant amount of money in current accounts and two apartments. Having assessed the disproportion between these assets and the women's income, the legal problem was whether the extension of preventive confiscation to individuals suspected of having committed crimes not connected to the mafia phenomenon apply retroactively to acts that occurred before 2008 or 2009 (ie when the amendments were introduced)?

On 2 February 2015, the Court *en banc*, in the *Spinelli* decision, decided to overrule the new interpretation of the law that originated with the *Occhipinti* decision. In particular, the decision underlined how, following the recent amendments, it is still absolutely necessary to assess the dangerousness of the offender when imposing preventive confiscation. According to the Supreme Court, the only requirement that was dropped was the necessity of dangerousness at the time of the application of the confiscation: repealing this prerequisite does not mean—according to the Court—that confiscation is no longer preventive in nature, since dangerousness would be objectively related to the assets, even if the owner has subsequently ceased to be dangerous. In brief, the illicit source of the assets would make them 'inherently dangerous' even if they were owned by a harmless person.[19]

In other words, following the amendments to the preventive confiscation regime, a chamber of the Italian Supreme Court initially started to reconsider the measure as a criminal penalty; however, more recently, the Court, in its full composition, returned to its previous interpretation, whereby preventive confiscation

[18] See Corte di cassazione, 25 March 2013, No 14044, *Occhipinti*.

[19] In particular, according to the *Spinelli* decision: 'Dangerousness is a characteristic of the asset because of its unlawful acquisition and it is a "genetic" characteristic of it, a permanent and undeletable one, and in the case of unlawfully acquired assets, dangerousness is connected to the subjective characteristics of the individual who has acquired the asset and not to the modes of acquisition or the structural characteristics of the asset itself. The social dangerousness of the individual who acquires the asset is mirrored in the asset itself not statically (as a mirror image of a subjective characteristic) but rather dynamically as the reflection of the objective dangerousness of the availability of the unlawfully acquired assets in the hands of individuals who are suspected to or belong to one of the relevant categories. The mentioned reflection takes objective shape and becomes a characteristic of the object, with consequences for its juridical condition.'

is just preventive and, therefore, does not amount to a penalty. For this reason, it can also be applied retroactively.

III. A Firm Answer to the Nature of Preventive Confiscation? The Shortcomings of the Recent Italian Case Law

Most likely, the recent *Spinelli* decision of the Supreme Court does not give a firm answer to the problem of the real nature of the Italian preventive confiscation. The reasoning followed by the Court to justify the preventive nature, indeed, is not totally watertight. In this section of the chapter, some critical remarks will be expounded, in particular as regards the identification of the purposes of confiscation.

First of all, it must be noted that the assessment of the individual's dangerousness in order to apply the measure is not very thorough. This seems to be plainly inconsistent with a 'preventive' label:[20] although it is true that certain criminal records strongly suggest a dangerous personality, according to the current legislation, the suspicion of commission of criminal activities may also concern crimes that are unrelated to the sphere of organised crime; and with regard to such a broad array of offences, the dangerousness should not be assumed, but carefully assessed.

Furthermore, it can be observed how confiscation does not depend on the purposes that assets were supposed to serve, but rather on the property's origin.[21] Even if one could say that the assets that are suspected of being unlawfully obtained could be reused in activities that are suspected to be criminal, we should also consider that confiscation could concern assets that surely cannot be re-employed in that sense.[22] This becomes particularly clear, once again, if we take into consideration the individuals who are accused of ordinary crimes, different from organised crime. For example, in the last Sezioni Unite decision, the confiscated assets were bank accounts and real estate belonging to two burglars: it was clear, in other words, that these assets could not be used to facilitate the continuation of further burglaries.

[20] This conclusion has been reached by several Italian authors. See F Bricola, 'Forme di tutela "*ante-delictum*" e profili costituzionali della prevenzione' [1974] *Politica del diritto* 374; P Nuvolone, 'Le misure di prevenzione nel sistema penale italiano' [1974] *Indice penale* 461; G Fiandaca, 'Misure di prevenzione (profili sostanziali)' in *Digesto delle discipline penalistiche*, VIII (Turin, Utet, 1994) 116; D Petrini, *La prevenzione inutile* (Naples, Jovene, 1996) 221.

[21] See A Mangione, *La misura di prevenzione patrimoniale fra dogmatica e politica criminale* (Padova, Cedam, 2001) 384.

[22] This is confirmed by recent studies showing that around half of the assets seized are real estate. Financial assets and companies account for only about 20%.

In that regard, the argument that unlawfully obtained assets should be confiscated (in a preventive way) does not seem so relevant, since they could damage free competition:[23] in fact, preventive confiscation is applied even when there is no such risk. Furthermore, the meaning of 'prevention' in this case seems to correspond to the need to curb the use of assets in the economic cycle, which is already fulfilled, for example, by the criminalisation of money laundering.

The argument that an asset's dangerousness derives from the individual's dangerousness at the time when the asset was unlawfully acquired sounds like a rhetorical artifice, which does not necessarily find empirical confirmation. Indeed, it is difficult to understand why the asset's unlawful origin should make it dangerous in a definitive way. Either an asset is objectively dangerous—in which case, it can be subject to an ordinary confiscation measure provided by the Criminal Code[24]—or it becomes dangerous because the person who can use it is dangerous, and therefore the asset can be reused in unlawful activities.

For this reason, the Sezioni Unite's reasoning seems quite weak in its strenuous defence of the preventive nature of confiscation. On this point, the reference made to the approach of the ECtHR is not decisive. In fact, the very words used by the Court of Strasbourg[25] confirm that the measure, to be preventive in nature, must involve a determination that the individual or an asset is dangerous at the moment of the application of the measure. Therefore, the conclusions of the Court seem to be no longer consistent with the amended statute, which now permits the imposition of confiscation even when the individual is not dangerous or deceased.

The recent evolution of preventive confiscation rather reveals that its nature has always been to 'restore' and 'compensate', in the sense that the objective of confiscation is to recover any asset deriving from the unlawful activity, independently from any evaluation of the dangerousness of the author.

This rationale was already underlined by the Sezioni Unite in an important 1996 decision, in which the Court decided that confiscation was applicable to heirs only by qualifying the measure as neither preventive nor punitive in nature, but

[23] This argument was recently maintained by Corte di cassazione, 23 September 2013, No 39204, *Ferrara*. On this point, see A Maugeri, 'Le Sezioni Unite devono prendere posizione sulla natura della confisca antimafia' [2014] *Diritto penale contemporaneo* 9, available at www.penalecontemporaneo.it.

[24] In particular, Art 240 of the Penal Code provides that, in addition to the proceeds deriving from the crime, it is possible to confiscate the tools used for the crime and those object whose detention is always unlawful.

[25] The measure 'is not comparable to a criminal sanction because it is designed to prevent the commission of offences. It follows that proceedings concerning it did not involve "the determination—of a criminal charge"': *Riela and others v Italy* App No 52439/99 (ECtHR, 4 September 2001). The same conclusion was reached by the Court with regard to the measure of special supervision in *Guzzardi v Italy* (1980) Series A No 39 §108; *Ciancimino v Italy* App No 12541/86 (ECtHR, 27 May 1991); *Raimondo v Italy* (1994) Series A No 281-A §43. See also, more recently, *Cacucci and Sabatelli v Italy* App No 29797/09 (ECtHR, 17 June 2014); *Capitani and Campanella v Italy* App No 24920/07 (ECtHR, 17 May 2011); *Leone v Italy* App No 30506/07 (ECtHR, 2 February 2010); *Bongiorno and others v Italy* App No 4514/07 (ECtHR, 5 January 2010).

rather as having a third purpose (*tertium genus*).[26] The Constitutional Court, on the other hand, while declaring that such a solution[27] is constitutionally permissible, held that the rationale of this type of confiscation includes, but goes beyond, the rationale of personal preventive measures, since in this case it consists of the definitive deprivation of the asset's ownership. Furthermore, contrary to the rationale of other preventive measures, in this case it goes beyond the prevention of a dangerous individual's behaviour, and therefore justifies the measure even beyond his or her lifetime.[28]

It must be noted, however, that even in the *Spinelli* decision there are passages in which the Court states that the goal of preventive confiscation is to eliminate from the economic cycle assets that were unlawfully acquired. In particular, the Court *en banc* links this goal to ethical reasons as well as economic goals connected to the protection of free competition. In that regard, it can be added that this aim is also related to the reparation for victims, as well as to general-prevention objectives. It would, indeed, consist of a message to potential and actual wrongdoers that not even their heirs will be able to profit from their criminal activities.[29]

Such a different purpose is also pursued by other measures provided for in the Italian legal system. For example, the above-mentioned value confiscation confirms that confiscation may not aim at the deprivation of specific assets because of their objective characteristics, but rather at the recovery of a certain value. Furthermore, the fact that the measure affects third parties as well as creditors who knew or should have known about the unlawful origin of the assets[30] confirms that the legislative goal is to neutralise every possible economic consequence of the committed crime, not to prevent the commission of further crimes. From a purely preventive point of view, there would be no reason to confiscate assets with respect to individuals who, even if they could have discovered that the assets were of unlawful origin, are nonetheless not involved in any criminal activity.

Finally, only by using this purpose-oriented perspective we can understand the recent judicial interpretative theory according to which confiscation can also be used with regard to the proceeds of tax evasion. These proceeds are not technically derived from an illicit activity, since the only illicit segment of conduct is the

[26] See Corte di cassazione, Sezioni Unite, 3 July 1996, No 18, *Simonelli*. Another recent decision of the Corte di cassazione stated that freeing confiscation from the requirement of 'actual dangerousness' has not changed the nature of confiscation with reference to its purposes. This amendment has, if anything, strengthened the tool's effectiveness with respect to its initial goal (Corte di cassazione, 17 May 2013, No 39204).

[27] See Decree No 92 of 2008; Art 18 of the Anti-mafia Code.

[28] See Corte costituzionale, Judgment No 21 of 2012, which confirms what was held in the previous Judgment No 335 of 1996. Recently, however, the Court has again stressed the preventive nature of confiscation, even though some ambiguity remains (see Corte costituzionale, Decision No 106 of 2015).

[29] Art 48 of the Anti-mafia Code states that confiscated sums can be used for the compensation of mafia-related crimes victims.

[30] Art 25 of the Anti-mafia Code.

failure to fulfil the tax obligation by transferring them to the state.[31] In this case, confiscation is used to recover all unlawfully obtained proceeds, in parallel with the instruments provided by tax law.

In conclusion, one may observe that several forms of confiscation of 'tainted property' share similar purposes. What differs among them is their incisiveness, especially as regards the following aspects: (i) the general provision contained in the Criminal Code can only be applied if the crime is proved and the proceeds are exactly identified; (ii) value confiscation enables the recovery of an equivalent amount of assets, if it is impossible to secure the crime proceeds; (c) extended confiscation is based upon a presumption of unlawful origin of the assets owned by the individual who has been convicted of certain crimes; and (d) preventive confiscation permits the use of such a presumption even if there is nothing more than a suspicion that such crimes have been committed (ie a conviction is not needed).

IV. Does the 'Compensatory' Purpose Fall within the Scope of Criminal Sanctions?

On the basis of these considerations, one may wonder how we should qualify all these measures having the objective of recovering ill-gotten gains, and consequently which safeguards should be provided. In particular, we should try to understand whether the goals of 'compensation' and 'reparation' are different from punishment—as suggested by the label 'civil asset forfeiture' adopted in different countries[32]—and, if so, whether such a difference justifies exceptions to the presumption of innocence, as well as interpretative solutions borrowed from civil law, such as its application to the heirs and third parties 'in bad faith' (*mala fides*). In this regard, in the literature, some have argued that confiscation of unlawful proceeds would really represent a 'third option' compared with criminal penalties and preventive measures.[33]

First of all, it should be pointed out that, to be truly reparative, confiscation should be subsidiary to other legal tools whose goal is the compensation of monetary damages caused by the unlawful conduct (ie confiscation should be adopted

[31] See Corte di cassazione, Sezioni Unite, 29 May 2014, No 33451.

[32] See J Boucht, 'Civil Asset Forfeiture and the Presumption of Innocence under Article 6(2) ECHR' [2014] *New Journal of European Criminal Law* 225, who points out that the measure is usually qualified either as 'preventive' or 'reparative'.

[33] See V Mongillo, 'La confisca del profitto nei confronti dell'ente in cerca d'identità: luci e ombre della recente pronuncia delle Sezioni Unite' [2008] *Rivista italiana di diritto e procedura penale* 1779. See also A Maugeri, *Le moderne sanzioni patrimoniali tra funzionalità e garantismo* (Milan, Giuffrè, 2001) 503; Maugeri (n 23) 12.

only if these tools do not allow the full recovery of the dirty assets). Provided that confiscation can be applied, for example, to individuals suspected of tax evasion, it should be determined how to apply it concurrently with tax instruments whose function is to recover the unpaid amount. The risk, otherwise, is a double restitution, which is not justifiable from a reparative point of view. In the Italian system, the subsidiary application is expressly provided only in a few cases[34] and, most importantly, is not provided with respect to preventive confiscation.

The crucial point, however, is to understand whether asset recovery can be justified only by reparative purposes. If no damage is caused to third parties, does asset recovery really fulfil a restorative purpose? The idea of recreating the situation as it was before the unlawful conduct is one of the pillars of retributive conceptions of punishment where, for this reason, the proportionality between unlawful conduct and sanction is emphasised. In this sense, the confiscation of proceeds would almost look like a natural form of punishment for crimes in which the economic element is predominant. In other words, within the limits of what has been obtained through the criminal conduct, the adverse consequences imposed by confiscation are neither an indirect outcome of a request for compensation originating from a civil suit brought into a criminal trial nor a strategy to tackle the dangerousness of a certain person. On the contrary, they seem to be purposefully applied to deter and intimidate through the message 'crime does not pay', exposing their punitive nature.

On the other hand, this is the idea expressed in the important *Welch* decision of the ECtHR:

> [T]he preventive purpose of confiscating property that might be available for use in future drug-trafficking operations as well as the purpose of ensuring that crime does not pay are evident … However it cannot be excluded that legislation which confers such broad powers of confiscation on the courts also pursues the aim of punishing the offender. Indeed the aims of prevention and reparation are consistent with a punitive purpose and may be seen as constituent elements of the very notion of punishment.[35]

Moreover, even if arguably the reason behind its statement was the justification of the necessary legal basis, the Committee on Civil Liberties, Justice and Home Affairs of the EU Parliament (LIBE), in amending the proposal of the Commission for a new Directive of freezing and confiscation, wrote that confiscation without

[34] In Italian legislation, in particular, this form of subsidiarity emerges only from Art 6 of Legislative Decree No 231 of 2001, which concerns the regulation of crime-related liability of legal persons. In case law, this is the solution adopted for tax crimes.

[35] See *Welch v United Kingdom* App No 17440/90 (ECtHR, 9 February 1995) §30. At first, it seems that this position is in contrast to the approach of the Court, which usually divides these legal tools into three categories according to their preventive, restorative and punitive functions. However, if we put the need to contrast dangerousness and restitutions in the background, the Court seems to correctly note that prevention and reparation tend to lose their meaning in this context and approach the idea of punishment.

conviction is penal in nature.[36] In that perspective, it should be stressed that any form of retroactive application should be considered invalid, as should any violations of the presumption of innocence. Only in that case would the validity of such a confiscation be preserved.

V. Assuming that Preventive Confiscation is not Punitive, What Other Principles Should be Respected?

Even accepting the definition of the purpose of preventive confiscation as non-punitive, it is worth clarifying that the compensatory function may be limited by general principles whose application—unlike the presumption of innocence[37]—is not limited to criminal law. In particular, I am referring to the principles of legality and proportionality, which, pursuant to Article 1 Protocol 1 of the European Convention on Human Rights (ECHR), are relevant for any restriction of private property made by a public authority.

First of all, assuming that legality has the same meaning as in the context of Article 7 of the ECHR—as the ECtHR has sometimes suggested[38]—any retroactive application of confiscation should be forbidden. However, in provisions other than Article 7, the 'law provision' requirement seems to have the different meaning of *prééminence du droit*, according to which it suffices to have a legal basis at the moment of the court's decision.[39] Therefore, the recent amendments to Italian preventive confiscation seem to satisfy this requirement, since many of the

[36] The end of Amendment No 33 states: 'Such confiscation is to be considered of criminal nature according, amongst others, to the following criteria: (i) the legal classification of the offence under national law, (ii) the nature of the offence and (iii) the degree of severity of the penalty that the person concerned risks incurring and shall also be in line with national constitutional law'. The reasoning, however, makes it clear that: 'Notwithstanding its denomination in national law as civil confiscation, Article 83(1) TFEU does not exclude this type of confiscation, as long as it can be qualified as "criminal sanction" according to the criteria developed by the ECtHR in *Engel* judgment (be of a criminal nature, the severity of the penalty). The "criminal nature" of such a confiscation is a condition for any harmonisation under Article 83(1) TFEU.'

[37] It is a matter of debate whether the presumption of innocence may be applied even to 'non-criminal' measures, but we would agree with the contrary opinion expressed by Boucht (n 32) 234.

[38] In some decisions, the Court seems to be saying that the legal basis required by Art 1, Protocol 1 ECHR imposes compliance with the requirements of accessibility and predictability (in applying the measure) to be assessed at the moment when the conduct happened (see *Sud Fondi srl and others v Italy* App No 75909/01 (ECtHR, 20 January 2009); *Sun v Russia* App No 31004/02 (ECtHR, 5 February 2009) §26; *Oao Neftyanaya Kompaniya Yukos v Russia* App No 14902/04 (ECtHR, 20 September 2011) §559).

[39] The difference in meaning emerges from the text of the Convention as well as from other decisions of the Court concerning Art 1, Protocol 1, such as *Khuzhin and others v Russia* App No 13470/02 (ECtHR, 23 October 2008) §126.

courts' decisions based on a 'compensatory' conception of confiscation have been adopted according to laws enacted after the commission of the criminal conduct.[40]

The real debated point, however, concerns the principle of proportionality, according to which the limits of asset recovery policies should be clearly determined. The ECtHR, indeed, underlined that, since in these cases the presumption of innocence does not apply, the proportionality principle must also be used when imposing preventive confiscation, namely as regards the burden of proof.[41] This is also the approach adopted by domestic decisions, including the recent *Spinelli* case, in which the Supreme Court clarified that the burden of proof concerning the lawful obtainment of assets only concerns those assets acquired during the period in which the individual is supposed to have carried out criminal activities (the so-called 'temporal correlation' principle). However, this solution derives from the qualification of confiscation as preventive, while it would probably be more appropriate to link it with the proportionality principle, which requires that even the presumptions should be contained within reasonable limits.

Conclusion

The trend of expanding the scope of confiscation measures is not only typical of the Italian legal system, but can be observed also at the supranational level.[42] The EU debate also draws inspiration from the Italian developments. In particular, the discussion about the adoption of a non-conviction-based confiscation model was strongly influenced by the Italian approach. Even if eventually they were not included in the adopted Directive 2014/42/EU,[43] the amendments tabled by LIBE clearly referred to the Italian legislation, once again demonstrating how non-conviction-based confiscation is being increasingly considered a key instrument for asset recovery policies.

[40] As a matter of fact, innovative judicial interpretations are still being registered in the field of confiscation (such as the decision mentioned earlier concerning the applicability of confiscation in case of tax evasion), which seem to lack the 'legal basis' required by Art 1, Protocol 1 of the Convention.

[41] See recently *Cacucci and Sabatelli* (n 25) §35.

[42] On European Union tools providing value and extended confiscation, see N Selvaggi, 'On Instruments Adopted in the Area of Freezing and Confiscation' [2015] *Diritto penale contemporaneo*, 31 July 2015, available at www.penalecontemporaneo.it.

[43] See Amendment No 33, deriving from Art 5 of the Directive, according to which: 'Each Member State shall take the necessary measures to enable judicial authorities to confiscate, as a criminal sanction, proceeds and instrumentalities without a criminal conviction where a court is convinced on the basis of specific circumstances and all the available evidence that those assets derive from activities of a criminal nature, while fully respecting the provisions of article 6 of the ECHR and the European Charter of Fundamental Rights'. In the final draft of the Directive, a non-conviction-based confiscation appears only in Art 4(2), which does not seem to create a new, different model of confiscation, as observed by M Simonato, 'Directive 2014/42/EU and Non-Conviction Based Confiscation. A Step Forward on Asset Recovery?' [2015] *New Journal of European Criminal Law* 222.

Looking at the Italian system, on the one hand, it is clear that such an expansion makes the qualification of confiscation as preventive very precarious (since, as has been said, not every crime can be considered as a symptom of 'social dangerousness'); on the other hand, such a development can be considered coherent with the compensatory function that confiscation serves with regard to any kind of offence. However, if we consider that the same purpose is also pursued by other models of confiscation, the selection among these models should be strictly linked to a correlation between the incisiveness of confiscation and the seriousness of the criminal activity. In other words, if the goal of the various forms of confiscation does not vary, one could wonder whether the presumptions regarding the unlawful origin of assets are proportionate even when the underlying crimes are not connected to organised crime.

Maybe it would be reasonable to argue for the ECtHR to follow a safer approach, starting from the upcoming decision on the possibility of ordering the confiscation of real estate provided for by the Italian legislation (*confisca urbanistica*) even when the offence of unlawful property subdivision (*lottizzazione abusiva*) is time barred.[44] This case may lead the Court of Strasbourg to assess the general limits of non-conviction-based confiscation, irrespective of a costly requalification of the measure as criminal in nature. On several occasions the ECtHR has held that:

> the enormous profits made by these organisations from their unlawful activities give them a level of power which places in jeopardy the rule of law within the State. The means adopted to combat this economic power, particularly the confiscation measure complained of, may appear essential for the successful prosecution of the battle against the organisations in question.[45]

Following this approach, if confiscation does not concern organised crime, the assessment of proportionality would potentially reach a different result. To date, however, the Court of Strasbourg has been quite conservative. For example, in the recent *Gogitidze* judgment on a case concerning a form of civil forfeiture applicable in case of bribery, it held that:

[44] In particular, since the public hearing of 2 September 2015, a decision of the Grand Chamber is expected on the case *Hotel Promotion Bureau S.r.l. and Rita Sarda Srl v Italy* (No 34163/07), which concerns the same problem as emerged in *Varvara v Italy* App No 17475/09 (ECtHR, 29 October 2013). Even if the Grand Chamber is concerned with this specific issue, it could take the chance to consider the general problem of non-conviction-based confiscation (also considering the dissenting opinion of J Pinto de Albuquerque in *Varvara*, who remarked that: 'Under the *nomen juris* of confiscation, the States have introduced *ante delictum* criminal prevention measures, criminal sanctions (accessory or even principal criminal penalties), security measures in the broad sense, administrative measures adopted within or outside criminal proceedings, and civil measures *in rem*. Confronted with this enormous range of responses available to the State, the Court has not yet developed any consistent case-law based on principled reasoning').

[45] See *Bongiorno and others* (n 25) §45; more recently, see *Cacucci and Sabatelli* (n 25) §41.

> having regard to the Georgian authorities' wide margin of appreciation in their pursuit of the policy designed to combat corruption in the public service and to the fact that the domestic courts afforded the applicants a reasonable opportunity of putting their case through the adversarial proceedings, the Court concludes that the civil proceedings *in rem* for the forfeiture of the applicants' property, based on a procedure which was moreover in line with the relevant international standards, did not upset the requisite fair balance.[46]

In this approach, it is possible to discern a general tendency to allow a sort of 'parallel' criminal justice policy when burdensome measures concern assets instead of personal freedom. The risk, however, it to unduly overlook all criminal law safeguards just because of such a different scope.

[46] See *Gogitidze v Georgia* App No 36862/05 (ECtHR, 12 May 2015) §114.

5

Extended Confiscation: Criminal Assets or Criminal Owners?

JOHAN BOUCHT*

Introduction

The 'traditional' way of depriving offenders of their ill-gotten gains is by way of what in this context is referred to as regular criminal confiscation (of criminal proceeds). Typical for this kind of confiscation is that it follows on a conviction of a criminal offence, either in separate proceedings or together with the criminal proceedings, that is liable to produce gain, and that the assets in question are causally linked to that offence.

These requirements mean that regular criminal confiscation may not always be a successful means of removing illicit proceeds from circulation in situations where it is difficult to prove a requisite causal connection between the assets and a particular criminal offence.[1] This may be the case, for example, where individuals, who are suspected of being involved in more serious criminality, committed with the intent of achieving economic profit, than what they have been convicted of, possess property to an extent which does not reasonably correspond to their lawful income. Although it may appear likely that the property in question originates from criminal conduct, a confiscation claim may be rejected if the state cannot show that the property derives from a particular criminal offence of which the

* Professor Dr at the University of Oslo, Norway. I would like to thank Gustaf Almkvist as well as the editors for useful comments on earlier drafts of this article. This article is based on the corresponding sections in my forthcoming book *The Limits of Asset Confiscation* (Hart Publishing, Oxford, 2017).

[1] N Jayawickrama, J Pope and O Stolpe, 'Legal Provisions to Facilitate the Gathering of Evidence in Corruption Cases: Easing the Burden of Proof' (2002) 2 *Forum on Crime and Society* 23, 25 note that regular criminal confiscation, due its strict conditions of application, easily becomes a '"toothless tiger", especially in the case of an offender whose illicit wealth has been accrued systematically over a long period of time and who, though found guilty of a criminal act, is able to demonstrate that his or her wealth was not derived from that one criminal act'. On the other hand, it may be noted that comprehensive financial investigations may reduce the 'toothlessness' of regular criminal confiscation, that is, in many cases a thorough financial investigation may reduce the need of alternative confiscation measures.

defendant has been duly convicted. A similar scenario may arise where, in the course of investigating an offence, suspicious assets, the origin of which cannot be plausibly explained, are found in the defendant's possession. Thus, and to the extent that the assets exceed the gain of that particular offence, they cannot normally be confiscated by way of regular criminal confiscation.

In order to address these cases and to make it easier for the state to successfully claim confiscation, rules on so-called extended confiscation, in respect of which traditional criminal procedural safeguards were watered down, were introduced in many jurisdictions.[2] The introduction of these confiscation measures were largely motivated by the fight against organised crime and serious economic criminality. At EU level, for example, extended confiscation was introduced by Article 3 of the 2005 Framework decision on the confiscation of crime-related proceeds, instrumentalities and property (2005/212/JHA). However, implementation of the measure, as well as its effectivity in the sense of increasing asset recovery in the EU, did not match expectations. In 2012, seven years after extended confiscation was introduced at EU level, the Commission noted that:

> although regulated by EU and national laws, confiscation of criminal assets remains underdeveloped and underutilised. The overall amount recovered from crime in the EU remains modest compared to the estimated revenues of organised criminal groups. For example, in 2009 confiscated assets amounted to €185 million in France, £154 million in the United Kingdom, €50 million in The Netherlands and €281 million in Germany. … The 2009 Stockholm Programme calls the Member States and the Commission to make the confiscation of criminal assets more efficient and to strengthen the cooperation between Asset Recovery Offices.[3]

[2] The evolution of confiscation regimes varies between countries. For example, in the Nordic countries, regular criminal confiscation has been an essential part of the criminal justice system since the 1940s. The introduction of extended confiscation thus represented a dramatic expansion of the courts' 'traditional' confiscatory powers. In the UK, by contrast, no proper confiscation regime intended for proceeds of crime was apparently put in place before the Drug Trafficking Offence Act 1986 (DTA) entered into force (see eg *R v Cuthbertson* [1981] 1 AC 470). With the DTA, confiscation and extended confiscation of criminal proceeds from drug offences were introduced in one go. Since then, various parallel confiscation regimes have been consolidated under the Proceeds of Crime Act 2002. For the situation in English law before 1986, see D Hodgson, *Profits of Crime and Their Recovery: Report of a Committee Chaired by Derek Hodgson*, Cambridge Studies in Criminology 52 (London, Heinemann, 1984) 3.

[3] COM (2012) 85 final (12 March 2012), 2–3. In this connection, it may be noted that the relevance of absolute sums as an indicator of the overall effectiveness of confiscation regimes is limited. RT Naylor, 'Wash-out: A Critique of Follow-the-Money Methods in Crime Control Policy' [1999] *Crime, Law & Social Change* 15, 16 observes that, in order to truly determine if confiscation regimes have any impact in the criminal market place, two kinds of calculations are required. First, to find the ratio of seized criminal wealth to total criminal wealth, both at the beginning and at the end of a certain test period. Secondly, to make a comparison between the rate of growth of criminal income relative to legal income to ascertain if the part being taken out of criminal wealth is actually affecting adversely the ability of illegal markets to service their clientele. Both calculations may, however, be difficult to make due to limited access to reliable data as well as methodological difficulties. For a similar position, see A Freiberg and R Fox, 'Evaluating the Effectiveness of Australia's Confiscation Laws' [2000] *Australian and New Zealand Journal of Criminology* 239, 250.

This provision was passed on, with some amendments broadening the scope of it, in Article 5 of the EU Directive on the freezing and confiscation of criminal proceeds of 2014 (2014/42/EU).[4] Member States should have brought into force the laws, regulations and administrative provisions necessary to comply with this Directive by 4 October 2015.

In the following, I will first look at some of the characteristics of extended confiscation schemes. Thereafter, I will look at certain potential problems that may exist in regard to traditional principles of criminal law and criminal procedural law. More specifically, I will look at three aspects: the legitimacy of reversing the burden of proof and lowering the standard of proof, which are the keystones to extended confiscation, and the issue of quantification.

I. What is Extended Confiscation?

Extended criminal confiscation is conviction-based confiscation introduced for situations where the causal link between the assets and the (prior) offence(s) is not clearly established, but the assets nonetheless are assumed to be illicit. The rules were originally intended to mainly target individuals leading a so-called criminal lifestyle, ie were career criminals.[5]

The Finnish Supreme Court case *2006:9* may be used to illustrate one typical scenario. In this case, X was convicted of drug trafficking. In connection with his arrest, cash in various currencies to the value of some €30,000 were discovered in his flat, and consequently seized. The gain from the drug offence of which X was convicted was calculated at some €18,000. These means were confiscated by way of regular criminal confiscation. X explained, without substantiating his claims, the provenance of the exceeding assets, some €12,000, as legitimate income from selling wood carvings and phone cards, as well as income from the maintenance of summer kiosks and an inheritance of some €33,000 from Gambia. Even if the court found the explanation unlikely, the difference between the value of the money seized and the calculated gain from the drug trafficking offence of which he was convicted could not be confiscated by applying regular confiscation rules. However, using the rules on extended confiscation, the Supreme Court concluded

[4] The original proposal also included a provision (Art 5) on non-conviction-based confiscation with a view to addressing cases where criminal prosecution cannot be exercised, see COM (2012) 85 final (n 3). However, it was considered too controversial for some Member States at the time and was therefore abandoned in the final version of the Directive.

[5] The term 'criminal lifestyle' is unfortunate as a legal criterion. In a criminal law setting, one should be careful about linking criminal sanctions to criteria contingent on the individual's character, personality, lifestyle, etc rather than act-related facts. To the extent that the notion of a criminal lifestyle is employed in this context, it is done so only with the purpose of functioning as an umbrella concept for the group of individuals targeted, not as a legal criterion.

that it was likely, considering the substantial amount of money seized in X's flat and the unusual way the money was stored, that the money originated from criminal activities. Consequently, the Court ordered the money forfeit.

But extended confiscation may also, for example, be useful where, in the course of investigating an offence, suspicious assets, the provenance of which cannot be plausibly explained and which do not correspond to his legitimate income, are found in the defendant's possession. Extended confiscation may also be used for depriving the defendant more generally of gain obtained through prior unspecified criminal conduct.

What, then, are the main characteristics of extended confiscation compared to regular criminal confiscation? The specifics of extended confiscation schemes vary between (European) jurisdictions, but certain characteristics are discernible. In order to order extended confiscation, first, a predicate conviction of an offence liable to produce gain is normally required. In order to limit the applicability of extended confiscation, the target area (ie who can be targeted and in which situations) is often (somewhat) narrowed down compared to regular confiscation, for example so that only certain more serious predicate offences trigger confiscation. There are indications, however, that the target area is gradually made wider in several jurisdictions, and also at EU level.

Secondly, the requirement for the state to concretise the criminal offence from which the assets originate is moderated. Rather than focusing on a particular predicate offence, extended confiscation schemes are designed to target proceeds from vaguer prior 'criminal activity'. In this sense, extended confiscation is based on a presumption of prior criminality of which the defendant has in fact not been convicted. Certain procedural safeguards may be watered down regarding the provenance of the assets, for example, by employing a reversed burden of proof or a lower standard of proof. Thus, rather than being concerned with the relationship between the confiscation object and the unlawful conduct, extended confiscation focuses on that between the confiscation subject and the confiscation object.[6] In effect, it may be said that extended confiscation is mainly an instrument of relaxing the otherwise strict standards for the rules on evidence in criminal proceedings.

Extended confiscation may, thirdly, be value based or *in specie* (see Section II.D below). Value confiscation means that the defendant is obliged to pay an amount of money as specified in the confiscation order, which corresponds to the value of the benefit he has obtained. This approach can be found in English confiscation law under Part II of the Proceeds of Crime Act 2002 (POCA 2002).[7] Extended confiscation is an extension of regular criminal confiscation and may be invoked where the defendant is considered to have a criminal lifestyle. Confiscation is not

[6] G Almkvist, *Förverkande av egendom* (Uppsala, Iustus förlag, 2013) 112.

[7] See generally P Alldridge, *Money Laundering Law. Forfeiture, Confiscation, Civil Recovery, Criminal Laundering and Taxation of the Proceeds of Crime* (Oxford, Hart Publishing, 2003) 127. It may be noted that the UK is not bound by EU Directive 2014/42/EU.

limited to assets retained by the defendant. What makes confiscation 'extended' is that a particular set of extra harsh quantification rules come into play for the purpose of determining the benefit obtained by the unlawful conduct in question. These rules take the shape of statutory presumptions (see section 10 POCA 2002) under which, inter alia, all property transferred to the defendant during the relevant six-year period, any property held by him after being convicted of the predicate offences and any expenditure incurred by him at any time after the start of the six-year period are considered to have been obtained as a result of his general criminal conduct.[8] However, according to section 9 POCA 2002, the actual confiscation order is limited to the value of all free property held by the defendant at the time when the confiscation is made (the recoverable amount), although the burden of proof is reversed at this stage.

In specie confiscation, on the other hand, means that the confiscation order targets certain identified pieces of property which represent the illicit benefit, and which the defendant holds in his possession. The difficulties inherent in proving a link between the assets and unspecified prior criminal activity mean that the essence of the assessment in fact relates to whether the magnitude of the assets in question are such that they appear unrealistic for the defendant, in view of his legitimate income, to have acquired legitimately. This model seems common amongst continental European states and is found, for example, in Finnish, German, Norwegian and Swedish law, but also in EU law.[9] In regard to the provenance of the assets, confiscation is typically based on a lower standard of proof or a reversed burden of proof.

II. Potentially Problematic Aspects of Extended Confiscation

A. Prelude

Even if extended confiscation was perceived by many as controversial when first introduced, confiscation schemes with various watered-down safeguards today

[8] Whether or not the lifestyle rules apply may have a significant impact on the magnitude of the confiscation order. One example of this is *R v Molloy* [2013] EWCA Crim 682, in which case the trial judge found M to have had a criminal lifestyle and imposed a confiscation order of £46,502. M had entered into an agreement to conduct a series of thefts of significant quantities of cigarettes. The offence was not in Schedule 2 of the Act, but extended to a period in excess of six months. Having pleaded guilty, M limited his involvement to a period of about a month. As s 75(2)(c) POCA related to the period of the particular accused's involvement and not to the total length of the conspiracy, it was not applicable. The Court of Appeal thus substituted the confiscation order with one set at £3,200, ie less than one-tenth of the original order. According to s 75(4) POCA 2002, the relevant threshold for initiating confiscation proceedings is that the defendant obtains relevant benefit of not less than £5,000.

[9] Regarding EU law, see Art 5(1) of the EU Directive (2014/42/EU) on the freezing and confiscation of instrumentalities and proceeds of crime in the European Union.

appear to be commonplace in many European jurisdictions. In spite of its merits as a measure of potentially high efficacy, it is clear that there is a tension between certain aspects of extended confiscation and basic principles of criminal law and criminal procedural law, such as the presumption of innocence. Even if the overarching objective of fighting organised crime and serious economic crime is important, these concerns deserve to be taken seriously. The maxim that 'the goal justifies the means' should not apply without reasonable limitations.

The point of departure in criminal confiscation proceedings should be to deprive the defendant only of the actual benefit he has obtained in connection with a criminal offence (although schemes today go further than this). Confiscation is to this extent of a restitutionary nature.[10] The same logic should in principle apply to extended confiscation: the point of departure is that only illicit property is targeted, ie property which has been obtained by way of unlawful conduct, and that confiscation thus serves to restore the status quo ante. Where confiscation goes no further than what is required to achieve a restorative aim, it is difficult to see how such confiscation could be synonymous with punishment per se, even if the confiscation order may be very large indeed. The main problem with extended confiscation is the risk that, due to watered down legal safeguards, the extended confiscation order goes beyond restoring the status quo ante and also targets licit property. As the purpose of extended confiscation is to target assets which may not be easy to causally connect with an offence of which the defendant has been convicted, the key issue here is not whether or not confiscation goes beyond actual enrichment, but how big a risk of doing so may be accepted.

When discussing efficacy-related matters in asset confiscation, it is also important to maintain focus on the confiscation system as a whole and not only on the legal powers conferred on the courts. The effectivity of asset confiscation regimes is contingent not only on these powers, but also on other parts of the confiscation process being effectuated. One important aspect of this is the tracing and

[10] G Virgo, *The Principles of the Law of Restitution*, 2nd edn (Oxford, Oxford University Press, 2006) 548 writes: 'Disgorgement of the proceeds of crime to the State should be considered to fall within the law of restitution, since, by committing a crime, the offender has committed a wrong against the State by breaching his or her duty to abide by the criminal law of the land.' Confiscation should ideally go no further than requiring the defendant to disgorge the profits he obtained by unlawful conduct, ie his net profits: see Hodgson (n 2) 74–75. However, this may be too simplified a position. It is, moreover, commonplace for many national confiscation regimes to go further by not permitting deductions for costs connected with the obtaining of profit (hence the reference 'proceeds' rather than 'profits'). However, it may be reasonable not to apply this rule absolutely but, for example, to make a distinction between predatory and market-based offences which are inherently illegal (such as drugs offences) on the one hand and commercial offences which are carried out legitimately but with illegitimate means on the other. See D Fried, 'Rationalizing Criminal Forfeiture' [1988] *Journal of Criminal Law and Criminology* 375; for the distinction between types of offences, see RT Naylor, 'Towards a General Theory of Profit-Driven Crimes' (2003) 43 *British Journal of Criminology* 81, 84. This is a complex issue connected with many difficult policy issues. It is also closely linked to the law on restitution. It will therefore not be pursued here.

identification of assets during prior financial investigations. It would seem that many shortcomings in recovering criminal proceeds may often (but not always) have more to do with assets not having been identified and traced (both domestically and internationally) than on the inadequacy of the legal powers conferred on the courts.[11] This calls for caution when it comes to attempts to redress failing efficacy with more legal powers to the courts.[12]

In the following, I will look at three potentially problematic aspects of extended confiscation: reversing the burden of proof; lowering the standard of proof in extended confiscation proceedings; and the issue of quantification of extended confiscation orders.[13]

B. Reversing the Burden of Proof

Reversing the burden of proof in extended confiscation proceedings means that the defendant has to prove the licit origin of the assets in order to avoid confiscation.

The onus in extended confiscation proceedings can be shifted both in systems employing value-based confiscation and in systems confiscating *in specie*. The burden can be reversed either generally or by way of statutory presumptions. In the former case, the defendant will have to prove the legitimate provenance of

[11] See also, eg, M Levi and L Osofsky, *Investigating, Seizing, and Confiscating the Proceeds of Crime*, Crime Detection and Prevention Series No 61 (London, Home Office Police Department, 1995) 38. Many factors may inhibit the effectivity of financial investigations. The mind-set of investigating police officers, even of officers specialising in economic crime, may be focused more on investigating the criminal offence than on the proceeds it has generated (financial investigations may even be considered a distraction as they divert time and resources from the criminal investigation). They may be initiated too late in the process (or not at all), rather than being carried out in parallel with the criminal investigation. There may be a lack of resources in investigating units, so that when the money trail is complicated and the benefit involved does not appear considerable, other tasks may have to be prioritised. And access to crucial information, essential for successfully carrying out financial investigations, may be inadequate between government bodies as the free flow of information from government agencies (such as tax or social welfare authorities) to the investigating authorities may be hampered by 'watertight bulkheads' between bodies. See also J Boucht, 'European Cooperation in Financial Investigations. An Overview of the Legal Framework and Future Challenges' in Z Durdevic and E Ivicevic Karas (eds), *European Criminal Procedure Law in the Service of the Protection of European Union Financial Interests* (Zagreb, Croatian Association of European Criminal Law, 2016) 117.

[12] See also M Levi, 'Following the Criminal and Terrorist Money Trails' in P van Duyne, K von Lampe and JL Newell (eds), *Criminal Finances and Organizing Crime in Europe* (Nijmegen, Wolf Legal Publishers, 2003) 115. See also Freiberg and Fox (n 3) 239. In Norway, it seems that the reversed burden of proof in extended confiscation proceedings has not increased the efficacy of the scheme: see J Boucht, 'Utvidgat förverkande enligt norska straffeloven § 34a—ökad funktionalitet eller obefogat avsteg från hävdvunna rättssäkerhetskrav?' [2012] *Tidsskrift for strafferett* 410.

[13] There are other issues as well, such as the target area of extended confiscation, which involves not only who may be targeted, but also which predicate offences may trigger confiscation. I will not, however, address these issues here. For a discussion on this, I refer to J Boucht, *Limits of Assets Confiscation. On the Legitimacy of Extended Appropriation of Criminal Proceeds* (Oxford, Hart Publishing, 2017 forthcoming).

the assets he holds in order to avoid confiscation. An example is section 68(1)(a) of the Norwegian Penal Code. According to this provision, extended confiscation may be ordered when the defendant is convicted of a predicate offence which carries a penalty of six years' imprisonment provided that the offence is of a nature liable to produce considerable gain.

Statutory legal presumptions, on the other hand, may be used in value-based confiscation regimes because of the difficulty connected with quantifying benefit obtained from unspecified unlawful conduct. Statutory presumptions mandate courts to presume or conclude *q*, given proof *p*, even though *p* would not, by the standards of ordinary reasoning, amount to proof of *q*.[14] Presumptions may be mandatory or facultative. An example of mandatory legal presumptions, which are to be deployed when the defendant is considered to have a criminal lifestyle under section 75, can be found in section 10 of the UK's POCA 2002. Facultative legal presumptions may be invoked under section 36e(3) of the Dutch Penal Code.

The reversal of the onus can, moreover, be either automatic or non-automatic. It is automatic if the burden shifts without the state first having to discharge an initial burden regarding the claims that the property in question represents unlawful benefit provided. An example of a more or less automatic presumption can be found in section 68(1)(a) of the Norwegian Penal Code. Under this section, it suffices for confiscation that the defendant is convicted of a relevant offence that is of a kind liable to produce considerable gain (although the state has to prove that the defendant holds the relevant property). Similarly, under section 75(2)(a) POCA 2002, the presumptions in section 10 apply when the defendant is convicted of an offence specified in Schedule 2 of the Act. In practice, the state has no evidential burden whatsoever to discharge in these cases (although the state will have to prove that the defendant has obtained the benefit/retains the assets). In a non-automatic scheme, the state would first have to prove, for example on the balance of probabilities, that the assets derive from unlawful conduct. Only if the state succeeds in discharging this initial burden (and the defendant is convicted of a relevant offence) will the onus would shift.[15]

The main arguments invoked in support of reversing the burden on proof in extended confiscation proceedings relate to crime prevention and making the recovery of ill-gotten gains more effective.[16] It is clear that there may be

[14] See RA Duff, *Answering For Crime. Responsibility and Liability in the Criminal Law* (Oxford, Hart Publishing, 2009) 239.

[15] This has been described as a partial sharing of the burden of proof rather than a reversed burden of proof. See G Stessens, *Money Laundering. A New International Law Enforcement Model* (Cambridge, Cambridge University Press, 2000) 70. A reversed burden of proof can also be either legal or evidential. A legal burden requires the defendant to prove, to the requisite standard of proof, that the assets are legitimate. In the latter case, the state has to discharge an initial burden (a substantiated claim) before the burden is reversed onto the defendant. In extended confiscation proceedings the burden is often legal.

[16] In Finland, for example, where the burden of proof has been on the state in extended confiscation proceedings, a working group has proposed, without further explanation, that a reversed burden

considerable evidential difficulties involved in showing that the property in question is unlawful, for example in regard to victimless offences, where the assets have been generated by violations of the criminal law of a foreign state or where the organisational structure of the perpetrators makes it difficult to target the 'backmen'.[17] Effectivity in this context normally refers to making it easier for the state to make successful claims. But 'effectivity' may also denote 'the impact of raising the financial risks from crime upon the local level of crime and upon its level of organisation';[18] in other words, if criminals scale down their ambitions or move elsewhere due to the risk of confiscation, this may also be viewed as an effective result.

There is also some institutional support for reversing the burden of proof in confiscation proceedings. For example, Article 5(7) of the UN Convention against Illicit Traffic in Narcotic Drugs and Psychotropic Substances (1988) states that each party may, to the extent that such action is consistent with the principles of its domestic law and the nature of judicial or other proceedings, consider ensuring that the onus of proof be reversed regarding the lawful origin of alleged proceeds or other property liable to confiscation. Similar wording can also be found in Article 31(7) of the UN Convention against Corruption (2003).[19]

Reversed burdens of proof in criminal proceedings are, however, generally controversial. This is particularly so if they relate to the establishment of criminal responsibility; it is an essential element of the presumption of innocence under Article 6(2) of the European Convention on Human Rights (ECHR) that the burden of proof is on the prosecution.[20] Confiscation proceedings, however, do not concern the establishment of criminal liability, but are directed against assets suspected of being obtained by unlawful conduct and are often described as being part of the sentencing process.[21] Because of this, it is sometimes considered less controversial to reverse the onus in such proceedings; it is seen as a matter of sharing the burden of proof, as it is only fair to expect the defendant, who is normally in the best place to do so, to explain the provenance of his assets.[22]

It may not necessarily be unfair to put the burden of explanation on the defendant at some stage in the confiscation proceedings relating to certain kinds of

of proof be introduced in extended confiscation proceedings in Finnish law in order to make confiscation more effective. See *Rikoslain menettämisseuraamuksia koskevien yleissäännösten tarkistaminen*, Oikeusministeriö, mietintöja ja lausuntoja 3/2015, 72–73.

[17] See Stessens (n 15) 67.

[18] M Levi, 'Reversal of the Burden of Proof in Confiscation of the Proceeds of Crime: A Council of Europe Best Practice Survey', Best Practice Survey No 2 (Strasbourg, Council of Europe, 2000) 10–11.

[19] See also Art 12(7) of the UN Convention against Transnational Organised Crime (1994).

[20] See, eg, *Barberà, Messegué and Jabardo v Spain* App No 10590/83 (European Court of Human Rights (ECtHR), 6 December 1988) para 77.

[21] *Phillips v the United Kingdom* App No 41087/98 (ECtHR, 5 July 2001) para 40.

[22] This was, for example, the position of the standing committee on constitutional matters of the Finnish Parliament. See Opinion GrUU 33/2000 rd.

offences, for example if the defendant has been convicted of a relevant predicate offence and has prior convictions of similar kind, if it can be further shown that he either holds or has held the assets in question.[23] A general reversal of the burden of proof in extended confiscation proceedings is nonetheless not unproblematic. Not only may the consequences of extended confiscation be severe and confer considerable hardship on the defendant as well as his family, but there is undoubtedly also a close connection to the criminal trial.[24]

Another unsettling aspect of extended confiscation is the risk of licit property being targeted, whereby the right to property is also in principle violated. Even if the point of departure is to restore the status quo ante, there is nonetheless an inherent risk due to watered down legal safeguards that licit property may be targeted. Reversing the onus of proof considerably increases that risk.[25] The question is therefore how big a risk may be considered acceptable. Moreover, the fact that extended confiscation may function on a presumption of prior criminality based on the conviction of a single offence obviously does not sit very well with the presumption of innocence.

Reversed burdens of proof have been under scrutiny by the ECtHR on several occasions, and on most occasions have been considered compatible with Article 6. A leading case is *Phillips v the United Kingdom*, in which a considerable criminal confiscation order was imposed on the applicant after, but in conjunction with, him being sentenced to nine years' imprisonment for drug offences. As regards the presumption of innocence, the Court held that extended confiscation does not constitute a 'criminal charge' under Article 6(2): since the purpose of the procedure was to enable the national court to assess the amount at which the confiscation order should properly be fixed, the procedure involved 'was analogous to the determination by a court of the amount of a fine or the length of a period of

[23] See Hodgson (n 2) 75 and 82–84. On the need to show that the defendant actually has held the assets in question, see *Geerings v the Netherlands* App No 30810/03 (ECtHR, 1 March 2007).

[24] Indeed, it has been argued that as extended confiscation factually involves confiscating more than what can be derived from a particular crime, it is in fact a penalty, which ought to abide by the same rules as criminal proceedings. See PO Träskman, 'Omvänt eller bakvänt. Om konststycket att lägga bevisbördan i brottmål på den tilltalade, utan att det kommer bak på människorättigheterna' [1998] *Nordisk Tidsskrift for Kriminalvidenskab* 363. Although this argument may not be rock solid, it may in this connection be recalled that the ECtHR has found that extended value confiscation may, depending on the circumstances of the case, amount to a penalty for the purposes of Art 7 of the ECHR (confirmed in *Phillips* (n 21)). The ECtHR has, however, apparently reserved the judgment against wide-reaching implications for the confiscation of proceeds of crime. In para 36 of the judgment, the Court stresses 'that this conclusion concerns only the retrospective application of the relevant legislation and does not call into question in any respect the powers of confiscation conferred on the courts as a weapon in the fight against the scourge of drug trafficking'.

[25] Similarly, Alldridge (n 7) 146 notes that '[a]ny rules that place the burden upon the defendant to show something not to have been will generate more incorrect findings of guilt or confiscation orders than where the burden is on the prosecution'.

imprisonment to be imposed on a properly convicted offender'.[26] The Court said that Article 6(2) could not in any case have any application to confiscation proceedings as it applies in connection with the particular offence charged, and once the defendant had properly been proved guilty of that offence Article 6(2) applies only if the accusations are of such a nature and degree as to amount to the bringing of a new 'charge'.[27]

However, the Court nonetheless considered that a person's right in a criminal case to be presumed innocent and to require the prosecution to bear the onus of proving the allegations against him also forms part of the general notion of a fair hearing under Article 6(1).[28] Reiterating the principle laid down in *Salabiaku v France*,[29] the Court found that presumptions of fact or of law, which operate in every criminal law system, are not prohibited in principle by the ECHR so long as states remain within certain limits, taking into account the importance of what is at stake and maintaining the rights of the defence.[30] A reversed burden of proof by way of statutory presumptions was not considered to deprive the defendant of a fair hearing under Article 6(1) as the safeguards provided for by English system were sufficient. The Court noted, however, that the position might be otherwise in circumstances where the amount of a confiscation order was based on the value of assumed hidden assets.[31]

As criminal confiscation represents an interference with an individual's right to peaceful disposal of his property, it also engages the right to property under Article 1 of Protocol 1 ECHR (A1P1). Criminal confiscation of property has, in the jurisprudence of the ECtHR, normally been seen to constitute control of the use of property under the second paragraph of A1P1.[32] To comply with this paragraph, an interference has to satisfy three requirements: it has to be lawful, it has

[26] *Phillips* (n 21) para 34. This position has been confirmed in subsequent case law. See, eg, *van Offeren v the Netherlands* App No 19581/04 (ECtHR, 5 July 2005); *Grayson and Barnham v the United Kingdom* App Nos 19955/05 and 15085/06 (ECtHR, 23 September 2008).

[27] *Phillips* (n 21) para 35.

[28] See *Phillips* (n 21) paras 39 and 40. See also D Harris, M O'Boyle, E Bates and C Buckley, *Harris, O'Boyle and Warbrick Law of the Convention of the European Convention on Human Rights*, 2nd edn (Oxford, Oxford University Press, 2014) 421.

[29] *Salabiaku v France* App No 10519/83 (ECtHR, 7 October 1988).

[30] *Phillips* (n 21) paras 40–47.

[31] I Smith, T Owen and A Bodnar, *Asset Recovery. Criminal Confiscation and Civil Recovery* (Oxford, Oxford University Press, 2012) II.2.131 note that *Phillips* (n 21) concerned the Drug Trafficking Act 1994, where the link between the subject matter of the indictment and the subject matter of the confiscation inquiry was close in that, upon conviction of drug trafficking, the court was to establish the defendant's benefit from drug trafficking. Thus, they argue, it was more understandable that the confiscation claim was not considered to be a separate criminal charge. However, determining that the defendant has a criminal lifestyle under POCA 2002 does not have to have any connection with the subject matter of the indictment, ie it is assumed that the defendant has committed unspecified criminality in the past. Thus they question whether the principle laid down in *Phillips* would readily also support the POCA confiscation scheme.

[32] See, eg, *Borzhonov v Russia* App No 18274/04 (ECtHR, 22 September 2009) para 57.

to pursue a legitimate aim and it must strike a fair balance between the interests of the state and general community and those of the individual's fundamental rights.[33] The latter requirement means that there must be a reasonable relationship of proportionality between the means employed by the state in depriving an individual of property as a form of penalty and the legitimate aim that is sought to be realised by the deprivation. Provided that the interference is based on a legitimate aim, for example crime control, A1P1 awards a wide margin of appreciation with regard both to choosing the means of enforcement and to ascertaining whether the consequences of enforcement are justified as being in the general interest for the purpose of achieving the object of the law in question.

The proportionality requirement inherent in A1P1 requires that a fair balance be struck between the interests of the state and those of the individual. This also includes a procedural dimension. Even if there is an affinity between Article 6(1) and A1P1 so that many procedural guarantees overlap,[34] there is nonetheless a difference in purpose. Whereas the safeguards of Article 6(1) are strictly procedural as such, the procedural requirement of A1P1 is ancillary to the wider purpose of ensuring respect for the right to the peaceful enjoyment of one's possessions. This requirement is necessary in order to ensure that the operation of the system and its impact on the person's property rights is neither arbitrary nor unforeseeable.[35]

In *Phillips*, the ECtHR also addressed the confiscatory powers exercised by the English court in the light of A1P1. The Court concluded that they were not unreasonably extensive or in breach of A1P1. In so finding, the Court took note of the fact that the confiscated sum, although extensive, corresponded to the amount which the national court had found the applicant to have benefited by through drug trafficking over the preceding six years and was a sum which he was able to realise from the assets in his possession. The Court also referred to the importance of the aim pursued (to combat the serious problem of drug trafficking), as well as its finding in connection with Article 6(1) that the procedure followed in the making of the order was fair and respected the rights of the defence.

The decision in *Phillips* has been criticised. Judges Bratza and Vajic submitted a powerful dissent regarding the conclusion that Article 6(2) did not apply, as this would be to take too narrow a view of the role of Article 6(2) in the context of proceedings relating to a criminal charge (although they agreed with the fact that Article 6(2) had not been violated).[36] Trechsel, on his part, argues that not only

[33] See, amongst others, *Borzhonov* (ibid) para 59; *Silickiene v Lithuania* App No 20496/02 (ECtHR, 10 April 2012) para 63; *AGOSI v the United Kingdom* App No 9118/80 (ECtHR, 24 October 1986) para 52.

[34] See, eg, *Borzhonov* (n 32).

[35] *Borzhonov* (n 32) para 60.

[36] See S Trechsel, *Human Rights in Criminal Proceedings* (Oxford, Oxford University Press, 2005) 34–35, who argues that not only should Art 6(2) have applied, but it was also in fact violated in view of the fact that the presumptions applied went back several years in time and that the defendant has not previously been found guilty of drug offences, whereby the 'proceedings implicitly but unmistakably' were based on a presumption of prior criminality.

should Article 6(2) have applied, but it was in fact also violated. The presumptions applied went back several years in time and the defendant had not previously been found guilty of drug offences, so the proceedings 'implicitly but unmistakably' were based on a presumption of prior criminality. Smith et al, moreover, observe that *Phillips* concerned the Drug Trafficking Act 1994, where the link between the subject matter of the indictment and the subject matter of the confiscation inquiry was close in that, upon conviction of drug trafficking, the court was to establish the defendant's benefit from drug trafficking. Thus, they argue, it was more understandable that the confiscation claim was not considered to be a separate criminal charge. However, determining that the defendant has a criminal lifestyle under POCA 2002 does not have to have any connection with the subject matter of the indictment, ie it is assumed that the defendant has committed unspecified criminality in the past. Therefore, they argue, it may be questioned whether the principle laid down in *Phillips* needs to be reconsidered in view of the POCA scheme. As regards A1P1, it may also be noted that the Court placed considerable emphasis on the fact that the case concerned drug trafficking, an area in which the court has awarded Member States a considerable margin of appreciation. This means that the extent to which the Court's conclusions apply outside drug offences is not unequivocal. Moreover, the Court did not seem to consider the risk of confiscating lawful property as such.

In spite of the position of the ECtHR, there is a tension between a reversed burden of proof in extended confiscation proceedings and the presumption of innocence (even if confiscation proceedings lie at the periphery of criminal charges) and the right to property.[37] In cases where confiscation is triggered by the conviction of a single offence, the confiscation measure is clearly based on a presumption of prior criminality (see also the point raised by Smith et al above).[38] In regard to the right to property again, the tension seems to arise from the risk of confiscating licit property, particularly where statutory presumptions are used which go back in time several years.[39] Reversing the onus should therefore be done with caution. At the same time, the important interest of crime prevention,

[37] See, eg, A Schönke and H Schröder, *Strafgesetzbuch. Kommentar*, 27th edn (Munich, Verlag CH Beck, 2006) §73d rdnr 2 concerning the relationship with the German Constitution.

[38] Thus, Smith et al (n 31) II.2.136 argue, regarding the English confiscation legislation, that in cases where conviction of a single offence facilitates the establishment of a criminal lifestyle for the purposes of s 10 POCA 2002, the judge should inquire into the circumstances of the case as a whole and if, on the evidence, he is satisfied that the defendant is in fact not a career criminal, there is a risk of injustice under s 10(6) POCA 2002 if the presumptions are made. In situations where the defendant has been convicted in the past of similar offences, this tension seems to be reduced. In regard to the presumption of innocence, it should also be noted that the Court has rightly recognised in *Jussila v Finland* App No 73053/01 (ECtHR, 23 November 2006) para 43 that there are criminal cases which do not entail the level of stigma that 'core cases' may entail, which means the criminal-head guarantees will not necessarily always apply with their full stringency.

[39] This also touches on the way in which statutory presumptions may be rebutted: by raising a reasonable doubt, by requirement to adduce sufficient evidence to bring into question the truth of the presumed fact and by burden to prove on a balance of probabilities the non-existence of the relevant fact. See Jayawickrama et al (n 1) 28.

particularly organised crime and serious economic crime, must of course be taken into consideration.

In light of this discussion, there seems to be normative support for the proposition that the point of departure should be that the burden of proof is on the state, but that there is room for reversing the onus of proof in extended confiscation proceedings within narrow margins.[40] The tension in regard to the presumption of innocence and the right to property should be taken seriously.

As already noted, it is probably not unreasonable to put the burden of explanation on the defendant at some stage in the proceedings, provided that sufficient procedural safeguards are in place, but this should not be done generally. Fairness is generally perceived as being essential in criminal law,[41] and there is no reason why this should not also apply to confiscation.

Which cases would then be of a nature that might justify reversing the onus? It seems to me that a justified reversal requires that the policy interests involved are particularly strong. Merely invoking an unsubstantiated claim of the need to increase effectivity should not be sufficient. Nor should the mere fact that the individual may be in a better position to explain certain facts suffice per se. It may be that a reversed burden of proof can be justifiable concerning certain kinds of offences in regard to which difficulties of proving the unlawful provenance of the assets may be particularly evident and where the criminal justice policy interests are acute. This might involve, for example, corruption cases, particularly where state officials are involved, large drug trafficking cases and, possibly, offences related to organised crime.[42] Reversing the burden of proof in regard to other defendants, for example individuals who have only been convicted of a single offence, would appear unfair.

C. The Standard of Proof

The standard of proof may be relevant in extended confiscation proceedings in two ways: first, regarding whether or not the defendant has obtained (and retains) certain assets; and secondly, whether or not the provenance of that benefit is unlawful. As discussed in Section II.B above, some confiscation schemes employ a reversed burden of proof in regard to the latter. As suggested above, however, reversing the burden of proof should be done with discernment. The focus here is on the latter.

[40] It may be noted that a reversed burden of proof in extended confiscation proceedings was disqualified as contrary to the presumption of innocence in both Finland and Sweden when the 2005 Framework Decision was implemented. See Committee Opinion LaUB 14/2001 rd detaljmotivering SL 10:3 (Finland); Legislative Report SOU 1999:147, 125 (Sweden).

[41] See, eg, A Ashworth and J Horder, *Principles of Criminal Law*, 7th edn (Oxford, Oxford University Press, 2013) 162.

[42] As regards corruption, see Jayawickrama et al (n 1) 23. Organised crime could become a relevant category, provided that the notion of organised crime is defined in a sufficiently precise manner.

The standard of proof varies between jurisdictions. For example, under section 6(7) of POCA 2002, the standard of proof regarding the first inquiry is the balance of probabilities (the second inquiry is based on statutory presumptions).[43] Regarding the second inquiry, the origin of the assets, section 73d of the German Penal Code (StGB), for example, states that extended confiscation is to be ordered 'if the circumstances justify the assumption that these objects were acquired as a result of unlawful acts'. This section has been interpreted as requiring the judge to be convinced, having considered all the evidence, of the illicit origin of the assets in question, although he does not have to identify the suspected crimes in detail.[44] This comes close to the standard set out in Article 3(2) of the previous EU Framework Decision on confiscation (212/2005/JHA), which required the national court to be 'fully convinced' of the unlawful provenance of the property before extended confiscation could be ordered. Under chapter 36, section 1b of the Swedish Penal Code, again, the standard is set at a qualified balance of probabilities (a probability of 70–80 per cent), whereas chapter 10, section 2 of the Finnish Penal Code sets it as low as 'reasons to believe that the property is fully or partially derived from criminal activity that is not to be considered insignificant'.[45]

It is, of course, challenging to clearly state what the correct standard should be. A higher standard implies a lower risk of wrongful confiscations being made, but also entails a larger number of rightful confiscation claims being denied. A lower standard may be supported with efficiency arguments. On the other hand, as with the burden of proof, the standard of proof has a direct bearing on the risk of confiscating licit property and a higher standard means that this risk is reduced. On a general balance, it is important to take the objective of avoiding confiscation of licit property seriously.

It may also be possible to take some guidance from A1P1. As with the reversed burden of proof, there is arguably a tension between a low standard of proof and the right to property. As noted above, the proportionality requirement of A1P1 means that there must be a reasonable relationship of proportionality between the

[43] However, according to English law, some cases may require more careful consideration before the court is satisfied of the matter which has to be established to a requisite standard, even if that standard in itself is finite and unvarying. In *Re D* [2008] 1 WLR 1499, para 28, Lord Carswell, with whom the other Law Lords concurred, noted that '[s]ituations which make such heightened examination necessary may be the inherent unlikelihood of the occurrence taking place … the seriousness of the allegation to be proved or, in some cases, the consequences which could follow from acceptance of proof of the relevant fact'. In this context, I only discuss the standard of proof, not the cogency of the evidence required in order to satisfy a particular standard of proof. See also Lord Hoffman in *Re D (Children)* [2008] 3 WLR 1, para 13. In view of this, Smith et al (n 31) II.2.253–54 argue that the court should require cogent evidence before finding it proved that the defendant has benefited from criminal conduct.

[44] See the German Bunderverfassungsgericht decision BVerfG 2 BvR 564/95, 14 January 2004, para 92. See also below at nn 46 and 47.

[45] It should be noted that the German, Swedish and Finnish schemes all require that the defendant has been convicted of a relevant predicate offence before confiscation may be ordered.

means employed by the state in the deprivation of property as a form of penalty and the legitimate aim which is sought to be realised by the deprivation.

It would seem possible to argue that unless it can fairly be said in light of the evidence available that the assets in all probability are illicit, which can only be said where the standard of proof is sufficiently high, it cannot be necessary to confiscate them. The tension in regard to the presumption of innocence discussed above may further support this proposition. This kind of reasoning seems in fact to have been employed by German courts in interpreting section 73d of the StGB (see above). In a case from 1994, the Bundesgerichtshof (BGH) concluded that extended confiscation was compatible with the Constitution (Article 1 I on the schuldprinzip and the presumption of innocence and Article 14 I on the right to property), provided that the statute is narrowly interpreted so as to mean that the trial judge is 'unrestrictedly convinced' of the illicit origin of the assets in question.[46] In 2004, the Bundesverfassungsgericht (BVerfG), upon application, approved the interpretation by the BGH. Indeed, the BVerfG did not explicitly state that the constitutional dimension required the standard of proof to be set at 'unrestrictedly convinced', but there are some indications in the judgment to suggest this. The BVerfG concludes its proportionality assessment by saying that, by interpreting the statute narrowly, the court limits the scope of confiscation to assets which are verifiably obtained through unlawful conduct, and thereby ensures that the system of property ownership is only corrected where this is necessary in order to remove the disruption in ownership caused by the offence.[47]

This kind of reasoning, with which I am sympathetic, seems to provide arguments in support of a suggestion that the standard of proof should be reasonably high. Indeed, in view of the purpose of extended confiscation to facilitate confiscation in cases where the origin of the property cannot be proved at a criminal standard, the criminal standard 'beyond reasonable doubt' can hardly be required. This would easily defeat the purpose of extended confiscation. However, there seem to be reasons to argue that the risk of faulty decisions connected with a standard lower than a 'balance or probabilities', for example 'reasons to believe' (as in the Finnish scheme), is problematic in view of A1P1. If the unlawful origin

[46] See NStZ 1995, 125: 'Die Anordnung des erweiterten Verfalls kommt nur in Betracht, wenn der Tatrichter aufgrund erschöpfender Beweiserhebung und -würdigung … die uneingeschränkte Überzeugung gewonnen hat, daß der Angekl. die von der Anordnung erfaßten Gegenstände aus rechtswidrigen Taten erlangt hat, ohne daß diese selbst im einzelnen festgestellt werden müßten.' It seems that the lawmaker originally set the standard at 'a high level of probability' ('ganz hohe Wahrscheinlichkeit'). See H Tröndle and T Fischer, *Strafgesetzbuch und Nebengesetze*, 51st edn (Munich, Verlag CH Beck, 2003) § 73d rdnr 11.

[47] BVerfG 110, 14 January 2004, para 97: 'Die restriktive Auslegung des § 73d Abs. 1 Satz 1 StGB durch den Bundesgerichtshof entspricht auch den vom Gesetzgeber mit der Vorschrift verfolgten weitergehenden Zielen der Gewinnabschöpfung (vgl dazu bereits oben C. I. 1. b) bb). Sie konzentriert den Anwendungsbereich des erweiterten Verfalls auf nachweisbar deliktisch erlangte Gegenstände und stellt damit sicher, dass die Eigentumsordnung nur dort korrigiert wird, wo dies erforderlich ist, um deliktisch verursachte Störungen zu beseitigen.'

of the property is not established with a high degree of certainty, it is doubtful whether confiscation can be proportionate in the meaning of A1P1.

It would thus seem that the standard should be higher than a balance of probabilities but below 'beyond reasonable doubt'. At least where 'the contextual assumption' is weak, ie where the individual has been convicted only of a single offence, the standard of proof, regarding both whether or not the defendant has obtained benefit and the provenance of that benefit, should be higher than a balance of probabilities. However, for the reasons put forward above, there also seem to be reasons to argue that this should apply generally. A suitable standard of proof in these cases would seem to be a qualified balance of probability (which, at 70–80 per cent, is lower than the criminal standard but higher than a balance of probabilities).[48] This standard would require that the court, based on the complete picture of the circumstances of the case, finds it clearly more probable than not that the property in question constitutes benefit of unlawful conduct. It should not, however, be required to specify the offences in detail.

D. Quantification

A third issue that may arise is whether or not extended confiscation should target the calculated value of the benefit obtained unlawfully by unspecified prior criminality (value confiscation) or specific property (*in specie*), including cash, which the defendant retains. Value confiscation means that the defendant is obliged to pay an amount of money, as specified in the confiscation order, which corresponds to the value of the benefit he has obtained. *In specie* confiscation, on the other hand, means that the confiscation order targets certain pieces of property, which represent the illicit benefit.[49]

The guiding principles vary between jurisdictions. In the UK, extended confiscation is value based and the benefit of the defendant's prior criminal activity is calculated by way of legal presumptions.[50] However, the actual confiscation order is limited to assets which the defendant still retains (identified available assets),

[48] Such a standard is not unheard of in confiscation proceedings. Besides the high standard required in German law, under Swedish law (ch 36, s 1b of the Swedish Penal Code) extended confiscation may only be decided where it is clearly more probable than not that the assets in question have been obtained by unlawful conduct. In the report commissioned by the Swedish government, SOU 2015:67 ('För att brott inte skall löna sig'), where the extended confiscation scheme has been assessed, this standard of proof has been proposed to be continued. It may, perhaps, be said that in the case of the defendant having been convicted of prior offences, the evidence-related 'inherent probability' is higher, which may mean that less evidence is required in order to pass the threshold compared to situations where the anterior probability is low(er).

[49] *In specie* confiscation may be limited to property which the defendant still retains, or it may extend to property which is proved to have been in his possession but has subsequently been disposed of. In the latter case, value confiscation may be decided for this property.

[50] POCA 2002, ss 76(4) and 76(7).

provided that the defendant shows, to a balance of probabilities, that the available amount is less than the calculated benefit obtained through unlawful conduct.[51] As the benefit calculation is value based, also legitimate property which the defendant holds may be confiscated. In Finnish law, extended confiscation is decided *in specie* (which may involve both cash and property) against property which the defendant holds in his possession.[52] Under both Danish and Swedish law, the point of departure is *in specie* confiscation, although an amount corresponding to the value of that property may be confiscated in place of certain property.[53]

Both models seem to have their own advantages and disadvantages. To start with, it might be said that *in specie* confiscation may be perceived as being more 'concrete' in the sense that it is limited to property which the defendant actually holds. On the other hand, where confiscation is based on vague prior criminal activity, and the individual has had both lawful and unlawful income which he has disposed of as he has found fit, it may be difficult to ascertain whether or not a particular car, boat or real estate has been obtained with solely unlawful, or partially lawful and partially unlawful, means.[54] One may ask how specific one has to be regarding the origin of the property and whether the chain of a specific chattel must be traced. It could, for example, be said that the property in question simply manifests the disproportion between the defendant's lawful income and his available assets. But even so, the problem remains in principle that there is a tension with A1P1 to the extent that a chattel is acquired using both licit and illicit means, and how this tension is solved ought to be addressed by the policy makers. Another way of dealing with the problem is to say that, to the extent that the defendant's legitimate income does not exceed his (and his family's) basic living costs, the property is assumed to be obtained by unlawfully conduct.[55] Moreover, the effect of *in specie* confiscation may be limited in situations where the benefit of prior criminal activity has been spent on consumption. Hidden assets, ie assets

[51] See POCA 2002, ss 7 and 9. In *R v May* [2008] 1 AC 1028, the House of Lords concluded that the defendant 'cannot be ordered to pay a sum which it is beyond his means to pay'. This means, however, that the burden of showing the extent and value of his assets is shifted onto the defendant. In extended confiscation proceedings, the burden is thus on the defendant not only to rebut the statutory presumptions that the court has to apply, but also to show that the amount available is less than the calculated benefit obtained.

[52] Finnish Penal Code, ch 10, s 3. See also P Viljanen, *Konfiskaatio rikosoikeudellisena seuraamuksena* (Helsinki, Edita Publishing, 2007) 215–16.

[53] Danish Penal Code, s 76a(5); Swedish Penal Code, ch 36, s 1b.

[54] The difficulty in satisfying the burden of individualising the property subjected to confiscation obviously depends on the standard of proof required. If, as under Finnish law, the state only has 'reasons to suspect' that the property is unlawfully obtained, it is probably quite easily discharged. If, however, the standard of proof required is a qualified balance of probabilities, it will be considerably more difficult to individualise the property in question. This is particularly so in view of the fact that the state's claim is probably primarily based on a general finding that, for example, 40% of the individual's assets exceed his legal income. Unless certain posts can be traced directly to the purchase of certain property, individualisation may be very difficult.

[55] This is the position of the Norwegian Supreme Court; see, eg, case Rt 2003 s 1096.

which the defendant keeps hidden, for example by using complex offshore entities, may also be problematic.

Value-based extended confiscation, on the other hand, is based on appraisal of the benefit obtained by the defendant through unlawful conduct. As extended value confiscation also targets prior unspecified criminality, it is encumbered with the problem of specifying the value of that prior criminality. That is, as the preceding criminal activity in which the assets originate is merely assumed and not proved, the question arises how properly to quantify the value subjected to confiscation. This may obviously be a difficult task.[56] In order to facilitate quantification, recourse may, as in English law under POCA 2002, be had to statutory presumptions. Such presumptions may, for example, specify that any income or any expenses incurred during a certain statutory period of time will be presumed to have been derived from unlawful conduct. However, the use of presumptions involves a considerable risk of striking too broadly, which may result in wrongful confiscation decisions, and of putting the defendant in a procedurally problematic position. Also, the longer the period the presumptions cover, the greater the uncertainty of the origin of the property is likely to be, and consequently the more difficult it will be for the defendant to rebut them.[57] Value confiscation of this kind may also result in confiscation orders of considerable magnitude.

On the other hand, value confiscation requires in principle the defendant to disgorge all the benefit he has obtained as a result of his assumed unlawful activity, not just the assets he retains at the time the confiscation proceedings are initiated. However, the confiscation order may be limited to assets actually held by the defendant (which may be considerably less than the benefit obtained), such as in the English system. This means that possible unreasonableness is mainly linked to the quantification rules as regards the benefit obtained.

The choice between value-based and *in specie* confiscation may in part depend on what the national jurisdiction in question considers the purpose of (extended) confiscation to be. Should confiscation only target property which the defendant holds in his possession, ie should it be confined to removing only the most blatant injustice caused by permitting the defendant to retain property obtained by palpably unlawful means? This would seem to be the Nordic approach. Or should it strive to remove the total value of all assets which the defendant has obtained through unlawful conduct, irrespective of whether or not he retains them?[58] This is the UK approach.

[56] See, eg, the Swedish Supreme Court case NJA 2010 s 374.

[57] For example, temporally very broad presumptions in extended confiscation proceedings which state that, say, all assets obtained during 25 years prior to the proceedings will be considered unlawful are clearly problematic as they are very difficult to rebut.

[58] An example of this is Lord Bingham's statement in his Endnote (para 48) in *R v May* [2008] 1 AC 1028: 'The legislation is intended to deprive defendants of the benefit they have gained from

I am sympathetic to the *in specie* approach as a point of departure. The primary target area of confiscation should arguably be to deprive defendants of property which is found to be in their possession and which sufficiently clearly represents benefit obtained through unlawful conduct. However, this approach is open to criticism, as it would induce criminals to spend as much as possible of their ill-gotten gains. So-called hidden assets may also be problematic. Ultimately, the choice is policy based.

Conclusion

It is clear that sufficient confiscatory powers are required in order to achieve effective confiscation of illicit assets. Extensive confiscation schemes which do not require a clear causal connection to be established between the predicate offence and the assets in question may be useful tools for law enforcement authorities. These tools have also been surrounded by principled controversies and arguments that they circumvent fundamental safeguards of criminal law and criminal procedural law.

Assuming that the assets targeted, and subsequently confiscated, represent unlawful benefit, extended confiscation is perfectly legitimate. In this case, the individual is deprived of assets to which he has no proper title. The measure thus resembles rectification of unjust enrichment by restoring the status quo ante. However, the heart of the problem with all extensive confiscation schemes seems to be the risk of confiscating licit property. The crucial question is thus what level of risk may be acceptable.

It may be argued that the risk caused by these measures is negligible in view of the importance of the overarching policy ambition of fighting serious economic crime. Indeed, it is not unimaginable that criminal law is just an 'old machine', which is incapable of functioning effectively in areas such as organised crime and serious economic crime if strict adherence to the traditional safeguards and principles of law is always insisted upon. Moreover, the aim of preventing organised crime and serious economic criminality is an important one. However, the maxim that 'the goal justifies the means' should not apply without reasonable limitations.

As seen above, there are aspects of current schemes which may not be readily reconcilable with fundamental principles underlying criminal and criminal procedural law. The fact that certain moderations of traditional safeguards may be necessary in this field is probably not controversial per se. Rather, the question is how far it is legitimate to go in diluting these safeguards. I believe there are good

relevant criminal conduct, whether or not they have retained such benefit, within the limits of their available means. It does not provide for confiscation in the sense understood by schoolchildren and others, but nor does it operate by way of a fine. The benefit gained is the total value of the property or advantage obtained, not the defendant's net profit after deduction of expenses or any amounts payable to co-conspirators.'

reasons for requiring, as a point of departure, a fairly low risk, although this may be adjusted depending on the context. For example, where the individual has, say, during a period of six years, been convicted of a number of similar offences liable to produce gain, there is probably a fairly strong, and fair, assumption that the property in question may represent unlawfully obtained benefit. In this case, it seems to be less controversial to dilute certain safeguards as the underlying probability ('anterior probability') of the assets being illicit is higher. Where, on the other hand, the individual has only been convicted of a single offence, the contextual assumption appears much weaker and the safeguards required should reflected this.

How, then, should extended confiscation schemes be constructed in order to best achieve a reasonable balance between the interests of the state and those of the individual? First of all, the burden of proof should, as a point of departure, be on the state, perhaps with the exception of cases where the policy interests involved in support of reversing the onus are particularly robust. Secondly, the standard of proof regarding the illicit nature of the property in question should be reasonably high, at least in regard to defendants without prior convictions relating to acquisitive crime. A suitable standard would in principle seem to be a qualified balance of probabilities (70–80 per cent probability).

Can it, then, be said that extended confiscation is more about targeting criminal proceeds than criminal owners? In a way, it probably can, as the focus is on depriving the individual of assets which are suspected of representing unlawfully obtained proceeds even though they cannot be linked to the predicate offence of which the defendant is convicted. However, as extended confiscation is decided within the framework of criminal proceedings and requires the existence of a predicate criminal conviction, it is still probably more accurate to say that, ultimately, it is still about criminal owners, in a similar way as regular criminal confiscation, rather than only criminal assets.[59]

Against the background set out above, I believe there are in fact reasons to question if extended confiscation could in fact, in many cases, successfully be replaced by other schemes better fitted for its purpose. Civil confiscation (civil recovery or non-conviction-based confiscation), which has been embraced by many jurisdictions, may be an interesting alternative in many situations,[60] provided that sufficient safeguards are put in place. The purpose is similar to that of extended confiscation: to be able to deprive individuals of property which is unlawful in nature to which the individual therefore can have no title. The focus is thus not so much on whether the holder has committed an offence, but if the property in question is criminal. This scheme is truly about the property, not the criminal owners.

[59] Extended confiscation may in this regard be compared with civil confiscation (or recovery), which is wholly detached from criminal proceedings and is pursued within civil proceedings. Here I believe it may be fairer to argue that it is about criminal assets rather than criminal owners. On civil confiscation, see eg J Boucht, 'Civil Asset Forfeiture and the Presumption of Innocence' [2014] *New Journal of European Criminal Law* 222, 227.

[60] See, eg, the contributions by King and Cassella in this publication (Chapters 3 and 11, respectively).

6

Modern Forms of Confiscation and Protection of Third Parties

ISIDORO BLANCO CORDERO*

Introduction

EU Directive 2014/42/EU (the Directive) on the Freezing and Confiscation of Instrumentalities and Proceeds of Crime in the EU sets the minimum rules to be applied in the Union, with the aim of establishing a set of common minimum standards in order to recover the proceeds of crime. This instrument is part of the EU's efforts to approximate substantive criminal law, in order to facilitate the co-operation in criminal matters inside the EU. The international co-operation in depriving criminals of their resources or proceeds of crime is an important aspect of the EU criminal policy[1] in order to fight crimes that are essentially profit-driven. The approximation of confiscation systems should contribute to ensuring the compatibility of rules applicable in the Member States and to facilitating co-operation between competent authorities.

On the basis of the Lisbon Treaty, the old Framework Decisions on confiscation, adopted under the former third pillar of the EU, have been 'Lisbonised',[2] ie they have been replaced—totally or in part—by the Directive /42/EU. This instrument is fully integrated into the supranational framework of the post-Lisbon Union.[3] The Directive has replaced Joint Action 98/699/JHA of 3 December 1998

* Professor at the University of Alicante. This chapter is included in the research project 'Adaptación del Derecho penal español al Derecho penal europeo' (DER2013-43883-P), funded by the Ministry of Economy and Competitiveness of the Spanish Government.

[1] See M Simonato, 'Directive 2014/42/EU and Non-Conviction Based Confiscation: A Step Forward on Asset Recovery?' (2015) 6(2) *New Journal of European Criminal Law* 213, 214.

[2] See 'Revised Preliminary List of the Former Third Pillar Acquis', Commission Staff Working Document 14 May 2014 (SWD(2014)166 final).

[3] Although in recent years some authors have seen a process of 'de-Lisbonisation' of the EU Area of Freedom, Security and Justice, as a consequence of the Strategic Guidelines for Legislative and Operational Planning for the coming years within the EU's Area of Freedom, Security and Justice (AFSJ). See, in this sense, S Carrera and E Guild, 'The European Council's Guidelines for the Area of Freedom, Security and Justice 2020: Subverting the "Lisbonisation" of Justice and Home Affairs?', *CEPS Essay* No 13, 14 July 2014.

adopted by the Council on the basis of Article K.3 of the Treaty on European Union on money laundering and the identification, tracing, freezing, seizing and confiscation of instrumentalities and proceeds from crime.[4] The Directive has also amended Council Framework Decision 2001/500/JHA of 26 June 2001 on money laundering and the identification, tracing, freezing, seizing and confiscation of instrumentalities and the proceeds of crime,[5] and Council Framework Decision 2005/212/JHA of 24 February 2005 on confiscation of crime related proceeds, instrumentalities and property.[6] However, Articles 2, 4 and 5 of Framework Decision 2005/212/JHA remains in force for criminal activities falling outside the scope of the Directive.[7] Far from simplifying the legal framework on confiscation, the Directive has created a sensation of fragmentation.[8] Only Joint Action 98/699/JHA is repealed in its entirety, while only a limited number of provisions of Framework Decision 2001/500/JHA[9] and of Framework Decision 2005/212/JHA[10] are replaced by the provisions of the Directive. Finally, only 26 Member States are bound by the Directive, the other two Member States not being bound by special statute under the Treaty of Lisbon. In conclusion, the Lisbonisation process has given the opportunity to the EU to evaluate and revise existing harmonising instruments, namely by improving provisions of doubtful quality.[11] Nevertheless, one could say that in this case the Lisbonisation process has complicated the legal framework rather than simplifying it.

The EU legislator has been inspired by the objective that 'crime does not pay',[12] ie offenders should not be allowed to benefit from crime.[13] The risk of being deprived of their assets, however, might convince criminals to distance themselves

[4] See Joint Action 98/699/JHA of 3 December 1998 adopted by the Council on the basis of Article K.3 of the Treaty on European Union, on money laundering, the identification, tracing, freezing, seizing and confiscation of instrumentalities and the proceeds from crime [1998] OJ L333/1.

[5] Council Framework Decision 2001/500/JHA of 26 June 2001 on money laundering, the identification, tracing, freezing, seizing and confiscation of instrumentalities and the proceeds of crime [2001] OJ L182/1.

[6] See Council Framework Decision 2005/212/JHA of 24 February 2005 on confiscation of crime-related proceeds, instrumentalities and property [2005] OJ L68/49.

[7] We need to remember that the Framework Decision refers to all criminal offences punishable by deprivation of liberty for more than one year; see G Arcifa, 'The New EU Directive on Confiscation: a good (Even if Still Prudent) Starting Point for the Post-Lisbon EU Strategy on Tracking and Confiscating Illicit Money', available at https://free-group.eu/2014/03/25/the-new-eu-directive-on-confiscation-a-good-even-if-still-prudent-starting-point-for-the-post-lisbon-eu-strategy-on-tracking-and-confiscating-illicit-money/.

[8] A Mura, 'Towards Greater Cooperation in Freezing and Confiscation of the Proceeds of Crime: A Practitioners Approach' (Eurojust Strategic Seminar, the Hague, 11 December 2014) 2.

[9] Point (a) of Art 1 and Arts 3 and 4.

[10] The first four paragraphs of Art 1 and Art 3.

[11] H Satzger, 'Study on Police and Justice Cooperation in the European Union', available at www.janalbrecht.eu/fileadmin/material/Dokumente/SATZGER__Study_on_Police_and_Justice_Cooperation_28_11_13_final.pdf.

[12] Communication from the Commission to the European Parliament and the Council of 20 November 2008—'Proceeds of Organised Crime: Ensuring that "Crime Does Not Pay"' COM (2008)766 final.

[13] For a critical appraisal of this approach, see RT Naylor, 'Wash-out: A Critique of Follow the Money Methods in Crime Control Policy' (1999) 32 *Crime, Law and Social Change* 1; RT Naylor, 'License to Loot? A Critique of Follow-the-Money Methods in Crime Control Policy' (2001) 28 *Social Justice* 121.

from their illicit gain, and transfer their criminal property to third parties—usually relatives, family members, girlfriends and other close friends[14]—with the intention of avoiding confiscation.

As a general rule, confiscation provisions only apply to property owned by a person who has committed a crime. However, this rule might have an important exception, in so far as interests of 'third parties'[15] who are not involved in the same criminal activity are affected. As a result, confiscation laws may operate to the detriment of innocent third persons whose property could be subject to confiscation because it was either used in the commission of or derived from a crime. In this case, third parties are 'caught in the crossfire'.[16] Needless to say, the deprivation of innocent persons' assets affects their fundamental rights, especially the right to property.

For example, a car bought with money earned through criminal conduct can be confiscated as a proceed of crime. But what if the car is jointly owned by the offender and his spouse? What if the car is held by a nominee, or the defendant holds the car as a nominee for someone else? Imagine that the car is sold: should the buyer's interest be affected by the confiscation?

I. Two Ways to Recover Assets from Third Parties

Third parties who are not responsible for the criminal activity that has motivated the confiscation can be deprived of their assets in two ways. First, consider that the third party is responsible for a new crime when he/she receives the assets, normally with knowledge of their illicit origin. In this case, the confiscation can be based upon the crime of receiving illicit goods, or money laundering. The person is no longer a third party separate from the offender, but he/she is a first (or maybe second) party, ie he/she is considered as the perpetrator of a new crime. The confiscation, therefore, can be ordered in a new criminal process against the person who has acquired the assets from the suspected or accused person. Of course, new criminal proceedings take more time and require more resources, and trigger the application of the whole set of criminal procedural safeguards. This could make asset recovery quite difficult.

For this reason, if separate criminal charges are not brought, confiscation can also be ordered against a third party who is not responsible for the crime from which property is derived. In this case, the third party is not accused of a crime, he/she is not a defendant in the criminal proceedings and criminal responsibility cannot be declared. Such a person cannot be sentenced to any penalty, and

[14] SD Cassella, 'The Uniform Innocent Owner Defense to Civil Asset Forfeiture' (2001) 89(3) *Kentucky Law Journal* 653.

[15] These third parties can be both natural and legal persons.

[16] AM O'Brien, '"Caught in the Crossfire": Protecting the Innocent Owner of Real Property from Civil Forfeiture Under 21 U.S.C. § 881(a)(7)' (2012) 65 *St John's Law Review* 521.

nothing is mentioned in his/her criminal record. Nonetheless, confiscation can be imposed, and this may adversely affect his/her fundamental human rights and freedoms, particularly the right to property.[17]

This chapter will focus on the latter situation, ie when the third party is not responsible for the crime but the property he/she has acquired from the suspected or accused person of a crime can be subject to confiscation. In particular, the chapter will analyse features and limits of the EU legal framework on third-party confiscations, exploring some possibilities to transpose it into effective and reasonable national laws. When relevant, the EU approach is compared with the one adopted by other jurisdictions, particularly the USA.

A third party affected by confiscation is somebody who is not responsible for the criminal activity that has justified the confiscation[18] but is the owner of the assets, or has a right or legal interests in them. It could also be a person who has acquired an interest in the confiscated property after the commission of the crime.

A third party who holds legal interests in the assets subject to confiscation can be the person to whom the property belongs, as in the case of a home jointly owned by an offender and his/her spouse. In this event, the confiscation can affect the legal rights of the spouse, so he/she has a direct interest against the confiscation.[19]

In other cases, the third party can have a right over the assets which belong to another person. For instance, the person can have a right *in rem* over the property, eg a right to use and get benefit from it. If the property enters under the disposition of the state as a consequence of the confiscation, the legal right of the third party can be affected because its use or benefit can depend on the asset's owner. The same occurs with other rights, for example if the property has been leased or lent by an offender to a third party, or the property has a credit over it. And even if the property subject to confiscation is a company, third parties with interests could still be the shareholders, and the employees would also be interested in the continuation of the company's economic activity.

II. Confiscation from a Third Party in the Directive

A great innovation of the Directive is that it should increase the capacity of EU Member States to confiscate assets that have been transferred to third parties. According to Article 6(1):

> Member States shall take the necessary measures to enable the confiscation of proceeds, or other property the value of which corresponds to proceeds, which, directly or

[17] See R Ivory, *Corruption, Asset Recovery, and the Protection of Property in Public International Law* (Cambridge, Cambridge University Press, 2014).

[18] KE Davis, 'The Effects of Forfeiture on Third Parties' (2003) 48 *McGill Law Journal* 183, 185.

[19] See M Antinucci, 'The Principles of Patrimony Due Process of Law: The Punitive Confiscation and the Protection of Third Parties Misrelated to the Crime' (2015) *Iliria International Review* 127.

> indirectly, were transferred by a suspected or accused person to third parties, or which were acquired by third parties from a suspected or accused person, at least if those third parties knew or ought to have known that the purpose of the transfer or acquisition was to avoid confiscation, on the basis of concrete facts and circumstances, including that the transfer or acquisition was carried out free of charge or in exchange for an amount significantly lower than the market value.

Article 6 of the Directive allows confiscation from a third party if some listed conditions are met. Furthermore, as a final clause, paragraph 2 states that the confiscation should not prejudice the rights of bona fide third parties, therefore national law should make sure to adequately protect third bona fide parties' interests.

With this provision, the Directive introduces in the EU legal framework a binding rule on the confiscation of property transferred to third parties. Member States, according to their national law, are free to define third party confiscation as subsidiary or alternative to direct confiscation.[20] The purpose of Article 6 is to prevent criminals from shielding their property from confiscation by transferring it to someone else. Indeed, 'the practice by a suspected or accused person of transferring property to a knowing third party with a view to avoiding confiscation is common and increasingly widespread'.[21] This provision, therefore, obliges EU Member States to overcome the problems faced when a suspect transfers his/her properties to another person in order to avoid freezing and confiscation. Confiscation from these third parties will be possible if their lack of bona fide is proved.

To some extent, such an approach may resemble the American 'relation back doctrine'[22] (or 'the taint doctrine'), according to which any property derived from a criminal offence remains subject to forfeiture in spite of the defendant's attempt to transfer the property to a third party.[23] The underlying theory behind this doctrine is that property involved in criminal behaviour is itself tainted by the wrongdoing.[24] The relation back doctrine is a legal fiction, whereby the law considers confiscation to have occurred at the time of the illegality, thereby disregarding subsequent transfers to third parties.[25] The crime, indeed, is not a licit way to acquire rights on the property, so when the suspected or accused person commits the crime, he/she cannot claim any legitimate title. When property is transferred from the suspected or accused person to a third party, the receiver can obtain no better title than the transferor has to give.[26] In other words, the suspected or

[20] Recital 25 of Directive 2014/42/EU.

[21] ibid.

[22] An explanation of the relation back doctrine can be found in JAE Vervaele, 'La saisie et la confiscation à la suite d'atteintes punissables au droit aux Etats-Unis' (1998) 78 *Revue de Droit Pénal et de Criminologie* 974, 996.

[23] See the evolution of the US case law in SD Cassella, *Asset Forfeiture Law in the United States*, 2nd edn (New York, Juris, 2013) 619.

[24] M Goldsmith and MJ Linderman, 'Asset Forfeiture and Third Party Rights: The Need for Further Law Reform' (1989) *Duke Law Journal* 1254, 1261.

[25] MA Jankowski, 'Tempering the Relation-Back Doctrine: A More Reasonable Approach to Civil Forfeiture in Drug Cases' (1990) 76, 1 *Virginia Law Review* 165.

[26] Cassella (n 14).

accused person has no legitimate title that he/she can transfer to a third party, and the third party has no interest that he/she could assert in the confiscation proceedings.

According to US federal law, therefore, property derived from (or used in) a criminal act belongs to the state even if the actual owner did not commit the act. Nevertheless, this doctrine should not apply to deprive a person of the property acquired as a bona fide purchaser, ie purchased without reason to believe that the property was subject to confiscation. In criminal forfeiture cases, the relation back doctrine is codified at 21 USC 853(c), which provides that all right, title and interest in property subject to forfeiture vests in the government upon the commission of the crime giving rise to the confiscation, and subsequent transfers to third parties are therefore void 'unless the transferee establishes … that he is a bona fide purchaser for value'. The confiscation provision takes effect immediately upon the commission of the crime. At that moment, the right to the property vests in the government, and when confiscation is ordered, it relates back to that time and disregards all intermediate transfers of the property. In this sense, the relation back doctrine vests title in the state as of the date of the offence.

A. The Conditions Required to Admit a Confiscation from a Third Party

(i) Who is a Bona Fide Third Party?

In private law, usually 'bona fide third party' refers to a person who purchases an object from a seller thinking that he/she can transfer it without any impediment because he/she is the legitimate owner, ie without knowing that the seller's title in that object is invalid in some way. In such a situation, the bona fide purchaser obtains good title, so he/she can freely transfer it to others.

In the context of the criminal confiscation laws, the Directive establishes some requirements in order to consider a person as a bona fide third party. It is therefore worth analysing such requirements provided for by the Directive in order to admit a confiscation from a third (mala fide) party.

(ii) Object of Confiscation: Proceeds or Value Confiscation

The traditional types of confiscation used among EU Member States are: (i) confiscation of the instruments (*instrumentum sceleris*) or the subject of crime (*objectum sceleris*); (ii) confiscation of the proceeds from crime (*producta/fructa sceleris*);[27] and (iii) value confiscation, ie the deprivation of property whose value corresponds to the proceeds of crime. According to Article 6 of the Directive, third

[27] G Stessens, *Money Laundering. A New International Enforcement Model* (Cambridge, Cambridge University Press, 2000) 4.

party confiscation is only allowed as regards the proceeds of a crime or the value corresponding to those proceeds.

There is no reference to the confiscation of 'instrumentalities' (ie any property used or intended to be used, in any manner, wholly or in part, to commit a criminal offence or criminal offences). Consider, for example, a situation in which a car owned by A is used by B as an instrument for the commission of a crime. According to US criminal law, the car could be confiscated as an instrument of the crime. In the EU, although the European Parliament attempted to include a reference to the instrumentalities,[28] the final version of the Directive does not contain any provision concerning the confiscation of instrumentalities which belong to a person other than the offender. In any case, Member States are free to implement stricter measures, and they can even allow the confiscation of instrumentalities owned by a third party. If this is the case, the automobile could be confiscated any time after B's intervention, to the prejudice of A, if the mental requirements (knowledge or negligence) are all met (see Section II.A(v) below).

The Directive does not refer to confiscation of other goods on the basis of the extended confiscation or on the basis of a non-conviction-based confiscation. In both cases, the confiscation refers to the proceeds of crime, so it should be possible to confiscate the property when it is transferred or acquired by mala fide third parties.

According to the Directive (as well as to the American relation back doctrine), the transfer of proceeds directly obtained from the crime to a third party is void because the state had a legitimate interest in those proceeds before the transfer occurred. The same is true concerning the transfers of substitute assets to third parties. In this case, transfer of substitute assets to third parties may be voided if this transfer occurred after the commission of the crime.[29]

As said, when the property subject to confiscation from the defendant cannot be traced, the court may order the deprivation of property, the value of which corresponds to the proceeds from crime ('value confiscation'). The problem arises when the third parties claim property rights. Imagine that the value confiscation against the defendant is ordered over the marital residence owned also by the spouse. In this case, it is difficult to justify the application of the relation back doctrine and affirm that the state has an interest in it since the time of the offence. It could also happen that the property of equivalent value may not have even existed at the time the crime was committed. The question here is: when can the state claim its interest over that property? The most reasonable solution should be to consider that no one should be able to acquire an interest in property once it has been indicated in an order as property subject to value confiscation. From that

[28] Report on the proposal for a Directive of the European Parliament and of the Council on the freezing and confiscation of proceeds of crime in the European Union (COM(2012)0085—C7-0075/2012—2012/0036(COD)), 20 May 2013, amendment 34.

[29] See American case law in SD Cassella, 'Criminal Forfeiture Procedure in 2012: An Annual Survey of Developments in the Case Law' (2012) 48, 5 *Criminal Law Bulletin* 863, 891.

moment, any third party could not acquire the property because of the intent of the state to confiscate the property.

Another issue concerns the possibility of confiscating property that the suspected or accused person has transferred to a third party, who has then transformed it in other assets. For example, the accused person transfers to his wife a car which constitutes the proceeds of a crime. Let us assume that the state could void the transaction and get the car back from the wife. But imagine that the wife has already sold the car. The problem that arises in this situation is whether the state can confiscate the money that the wife has received in return for the car. As an alternative, could the state apply value confiscation (targeting the value of the money received for the car)? According to the wording of the Directive ('proceeds, or other property the value of which corresponds to proceeds, which … were transferred by a suspected or accused person to third parties'), it seems that value confiscation applies only to the suspected or accused person; it cannot be invoked to recover any property from a third party. So if the wife has sold the car and spent the money, nothing can be confiscated. It still remains unresolved whether the state can confiscate whatever property that the third party had received in return for the property. In other words, can the state confiscate the substitute assets—the money that the wife has received in return for the car?[30]

(iii) Proceeds Directly or Indirectly Transferred to or Acquired by Third Parties

The proceeds (or value) should be transferred to or acquired by third parties. The transfer and acquisition are two sides of the same coin. The transfer refers to the behaviour of the suspected or accused person, who transfers the assets to a third party. The acquisition refers to the behaviour of the third party, who obtains a right over the tainted assets. This implies a transfer or an acquisition of assets that in many cases will be 'fictitious'. For example, if the third party buys the assets knowing the offender's intention to avoid confiscation, he/she is no longer a bona fide party. The Directive only clarifies the behaviour of acquisition by way of example:

> acquisition by a third party refers to situations where, for example, property has been acquired, directly or indirectly, for example through an intermediary, by the third party from a suspected or accused person, including when the criminal offence has been committed on their behalf or for their benefit, and when an accused person does not have property that can be confiscated. (Recital 24)

The third party must establish an ownership or similar legal interest in the property. It does not suffice to be a general unsecured creditor[31] or defrauded investor, since they have no pre-existing interest in any specific asset of the defendant.[32]

[30] The American experience shows that this last solution is admissible, see SD Cassella, 'Third Party Rights in Criminal Forfeiture Cases' (1996) 32, 6 *Criminal Law Bulletin* 499.

[31] This is the opinion of the US case law, see Goldsmith and Linderman (n 24) 1277.

[32] CJ Linn, 'Recovering Assets in Investment Fraud Cases' (2009) 45(5) *Criminal Law Bulletin* 744.

It seems necessary to establish a more direct interest in the property. For example, ownership or other rights of enjoyment: usufruct, use, habitation, servitude, etc.

(iv) Proceeds Transferred by an Already Suspected or Convicted Person

Third party confiscation should be applied when the assets have been transferred by an already suspected or convicted person. This might cause problems if the property was owned by relatives or other close persons before they knew that the person was suspected or accused,[33] or even if the property was originally owned by third parties (ie when there is no transfer from the defendant to the third party). In this last situation, the suspected or accused person may have control over the assets through his/her influence over the relatives or friends who actually own the property. However, confiscation would not be possible because the property was not transferred by the suspected or accused person to the third party, as the wording of Article 6 requires. In order to address this problem, Eurojust suggested an amendment to the Proposal of the Directive in order to include a presumption whereby 'any asset held by heirs or close friends has been transferred if the owner cannot explain the licit origin of those assets'.[34] This proposal, however, was not adopted.

Eurojust also proposed to keep in the Directive the notion of 'controlling influence' contained in Article 3(3) of Council Framework Decision 2005/212/JHA and to make it obligatory rather than optional. Whilst this proposal seems to refer to property controlled through the influence over closest relatives of the person concerned, it should be noted that this concept was established in the 2005 Framework Decision in relation to property transferred to a legal person in respect of which the person concerned has a controlling influence. In any case, this proposal was not adopted and the notion of 'controlling influence' has not been included in the Directive.

(v) At Least if the Third Parties Knew or Ought to Have Known that the Purpose of the Transfer or Acquisition Was to Avoid Confiscation

The mere fact that a person has not been convicted of an offence will not necessarily allow him/her to claim bona fide status for the purposes of the confiscation provisions. Moreover, the references to good faith seem to exclude third parties who do not hold legitimate interests in the property subject to confiscation. According to the Directive, parties who knew or ought to have known that the purpose of the transfer or acquisition was to avoid confiscation should not be considered persons who could purchase the property in good faith. The expression 'at least' means that

[33] See Eurojust's opinion on the proposal of the EU Commission for a directive on the freezing and confiscation of proceeds of crime in the EU (2012) 7.

[34] ibid.

Member States can impose stricter requirements concerning the mental element in order to be considered a person who acquires the property in good faith.

The expression 'knew or ought to have known' refers to the mental element of the mala fide third party. The Directive makes it clear that this state of mind should be determined at the time the third person acquired his/her interest in the property.[35]

Knowledge

It does not seem logical to confiscate the property of a bona fide purchaser who paid the full value for an asset and neither knew nor had any reason to know of any previous illicit origin. However, it is possible to order the confiscation of the assets transferred or acquired by a third party who did know about the intention of the offender to avoid the confiscation. In other words, the point of reference of the knowledge is not the illegal origin of the assets, but the intention of the offender. Under the wording of Article 6 of the Directive, the knowledge requirement should embrace the intention of the transferor to avoid confiscation; there is no reference to the knowledge of the illegal origin of the assets. Nevertheless, it can be argued that knowledge of the intention to avoid confiscation by the transfer implies awareness of the illegal origin of the property transferred. Thus, it seems that the knowledge standard includes the so-called *dolus eventualis* (ie when the third party foresees the possibility that his/her acquisition could evade the confiscation).

As we have said before, the behaviour of a third party who has knowledge of the illegal origin of the property, and of the purpose of the suspected or accused to avoid confiscation by the transfer, could be considered as a money laundering crime (so the purchaser could be not considered a third party not responsible for a criminal activity).

Finally, it is worth mentioning that the European Parliament proposed the introduction of a new offence in order to prosecute persons who fictitiously attribute ownership and availability of property to third parties with the intention of avoiding seizure or confiscation measure.[36] Usually, this person will be the suspected or accused person who could be prosecuted for the criminal offence which generates the property and, in some countries, also for money laundering. According to this proposal, such person could be prosecuted for a new criminal offence. This amendment, however, was not adopted.

Ought to Have Known

This expression contains an element of criminal negligence, which implies that the third party does not have actual knowledge of the purpose of the transfer or

[35] See the debate in the American case law in Cassella (n 14).
[36] See n 28, amendment 43 (Art 6a).

acquisition (to avoid confiscation) but he/she should have known. In this way, the Directive encourages confiscation against third parties who have failed to exercise reasonable diligence in the acquisition of the criminal proceeds.

In this regard, it seems necessary to ascertain whether the party has a 'duty of care' concerning the transfer, and whether he/she has breached such duty. The duty of care can have different sources. Apart from the case in which the law clearly provides for it, in order to determine whether there is a duty of care, all the factors and circumstances of the transaction should be considered. As a general rule, a duty of care arises when the party is confronted with a risk that suggests that the acquisition/transaction of an asset pursues the objective of avoiding confiscation. In this case, a reasonable individual in that position would have taken some precautions against this risk. What precautions can be considered reasonable will vary according to the circumstances; refraining from acquiring the assets is one of them. The considerations that a reasonable person would have made in deciding to take precautions against a risk will depend on the factors and circumstances of the specific case; and in the case of legal persons, compliance programmes can play an important role (see Section II.B(i) below).

The Purpose to Avoid Confiscation

It is even more difficult to analyse what the third party should know or have known, ie that the purpose of the suspected or accused person in transferring the assets is to avoid confiscation. Therefore, it does not suffice that the person knows the illicit origin of the property; an additional requirement must be proved (the knowledge of the purpose). This requirement clearly reduces the scope of application of third party confiscation, since it might be the case that the principal aim of the suspected person with the transfer was not to avoid confiscation but to achieve other goals, for example, to pay for a lawyer or to pay a debt.

The Directive has identified a number of facts and circumstances that should be considered in assessing the behaviour of the third party who acquires the tainted property. In particular, and by way of example, the Directive mentions as circumstances: (i) that the transfer or acquisition was carried out free of charge; or (ii) that it was carried out in exchange for an amount significantly lower than the market value. It seems that the Directive is aimed at limiting the confiscation provisions to sham or fraudulent transactions and is not intended to be applied to the compensation legitimately paid for goods or services. Therefore, the Directive excludes from confiscation the so-called bona fide purchase for value,[37] and the third party can prove his/her legitimate right or interest in the property subject

[37] US case law considers that a bona fide purchaser is a person who gives something of value in exchange for the property interest. See A Martucci, 'Advocating for Asset Forfeiture in the Post-Madoff Era: Why the Government, Not a Bankruptcy Trustee, Should Be Responsible for Recovering and Redistributing Assets from Feedere Funds and Net Winners' (2012) 63 *Case Western Reserve Law Review* 599, 624.

to confiscation by demonstrating that he/she is a bona fide purchaser for value, ie that a purchase was made, that the good was received in an arm's-length transaction and that, from a subjective point of view, there was no reason to know that the property was subject to confiscation.

This could lead to an inversion of the burden of proof.[38] In this sense, a person who acquired the property after the offence giving rise to the confiscation could be obliged to prove that he/she was a bona fide purchaser who had no reason to know that the property was subject to confiscation. In the case of a donation, the burden of proof of the good faith is on the beneficiary (donee): a donee who acquires his title in the property as a gift after the commission of the crime should prove that at the moment of the acquisition he/she did not know—nor had reason to know—that the property was transferred in order to avoid confiscation.[39] In my view, it would be advisable to shift the burden of proof to the accuser.

In the USA, one can observe in the case law a tendency to presume that creditors, persons who received gifts and persons with causes of action against the defendant are not bona fide purchasers. So, a woman who accepts property from her suspected or accused husband in a divorce settlement is not a bona fide purchaser because she did not pay any price for the property.[40] Similarly, a trade creditor to whom the suspected or accused owes a debt is not the bona fide purchaser of any asset subject to confiscation because he/she has no property rights over it.

B. Some Problematic Cases

(i) Confiscation of Assets of Legal Persons

Imagine that the suspected or accused person sets up a company and transfers all his/her illegal assets to the new entity. This is clearly a fraudulent transaction, and therefore confiscation of the assets should be possible because the operation was carried out with the intention of avoiding confiscation. In order to ensure the effectiveness of the confiscation provisions, it is necessary to allow the confiscation of the property acquired by legal persons, which in this case are third parties. According to the Directive, indeed, 'the rules on third party confiscation should extend to both natural and legal persons'.[41]

[38] In the case of the Spanish Criminal Code, it presumes that the third party has knowledge of or reasons to know when the transfer or acquisition was carried out free of charge or in exchange for an amount significantly lower than the market value (Art 127-*quater* of the Spanish Criminal Code, as amended in 2015).

[39] According to the American literature, innocent donees are not protected by the law, so the property transferred can be confiscated, see D Pimentel, 'Forfeitures Revisited: Bringing Principle to Practice in Federal Court' (2012) 13(1) *Nevada Law Journal* 1, 18.

[40] Cassella (n 30).

[41] Recital 24 of the Directive 2014/42/EU.

In commercial situations, legal persons can be third parties who can claim good faith because they have purchased an asset without knowing the intention of the seller to avoid confiscation. In this situation, it is more complicated to assess the negligence standard established by the Directive. For example, suppose that a legal person (company) buys the asset from the suspected or accused person without knowledge that the purpose of the transfer is to avoid confiscation. In this case, the company can be considered as a person who purchases the property in good faith. But the negligent standard can change this conclusion if the company has not adopted adequate precautionary measures to avoid the acquisition of those assets subject to confiscation and there is a duty of care concerning the transfer. There are different scenarios in which this could happen. Imagine a company that is dedicated to buying and selling works of art but does not ask the seller for the documents proving their licit origin. In this case, it could be held that the company has not adopted adequate precautionary measures (and usually there is an obligation to ask for the traceability of the piece of art). In order to assess the adequacy of the adopted measures, it should be taken into account whether an effective compliance programme is in place. This is important, for example, in the case of financial institutions and other business activities, which are legally obliged to take measures to monitor transactions for avoiding money laundering and the financing of terrorism.[42]

(ii) *Confiscation of Attorney's Fees for Legal Services*

One important issue surrounding asset freezing and confiscation is access to a lawyer. It is possible that if a defendant's assets are frozen during trial, he/she will have no money with which to pay his/her lawyer.[43] The point in this case is whether the fundamental right to a lawyer must allow the defendant to use his/her property to pay for one. In the USA, according to a recent judgment of the Supreme Court, the pre-trial freezing of 'untainted' assets violates the Sixth Amendment to the United States Constitution, which guarantees that, in all criminal cases, the defendant has a right 'to the assistance of counsel for his defence'.[44]

I will not consider this question further here because it is not the exact subject of this chapter; it is,however, strongly connected with the issues addressed herein because the lawyer—who receives criminal proceeds as payment of his/her fees—could be considered a third party. The question, therefore, is whether the lawyer is a bona fide third party; if not, the fees can be confiscated. In the EU, as a consequence of the Directive, any confiscation of assets transferred to lawyer as fees for legal services should be reviewed carefully in order to determine whether

[42] See I Blanco Cordero, *El delito de blanqueo de capitales*, 4th edn (Pamplona, Aranzadi-Thomson Reuters, 2015).

[43] See MR Lasky, 'Imposing Indigence: Reclaiming the Qualified Right to Counsel of Choice in Criminal Asset Forfeiture Cases' (2014) 104 *Journal of Criminal Law and Criminology* 165.

[44] See Supreme Court of the United States, *Sila Luis v United States*, decided on 30 March 2016.

the transfer is a fraudulent transaction designed to shield criminal assets from confiscation.

The lawyer who provides legal services in exchange for payment that he/she has no reason to believe is connected to criminal activity can be considered a bona fide third party. The fees cannot be confiscated because he/she has received the money in exchange for legal services actually rendered. In this case, the aim of the suspected or accused person in making the payment is not to avoid confiscation and therefore he/she has the right to use the alleged proceeds of crime to pay legal fees. It can be discussed whether the amount of money paid for the legal fees is unreasonably large, especially in a context in which lawyers are free to charge their own fees. In any case, if the lawyer is considered a bona fide third party, the fees received cannot be confiscated. However, the state could confiscate the property of the accused person, and in this case it could apply the value confiscation because the proceeds have been transferred to a third party who has acted in good faith.

In contrast, if the lawyer is aware that he/she is being paid with criminal proceeds, or should have known it, in principle his/her fees could be subject to confiscation. In this case, according to the Directive, he/she could be considered a mala fide purchaser. As a consequence, any lawyer would be hesitant to take on a client whose property could be confiscated, since he/she might encounter several risks: first, the risk of not being paid; secondly, the risk of being considered as a mala fide third party and having his/her fees confiscated; and thirdly, the risk of being charged with money laundering.

One may conclude that it is very difficult to establish when the lawyer has knowledge that the assets that he/she received might be subject to confiscation because the payment was done for the purpose of avoiding confiscation. In any case, the consequences of broad provisions on third party confiscation for criminal defence lawyers and their potential clients may be very serious. The possibility of confiscating attorney's fees may mean that private lawyers refuse to take on the defence of potential defendants who may be accused of profit-driven crimes. This situation could have a direct impact on the right to a fair trial because the defendant would be unable to afford a legal defence of his/her choice, thereby limiting the effectiveness of the right to a lawyer. In such a scenario, a public defender would become the only option for the defendant, and it is well known that they are not always well enough equipped to deal with complex cases that require more resources and specialisation.[45] One possible solution in this regard could be to allow the court, after a hearing,[46] to decide to exempt the attorney's fees from the property subject to freezing or confiscation. Alternatively, Member States could consider providing a legal exemption from freezing and confiscation for a certain amount of funds to pay reasonable lawyer's fees.

[45] Lasky (n 43) 168.

[46] M Hardy, 'Sixth Amendment—Applicability of Right to Counsel of Choice to Forfeiture of Attorneys' Fees' (1990) 80 *Journal of Criminal Law and Criminology* 1154, 1189.

III. Rights of Third Party in Confiscation Process

Normally, confiscation is part of the criminal trial itself. Since bona fide third parties are not involved in this trial, they may not claim their rights on confiscated assets before the trial has been completed.[47] Due to the complexity of such cases, the litigation may take several years, during which time third parties who are doing business with the offender face the risk of losing their rights over the assets acquired.[48]

The Directive pays particular attention to the procedural safeguards of those involved in the confiscation proceedings. Article 8 defines the measures in order to ensure that the persons affected by confiscation (including third parties and victims)[49] have the right to an effective remedy and a fair trial in order to uphold their rights. It lists several guarantees that shall be ensured, irrespective of the ownership at the time of confiscation. Concerning third parties, the safeguards include, among others, the right to an effective remedy and a fair trial; the right to a communication of the freezing order and the confiscation order; the right to challenge the freezing and confiscation order before a court; and the right of access to a lawyer and to be informed of this right.

In order to respect these rights, before a confiscation order can be made, notice must be provided to any person who appears to have a valid interest in the property. There are different ways to do this: if the interested parties are known, the simplest option is to send direct notice of the confiscation to third parties; another possibility is to publish notice of the confiscation order. Various models are available to give third parties the opportunity to establish that they have an interest in the asset and that it must be recognised. For example, in the USA, an ancillary proceeding is provided for criminal forfeiture; in other countries, in enforcement proceedings, any person holding an interest in the assets can claim title of ownership or other property rights.

Conclusion

The aim to ensure that crime does not pay has expanded the scope of application of confiscation provisions to third parties. The commission of a crime taints the proceeds obtained in such a way that the suspected or accused person cannot

[47] Cassella (n 23) 631.

[48] Goldsmith and Linderman (n 24) 1264.

[49] In the case of victims, if they have claims against the person who is subject to a confiscation measure, Member States shall take the necessary measures to ensure that the confiscation measure does not prevent those victims from seeking compensation for their claims (this is in accordance with the European victims' rights law).

safely transfer his/her assets to third parties. Preventing the alleged offender from transfer his/her property, however, means also preventing him/her from doing business with other persons. One may imagine that, following the implementation of the Directive in the EU Member States, third parties will have to be even more cautious in establishing commercial/economic relationships with suspected criminals. In the literature, it has been even feared that suspected or accused persons might become socially and economically isolated, treated as 'economic pariahs'.[50]

Despite such drawbacks, however, there are several reasons to affirm that Directive 2014/42/EU represents a significant step forward in regulating the position of third parties in the context of confiscation measures. Perhaps the most important aspect is the negligent standard, ie the description of the requirements that must be fulfilled for a party to be considered as a mala fide third party. The EU's approach might well pose problems for some parties, such as lawyers. It is now up to the Member States to transpose the Directive into reasonable and balanced national laws.

[50] Goldsmith and Linderman (n 24) 1256.

Part II

Not Only About Confiscation: Towards Comprehensive Policies on Asset Recovery

7

Tax, Money Laundering and Offshore: The HSBC Suisse Affair

PETER ALLDRIDGE*

Introduction. The Leaks

This chapter traces a series of events in 2015, arising from the leaking of the HSBC Suisse account information from 2007 and 2008, and their effect upon the UK laws of tax evasion and money laundering.

In 2006–07, Hervé Falciani began surreptitiously extracting client data from inside HSBC Suisse. In December 2008, he was arrested in Geneva, bailed and fled to France with the files. HSBC revealed that data had been stolen from its Swiss arm, affecting 30,000 accounts. In January 2009, the French authorities refused a Swiss extradition request and launched their own investigation into the data. In November 2015, Falciani was sentenced *in absentia* to five years' imprisonment for breach of Swiss banking secrecy laws.[1]

Early in 2010, the French tax authorities began informing other tax authorities around the world of the existence of the HSBC files. In April 2010, the UK's HM Revenue & Customs (HMRC) received the HSBC files. In July 2010, the *Financial Times* reported that HSBC had asked the French courts to prevent the country's tax authority from handing files to HMRC. In September 2011, Dave Hartnett, Head of HMRC, told the House of Commons Treasury Select Committee: 'I think the whole nation probably knows that our department has a disc from the Swiss—from the Geneva branch of a major UK bank—with 6,000 names, all ripe for investigation.'[2] It turned out that HMRC was in the process of acting on information from the Falciani list, which it received from the French in 2010, of 130,000 potential tax evaders using the Geneva branch of HSBC. HMRC identified from this list 3,600 potentially non-compliant UK taxpayers. It has since

* Drapers' Professor of Law, Queen Mary, University of London.

[1] 'HSBC Whistleblower Jailed in Absentia by Swiss Court', *BBC News*, 27 November 2015.

[2] In January 2013, six months after retiring from HMRC, Hartnett joined HSBC as a consultant.

recovered £135 million of unpaid taxes and penalties, and has secured one criminal conviction.[3] In November 2014, French judges placed HSBC under official investigation for 'illicit financial and banking practices'. Belgium charged HSBC with money laundering and fraud in connection with its Swiss arm, and is seeking to reclaim €540 million in taxes. Argentina charged HSBC with aiding tax evasion via its Swiss arm. And so on.

In February 2015, media organisations around the world, working under the co-ordination of the International Consortium of Investigative Journalists, began to publish revelations from the leaked files. In March 2015, the French financial state prosecutor formally requested that HSBC's Swiss private bank be sent to criminal trial over tax fraud allegations.[4] In April 2015, France widened its HSBC Swiss bank inquiry to its global holding company.[5] In April 2015, Arlette Ricci was convicted in France of evasion and the judge condemned her conduct as a breach of the '*Pacte rẻpublicain*'.[6]

These events did not come to light at a good time for banks. The market manipulation scandals to do with Libor[7] and Forex were very serious. In June 2015, HSBC paid out £27.8 million (SFr 40 million) over money-laundering claims.[8] It is undoubtedly the case that during the period to which the records relate the bank was the repository for huge amounts of money being hidden from domestic authorities, some of dubious provenance, some because of uncertainties occasioned by the domestic authorities, some lawfully and some unlawfully to avoid paying tax domestically.

The sheer size of the HSBC deposits is noteworthy. The total amount of money acquired by the state in England and Wales by confiscating the proceeds of crime in any given year is about £150 million.[9] This pales into insignificance compared to the amounts stashed in just one bank in just one country. It raises an important question about priorities. If the objective of the law enforcement efforts directed against proceeds of crime is to acquire money for the state, and if crime for these purposes is to extend to tax evasion, then the most lucrative area by far will be tax evasion.

[3] Margaret Hodge (Chair), House of Commons Public Accounts Committee, Fiftieth Report, 'Improving Tax Collection' (2015) paras 9–11 and Qq 16–18. In July 2012, Michael Shanly pleaded guilty to tax evasion worth £430,000 in connection with the HSBC Swiss list. He was ordered to pay £469,444 in fines and costs for failing to pay tax on money hidden in a Swiss bank account.

[4] 'HSBC's Swiss Private Bank: French Prosecutor Formally Requests Trial', *The Guardian*, 13 March 2015.

[5] 'France Widens HSBC Swiss Bank Inquiry to Global Holding company', *The Guardian*, 9 April 2015.

[6] 'Affaire HSBC: Prison Ferme pour Arlette Ricci', *Le Monde*, 14 April 2015. The use of the expression '*Pacte rẻpublicain*' is most telling because of its significance in French constitutional discourse. It connotes equal treatment for all, within the terms especially of Art 2 of the French Constitution.

[7] *R v Hayes* [2015] EWCA Crim 1944.

[8] 'Geneva Prosecutor Agrees to Close Investigation into HSBC in Return for the Financial Settlement', *The Guardian*, 4 June 2015.

[9] 'CPS Asset Recovery Strategy' (London, Crown Prosecution Service, June 2014).

I. Addressing Evasion

Did the customers of HSBC Suisse commit tax evasion offences? Some did, undoubtedly. While some of the money in the bank may have been entirely legitimate, or there lawfully to avoid tax, and some the proceeds of crimes other than evasion, the suspicion is that the preponderance of it had been housed in the bank as a means by which its owners could escape being assessed to tax upon it.

Did the bank or its employees commit offences? From what has been published to date (January 2016), there is no 'smoking gun' providing compelling evidence of complicity by the bank or its employees in illegal tax evasion (and/or money laundering). The closest might be that a particular transfer was said to be arranged 'for ESD reasons' (ie because of the European Savings Directive).[10] While, upon the publication of the reports, there was a further referral to the Serious Fraud Office, there have so far been no further arrests or charges. No further prosecutions under English law are likely.[11] On the other hand, there is evidence of behaviour by the bank that is vastly different from the passive model of the reactive domestic bank. But addressing the personal liability of the bankers may have to wait.[12]

There is a range of approaches the state might adopt in respect of the taxpayer who is found to have evaded tax:

1. *Impose a civil penalty*. This can be done under a procedure designed to encourage candour from a defendant. Since the birth of the income tax, the preference of HMRC has been to use civil penalties, because the proceedings are faster and cheaper, and the results more predictable.
2. *Bring criminal proceedings with a view to obtaining a conviction and the imposition of a confiscation order*. The prosecution might do this for one of a wide range of offences—cheating the revenue, fraudulent evasion of tax, false accounting, conspiracy to defraud, and a number of inchoate versions and types of complicity. Confiscation proceedings follow convictions. Confiscation proceedings are criminal in nature, but the standard of proof is the civil one—the balance of probabilities.[13] The rules of evidence are apparently those of a sentencing hearing. The 'strict'[14] rules of criminal evidence do not apply,[15] and the Criminal Justice Act 2003 hearsay regime does not apply

[10] Council Directive 2014/48/EU of 24 March 2014 amending Directive 2003/48/EC on taxation of savings income in the form of interest payments [2014] OJ L111/50. See also 'HSBC Files: Swiss Bank Aggressively Pushed Way for Clients to Avoid New Tax', *The Guardian*, 10 February 2015.

[11] 'HMRC Failed to Prosecute Tycoon over Tax Evasion', *BBC News*, 13 February 2015.

[12] B Ferguson, 'The Personal Accountability of Bankers' (2015) 9 *Law and Financial Markets Review* 40.

[13] Proceeds of Crime Act 2002, s 6(7).

[14] Criminal Justice Act 2003, s 134(1) defines 'criminal proceedings' as 'criminal proceedings to which the strict rules of evidence apply'.

[15] *R* v *Silcock & Levin* [2004] EWCA Crim 408, [2004] 2 Cr App R (S) 323, in which, at para 69, the Court of Appeal declined even to certify this question as being of general public importance. *Silcock & Levin* decides that they do not, and this was affirmed in *R v Clipston* [2011] EWCA Crim 446.

'strictly and directly', but may apply by analogy in ensuring the fairness of the proceedings.[16] Confiscation proceedings are not necessarily penal,[17] so do not attract the protection of Article 6(2) and 6(3) of the European Convention on Human Rights (ECHR),[18] even when the 'lifestyle' rules are triggered.[19]

3. *Bring civil recovery proceedings*—in rem *proceedings under Part 5 of the Proceeds of Crime Act—in respect of identified property*. This procedure, for non-conviction-based forfeiture, has been deployed since the Proceeds of Crime Act 2002 came into force. It can be useful, particularly when large amounts of cash are involved.
4. *Exercise the tax jurisdiction under the Proceeds of Crime Act 2002*[20] *to raise assessments to tax*. This is easier for the National Crime Agency because, unlike the regular tax collection body, HMRC, it does not have to ascribe the income (or capital gains) to a year or a source, and in the exercise of that jurisdiction can simply raise an assessment to tax, which places the burden on the taxpayer to prove the contrary.
5. *Use regulatory activity directed against the laxness in the way in which the corporation conducted its activity*. Regulators will say that this option is quicker, easier, less contentious and less likely to fail than the other options.

The measures laid out in a policy statement of the Director of Public Prosecutions in 2013, setting out to raise the numbers of tax evasion prosecutions brought in England and Wales, have been implemented.[21] There is a complex calculation to be made between the enforcement options, reconciling the chances of losing, the burden and standard of proof, the rules of evidence, relevant rules on quantum and deductions, publicity, elementary fairness. A report by the National Audit Office has in general given the HMRC policy a clean bill of health.[22]

II. The Line Between Avoidance and Evasion

The traditional approach to evasion and avoidance is that they can be differentiated quite clearly. They are two different phenomena, requiring different approaches.

[16] *R v Clipston* at para 64(b), a notion that might apply to other types of evidence that would be excluded under the criminal rules.

[17] Proceeds of Crime Act 2002 (POCA) s 13(4).

[18] *HM Advocate v McIntosh (Sentencing)* [2001] UKPC D1, [2001] 3 WLR 107 paras 14 *et seq*; *Phillips v United Kingdom* (2001) 11 BHRC 280; *R v Rezvi* [2002] UKHL 1, [2003] 1 AC 1099; *R v Benjafield* [2002] UKHL 2, [2003] 1 AC 1099.

[19] POCA, s 10.

[20] POCA, Part 7.

[21] See www.govuk/government/policies/reducing-tax-evasion-and-avoidance.

[22] National Audit Office, *Tackling Tax Fraud: How HMRC Responds to Tax Evasion, the Hidden Economy and Criminal Attacks* (HC 610, Session 2015–16). Part Three sets out HMRC's approach to prosecutions.

Avoidance is lawful, evasion is criminal, and that is the end of it. Attention to financial crime arising from the crisis following the collapse of Lehmann Brothers, coupled with increased attention to the mechanisms used by international companies to reduce their tax liabilities, has led to increased attention being given to the financial sector and the possibility of increased use being made there of the criminal law. This has involved the possibility of challenging the traditionally accepted version of the distinction between avoidance and evasion, by reference to the lawfulness or unlawfulness of the conduct (avoidance is lawful, evasion is not), which has been threatened in at least five ways.

First, the limits of the criminal offence of cheating the public revenue are so indistinct,[23] and depend so heavily upon the notion of dishonesty in *Ghosh*,[24] that the offence can be used to extend to cases which might previously have been called avoidance.[25]

Secondly, investigations may be carried on in such a way as to suggest that some very serious crime is in point. *Rossminster*,[26] in which no criminal charges followed a dawn raid that was generally seen as overzealous,[27] remains the clearest case in point. More recently, the failed prosecution against the football manager, Harry Redknapp, started with an unlawful search and ended with a jury acquittal.[28] Both are instances of HMRC overplaying not especially powerful hands, and investigating what might have been avoidance as though it was evasion.

Thirdly, statutory extensions to the criminal law of evasion might make the distinction between evasion and avoidance otherwise than on the basis of the mental state of the defendant. In particular, the idea that there could be a non-deliberate evasion[29] is a radical departure. If one can evade by mistake but avoid only deliberately, it is difficult to see why evasion should be regarded more seriously.

Fourthly, there are those who talk about evaders and avoiders as though they are the same category. This habit is not restricted to the media or to politicians,[30]

[23] Above, 66.

[24] *R v Ghosh* [1982] QB 1053, 75 Cr App R 154.

[25] *R v Charlton* [1996] STC 1418; R Rhodes and R Bosworth-Davies, '*Regina v Charlton, Cunningham, Kitchen and Wheeler* [1995]' (1999) 2 *Journal of Money Laundering Control* 197.

[26] *R v IRC, ex p Rossminster Ltd* [1980] AC 952, (1980) 70 Cr App R 157; see this volume, Chapter 4. See also *R v Dimsey; R v Allen* [2001] UKHL 46, [2002] 1 AC 509.

[27] As Moses J put it, 'when searching for needles indicative of tax fraud the Revenue took haystacks': *Regina v Middlesex Guildhall Crown Court and another* [2000] 1 WLR 453, 460.

[28] *R (on the application of Redknapp) v Commissioner of the City of London Police* [2008] EWHC 1177 (Admin), [2009] 1 WLR 2091.

[29] HMRC Consultation, 'Tackling Offshore Tax Evasion: A New Criminal Offence' (London, HMRC, 2014).

[30] R Watson, 'PM Seeks Global Action to Tackle Tax Avoiders' *The Times*, 25 April 2013: '[David Cameron] urged Europe's leaders to use next month's EU summit in Brussels to agree new rules and help to restore public confidence in European tax systems. "Tax evasion and aggressive tax avoidance are global problems that require truly global solutions", Mr Cameron said. "Otherwise tax evaders will simply play the system."' 'Playing the system' is a standard condemnation of avoidance. It lies especially badly in the mouths of those responsible for the system being as it is.

but can also be heard from judges[31] and academics.[32] This blurring of categories should be resisted.[33] The development of the category of disapproved 'aggressive'[34] avoidance is in this context problematic. An attitude that says 'we disapprove of tax avoidance so we should prosecute more evaders' lacks focus.

Fifthly, the same people (tax advisers and financial institutions) might be involved both in avoiding and evading.

Their clientele may well care little but to see the liability to taxation reduced. Take, for example, the reliance placed by Chris Moyles, a DJ, on the false factual proposition that he was a used car dealer for the purposes of a tax avoidance scheme.[35] Or that of Amazon, whose tax avoidance relied on the factual proposition that its Luxembourg and UK entities have operations neatly split into trading on the one hand and auxiliary functions on the other, when in reality the operations of the two companies are so mixed up together that one of them has been found liable for the other one's tort.[36]

While the line has certainly been blurred a few times, those who want to equate avoidance and evasion should be careful who their friends are. Russian law does not differentiate between evasion and avoidance. The original tax proceedings against Yukos[37] were driven by a numbers of factors, including a crackdown on avoidance by using the favourable tax position of a particular area of Russia, which subsequently was held to fall foul of Article 6. In *Yukos v Russia*,[38] the European Court of Human Rights (ECtHR) held that, although having a basis in law, the speed with which enforcement measures were taken by the Russian tax authorities against a company which had consequently gone into liquidation, and the failure of the authorities to have sufficient regard to the economic and social implications of those measures on the company and its stakeholders, meant that the authorities

[31] Lord Templeman in *Fitzwilliam v IRC* [1993] 1 WLR 1189, [1993] 3 All ER 184, 1226, stated: 'I regard tax-avoidance schemes of the kind invented and implemented in the present case as no better than attempts to cheat the revenue.' See also his judgment in *Ramsay (CA)—WT Ramsay Ltd v IRC* [1979] 3 All ER 213, [1979] STC 582; see, extrajudicially, Lord Templeman, 'Tax and the Taxpayer' (2001) 117 *Law Quarterly Review* 575.

[32] D McBarnet, 'Legitimate Rackets: Tax Evasion, Tax Avoidance, and the Boundaries of Legality' (1992) 3 *Journal of Human Justice* 56.

[33] See *R v Quillan* [2015] EWCA Crim 538, [2015] Lloyd's Rep FC Plus 20, in which the Court of Appeal was critical of prosecution attempts to present a scheme involving the claiming of relief at source on pension contributions as a sham.

[34] 'Aggressive tax avoidance is the practice of seeking to minimise a tax bill by attempting to comply with the letter of the law whilst avoiding its purpose or spirit': R Jenkins and P Newell, 'CSR, Tax and Development' (2013) 34 *Third World Quarterly* 378.

[35] The 'Working Wheels' Scheme: *Flanagan, Moyles and Stennett v Commissioners for HMRC* [2014] UKFTT 175 (TC). Another scheme, 'Liberty' began in 2005 and was closed down in 2009.

[36] See David Quentin's Tax and Law Blog, 27 February 2015, http://dqtax.tumblr.com/page/2.

[37] D Gololobov, 'The Yukos Tax Case or Ramsay Adventures in Russia' (2008) 7 *FSU Business Review* 165.

[38] *OAO Neftyanaya Kompaniya Yukos v Russia*, App No 14902/04 (ECtHR, 20 September 2011). See also *Yukos Universal Ltd (Isle of Man) v The Russian Federation* Permanent Court of Arbitration Case No AA 227 (2014).

had failed to strike a fair balance between the legitimate aim of enforcing a tax liability and the measures employed to achieve that aim.

It is possible to overcomplicate the avoidance/evasion distinction. Whilst it is unhelpful (because circular) to say that the difference between evasion and avoidance is 'the thickness of a prison wall',[39] there is a simple test that does differentiate. It is that if the taxpayer lies to HMRC with a view to reducing his/her liability, then that is evasion. If the taxpayer does not lie, however much his/her conduct might attract opprobrium, it is not. Many anti-avoidance provisions are directed towards reducing the possibility for the taxpayer to lie.

McBarnet's critique[40] holds that the process of legislation, then the generation of avoidance mechanisms, then the blocking of particular avoidance routes and the search for others is not so much a failure by lawmakers, law enforcers and judges to put in place bullet-proof law as an inevitable dynamic process involving 'constructive compliance' by taxpayers and a continuing attempt by legislation not to be left too far behind. There is much in this, particularly in the notion that there is no 'magic bullet', but just continuing countervailing efforts of those committed to falling outwith the charge to tax and those trying to bring them within it.

III. New Crimes of Offshore Evasion

The UK government's 'no safe haven' programme deals with the increasing concerns raised by the use of secrecy jurisdictions to reduce liability to tax.[41] The first consultation on new offences was in 2014, and included the suggestion that some forms of avoidance be made criminal. A second consultation took place in 2015, after the General Election, and the policy and draft legislation was announced in December 2015.[42]

There were to have been two distinct new offences proposed: one of offshore evasion[43] and the other of failure by a corporation to prevent offshore evasion

[39] Generally attributed to Denis Healey: E Craig 'The Thickness of a Prison Wall—When Does Tax Avoidance Become a Criminal Offence?' (2011) 17 *New Zealand Business Law Quarterly* 441 cites 'Holes in the Net: Tax Avoidance' (2000) 354 *The Economist* 8152 (2000) 186.

[40] Expressed particularly in D McBarnet, 'Law, Policy, and Legal Avoidance: Can Law Effectively Implement Egalitarian Policies' (1988) 15 *Journal of Law and Society* 113; D McBarnet, 'Legitimate Rackets: Tax Evasion, Tax Avoidance, and the Boundaries of Legality' (1992) 3 *Journal of Human Justice* 56; D McBarnet, 'It's Not What You Do but the Way that You Do It: Tax Evasion, Tax Avoidance and the Boundaries of Deviance' in D Downes (ed), *Unravelling Criminal Justice* (London, MacMillan, 1992) 247.

[41] See www.gov.uk/government/publications/no-safe-havens.

[42] HMRC, 'Tackling Offshore Tax Evasion: A New Criminal Offence for Offshore Evaders: Summary of Responses' (London, HMRC, December 2015).

[43] HMRC, 'Tackling Offshore Tax Evasion: A New Criminal Offence for Offshore Evaders' (London, 2015), responding to the responses to HMRC Consultation, 'Tackling Offshore Tax Evasion: A New Criminal Offence' (n 14).

by an employee.[44] The offshore evasion offence[45] now extends the criminal law to cover three possible cases (in each case where this leads to an understatement or underpayment of tax relating to relevant offshore income, assets or activities): failing to notify HMRC of chargeability to tax; failing to file a return; and filing an inaccurate return.[46] The offence should apply only to income tax and capital gains tax (though this could be reviewed at a later date), and should apply to all offshore income and gains, not just to under-declared investment returns. The threshold will apply to each tax year separately. There is to be an option for a prison sentence of up to 12 months.[47]

One aspect of the proposed new offence that seems particularly unusual is a defence of *de minimis* being restricted to crimes to evasion above a given sum.[48] This would be extremely unusual. The possibility of introducing a general *de minimis* defence in criminal law is considered from time to time, but is always firmly rejected. Such a defence, were it to exist, might cover theft of small amounts, possession of very small amounts of drugs, exceeding the speed limit by a very small amount and very small violations of proscriptions related, for example, to the age of one of the participants.

While the matters involved may influence the exercise of a prosecutorial discretion, there is no suggestion elsewhere in criminal law theory that any of them may provide a substantial criminal defence of *de minimis*. It is particularly surprising to see a proposal for a *de minimis* defence coming from HMRC. It has never been suggested that *de minimis* should provide a defence in the case of small failures to discharge a liability to pay tax. It would be inappropriate to institute such a defence for the new offence, for which the main test of criminal liability will be that of liability to pay the tax.

As to the basis of liability, the offence is not a strict liability offence as such. There is an affirmative defence for a person to demonstrate that they had taken reasonable care in conducting their tax affairs,[49] but this, unlike the existing common law and statutory evasion offences, would no longer require dishonesty or any more active culpability. The history of the expansion of English criminal law is of the creation of exceptional liability for cases presented as particularly dangerous, then extension subsequently being applied throughout, for reasons of consistency. It may be, therefore, that this presages the abolition of the dishonesty threshold for liability and its replacement with a negligence threshold. If that is to happen, then it should not happen incrementally.

[44] HMRC, 'Tackling Offshore Tax Evasion: A New Corporate Criminal Offence of Failure to Prevent the Facilitation of Evasion' (London, HMRC, 2015).

[45] Finance Act 2016, s 166, inserting Taxes Management Act 1970, ss 106B–H.

[46] Taxes Management Act 1970, ss 106B–D, inserted by Finance Act 2016, s 166.

[47] Taxes Management Act 1970, s 106G.

[48] The original proposal was £5,000, which was subsequently raised to £25,000. This will now be dealt with in regulations under s 106H.

[49] Taxes Management Act 1970, s 106D(2).

Initially the earlier proposal to put in place a new 'failure to prevent' offence for advisers, modelled on section 7 of the Bribery Act 2010, was not pursued. The same view was taken as to financial crimes more generally.[50] This is a reflection of a more relaxed approach to corporate misconduct after the 2015 General Election returned a majority Conservative government. The failure to prevent an offence was restored to the legislative programme as part of the Criminal Finances Bill, trailed in the Queen's Speech of April 2016, but not introduced into Parliament until October 2016.

IV. The Expansion of Laundering

The events are further evidence of the continuing expansion of the money laundering industry. Anti-money laundering (AML) grew up as a result of the failure of the 'war on drugs'. Drug-related crime was the law enforcement priority when AML was introduced in the 1980s. If, at any time before the expansion of the AML industry beyond drugs, a decision had been taken to decriminalise drugs instead of prosecuting the 'war', then the proceeds of drug dealing would no longer have been obtained by crime, and the need for the industry would have disappeared. Now, while the recent changes in places such as Uruguay and Colorado[51] are welcome, we are still far from seeing the sort of global impetus that would lead to widespread decriminalisation. The moment has been missed. In terms of seizures, and with the exception of cocaine, which experienced a sharp rise in the years immediately after 2003 but is now declining, the figures have been showing a consistent downward trend for at least 10 years.[52] Recorded instances of drug trafficking and possession are also moving steadily downwards.[53]

We do not hear calls to be less concerned about the general issue of profits from crime as a result of this diminution, nor do we hear claims that the reductions in levels of burglary or drug crime are due to POCA and associated legislation. If the case for AML had been argued under present conditions (as it was in the late 1980s) solely as a means of prosecuting the war on drugs, the argument would probably fail. This is why the AML industry[54] turned to other areas, and that move

[50] 'MoJ Drops "Failure to Prevent Economic Crime" Offence Plans', *Law Gazette*, 29 September 2015.

[51] R Room, 'Legalizing a Market for Cannabis for Pleasure: Colorado, Washington, Uruguay and Beyond' (2014) 109 *Addiction* 345.

[52] K Coleman, *Seizures of Drugs in England and Wales, 2012/13*, Home Office Statistical Bulletin 04/13 (London, Home Office, 2013).

[53] Office for National Statistics, *Key Annual Trend and Demographic Tables—Crime in England and Wales, Year Ending March 2014*. It may be that fashion, internet markets, currencies like bitcoins and the widespread availability of 'legal highs' also contribute.

[54] See A Verhage, *The Anti Money Laundering Complex and the Compliance Industry* (London, Taylor & Francis, 2011).

was made without asking two important questions: first, whether there is a victim who might take action; and secondly, whether there is some state agency that might act. The areas the industry turn to, in order, were organised crime, terrorism, corruption, organised crime (again) and tax. Again, with political advantage very much to the fore, David Cameron attempted to extend the proceeds of crime legislation to the income of illegal immigrants—not least because the legislation might well run contrary to the ECHR and thus trigger arguments about whether or not the UK should remain a signatory of the Convention.[55]

V. Tax Evasion Offences and AML

The Financial Action Task Force (FATF) caused the AML regime to be extended to cover taxation in the early years of the century. The idea that tax law might provide a mechanism by which to deal with crime is not a new one, but the advent of money laundering changes the dynamic.[56] The great advantages of the crime of tax evasion as a focus for those invested in the AML industry is that, once tax offences are regarded as appropriate predicates, then, first, the amounts of money involved in the AML narrative will increase sharply, and, secondly, more or less any criminal enterprise by which property is acquired will be covered, and it will not be necessary to establish another, more specific, type[57] of predicate in order to show laundering. Somebody making a living from dealing drugs will almost always not be declaring the income. Therefore, where it is straightforward to prove that they received the income, treating the evasion of tax, rather than the dealing, as the predicate, simply because of the aggregation of wealth, avoids the need to be more specific about the provenance.

From 2005 onwards, the law in England and Wales came to include tax offences as predicates to laundering, and this was made obligatory worldwide by FATF in the 2012 redraft of the Forty Recommendations.[58] This has led to an unnecessary and complex blurring between tax and criminal justice. It also renders the amounts of money that can be ascribed to laundering far higher, broadens the

[55] Immigration Bill 2015. See P Alldridge, *What Went Wrong with Money Laundering Law?* (London, Palgrave, 2016).

[56] There is a significant body of literature around Capone: see *Capone v United States* (1931) 56 F 2d 927, cert denied, 286 US 553, 76 LEd 1288, 52 SCt 503 (1932); *United States v Capone* 93 F 2d 840 (1937), cert denied, 303 US 651, 82 LEd 1112, 58 SCt 750 (1938). More generally, see R Baker, 'Taxation: Potential Destroyer of Crime' (1951) 29 *Chicago-Kent Law Review* 197; M Gallant, 'Tax and the Proceeds of Crime: A New Approach to Tainted Finance?' (2013) 16 *Journal of Money Laundering Control* 119; PH Bucy, 'Criminal Tax Fraud: The Downfall of Murderers, Madams and Thieves' (1997) 29 *Arizona State Law Journal* 639.

[57] On a charge of a POCA laundering offence, the prosecution does not have to prove a specific predicate offence but a type of offence to give the mental state for the purposes of POCA laundering offences. *R v Kuchhadia* [2015] EWCA Crim 1252.

[58] FATF, *Interpretive Note to Recommendation 3* (Money Laundering Offence) para 4.

margins for error in any claims as to the size of the problem and increases the proportion that can be allocated to the transnational component of the global sum claimed to be laundered.

In English law, the 'criminal property' is deemed to exist in the hands of the tax evader, and defendants have been held to launder the proceeds of the crime of evasion. In *R v William, William & William*,[59] the Court of Appeal held that where a taxpayer cheated HMRC by falsely representing the turnover of a business, he obtained a pecuniary advantage and was taken to have obtained a benefit equal to tax due on the undeclared turnover. Moreover, the 'criminal property' was the entirety of the undeclared turnover, not merely the tax due. Once the law commits to the fiction that the tax evader actually has in his/her possession property that he/she does not have and uses that as a basis for conviction, there is no obvious point to stop. If tax evasion is a predicate offence to criminal laundering, then, since almost all income from unlawful sources is taxable profits, there is a danger that the chosen enforcement mechanism—against, for example, drug dealers—will be to treat their money as the proceeds of tax evasion and charge laundering of that, rather than have to prove the predicate. If the prosecution need only establish that money was undeclared income, then, unless the sentences for laundering vary according to the predicate offence, there is no point in proving any other, more serious, 'criminal conduct' as a predicate. English law has no restriction preventing liability for 'self-laundering' (ie laundering the proceeds of one's own crime),[60] so the effect of these developments is that it is now very unlikely that any defendant who commits an evasion offence will not also be liable for a laundering offence. This trend is exemplified by *R v Kuchhadia*,[61] in which the defendant's lifestyle was taken as evidence of a number of possible predicates, of which evasion was one, and the most easily proven.

VI. Changing the Position of Institutions and Advisers

So far as concerns laundering, the reporting obligation imposed upon financial institutions is to report suspicion of money laundering.[62] It is not to report that they think particular clients are crooks. Money laundering has as an element 'criminal property'. If the state cannot identify the property, there is no crime of laundering, and if the financial institution cannot identify any criminal property, there is no need to report. The problem in the case of tax evasion is that, while

[59] *R v William, William & William* [2013] EWCA Crim 1262, approving and expanding upon *R v Gabriel* [2006] EWCA Crim 229, [2007] 2 Cr App R 11; *R v K* [2007] EWCA Crim 491, [2008] STC 1270; *Serious Organised Crime Agency v Bosworth* [2010] EWHC 645 (QB).

[60] German and Austrian law both exclude liability for self-laundering. See §261 and §165 StGB of the respective Criminal Codes.

[61] *R v Kuchhadia* [2015] EWCA Crim 1252, [2015] Lloyd's Rep FC 526.

[62] Proceeds of Crime Act 2002, s 330.

some cases will give rise to easily identifiable proceeds, whether for the purposes of property-specific or value-based asset seizure schemes,[63] other cases will not. In the case where a defendant has more property than he/she would otherwise have as a consequence of under-declaration, it is not clear that any specific property in his/her possession will be the product of that under-declaration.

Beyond that, note that the trigger for the reporting requirement in English law is 'suspicion', which in this context is widely defined. The leading English case, *R v Da Silva*,[64] speaks of 'any inkling or fleeting thought that the money being paid into her account … might be the proceeds of criminal conduct will suffice for the offence against her to be proved'. This has the effect that if the person in the regulated sector has an inkling that the client has an inkling that the property in question is of dubious provenance, then reports should be made.[65] The consequence is that far more reports are made in the UK than in comparable jurisdictions. There is also the possibility that the bank will not merely have failed to discharge duties imposed on it as a regulated institution but will also have committed criminal offences.

VII. How Does the Extension of Tax Evasion Law Affect Money Laundering Law?

Banking secrecy and corporate anonymity are both important because if the authorities do not know who controls what money in which overseas bank account, then any system of taxation of capital and income which relies upon aggregation of spending and saving as its measure will fail. Taxpayers will be able to park their money outside the reach of the authorities. The extension of laundering law, and its reporting requirements, into tax evasion will become yet more serious if the proposal for a strict liability offence of offshore tax evasion were to become law.[66] It would be very difficult to commit the new evasion offence without also committing the offence of laundering.

If this is really what is intended, this should at least be made explicit. If people do evade tax, whether by under- or non-declaration or other means, they will have more money than otherwise they would have had, but that does not necessarily

[63] Per Hughes LJ in *Re Stanford International Bank Ltd* [2010] EWCA Civ 137, [2011] Ch 33, para 162, distinguishing: 'A system such as ours is sometimes referred to as a "value-based" regime; one relying on tracing is sometimes referred to as a "specific property-based" regime.'

[64] *R v Da Silva* [2006] EWCA Crim 1654, [2007] 1 WLR 303.

[65] And note the duty on banks to make enquiries: *Crédit Agricole Corporation and Investment Bank v Papadimitriou* [2015] UKPC 13 (Gibraltar).

[66] The suggestion first made in HMRC Consultation, 'Tackling Offshore Tax Evasion: A New Criminal Offence' (n 14). See now HMRC, 'Tackling Offshore Tax Evasion: A New Criminal Offence for Offshore Evaders. Summary of Responses and Further Consultation' (London, HMRC, 2015).

mean that it concerns any act that might fall within the definition of the major laundering offences.[67] Notwithstanding arguments to the contrary,[68] in English law the relevant deeming provision[69] has been construed, where the pecuniary advantage is the deferral of a debt, to impute to the defendant the value of the debt, not the value of the deferral. In the case of tax fraud by under- or non-declaration,[70] it is clear that the taxpayer will have more property, but there will not necessarily be any identifiable property arising from the evasion to which a laundering charge can be attached. Even if there is identifiable property, the defendant will not necessarily hold the required mental state for conviction (ie knowledge that or suspicion as to whether the property in question 'represented or constituted'[71] the proceeds of an offence of the type of the predicate offence), but the conceptual problems raised as to the quantity and identity of the criminal property have consistently been ducked in the laundering case law of England and Wales.

Naylor described this extension of laundering law into the area of tax thus:

> [O]ne of the many bad ideas to circulate from time to time in official Washington circles is the notion of making tax evasion a predicate offense for money laundering. … This represents a major step toward creating a de facto merger of criminal and fiscal enforcement, contrary to a long tradition in Anglo-Saxon legal practice that insisted on a division of those two functions.[72]

He gives seven reasons why this is a bad idea. Not all apply here, but one is that 'it is absurd to think of tax evasion as a predicate offense for money laundering charges—they are both post-dicate offenses, occurring only after a flow of income has been generated'.

The great triumph of the AML industry has been to dissociate the proceeds from the predicate offence. It is not drug money: it is criminal money. The shift from concern with the predicate to concern with the laundering has rendered the nature and gravity of the predicate irrelevant.[73]

The creation of the new offence of overseas evasion would broaden the scope of tax evasion offences, and consequently enlarge the scope of the offence of laundering the proceeds of tax evasion. This might have as a consequence that the introduction of a relatively minor offence would involve a significant change in

[67] POCA, ss 327–29.

[68] P Alldridge and A Mumford, 'Tax Evasion and the Proceeds of Crime Act 2002' (2005) 25 *Legal Studies* 353.

[69] POCA, s 76(5) (confiscation) and s 340(6) (criminal laundering): 'If a person obtains a pecuniary advantage as a result of or in connection with conduct, he is to be taken to obtain as a result of or in connection with the conduct a sum of money equal to the value of the pecuniary advantage.'

[70] But not falsely claiming rebates.

[71] A legal judgment is implied in 'constituted'; consequently, mistake or ignorance in that regard should, in principle, provide a defence: *R v Smith (DR)* [1974] QB 354.

[72] RT Naylor, *Counterfeit Crime Criminal Profits, Terror Dollars, and Nonsense* (Montreal/Kingston, McGill-Queens University Press, 2015) 110.

[73] See P Alldridge, 'Money Laundering and Globalization' (2008) 35 *Journal of Law and Society* 437.

the criminal law. As things stand, the minimum mental state required for conviction for laundering the proceeds of tax evasion is suspicion as to whether the property in question was obtained by evasion, and that suspicion[74] must address the relevant mental state (dishonesty or a fraudulent intent of some sort), as well as the acquisition of the actual funds.

The mental state required for conviction of laundering the proceeds of the new offence would be knowledge that or suspicion as to whether the property in question 'represented or constituted' the proceeds of the offence, and that suspicion will no longer need to advert to a relevant serious mental state, but simply as to whether the offence was committed, albeit blamelessly, or, if a defence is provided, of a reasonable care. Under the new offence, the taxpayer would be liable for laundering if he/she considered the possibility that the offence had been committed—that is, that he or she, or somebody acting on his or her behalf, had made a mistake when completing the tax forms. There can be few people who complete tax forms without considering such a possibility. So the introduction of a new offence would not only install a new band of liability below the existing criminal offence of evasion, but it would also radically broaden the scope of the offence of laundering the proceeds of evasion, which is a much more serious offence. On the face of it, the penalties for this offence would not have been significantly different from those for any other laundering offences.[75]

The English law definition of laundering now extends, in particular, to include activity directed towards the disposal of money which is the product of tax evasion. Almost all undeclared income from crime is taxable. The consequence of this is that at least as much money will be laundered in any given economy as is equivalent to the entire black economy of the jurisdiction in question, plus some (because honest mistakes will occur too). The same applies globally. Far from being a slight change, the introduction of the proposed offence would be a huge one, which, at the very least, should have been considered. It is easy to say that tax evasion is a crime (or even a serious crime) and that it should be treated equally with other serious crimes as a predicate to laundering. It is less easy to see that the 'de facto merger'[76] of criminal justice and taxation might have significant harmful consequences.

The argument for including tax evasion as a predicate is clear. Money laundering should have as its predicate a range of serious property offences. Tax evasion is a serious offence. What is the problem? The prosecution policy has always been to treat tax evasion rather differently from other frauds that may be considered equivalents. Partly because of the availability of civil sanctions, partly because

[74] See *Shah v HSBC Private Bank (UK) Ltd* [2010] EWCA Civ 31, [2010] 3 All ER 477; *K Ltd v National Westminster Bank Plc* [2006] EWCA Civ 1039, [2007] 1 WLR 311.

[75] In the early sentencing cases on laundering the courts were strongly influenced by the gravity of the predicate offence: *R v Goodyear* [2005] EWCA Crim 888, [2005] 1 WLR 2532; *R v Yoonus* [2004] EWCA Crim 1734, [2005] 1 CAR (S) 46; *Attorney General's Reference No 48 of 2006 (Andrew Farrow)* [2006] EWCA Crim 2396. Since then there has been a move away from that position: Sentencing Council, 'Fraud, Bribery and Money Laundering Offences: Definitive Guidelines' (2014).

[76] Naylor (n 71) 110.

of the powerful enforcement mechanisms, partly because it is not universally regarded as being as bad as other frauds and partly out of habit, the rate of prosecutions has always been low.[77]

Nonetheless, there has always been ambivalence about the relationship between tax evasion, other crimes and laundering. Tax evasion is serious for some purposes, but for others it is not serious. It has been argued cogently[78] that the introduction of tax evasion reporting to the AML scheme was to encourage the financial sector into making disclosures in revenue cases where no underlying criminal activity is involved, by taking advantage of the ambiguity which hovers over the line between lawful tax avoidance and dishonest tax evasion. Fisher traces this development to a G7 meeting in 1998.[79] The underlying ambivalence towards evasion is most clearly seen in the amnesty schemes dealing with tax evasion by British taxpayers in Liechtenstein and three British Crown dependencies.[80] Those schemes do not apply to 'criminal property' within the POCA definition unless the money is criminal property only by reason of tax evasion—in which case the taxpayer gets the benefit of the amnesty scheme.

VIII. Why Are We Doing AML?

The AML industry has grown organically without reconsideration of its rationale at every point in its growth. A fundamental reconsideration might ask what the purpose of the industry is, and how the satisfaction of that purpose would provide limits to the enterprise. First, AML might be worthwhile because, on a proper economic costing, AML and counter-terrorism financing more than pays for itself in property seized and reductions in other crimes (by preventing reinvestment or reducing the incentives), and the state can use the money thereby acquired to build hospitals, schools and prisons. Alternatively, it might be thought valuable for reasons to do with moral entrepreneurship—because careers are to be had and because there is a political advantage to be gained. In his day, Tony Blair did very well out of profits of crime, and David Cameron followed suit.[81] Or the crusade against laundering might be thought of as an end in itself—because, like Kant's famous example of the murderers on the island[82] that is being vacated, it should be done whatever the cost.

[77] For an apologia see J Fisher, 'HSBC, Tax Evasion and Criminal Prosecution', *Tax Journal*, 2 March 2015.

[78] By J Fisher, 'The Anti-Money Laundering Disclosure Regime and the Collection of Revenue in the United Kingdom' (2010) *British Tax Review* 235.

[79] ibid 246.

[80] See www.gov.uk/offshore-disclosure-facilities.

[81] Immigration Bill 2015.

[82] I Kant, *The Metaphysical Elements of Justice* (Indianapolis, Bobbs-Merrill, 1065) 102.

Regarding the first reason—that AML actually causes economic benefits—proper economic costing would be crucial. If we do not know—and we do not—that AML pays for itself, it should be reassessed. A report written for the International Monetary Fund (IMF) was unequivocal:

> To date there is no substantial effort by any international organization, including the IMF, to assess either the costs or benefits of an AML/CFT regime. The FATF system has proceeded as if it produces only public and private goods, not public or private 'bads' or adverse by-products against which the 'goods' have to be weighed. ... There needs to be more open acknowledgement of actual and potential financial costs of AML/CFT controls, their potential misuse by authoritarian rulers, and possible adverse effects on populations that rely on remittances and the informal economy, as well as potential negative impacts on NGOs and parts of civil society. Likewise the benefits, including a more universally compatible mutual legal assistance scheme, laundering prevention and better proceeds of crime detection and recoveries, need to be articulated more clearly.[83]

The choice is clear: either include tax evasion, and in particular offshore evasion, within the scope of the AML industry, in which case it takes it over (worry, if you like, about racehorses, yachts, Bentleys and mansions owned by Mafiosi, deposits by despots in Cypriot banks or Colombian drug barons, or whatever it is, but you will not get within two orders of magnitude of the amount of tax evaded by people with money in Swiss banks); or do not include evaded tax, in which case the AML industry is probably not paying for itself and the only justification could be its success in reducing crimes other than laundering (and whether and to what extent it does so is a question to which we do not really know the answer).

Conclusion—Responses

The unspoken assumption governing the growth of the AML industry, on the one hand, and of the regulation of banking and the growing imposition upon banks of duties to report for tax purposes, on the other, seems to be that it is probably a good thing, and at least cannot be a bad thing, if one set of arrangements devised to prevent the banking system being used for the laundering of dirty money and another to prevent the international financial system being used for hiding money from the tax authorities operate at the same time.

One alternative would be to treat the whole issue of offshore as a tax issue, rather than as a laundering issue. Common reporting standards involving full automatic disclosure of the relevant information between jurisdictions is planned from 2018. If they operate successfully, further intervention in respect of laundering would be unnecessary.

[83] T Halliday, M Levi and P Reuter, *Global Surveillance of Dirty Money* (Illinois, Centre for Law and Globalization, 2014) 9.

The initial response of the UK government to the HSBC Suisse affair[84] was that the fact that there had been so few prosecutions was a function of its general policy of using civil penalties and other mechanisms to recover the tax, which was their priority. Consistent with this, the Serious Fraud Office had known about the HSBC Suisse affair at least as early as 2012 and had decided to take no action. After the 2015 General Election, and the return of a Conservative majority, the mood music changed. The Financial Conduct Authority enquiry into the culture of banking was cancelled.[85]

HSBC's own response was to acknowledge that mistakes had been made during the period covered by the leaks, that controls were lax, that practices were inappropriate and that the organisation's structure was flawed, but that it was not their fault, and they have been, and still are, working hard to put things right—from the time it had come into possession of the information, it had used it for the purpose of enforcing the payment of owing tax. This was a case in which the usual policy of HMRC on prosecution, which was to incline against using criminal proceedings, applied. HMRC wanted its money—and it had used the information in the Falciani leaks to get a good deal of it.

The bank now says that that was then and this is now. It has implemented 'numerous initiatives designed to prevent its banking services being used to evade taxes or launder money'.[86] The Code of Practice on Taxation for Banks (which, anecdotally at least, appears to have been effective) has placed 'voluntarily' obligations upon banks.[87] HSBC wrote to all holders of accounts[88] in Jersey informing them that, unless they can explain their need for the facility in Jersey, their accounts will be closed, and is restructuring its private banking.[89] HSBC announced in June 2015 that it might move its headquarters back to Asia, losing 50,000 jobs worldwide in the next two years. It announced in December 2015 that its private banking activities were to be revised.[90] The UK government is keen to retain the bank's headquarters in London. Business as usual—that is, the UK lurching from scandal to indignation and the introduction of repressive measures, to the UK recognising its economic self-interest—seems to have been resumed.[91]

[84] 'Statement by HMRC on Tax Evasion and the HSBC Suisse Data Leak' (HMRC, 14 February 2015).

[85] The enquiry is described at www.fca.org.uk/static/documents/foi/foi4350-information-provided.pdf, and its termination in 'UK Draws Line under "Banker Bashing" after Scrapping Assessment', *Financial Times*, 30 December 2015.

[86] HSBC's Swiss Private Bank Progress Update—January 2015.

[87] 'Such is the heightened state of paranoia in the banks at the moment that any tax planning which could be erosive of the UK tax base—including some fairly anodyne transactions—tends to get killed off pretty quickly, if not by a nervous internal committee, then following a friendly chat with HMRC': H Lethaby, 'Reflections on Tax and the City' (2014) 1220 *Tax Journal* 10, 11.

[88] Except for those falling within its expat business unit.

[89] 'HSBC Reviews Jersey Accounts of UK Customers', *Financial Times*, 17 March 2015.

[90] 'HSBC Appoints Rothschild for Restructuring of Private Banking Arm', *Financial Times*, 20 December 2015.

[91] 'UK Draws Line under "Banker Bashing" after Scrapping Assessment', *Financial Times*, 30 December 2015.

8

Asset Recovery in Four Dimensions: Returning Wealth to Victim Countries as a Challenge for Global Governance

RADHA IVORY*

Introduction

The challenge of asset recovery in grand corruption cases is a challenge of global governance in its practical and normative dimensions. Asset recovery is, at once, a functionalist and radical agenda. It presents a world that is full of injustice. It argues for a redistribution of wealth between rich and poor states. And it asks us to imagine a future in which high-level public officials are less able to move illicit wealth through the international financial system and countries are better able to 'get the money back' when it is transferred abroad. Supplementing weak domestic revenue sources and diminishing foreign aid, recovered funds enable the governments of developing or post-transition states to achieve their socio-economic objectives. This is a cosmopolitan vision. But it is to be achieved through legal measures more familiar from regulations on banking supervision or corporate insolvency than public international law. At several points, they seem to require departures from protections for individual rights to property and due process. To the extent that its objectives can be clearly formulated and 'outputs' measured,

* University of Queensland, Australia. My sincere thanks to Jonathan Crowe, Terrence Halliday and Jason Sharman for reading and commenting on drafts of this work. Sruthy John, Sam Hickey and Maria Dolhare provided excellent research assistance, from near and far, and Pedram Rashidi much encouragement and inspiration at home. The initial presentation for the University of Luxembourg conference 'Chasing Criminal Money in the EU: New Tools and Practices?' was prepared during a visit to the Basel Institute on Governance in the summer of 2015. That visit was funded by UQ's Faculty of Business, Economics and Law as part of my project, 'Governing Good Governance: Corporate Corruption and the Regulation of Transnational Crime'. The research for this chapter was finalised on 30 October 2015.

there are very few signs of success. When states engage in asset recovery, they may be fighting transnational crime and pursuing 'good' governance, but they are also co-operating in everyday bureaucratic matters and paradoxically in tension with principles of effectiveness and fairness, rationality, and the rule of law.

The facets of asset recovery as a discourse of governance are evident in the concept of asset recovery in international law. Asset recovery is both a promise and practice and a purpose and process under the United Nations Convention against Corruption (UNCAC), the most widely subscribed and recent anti-corruption treaty.[1] It would appear from that convention that asset recovery is a goal of preventing and reversing illicit financial flows generated by acts of grand corruption, as well as a set of procedures that are intended to achieve key aspects of that agenda.[2] States are to require their financial institutions to detect and disclose suspicious transactions, which are connected with certain high-level customers and high-value accounts.[3] They are also to assist each other to obtain ownership of assets that are the proceeds, instrumentalities or objects of a convention offence or assets that, directly or indirectly, represents such wealth.[4] 'Co-operative confiscation' is the quintessential reactive process in international asset recovery law. It occurs when a state with enforcement jurisdiction over things (the 'haven' state) compulsorily acquires illicit wealth at the behest of a state with legislative and judicial competence over the alleged offence (the 'victim' country).[5] In addition, state parties are to permit each other to claim ownership of those assets or seek compensation for the harms caused by corruption in domestic civil courts. On this definition, asset recovery is a feature not just of the UNCAC, but also of other treaties and instruments on anti-corruption and anti-money laundering (AML), mutual legal assistance (MLA) and transnational crime control.[6]

Though asset recovery is a concept within international law, the challenges of asset recovery cut across international law and other disciplines and fields of practice.[7] This chapter presents the issue of asset recovery in these several dimensions. It begins, in Sections I and II, with a description of the international legal framework for preventing transfers of illicit wealth and enforcing anti-corruption and AML laws. I explain why international rules on corruption seemed necessary and how asset recovery rules have worked (or not) in the real world.

[1] New York, 31 October 2003, in force 14 December 2005, 2349 UNTS 41, (2004) 43 International Legal Materials 37.

[2] R Ivory, *Corruption, Asset Recovery, and the Protection of Property in Public International Law: The Human Rights of Bad Guys* (Cambridge, Cambridge University Press, 2014) 22. For a similar observation about the concept of 'development', see also J Salacuse, 'From Developing Countries to Emerging Markets: A Changing Role for Law in the Third World' (1999) *The International Lawyer* 875, 876.

[3] Ivory (ibid) 23.

[4] Ivory (n 2) 27.

[5] Ivory (n 2) 28.

[6] Ivory (n 2) 28.

[7] See also C King and C Walker, 'Emerging Issues in the Regulation of Criminal and Terrorist Assets' in C King and C Walker (eds), *Dirty Assets: Emerging Issues in the Regulation of Criminal and Terrorist Assets* (Farnham, Ashgate Publishing, 2014) 5.

Some states with important financial centres do appear to be following the new norm. A small international bureaucracy provides technical assistance to developing and transition states on asset recovery matters. Yet, even by the estimates of these institutions, only a small fraction of the assets 'stolen' have been returned since international efforts against corruption began in earnest after the Cold War. When proceedings have taken place, they have typically been complex, multi-stage litigations involving a mixture of unilateral and consensual measures (sanctions and settlements), and ex post hoc (tailor-made) asset recovery laws—hardly a seamless international division of labour in criminal procedure.[8]

The challenges of asset recovery are then discussed in Sections III–VI. The first challenge (Section III) is to overcome official ambivalence towards the asset recovery cause. The Stolen Asset Recovery Initiative (StAR) identifies almost 30 laws, practices and attitudes that inhibit the restraint and ultimate transfer of illicit wealth to victim countries. Of particular concern are broad powers on the part of haven states to refuse requests for assistance and narrow powers on the part of victim or haven countries to convict apparently enriched officials or confiscate illicit wealth. Can states be persuaded to use the international rules and undertake domestic reforms? The second challenge (Section IV) follows from the first. There is an apparent contradiction between international laws that require states to 'enhance' their powers for confiscation and co-operation in corruption cases and international standards that require governments to ensure individual civil and political rights. Will states infringe 'the human rights of bad guys' if they 'lower the barriers to recovery'? The European Court of Human Rights (ECtHR) has permitted many of the measures that states are encouraged or required to take against grand corruption and for asset recovery. Other human rights bodies and scholars have cited these decisions in advocating presumptions of illicit acquisition and non-conviction-based (NCB) confiscation rules. Strasbourg's reasoning is hard to follow, however, and its judgments fail, as a rule, to engage with the underlying normative (or norm conflict) issues. Meanwhile, the effectiveness of asset recovery is doubted. The third challenge (Section V) is to demonstrate that the international standards on asset recovery achieve their objectives. Evaluating any anti-corruption programme is difficult: what is corruption? How to detect corruption? Do the policy interventions cause people to be less corrupt and, if so, at what cost? The methodological difficulties increase when the 'programme' takes the form of international standards: what constitutes compliance? Does treaty ratification cause compliance? Does country-level compliance affect the behaviour of individuals and firms? Is the process for behavioural change top-down or more recursive? Only a few scholars have attempted to answer these empirical questions for the international law on corruption; still fewer have posed them for

[8] W Schomburg et al, 'Einleitung' in W Schomburg et al (eds), *Internationale Rechtshilfe in Strafsachen (International Cooperation in Criminal Matters)*, 5th edn (Munich, Verlag CH Beck, 2012) 97 (ein 'international-arbeitsteiliges Strafverfahren').

asset recovery rules. Those who do soon encounter the fourth set of challenges (Section VI): what are the 'real' reasons for the international legal standards on asset recovery? Are quantitative criteria (less crime, more revenue) the 'real' measures for success? Constructivist and critical scholars see much in international anti-corruptionism that derives from Western liberal thought and neoliberal ideology. States (and citizens) may perceive certain transactions as corrupt because they have been socialised to distinguish between 'public' and 'private' life; they perceive asset recovery as desirable because they regard individuals as autonomous moral agents and the primary units for social control. As a case study of the (neo) liberal influence in anti-corruption, asset recovery would seem to have plenty to offer the critics—but there is also evidence that asset recovery is sometimes a Second or Third World preference.

I conclude with a detailed summary of my findings and an agenda for future research. Readers who are short on time can use that section as a quick précis of the argument in this chapter. But a warning: the challenges are not overcome, the perspectives do not become problems, and viewpoints are not allocated to a respective discipline or category of actor in that final part. Rather, each challenge ends up presupposing the others and all turn out to be acknowledged (though given different emphasis) by international policy makers, international lawyers, socio-legal scholars and critics of 'transnational crime'. In fact, I describe the challenges in 'dimension' to convey their discreteness and interconnection, as well as to decouple them from a particular institutional or academic point of view. Even the term 'challenge' is used flexibly to denote the difficulties of carrying out asset recovery for co-operating states, as well as the difficulties presented by asset recovery for those interested in the pragmatics and morality of global governance.[9] The contribution itself is a snapshot a rapidly moving field.

I. The International Legal Framework for Asset Recovery

The international legal framework for asset recovery is set forth in a network of treaties and supranational legislative instruments concluded during the first two decades after the Cold War.[10] International relations scholars have observed the rapid development and legalisation of the 'global anti-corruption norm'

[9] I am indebted to Terrence Halliday for this expression of the problem.

[10] Ivory (n 2) 3–4, 11–23 and ch 4. The language of 'international legal frameworks' in this area is that of JB Terracino, *The International Legal Framework against Corruption: States' Obligations to Prevent and Repress Corruption* (Oxford, Intersentia, 2012). See also J Wouters, C Ryngaert and AS Cloots, 'The International Legal Framework against Corruption: Achievements and Challenges' (2013) 14 *Melbourne Journal of International Law* 205.

in those years.[11] Between 1995 and 2005, international co-operation organisations oversaw the creation of 14 binding multilateral instruments on the topics of 'corruption', 'bribery' and 'fraud'.[12] Within Europe alone, states concluded four conventions,[13] three additional protocols[14] and one Framework Decision on public and private corruption under the auspices of regional economic and political co-operation organisations, the European Union (as it became) and the Council of Europe (CoE).[15] The Organisation for Economic Co-operation and Development's Convention on the Bribery of Foreign Public Officials in International Business Transactions (OECD Convention) now binds 41 OECD and non-OECD countries to a small number of regularly peer-reviewed anti-foreign bribery norms.[16] The UNCAC covers 177 party states and a broader range of matters.[17] In 71 articles and eight chapters, it prescribes measures for the prevention and criminalisation of corruption, co-operation in criminal and administrative matters, and implementation at the national level. In this way, it facilitates legal harmonisation between developed and developing countries and across the areas covered by the previous treaties and 'soft laws'. The UN Convention on Transnational Organised Crime (UNTOC) performs a similar function with respect to some

[11] J McCoy and H Heckel, 'The Emergence of a Global Anti-Corruption Norm' (2001) 38 *International Politics* 65; K Abbott and D Snidal, 'Values and Interests: International Legalization in the Fight Against Corruption' (2002) 31 *The Journal of Legal Studies* S141, S157–76; A Jakobi, *Common Goods and Evils? The Formation of Global Crime Governance* (Oxford, Oxford University Press, 2013) ch 5.

[12] See generally: I Androulakis, *Die Globalisierung der Korruptionsbekämpfung* (Baden-Baden, Nomos, 2007), 219–245; M Pieth, 'Introduction' in M Pieth, L Low and N Bonucci (eds), *The OECD Convention on Bribery: A Commentary*, 2nd edn (Cambridge, Cambridge University Press, 2014) 8–30; A Posadas, 'Combating Corruption under International Law' (2000) 10 *Duke Journal of Comparative and International Law* 345.

[13] Convention drawn up on the basis of Article K.3 of the Treaty on European Union, on the protection of the European Communities' financial interests, Brussels, 26 July 1995, in force 17 October 2002 [1995] OJ C316, 49; Council Act of 26 May 1997 drawing up, on the basis of Article K.3(2)(c) of the Treaty on European Union, the Convention on the fight against corruption involving officials of the European Communities or officials of Member States of the European Union, Brussels, 26 May 1997, in force 28 September 2005 [1997] OJ C195, 2; Criminal Law Convention on Corruption, Strasbourg, 27 January 1999, in force 1 July 2002, 2216 UNTS 225, 173 ETS; Civil Law Convention on Corruption, Strasbourg, 4 November 1999, in force 1 November 2003, 2246 UNTS 3, 174 ETS.

[14] Protocol drawn up on the basis of Article K.3 of the Treaty on European Union to the Convention on the protection of the European Communities' financial interests—Statements made by Member States on the adoption of the Act drawing up the Protocol, Brussels, 27 September 1996, in force 17 October 2002 in accordance with Art 11 [1996] OJ C313, 2; Second Protocol, drawn up on the basis of Article K.3 of the treaty on European Union, to the Convention on the protection of the European Communities' financial interests—Joint Declaration on Article 13(2)—Commission Declaration on Article 7, Brussels, 19 June 1997, in force 19 May 2009 [1997] OJ C221, 12; Additional Protocol to the Criminal Law Convention on Corruption, Strasbourg, 15 May 2003, in force 1 February 2005, 2466 UNTS 168, 191 ETS.

[15] Council Framework Decision 2003/568/JHA of 22 July 2003 on combating corruption in the private sector, 22 July 2003, in force 31 July 2003 [2003] OJ L192, 54.

[16] Convention on Combating Bribery of Foreign Public Officials in International Business Transactions, Paris, 17 December 1997, in force 15 February 1999, (1998) 37 International Legal Materials 1.

[17] United Nations Convention against Corruption, New York, 31 October 2003, in force 14 December 2005, 2349 UNTS 41, (2004) 43 International Legal Materials 37.

acts of public bribery 'that are transnational in nature and involv[e] an organized criminal group'.[18] Anti-corruption is now squarely a focus of *international* law and, I submit, a prime example of *transnational* law, understood as a body of rules applying to cross-border situations, a process of legal ordering between and beyond states, or a non-statist perspective on normative statements.[19]

The so-called 'corruption eruption'[20] can be read as a rational response to key social and economic problems of the late twentieth century.[21] From the mid-1970s, attitudes towards corruption shifted from permissive to condemnatory among development academics and within the development institutions.[22] Once thought to 'grease the wheels' of commerce in 'modernising' states,[23] bribery (and corruption in all forms) was recast as a source of economic inefficiency, distributive injustice, and political and social instability in developing countries.[24] The collapse of the USSR had ended the West's incentive to patronise oppressive anti-communist regimes,[25] and simultaneously focused attention on corruption in the former East. It also accelerated processes of economic globalisation that, it has been said, increased opportunities for self-dealing: in post-communist 'capture' economies, officials could collude with newly rich oligarchs to privatise government

[18] United Nations Convention against Transnational Organized Crime, New York, 15 November 2000, in force 19 September 2003, 2225 UNTS 209, Arts 3(1) and 8.

[19] G Shaffer, 'Transnational Legal Ordering and State Change' in G Shaffer (ed), *Transnational Legal Ordering and State Change* (Cambridge, Cambridge University Press, 2013) 3–7; K Tuori, 'Transnational Law: On Legal Hybrids and Perspectivism' in M Maduro, K Tuori and S Sankari (eds), *Transnational Law: Rethinking European Law and Legal Thinking* (Cambridge, Cambridge University Press, 2014).

[20] M Naim, 'The Corruption Eruption' (1995) 2 *The Brown Journal of World Affairs* 245; P Glynn, S Kobrin and M Naim, 'The Globalization of Corruption' in K Elliot (ed), *Corruption and the Global Economy* (Washington, DC, Institute for International Economics, 1997) 7–27.

[21] See, eg, P Delaney, 'Transitional Corruption: Regulation across Borders' (2006) 47 *Virginia Journal of International Law* 413; P Nichols, 'Are Extraterritorial Restrictions on Bribery a Viable and Desirable International Policy Goal under the Global Conditions of the Late Twentieth Century: Increasing Global Security by Controlling Transnational Bribery' (1998) 20 *Michigan Journal of International Law* 451; Wouters et al (n 10) 207–19.

[22] For a general definition of this contentious concept, see B Crow, 'Development and Underdevelopment: Definitions' in PA O'Hara, *Encyclopedia of Political Economy* (London, Routledge 2001) 206 ('Within political economy "development" is most frequently used to delineate the sets of social changes associated with social and economic progress in the Third (or developing) World. This use of the term became widespread after the Second World War, when the Marshall Plan for the reconstruction of Europe provided a model for directed reconstruction of production and livelihoods and much of colonial Asia and Africa gained independence').

[23] D Kaufmann and SJ Wei, 'Does "Grease Money" Speed up the Wheels of Commerce?' (1999) National Bureau of Economic Research Working Paper No 7093, 1–2, available at www.nber.org/papers/w7093, citing N Leff, 'Economic Development Through Bureaucratic Corruption' (1964) 8 *American Behavioral Scientist* 8, 11; S Huntington, *Political Order in Changing Societies* (New Haven, Yale University Press, 1968) 386.

[24] For surveys of this literature, see also JG Lambsdorff, 'Consequences and Causes of Corruption: What Do We Know from a Cross-Section of Countries?' [2005] *Passauer Diskussionspapiere: Volkswirtschaftliche Reihe*, No V-34–05, Part II, available at www.econstor.eu; D Treisman, 'What Have We Learned about the Causes of Corruption from Ten Years of Cross-National Empirical Research?' (2007) 10 *Annual Review of Political Science* 211; K Kis-Katos and GG Schulze, 'Corruption in Southeast Asia: A Survey of Recent Research' (2013) 27 *Asian-Pacific Economic Literature* 79.

[25] Glynn et al (n 20) 9–11.

assets at an undervalue.[26] In post-colonial states,[27] particularly in Africa, high-level officials could charge (more or higher) rents to multinational enterprises bidding for government procurement contracts or natural resource concessions.[28] Quite aside from the corrupt opportunities created by investment, weak political institutions were seen to enable such officials to enrich themselves unilaterally.[29] Meanwhile, there were fears that transnational crimes of all sorts had become easier to perpetrate with improvements in technology and the relative liberalisation of immigration and financial controls.[30] 'Globetrotting' criminals could move themselves and their assets more easily across borders; states remained constrained to enforcing laws within their territories and through cumbersome processes of co-operation with other sovereigns or international organisations.[31]

Though corruption appears to be a classic global governance (or collective action) problem,[32] states did not globalise (or collectivise) their powers of corruption control. The anti-corruption treaties are suppression conventions, as defined and described by Neil Boister in his work on the architecture of transnational criminal law.[33] As such, they neither create an international crime (or crimes) of corruption nor empower international courts or tribunals to investigate, sanction and prosecute corrupt conduct.[34] Rather, they call on state parties to criminalise particular acts or omissions within their jurisdictions and to co-operate in criminal

26 J Hellman, G Jones and D Kaufmann, 'Seize the State, Seize the Day: State Capture, Corruption and Influence in Transition' (2002) World Bank Policy Research Working Papers No 2444. See, eg, P Nichols, '*United States v Lazarenko*: The Trial and Conviction of Two Former Prime Ministers of Ukraine' [2012] *University of Chicago Legal Forum* 41, 63.

27 Salacuse (n 2) 884.

28 D Hall, 'Privatisation, Multinationals, and Corruption' (1999) 9 *Development in Practice* 539; J Coolidge and SR Ackerman, 'High-Level Rent-Seeking and Corruption in African Regimes: Theory and Cases' (1997) World Bank Policy Research Paper No 1780, 21–23, 37–40; S Hawley, 'Exporting Corruption: Privatisation, Multinationals & Bribery' (2000) The Corner House Briefing No 19, available at www.thecornerhouse.org.uk/resource/exporting-corruption-0. See also T Burgis, *The Looting Machine: Warlords, Oligarchs, Corporations, Smuggler and the Theft of Africa's Wealth* (New York, PublicAffairs, 2015).

29 Perhaps the most graphic example comes from Nigeria under the leadership of General S Abacha. E Monfrini, Nigeria's Swiss lawyer, recounts that '[f]unds were removed in cash from the Central Bank, sometimes by the truck-load': E Monfrini, 'The Abacha Case' in M Pieth (ed), *Recovering Stolen Assets* (Bern, Peter Lang, 2008) 42.

30 M Levitsky, 'The Dark Side of Globalization' (2003) 5 *International Studies Review* 253; M Naim, *Illicit: How Smugglers, Traffickers and Copycats are Hijacking the Global Economy* (New York, Doubleday, 2005) Introduction and ch 1, esp 3–4 and 18–24.

31 P Andreas, 'Illicit Globalizations: Myths, Misconceptions, and Historical Lessons' (2011) 126 *Political Science Quarterly* 403, 404; P Andreas, *Smuggler Nation: How Illicit Trade Made America* (Oxford, Oxford University Press, 2013) 331.

32 H Wang and J Rosenau, 'Transparency International and Corruption as an Issue of Global Governance' (2001) 7 *Global Governance* 25. See also M Pieth, 'Collective Action and Corruption' in M Pieth (ed), *Collective Action: Innovative Strategies to Prevent Corruption* (Zurich, Dike, 2012).

33 See, eg, N Boister, '"Transnational Criminal Law"?' (2003) 14 *European Journal of International Law* 953. On the corruption treaties as transnational criminal law, see, eg, N Boister, *An Introduction to Transnational Criminal Law* (Oxford, Oxford University Press, 2012), ch 8; Ivory (n 2) 12–15.

34 B Harms, 'Holding Public Officials Accountable in the International Realm: A New Multi-Layered Strategy to Combat Corruption' (2000) 33 *Cornell International Law Journal* 159, 195–204;

matters when individuals, corporations or assets are within the judicial or enforcement power of another state. The anti-corruption treaties contain slightly different catalogues of offences, which they define in somewhat different terms. Only some of those offences must be criminalised; only some are labelled 'corrupt'. However, all of the conventions require state parties to sanction behaviours that are corrupt according to the standard international definition,[35] or are judged to enable such acts of corruption according to mainstream theories of corruption control.[36] Various forms of bribery and embezzlement are on the global and regional criminalisation lists, as are money laundering and the obstruction of justice.[37]

As a form of suppression convention, the anti-corruption treaties generally leave prosecution policy and the specifics of sanctioning to party states; however, they do foresee confiscation in connection with their crimes and co-operation in confiscation matters.[38] The OECD Convention and the CoE Criminal Law Convention on Corruption (CoECrimCC) require states to enable confiscation and provide mutual legal assistance in criminal matters in two terse provisions:[39] these are interpreted by the respective convention monitoring bodies as creating duties to co-operate with state requests for assistance in confiscation matters ('co-operative confiscation').[40] The EU treaties on corruption say nothing about confiscation but are complemented, on paper and in practice, by an EU convention on mutual legal assistance,[41] two CoE money laundering

Transparency International, 'Putrajaya Declaration: Zero Tolerance for Impunity' (4 September 2015), available at www.transparency.org/news/feature/the_putrajaya_declaration (recommendation of the 16th International Anti-Corruption Conference that 'Grand corruption should become a crime of international law. This will enable international institutions and alliances to prosecute offenders, as well as develop additional international mechanisms to apprehend, prosecute, judge, and sentence those who have committed crimes of grand corruption').

[35] That is, a misuse of (public) power or office for private gain: Ivory (n 2) 17–22. P Nichols, 'Corruption as an Assurance Problem' (2004) 19 *American University International Law Review* 1308 attributes the definition to J Nye, 'Corruption and Political Development: A Cost Benefit Analysis' (1967) 61 *American Political Science Review* 417, 419. For international permutations of the definitions, see, eg, World Bank Group, 'Helping Countries Combat Corruption: Poverty Reduction and Economic Management (1997) 8, available at www1.worldbank.org/publicsector/anticorrupt/corruptn/coridx.htm; Transparency International, 'The Anti-Corruption Plain Language Guide' (2009) 14, available at www.transparency.org/whatwedo/pub/the_anti_corruption_plain_language_guide.

[36] United Nations Office on Drugs and Crime Division for Treaty Affairs (UNODC), *Legislative Guide for the Implementation of the United Nations Convention against Corruption* (New York, United Nations, 2006) paras 222–24 and 252, available at https://www.unodc.org/pdf/corruption/CoC_LegislativeGuide.pdf.

[37] See further Ivory (n 2) 20–22 and 63–90.

[38] See generally Ivory (n 2) ch 4.

[39] CoECrimCC, Arts 19(3) and 25(1); OECD Convention, Arts 3 and 9.

[40] Ivory (n 2) 102, but see also 28–29 (defining 'cooperative confiscation' as 'the compulsory assumption of ownership of illicit wealth by a state with jurisdiction over those things (the "haven state") at the behest of a state with legislative and judicial competence over the alleged offence (the "victim state")').

[41] Council Act of 29 May 2000, establishing in accordance with Article 34 of the Treaty on European Union the Convention on Mutual Assistance in Criminal Matters between the Member States of the European Union, Brussels, 29 May 2000, in force 23 August 2005 [2000] OJ C197, 1, Art 8(1).

conventions,[42] and several EU legislative instruments on co-operation and confiscation.[43] There are broadly equivalent duties under the other anti-corruption and related MLA treaties,[44] although the Inter-American and Southern African treaties only refer to 'forfeiture' and 'confiscation', respectively, and the pan-African treaty does not provide a clear basis for co-operative confiscation, in my view.[45]

The UNCAC and UNTOC incorporate this detail, the UNCAC adding the concept of 'asset recovery' in its preamble, purposive provision and the heading of its fifth chapter (Articles 51–59). UNCAC state parties must enable confiscation with respect to convention offences under Article 31 and assist each other with confiscation under Article 55(1). To permit this form of assistance, under Article 54(1), they must enable their competent authorities to give effect to another party's judicial confiscation orders or to confiscate 'such property of foreign origin' by adjudicating related local offences, like money laundering: states may provide other confiscation procedures under local law. When making and assessing requests for assistance in confiscation matters, UNCAC states may rely on the 'mini-MLAT' within Article 46 or create new agreements or arrangements pursuant to Article 59. In disposing of confiscated illicit wealth, Article 57 UNCAC sets forth modifications to the *locus regit actum* rule.[46] Amongst other things, UNCAC state parties are to give 'priority consideration' to '[the] retur[n] of confiscated property to the requesting State Party, [the] retur[n] [of] such property to its prior legitimate owners or [the] compensati[on] [of] the victims of the crime'.[47] Article 53 is an obligation on each state party to permit other state parties to bring civil actions

[42] Convention on Money Laundering, the Confiscation, Search and Seizure of the Proceeds of Crime 1990, Strasbourg, 8 November 1990, in force 1 September 1993, 1862 UNTS 69, 141 ETS; Council of Europe Convention on Laundering, Search, Seizure and Confiscation of the Proceeds from Crime and on the Financing of Terrorism, Warsaw, 16 May 2005, in force 1 May 2008, 198 ETS.

[43] Council Framework Decision 2003/577/JHA of 22 July 2003, on the execution in the European Union of orders freezing property or evidence [2003] OJ L196, 45, Arts 1 and 5(1); Council Framework Decisions 2006/783/JHA of 6 October 2006, on the application of the principle of mutual recognition to confiscation orders [2006] OJ L328, 59, Arts 6–7; Council Decision 2007/845/JHA of 6 December 2007, concerning cooperation between Asset Recovery Offices of the Member States in the field of tracing and identification of proceeds from, or other property related to crime [2007] OJ L332, 103, Arts 1(1) and 3(1); Directive 2014/42/EU of the European Parliament and of the Council of 3 April 2014, on the freezing and confiscation of instrumentalities and proceeds of crime in the European Union [2014] OJ L127, 39.

[44] African Union Convention on Preventing and Combating Corruption, Maputo, 11 July 2003, in force 5 August 2006, (2004) 43 International Legal Materials 1, Arts 16(1)(b), 18(1); Inter-American Convention against Corruption, Caracas, 29 March 1996, in force 6 March 1997, (1996) 25 International Legal Materials 724, Art XV(1); Protocol Against Corruption to the Treaty of the Southern African Development Community, Blantyre, 14 August 2001, in force 6 July 2005, Arts 8(1)(a) and 8(4), available at www.sadc.int/about-sadc/overview/sa-protocols. See also Inter-America Convention on Mutual Assistance in Criminal Matters, Nassau, 23 May 1992, in force 14 April 1996, OASTS 75; Protocol on Mutual Legal Assistance in Criminal Matters to the Treaty of the Southern African Development Community (SADC-MLAP), Luanda, 3 October 2002, in force 1 March 2007, Art 22(1), available at www.sadc.int/about-sadc/overview/sa-protocols.

[45] Ivory (n 2) 104–05, 115 and 125–26.

[46] G Stessens, *Money Laundering: A New International Law Enforcement Model* (Cambridge, Cambridge University Press, 2000), 416–18.

[47] UNCAC, Art 57(3)(c).

so as to establish proprietary interests in proceeds and to enable domestic civil law courts to award the corresponding remedies.[48]

But, for all its prominence, the term 'asset recovery' is not expressly defined in the UNCAC and has two implicit definitions in the convention, as I have argued elsewhere.[49] Firstly and narrowly, asset recovery is a set of legal processes by which states use each other's coercive powers to obtain or regain ownership of proceeds and objects of corruption or substitute assets. This meaning is borne out in the statement of principle in Article 51, the substantive provisions on co-operative confiscation and civil suits by foreign sovereigns in chapter V, and some subsequent usage by interested states and international organisations.[50] Later drafts of the UNCAC defined 'recovery of assets' tellingly as:

> the procedure for the transfer or conveyance of all the property or assets, their proceeds or revenue, acquired through acts of corruption covered by this Convention from the receiving State Party where the assets are located to the affected State Party, even if they have been transformed, converted or disguised.[51]

Secondly and more broadly, asset recovery is the dual goal of preventing senior public officials, their relatives and close associates from moving corruption-related assets through the international financial system, as well as enabling victim states to regain or obtain assets or substitute items that are moved abroad.[52] This second meaning is apparent from the remaining articles of chapter V, which require states to establish regulatory regimes for suspicious transaction reporting.[53] Financial institutions are to know their customers and to exercise varying levels of diligence in managing high-value accounts and high-level account holders.[54] To this end, governments have duties to advise financial institutions of the people, deposits and transactions that attract additional attention.[55] Banks must be required to keep the appropriate records and officials may be obliged to disclose their finances and foreign account holdings.[56] States are to prohibit the establishment of 'shell banks' in their territories;[57] they are to consider empowering financial intelligence units to receive and analyse suspicious transaction reports and, perhaps, to exchange information spontaneously.[58] An overall purpose of the Convention is to 'promote,

[48] For a discussion of civil law causes of action and Art 53, see E van der Willebois and P Brun, 'Using Civil Remedies in Corruption and Asset Recovery Cases' [2013] *Case Western Reserve Journal of International Law* 615.

[49] Ivory (n 2) 22–29.

[50] Ivory (n 2) 27–28, 124.

[51] Ad hoc Committee, Revised Draft UNCAC A/AC.261/3/Rev3–A/AC.261/3/Rev5, each at Art 2(p).

[52] Ivory (n 2) 23–27. See also I Carr and R Jago, 'Corruption, the United Nations Convention against Corruption ("UNCAC") and Asset Recovery' in King and Walker, *Dirty Assets* (n 7) 211–16.

[53] See also UNCAC, Art 14; Carr and Jago (ibid) 219–23.

[54] UNCAC, Art 52(1).

[55] UNCAC, Art 52(2).

[56] UNCAC, Art 52(3), (5)–(6).

[57] UNCAC, Art 52(4).

[58] UNCAC, Art 56, 58.

facilitate and support international cooperation and technical assistance in the prevention of and the fight against corruption including in asset recovery'.[59]

On either definition, asset recovery is a topic not just of the UNCAC, but also of other international standards on transnational crime, financial sector 'integrity', and international co-operation in judicial and administrative matters.[60] The United Nations Convention against Illicit Traffic in Narcotic Drugs and Psychotropic Substances (UNCATND) provides the basic template for the UNCAC's confiscation provisions and its offence of money laundering.[61] The UNTOC then provides much of the wording for the UNCAC's detailed rules on international co-operation for the purposes of confiscation and mutual legal assistance.[62] The combination of repressive (enforcement) and preventive measures is likewise familiar from the UNTOC and the recommendations of the Financial Action Task Force (FATF) on money laundering. It would appear that the Task Force borrowed from the Basel Committee on Banking Supervision (BCBS) and the Wolfsberg Group of financial institutions, which in turn drew on models from national law.[63] Now, all three soft law standard setters require extra care when banks commence or review relationships with 'politically exposed persons' (PEPs).[64] Within Europe, the fourth EU Money Laundering Directive makes similar measures international 'hard' law.[65] Even Article 57 UNCAC has a parallel in Article 14 UNTOC on 'disposal of confiscated proceeds of crime or property', although it departs from the

[59] UNCAC, Art 1(b).

[60] Ivory (n 2) chs 2.2 and 4. On the relationship between international corruption and money laundering controls, see generally I Carr and M Goldby, 'Recovering the Proceeds of Corruption: UNCAC and Anti-Money Laundering Standards' [2011] *Journal of Business Law* 170, 179–87; D Chaiken and J Sharman, *Corruption and Money Laundering: A Symbiotic Relationship, Palgrave Series on Asian Governance* (New York, Palgrave Macmillan, 2009) ch 1.

[61] UNCATND, Arts 1(f), (l), (p) and (q), 2(b) and 5(1) and (2); UNCAC, Arts 2(d)–(g), 23 and 31(1) and (2). See also UNODC (n 36) paras 403 and 422.

[62] UNTOC, Arts 13 and 18; UNCAC, Art 46, 55.

[63] A Flohr, *Self-Regulation and Legalization: Making Global Rules for Banks and Corporations* (Houndmills, Palgrave Macmillan, 2014), 101–02, 116–19; A Jakobi, 'The OECD and Crime: The Fight against Corruption and Money Laundering' in K Martens and A Jakobi (eds), *Mechanisms of OECD Governance: International Incentives for National Policy-Making* (Oxford, Oxford University Press, 2010) 149–50; M Pieth, 'International Standards against Money Laundering' in M Pieth and G Aiolfi (eds), *A Comparative Guide to Anti-Money Laundering: A Critical Analysis of Systems in Singapore, Switzerland, the UK and the USA* (Cheltenham, Edward Elgar, 2004) 6–10, 24–27 and 32; P Reuter and E Truman, *Chasing Dirty Money: The Fight against Money Laundering* (Washington, DC, Institute for International Economics, 2004), ch 4, esp Table 4.1.

[64] BCBS, 'Sound Management of Risks Related to Money Laundering and Financing of Terrorism' (2014), available at www.bis.org/publ/bcbs275.htm; FATF, 'International Standards on Combating Money Laundering and the Financing of Terrorism & Proliferation: The FATF Recommendations' (2012) Pt D, Glossary, available at www.fatf-gafi.org (FATF Recommendations); The Wolfsberg Group, 'Wolfsberg Anti-Money Laundering Principles for Private Banking' (2012) para 2.3, available at www.wolfsberg-principles.com/pdf/standards/Wolfsberg-Private-Banking-Prinicples-May-2012.pdf.

[65] Directive EU 2015/849 of the European Parliament and of the Council of 20 May 2015 on the prevention of the use of the financial system for the purpose of money laundering and terrorist financing, amending Regulation (EU) No 648/2012 of the European Parliament and of the Council, and repealing Directive 2005/60/EC of the European Parliament and of the Council and Commission Directive 2006/70/EC [2015] OJ L 141/73, Arts 3(9)–(11), 20–23.

rule that the requested state determines the allocation of confiscated assets *locus regit actum*.[66] There is a rough analogue to Article 53 UNCAC, too, in the CoE's Civil Law Convention against Corruption.[67]

II. Asset Recovery: The Anecdotal Report Card

From the above, it is clear that the challenge of asset recovery is not the challenge of convincing states that corruption is a problem worthy of global regulation, nor is it the novelty of asset recovery rules in international law. To the contrary, the number and diversity of anti-corruption and AML instruments would seem to demonstrate an international consensus on the criminal nature of corruption-related money laundering and the need for international co-operation in the prevention and reversal of related illicit financial flows. The anti-corruption treaties are widely and diversely subscribed, moreover, and reinforced by a network of bilateral and multilateral agreements on MLA.[68] Through overlapping 'peer review' processes, states have agreed to police each other's efforts to implement the OECD, UN, FATF and regional standards: a standard-setting and review process now also takes place among the Group of 20 (G20).[69] To 'encourage and facilitate more systematic and timely return of assets stolen by politically exposed persons through acts of corruption', the World Bank and the UNODC established StAR.[70] Avowedly not engaged in case work,[71] StAR researches and campaigns on the issue of asset recovery, 'raising awareness', 'building capacity' and 'facilitat[ing]' 'collaboration

[66] UNODC (n 36) para 673.

[67] L Low, 'The United Nations Convention against Corruption: The Globalization of Anti-Corruption Standards' ('The Awakening Giant of Anticorruption Enforcement' conference, London, 4–5 May 2006), available at www.steptoe.com/assets/attachments/2599.pdf.

[68] See, eg, UN General Assembly Resolution 54/117, Model Treaty on Mutual Assistance in Criminal Matters, UN Doc A/RES/45/117 (3 April 1991), subsequently amended by GA Resolution 53/112, Mutual Assistance and International Cooperation in Criminal Matters, UN Doc A/53/112 (20 January 1999); see further Ivory (n 2), 134–35.

[69] 2015–16 G20 Anti-Corruption Action Plan, available at https://g20.org/wp-content/uploads/2014/12/2015-16%20_g20_anti-corruption_action_plan_0.pdf. See generally H Jorgensen, 'Hard Graft: The G20 and Anti-Corruption' (2013) *G20 Monitor* No 6, available at www.lowyinstitute.org/files/g20_monitor_october_2013.pdf. See also M Larionova and J Kirton, 'G7/8 and G20 Accountability' in M Larionova and J Kirton (eds), *The G8–G20 Relationship in Global Governance* (Farnham, Ashgate Publishing, 2015), 220.

[70] World Bank and UN Office on Drugs and Crime (UNODC), 'Partnership Charter' (7 November 2008), para 4, available at http://star.worldbank.org/star/sites/star/files/StAR_Partnership_Charter_1_0.pdf.

[71] cp the International Centre for Asset Recovery (ICAR) at the Basel Institute on Governance, 'Asset Recovery/ICAR', website available at www.baselgovernance.org/themes/icar ('ICAR assists national enforcement authorities in partner countries with handling concrete and complex international corruption and/or money laundering cases with an asset recovery angle').

and dialogue' among supporting states.[72] Corruption and illicit financial flows have also become issues of concern within the UN human rights system, with the Human Rights Council passing several resolutions on 'the negative impact of the non-repatriation of funds of illicit origin' and tasking an Independent Expert on the effects of foreign debt to investigate the issue.[73] More recently still, states have committed to 'significantly reduc[ing] illicit financial and arms flows, [and] strengthen[ing] the recovery and return of stolen assets and combat all forms of organized crime' by 2030 as a step towards achieving the 2015 Sustainable Development Goals.[74]

There is some anecdotal evidence that states have changed their behaviour to comply with the international asset recovery rules. In the words of StAR, 'Countries with established asset recovery policies and solid legal and institutional frameworks continue to achieve success in returning the proceeds of corruption'.[75] Surveying 34 OECD states for the period 2010–12, StAR cites an increase in the total volume of assets frozen since its first report of 2006–09, as well as consistency in the amounts returned over its two reporting periods.[76] Within the group of asset recovery 'active' jurisdictions, the USA, the UK and Switzerland are singled out for praise.[77] Their efforts account for more than 95 per cent of the amounts frozen and all of the assets returned by the surveyed countries between 2010 and 2012.[78] Prominent recent actions concern the so-called 'Arab Spring' states and Ukraine.[79] Giving further weight to those figures, the USA, the UK and

[72] World Bank and UNODC, 'StAR Partnership Charter', paras 6–8 and 33(iii) and 'Our Work', available at http://star.worldbank.org/star/about-us/our-work.

[73] See, eg, The Negative Impact of the Non-repatriation of Funds of Illicit Origin on the Enjoyment of Human Rights, Final report of the Independent Expert on the effects of foreign debt and other related international financial obligations of States on the full enjoyment of all human rights, particularly economic, social and cultural rights, C Lumina, UN Doc A/HRC/25/52 (7 May 2014); Resolution adopted by the Human Rights Council 28/5, 'The Negative Impact of the Non-repatriation of Funds of Illicit Origin to the Countries of Origin on the Enjoyment of Human Rights, and the Importance of Improving International Cooperation', A/HRC/RES/28/5 (10 April 2015).

[74] UN General Assembly, 'Draft Outcome Document of the United Nations Summit for the Adoption of the Post-2015 Development Agenda', A/69/L.85 (12 August 2015) Annex, Goal 16.4. See also Busan Partnership for Effective Development Co-operation, 'Fourth High Level Forum on Aid Effectiveness, Busan, Republic of Korea' (9 November–1 December 2011) para 33(b), available at www.oecd.org/dac/effectiveness/49650173.pdf.

[75] L Gray et al, *The Hard Facts on Stolen Asset Recovery* (Washington, DC, The International Bank for Reconstruction and Development (IBRD)/World Bank and Organisation for Economic Cooperation and Development (OECD), 2014) 2, available at http://star.worldbank.org/star/publication/few-and-far-hard-facts-stolen-asset-recovery.

[76] ibid 1–2 and 18–23.

[77] Gray et al (n 75) 18–22.

[78] Gray et al (n 75) 19.

[79] There are others. See, eg, B Hope and T Wright, 'Malaysia Fund 1MDB's Missing Money Problem Grows', *Wall Street Journal*, 18 September 2015, available at www.wsj.com/articles/malaysia-fund-1mdbs-missing-money-problem-grows-1442547656?mod=trending_now_1; C Fellstrom and P Peachey, 'Ex-Prime Minister of Mauritius under Investigation by UK

Switzerland host major financial centres and are favoured sites for investment and spending by (ultra-)high-net-worth individuals.[80] Each of these governments has established special initiatives and strategies for asset recovery[81] and, in the case of Switzerland, a special-purpose asset recovery law.[82] At the diplomatic level, the USA led the drafting of chapter V UNCAC along with Peru;[83] the UK lobbied the G8 for so-called 'beneficial ownership' rules;[84] and Switzerland championed StAR (and asset recovery) with a series of international conferences and meetings.[85]

All that said, the practice of asset recovery does not yet conform to the ideal in the UNCAC, even among the few countries that are engaged in the cause. According to StAR, the 'US$147.2 million … returned by OECD members between 2010 and June 2012, and US$276.3 million between 2006 and 2009, [is] a fraction of the $20–40 billion estimated to have been stolen each year'.[86] The UN's Independent

Anti-Corruption Unit', *The Independent*, 4 October 2015, available at www.independent.co.uk/news/uk/crime/ex-prime-minister-of-mauritius-under-investigation-by-uk-anti-corruption-unit-a6679111.html. On the 2016 US civil forfeiture complaints, see US Department of Justice, 'United States Seeks to Recover More Than $1 Billion Obtained from Corruption Involving Malaysian Sovereign Wealth Fund' (press release) (20 July 2016), available at www.justice.gov/opa/pr/united-states-seeks-recover-more-1-billion-obtained-corruption-involving-malaysian-sovereign.

[80] JC Sharman, *The Despot's Guide to Wealth Management: On the International Campaign against Grand Corruption* (Ithaca, Cornell University Press, forthcoming) Introduction.

[81] US Department of Justice, 'Attorney General Holder at the African Union Summit, Kampala Uganda, Sunday, July 25, 2010' (press release), available at www.justice.gov/opa/speech/attorney-general-holder-african-union-summit (announcing the establishment of the 'Kleptocracy Asset Recovery Initiative'); Department for International Development and The Rt Hon Justine Greening MP, 'New Crime Unit to Investigate Corruption Affecting Developing Countries' (press release) (9 August 2015), available at www.gov.uk/government/news/new-crime-unit-to-investigate-corruption-affecting-developing-countries. See also Federal Department of Foreign Affairs of the Swiss Confederation (FDFA), 'Illicitly acquired assets (PEPs)' (website), available at www.eda.admin.ch/eda/en/fdfa/foreign-policy/financial-centre-economy/illicit-assets-pep.html (referring to an 'FDFA Task Force Asset Recovery' as the point for further information).

[82] *Bundesgetz über die Rückerstattung unrechtmässig erworbener Vermögenswerte politisch exponierter Personen (RuVG) vom 1. Oktober 2010 (Stand am 1. Februar 2011)* (SR 196.1), available in unofficial English translation at www.eda.admin.ch/eda/en/fdfa/foreign-policy/financial-centre-economy/illicit-assets-pep/praevention.html. See further, Schweizerischer Bundesrat, *Botschaft zum Bundesgesetz über die Rückerstattung unrechtmässig erworbener Vermögenswerte politisch exponierter Personen (RuVG)* (28 April 2010) Annex 1, available in unofficial English translation at www.eda.admin.ch/eda/en/home/topics/finec/poexp.html (Dispatch on the RIAA).

[83] Informal Preparatory Meeting of the Ad Hoc Committee for the Negotiation of a Convention against Corruption Buenos Aires, 4–7 December 2001, Proposals and Contributions Received from Governments, UN Docs A/AC.261/IPM/11 (12 November 2001) and A/AC.261/IPM/19 (3 December 2001). See also Sharman (n 80) USA chapter.

[84] Prime Minister's Office, 'G8 Action Plan Principles to Prevent the Misuse of Companies and Legal Arrangements' (policy paper) (18 June 2003), available at www.gov.uk/government/publications/g8-action-plan-principles-to-prevent-the-misuse-of-companies-and-legal-arrangements.

[85] See, eg, FDFA, 'Federal Councillor Calmy-Rey Attends International Conference on the Restitution of Illegal Assets in Paris' (4 June 2010), available at www.eda.admin.ch/eda/en/home/recent/media.html; 'Restitution of Illicit Assets in the Context of the Arab Spring: Meeting of Experts in Lausanne (press release) (4 January 2012), available at www.news.admin.ch/message/index.html?lang=en&msg-id=43127.

[86] Gray et al (n 75) 2 and 18–23.

Expert cited estimated repatriation rates of about two per cent.[87] The continued detection of PEP wealth in financial centres also indicates ongoing difficulties with corporate or national systems for discouraging and identifying inflows to financial institutions.[88] Crunching the numbers for the FATF and FATF-style body reports, StAR calculated that only three of 124 jurisdictions were 'fully compliant' with Recommendation 6 (as it then was) on enhanced due diligence for PEPs.[89] These findings are—to some extent—corroborated by regulators. In 2015, HM Treasury found persistent problems of careless bank 'onboarding' of high-risk PEPs, as well as intelligence gaps with respect to 'high-end' money laundering risks.[90] The Swiss were somewhat more sanguine about their banks' performance in their first inter-agency report of the same year.[91] Global Witness, a non-government organisation (NGO), criticises the UK and Switzerland for the low level of corporate penalties for banks that breach AML regulations with respect to PEPs. It also points out that apparently impressive fines in the USA are actually sums paid to defer prosecution or avoid indictment.[92] Individual executives are not prosecuted and banks avoid the stigma of criminal sanctions, if not the financial effects of penalties.

[87] Human Rights Council, The Negative Impact of the Non-repatriation of Funds of Illicit Origin on the Enjoyment of Human Rights, Interim report by the Independent Expert on the effects of foreign debt and other related international financial obligations of States on the full enjoyment of all human rights, particularly economic, social and cultural rights, Cephas Lumina, UN Doc A/HRC/22/42 (21 February 2013) para 15.

[88] See, eg, the acerbic commentary on the Swiss in the German financial press: Frankfurter Allgemeine Zeitung, 'Das Sündenregister der Schweizer Banken', *Frankfurter Allgemeine Zeitung*, 23 May 2014, available at www.faz.net/-gqe-7pj5v ('Inzwischen rühmen sich die Eidgenossen ihres strikten Geldwäschgesetzes und der Potentatenbekämfung. Doch sobald ein Diktator irgendwo auf der Welt seine Macht verliert, stellt sich noch immer oft heraus, dass er in der Schweiz ein Vermögen bunkert. Im Kontensperren von Despoten hat das Land mittlerweile Routine').

[89] T Greenberg et al, *Politically Exposed Persons: Preventative Measures for the Banking Sector* (Washington, DC, IBRD/World Bank, 2010), available at http://star.worldbank.org/star/sites/star/files/Politically%20Exposed%20Persons_0.pdf, 7.

[90] HM Treasury and HM Home Office, *UK National Risk Assessment of Money Laundering and Terrorist Financing* (2015), available at www.gov.uk/government/uploads/system/uploads/attachment_data/file/468210/UK_NRA_October_2015_final_web.pdf, Executive Summary, 9, paras 6.7 and 6.31. See also Financial Services Authority, 'Banks' Management of High Money-Laundering Risk Situations' (2011), available at www.fsa.gov.uk/pubs/other/aml_final_report.pdf. See also United States Senate, Permanent Subcommittee on Investigations, Committee on Homeland Security and Governmental Affairs, 'Keeping Foreign Corruption out of the United States: Four Case Histories' (2010), available at www.hsgac.senate.gov/download/report-psi-staff-report-keeping-foreign-corruption-out-of-the-united-states-four-case-histories.

[91] Interdepartementalen Koordinationsgruppe zur Bekämpfung der Geldwäscherei und der Terrorismusfinanzierung (KGGT), *Schweizerische Eidgenossenschaft, Bericht über die nationale Beurteilung der Geldwäschereiund Terrorismusfinanzierungsrisiken in der Schweiz* (2015) 5, 62 and 67, available at www.news.admin.ch/NSBSubscriber/message/attachments/42572.pdf (identifying increased exposure to high-risk PEPs as a risk factor for 'universal' banks, but finding that those institutions contributed to the efficient minimisation of AML or counter-terrorist financing (CTF) risks in Switzerland with its risk-based system of regulation).

[92] Global Witness, 'Banks and Dirty Money: How the Financial System Enables State Looting at a Devastating Human Cost' (2015) 16–17, available at www.globalwitness.org/reports/banks-and-dirty-money.

Co-operative processes for asset restraint and confiscation are questionable as the main mode for recovering illicit wealth.[93] In Switzerland, unilateral executive freezes are routinely used to prevent the dissipation of assets ahead of MLA requests or domestic criminal investigations.[94] Such measures have a precedent in economic sanctions 'targeted' to prevent breaches of international peace and national security; however, they are not easily read into the UNCAC or the related MLA treaties. As for the returns themselves, unilateral NCB confiscation proceedings and AML prosecutions resulted in repatriations from the USA and the UK to Nigeria, Nicaragua, Peru and pre-Maidan Ukraine.[95] Settlements and supervised asset repatriation processes have been important but controversial parts of Swiss and US asset recovery practice.[96] There have also been some notable co-operative confiscation failures. In 2009, Switzerland lifted a freeze that it had imposed with respect to Zaire's Mobutu Seso Seko due to the expiry of the statute of limitations.[97] The Restitution of Illicit Asset Act (RIAA) was introduced to enable the repatriation of funds to Haiti, a state where weak institutions were judged to have stymied confiscation and co-operation in criminal matters.[98] So far, the 'Lex Duvalier' has not helped the Swiss to respond to the Arab Spring, despite the fact that some Egyptian and Tunisian convictions and confiscation orders have been annulled.[99] A proposal for a broader asset recovery law (the so-called 'Lex Ben Ali') has encountered opposition from lawyers and liberal/conservative politicians, who claim that it is contrary to the Swiss principles of legality, due process and property.[100]

[93] See also Gray et al (n 75) 2 and 26–28.

[94] Ivory (n 2) 38–55.

[95] Nichols (n 26); Sharman (n 80) ch UK and USA.

[96] N Ridadu, 'Challenges and Opportunities of Asset Recovery in a Developing Economy' in Pieth, *Recovering Stolen Assets* (n 29), 36 (disputing Switzerland's authority to insist on World Bank monitoring of returned Abacha); I Jimu, 'Managing the Proceeds of Asset Recovery: The Case of Nigeria, Peru, the Philippines and Kazakhstan' (2009) Basel Institute on Governance Working Paper Series No 6, available at www.baselgovernance.org/fileadmin/docs/publications/working_papers/Managing_Prodceeds_of_AR_Final.pdf (questioning the effectiveness of monitoring procedures).

[97] Federal Department of Foreign Affairs of the Swiss Confederation, 'Switzerland is Forced to Unfreeze Mobutu Assets' (press release) (16 July 2009), available at www.swissinfo.ch/eng/politics/Switzerland_forced_to_unfreeze_Mobutu_assets.html?cid=986866.

[98] Schweizerischer Bundesrat (n 82) Annex 1, 22.

[99] T Amara, 'Tunisian Court Annuls Confiscation of Ousted President's Assets', *Reuters*, 10 June 2015, available at www.reuters.com/article/2015/06/10/us-tunisia-corruption-idUSKBN0OQ19A20150610; B Bruppacher, 'Bundesanwalt Lauber krebst zurück', *Neue Zürcher Zeitung*, 22 June 2015, available at www.nzz.ch/schweiz/bundesanwalt-lauber-krebst-zurueck-1.18567077.

[100] A Burri, 'Bürgerliche fordern mehr Rechtsschutz für Ex-Dictatoren', *Tages Anzeiger*, 5 June 2015, available at www.tagesanzeiger.ch/schweiz/standard/Buergerliche-fordern-mehr-Rechtsschutz-fuer-ExDiktatoren--/story/13940787; 'Nationalrat schwächt "Lex Ben Ali" ab', *Neue Zürcher Zeitung*, 10 June 2015, available at www.nzz.ch/schweiz/nationalrat-schwaecht-lex-ben-ali-ab-1.18559390. See also F Meyer, 'Auch Potentaten haben Rechte', *Neue Zürcher Zeitung* (28 June 2015) available at www.nzz.ch/meinung/kommentare/die-rechte-von-potentaten-ld.791. The *Bundesgesetz über die Sperrung und die Rückerstattung unrechtmässig erworbener Vermögenswerte ausländischer politisch exponierter Personen* (SRVG) was passed on 18 December 2015 and entered into force on 1 July 2016.

III. The First Dimension: Barriers to Recovery

The difficulties experienced by co-operating states are presented by global policy makers as 'barriers' to asset recovery.[101] Roughly defined, these are the laws, practices and attitudes that inhibit the restraint and ultimate transfer of illicit wealth by the haven state to the victim country—and result in its release to individual PEPs or associated beneficiaries. Presenting the findings of research obtained through the Swiss-led 'Lausanne Process', StAR names the 'key impediment' as weak 'political will': 'a lack of a comprehensive, sustained, and concerted policy or strategy to identify asset recovery as a priority and to ensure alignment of objectives, tools, and resources to this end'.[102] StAR then identifies 29 specific factors, which it discusses in three groups.[103]

The first set of 'general barriers and institutional issues' covers matters like mistrust between national authorities due to cultural differences or past political disputes, deficient resourcing and weak political support for the preventative and reparative goals of asset return.[104] Lax enforcement of AML and counter-terrorist financing laws appear under this heading, with both financial institutions and regulators being named as underperforming institutions.[105] Secondly, under 'legal barriers and requirements that delay assistance' are a host of mainly procedural obligations that are judged to impede the removal of wealth, through MLA processes or otherwise, or to increase the time taken to restrain or achieve 'returns'. Non-conviction and value-based confiscation laws figure on this wish list, as do longer statutes of limitation and executive powers to restrain assets and exchange information, independently of criminal charges and MLA requests.[106] StAR has elsewhere advocated the criminalisation of illicit enrichment, as well as asset reporting systems for public officials and related parties.[107] The third group

[101] K Stephenson et al, *Barriers to Asset Recovery: An Analysis of the Key Barriers and Recommendations for Action* (Washington, DC, IBRD/World Bank Group, 2011). See also A Suarez-Martinez, 'Closing Down the Safe Havens: Ending Impunity for Corrupt Individuals by Seizing and Recovering their Assets in the UK' (Transparency International UK, 2013), available at www.transparency.org.uk/publications/closing-down-the-safe-havens; M Pieth, 'Preface: Are We Recovering Any Assets Yet?' in G Fenner-Zinkernagel, C Montieth and P Gomes Pereira (eds), *Emerging Trends in Asset Recovery* (Bern, Peter Lang, 2013); Resolution adopted by the General Assembly on 18 December 2014, 69/199: Preventing and Combating Corrupt Practices and the Transfer of Proceeds of Corruption, Facilitating Asset Recovery and Returning such Assets to Legitimate Owners, in Particular to Countries of Origin, in Accordance with the United Nations Convention against Corruption, UN Doc A/RES/69/199 (5 February 2015) para 15.

[102] Stephenson et al (ibid) 3.

[103] Stephenson et al (n 101) 16–17.

[104] Stephenson et al (n 101) Barrier 1, 2.

[105] Stephenson et al (n 101) Barrier 4, esp 33.

[106] Stephenson et al (n 101) Barriers 10, 14–15 and 17.

[107] L Muzila et al, *On the Take: Criminalizing Illicit Enrichment to Fight Corruption* (Washington, DC, IBRD/World Bank Group, 2012); StAR, *Public Office, Private Interests: Accountability through Income and Asset Disclosure* (Washington, DC, IBRD/World Bank Group, 2012), both available at https://star.worldbank.org/star/?q=publications&keys=&sort_by=field_date_value&sort_order=DESC&items_per_page=20.

of 'operational barriers and communication issues' frustrate the utilisation of otherwise sound asset recovery laws by well-intended practitioners: they necessitate two broad sets of reforms. States are encouraged to provide their operational staff with discretions in applying existing MLA requirements, on the one hand; on the other, they are to establish clear chains of command, publicise financial and legal information, and enhance access to their justice systems for less well-resourced countries.[108]

StAR's barriers to recovery reflect the regulatory approach of the anti-corruption treaties, as exemplified by the UNCAC. First, to encourage states to implement (comply with) the treaty terms, the UNCAC establishes a Conference of State Parties (COSP), which it empowers to promote the exchange of information between states and to create an 'appropriate mechanism or body to assist in the effective implementation of the Convention', if necessary.[109] Secondly, to help states to restrain and remove illicit wealth, the UNCAC foresees a series of changes to the grounds for restraining and confiscating assets and assessing requests for assistance.[110] Offenders may be 'require[d] … [to] demonstrate the lawful origin of … property liable to confiscation' under Article 31(8) and public officials may be required to explain significant increases in assets—or face conviction for illicit enrichment pursuant to Article 20.[111] Further, confiscation may occur without conviction pursuant to optional Article 54(1)(c) 'in cases in which the offender cannot be prosecuted by reason of death, flight or absence or in other appropriate cases'. Thirdly, other 'operational' barriers are addressed in chapters IV, VI and VII on international co-operation, technical assistance and treaty implementation, respectively. Anticipating the divergence in labelling of UNCAC crimes in domestic law, Article 43(2) deems the requirement of dual criminality to be fulfilled whenever offences are substantively congruent.[112] Then, foreseeing divergent capacities for implementation, Article 62(2)(c) requires state parties to assist 'developing countries and countries with economies in transition' with the treaty implementation. 'To that end, State Parties shall endeavour to make adequate and regular voluntary contributions to an account specifically designated for that purpose in a United Nations funding mechanism.'[113]

In short, for actors like StAR and the drafters of the UNCAC, the challenge of returning wealth to victim countries in grand corruption cases is the challenge of persuading state officials (and non-state 'gatekeepers') to comply with their existing legal obligations—and to adopt other laws and practices that promote the goal

[108] Stephenson et al (n 101) 107–11.

[109] UNCAC, Art 63(7).

[110] Stephenson et al (n 101) 103–07 (recommendations to Barriers 7–20).

[111] UNODC (n 36) para 297.

[112] See also UNCAC, Art 46(9) (requiring that state parties, 'in responding to a request for assistance pursuant to this article in the absence of dual criminality, take into account the purposes of this Convention, as set forth in article 1').

[113] UNCAC, Art 62(2)(c).

of asset return. It is presumed that high-level senior public officials are broadly committed to implementing chapter V; however, they have failed to garner sufficient domestic political support to ensure compliance with international asset recovery standards by the states as legal entities. Operational staff are similarly well intentioned, but lack the information, resources and/or discretions to identify and exploit opportunities for return. Fundamental rights must be respected, but parochial constructions of criminal procedures, international co-operation and immunity rules may unduly inhibit asset recovery and the related objectives of development and (democratic) political control.[114] In the conditions of global economic integration, there is a perceived risk that individual guarantees will be rendered inimitable to the common good. Rather than protecting vulnerable people and their livelihoods from autocratic authorities, they protect unaccountable leaders and economic actors from the developmental objectives of the people.

IV. The Second Dimension: Human Rights

In this way, the first challenge of asset recovery for global public policy makers becomes the second challenge of asset recovery for public international lawyers. States have duties to prevent and suppress corruption, as well as to ensure the equal protection 'of individuals vis-à-vis the state, … [in their] fundamental characteristics [as] human person[s] and … [in their] dignity in peacetime and in times of armed conflict'.[115] Limitations based on a person's location or alleged crime (or association with a sort of alleged criminal) sit uneasily with the notions of universal and inalienable entitlements and individual guilt. Measures that enhance confiscation would seem to jeopardise legal certainty and proportionality for instrumental ends.[116] Through acts of co-operation in criminal matters, states coerce people who do not help choose the authorising norm in the haven state and who may contest the political neutrality of procedures or measures in the victim country. Yet, corruption would itself seem to place a range of human rights at risk. Some acts of corruption simultaneously infringe civil and political liberties, whilst others motivate or enable separate abuses against property, political participation

[114] See also V Pujas, 'Immunity and Extradition: Obstacles to Justice' in R Hodess et al (eds), *Transparency International: Global Corruption Report 2004* (London, Pluto Press, 2004).

[115] W Kälin and J Künzli, *The Law of International Human Rights Protection* (Oxford, Oxford University Press, 2009) 32.

[116] J Boucht, 'Extended Confiscation and the Proposed Directive on Freezing and Confiscation of Criminal Proceeds in the EU: On Striking a Balance between Efficiency, Fairness and Legal Certainty' (2013) 21 *European Journal of Crime, Criminal Law and Criminal Justice* 127; C King, 'Civil Forfeiture and Article 6 of the ECHR: Due Process Implications for England & Wales and Ireland' (2014) 34 *Legal Studies* 371; M Simonato, 'Directive 2014/42/EU and Non-Conviction Based Confiscation: A Step Forward on Asset Recovery?' (2015) 6 *New Journal of European Criminal Law* 213.

and bodily integrity.[117] If imputed to a state, corrupt acts may constitute failures in national duties to progressively achieve full realisation of social, economic and cultural guarantees.[118] Corruption is often described as discriminatory and regressive, since the poor and otherwise marginalised tend to be more reliant on public services and least able to pay surcharges in the form of bribes.[119] Moreover, when committed on a large scale, corruption has been characterised as a threat to collective rights of self-determination, permanent sovereignty over wealth and resources, and development.[120] States have existing duties to co-operate in the realisation of these global norms; asset recovery appears to be a logical extension of these obligations.[121]

Thus, in committing themselves to enabling asset recovery, as foreseen by the anti-corruption treaties, states seem to place themselves in a position of conflict between their international duties.[122] They have discretion to adapt their confiscation and MLA laws to their fundamental legal principles, domestic laws and legal systems under the anti-corruption treaties. Relying on such provisions, national institutions may pre-empt or resolve any conflicts (or 'tensions') by reference to constitutional rules or principles of statutory interpretation.[123] However, international human rights standards are not an express constraint on implementation or co-operation in the UNCAC.[124] In fact, the UN has described the confiscation provisions in the narcotics trafficking convention as 'deliberately draconian' and

[117] See, eg, M Boersma, *Corruption: A Violation of Human Rights and a Crime under International Law?* (Cambridge, Intersentia, 2012); C Raj Kumar, *Corruption and Human Rights in India: Comparative Perspectives on Transparency and Good Governance* (New Delhi, Oxford University Press, 2011) 42–43: International Council on Human Rights Policy (ICHRP) and Transparency International, 'Corruption and Human Rights: Making the Connection' (report) (2009), available at www.ichrp.org/en/projects/131; A Peters, 'Korruption und Menchschenrechten' [2015] *Juristen-Zeitung*, English version available at http://ssrn.com/abstract=2635443, 5; K Olaniyan, *Corruption and Human Rights Law in Africa* (Oxford, Hart Publishing, 2014) 202–46; M Robinson, 'Corruption and Human Rights' in Hodess et al (n 114). See also AB Spalding, 'Corruption, Corporations, and the New Human Right' (2013) 91 *Washington University Law Review* 1365.

[118] ICHRP and Transparency International (ibid) 46–47; Olaniyan (ibid), 201 and 246–58.

[119] See, eg, ICHRP and Transparency International, (n 117) 7–10; Olaniyan (n 117) 199–200; Peters (n 117) 17.

[120] N Kofele-Kale, *The International Law of Responsibility for Economic Crimes: Holding State Officials Individually Liable for Acts of Fraudulent Enrichment*, 2nd edn (Aldershot, Ashgate Publishing, 2006) 107–11; Kumar (n 117) 54–57; Olaniyan (n 117) 295–303. See also A/HRC/RES/28/5 (n 73) Preamble.

[121] A/HRC/25/52 (n 73) paras 35–41.

[122] N Kofel-Kale, *Combating Economic Crimes: Balancing Competing Rights and Interests in Prosecuting the Crime of Illicit Enrichment*, Routledge Research in Transnational Crime and Criminal Law (Abingdon, Routledge, 2012), 132. On norm conflicts in human rights, see generally M Milanovic, 'Norm Conflict in International Law: Whither Human Rights?' (2009) 20 *Duke Journal of Comparative & International Law* 69, 73; cp Ivory (n 2) 170–72.

[123] N Boister, 'Human Rights Protections in the Suppression Conventions' (2002) 2 *Human Rights Law Review* 199, 208–09 and 217.

[124] cp African Union Convention on Preventing and Combating Corruption, Arts 3(2) and 14; Directive 2014/42/EU, Art 8.

rights-restricting;[125] in that convention, and the anti-corruption one, states may even 'adopt more strict or severe measures'.[126] International monitoring bodies have generally failed to consider the broader, rights-related consequences of international AML/CFT and anti-corruption confiscation regimes.[127] At the international level, there is no clear hierarchy of norms and no centralised mechanism for deciding which rule takes precedence.[128] Do states place individual human rights at risk when they co-operate for the purposes of asset recovery? Have the anti-corruption and international human rights regimes fragmented?[129] Who is responsible for answering these questions and what solutions do they present?

The ECtHR has found a range of confiscation orders compatible with the due process rights in the Convention for the Protection of Human Rights and Fundamental Freedoms (ECHR) and the right to property in the Protocol (ECHR-P1).[130] NCB ('civil') confiscation orders may not be punitive within the meaning of Article 7 ECHR, which prohibits retrospective 'penalties', if they merely remove the benefit from past wrongdoing.[131] Post-conviction confiscation orders have been found to punish offenders; however, in the Court's view, they generally do not 'charge' individuals with crimes so as to trigger the more exacting procedural guarantees of Article 6(2) and (3) ECHR.[132] The ECtHR cites a list of factors in justifying this non-criminal designation, the absence of a clear pronouncement of guilt and the state's non-punitive (preventative and restorative) objectives being particularly

[125] Commentary on the United Nations Convention Against Illicit Traffic in Narcotic Drugs and Psychotropic Substances (New York, UN, 1998), UN Doc E/CN.7/590.

[126] UNCATND, Art 24; UNCAC, Art 65(2).

[127] TC Halliday, M Levi and P Reuter, 'Global Surveillance of Dirty Money: Assessing Assessments of Regimes to Control Money Laundering and Combat the Financing of Terrorism' (Center on Law & Globalization, 2014) 7, available at www.lexglobal.org/files/Report_Global%20Surveillance%20of%20 Dirty%20Money%201.30.2014.pdf. cp Ivory (n 2) 119–20 (noting some differentiation in the discussion of human rights impacts of third party confiscation provisions by anti-corruption monitoring bodies).

[128] D Shelton, 'International Law and "Relative Normativity"' in M Evans (ed), *International Law*, 4th edn (Oxford, Oxford University Press, 2014) 138.

[129] Fragmentation of International Law: Difficulties Arising from the Diversification and Expansion of International Law, Report of the Study Group of States against Corruption the International Law Commission Finalized by M Koskenniemi, UN Doc A/CN.4/L.682/Add. 1 (13 April 2006).

[130] Convention for the Protection of Human Rights and Fundamental Freedoms, as amended by Protocols No 11 and 14, Rome, 4 November 1950, in force 3 September 1953, 5 ETS read with the Protocol to the Convention for the Protection of Human Rights and Fundamental Freedoms as amended by Protocol No 11, Paris, 20 March 1952, in force 18 May 1954, 9 ETS; Protocol to the Convention for the Protection of Human Rights and Fundamental Freedoms as amended by Protocol No 11, Paris, 20 March 1952, in force 18 May 1954, 9 ETS.

[131] *Dassa Foundation and Others v Liechtenstein*, App No 696/05 (ECtHR, 10 July 2007) 'The Law', para C.

[132] See especially *Welch v UK*, App No 17440/90 (1995) 20 EHRR 247, esp para 35; *Phillips v UK*, App No 41087/98 (2000) 30 EHRR CD 170; *van Offeren v Netherlands*, App No 19581/04 (ECtHR, 5 July 2005). cp *Geerings v Netherlands*, App No 30810/03 (ECtHR, 1 March 2007). See MM Gallant, *Money Laundering and the Proceeds of Crime: Economic Crime and Civil Remedies* (Cheltenham, Edward Elgar, 2005) 34–38; Ivory (n 2) 189 and 230–34; Stessens (n 46) 64–65 and 68.

persuasive.[133] It still reviews both conviction and NCB confiscation orders under the civil limb of Article 6(1) ECHR,[134] but it finds these proceedings fair, on the whole. Reversed burdens of proof, civil standards of proof and third party confiscation are permissible when accompanied by adequate procedural safeguards.[135]

Similar arguments justify confiscation orders under the right to property. The Court reasons that a person may have a protected interest in proceeds, instrumentalities, objects of crime or substitute items under Article 1 ECHR-P1; however, such interferences are generally mere 'controls of the use of possessions' or measures to secure the payment of penalties.[136] They are justified, moreover, when they are lawful—ie authorised by a domestic legal norm that is itself compatible with the rule of law—and proportionate to the general interest—such as deterring money laundering or its predicate offences.[137] Generally, a measure is within the margin of appreciation when the affected party has had an opportunity to challenge the confiscation order before an independent and impartial judicial tribunal in a proceeding that was otherwise fair under Article 6(1) ECHR.[138] For example, in *Gogitidze and Others v Georgia*, the ECtHR cited a battery of 'internationally acclaimed standards' in upholding the 'civil *in rem* confiscation' of property from a former public official and his relatives.[139] 'Articles 31 and 54 § 1 (c) of [the UNCAC] … set forth the principle of universal recognition of confiscation of property linked to corruption, or proceeds of crime derived from corruption offences.'[140] The FATF Recommendations and CoE Money Laundering Conventions confirmed the 'common European and even universal' nature of the civil *in rem* confiscation provisions.[141] They had been imposed, in this case, as 'an essential

[133] Ivory (n 2) 248–49; King (n 116) 378–79 and 387–88.

[134] See, eg, *Phillips* (n 132) paras 42–46.

[135] On objects and instrumentalities, see, eg, *Allgemeine Gold- und Silberscheideanstalt AG (AGOSI) v UK*, App No 9118/80 (1987) 9 EHRR 1, para 63–67; *Air Canada v UK*, App No 18465/91 (1995) 20 EHRR 150, para 49–63. On *in rem* confiscations of proceeds, see, eg, *Arcuri and Others v Italy*, App No 52024/99 (ECtHR, 5 July 2001) 'The Law', para 1; *Honecker and Others v Germany*, App Nos 54999/00 and 53991/00 (ECtHR, 15 November 2001) 'The Law', para 3; *Silickienė v Lithuania*, App No 20496/02 (ECtHR, 10 April 2012) para 48–50; *Gogitidze and Others v Georgia*, App No 36862/05 (ECtHR, 12 May 2015) paras 116–27. cp *Rummi v Estonia*, App No 63362/09 (ECtHR, 15 February 2015) paras 80–86.

[136] See, eg, *Handyside v UK*, App No 5493/72 (1979–80) 1 EHRR 737, para 62–63; *AGOSI* (ibid) para 51; *Air Canada* (ibid) para 32–34; *Raimondo v Italy*, App No 12954/87 (1994) 18 EHRR 237, para 29; *Gogitidze* (ibid) paras 92–93; *Paulet v UK*, App No 6219/08 (ECtHR, 13 May 2014) para 64. cp *Konovalov v Russia*, App No 43626/02 (ECtHR, 24 May 2007) para 41; *Frizen v Russia*, App No 58254/00 (2006) 42 EHRR 19, para 29; *Waldemar Nowakowski v Poland*, App No 55167/11 (ECtHR, 24 July 2012) para 46. See further Ivory (n 2) 173–96.

[137] See, eg, *Handyside* (ibid) paras 62–63; *AGOSI* (n 135) paras 52–61; *Air Canada* (n 135) para 35–49; *Raimondo* (ibid) paras 30; *Gogitidze* (n 135) paras 109–13; *Silickienė* (n 135) para 65–70. cp *Denisova and Moiseyeva v Russia*, App No 16903/03 (ECtHR, 1 April 2010) paras 61–65; *Paulet v UK*, App No 6219/08 (ECtHR, 13 May 2014) para 67–68; *Dimitrovi v Bulgaria*, App No 12655/09 (ECtHR 03 March 2015) paras 39–56. See further Ivory (n 2) 196–218 and 222–58.

[138] Ivory (n 2) 248–54.

[139] *Gogitidze* (n 135) paras 55–73 and 105. cp *Dimitrovi* (n 137) paras 32 and 52–55.

[140] *Gogitidze* (n 135) para 56.

[141] *Gogitidze* (n 135) para 105.

part of a larger legislative package aimed at intensifying the fight against corruption' following the 2004 'Rose Revolution'.[142]

Already criticised for their obscurity and inconsistency in domestic matters,[143] these principles are still harder to apply to co-operative confiscations. From *Soering* to *Othman* to *Husayn*,[144] there is authority for the proposition that state parties violate fair trial rights when they expose individuals to flagrant denials of justice abroad.[145] Those cases concerned extradition, expulsion, rendition and prisoner transfer. It is not clear whether the 'stringent test' applies to confiscation orders that emanate from third states, especially those that are 'in transition'.[146] In *Saccoccia v Austria*, a substantial forfeiture order had been imposed on assets found in the applicant's Austrian apartment and determined by a US court to be the proceeds (or substitutes) of 'large-scale' drug money laundering.[147] The ECtHR's First Section found that it was not 'called upon to decide in the abstract which level of review was required' under the Convention: the Austrian MLA law 'required the Austrian courts to satisfy themselves that the decision to be enforced was given in proceedings complying with the principles of Article 6 of the Convention'. '[T]he Austrian courts, before authorising the enforcement of the [US] forfeiture order, [had] duly satisfied themselves that the decision at issue was not the result of a flagrant denial of justice.'[148] Furthermore, the applicant's representatives were afforded ample opportunity to make submissions to the Vienna Court of Appeal, which were considered in a detailed decision.[149] Hence, the Austrian *exequatur* order was not only a lawful and fair but also a proportionate interference with the applicant's right to property.[150] The Court did not mention the 'flagrant denial of justice' in adjudicating the applicant's complaints under Article 1 ECHR-P1: whether

[142] *Gogitidze* (n 135) paras 8–9 and 101.

[143] Gallant (n 132) 34–38 and 124–32; Ivory (n 2) 249–51; King (n 116) 394.

[144] *Soering v UK*, App No 14038/88 (1989) 11 EHRR 439, paras 81–91; *Drozd and Janousek v France and Spain*, App No 12747/87 (1992) 14 EHRR 745, paras 108–10; *Othman (Abu Qatada) v UK*, App No 8139/09 (2012) 55 EHRR 1, paras 236–87; *Husayn (Abu Zubayda) v Poland*, App No 7511/13 (2015) 60 EHRR 16, paras 551–61; *Al Nashiri v Poland*, App No 28761/11, (2015) 60 EHRR 16, paras 552–69. See also *El-Masri v Macedonia*, App No 39630/09 (2013) 57 EHRR 25, para 239.

[145] J Dugard and C van den Wyngaert, 'Reconciling Extradition with Human Rights' (1998) 92 *American Journal of International Law* 187; A van Hoek and M Luchtman, 'Transnational Cooperation in Criminal Matters and the Safeguarding of Human Rights' (2005) 1 *Utrecht Law Review* 1, 6–19; G Gilbert, *Responding to International Crime* (Leiden, Martinus Nijhoff Publishers, 2006) 163–67; C Michaelsen, 'The Renaissance of Non-Refoulement? The Othman (Abu Qatada) Decision of the European Court of Human Rights' (2012) 61 *International and Comparative Law Quarterly* 750.

[146] R Ivory, 'The Right to a Fair Trial and International Cooperation in Criminal Matters: Article 6 ECHR and the Recovery of Assets in Grand Corruption Cases' (2013) 9 *Utrecht Law Review* 147. See also Case C-396/11 *Proceedings Relating to the Execution of European Arrest Warrants Issued against Ciprian Vasile Radu* (29 January 2013) paras 28–34; cp Case C-396/11 *Ministerul Public—Parchetul de pe lângaă Curtea de Apel Constanța v Ciprian Vasile Radu*, Opinion of Advocate General Sharpston (18 October 2012) para 82 (the flagrant denial and 'mutual recognition' within the EU).

[147] App No 69917/01 (ECtHR, 5 July 2007) 'The Law', para 2. See also *Saccoccia v Austria* (2010) 50 EHRR 11; *Duboc v Austria*, App No 8154/04 (ECtHR, 5 June 2012).

[148] *Saccoccia* (ECtHR, 5 July 2007) 'The Law', para 2, discussed further in Ivory (n 2) 152–54.

[149] *Saccoccia* (2010) 50 EHRR 11, paras 89–91 (Art 1 ECHR-P1).

[150] *Saccoccia* (2010) 50 EHRR 11, paras 85–91. See further, Ivory (n 2) 198–99 and 228–30.

the flagrant denial of justice standard would be used to assess compliance with the right to property in co-operative confiscation cases is an open question.[151]

The recent judgment in *Al-Dulimi and Montana Management Inc v Switzerland*[152] may indicate a stricter approach to review when asset recovery measures take the form of international economic sanctions. At issue in *Al-Dulimi* were a series of UN Security Council Resolutions that provided for the listing of senior Iraqi officials and the freezing and eventual transfer of associated wealth to a 'Development Fund for Iraq'.[153] Switzerland had implemented the Resolutions by ordering the administrative restraint and confiscation of bank deposits connected to the former finance chief for the Baathist secret service and a Panamanian company which he had managed.[154] The Swiss court found it had no jurisdiction to review the Security Council's listing decision and that the applicants had otherwise received a fair hearing under Article 6 ECHR, Article 14 ICCPR and the procedural aspects of the Swiss constitutional right to property.[155] Distinguishing *Nada v Switzerland*,[156] the ECtHR held that Switzerland was obliged to give effect to the Resolutions strictly according to their terms;[157] Switzerland had no discretion to implement the decision in conformity with its obligations under the ECHR. However, the Swiss courts had failed to secure the applicant's right to access a court under Article 6(1) ECHR[158] because the UN's 'Focal Point' procedure did not provide 'equivalent protection' for Convention guarantees.[159] The freezing and confiscation orders were a significant interference with the applicant's civil rights, not least because they had been in place for some 20 years. In language reminiscent of the EU courts' most strident *Kadi* decision,[160] it found that the measures were not proportionate to the general interest of (merely) 're-establishing the autonomy and sovereignty of the Iraqi Government and of securing the right of the Iraqi people freely to determine their own political future and control their own natural resources' in a post-conflict situation.[161] '[M]ore differentiated and specifically targeted measures would probably have been more conducive to the effective implementation of the resolutions.'[162]

[151] Ivory (n 2) 243–45.
[152] App No 5809/08 (ECtHR, 26 November 2013) (referred to Grand Chamber on 4 April 2014).
[153] ibid para 14.
[154] *Al-Dulimi* (n 152) paras 1, 10, 32.
[155] *Al-Dulimi* (n 152) para 38. Switzerland has not ratified ECHR-P1.
[156] App No 10593/08 (2013) 56 EHRR 18, paras 172–76, 197. See further S Hollenberg, 'The Diverging Approaches of the European Court of Human Rights in the Cases of Nada and Al-Dulimi' (2015) 64 *International and Comparative Law Quarterly* 445.
[157] *Al-Dulimi* (n 152) para 117.
[158] *Al-Dulimi* (n 152) paras 123–35.
[159] *Al-Dulimi* (n 152) paras 118–21.
[160] Cases C-402/05 P and C-415/05 P *Yassin Abdullah Kadi and Al Barakaat International Foundation v Council of the European Union and Commission of the European Communities* [2008] ECR I-06351, paras 357–58 (*Kadi No 2*).
[161] *Al-Dulimi* (n 152) paras 118–21.
[162] *Al-Dulimi* (n 152) para 130.

The Second Section's judgment in *Al-Dulimi* is now on appeal to the Grand Chamber. Whatever the outcome,[163] it is likely to have effects further afield. Already, it is apparent that other human rights bodies are borrowing from the ECtHR's rulings on the 'balance' between security and liberty in transnational crime control cases. Under the EU Charter, fundamental rights have the same 'meaning and scope' as they do under the ECHR and its protocols.[164] The European Court of Justice cited the ECtHR in its *Kadi* decisions[165] and in a recent opinion on cross-border cash disclosure requirements.[166] Luxembourg has also rejected requests for the annulment of sanctions imposed on members of the Mubarak and Assad regimes, as well as their relatives and associates.[167] In so doing, the EU judges have commented on the concept of penalties,[168] the use of presumptions[169] and the European rights to property,[170] sometimes with reference to Strasbourg's decisions.[171]

Outside Europe, international human rights bodies have taken a permissive approach from the ECtHR confiscation case law. The Inter-American Commission on Human Rights used *Raimondo v Italy*, an anti-mafia matter, in its 2002 report on counter-terrorism:

> [W]hile each case must be evaluated in its own circumstances in light of the principles of proportionality and necessity, restrictions on the use or enjoyment of property may well be necessary in the general interest, to effectively investigate and deter criminal activity and to ensure that the property does not provide criminal defendants with advantages to the detriment of the community at large.[172]

[163] The Grand Chamber eventually found a violation of Art 6(1) by a majority of 15 votes to 2, albeit in a judgment with several concurring opinions: *Al-Dulimi and Montana Management Inc v Switzerland* (ECtHR, App No 5809/08, 21 June 2016).

[164] Charter of Fundamental Rights of the European Union, Strasbourg, 12 December 2007, in force 1 December 2009 [2010] OJ C83, 2, Art 52(3).

[165] See, eg, *Kadi No 2* (n 160) para 334 citing *Chahal v UK*, App No 22414/93 (1997) 23 EHRR 413, para 131.

[166] Opinion of Advocate General Wathelet, C-255/14, *Robert Michal Chmielewski v Nemzeti Adóés Vámhivatal Dél-alföldi Regionális Vámés Pénzügyőri Főigazgatósága* (7 May 2015) paras 35–64, citing *Ismayilov v Russia*, App No 30352/03 (ECtHR, 6 November 2008), *Grifhorst v France*, App No 28336/02 (ECtHR, 26 February 2009) and *Moon v France*, App No 39973/03 (ECtHR, 9 July 2009).

[167] See especially Case T-383/11 *Makhlouf v Council* (13 September 2013); Case T-256/11 *Ezz and Others v Council of the EU* (27 February 2014) affirmed in Case C-220/14P *Ezz and Others v Council of the EU* (5 March 2015); Case T-202/12 *Al-Assad v Council of the EU* (12 March 2014); Case T-592/11 *Anbouba v Council of the EU* (13 September 2013) affirmed in Case C-630/13P *Anbouba v Council of the EU* (21 April 2015).

[168] Case T-256/11 *Ezz* (ibid) paras 70–81; Case T-203/12 *Alchaar v Council of the EU* (3 July 2014) para 142.

[169] Case C-630/13P *Anbouba* (n 167) paras 45–55; Case T-256/11 *Ezz* (n 167), 82–84; *Alchaar* (ibid) paras 144–71; Case T-579/11 *Akhras v Council of the EU* (12 February 2015) paras 109–19.

[170] See, eg, *Makhlouf* (n 16) paras 86–107; Case T-256/11 *Ezz* (n 167) paras 186–217; Joined Cases T-307/12 and T-408/13 *Mayaleh v Council of the EU* (5 November 2014) paras 172–81; Case T-593/11 *Al Chihabi v Council of the EU* (30 April 2015) paras 89–105.

[171] See especially Case T-563/11 *Anbouba v Council* (13 September 2013) para 36 citing *Salabiaku v France*, App No 10519/83 (ECtHR, 7 October 1988) and *Klouvi v France*, App No 30754/03 (ECtHR, 30 June 2011).

[172] Report on Terrorism and Human Rights (2002), paras 365–71, esp para 368, available at www.cidh.oas.org/Terrorism/Eng/toc.htm, citing *Raimondo* (n 136) para 30.

In its recent first case on extradition, the Inter-American Court of Human Rights (IACtHR) appears to have taken a narrow interpretation of 'flagrant denials of justice' from the ECtHR's judgment in *Othman*.[173] More relevant still, the UN High Commissioner for Human Rights cited the ECtHR as the authority for the proposition that NCB confiscation powers and presumptions of illicit acquisition can be aligned.[174] The Commissioner advocates a 'human rights-based approach to the asset recovery process' in which 'countries of origin make every effort to achieve the recovery and repatriation of proceeds of corruption for implementation of their international human rights obligations, [and] recipient countries understand repatriation not as a discretionary measure but also as a duty derived from the obligations of international cooperation and assistance'.[175] 'When appropriate, recipient countries of funds of illicit origin should de-link confiscation measures from a requirement of conviction in the country of origin…'.[176] StAR took a similar view in its report on the discretionary obligation to criminalise illicit enrichment,[177] as did Transparency International and the International Council for Human Rights Policy in their joint work.[178] The academic Nvida Kofele-Kale goes further still, arguing that a 'right to a corruption-free society' is emerging in customary international law.[179] For Kofele-Kale, the European Court has confirmed that international human rights law permits 'derogation from the presumption of innocence' so as to protect that core collective interest.[180]

Of course, the ECtHR is not the last word on the relationship between civil and political rights and asset recovery measures. In 2013, the EU's General Court found an insufficient basis for claims that some members of the Ben Ali family were associated with, or responsible for, misappropriations of Tunisian state funds (they were only being investigated for money laundering).[181] With respect to Syrian and Libyan parties, the Court has since ordered annulments due to the

[173] *Case of Wong Ho Wing v Peru* (Preliminary Objection, Merits, Reparations and Costs), Series C No 297 (IACtHR, 30 June 2015) para 136, 154 citing *Othman* (n 144) paras 258–60. See further Ivory, 'Fair Trial' (n 146); Ivory (n 2) 267–69. In *Wong Ho Wing*, the Inter-American Court discussed the flagrant denial of justice solely in connection with the risk of the use of torture evidence by the requesting state and the risk of procedural irregularities in capital cases; it may be that the applicant only pleaded the 'flagrant denial' in these terms.

[174] Comprehensive study on the negative impact of the non-repatriation of funds of illicit origin to the countries of origin on the enjoyment of human rights, in particular economic, social and cultural rights: Report of the United Nations High Commissioner for Human Rights, UN Doc A/HRC/19/42 (14 December 2011) paras 46–48, nn 39–41.

[175] ibid para 26.

[176] A/HRC/19/42 (n 174) Recommendations, para 63(a)(iv).

[177] Muzila et al (n 107) 31.

[178] International Council on Human Rights Policy and Transparency International, 'Integrating Human Rights in the Anti-Corruption Agenda: Challenges, Possibilities and Opportunities' (report) (2010), available at www.ichrp.org/en/projects/131, 65–66.

[179] Kofele-Kale (n 122) ch 6, esp 137–44. See also Spalding (n 117) 1366.

[180] N Kofele-Kale, 'Presumed Guilty: Balancing Competing Rights and Interests in Combating Economic Crimes' (2006) 40 *The International Lawyer* 909, 933–34.

[181] Case T-187/11 *Trabelsi and Others v Council of the EU* (28 May 2013) 74–117; Case T-200/11 *Al Matri v Council of the EU* (28 May 2013) paras 38–54; Case T-188/11 *Chiboub v Council of the EU*

failure of the Council to state its reasons and to correctly assess the evidence.[182] The African Court of Human and Peoples' Rights has provisionally ordered Libya to refrain from executing a death sentence against one of the surviving Gaddafi sons and to ensure his 'internationally recognised' fair trial rights.[183] Previously, the IACtHR and African Commission on Human and People's Rights had interpreted the proportionality requirement more strictly in property and confiscation cases—and been more willing to openly recognise collective entitlements as protected by their Conventions' property guarantees.[184] In this way, they have provided greater scope for arguments about the impact of asset recovery measures on the rights of individuals with questionable connection to those things—and of the (potential) importance of asset recovery for people within developing states.

As an academic, I have called for explicitly relational interpretations of collective (anti-corruption) and individual (human rights) norms.[185] The ECtHR's deference to Member States in international co-operation situations has effectively created a third category of proceeding under Article 6 ECHR; its obscure and parochial construction of Article 1 ECHR-P1 risks reducing the property guarantee to a procedural entitlement unable to metabolise cross-border economic claims.[186] Kofele-Kale's presentation of an irreconcilable norm conflict ignores the enabling relationship between collective and individual guarantees in development, I argue.[187] His language of a 'global war against corruption'[188] is an unwelcome attempt to 'securitise' the human rights and anti-corruption discourse.[189]

(28 May 2013) paras 46–91. See also Case T-133/12 *Ben Ali v Council of the EU* (2 April 2014) paras 64–75. The court reached a similar conclusion in Case T-290/14 *Portnov v Council of the EU* (26 October 2015) 35–51, and in a series of 2016 cases on the EU Ukraine sanctions regime, eg, Case T-494/14 *Klymenko v Council of the EU* (10 June 2016) 54–73.

[182] Case T-653/11 *Jaber v Council of the EU* (13 November 2013) paras 78–86; Case T-293/12 *Syria International Islamic Bank v Council* (11 June 2014) paras 45–66; Joined Cases T-329/12 and T-74/13 *Al Tabbaa v Council* (9 July 2014) paras 65–99; Case T-348/13 *Kadhaf Al Dam v Council of the EU* (24 September 2014) paras 50–99; Case T-572/11 *Hassan v Council of the EU* (16 July 2014) paras 86–95; Case T-579/11 *Akhras* (n 169) paras 53–73; Case T-652/11 *Sabbagh v Council* (26 February 2015) paras 30–51.

[183] *African Commission on Human and Peoples' Rights v Libya*, App No 002/2013 (Order of Provisional Measures, No 2) (AfCtHPR, 10 October 2015).

[184] Ivory (n 2) ch 6.

[185] Ivory (n 2) 286–88.

[186] Ivory, 'Fair Trial' (n 146) 158; Ivory (n 2) 299.

[187] A Sen, *Development as Freedom* (Oxford, Oxford University Press, 1999). Sen is reported to have commented on the recent Indian anti-corruption movement in G Goris, 'Amartya Sen on Elections, Communal Politics and Inequality in India', *Mondiaal Nieuws*, 8 April 2014, available at www.mo.be/en/interview/amartya-sen-elections-communal-politics-and-inequality-india.

[188] Kofele-Kale, 'Presumed Guilty' (n 180) 933 and 936; Kofele-Kale, *Combating Economic Crimes* (n 122) 9, 29, 96, 110 and 142.

[189] L Campbell, 'Organized Crime and National Security: A Dubious Connection?' (2014) 17 *New Criminal Law Review* 220, esp 247–50.

V. The Third Dimension: Effectiveness

The conundrum of lowering barriers to asset recovery whilst protecting human rights easily obscures a further challenge to the return of illicit wealth: effectiveness. When international organisations and NGOs campaign for more political will and fewer barriers to return, they accept the international consensus as genuine, the goal of asset recovery as realistic and the means described in the UNCAC as adapted to achieving that end. Lawyers tend to make similar assumptions when they debate the limits on co-operative confiscation imposed by human rights to property and due process in positive international law.[190] For other scholars of international law and anti-corruption, asset recovery cannot be assumed to be a genuine promise or a workable practice—even with more effort by states or more finely nuanced protections for individuals. In the third dimension, the challenge of returning wealth to victim countries is the challenge of demonstrating that international asset recovery laws motivate state actors to engage in asset recovery practices—and that national asset recovery law and practices motivate non-state actors to refrain from grand corruption and associated acts of money laundering.

There are significant methodological difficulties in proving that anti-corruption programmes and AML controls are 'effective'. This is not the place to review those issues—save to say that they range from difficulties in defining the crime for the purposes of measurement to determining the measures of success.[191] They increase, moreover, when the putative cause of individual (or corporate) compliance is the international regime for ensuring domestic law reform. Social scientific accounts of international anti-corruption regulations are still relatively rare;[192] studies focusing on the asset recovery component of the order are even harder to find.[193] Sharman's *The Despot's Guide to Wealth Management* promises to be an important exception, though it was still in manuscript form at the time of

[190] King (n 116) 391–93.

[191] See, eg, M Levi and P Reuter, 'Money Laundering' (2006) 24 *Crime and Justice* 289, 347–64; J Johnsøn, N Taxell and D Zaum, 'Mapping Evidence Gaps in Anti-Corruption: Assessing the State of the Operationally Relevant Evidence on Donors' Actions and Approaches to Reducing Corruption' [2012] *Christian Michelsen Institute, U4* Issue 7, 6–8, available at www.u4.no/publications.

[192] As exceptions, see, eg, W Cole, 'Institutionalizing a Global Anticorruption Regime: Perverse Effects on Country Outcomes, 1984–2012' (2015) 56 *International Journal of Comparative Sociology* 53; K Davis, 'Does the Globalization of Anti-Corruption Law Help Developing Countries?' in J Faundez and C Tan (eds), *International Economic Law, Globalisation and Developing Countries* (Cheltenham, Edward Elgar, 2010) 296–305; N Lord, *Regulating Corporate Bribery in International Business: Anti-Corruption in the UK and Germany* (Aldershot, Ashgate Publishing, 2014). See also A Cuervo-Cazurra, 'Who Cares about Corruption?' (2006) 37 *Journal of International Business Studies* 807 (OECD Convention membership and foreign direct investment patterns).

[193] See also P Reuter, 'Introduction' in P Reuter (ed), *Draining Development? Controlling Flows of Illicit Funds from Developing Countries* (Washington, DC, IBRD/World Bank, 2012) 5; M Levi, 'How Well Do Anti-Money Laundering Controls Work in Developing Countries?' in Reuter, *Draining Development?* (ibid) 404.

writing.[194] International organisation or NGO studies of particular cases or overall levels of asset recovery do not fill this gap despite their best efforts to work empirically.[195]

Meanwhile, the 'success' of the sister FATF process is somewhat dubious. There has been a rapid uptake in membership in the FATF bodies, as well as some efforts on the part of the Task Force 'to deliver systematic and evidence-based advice'.[196] However, in Jakobi's words, 'there is still no reliable data on the magnitude of laundering or the extent to which the regime has actually influenced the capability of money launderers'.[197] Similarly, Halliday, Levi and Reuter find a lack of rigour in the FATF methodologies and a failure, on the part of the Task Force, to articulate its objectives and to demonstrate that membership contributes to those goals, as they could be understood. The authors also note a lack of evidence that participation in the FATF process lowers financial crime or increases financial stability, and a lack of consideration as to how AML/CTF policies may generate other costs for political participation, financial services access or civil society.[198] As Tsingou likewise observes, 'despite the ambitions of the regime, its achievements with respect to its goals remain modest at best, while numerous significant side-effects raise serious concerns about its role, efficiency and legitimacy'.[199] As for the compliance effects of the standards, Machado's recent study of AML and CTF law reform in Argentina and Brazil suggests that the proximate cause of state change may be domestic factors, rather than transnational pressure alone.[200] The international rules on money laundering may then be indicative of a transnational legal process, not generative of one.[201] To the extent that international treaties have enabled international enforcement in tax matters, the UN's Independent Expert raises the possibility that they may merely encourage the diversion of illicit financial flows to less regulated jurisdictions.[202]

[194] Sharman (n 80). See also Reuter and Truman (n 63) 148–55.

[195] By their own account, StAR struggled to gather responses to its 2012 questionnaire: Gray et al (n 75), 9.

[196] Jakobi (n 63) 153.

[197] Jakobi (n 63) 153.

[198] Halliday et al (n 127) 4–15.

[199] E Tsingou, 'Global Financial Governance and the Developing Anti-Money Laundering Regime: What Lessons for International Political Economy?' (2010) 47 *International Politics* 617, 618.

[200] M Machado, 'Similar in Their Differences: Transnational Legal Processes Addressing Money Laundering in Brazil and Argentina' in G Shaffer (ed), *Transnational Legal Ordering and State Change* (Cambridge, Cambridge University Press, 2013).

[201] See also TC Halliday and G Shaffer, 'Transnational Legal Orders' in TC Halliday and G Shaffer (eds), *Transnational Legal Orders* (Cambridge, Cambridge University Press, 2015) 36–42 ('Transnational Recursivity Theory').

[202] A/HRC/22/42, para 22 citing N Johannesen and G Zucman, 'The End of Bank Secrecy? An Evaluation of the G20 Tax Haven Crackdown' (2012) Paris School of Economics Working Paper No 2012-4.

VI. The Fourth Dimension: (IR)rationality

Investigations of state compliance with international asset recovery norms open up a fourth challenge of asset recovery: its apparent irrationality. Why would states conclude (and continually advocate) norms that they are then reluctant to consistently follow? Writing with Kim, Sharman finds that neither realpolitik nor enlightened self-interest accounts for the development of this aspect of international anti-corruption law.[203] A norm that high-level officials (from developing states) should not be allowed to sequester money abroad inhibits the pursuit of absolute self-interest by powerful (developed) countries.[204] And there are few, if any, payoffs for haven states in absolute terms: 'There are no joint gains to be captured, or losses from opportunism to be feared, when the leaders of other states either refrain from or engage in embezzlement or bribery.'[205] Rather, the development of the asset recovery norm is best seen as a product of a liberal 'culture of modernity' within contemporary international relations. 'Rationalised impersonal authority' is the source of legitimate governance; rational, rights-endowed individuals are the primary objects for protections and units for decision. The use of public power for private ends is therefore an act of corruption and a transgression on the part of the individual wrongdoer.[206] With its focus on the highest and least constrained office holders and their economic reasons for action, asset recovery appears to be both a rational response to the corruption and a moral 'good' regardless of its actual 'outcomes'. That it fails in practice is indicative of the persistence of interests (or norms about the importance of absolute and relative interests) in the international relations of international law.

The constructivist account of the asset recovery in international relations echoes the sceptical literature on anti-corruption in political economy and geography,[207] development studies,[208] sociology, anthropology and social psychology.[209] For these critical 'corruptologists', the dominant definition of corruption as an

[203] HJ Joon Kim and JC Sharman, 'Accounts and Accountability: Corruption Human Rights, and Individual Accountability Norms' (2014) 68 *International Organization* 417.

[204] Sharman (n 80) Introduction.

[205] Kim and Sharman (n 203) 420–21.

[206] Kim and Sharman (n 203) 435–36.

[207] E Brown and J Cloke, 'Neoliberal Reform, Governance, and Corruption in the South: Assessing the International Anti-Corruption Crusade' (2004) 36 *Antipode* 272; E Brown and J Cloke, 'Neoliberal Reform, Governance, and Corruption in Central America: Exploring the Nicaraguan Case' (2005) 24 *Political Geography* 601; M Bukovansky, 'The Hollowness of Anti-Corruption Discourse' (2006) 13 *Review of International Political Economy* 181.

[208] T Polzer, 'Corruption: Deconstructing the World Bank Discourse' (2001) DESTIN Development Studies Institute Working Paper No 1, available at www.lse.ac.uk/internationalDevelopment/pdf/WP/WP18.pdf; R Theobold, *Corruption, Development and Underdevelopment* (Durham, NC, Duke University Press, 1990).

[209] G Anders and M Niujten, 'Corruption and the Secret of the Law: An Introduction' in M Niujten and G Anders (eds), *Corruption and the Secret of the Law: A Legal Anthropological Perspective* (Farnham, Ashgate Publishing, 2007); M Levi and D Nelken, 'The Corruption of Politics and the

abuse of public office or power is culturally and politically biased.[210] It relies on dualisms in Enlightenment thought between the public and private, state and civil society, institution and individual, and rational and moral.[211] It also stigmatises the types of informal transactions that are more prevalent in the global south,[212] distracting from the forms of financial malfeasance that predominate in the north.[213] Because they locate corruption in the state, mainstream anti-corruption strategies lead to policies that reduce government capacity and legitimacy and weaken formal political controls (to say nothing of their potential to justify repressive politics).[214] Because they treat corruption as an individual crime, they distract from the structural factors that enable rent-seeking and embezzlement. Here, too, Western countries are partly to blame: during the colonial period, they created many of the bureaucratic institutions in which corruption now occurs; latterly, they have supported neoliberal economic 'reforms' that have caused further social dislocation and generated opportunities for graft and asset transfer.[215] In fact, the failure of structural adjustment programmes in the former USSR, Latin America and sub-Saharan Africa in the 1980s and 1990s is said to have created the need for explanations of 'state failure' and 'underdevelopment' that corrupt local institutions conveniently filled.[216] To present corruption as human rights issue is to co-opt an emancipatory discourse that could otherwise be used to oppose neoliberal reform.[217]

Politics of Corruption: An Overview' in M Levi and D Nelken (eds), *The Corruption of Politics and the Politics of Corruption* (Oxford, Blackwell, 1996); M Zaloznaya, 'Beyond Anti-Corruptionism: Sociological Imagination and Comparative Study of Corruption' (2013) 12 *Comparative Sociology* 1; M Zaloznaya, Social Psychology of Corruption: Why It Does Not Exist and Why It Should' (2014) 8 *Sociology Compass* 187.

[210] E Brown and J Cloke, 'Critical Perspectives on Corruption: An Overview' (2011) 7 *Critical Perspectives International Business* 116, 117–18; E Brown and J Cloke, 'The Critical Business of Corruption' (2006) 2 *Critical Perspectives International Business* 275, 277–78 and 281–84; Zaloznaya, 'Beyond Anti-Corruptionism' (ibid); Zaloznaya, 'Social Psychology of Corruption' (ibid).

[211] Anders and Niujten (n 209) 11; Brown and Cloke, 'Neoliberal Reform, Governance, and Corruption in the South' (n 207) 282–85; Brown and Cloke, 'Neoliberal Reform, Governance, and Corruption in Central America' (n 207) 609–11; Brown and Cloke, 'The Critical Business of Corruption' (n 210) 287–288; Bukovansky (n 207) 182–86; Polzer (n 208) 15–23. See also A Gupta, 'Blurred Boundaries: The Discourse of Corruption, the Culture of Politics, and the Imagined State' (1995) 22 *American Ethnologist* 375. cp Theobold (n 208) 8–10.

[212] Brown and Cloke, 'Critical Perspectives on Corruption' 118–19; Zaloznaya, 'Beyond Anti-Corruptionism' (n 209) 710.

[213] Anders and Niujten (n 209) 3; Brown and Cloke, 'The Critical Business of Corruption' (n 210) 283; Brown and Cloke, 'Critical Perspectives on Corruption', 118.

[214] Levi and Nelken, 'The Corruption of Politics' (n 209) 2–3; Polzer (n 208) 17–18 citing Theobold (n 208) 9. See also Theobold (n 208) 139; G Walton, 'The Limitations of Neoliberal Logic in the Anti-Corruption Industry: Lessons from Papua New Guinea' (2013) 60 *Crime, Law and Social Change* 147.

[215] Brown and Cloke, 'Neoliberal Reform, Governance, and Corruption in the South' (n 207) 285–89; Polzer (n 208) 19.

[216] Brown and Cloke, 'The Critical Business of Corruption' (n 210) 288–90; Polzer (n 208) 8–9.

[217] See also M Goodwin and K Rose-Sender, 'Linking Corruption and Human Rights: An Unwelcome Addition to the Development Discourse' (2010) 12 Tilburg Law School Research Paper No 12, available at http://papers.ssrn.com/sol3/papers.cfm?abstract_id=1623225. See also JT Gathii, 'Defining the Relationship between Human Rights and Corruption' (2009) 31 *University of Pennsylvania Journal of International Law* 161.

As a case study of the (neo)liberal influence in anti-corruption, asset recovery would seem to have plenty to offer the 'crits'—and their own potential critics. To borrow from Harvey, neoliberalism is 'a theory of political economic practice that proposes that human well-being can be advanced by liberating individual entrepreneurial freedoms and skills within an institutional framework characterized by strong private property rights, free markets, and free trade'.[218] On the one hand, the discourse of asset recovery privileges a view of global income inequality as a consequence of particular acts of individual wrong-doing—by leaders in developing countries and their 'bad apple' bankers in developed states. The solution to the problem, so constructed, lies in the initiative of individual governments which avail themselves of opportunities for redress provided by international law. The legal system itself is presumed to be equally accessible to all participants and legitimate, in so far as it is the product of sovereign states' consent. Treaties like the UNCAC and initiatives like StAR use the language of collective solutions—witness the 'Trust Fund' of StAR and the funding mechanism foreseen by chapter VI UNCAC; however, they stipulate that contributions are voluntary and/or conditional on successful returns. They are hardly standing mechanisms of wealth redistribution between countries. Are they, rather, an alibi or a decoy for broader claims to reparations for colonial wrongs, global trade or taxation law reforms?[219]

On the other hand, the rules on asset recovery would appear to reflect an alternative conception of corruption as a crime facilitated by the North through its possession of the social and economic spaces that are attractive to investment from the South. As provided for by the UNCAC, asset recovery not only aims to 'repatriate' wealth 'stolen' (embezzled or misappropriate) by Second and Third World officials; it also empowers those governments to demand a stake in the proceeds of the foreign public bribes that enrich First World corporations.[220] In this way, asset recovery is a continuation of efforts to link anti-corruption to a New International Economic Order and a code of conduct for transnational companies.[221] At least some southern governments and citizens would also appear to support the cause. Official commitment is reflected in the 'other' regional anti-corruption

[218] D Harvey, *A Brief History of Neoliberalism* (Oxford, Oxford University Press, 2005) 5.

[219] For calls to such reforms, see, eg, Declaration from the Addis Ababa Civil Society Forum on Financing for Development (12 July 2015), available at www.un.org/esa/ffd/ffd3/documents.html. See also Oxfam, 'Rich Countries Provide a Poor Outcome at Addis Financing for Development Conference: Oxfam' (press release) (15 July 2015), available at http://oxf.am/ZPkE.

[220] JA Oduor et al, *Left Out of the Bargain: Settlements in the Foreign Bribery Cases and Implications for Asset Recovery* (Washington, DC, IBRD/World Bank, 2014). On the 'proceeds-not-profits' rule, see P Alldridge, *Money Laundering Law: Forfeiture, Confiscation, Civil Recovery, Criminal Laundering and Taxation of the Proceeds of Crime* (Oxford, Hart Publishing, 2003), 259–260,

[221] See, eg, UN General Assembly Resolution 3514 (XXX), Measures against corrupt practices of transnational and other corporations their intermediaries and others involved, UN Doc A/RES/3514 (15 December 1975); ESC, Report of the Ad hoc Intergovernmental Working Group on the Problem of Corrupt Practices on its First, Second, Third and Resumed Sessions, UN Doc E/6006 (5 July 1977) reprinted (1977) 16 International Legal Materials 1236. See further M Salomon, 'From NIEO to Now and the Unfinishable Story of Economic Justice' (2013) 62 *International and Comparative Law Quarterly* 31.

treaties in Africa and the Americas,[222] and the resolutions on asset recovery within the UN Human Rights Council.[223] Popular dissatisfaction with corruption would seem evident in the protests that preceded those transitions.[224] As the Croatian contribution to this volume shows, asset recovery may be perceived to be a crucial element in post-conflict political and constitutional reforms: social justice and legitimate state building may also be goals of confiscation.[225]

The critical critique of anti-corruption may thus be plausibly applied to asset recovery, but it is also potentially vulnerable to allegations of paternalism, if not economic rationalism, in conceptions of transitional justice. Perhaps the measure of asset recovery is not the extent to which states actually increase the pool of funds for development or change the behaviour of high-level officials. Perhaps asset recovery is a means of signalling commitment to second- and third-generation human rights, or the accountability of high-level public officials to citizens in times of increasing globalisation and cosmopolitan identification.[226] Perhaps successful cases, no matter how rare, serve to encourage 'grass roots' campaigners to pursue their accountability work.[227] Asset recovery may have value in so far as it enhances legitimacy of local or global legal orders and, with that, development outcomes and compliance.[228] Or perhaps asset recovery has value irrespective of its instrumental impacts—just because it is, or it is perceived to be, 'the right thing to do'. As has been observed of a controversial new form of class action in national private law:

> Not only can cy-près distribution deter wrongdoing ..., *but it can align closely with victims' remedial preferences*, since one of the things victims appear to want (perhaps as much, or even more, than monetary compensation) is an *acknowledgement by a wrongdoer that wrong has been done, education and a change* in the wrongdoer's future behaviour.[229]

In a regulatory environment as diverse as the entire world, which ethical system should provide the answer to the normative versions of this question?

[222] See above (n 44).

[223] See, eg, Resolution adopted by the Human Rights Council 22/12, The negative impact of the non-repatriation of funds of illicit origin to the countries of origin on the enjoyment of human rights, and the importance of improving international cooperation, UN Doc A/HRC/22/12 (10 April 2013); Resolution adopted by the Human Rights Council 25/9, The negative impact of the non-repatriation of funds of illicit origin to the countries of origin on the enjoyment of human rights, and the importance of improving international cooperation, UN Doc A/HRC/RES/25/9 (15 April 2014).

[224] Peters (n 117); Sharman (n 80) Conclusions.

[225] EI Karas and SR Vidlička, 'The Relevance of Asset Recovery Policies in Transitional Societies: The Croatian Perspectives', Chapter 10 in this volume.

[226] See also Sharman (n 80) Conclusion.

[227] C Holzmeyer, 'Human Rights in an Era of Neoliberal Globalization: The Alien Tort Claims Act and Grassroots Mobilization in *Doe v Unocal*' (2009) 43 *Law & Society Review* 271.

[228] T Tyler and J Jackson, 'Popular Legitimacy and the Exercise of Legal Authority: Motivating Compliance, Cooperation, and Engagement' (2014) 20 *Psychology, Public Policy and Law* 78.

[229] K Barker, 'Private Law: Key Encounters with Public Law' in K Barker and D Jensen (eds), *Private Law: Key Encounters with Public Law* (Cambridge, Cambridge University Press, 2013) 35–36 (emphasis added).

Alternatively, if 'right' (or 'legitimate') is a sociological fact, whose perceptions count—or count more? Does a globalised sense of outrage and threat from corruption perhaps drown out the views of affected Second and Third World peoples, which should actually carry more weight?

Conclusions

Since the end of the Cold War, anti-corruption has been considered a component part of efforts to improve governance. Once regarded as the efficient grease of modernising markets, corruption was reconfigured as a danger to economic growth and foreign investment, social stability and the rule of law. Development institutions changed their policies and programmes, and states concluded international treaties to 'prevent and suppress' misuses of power or office for private gain. Various forms of bribery were to be criminalised, as were unilateral acts like embezzlement. Attributed to all societies and all levels of government, such corruption was considered of particular concern when it occurred in developing or transition countries at the level of heads of state or other 'politically exposed persons'. Those individuals pose a particular risk to 'good' governance due to their broad discretionary powers and ability to exploit the conditions of economic globalisation. They may receive or solicit bribes from multinational enterprises and other corporate actors, and they may conceal and enjoy their wealth through their access to financial centres and markets. Thus, chapter V UNCAC prescribes national laws intended to prevent the transfer of illicit wealth to financial institutions, on the one hand, and to help victim countries to enforce claims to transferred assets, on the other. Familiar from earlier instruments on money laundering, prudential regulation and drug control, such measures are presented as removing the incentives and capital for crime. These are retributive and remedial goals. Given the label of 'asset recovery' in the UNCAC, the measures are also seen to 'fight impunity' of public officials and realise a range of individual and collective human rights objectives.

As yet, there are few signs of consistent state or non-state compliance with the standards. The USA, the UK and Switzerland have been important 'early adopters' of the programme. They have departed from their apparent interests in protecting their financial centres and restrained, confiscated or otherwise helped in the restitution of wealth to Africa, Asia, Eastern Europe and Latin America. They have also instituted and reviewed their preventative AML laws. However, the totals intercepted and returned are still dwarfed by estimates of the amounts taken. On this basis alone, there are reasons to doubt that the lack of progress can be usefully ascribed to 'lack of political will' or high 'barriers to return'. Asset recovery practices are criticised for their weak evidentiary basis and departures from important principles of criminal procedure and public law: there are long-standing empirical critiques of the effectiveness of AML and associated 'proceeds of crime' laws in deterring and incapacitating offenders; there are renewed concerns with the compatibility of 'enhanced' methods of asset recovery with human rights standards. If recent debates in Switzerland over the proposed Lex Ben Ali are any guide, protection of fundamental principles may be a point of resistance in haven countries, traditional 'liberal' constituencies opposing pragmatic cosmopolitan law reform. It is somewhat ironic, then, that the broader programme of 'global anti-corruption' is also relativised—even criticised—as demonstrating a Western (neo) liberal bias.

Overall, the challenge of asset recovery is not merely a challenge of deciding on, and assessing against, measures of policy performance. By extension, it is not merely a challenge of persuading domestic officials to implement the necessary law reforms. Equally, it is a challenge of justifying the apparently restrictive effect of asset recovery measures on individual civil and political rights—in light of questions about the existence of constitutional norms in public international law and weak empirical evidence. Studies of effectiveness would bolster the permissive position of the ECtHR, but would not end the arguments from a critical point of view. These critiques have superficial application to 'asset recovery', though they do not entirely account for 'indigenous' Second and Third World support for the new norm.

In this way, the 'challenge' of asset recovery highlights the indeterminacy of standards and methodologies for evaluating efforts at global governance that are set forth in international law. At the global level of abstraction and diversity, benchmarks like 'effectiveness', 'community support', 'proportionality' and 'legitimacy' become unstable and break down easily. Resting on prior understandings of good regulation, these ideas beg questions of how (for whom) the standards came into being and whether (and how) they can be assessed against. There is a political and an epistemological challenge embedded within the problem of asset recovery. To confront a challenge like asset recovery is to open up the underlying meta-concepts for review. It is then to go a step further and include the views of multiple actors in assessments and to seek their views about the efficacy and defensibility of that work. Last but not least, it is to treat the setting of standards for assessment as a self-conscious and inductive activity.

Scholars in the legal pluralists tradition have already undertaken macro- and microstudies of individual accountability norms,[230] and there are ongoing efforts to gather beneficiary views on the efficacy, accountability and impact of other forms of international assistance, particularly in humanitarian situations.[231] It is now time to explore how similar methodologies could be used to enrich more traditionally socio-legal studies of effectiveness and more narrowly 'legal theoretical'

[230] SE Merry, *Human Rights and Gender Violence: Translating International Law into Local Justice* (Chicago, University of Chicago Press, 2010).

[231] See, eg, C Abu-Sada (ed), *In the Eyes of Others: How People in Crises Perceive Humanitarian Aid* (Médecins Sans Frontières/Humanitarian Outcomes/NYU Center on International Cooperation, 2012), available at www.doctorswithoutborders.org/eyes-others-how-people-crises-perceive-humanitarian-aid (describing the 'Perceptions Project'); M Anderson, D Brown and I Jean, *Time to Listen:*

or doctrinal works on global efforts to control economic crime. What is missing is a method that allows for critical reflection of asset recovery as a promise and practice, and permits a range of conventional and radical perspectives on what is or could be right. If it is any one thing, the challenge of asset recovery is the challenge of justifying particular attempts to regulate for the common good in conditions which encourage scepticism about the (pragmatic) means and measures, and the (moral) ends and standards for regulation.

Hearing People on the Receiving End of International Aid (Cambridge, MA, CDA Collaborative Learning Projects, 2012) (describing the 'Listening Project'), available at cdacollaborative.org/media/60478/Time-to-Listen-Book.pdf; Humanitarian Accountability Partnership, 'Humanitarian Accountability Standards 2010', available at www.hapinternational.org/pool/files/2010-hap-standard-in-accountability.pdf.

9

Restitution of Dirty Assets: A Swiss Template for the International Community

FRANK MEYER*

Introduction

Swiss Banks currently have approximately SFr 6,656 billion[1] under management. About 51 per cent of the deposits come from abroad, making Switzerland the world's number one country for cross-border asset management, with a massive 25 per cent market share. It may come as no surprise that a considerable part of this money is thought to be of illicit origin. Dictators, corrupt officials, shady businessmen, tax evaders and money launderers habitually (ab)use offshore financial centres to hide their ill-gotten wealth. Swiss banks are no exception. Counting on bank secrecy and a long-lived primacy of profit-orientation, so-called potentates and criminals have made vast use of the financial sector to stash away the fruits of their illegal acts,[2] imagining that their money is and will remain safe. This might have been a misperception.

Beginning with the ground-breaking *Marcos* case in 1986,[3] Swiss authorities have increasingly strengthened their efforts to identify and repatriate illegal assets. Having turned a blind eye to this problem before, the inflow of dirty assets has

* Prof Dr iur, LLM (Yale), Chair of Criminal Law and Procedure including International Criminal Law, University of Zurich.

[1] www.swissbanking.org/home/finanzplatz-link/facts_figures.htm.

[2] The (pro-active) acquisition of ill-gotten assets was a very common practice among Swiss fund managers until the 1970s, M Pieth (ed), *Recovering Stolen Assets* (Bern, Lang, 2008) 3.

[3] Ferdinand Marcos and his wife Imelda dominated Philippine politics from 1965 until a military and popular uprising removed him from the presidency in February 1986. Anticipating political developments, in March 1986, the Swiss Federal Council unilaterally froze hundreds of millions of US dollars held by Marcos, his family and associates in Swiss bank accounts. The amounts were emitted to an escrow account at the Philippine National Bank in 1998 and released in 2003 after the Philippine Supreme Court found in favour of the Republic in a confiscation action. As a result, the Philippines received $683 million from Switzerland. For more details, see SV Marcelo, 'The Long Road from Zurich to Manila: the Recovery of the Marcos Swiss Dollars Deposit' in Pieth (ibid) 89.

been recognised as a pivotal political concern ever since.[4] With growing awareness of the magnitude of the problem and of the immense reputational risks that abusive practices in its financial centres entail, policy makers have understood that continued inactivity could have threatened the integrity of the entire financial centre. Of late, further policy threads have been woven into the overall strategy to combat illegal assets. Tracing and restitution activities have been put in context with broader development policies (seeking to improve the lot of affected communities and to promote good governance) and the fight against impunity (and corruption) at large.

In response to this challenge, Switzerland follows a two-pronged approach, comprising preventive and repressive elements. In terms of prevention, domestic money laundering provisions and administrative regulations for the financial sector adopted by the Swiss Financial Market Supervisory Authority (FINMA) legally oblige banks and financial intermediaries to identify their customers and beneficial owners. With respect to politically exposed persons (PEPs), enhanced diligence is due under Swiss law.[5] Suspicious activities have to be reported to the Money Laundering Report Office Switzerland (MROS), the national financial intelligence unit.

As the many instances of illicit assets detected in Switzerland imply that this first prong is obviously not sufficient, repressive instruments play a much more important part in Switzerland's action plan against illicit assets. Over the years, the legal machinery has been refined and diversified to be able to better cope with the huge variety of scenarios and challenges. The latest addition to the line-up was introduced in 2011: the Restitution of Illicit Assets Act (RIAA),[6] which provides for an administrative non-conviction-based forfeiture. Today, repressive measures encompass precautionary seizures, legal assistance for foreign criminal investigations, enforcement of foreign confiscation orders, and criminal and administrative confiscations at the domestic level.

Deliberately deviating from traditional international practice to channel confiscated proceeds of crime into state coffers even if they might be of foreign origin, Switzerland had adopted a policy of returning assets confiscated by way

[4] Federal Council, Strategic directions for Switzerland's financial market policy, Report in Response of the Graber postulate, 16 December 2009 (09.3209), 4; HP Bauer, 'How to Deal with Politically Exposed Persons' in Pieth (n 2) 197. Switzerland started to demand heightened scrutiny of customers from the financial sector and later passed anti-money-laundering legislation to actively defend its financial market against dirty assets—the Swiss Act against Money Laundering of 1997 (Bundesgesetz über die Bekämpfung der Geldwäscherei und der Terrorismusfinanzierung im Finanzsektor of 10 October 1997, SR 955.0).

[5] Art 2 RIAA defines politically exposed persons as persons who exercise or have exercised prominent public functions in a foreign state, in particular heads of state or heads of government, high-ranking politicians, high-ranking civil servants in the executive branch, the judiciary, the military, high-ranking officials of national parties and senior executives of state-owned enterprises of national importance.

[6] Federal Act on the Restitution of Illegally Gained Assets of Politically Exposed Persons (Bundesgesetz v 1.10.2010 über die Rückerstattung unrechtmässig erworbener Vermögenswerte politisch exponierter Personen (RuVG) SR 196.1).

of any of the aforementioned instruments to the country of origin long before the United Nations Convention against Corruption (UNCAC) came into effect. Swiss agencies, in concert with receiving states and international organisations, have developed an assorted array of disposal mechanisms whose main function and common denominator is to guarantee the co-ordinated and transparent reuse of confiscated assets for purposes of public interest. Since the mid-1980s, Swiss authorities have made use of the full panoply of instruments and remitted several billion dollars to states whose economies and treasuries had been looted by politicians and organised criminals.[7] While these efforts for decades were perceived as being primarily specific concerns of Swiss financial centres, public perception has changed considerably of late. The Arab Spring may be seen as an international watershed moment in this regard. It has led to the accelerated conclusion of a gradual change of dimension and paradigm. The scope of the measures was expanded to the entire ensemble of persons and entities mired in the nepotistic and exploitative practices of rogue regimes.[8] More importantly, the fight against potentate funds has gained political importance and become a joint international concern in its wake. At the UN and especially in the EU,[9] instruments have been adopted that directly target such funds.[10]

Whereas the freezing of property is a measure entrenched in international security law (eg embargos, prevention of financing terrorism), its reallocation was not. It is therefore no surprise that most states have effective freezing mechanisms in place but lack powerful tools and executive clout to effect confiscations and returns of potentate funds.[11] For this approach to get off the ground and gain momentum, the actors need effective instruments and operational expertise. Switzerland provides a good example of both. The country has been at the

[7] For an overview of groundbreaking cases, see F Zinkernagel and K Attisso, *Returning Stolen Assets—Learning from Past Practice: Selected Case Studies* (Bern, Basel Institute on Governance, 2013); for greater detail of the early cases, see D Richter, 'Potentatengelder in der Schweiz: Rechtshilfe im Spannungsfeld der Menschenrechte von Tätern und Opfern' [1998] *Zeitschrift für ausländisches öffentliches Recht und Völkerrecht ZaöRV* 541.

[8] See generally Federal Department of Foreign Affairs, Directorate of International Law (EDA-Direktion für Völkerrecht), commentaries to the Preliminary Draft Act on the Freezing and Restitution of Potentates' Assets (Bundesgesetz über die Sperrung und die Rückerstattung unrechtmässig erworbener Vermögenswerte politisch exponierter Personen SRVG) 8 May 2013, 7 and 9.

[9] See, eg, Council Act of 26 May 1997 drawing up, on the basis of Article K.3 of the treaty on European Union, the Convention on the fight against corruption involving officials of the European Communities or officials of Member States of the European Union, Brussels, May 26, 1997, in force 28 September 2005 [1997] OJ C195, 2.

[10] For instance, at the outbreak of the uprising in Libya, the UN Security Council required all member states to freeze the assets and other economic resources owned or controlled by individuals or entities named on an annexed list, as well as those of the Libyan authorities, as designated, and individuals and entities acting on their behalf or at their direction, or entities owned or controlled by them: SC Res 1970 (2011), adopted by the Security Council at its 6491st meeting, 26 February 2011, UN Doc S/Res/1970(2011), §17; SC res 1973 (2011), adopted by the Security Council at its 6498th meeting, 17 March 2011, UN Doc S/Res/1973 (2011), §19.

[11] See EDA, commentaries to the Preliminary Draft SRVG, 8 May 2013, 12.

forefront of the fight against potentate funds, and features the internationally most developed and time-tested system. As such, the Swiss example is a valuable point of reference for all countries that struggle with the confiscation and restitution of illegally obtained assets. In the subsequent sections, the relevant restitution instruments at the disposal of Swiss institutions to confiscate assets will be presented summarily, together with those restitution mechanisms that have been tested so far. The chapter concludes with a brief exploration of challenges and problems encountered throughout the implementation process.

I. Options

As the inevitable first step in the restitution process, suspicious assets can be frozen. Swiss authorities usually act quickly when it comes to the freezing of assets deposited in Switzerland. Since Swiss law provides for multiple overlapping seizure powers[12] conferred on different actors,[13] these assets could be subject to multiple seizure warrants. In practice, such provisional measures may last for an extremely long time without measurable prospects of successfully challenging individual freezing orders before federal courts. At the time of writing, five billion Swiss francs' worth of assets remain frozen.[14] Whereas seizures are imposed with minimal delay, the ultimate disposal of frozen assets may take years. The extraordinary length of proceedings for the most part is due to the complicated operation of the restitution instruments. The following subsections outline the various mechanisms Swiss authorities have used in the past to facilitate the return of dirty assets to victim countries.

A. Execution of Foreign Judgments and Civil Proceedings

Among these instruments, the classic (and internationally common) execution of foreign judgments subsequent to an exequatur process has become virtually irrelevant.[15] Equally futile ways for foreign countries would be to intervene as a civil

[12] Namely, administrative preventive measures based on constitutional emergency clauses, provisional measures based on mutual legal assistance statutes, regular seizure pursuant to domestic criminal procedure.

[13] Namely, the Federal Council (the Swiss Government/Bundesrat), the Federal Office of Justice (Bundesamt für Justiz/BJ) and the Federal Public Prosecutor (Bundesanwaltschaft/BA).

[14] For instance Petrobras: SFr 400 million; Yanukovich: SFr 100 million.

[15] It still plays a role for value-based confiscation, Federal Criminal Court (BStGer) 15 April 2009, RR.2008.244, E. 4.2. The applicable procedure is regulated in Art 94 et seq. IMAC. Execution of value-based confiscations would require a domestic exequatur decision. Such authorisation is ruled out categorically, however, for specific types of offences, namely fiscal, political and military offences, decision of the Federal Court of Justice BGE 133 IV 215, 221, E.2.2.2.

party to the criminal proceedings or to seek enforcement through civil actions in Switzerland.[16] Instead, mutual legal assistance plays the most important role.[17]

B. Mutual Legal Assistance

The central position of mutual legal assistance results from an innovative provision in Article 74a of the Federal Act on International Mutual Assistance in Criminal Matters (IMAC) that allows the return of illicit proceeds of crime without a prior exequatur decision in reaction to foreign confiscation efforts (be they of a criminal, administrative or civil nature).[18] Said provision was conceived of with a double purpose. It was meant to alleviate procedural incompatibilities that resulted from specific types of foreign decisions or evidential standards not known or insufficient in Swiss proceedings (which thus would have precluded exequatur decisions). Article 74a IMAC was also supposed to statutorily align an established but perfunctory prior practice of handing over assets for the purpose of forfeiture or return.[19] The Article was passed by the legislature with politically sensitive cases of former dictators in mind. Article 74a IMAC does not make this concern explicit though; consequently, it applies to all types of crime. By virtue of Article 74a paragraph 1 IMAC, 'On request, objects or assets subject to a precautionary seizure may be handed over to the competent foreign authority after conclusion of the mutual assistance proceedings for the purpose of forfeiture or return to the person entitled'.[20] Paragraph 3 adds that this handing over may take place at any stage of the foreign proceedings, normally but not necessarily based on a final and executable decision from the requesting state.[21] This restriction meets concerns about the severity of the civil rights infringement that this combination of expatriation and expropriation of property constitutes, especially when assets of persons who have not (yet) been convicted are concerned.[22]

[16] eg the case of *Schah Mohammed Reza Pahlavi*, 1979; on advantages and disadvantages of civil proceedings, see T Daniel and J Maton, 'Civil Proceedings to Recover Corruptly Acquired Assets of Public Officials' in Pieth (n 2) 243, 248.

[17] Over the last five years alone, Switzerland has returned SFr 126 million by virtue of Art 74a IMAC; most cases concerned fraud. Not surprisingly, Switzerland's reliance on the MLA track has expedited the conclusion of new bilateral mutual legal assistance treaties with countries of origin such as the Philippines (Marcos), Peru (Fujimori), Mexico (Salinas) and Egypt.

[18] Federal Court of Justice, case BGE 132 II 178, 182, E. 3–5. Art 74a IMAC was introduced in 1997.

[19] Federal Court of Justice, case BGE 123, 595 S. 602; M Aepli in *Basler Kommentar Internationales Strafrecht BSK/IMAC* (Basel, Helbing, 2015), Art 74a, margin no 2 referring to the leading cases BGE 115 Ib 517 (*PEMEX*) and BGE 116 Ib 452 (*Marcos*).

[20] The objects or assets referred to include instruments which were used to commit the offence, products of or profits from the offence, their replacement value and any unlawful advantage, gifts and other contributions which served to instigate the offence or recompense the offender, as well as their replacement value.

[21] F Meyer, 'Ergänzende Kommentierung "Schweiz": kleine Rechtshilfe' in K Ambos, S König and P Rackow (eds), *Rechtshilferecht in Strafsachen* (Baden-Baden, Nomos, 2015) 1001.

[22] Federal Court of Justice, case BGE 115 Ib 517, 556.

(i) Early Release

This standard rule does not exclude the possibility of an early release.[23] In fact, the competent Swiss authorities enjoy considerable discretion—in particular, in preventing Switzerland from becoming a safe haven for dirty money.[24] However, they usually grant restitution only under strict conditions when no doubt could be entertained about the illegal origin of the funds and a proper subsequent confiscation proceeding consistent with essential human rights standards was guaranteed.[25] This exception is handled very strictly.[26] A more permissive practice would run the risk of side-stepping the decision taken by the legislature that sought to limit restitutions (without previous foreign judgment to act on) to exceptional cases, while not entirely excluding them.

(ii) Criminal Organisations

Another possible case of application for an early release concerns assets which belong to criminal organisations,[27] if the conduct at the heart of the request qualifies as participation in a criminal organisation under Swiss criminal law.[28] Article 72 of the Criminal Code (Strafgesetzbuch; StGB) provides for the confiscation of all assets over which criminal organisations have control without positive proof of their criminal provenance. Furthermore, assets belonging to individuals who participated in or contributed to this criminal organisation are presumed to be controlled by the organisation (Article 72, paragraph 2 StGB).[29] Said provision effectively loosens the otherwise necessary link between asset and actual crime based on the relatively thin concept of criminal organisation. The Federal Court of Justice (Bundesgericht) nevertheless condoned this innovative approach in the *Abacha* case.[30] However,

[23] Aepli *IMAC*(n 19) Art 74a, margin no 48; M Dannacher, *Diktatorengelder in der Schweiz* (Basel, Helbing, 2012) 79; Even though the approval of an early release should not undermine the general requirement of a legally binding decision, Federal Court of Justice, case BGE 123 II 595 E. 4f.

[24] Aepli *IMAC*(n 19) Art 74a, margin nos 10 and 12.

[25] Federal Office of Justice, *Die internationale Rechtshilfe in Strafsachen, Wegleitung* (*Guidelines of the Federal Office of Justice*), 9th edn (Federal Office of Justice, 2010) 68; Federal Court of Justice, cases BGE 123 II 134, 137ff, E. 5b; BGE 123 II 595, 605, E. 4e; earlier cases: BGE 115 1b 517, E. 7d; 116 1b 452, E. 5b.

[26] The source of the seized fortune must be almost self-evident; doubts exclude early release; Federal Court of Justice, case BGE 123 II 595, 605, E. 4f; R Zimmermann, *La coopération judiciaire internationale en matière pénale*, 4th edn (Bern, Stämpfli, 2014) 337.

[27] Aepli *IMAC*(n 19) Art 74a, no 37; Dannacher (n 23) 81–82.

[28] Zimmermann (n 26) 339.

[29] Dannacher (n 23) 76–77.

[30] Federal Court of Justice, case BGE 131 II 169, 184, E. 9.1; for more information on this case, see E Monfrini, 'The *Abacha* Case' in Pieth (n 2) 41; T Daniel and J Maton, 'Recovering the Proceeds of Corruption: General Sani Abacha—A Nation's Thief' in Pieth (n 2) 63. After the death of General Sani Abacha in 1998, his successors decreed the return of his foreign assets and charged two of his sons and an associate with property offences. The Nigerian authorities sought the help of—among others—Switzerland in gathering evidence and tracing, restraining and confiscating suspected illicit wealth. The Federal Court of Justice affirmed that funds could be repatriated without a final and executable Nigerian order because they were clearly of criminal origin. The Federal Court of Justice applied the

with the exception of *Duvalier*,[31] it has hardly ever been practised since. The Federal Public Prosecutor revived the concept in a recent case, but the handing order was ultimately deemed illegal by the Federal Criminal Court (Bundesstrafgericht) for other reasons.[32]

That implies that this option is not moot. However, it has not been pushed decisively to test its limits, and awaits further substantiation (in Federal Court jurisprudence). While proving the existence of a criminal organisation already poses a formidable legal challenge, the situation is even more complicated in the context of PEPs. Declaring corrupt political elites a criminal organisation might be tempting, and seems natural for journalists or human rights activists. It is much less so for lawyers, who must establish the required legal elements. This manoeuvre is even more troubling from a more abstract perspective, given its obvious functionalist rationale. Proponents want to cast a wide net over PEPs and all affiliated persons,[33] thus tainting all assets at their disposal. This would in effect be tantamount to a complete reversal of the burden of proof for all PEPs, including their entire entourage, which—with a view to the deep entanglement of politics, business and security apparatus in highly corrupt countries, and bearing in mind the broad definitions of PEPs and affiliated persons—might affect and perhaps paralyse large parts of the national economy.

(iii) Practical Limitations

As a result, Article 74a IMAC does not open a fast track to restitution. Early releases have been limited to rare instances. As a matter of standard operating procedure, requesting states still have to furnish a final confiscation order or equivalent decisions. This statutory requirement causes a host of problems, particularly in PEP cases. Foreign requests have to establish a link (paper trail) between asset and criminal act.[34] Requesting states often fail to sufficiently substantiate that assets located in Switzerland originate from a specific criminal act. These problems are partly caused by the fact that Article 74a IMAC does not allow for value-based

rebuttable presumption that assets of a participant or supporter of a criminal organisation were actually at the organisation's disposal, assuming that Abacha and his closest persons around him had established a criminal organisation (with a criminal structure), the aim of which was to profit from corrupt actions. The Swiss Court therefore held that frozen assets in the amount of $508 million could be repatriated, as no evidence of the legal origins of the funds was forthcoming.

[31] Federal Court of Justice, case BGE 136 IV 4. The Federal Public Prosecutor of Switzerland had ordered the funds to be returned to Haiti for use in humanitarian projects, reasoning that the Duvalier Clan was a criminal organisation and that the assets had not been shown to have a legal origin.

[32] BStGer, 9 December 2014, RR.2014.150–52, E.4.3.

[33] The inclusion of affiliated persons in particular raises concerns because it is not comparable with membership in a criminal organisation and thus not a convincing proxy for the criminal origin of their wealth.

[34] See Federal Court of Justice, case BGE 115 Ib 517, 534, E. 7d.

confiscations,[35] albeit foreign authorities are sometimes not even in a position to prove an offence. Generally, it can be said that many jurisdictions that are seriously affected by organised crime and (former) corrupt elites have difficulty meeting formal mutual legal assistance (MLA) minimum requirements. On a more emotional level, relations between societies and agencies involved may become strained if operational and technical problems go hand in hand with exaggerated (public) expectations in requesting states. Seized amounts often fall behind estimates that circulate in the public sphere. This is partly due to a lack of reliable data, so that estimates rather resemble informed guesses.

Against this backdrop, Swiss authorities have resorted to other pragmatic means in order to make the MLA track more effective. They offer co-operation, training and counselling as part of a larger strategy to alleviate the problems occurring at the various stages of the confiscation process. Most importantly, the Federal Bureau of Justice may second its own staff or dispatch cantonal magistrates, prosecutors or attorneys to support foreign magistrates throughout the crucial investigative phase. This is the stage that makes the greatest difference in the end, assuming that no more asset tracing takes place in the later stages of the process and that requested states generally rely on information provided by the requesting state.

Furthermore, issuing a sufficiently substantiated restitution request gives rise to additional difficulties. Both the crime and the paper trail must be demonstrated in a conclusive and detailed manner. Here, again, the Federal Office of Justice provides guidance and offers to unofficially review draft versions of the foreign request prior to its official submission. It is also possible (though rare, and contingent on whether domestic jurisdiction exists) that Federal or Cantonal Public Prosecutors will open own investigations to gather evidence with a view to transferring it to the requesting state later on in order to enable the requesting state to establish elements of the crime and paper trail.

It is obvious, however, that lack of training and resources, and sometimes (for reasons of personal or national pride) unaccommodating attitudes of foreign partners or even a lack of political will[36] to investigate against former regime members, stand in the way of making MLA more effective.

[35] See n 8 above. According to the prevailing opinion, confiscations to enforce foreign (value-based) compensation orders called 'Ersatzforderung' are not possible; *cf* A Donatsch, S Heimgartner, F Meyer and M Simonek, *Internationale Rechtshilfe unter Einbezug der Amtshilfe im Steuerrecht*, 2nd edn (Zurich, Schulthess, 2015) 44; for a different view, see Zimmermann (n 26) 333. Consequently, Art 74a IMAC does not allow the transfer of assets when the confiscation order does not contain sufficient information about the nexus between crime and property, Federal Court of Justice, cases BGE 133 IV 215, 220, E. 2.2.1; BGE 129 II 453,461, E. 4.1.

[36] In some countries, old power networks might still be able to exert influence on all branches of government. Such interferences could have the potential to paralyse the entire confiscation process.

C. Domestic Prosecutions

An alternative is the initiation of own domestic prosecutions and subsequent confiscations pursuant to national criminal law.[37] This avenue presupposes own jurisdiction and a willingness to invest an increased amount of own resources. Despite the domestic nature of these proceedings, assets expropriated in this way can be returned to the state of origin based on international sharing agreements (so-called 'fake sharing').[38]

D. Third State Confiscation Requests

Likewise, requests by third states capable of passing adequate confiscation orders may ultimately lead to a handing over of assets seized in Switzerland to the state of origin. The pivotal conduit that permits requested and requesting states to return property to another country is a subsequent trilateral sharing agreement between all of the countries involved.[39]

E. Settlements

Finally, settlements between property holders and Swiss authorities allow for a simplified restitution of illicit assets. Such settlements and waivers of property rights can be induced by offering a reduced sentence in the country of origin and can be negotiated as part of a plea agreement. Such haggling may entail negative side effects, of course. At times, authorities might feel impelled to leave fractions of illicitly acquired funds to notorious looters in order to reach an agreement.

F. Administrative Confiscations

(i) Legislative History

With increasing experience, it became clear that more efficient instruments were needed,[40] the Arab Spring and various expert reports (eg the OECD

[37] This happened in the Angolan cases and facilitated the repatriation of huge amounts held by Montesinos or his associates. In the Peruvian case, neither criminal convictions nor confiscation orders followed from the prosecution. Instead, the repatriation of frozen assets was based on the declaration of waivers by the property holders.

[38] 'Fake' in the sense that assets are not shared but returned in their entirety if they can be linked to a foreign country of origin.

[39] Kazakhstan is a good example of this practice. In this case, a US request for MLA in a corruption case also triggered money laundering investigations that led to the confiscation of $48 million.

[40] Y Morier, 'Is Autonomous Confiscation the Acme of Asset Recovery?' in Pieth (n 2) 267 and 276.

Report on Corruption) having exposed the shortcomings of the available toolkit. Despite all co-operative efforts, MLA standards might still turn out to be too demanding to comply with.[41] This proved particularly true for failed or failing states such as Haiti and Libya, especially in the aftermath of dramatic overthrows. Without proper investigations into crimes of former potentates, their countries of origin run the risk that a statute of limitations will eventually forbid prosecutors from charging those crimes. Switzerland experienced this exasperating outcome in the epic *Duvalier* case.[42] Statutes of limitation generally pose a serious problem in PEP cases. Since many potentates manage to stay in power for lengthy periods of time (and often for life), a substantial portion of their crimes (typically corruption) will have become time-barred even before their regimes are toppled.[43]

It thus became evident that authorities run out of options once MLA stalls. In response, Switzerland decided to expand its arsenal in the fight against potentate funds. The RIAA, which came into force on 1 February 2011 (but was applied retroactively to the *Duvalier* case), introduces an administrative non-conviction-based forfeiture of funds of PEPs obtained by unlawful means.[44] The RIAA is no magical wand, though; rather, it is a subsidiary tool. The Federal Council may only resort to this instrument once MLA fails due to the failure or even breakdown of the justice system in the state of origin.[45] It authorises the freezing, forfeiture and restitution (repatriation) of illicit assets in the hands of PEPs or their associates only under these narrow conditions.

[41] Dannacher (n 23) 88–89.

[42] The *Duvalier* case started in 1986, when Haitian authorities submitted an official request for mutual legal assistance and asked for a provisional seizure of the assets of former state president Jean-Claude Duvalier. It took until 2002 to reach a decision. The mutual legal assistance proceedings were then closed after Haiti was unable to rectify several deficiencies in its request. In 2008, Haiti reiterated its request for assistance. It was granted by the BJ in 2009 and later confirmed by the Appeals Chamber of the Federal Criminal Court. By contrast, the Federal Court found that mutual legal assistance had become impermissible with the expiry of the period of limitation. According to the Federal Court, the further actions had been time-barred already when the 2002 decision was taken.

[43] G Fiolka, in *BSK/IMAC* (2015) Art 5, margin no 76. The *Mobutu* example is a case in point. In the end, frozen property had to be returned to his heirs. Short periods of limitation are a main reason why authorities attempt to define PEP and their entourage as criminal organisations. This has the immediate advantage that the statute of limitation does not become applicable before the regime (that is, the criminal organisation) dissolves; Federal Court of Justice, case BGE 136 IV 4, 10, E. 6.5.

[44] Bundesgesetz v 1.10.2010 über die Rückerstattung unrechtmässig erworbener Vermögenswerte politisch exponierter Personen (RuVG), SR 196.1; R Adam and V Zellweger, 'The Proposed Swiss Comprehensive Act on Asset Recovery' in G Zinkernagel, C Monteith and G Pereira (eds), *Emerging Trends in Asset Recovery* (Bern, Lang, 2013) 173, 176; U Cassani, 'Les avoirs mal acquis, et après la chute du "potentat"' (2010) 4 *Schweizerische Zeitschrift für internationales und europäisches Recht* 465; Dannacher (n 23); F Bianchi and S Heimgartner, 'Die Rückerstattung von Potentatengeldern' [2012] *Aktuelle Juristische Praxis* 353.

[45] This condition is modelled on Art 17, para 3 of the Rome Statute.

(ii) Scope and Functioning of the RIAA

Once MLA efforts have definitely failed, the Federal Council is entitled to freeze tainted assets of PEPs and associated persons[46] in order to facilitate their eventual administrative confiscation (Article 2 RIAA), though only under the condition that these assets had already been seized (by either the Federal Council or the Federal Office of Justice) and continuation of the measure is in the national interest.[47] These assets could then be put up for confiscation. Upon request by the Federal Council, the Federal Department of Finance is to file an application for confiscation with the Federal Administrative Court (Article 5, paragraph 1 RIAA). Article 5, paragraph 2 RIAA spells out the legal requirements: first and foremost, the court must satisfy itself with the illicit origin of all items listed in the request. Admittedly, this is easier written into law than actually done. Therefore, a key element of the new procedure is the reversal of the burden to prove the illicit origin of the assets foreseen in Article 6 RIAA.[48] Without such arrangements, it would often be next to impossible to establish criminal conduct and a paper trial. The reversal rests on the assumption that assets have been acquired illegally if the property holder is a PEP or an associate, if the PEP's wealth increased exceptionally during his term in office (lit a)[49] and if the country of origin was known for a notoriously high level of corruption throughout this period (lit b).[50] If the Federal Department of Finance succeeds in demonstrating these elements, the PEP or his/her associates are to rebut this presumption by proving the legal acquisition of the funds.[51] Third parties may also claim (limited) rights to the property at this stage (Article 7 RIAA). The court is tasked with the examination of such claims.

As a result of the painful lesson from the *Duvalier* debacle, the criminal statutes of limitation do not apply to the activities from which the allegedly illicit wealth originated.[52] This decision is conceptually sound and in line with the

[46] Pursuant to the RIAA, the concept of associated persons comprises natural and legal persons who maintain familial or personal relationships or business connections with PEPs. Definitions used for the RIAA complied with the then applicable international standards as set by the UN and the FATF. Its successor, FRPA, contains an updated definition, seeking conformity with modified FATF recommendations.

[47] The term 'national interest' alludes to the foreign policy discretion of the Federal Council and allows for sufficient leeway in the decision-making process.

[48] This provision has, at least partly, been inspired by the concept of illicit enrichment in Art 20 UNCAC; for a brief exploration of this concept and its current state of implementation, see L Muzila, M Berger, M Mathias and M Morales, 'Illicit Enrichment: An Emerging Tool in the Asset Recovery Process' in F Zinkernagel, G Monteith and C Gomes (eds), *Emerging Trends in Asset Recovery* (Bern, Lang, 2013) 245.

[49] Which means that there is no plausible explanation for this increase apart from corruption; the onus is on the government to prove the implausibility, Explanatory Memorandum (Botschaft) RuVG, 3337.

[50] Studies published by the World Bank or Transparency International count as valid sources of information in order to verify this prerequisite, Explanatory Memorandum (Botschaft) RuVG, 3337 f.

[51] It is fair to say, though, that these terms are very vague and in dire need of substantiation.

[52] There has been controversy surrounding this issue during the parliamentary debates, though.

in rem nature of RIAA confiscations. In this respect, it suffices that it is demonstrated convincingly that the funds have been acquired illegally.

After confiscation, Switzerland may conclude an international agreement with the country of origin to finalise the restitution of assets and arrange for their disposal (Article 9, paragraph 2 RIAA). One of the core interests of the law—going back to the main policies underlying the asset restitution—is that assets are to be reused to strengthen the rule of law and to improve the lot of the local population. In late 2013, the new procedure reached an important milestone. The Federal Administrative Court authorised the first administrative confiscation of assets owned by the Duvalier family.[53] The court decision became final shortly afterwards since the Duvaliers did not appeal to the Federal Court.

(iii) Common Points of Criticism

Many points of criticism have been put forward against the new law. Criminal lawyers have lamented that the RIAA's retroactivity violates the constitution, as does the reversal of the burden of proof, which is said to be irreconcilable with the presumption of innocence.[54] Much of the critique is due to diverging legal classifications regarding the confiscation. Whereas most criminal lawyers assume that said confiscation satisfies the elements of a criminal charge under Article 6 ECHR,[55] others, including the Federal Administrative Court, hold the view that it does not.[56] Most importantly, the confiscation neither rests on a specific finding of individual criminal responsibility nor expresses blame or public censure against the property holder.[57]

The same holds true for the preconditions and underlying assumptions of the reversal of the burden of proof. RIAA confiscations have been devised as instruments *in rem*. Their qualitative impact is that of an administrative measure, not of a criminal sanction. The magnitude of the infringement of the right to property does not change this characteristic. The expropriated amount alone does not transform the legal nature of a confiscation. The ECtHR has never recognised or even identified a quantitative monetary threshold in its Article 6-related jurisprudence. Admittedly, the distinction between proceedings *in rem* and proceedings *in personam* might sound artificial, especially because it is the *raison d'être*

[53] Federal Administrative Court (Bundesverwaltungsgericht), 23 September 2013, C-1371/2010 and 24 September 2013, C-2528/2011.

[54] Dannacher (n 23) 148 and 159–60, Cassani (n 44) 465 and 478–79; Bianchi and Heimgartner (n 44) 366–7; by contrast Bundesverwaltungsgericht of 23 September 2013, C-1371/2010, E. 2 u 3, Bundesverwaltungsgericht of 24 September 2013, C-2528/2011, E. 7.

[55] Dannacher (n 23) 147–48 and 150; Bianchi and Heimgartner (n 44) 366.

[56] Donatsch et al (n 35) 67; Explanatory Memorandum (Botschaft) RuVG, 3347–48; Bundesverwaltungsgericht, 24 September 2013, C-2528/2011, Erw 6.4.3 and 6.5.

[57] Botschaft zum Bundesgesetz über die Sperrung und die Rückerstattung unrechtmässig erworbener Vermögenswerte ausländischer politisch exponierter Personen vom 24. Mail 2014 (BBl 2014 5265), 36 f; Bundesverwaltungsgericht of 24 September 2013, C-2528/2011, E. 6.2–6.4; Donatsch et al (n 35) 67.

of non-conviction-based forfeitures to fight crime and hit criminals even when convictions before criminal courts cannot be secured. This does not make the RIAA illegitimate, but it should caution the legislature to define the instances in which such mechanisms can be resorted to clearly and convincingly. Architects of administrative confiscation instruments must also guarantee the right to be heard and provide for effective procedural remedies that allow third parties to protect their property rights.

(iv) Federal Act on the Freezing and Restitution of Potentates' Assets

After just one case of application, the RIAA was already subjected to a general overhaul. A need for reform was exposed by the unexpected challenges that followed from the events of the Arab Spring.[58] For reasons of expedience and constitutional due process, new legislation was drafted that was to confer statutory seizure power on the Federal Council early in the run-up to future MLA requests.[59] It was also meant to improve the clarity and accessibility of the restitution process.[60] Notably, it sought to allow administrative confiscations even when MLA co-operation had to be abandoned for reasons of human-rights-based MLA restrictions.

After protracted discussions in both parliamentary chambers, a new Federal Act on the Freezing and Restitution of Potentates' Assets (FRPA) was passed on 18 December 2015.[61] The FRPA entered into force in July 2016. Apart from (failed) attempts to integrate a statute of limitations,[62] the new human rights exception proved to be a particularly controversial issue. Detractors considered it to be incompatible with the fundamental principles of Swiss law because the FRPA enables co-operation where the IMAC prohibits it.[63] The decisive counter-argument would run along conceptual lines. An administrative confiscation proceeding is not about human beings, but about money. This difference renders deficits in the area of the rule of law and human rights protection less problematic, provided that returned assets cannot be diverted to finance unacceptable human rights policies and practices. It must also be ensured that foreign agencies observe the strict purpose limitation with regard to any information Swiss authorities share with them for the furtherance of confiscation proceedings.

[58] R Ivory, *Corruption, Asset Recovery and the Protection of Property in Public International Law, the Human Rights of Bad Guys* (Cambridge, Cambridge University Press, 2014) 47.

[59] A Chablais, 'La nouvelle loi sur les valeurs patrimoniales d'origine illicite', *Jusletter*, 11 January 2016, 3.

[60] Adam and Zellweger (n 44) 173 and 175.

[61] Federal Act on the Freezing and Restitution of Potentates' Assets (Bundesgesetz über die Sperrung und die Rückerstattung unrechtmässig erworbener Vermögenswerte politisch exponierter Personen/ SRVG). The freezing, confiscation and restitution provisions in this Act are modelled on Swiss state practice (Federal Council) under Art 184, para 3 Swiss Federal Constitution and the RIAA and EDA, commentaries to the Preliminary Draft SRVG, 23–25; Chablais (n 59) 3.

[62] Chablais (n 59) 24.

[63] Dannacher (n 23) 135 and 139–40.

The restitution process pursuant to the new comprehensive act comprises four stages. It starts with administrative actions to block funds as a precautionary measure, taken with a view to securing subsequent mutual legal assistance proceedings.[64] It empowers the Federal Council to act expeditiously in situations of political turmoil and regime change (Article 3 FRPA). The next step is effective support for criminal investigations and for the initiation or preparation of mutual legal assistance proceedings in the country of origin, including capacity building and the secondment of experts.[65] These powers are geared at removing obstacles in the MLA-based restitution process and hence testify to the subsidiary nature of administrative confiscation; new Article 13 even provides for the proactive forwarding of information to the country of origin through its financial intelligence unit MROS (if it is assured that information will be used exclusively for the preparation of an MLA request).[66]

Once the legal assistance track has proved to be of no avail due to severe institutional deficiencies or because certain minimum requirements regarding the rule of law and procedural guarantees according to European and international human rights standards cannot be met (Article 4, paragraph 3 FRPA), an administrative proceeding for confiscation of the funds may be initiated to avoid incriminated assets having to be released. The FPRA authorises the Federal Council (Swiss government) to start the administrative confiscation process, which is structured to culminate in a decision of the Federal Administrative Court on the legality of confiscation. The Federal Administrative Court may forfeit the frozen assets if they are owned by a PEP or an associate and were illicitly obtained (Articles 14–15 FRPA). A presumption of illicit acquisition in terms almost identical to those in the RIAA will be included to facilitate the court's work. Once final, the judgment effectuates the expropriation and confers the property rights on the Swiss Federation. Afterwards the funds are to be returned to the country of origin. The details of the transfer and the appropriation of the funds for public purposes are to be worked out and laid down in an international agreement.

II. Asset Disposal

The disposal phase is of utmost importance for the success of the overall restitution policy. Over the years, Swiss authorities have tested multiple options and gained considerable experience. Their actions have been guided by a couple of

[64] The SRVG, unlike the RIAA, does not require that a freezing order has been issued previously in an MLA proceeding. The seizure can be upheld for a maximum period of ten years.

[65] For possible forms of co-operation, see Adam and Zellweger (n 44) 177–78.

[66] Donatsch et al (n 35) 64, 66 and 69 points out a number of concerns surrounding this provision. It is to be understood in connection with Art 7 SRVG, which requires financial institutions to report the assets of all persons designated by the Foreign Office as PEPs or their associates.

basic principles. Dirty assets shall not fall back into the hands of 'unsavoury' persons. Returned property shall be disbursed for public purposes. The OECD's Paris Declaration on Aid Effectiveness (2005)[67] and the Accra Agenda for Action (2008),[68] designed to strengthen and deepen the implementation of the Paris Declaration, serve as further guideposts. Looking at past practice, it becomes clear that tailor-made solutions dominate.[69] 'One size fits all' approaches are considered inappropriate in this highly sensitive area.

Returning and receiving states have a wide spectrum of possibilities for effecting restitution at their disposal. These range from escrow accounts, special national funds,[70] World Bank programmes and projects of the Swiss Agency for Development and Cooperation (DEZA),[71] to customised foundations.[72] All disposal mechanisms share certain key elements, though. In combination, these elements are to ensure the proper implementation of the basic guiding principles. The arrangements must include a sufficiently precise determination of the end use of the assets.[73] The disposal process must be transparent: transparency and accountability are indeed further core components. Recently, disposal agreements have also revealed a preference for multi-stakeholder approaches. Purely national mechanisms, such as those installed in the cases of Peru (*Montesinos*)[74] and Nigeria (*Abacha*),[75] have proven to be prone to abuse and inefficiency. Multilateral monitoring and independence from domestic governments achieve better results.

If executed properly, a visible and transparent social reuse has a high symbolic value, as it underscores that political structures have changed and strengthened civil society. In cases of fake sharing (as the example of Kazakhstan illustrates), it

[67] Available under www.oecd.org/dac/effectiveness/parisdeclarationandaccraagendaforaction.htm (accessed on 7 April 2016).

[68] ibid.

[69] Zinkernagel and Attisso (n 7) 3 describe different structures and their effectiveness; P Veglio and P Siegenthaler, 'Monitoring the Restitution of Looted State Assets: The Role of Multilateral Development Banks (MDBs)' in Pieth (n 2) 315 and 322–23; for some case studies see I Jimu, 'Managing Proceeds of Asset Recovery: The Case of Nigeria, Peru, the Philippines and Kazakhstan', Working Paper No 6 (Basel, Basel Institute on Governance, 2009) 7–11, available at www.baselgovernance.org/sites/collective.localhost/files/publications/biog_working_paper_06.pdf.

[70] Like FEDADOI (Fondo Especial de Administración del Dinero Obtenido Ilícitamente en perjuicio del Estado) in Peru.

[71] Cases concerning Angola funds were administered by DEZA.

[72] As regards Kazakhstan, Switzerland, the United States, the World Bank and the country of origin agreed on a restitution through the 'BOTA Kazakh Child and Youth Development Foundation', to which frozen assets were to be transferred.

[73] According to Arts 17–18 SRVG and Arts 8–9 RIAA, confiscated assets shall be used in programmes that aim to improve the living conditions of the population or they shall help strengthen the rule of law in the country of origin.

[74] Peru established a special national fund, FEDADOI, and put it in charge of the administration of forfeited proceeds; Decreto de Urgencia No122-2001 (27 October 2001), available at www.justiciaviva.org.pe/nuevos/2006/setiembre/07/decreto.pdf. Switzerland had no more influence over the destination of the returned assets. Later reviews also cast doubt on some spending allocations, Zinkernagel and Attisso (n 7) 3.

[75] Nigeria channelled the Abacha assets into its national budget; the lack of parallel/concomitant monitoring was diagnosed as a major shortcoming.

is possible to return assets to countries with suspect regimes even before the PEPs have been forced to resign. Some countries, however, might be unwilling to follow this script for various reasons,[76] while others might experience a usurpation of power by even worse succession governments. Both situations could create an unfortunate state of uncertainty. Once assets are forfeited, they are to be handed over to the country of origin; however, in these instances, this is not an option. The integrity of the government seeking repatriation therefore plays a key role in the disposal process. Even when states are co-operative, they might sometimes be incapable of absorbing exorbitant inflows of money for public projects.

That said, the short history of asset disposal is one of constant learning, revising and improvising. Case studies starting with the Peruvian example and ending with the challenges of the Arab Spring suggest that the disposal process is both onerous and at times quite cost-intensive. It requires long-term commitment on the part of the returning state to make things work right.

Conclusion: Shortcomings and Innovation Potential

A number of technical problems that could arise during the restitution process have already been highlighted above. The final section of this chapter will address general operational, conceptual and political aspects. As regards the operational side, the co-ordination and co-operation between Swiss actors[77] and foreign agencies could be much enhanced. There seems to be too little joint asset tracing and mutual exchange of intelligence.[78]

Conceptually, it appears objectionable that administrative confiscations have been introduced as subsidiary instruments only. The normative concept behind the administrative confiscation procedure provides a stand-alone justification for both confiscation and reversal. It does not depend on the loss of power of either government or individual leaders, or on the failure of mutual legal assistance. Its legitimacy is entirely (conceptually and functionally) detached from these aspects. Yet, the Swiss legislature has not taken the measures to decouple confiscation and mutual assistance that several non-government organisations have called for. Lawmakers continue to curtail its potential applicability significantly for political reasons that are equally debatable. While it makes sense from a realist standpoint not to expropriate potentate funds as long as their owners still hold office, such restraint is at odds with more idealistic thinking. The central issue with both the RIAA and the FRPA is that they combine hard-core realist thinking and

[76] One might be that old networks and social power structures are still in place and impede efforts to channel money to the poor and needy.

[77] There are many cooks involved, but they are sometimes not preparing the same dish.

[78] As mentioned above, the Swiss authorities rely on information provided by requesting states or reports filed by Swiss banks.

high-flying idealism. This makes a strange amalgam, in particular with a view to the inherent tensions that the provision on the reversal of the burden of proof in Article 6 RIAA (and soon Article 15 FRPA) creates. In essence, these provisions imply that PEPs' assets can be presumed illegal under certain conditions and can subsequently be expropriated. However, Swiss authorities will not be able to address unexplainable increases of wealth in the future as long as the PEPs stay in power.[79]

At closer inspection, the RIAA and the FRPA do not send as clear a message as many of its advocates would like. They do not prevent the continued courting of PEPs by bankers, brokers, business and politicians as long as the criminal origin of their money is not too obvious and they are still in office. The political sector and international organisations maintain working relationships with many known corrupt politicians, ignoring their sometimes ostentatious display of illegal wealth.[80] Superseding public interests and the realist rules of international politics serve as convenient justifications.

However, some experts would argue that this portrayal is unrealistic, given that international sanctions require freezing orders against many incumbent statesmen with tarnished reputations. Moreover, banks and financial intermediaries are said to have implemented sufficient safeguards out of self-interest to avert reputational damage. The rather small amounts seized in the *Yanukovych* and *Ben Ali* cases[81] are read as evidence for the assumption that Swiss banks have stemmed the tide of potentates' funds quite successfully.

While that may be the case, in practice the legal frameworks for the prevention of money laundering and for the restitution of illicit assets have not been coordinated. The reporting duties concerning incoming assets are not necessarily triggered in all situations that would later allow confiscation pursuant to the RIAA. The national banking authority has not issued guidelines that would require such a reading. The biggest deterrence would be to introduce proactive administrative confiscation powers in all cases that satisfy the requirements of Article 5, paragraph 2 and Article 6 RIAA.[82] That said, there are still a lot of things that can be improved. One of the most crucial questions in terms of legal policy remains the

[79] Immunity from prosecution may impede initiation or successful conclusion of criminal or confiscation proceedings in the victim state.

[80] Bauer (n 4) 195 and 216.

[81] Art 1, para 1 Federal Council Order 'Verordnung über Massnahmen gegen gewisse Personen aus der Ukraine', 26 February 2014; Art 1, para 1 Federal Council Order 'Verordnung über Massnahmen gegen gewisse Personen aus Tunesien', 19 January 2011.

[82] Admittedly, the implementation of such a step would face serious obstacles. It could create diplomatic tensions and might affect personal immunities to be respected under international law, P Gully-Hart, 'International Asset Recovery of Corruption-Related Assets: Switzerland' in Pieth (n 2) 165, 179. Restitution to the country of origin could be impossible for long periods of time, requiring Switzerland to administrate and manage these assets during this time. Such a proactive stance could also harm the economy if investors and wealthy individuals turn their back on Switzerland for fear of (in their mind) unjustified expropriations.

feasibility of a general non-conviction-based forfeiture. PEPs do not always pose the biggest challenge in the field of asset recovery.

Most illicit assets result from ordinary white-collar crime or transnational organised crime; their proceeds make up a far larger portion of hidden assets. Although PEPs' assets are the main driving force behind recent developments, given their sensitivity and the public attention they draw, non-conviction-based approaches and reversals of the burden of proof are not inherently linked to these categories of cases. The introduction of comprehensive non-conviction-based forfeiture models would be highly pertinent in other areas of crime as well.[83] These would include the presumably countless unlawful activities of the PEPs' compatriots that fall outside the scope of RIAA or FRPA. Kleptocratic societies are mired in corruption and cronyism, and involve large parts of the economy. Yet, the vast majority of dubious business actors are not close enough to the targeted circle of PEPs to become targets themselves. They rather fly under the radar of the latest legal innovations.

Introducing more extensive confiscation instruments would, therefore, not only mark a further shift towards depriving criminals of the proceeds of their crimes, but also enable public authorities to target this group even before a regime change. Such efforts could be part of a broader strategy to bring down the regime itself. It seems, however, as if the potential for reform will have been exhausted with the passage of the new FRPA. Politically, it should nevertheless be recognised that Switzerland embodies the avant-garde of dealing with potentates' funds and does much more than other equally exposed financial centres. It has acted exemplarily in its reaction to international pressures. Against this background, it is understandable that decision makers in Switzerland emphasise the necessity to level the playing field now. Indeed, it is high time for all countries that have publicly committed themselves to the return of illicit assets to their country of origin to act. The Swiss example is a good point of reference.

[83] F Meyer, '"Reformiert die Rückgewinnungshilfe!"—Denkanstöße für eine Generalüberholung der Vermögensabschöpfung' [2015] *Zeitschrift für die gesamte Strafrechtswissenschaft ZStW* 241, 256.

10

The Relevance of Asset Recovery Policies in Transitional Societies: The Croatian Perspective

ELIZABETA IVIČEVIĆ KARAS* AND SUNČANA ROKSANDIĆ VIDLIČKA**

Introduction

Transitional justice refers to the set of judicial and non-judicial measures that have been implemented by different countries in order to redress the legacies of massive human rights abuses (mainly, abuses of civil and political rights). These measures include criminal prosecutions, truth commissions, reparation programmes and various kinds of institutional reforms.[1] One of the most cited definitions of transitional justice is one by Ruti Teitel. Teitel defined transitional justice as 'the conception of justice associated with periods of political change, characterised by legal responses to confront the wrongdoings of repressive predecessor regimes'.[2] As Sharp described:

> Some influential articles by Guillermo O'Donnell and Samuel Huntington, canonized in Neil Kritz's seminal three-volume work, view the parameters of justice in times of

* Associate Professor, University of Zagreb Faculty of Law.

** Assistant Professor, University of Zagreb Faculty of Law. This work was supported in part by the Croatian Science Foundation under projects 8282, 'Croatian Judicial Cooperation in Criminal Matters in the EU and the Region: Heritage of the Past and Challenges of the Future', and 1949, 'Multidisciplinary Research Cluster on Crime in Transition—Trafficking in Human Beings, Corruption and Economic Crime'. In writing this chapter, findings of the PhD study of Sunčana Roksandić Vidlička, 'Criminal Responsibility for Severe Economic Crimes Committed in a Transitional Period', defended as an international dual doctorate (University of Zagreb and University of Freiburg) in 2015, were used to describe the context of the transitional period of Croatia. Therefore, the Introduction and Section I were written by Roksandić Vidlička, while Section II was written by Ivičević Karas. Writing this chapter was a joint idea, and opinions represented in herein are the opinion of both authors concerning this topic. The conclusions were jointly proposed and written.

[1] 'What is Transitional Justice? Factsheet, International Center for Transitional Justice 2009', available at http://ictj.org/sites/default/files/ICTJ-Global-Transitional-Justice-2009-English.pdf.

[2] R Teitel, 'Transitional Justice Genealogy' (2003) 16 *Harvard Human Rights Journal* 69.

> transition to democracy as a function of a series of bargains between elite groups, with more or less justice available depending on the extent to which elite perpetrator groups were able to dictate the terms of transition.[3]

Laplante rightly emphasised:

> Given the tensions inherent in balancing absolute traditional justice through criminal trials with political compromises like selective prosecutions and amnesties, the transitional justice approach has generated debates that have grown in complexity over the years, 'prompting continued development of transitional justice mechanisms.[4]

In general, the discipline recognises that, due to political and historical realities, traditional justice mechanisms may be inadequate during political transitions towards liberal democracy. One of the main problems is that often 'inadequate or corrupt judicial institutions give rise to or permit repression and political violence, and the same problems continue during political transitions'.[5] Similarly, as Hesse and Post underlined,

> traditional judicial mechanisms may simply be incapable of addressing episodes of massive human rights violations. While at the same time, political compromises and the quest for peace and reconciliation often require more leniency and less strict adherence to the norms of criminal justice.[6]

One can state that the ambition of 'transitional justice' is to assist 'the transformation of oppressed societies into free ones by addressing the injustices of the past through measures that will procure an equitable future'.[7] As Alexander Boraine pointed out, this calls for a 'holistic interpretation'. While not detracting from criminal justice, this approach 'offers a deeper, richer and broader vision of justice which seeks to confront perpetrators, address the needs of victims and assist in the start of a process of reconciliation and transformation'.[8] Arbour emphasises that it must reach for 'and go beyond the crimes and abuses committed during the conflict that led to transition, and must address the human rights violations that

[3] DN Sharp, 'Introduction: Addressing Economic Violence in Times of Transition' in DN Sharp (ed), *Justice and Economic Violence in Transition* (New York, Springer Science+Business Media, 2014) 1, 7.

[4] For further discussion, see generally N Roth-Arriaza and J Mariezcurrena (eds), *Transitional Justice in the Twenty-first Century: Beyond Truth Versus Justice* (Cambridge, Cambridge University Press, 2006) as cited also by LJ Laplante, 'On the Indivisibility of Rights: Truth Commissions, Reparations, and the Right to Development' (2004) 10 *Yale Human Rights and Development Journal* 145.

[5] J Benomar, 'Justice after Transitions' in N Kritz (ed), *Transitional Justice: How Emerging Democracies Reckon with Former Regimes* (Washington DC, United States Institute of Peace Press, 1995) 32.

[6] C Hesse and R Post, 'Introduction' in C Hesse and R Post (eds), *Human Rights In Political Transitions: Gettysburg To Bosnia* (New York, Zone Books, 1999) 20–21.

[7] L Arbour, 'Economic and Social Justice for Societies in Transition' (2007) 40(1) *New York University Journal of International Law and Politics* 1, 2.

[8] AL Boraine, 'Transitional Justice: A Holistic Interpretation' (2006) 60(1) *Journal of International Affairs* 17.

pre-dated the conflict that caused and/or contributed to it'.[9] In any case, criminal justice for human rights abuses committed during periods of political repression or dictatorship 'is one of the greatest challenges to post-conflict societies'.[10]

As Carranza[11] argued, while transitional justice promotes accountability by what it chooses to confront, it may reinforce impunity by what it chooses to ignore. Therefore, strengthening the protection of economic and social rights in transitional states, including adequately regulating economic crimes, can be considered a *conditio sine qua non* for fulfilling goals of transitional justice, especially in countries that have shifted from the socialist economic system to a free market economy, or are in one of the phases of a transitional period.[12]

Schmid and Nolan pointed out[13] that some authors have recently considered the term 'transformative justice' as an alternative to transitional justice; one that will enable us to pay more attention to socio-economic issues when addressing the legacies of an abusive past.[14] For instance, Lambourne called for 'a transformative justice model of transitional justice that brings together economic justice along with legal, psychosocial, and political justice in an effort to transform both structures and relation'.[15] In any case, in 2010, the United Nations Secretary General released a Guidance Note on the United Nations Approach to Transitional Justice[16] that contains the principle that calls on the United Nations to strive to ensure that transitional justice processes and mechanisms should take into account root causes of conflict and repressive rule, addressing violations of all rights, including economic, social and cultural rights, not just civil and political ones. The same was repeated and enhanced in a recent publication by the United Nations Human Rights Office of the High Commissioner.[17]

Therefore, it could be clearly stated that transition is an especially vulnerable period and incentives to commit widespread and systematic economic crimes are enticing. How to address those transitional economic crimes and succeed in asset recovery is the topic of this chapter. Are these transitional economic crimes serious

[9] Arbour (n 7) 3.

[10] WA Schabas, 'Introduction' in WA Schabas and S Darcy (eds), *Truth Commissions and the Court, the Tension between Criminal Justice and the Search for Truth* (Dordrecht, Kluwer Academic Publishers, 2004) 1.

[11] R Carranza, 'Plunder and Pain: Should Transitional Justice Engage with Corruption and Economic Crimes?' (2008) 2(3) *International Journal of Transitional Justice* 310.

[12] Teitel (n 2) 69.

[13] E Schmid and A Nolan, '"Do No Harm"? Exploring the Scope of Economic and Social Rights in Transitional Justice' (2014) 8(3) *International Journal of Transitional Justice* 1, 19.

[14] For Schmid and Nolan (ibid), the proposed adjective 'transformative' has interesting philosophical implications for the concept of justice as such, including situations outside transitions.

[15] W Lambourne, 'Transitional Justice and Peacebuilding after Mass Violence' (2009) 3(1) *International Journal of Transitional Justice* 28, cited in Schmid and Nolan (n 13) 19.

[16] United Nations Guidance Note on the United Nations Approach to Transitional Justice 2008.

[17] United Nations Human Rights Office of the High Commissioner, *Transitional Justice and Economic, Social and Cultural Rights* (New York, United Nations Publication, 2014).

enough to serve as an incentive for introducing a special model of asset recovery 'just for them', even when the crimes are statute barred? How can the proceeds of such crimes be confiscated despite the statute of limitations? These are questions that this chapter aims to answer. In order to find an answer, a case study of Croatia is taken as an example due to its unique legal solutions concerning transitional economic crimes. Moreover, Croatian transitional experience shows that it is necessary to address all human rights abuses on time through a transitional justice mechanism, while ignoring economic crimes committed during the transitional period could lead to long-lasting anomie, as will be discussed later on.

Therefore, in this chapter, when we refer to the notion of transitional economic crimes, we are referring to economic crimes committed during the privatisation and ownership transformation period that occurred in Croatia while the economic system was changing from a communistic one (*socijalističko samoupravljanje*) to capitalistic one. But this notion is broader when taken in the Croatian context.

I. Facing the Problem of Transitional Economic Crimes in Croatia

A. The Notion of 'Transitional Economic Crimes' and the Croatian Differentiating Factor

Croatia is, unfortunately, a perfect example of a legal 'playground' for testing different possibilities in approaching asset recovery policies in transitional societies of transitional economic crimes. As stated by Novoselec et al,[18] after the fall of the Berlin Wall in 1989, a political crisis in the former Yugoslavia reached a peak and led to the country's dissolution. During this time, at the turn of the 1990s, Yugoslavia still chaired the Non-Aligned Movement. From the 1990s, it was also subject to severe recession, which was temporary halted by Marković's economic policy. Although the annual inflation rate of 02,665 per cent at the end of 1989 (with an unemployment rate of 15 per cent) had fallen to below 0.2 per cent by June 1990, it then climbed until the end of 1993.[19] Out of eight countries

[18] P Novoselec, S Roksandić Vidlička and A Maršavelski, 'Retroactive Prosecution of Transitional Economic Crimes in Croatia—Testing the Legal Principles and Human Rights' in J Van Erp, W Huisman and G Wande Walle (eds), *The Routledge Handbook of White-Collar and Corporate Crime in Europe* (Abingdon, Routledge, 2015) 198, citing K Engelberg, 'Feuds Crippling Yugoslav Economy', *New York Times*, 20 Apri 1991, available at www.nytimes.com/1991/04/20/business/feuds-crippling-yugoslav-economy.html.

[19] ibid 198.

in transition, Croatia had the highest average inflation rate in the first phase of transition (1991–1993).[20]

In the decade that followed the dissolution, most countries of the former Yugoslavia, including Croatia, went through one of the most difficult transitions of all European countries. The changes in the political and economic systems during the 1990s have made Croatia comparable to other countries that have shifted to a market economy and have undergone the privatisation process (a common denominator with other countries of central, eastern and south-eastern Europe).[21] At the same time, however, Croatia experienced war and peaceful reintegration (a differentiating factor). This differentiating factor or 'local context'[22] has proven to be of a dominant nature for Croatian transitional society, at least in prioritising the protection of civil and political rights over economic ones. Therefore, when we use the notion of transitional economic crimes in the Croatian context, one should be aware that we are referring also to the period of the Croatian Homeland War and peaceful reintegration (1990–98). During and after the Homeland War (1991–95), Croatia suffered major financial losses due to the extensive armed conflict that had taken place. According to the findings of the State Audit Report, direct war damage in the period 1990–99 was DEM 65 billion, ie €32 billion.[23] An important part of that war damage was a result of war crimes and collateral damage.

Although Croatian war profiteers abused the state of war for personal financial gain (eg setting disproportionately high prices for basic products and the sale of state property substantially below its value), profiteering did not appear in the audit of the overall amount of war damage. Further, the amount the war profiteers earned has never been officially revealed.[24] Instead, one must refer to Michalowski and Kramer's[25] statements that state-corporate relations create 'a political culture and organizational framework that ultimately [led] to heinous acts that would not have occurred without that culture and those frameworks'.[26]

The above-mentioned contexts—experiencing war and peaceful reintegration while undergoing economic transition—determined two categories of transitional

[20] V Šonje & B. Vujčić, 'Hrvatska u drugoj fazi tranzicije 1994–1999' (Croatian National Bank, June 1999) 1. In the period 1990–1993, the annual inflation rate was 728.5% (max 1517%), with an unemployment rate of 195%, as cited in I Matutinović and M Latković, 'Povratna veza inflacije i deprecijacije na primjeru Hrvatske 1991–1993' (November 1998).

[21] See, eg, A Eser, U Sieber and J Arnold (eds), *Strafrecht in Reaktion auf Systemunrecht 1996–2011* (Freiburg, Max-Planck-Institut für ausländisches und internationales Strafrecht, 2000–2012).

[22] Teitel (n 2) 93.

[23] M Perković and V Puljiz, 'Ratne štete, izdaci za branitelje, žrtve i stradalnike rata u Republici Hrvatskoj' (2001) 8 *Revija za socijalnu politiku* 235.

[24] See further Novoselec et al (n 18) 198.

[25] RJ Michalowski and RC Kramer (eds), *State-Corporate Crime: Wrongdoing at the Intersection of Business and Government* (New Brunswick, Rutgers University Press, 2006) 9.

[26] Cited in G Barak, 'Towards an Integrative Study of International Crimes and State-Corporate Criminality: A Reciprocal Approach to Gross Human Rights Violations' in A Smeulers and R Haveman (eds), *Supranational Criminology: Towards a Criminology of International Crimes* (Antwerp, Intersentia, 2014).

economic crimes in Croatia: (i) war profiteering and (ii) crimes in the process of privatisation and ownership transformation. In many cases, perpetrators of these transitional economic crimes abused the vulnerability of both processes and took advantage of Croatia as a young democracy.[27] Therefore, when we use the term 'transitional economic crimes' in the context of Croatia, we are addressing those two categories of crimes.

The only practical example so far of what may be considered to be a war profiteer was given in the judgment of the Supreme Court of Croatia in the case of former Croatian Prime Minister Ivo Sanader, which lasted only 15 months, before the Republic of Croatia Constitutional Court quashed it, together with the first instance judgment, on several grounds (see below).[28] The Supreme Court defined what was considered to be war profiteering, especially relating to the behaviour of public officials:[29]

> A large part of the occupied territory, great destruction, hundreds of thousands exiled and displaced Croatian citizens, extremely difficult economic situation, the use of most of the budget for defence of the state and at the same time the necessity of purchasing the building of the Croatian Embassy in order to spread the truth in the World of aggression which is committed [upon Croatia] and the liberation character of the Homeland War. Although the basic content of the war includes armed struggle, the war, however, is not just about conflict. War is a broader, more complex phenomenon because it involves other forms of struggle (political, economic, information) which have great importance for the preparation and conduct of war. In this connection, a notorious fact is that war preparation and other forms of struggle, which do not involve the use of weapons, are carried on in an area that is not directly affected by the war. This is especially important because of the fact that Croatia, at an international level, was a young state that, except for military battles, led political ones for the recognition of its political status, credibility and political positioning in the international, primarily in the European, community. The efforts of all citizens of Croatia, including government officials, at that time were, or should have been, directed toward the same goal, the establishment of a sovereign, independent and democratic state based on generally accepted social values. The fact that the war should have been won on a political level, on which Croatia should have proven its integrity, maturity, democracy and reliability, makes the context in which criminalized behavior has the characteristics of war profiteering. Specifically since, in this atmosphere the defendant used his official powers for illicit purposes, as it was rightly concluded by the trial court. At that time, Croatia, and its diplomacy, were not known at an international level … The defendant was entrusted with particular tasks, which at that time were extremely important for Croatia, and he abused that fact … by putting his personal interests above those of Croatian citizens. In this way, the defendant, as the Deputy Minister in Government., in Croatia's darkest hour, undermined [Croatian] reputation, degraded the sacrifice of soldiers in the war and threatened the core values of Croatian

[27] See further Novoselec et al (n 18) 19.
[28] VSRH I Kž-Us 94/13–10, 3 April 2014.
[29] ibid 6.

> society. The proper conclusion of the trial court is that [by doing so] this defendant violated the public order. Given that, it is justifiably established by the trial court, that war profiteering does not only make only previously known forms of this phenomena, such as raising the price of goods due to shortages, selling weapons to defend the country with disproportionately high prices, but also the behavior of which the defendant is guilty of ... Taking the provision from the agreement [Loan agreement between K.L. & H. b. with the political support of Austria] by the person to whom the primary duty was to represent and defend the interests of Croatia and not to worry about his own illegal profit ... and bearing in mind all aforementioned circumstances which marked the incriminated period, [that action] cannot be described in any other way other than war profiteering.

In this excerpt from the judgment, the Croatian Supreme Court provides a very extensive interpretation of the term 'war profiteer'.

According to Teitel, two political dimensions determine what signifies the rule of law in periods of transition: the transitional context, specifically the circumstances relating to political and legal conditions associated with periods of political change; and other political factors, such as the local context.[30] Although set circumstances made Croatia's transition somewhat specific, political weakness in addressing the economic crimes in conflict and post-conflict societies is typical not only of Croatia.[31] As Cejp and Scheinost said of the Czech Republic, it was 'a result of the social disintegration and disorientation brought by fundamental and ongoing changes in values and behavioural patterns'.[32] As a comparable example, for Serbia it can be stated that:

> The Milošević-era economic system (1991–2000) was characterized by a war economy, large grey economic sector, the black market, an oligarchy of tycoons controlling the large state-owned and private business enterprises, state-driven hyper-inflation, state-sponsored smuggling, client-patron relationships, state-backed pyramidal schemes, inefficient fiscal system, and lack of investments. Not only was economic crime considered 'normal', it was also actively encouraged to the extent that it became the regime's unofficial arm. The lines between the 'official' and 'unofficial' blurred to such extent that the 'shadier' parts of society found welcome protection under the regime of Slobodan Milošević. The regime was kept on a network (a pyramid, rather) of client-patron relationships that encompassed the whole society.[33]

[30] Teitel (n 2) 93.

[31] See MC Bassiouni, 'Assessing Conflict Outcomes: Accountability and Impunity in the Pursuit of International Criminal Justice, A World Study on Conflicts, Victimization and Post-Conflict Justice' in MC Bassiouni (ed), *The Pursuit of International Criminal Justice: a World Study on Conflicts, Victimization, and Post-Conflict Justice* (Antwerp, Intersentia, 2010) 18. For Hungary, see E Inzelt, 'White-Collar Crime During the Political and Economic Transition in Hungary' (2011) 8 *US-China Law Review* 352.

[32] M Cejp and M Scheinost, 'Organized and Economic Crime: A Common Problem' in A Šelih and A Završnik (eds), *Crime and Transition in Central and East Europe* (London, Springer, 2012) 158. See more in Novoselec et al (n 18) 201.

[33] R Brunhart and N Gajic 'Policing the Economic Transition in Serbia: Assessment of the Serbian Police Service's Capacities to Fight Economic Crime' (OSCE Mission to Serbia and Montenegro, Belgrade, 2005) 12, available at http://polis.osce.org/library/f/2917/1049/OSCE-SRB-RPT-2917-EN-1049 (accessed on 2 November 2014). See also M Vujosević, S Zeković and T Marić, 'Post-Socialist Transition in Serbia and Its Unsustainable Path' (2012) 20 *European Planning Studies* 1708.

Adding insult to injury, the process of privatisation and ownership transformation, which actually began in 1988 (while Croatia was still part of the former Yugoslavia), was—like in Serbia—far from transparent and fully legal from the beginning. The initial concept of privatisation and ownership transformation in Croatia was to transfer a substantial part of the state-owned corporations' shares to the workers for a privileged price, but one of the typical scenarios when abuses occurred was that substantial amount of shares were purchased by 'hawkers' and 'peddlers', while corruption was omnipresent.[34]

The process of privatisation and ownership transformation also required a suitable criminal law response. However, the overall legal order did not manage to keep up with the new economic order.[35] The descriptions of most economic crimes in the Yugoslav criminal legislation were completely obsolete and were adverse to the new constitutional order in Croatia. In addition, there were a number of loopholes, as some criminal offences were missing from the legislation (eg subsidy fraud, bankruptcy).[36] These obsolete economic offences, based on so-called administrative socialism, survived in a somewhat changed form until an extensive reform of economic crimes took place with the adopted of the new Criminal Code in 2011. Like company law in Croatia, this reform of economic crimes, their definitions and conceptualisation was heavily influence from German law.

The reform of Croatian criminal law, including the amendment of economic offences, was associated with the accession of Croatia to the European Union in 2013[37] (the year in which the new Criminal Code entered into force), since the harmonisation of national criminal law especially in the area of economic crimes was an accession requirement. The harmonisation requirements included, for example, the legal protection of free-market competition from prohibited cartels; the suppression of fraud damaging the EU budget; the combating of active and passive bribery in business transactions; and the criminalization of insider trading. In the meantime, the Law on Responsibility of Legal Entities for Crimes was passed in 2003, enabling criminal prosecution of legal entities, but since substantive criminal legislation was inadequate, the new law was unable to address contemporary economic crimes committed by corporations.

There are several social and political reasons for these flaws in Croatian criminal law. Some are related to the state of war, which attracted the most political

[34] See V Grozdanić and I Martinović, 'Corruption as a Metaphor for Societies in Transition?' in Šelih and Završnik (n 32). A Leburić, R Matić and M Quien, *Mito i korupcija u hrvatskom društvu* (Redak 2010) 13; OECD, *No Longer Business as Usual: Fighting Bribery and Corruption* (OECD, Paris, 2000); D Derenčinović, *Mit(o) korupciji* (Zagreb, NOCCI 2001) 7.

[35] For the 'deeds of fallen dictatorship', see J Arnold and E Silverman, 'Regime Change, State Crime and Transitional Justice: A Criminal Law Retrospective Concentrating on Former Eastern Block Countries' (1998) 6 *European Journal of Crime, Criminal Law and Criminal Justice* 140.

[36] See more in Novoselec et al (n 18) 202.

[37] For a commentary on the new Croatian Criminal Code, see K Turković et al., *Komentar Kaznenog zakona* (Zagreb, Narodne novine, 2013).

attention, others are related to political unwillingness to pass new legislation due to the personal benefits of the status quo by certain high-ranking officials. In addition, there was a problem with some of the law commissions that drafted proposals for new legislation, since sometimes they were appointed according to political preference, meaning that they lacked enough power to introduce much needed changes.[38] Furthermore, the opinions of experts are not always paid much attention by officials in power. Even when the law commissions were appointed independently from politics, some Croatian legal experts lacked knowledge about the rules of the free market economy and how it works in practice.[39] This additionally contributed to flaws and frequent legislative amendments, which created legal uncertainty. Frequent legal amendments are typical of countries in transition, such as Russia, which has amended chapter 22 of its Criminal Code, regulating economic crimes, at least two dozen times[40] and, in the process, introduced an additional ten new business-related crimes.

The neglect of economic rights in Croatia led to a number of social, economic, political and legal problems in the years that followed, and created conditions for what Durkheim described as a state of anomie. Such anomie also occurred in other central and south-eastern European transitional states in the 1990s. Albrecht noted in 1999 that countries in transition tend to share a number of common characteristics: increases in the volume of crime, growing anomie, growing weakness of control mechanisms, emergence of new types of crimes, decrease in the efficiency of law enforcement, limited economic sources, perception of an erosion of the state monopoly of legitimate violence, omnipresent fear of crime and preoccupation with safety concerns, etc.[41]

B. Croatian Legal Solutions to Transitional Economic Crimes: The Possibility of Export to Other Transitional Countries?

Croatian society became aware of the problem more extensively only in the years following the war. The findings of the Croation State Audit Report that carried

[38] Novoselec et al (n 18) 203.

[39] Novoselec et al (n 18).

[40] PH Solomon Jr, 'Criminalisation, Decriminalization and Post-communist Transition: The Case of the Russian Federation in Building Justice' in K Goodall, M Malloch and B Munro (eds), *Post-Transitional Europe? Processes of criminalization within Central and Eastern European societies* (Abingdon, Routledge, 2013) 99.

[41] HJ Albrecht, 'Countries in Transition: Effects of Political, Social and Economic Change on Crime and Criminal Justice—Sanctions and Their Implementation' (1999) 7 *European Journal of Crime, Criminal Law and Criminal Justice* 448; HJ Albrecht and AM Getoš, 'Researching Terrorism and Organized Crime in Southeast Europe' in W Benedek, C Daase, V Dimitrijević and P Van Duyne (eds), *Transnational Terrorism, Organized Crime and Peace-Building—Human Security in the Western Balkans* (Basingstoke, Palgrave Macmillan, 2010) 117.

out revisions of the privatisation processes (hereafter the Transformation and Privatization Revision Report), which were publicly revealed in 2004,[42] led to a paradigm change in approach to transitional economic crimes. Following the publication of 2004 Report, a new approach has been explored in order to bring such cases before a court of justice. Returning illegally obtained gain should be included as part of the solution. However, at the first glance, from a criminal law point of view, the Report seemed to be irrelevant in most cases because the statute of limitations for economic crimes committed in the process of transformation and privatisation was either expiring soon or already had. Even the Transformation and Privatization Revision Report decisively stated the same.[43] In Croatia, the prosecution of violent crimes took priority, especially in the aftermath of war; nevertheless,there was a necessary reaction to the criminal policy because the constitutional quest for social justice[44] was important to the opinion makers in Croatia, and new solutions had to be found in reaction to the irregularities established in the Report. Ultimately, this resulted in constitutional amendments being passed in 2010 which allow for the retroactive prosecution of all transitional economic crimes. The Decision Proposal to Amend the Constitution of Croatia[45] to allow retroactive prosecution of transitional economic offences stated that, as transformation and privatisation did not have the expected economic outcome, they have had no significant positive impact on the economic development of Croatia.

On the contrary, the implementation of transformation and privatisation resulted in an increase in domestic and foreign debt, and caused a significant increase in unemployment, the disproportionate and fast enrichment of some individuals, and the unjust impoverishment of many. The implementation also caused a fall in wages and pensions in real terms, compared to the cost of living and a number of other consequences. It is just, and in the spirit of international law, to deny the perpetrators of such grave crimes the possibility of avoiding criminal liability by application of the statute of limitations. The basis for the statute of limitations is the guarantee of legal certainty to citizens, but—as stated in the

[42] 'Final State Audit Office Report on Revision of Ownership Transformation and Privatization' in *The Routledge Handbook of White-Collar and Corporate Crime in Europe* (Abingdon, Routledge, 2015) 2. The Report covers 1,556 companies that were transformed and privatised from May 2001 to September 2004. Banking, a major sector, was not covered in the revision. Regardless, 1,936 irregularities were established in 1,481 companies (95.2% revised!), of which 1,215 did not have characteristics of illegal actions, so sanctions were not proscribed. Of the remaining 721 irregularities, there was a reasonable doubt in 271 that they could qualify as criminal offences and 247 as misdemeanours, while 203 irregularities were no longer punishable after enactment of the new Law on Issuance of and Trade with Securities 1995. Only 75 companies have received a special opinion of the revision, confirming the correctness of their privatisation and transformation.

[43] Final State Audit Office Report on Revision of Ownership Transformation and Privatization (2004) 41.

[44] Art 3 of the Constitution of the Republic of Croatia.

[45] Decision Proposal to Amend the Constitution of Croatia, Government of Republic of Croatia, 2009, 8.

decision to amend the Constitution—'it is certain that this institute should not be the benefit for the perpetrators enabling them to practically legalise the effects of such acts through the statute of limitations'.[46]

No matter how 'right' the idea of passing such a constitutional amendment was, its effective application was not an easy task for prosecutors. According to the Venice Commission Report on the Rule of Law,[47] legal certainty also means that actions or promises given by the state to individuals should in general be honoured (the notion of 'legitimate expectation'). Moreover, 'legal certainty—and supremacy of the law—implies that the law is implemented in practice. This means also that it is implementable.'[48] However, these war profiteering crimes were committed long ago, witnesses lack credibility due to the time lapsed, many of the companies concerned no longer exist, financial documentation has been destroyed or is non-existent, there are difficulties in collecting evidence and ex post facto amendments to the statute of limitations create legal uncertainty. Additionally, financial accounting regulations state that accounting documents and financial reports must be kept for between seven and 11 years from the date issued. Furthermore, the problems that were emerging in the prosecution of transitional economic offences committed more than 20 years ago were not only legal in nature. There was also fierce opposition by political parties with financial interests, as well as the risk of political manipulation in prosecutorial discretion.

However, these risks were ignored and, after the constitutional amendment, the Law on Exemption from Statute of Limitations for War Profiteering and Crimes Committed in the Process of Ownership Transformation and Privatization (Law on Exemption) was passed in 2011, together with the new Criminal Code. One must, however, underline that the Law on Exemption identifies that the abolishment of the statute of limitations will apply only to those privatisation and ownership transformation crimes that took place in the transformation and privatisation process during: (i) the Homeland War; (ii) the peaceful reintegration; (ii) warfare; and (iv) a direct threat to the independence and territorial integrity of the state. Therefore, the Law on Exemption does not refer to all privatisation and ownership transformation crimes, but only to those offences committed in strictly defined time periods.

Subsequent developments have shown a number of positive changes, with 47 cases pending based on the Law on Exemption.[49] However, only around ten proceedings have been adjudicated to date,[50] and only one has had any real media

[46] ibid.

[47] European Commission on Democracy Through Law (Venice Commission) Report on the Rule of Law, 86th Plenary Session, Study No 512/2009, CDL-AD(2011)000rev, 2011, §48.

[48] ibid §51.

[49] Croatian State Attorney's Report for 2015, 92.

[50] According to the Croatian State Attorney's Report for 2015, 92, there were 84 persons in various stages of the proceedings. Out of those, the procedure against 47 persons was at the stage of indictments or hearing. The first instance judgment occurred against two persons in 2015. The appeal procedure was initiated against seven first instance judgments, during 2015. Seventeen cases are currently in the

attention (the case against the former Prime Minister of Croatia, Ivo Sanader, prosecuted more on accounts of abuse of position than on privatisation or war profiteering in the strict sense). According to data available from the State Attorney's Office, the application of the Law on Exemption from the Statute of Limitations is highly probable in 116 cases where investigations or criminal proceedings are underway.[51]

As the judges pointed out in the first instance judgment against Sanader, he abused his position as Prime Minister of the country for his own enrichment and not for the common good. According to the first judge, 'this judgment sends a message to people in power, current and future, that holding a public office must be performed for the common good and in the interest of society'.[52] Furthermore, according to the judges, Sanader's behaviour

> not only [harmed] vital strategic interests but also damaged the reputation of Croatia in the world … contributed to apathy and disillusionment of people in the system, created a belief among young people that honest labour does not pay, but the violation of the law and the morality of the society does.[53]

The judgment emphasised that Sanader was 'the architect of the system … that was an illusion of democracy'. Sanader was sentenced to eight and a half years' imprisonment.[54] This judgment expressed what has been stated in the Venice Commission on the relationship between political and criminal ministerial responsibility:

> An area of criminal law that may be of particular relevance for ministers is that of corruption, embezzlement and other forms of economic crime. It is of particular importance that such rules be strictly and effectively enforced against ministers and other publically appointed officials, since such offences are not only to be seen as criminal, but may also easily undermine public trust and the legitimacy and authority of the democratic system.[55]

The first instance judgment of the county court was then confirmed by the Supreme Court of the Republic of Croatia.[56]

As it was proclaimed to be the reason for amending the Constitution in the Decision Proposal to Amend the Constitution of Croatia,[57] which allows

appeal process. Out of the six cases appealed in 2015, in three cases the first instance judgment was confirmed and the other three cases went for retrial. S Škugor Hrnčević, 'Ovo su rezultati Zakona o nezastarjevanju kaznenih djela ratnog profiterstva i privatizacijskog kriminala!', *Index*, 30 June 2013, available at http://www.index.hr/vijesti/clanak/ovo-su-rezultati-zakona-o-nezastarijevanju-kaznenih-djela-ratnog-profiterstva-i-privatizacijskog-kriminala/710663.aspx accessed 19 July 2014.

[51] P Novoselec and D Novosel, 'Nezastarijevanje kaznenih djela ratnog profiterstva i kaznenih djela iz pretvorbe i privatizacije' (2011) 18 *Hrvatski ljetopis za kazneno pravo i praksu* 618.

[52] K-Us-26/11, Zagreb County Court Judgment, 2012.

[53] ibid.

[54] VSRH I Kž-Us 94/13-10, 3 April 2014.

[55] Venice Commission Report on the Relationship between Political and Criminal Ministerial Responsibility 2013, §97.

[56] VSRH I Kž-Us 94/13-10, 3 April 2014.

[57] Decision Proposal to Amend the Constitution of Croatia 2009, 8.

retroactive prosecution of transitional economic offences, Croatia made clear its position towards pecuniary gain: that the statute of limitations is the guarantee of legal certainty to citizens, but it should not enable perpetrators to benefit by effectively legalising the effects of their acts. The amendment clearly states that it is necessary for the proceeds of such offences to be confiscated.[58]

Therefore, one could claim that Article 31 of the Constitution could serve as an inspiration to all countries that have undergone through transition in 1990s. At least, it could have done until the most recent Constitutional Court decision on the *Sanader* case in July 2015, which not only quashed the first instance judgment of the Zagreb County Court and the second instance judgment of the Supreme Court, but also shed a new light on the retroactive application of the Law on Exemption, thereby forced us to consider other solutions to how to confiscate such ill-gotten gains. According to the Constitutional Court, if the statute of limitations had already expired for a crime at the time the amendments to the Constitution were adopted in 2010, that crime could not be prosecuted even after the Constitution was changed.

C. Another Change of Paradigm: The Croatian Constitutional Court Decision in July 2015

Almost five years after the introduction of the constitutional amendment, the Constitutional Court of the Republic of Croatia decided that the abolition of retroactivity could not apply to transitional economic offences for which the statute of limitations expired before 16 June 2010.[59] Thus, as stated in the previous section, if the statute of limitations had already expired for a crime at the time the amendments to the Constitution were adopted in 2010, that crime could not be prosecuted even after the Constitution was changed. Under the principle of the protection of the principle of legality, another Croatian constitutional principle lost the battle in this decision, namely the principle of 'social justice'.[60]

The most important consequence of this decision is that the ability to punish those crimes is significantly limited. For the great majority of privatisation

[58] See Art 31 of the Constitution: the statute of limitations shall not apply to the criminal offences of war profiteering, nor any criminal offences perpetrated in the course of economic transformation and privatisation and perpetrated during the period of the Homeland War and peaceful reintegration, during wartime and during times of clear and present danger to the independence and territorial integrity of the state, as stipulated by law, or those not subject to the statute of limitations under international law. Any gains obtained by these acts or in connection therewith shall be confiscated.

[59] USRH U-III-4149/2014, 24 July 2015.

[60] Constitution of the Republic of Croatia, Art 3: Freedom, equal rights, national and gender equality, peace-making, social justice, respect for human rights, inviolability of ownership, conservation of nature and the environment, the rule of law and a democratic multiparty system are the highest values of the constitutional order of the Republic of Croatia.

and ownership transformation scandals committed during the Homeland War, the statute of limitations has already expired. It appears, therefore, that Croatian society will not be allowed redress for the transitional crimes committed in the time of the war.

The Constitutional Court could have taken another path and not forgotten, while protecting the principle of legality and the rule of law, that these serious economic offences were committed during the transitional period. The basis for such reasoning can be found in the transitional justice jurisprudence of the European Court of Human Rights (ECtHR). The Constitutional Court, in our opinion, did not take into account the specific qualities of transitional societies when deciding what the rule of law in Croatia really means; in other words, it did not take into account the principle of social justice when balancing and looking at the Constitution as a whole.

Declaring the retroactive application of the exemption from the statute of limitations impossible actually legalised illegal enrichment, which is contrary to the judgments of the ECtHR and the Croatian legal system, and to the very explanation enacted in the constitutional amendments.

It must be noted that the ECtHR has an enormous number of cases pending regarding the assessment of legislative solutions of transitional countries and therefore has to balance principles and respect for human rights in transitional countries. A point of principle for transitional justice cases can be extracted from the judgment in *Holy Synod of the Bulgarian Orthodox Church (Metropolitan Inokentiy) and Others v Bulgaria*:[61] according to the ECtHR, transitional societies' common need to remedy unlawful acts of the past cannot, in a democratic society, justify disproportionate state action or further unlawful acts. Likewise, in relation to restitution, the Court has stressed that, although such policies may be legitimate, states should ensure that they do not create 'disproportionate new wrongs'.[62] Therefore, 'the width of the margin in particular cases will be tied to some combination of various factors, including the right at stake, the way that it is invoked, and the legitimate aim the restriction pursues'.[63] This means that Croatia could have proven that the law on exemption did not create 'disproportionate new wrongs', but that the principle of social justice and the principle that no one has the right to keep what is illegally acquired should have precedence. If we were to calculate the monetary amount Croatia could have received through privatisation—but eventually did not—the situation would not have been as simple as the Constitutional Court depicted.

[61] *Holy Synod of the Bulgarian Orthodox Church (Metropolitan Inokentiy) and Others v Bulgaria* App No 412/03 and No 35677/04 (ECtHR, 22 January 2009) §142.

[62] See *Velikovi and Others v Bulgaria* Nos 43278/98, 45437/99, 48014/99, 48380/99, 51362/99, 53367/99, 60036/00, 73465/01 and 194/02 (ECtHR 15 March 2007).

[63] J Sweeney 'Freedom of Religion and Democratic Transition' in A Buyse and M Hamilton (eds), *Transitional Jurisprudence and the ECHR: Justice, Politics and Rights* (Cambridge, Cambridge University Press, 2011) 119.

In any case, the Constitutional Court decided on the merits of the case in favour of Sanader's petition. Unless the Constitutional Court changes its opinion in some possible new ruling or the dissatisfied complainant then applies to the ECtHR for violation of Article 7 of the European Convention on Human Rights (ECHR), proclaiming that there can be no punishment without law, the ECtHR will not have the opportunity to make the decision on such important issue.[64] In our opinion, it is a huge shame that the questions surrounding the application of the law of exemption did not end up before the ECtHR, which would then have had the opportunity to carefully examine the components of Croatian transitional criminal law policy and ex post facto laws that were aimed at regulating the irregularities of privatisation and ownership transformation committed during the Homeland War.

II. How to Confiscate Despite the Statute of Limitations?

A. The Legal Nature and Forms of Confiscation Prior to the 2010 Constitutional and Legislative Reforms

In Croatian law, confiscation of pecuniary gain acquired through a criminal offence has traditionally been a measure *sui generis* (see the following subsection) pronounced with the conviction in criminal proceedings. Even before the 2010 political and legislative initiatives, there were discussions (mostly among academics) about other possible models of efficient confiscation.[65] The traditional regime of confiscation did not suit the new forms of crime, particularly serious economic crime, corruption and organised crime. The study of final judgments in cases of economic crimes conducted by Novosel, covering the period 1998–2006, found 'disastrous results'.[66] Confiscation was rarely pronounced despite the fact that the main motivation of perpetrators of economic crimes was acquiring unlawful pecuniary gain.[67] For that reason, but also in order to comply with European and international obligations, it was necessary to reform the confiscation regime.

64 For possible outcomes at the ECtHR see S Roksandić Vidlička, 'Possible Future Challenge For the ECtHR?: Importance of the Act on Exemption and the Sanader Case for Transitional Justice Jurisprudence and the Development of Transitional Justice Policies' (2014) 64(5–6) *Zbornik Pravnog Fakulteta u Zagrebu*.

65 See generally E Ivičević, *Oduzimanje imovinske koristi stečene kaznenim djelom* (Zagreb, Hrvatsko udruženje za kaznene znanosti i praksu, Ministarstvo unutarnjih poslova RH, 2004) 170.

66 D Novosel, 'Financijske istrage i progon počinitelja gospodarskog kriminaliteta' (2007) 2 *Hrvatski ljetopis za kazneno pravo i praksu* 743.

67 ibid.

Hence, the provisions on confiscation of pecuniary gain acquired through criminal offences are among the most frequently amended provisions of the former Criminal Code and the new Criminal Code (in force since 2013).

(i) Confiscation as a Measure Sui Generis

In Croatian criminal law, the confiscation of pecuniary gain has traditionally been regulated neither as a punishment, nor as a security measure, but as a measure *sui generis*.[68] Its purpose is to restore the state of property to as it was prior to the moment the crime was committed, not to punish the perpetrator. In a larger sense, it is not applied *in personam*, but *in rem*. This concept was developed under the influence of German doctrine and legislation, though it is also found in Swiss law.[69]

The Croatian Criminal Code, in its basic provisions, proclaims the principle of confiscation of pecuniary gain, stating that 'no one may retain a pecuniary gain acquired through illegal means'.[70] The message that 'crime does not pay' reflects the specifically restorative nature of the confiscation. Although the confiscation is normally pronounced within the conviction, the fact that it is applied *in rem* and not *in personam* implies that the element of guilt need not be established without exception. The Criminal Code prescribes that 'pecuniary gain shall be confiscated on the basis of a court decision establishing the commission of an unlawful act'.[71] So, if the perpetrator acted in a state of mental incapacity and committed an unlawful act defined in the Criminal Code, the pecuniary gain acquired through it shall be confiscated, even though the perpetrator may not be found guilty. The measure is nevertheless pronounced in the criminal proceedings, and the required standard of proof is 'beyond reasonable doubt'—the same standard as is required for the conviction.

Although declared as a restorative measure, confiscation of pecuniary gain acquired through a criminal offence also fulfils the preventive purpose of deterring persons from committing criminal offences.[72] The preventive purpose of confiscation is reflected in several provisions. The Croatian Criminal Code expressly proclaims the gross principle, stating that 'the confiscated pecuniary gain shall not be reduced by the value of resources invested in the criminal activity'.[73] This means that the confiscated pecuniary gain will not consist only of the pure profit acquired through a criminal offence, but also of any expenses that the perpetrator actually 'invested' in the commission of the offence, and therefore lost with the

[68] P Novoselec and I Bojanić, *Opći dio kaznenog prava* (Zagreb, Sveučilište u Zagrebu Pravni fakultet, 2013) 472.
[69] For the Swiss law, see generally S Schödler, *Dritte im Beschlagnahme-und Einziehungsverfahren* (Zurich, Schulthess, 2012) 12.
[70] Art 5 Criminal Code.
[71] Art 77(1) Criminal Code.
[72] Novoselec and Bojanić (n 68) 472.
[73] Art 77(5) Criminal Code.

confiscation. The fact that the crime shall not pay deters others from committing criminal offences. The law explicitly excludes the application of the net principle, which is immanent in the restorative dimension of the measure. Implications of the gross principle on the legal nature of the confiscation have been thoroughly discussed in the literature, and it may be concluded that the gross principle reflects the punitive dimension of the confiscation, since the perpetrator loses more that he or she gained through the criminal offence.[74]

Furthermore, the repressive purpose and punitive dimension of the confiscation reflects in the possibility of confiscation not only from the perpetrator, but also from a *mala fide* third party.[75] The third party who traded a certain value for the property acquired through a criminal offence shall be deprived of both the traded value and the gain acquired through the criminal offence, and therefore will be punished through the confiscation.

It should be concluded that the confiscation has a more complex legal nature than it might seem from its normative definition as a measure *sui generis* in Croatian criminal law. Swiss judicial practice adequately defined the confiscation as an *in rem* measure, which nevertheless reveals certain repressive features,[76] and it may also adequately describe the legal nature of the measure in Croatian law.

(ii) Extended Confiscation

The legal nature of confiscation as a restorative measure *sui generis* was challenged in 2006, when the legislation introduced the measure of extended confiscation, applicable in cases of criminal offences prosecuted by the Office for the Suppression of Corruption and Organized Crime (USKOK). Due to serious normative deficiencies concerning the lack of clarity and precision required by the principle of legality,[77] the extended confiscation regulation was amended on several occasions. With time, the scope of the criminal offences covered by extended confiscation has widened, and it now covers a relatively large scope of economic crimes.

Ever since its introduction, the measure of extended confiscation has been regulated within the criminal law regime. According to current regulation, if a

[74] See, eg, S Schödler (n 69) 13. See also G Mégevand, *Confiscation et corruption* (Basel, Helbing Lichtenhahn Verlag, 2013) 86. Not long before the law explicitly proclaimed application of the gross principle, there were some hesitations in Croatian jurisprudence, though the older jurisprudence, as well as the doctrine, clearly accepted the net principle, referring to a particular non-punitive character of confiscation. See, eg, Novoselec and Bojanić (n 68) 499. See also E Ivičevič Karas, 'Utvrđivanje imovinske koristi stečene kaznenim djelom primjenom bruto ili neto načela s obzirom na pravnu prirodu mjere (proširenog) oduzimanja imovinske koristi' (2010) 1 *Hrvatski ljetopis za kazneno pravo i praksu* 191.

[75] Schödler (n 69) 34. See Art 77(1) of the Criminal Code.

[76] Mégevand (n 74) 84.

[77] E Ivičević Karas, 'Kaznenopravno oduzimanje nezakonito stečene imovinske koristi' (2007) 2 *Hrvatski ljetopis za kazneno pravo i praksu* 687.

perpetrator is convicted for a criminal offence within the competence of USKOK, and he or she owns or owned property that is incommensurate with his or her legitimate income, it is assumed that the entire property represents a pecuniary advantage gained from a criminal offence and is to be confiscated, unless the perpetrator can show that it is probable that the property is of legitimate origin.[78] Therefore, on the one hand, the criminal offence must be proved beyond reasonable doubt and the perpetrator must be convicted in order to apply the presumption of criminal origin of the perpetrator's entire property, but, on the other hand, the standard of proof regarding the lawful origin of the property is much lower than 'beyond reasonable doubt'.

Although nominally conceived as a *sui generis* measure, and regulated under provisions for the basic, traditional form of confiscation measure, extended confiscation reveals typical features of punishment. First of all, the repressive character of the measure reflects in the fact that Croatian courts do not need to be completely convinced that the property was gained through criminal offences. In other words, the prosecutor does not have to prove the facts supporting the conclusion that the entire property of the perpetrator originates from criminal offences. It is enough to prove that the perpetrator 'owns or owned property that is incommensurate with his or her legitimate income' and the burden of proof is shifted to the defendant.[79] In contrast, regarding extended confiscation in German criminal law, the German Supreme Court clearly stated that the court must be completely convinced of the criminal origin of the property targeted with the measure of extended confiscation, though each concrete criminal offence need not be established.[80] Under such conditions, the extended confiscation does not have a punitive character, it does not imply the application of the principle of guilt and it is not contrary to the presumption of innocence.[81] Although the Croatian Constitutional Court has not yet judged the Croatian regime of extended confiscation, one may imagine that it could possibly apply the same reasoning as the German Constitutional Court. If it did so, the extended confiscation measure would be recognised as having a punitive nature.

Another punitive feature of the extended confiscation reflects in the possibility of confiscation from third persons. The pecuniary gain shall be confiscated from a family member 'irrespective of the legal basis on which he/she possesses it and regardless of whether he/she lives in a shared household with the perpetrator',[82] and 'from another person irrespective of the legal basis on which it was acquired

[78] Art 78 (2) Criminal Code.

[79] E Ivičević Karas, 'Utvrđivanje imovinske koristi stečene kaznenim djelom primjenom bruto ili neto načela s obzirom na pravnu prirodu mjere (proširenog) oduzimanja imovinske koristi' (2010) 1 *Hrvatski ljetopis za kazneno pravo i praksu* 209.

[80] BverG, Beschl. V. 14. 1. 2004—2 BvR 564/95 in H Tröndle and T Fischer, *Strafgesetzbuch und Nebengesetze* (Munich, Verlag CH Beck, 2006) 630.

[81] ibid.

[82] Art 78(4) Criminal Code.

unless this person makes it probable that he/she acquired the advantage in good faith and at a reasonable price'.[83] Due to the punitive character of the measure, the third persons must have procedural rights that in a great part comply with the rights of the defendants. In two decisions regarding the extended confiscation, the Supreme Court of the Republic of Croatia quashed the county court judgments for substantive violations of a criminal procedure consisting of inadequate reasoning of the decision, as the judgment was incomprehensible,[84] but also for inadequate procedural guarantees of the rights of third persons having an interest in the property concerned.[85] In both cases, the Supreme Court stressed that the extended confiscation concerned third parties—relatives of the defendant—to whom the property was transferred and who had legitimate interests in participating in the proceedings, through exercising their procedural rights, including the fair trial rights, and particularly the right to prove the lawful origin of their property. It is the punitive nature of the measure that imposes the need to provide fair trial guarantees not only for the defendant, but also for the third persons concerned.

Since the measure of extended confiscation was introduced in 2006, there seems to be only one final judgment that has applied such measure. In this case, the Croatian Supreme Court confirmed the first instance county court judgment, pronouncing the extended confiscation of a sum of money that was found in the closet of a police officer convicted for taking a bribe and for abuse of position and authority, who did not demonstrate that the money was of legitimate origin.[86] The scarce application of the measure shows that extended confiscation does not really work in practice. But even if it did, it could not be applied in cases of serious transitional economic criminal offences, due to its punitive legal nature and the requirements of the principle of legality: the measure was introduced only in 2006 and prohibition of its retroactive application is indisputable.

(iii) Other Confiscation Models?

Considering serious transitional economic crimes and the huge pecuniary gain acquired through those crimes, and looking beyond the message that 'crime does not pay', as Tanzi et al has pointed out, an efficient confiscation regime is needed to prevent the erosion of the rule of law.[87] Prior to the 2010 political and legislative initiative, there were other options of supplementing the traditional criminal law

[83] Art 78(5) Criminal Code.

[84] VSRH, I Kž-Us 106/10-8, 23 February 2012.

[85] VSRH, I Kž-Us 106/10-8, 23 February 2012 and I Kž-Us 11/12-2, 23 January 2013.

[86] VSRH, I Kž-Us 96/14-6, 10 September 2014.

[87] V Tanzi, PJ Quirk and LB Barlet, quoted in PC van Duyne, W de Zanger and FHG Kristen, 'Greedy of Crime-Money: The Reality and Ethics of Asset Recovery' in PC van Duyne, J Harvey, GA Antonopoulos, K von Lampe, A Maljević and A Marwkovska (eds), *Corruption, Greed and Crime Money: Sleaze and Shady Economy in Europe and Beyond* (Nijmegen, Wolf Legal Publishers, 2014) 235.

confiscation regime, including the possibilities of introducing a civil law confiscation regime and a criminal offence of illicit enrichment. However, disadvantages of both models prevented the legislator from introducing them in the Croatian legal system. Besides the danger of possible abuses for political purposes, the absence of a predicate criminal offence was stressed as a fundamental deficiency of introducing a new criminal offence of illicit enrichment.[88] However, regarding the transitional economic crimes, further debate would be pointless, knowing that introducing a new criminal offence of illicit enrichment in 2010, more than ten years after the completion of privatisation and the peaceful reintegration process, would not result in the prosecution of any serious economic crimes committed during that process, due to the requirements of the principle of legality—specifically, the prohibition of the retroactive application of criminal law.

Therefore, in 2010, the legislator decided to keep the traditional confiscation model, which required conviction prior to confiscation. The crucial problem, again, was that in 2010 some of the offences committed during the period of privatisation were already statute barred, due to relatively short limitations prescribed at the time they were perpetrated, so it was necessary to amend the normative framework, starting at the constitutional level.

B. The Possibility of Confiscation without Conviction

The same year that the constitutional amendment took place, there was another legislative initiative that introduced the possibility of confiscation without conviction. The Act on Proceedings of Confiscation of Pecuniary Gain Acquired through a Criminal Offence and Misdemeanours regulated not only confiscation within criminal proceedings, but also confiscation proceedings where there were circumstances that excluded criminal prosecution. The Act contained primarily procedural provisions, but also a few important substantive provisions: it expressly proclaimed the application of the gross principle, which is linked to the punitive nature of the confiscation even when it is nominally conceived as a measure *in rem*.[89]

The Act also implicitly excluded the possibility of applying extended confiscation within the regime of non-conviction-based confiscation, stating that the confiscation decision must contain the determination that the defendant committed a criminal offence, and that he or she gained a pecuniary advantage through that particular criminal offence.[90] In other words, in order to confiscate without a conviction, the court must establish that the concrete pecuniary gain

[88] D Derenčinović, 'Criminalization of Illegal Enrichment' (2009) 4 *Freedom from Fear Magazine* 21.
[89] Schödler (n 69) 13.
[90] Art 6(1) Act on Proceedings of Confiscation.

was acquired through a concrete criminal offence, and it may not presume that it was acquired through other criminal offences that have not been established before the court.

It should be concluded that extended confiscation, due to its punitive nature in Croatian law, may only be pronounced with a conviction. The traditional confiscation measure, despite some punitive features, has a predominantly restorative character and may be applied notwithstanding a conviction, though under somewhat strict procedural conditions prescribed in the Act on Proceedings of Confiscation of Pecuniary Gain Acquired through a Criminal Offence and Misdemeanours. This Act sets out quite a broad basis for confiscation without conviction, since it does not distinguish between real or factual reasons, on the one hand, and legal reasons preventing the possibility of conducting criminal proceedings and obtaining a conviction on the other hand. More concretely, the Act does not distinguish between procedural obstacles of a real nature, such as the death, absence or serious illness of the defendant, on the one hand, and procedural obstacles of a legal nature, such as the immunity from prosecution or *ne bis in idem*, on the other hand. Yet, the statute of limitations is explicitly exempted from other procedural obstacles which would allow confiscation without conviction.

The declared *in rem* nature of extended confiscation means that the confiscation proceedings may be carried out once the defendant has died, and the property may be confiscated from his or her descendants.[91] It is not required to establish the defendant's guilt, though all the other elements of the criminal offence must be proved beyond reasonable doubt. Therefore, the regime of confiscation is basically the same as the one prescribed in the criminal procedure, because the fundamental principles and rules of criminal proceedings apply, including the rules on the burden of proof and the standard of proof. Non-conviction-based confiscation may not be a solution in cases where there is insufficient evidence for a conviction, since the required standard of proof is the same as in criminal proceedings (ie beyond reasonable doubt).

As stressed, the possibility of non-conviction-based extended confiscation is excluded, and the burden of proof cannot be reduced or shifted, or shared between the prosecutor and the defendant, in any case. Regarding the transitional economic crimes, the practical problem of proving the criminal offence and the pecuniary gain acquired through it still remains. Moreover, the statute of limitations is explicitly exempted from other procedural obstacles which would allow confiscation without conviction. In cases where the prosecution of transitional economic crimes is already statute barred, ordinary conviction-based confiscation would have been possible by virtue of Article 31(4) of the Croatian Constitution, proclaiming that there is no statute of limitations for transitional economic crimes, if the Croatian Constitutional Court had not ruled that possibility out.

[91] Schödler (n 69) 58.

C. What Possible Solutions Remain?

The decision of the Constitutional Court in *Sanader* practically changed the provision of Article 31(4) of Croatian Constitution, since the decisions of the Constitutional Court brought upon constitutional complaints become sources of law[92] and are applied *erga omnes*, and not only *inter partes*.[93] Consequently, confiscation of pecuniary gain acquired through transitional economic crimes when the prosecution is already statute barred is practically impossible within the current criminal law regime: first, there can be no conviction, and secondly, non-conviction-based confiscation is explicitly excluded by law in cases where the prosecution of the criminal offence in question is already statute barred. Even though the Constitutional Court might change its jurisprudence in the future, what the possible confiscation models that remain must be reconsidered.

A solution might be found by amending the existing non-conviction-based confiscation regime in a way that does not require the statute of limitations to be excluded from procedural obstacles which allow non-confiscation-based confiscation proceedings to be conducted. If the legislator opted for such a solution, the statute of limitations would not prevent the confiscation proceedings either in general, or only for a catalogue of criminal offences provided in Article 31(4) of the Constitution and in the Act on Exemption from the Statute of Limitations for War Profiteering and Crimes Committed in the Process of Ownership Transformation and Privatisation. In that way, a conviction for transitional economic crimes would not be necessary in order to confiscate the pecuniary gain acquired through those crimes. But in that case, in order to comply with the reasoning the Constitutional Court gave in *Sanader*, the confiscation must not be conceived as a punishment, because otherwise the constitutional prohibition of retroactivity would apply. It also means that the extended confiscation would definitely be excluded, considering its significant punitive dimension. In any case, the prosecution would have to prove, beyond reasonable doubt, that particular property was acquired through the unlawful action specified in the charges.

It remains to consider the regime of civil recovery of pecuniary gain acquired through transitional economic crimes as a possible solution. On the one hand, some features of civil recovery, as it is regulated, for example, in English and Scottish law, are compatible with basic features of confiscation in Croatian criminal law: both are conceived as *in rem* and not *in personam* measures, and both may be pronounced without proving the perpetrator's guilt.[94] On the other hand, there are significant differences. Criminal confiscation is pronounced after a conviction, on the basis of a court decision establishing the commission of an unlawful act, or

[92] D Krapac, *Kazneno procesno pravo Prva Knjiga: Institucije* (Zagreb, Narodne novine, 2015) 56.

[93] See Z Đurđević, 'Suvremeni razvoj hrvatskoga kaznenog procesnog prava s posebnim osvrtom na novelu ZKP iz 2011' (2011) 2 *Hrvatski ljetopis za kazneno pravo i praksu* 322.

[94] HM Carmichael, *Confiscation and Civil Recovery* (Edinburgh, W Green & Son, 2013) 312.

without a conviction if there were some procedural obstacles preventing criminal proceedings, but always according to the rules of criminal proceedings, including the rules on burden of proof and the standard of proof 'beyond reasonable doubt'. It is, indeed, a confiscation within the criminal law regime.

Civil recovery may occur in many different guises. Though civil confiscation regimes in different countries differ in many respects,[95] they should have the same purpose. The purpose of civil recovery in English law is to deprive respondents of property obtained through unlawful conduct and to use it for the benefit of the community.[96] Comparing it to the existing model of non-conviction-based confiscation in Croatian criminal law, and looking at it through the perspective of the huge pecuniary gain acquired through transitional economic crimes committed over 20 years ago, its principal advantage is the retroactive applicability. That is, of course, on the condition that it is not conceived as a punishment due to its real nature. The ECtHR confirmed in *Dassa Foundation v Liechtenstein* that the retroactive applicability of the measure was in accordance with Article 7 ECHR, since the forfeiture was comparable to the civil law confiscation of illicit enrichment and was not a punishment.[97] The civil law character of the civil recovery proceedings was also confirmed in *Walsh v UK*.[98]

Another important advantage of the civil recovery regime is that, unlike the criminal law regime of non-conviction-based confiscation, civil recovery implies civil law rules and standards of evidence, which eases the burden of proof lying on the prosecutor. This is particularly important, bearing in mind that the criminal offences in question were perpetrated over 20 years ago and such a time lapse normally makes collecting evidence more difficult.

On the other hand, it must be pointed out that civil recovery regimes are subject to time limits. For example, in English law a 12-year limitation rule applies, and civil recovery proceedings can be brought only within that period, starting from the time the original property was generated by unlawful conduct.[99] The limitation period is one of the important safeguards needed to ensure fairness and compliance with the requirements of relevant civil law principles.[100] From the perspective of transitional economic crimes committed over 20 years ago, bearing in mind that in Croatian civil law the general limitation period is five years, although in some cases it is ten years, it remains to conclude that the civil recovery is not an answer to the question how to confiscate a pecuniary gain acquired through transitional economic crimes.

[95] B Vettori, *Tough on Criminal Wealth* (Oxford, Springer, 2010) 9.

[96] T Millington and M Sutherland Williams, *On the Proceeds of Crime* (Oxford, Oxford University Press, 2010) 360.

[97] *Dassa Foundation v Liechtenstein* App No 696/05 (ECtHR, 10 July 2007). See TS Greenberg, LM Samuel, W Grant and L Gray, *Stolen Asset Recovery: A Good Practices Guide for Non-Conviction Based Asset Forfeiture* (Washington, DC, World Bank, 2009) 46.

[98] *Walsh v UK* App No 43384/05 (ECtHR, 21 November 2006). See Carmichael (n 94) 316.

[99] Millington and Sutherland Williams (n 96) 367.

[100] Millington and Sutherland Williams (n 96).

Conclusions

Unlike what was proclaimed as the reason to amend the Constitution in the Decision Proposal to Amend the Constitution of Croatia—to allow retroactive prosecution of transitional economic offences on the basis that the

> statute of limitations is the guarantee of legal certainty to citizens, but it is certain that this institute should not be the benefit for the perpetrators enabling them to practically legalise the effects of such acts through the statute of limitations[101]

this is what may eventually occur after the Constitutional Court decision in the *Sanader* case. It is possible to conclude that Croatia failed to capitalise on its historical opportunity to become a transitional country that had enough courage to harden a path and solve the question of effective problem solving in (not) processing and (not) punishing the serious and systematic economic crimes that all transitional countries have, unfortunately, experienced. It failed to be the leading country in the region, and remains a country that is struggling with the consequences of privatisation and serious economic crimes committed in war conflict. What now?

Even though the Constitutional Court may change its jurisprudence, the fact is that its legal opinion is a source of law and binds the courts and other state organs. This means that state attorneys should not prosecute and propose confiscation, and the courts should not adjudicate in cases of transitional economic crimes, when the prosecution is already statute barred. Thus, we cannot simply expect that the Constitutional Court will have another opportunity to adjudicate on the same legal issue again.[102] Even though the question remains whether the Constitutional Court of the Republic of Croatia actually exceeded its jurisdiction when interpreting the constitutional provision on exemption from statute of limitations, since—as Omejec states—it is not within its jurisdiction to review the compliance of particular constitutional norms with the Constitution,[103] it seems that the only possible solution would imply redefining the provision of Article 31(4) of the Constitution in such a manner that it would expressly refer to cases where the criminal offences in question were already statute barred at the time the constitutional amendment entered into force. In that way, the Constitutional Court would not have any room to come to a different interpretation of the provision of Article 31(4) of the Croatian Constitution. Yet, this solution would require initiating a complicated procedure of constitutional amendments. Alternatively,

[101] Decision Proposal to Amend the Constitution of Croatia 2009, 8.

[102] In October 2016, the indictment against Gavrilović was confirmed, and this case might potentially bring back the Law on Exemption to the Constitutional Court.

[103] J Omejec, 'Kontrola ustavnosti ustavnih normi (ustavnih amandmana i ustavnih zakona)' (2010) 1 *Godišnjak Akademije pravnih znanosti Hrvatske* 27.

there is a possibility of requesting an authentic interpretation of the constitutional amendment from the Croatian Parliament.

Despite the present state of play, it can be stated that Croatia at least introduced legal mechanisms to address crimes committed in the transitional period, and it showed by example, rather than just in theory, that in today's globalised society it is becoming harder to argue that only violent crimes represent a threat to the well-being of humanity, and that only these crimes shock the conscience of mankind and justify the non-applicability of statutory limitations. However, the full success of the reform depends on the implementation of these mechanisms by all relevant and responsible bodies. If that will not work either, the Croatian experience additionally fuels the need for severe economic crimes (that violate economic, social and cultural rights) to be addressed at the international level in the future, in order to serve as a deterrent and avoid complicated legal exercises.[104]

[104] See more in Roksandić Vidlička (n 64).

11

The American Perspective on Recovering Criminal Proceeds in Criminal and Non-Conviction Based Proceedings

STEFAN D CASSELLA*

Introduction

The purpose of this chapter is to provide the American perspective on the following question: why, after more than a decade of effort to reconcile our respective procedures to accommodate requests to freeze assets and enforce confiscation orders, is it still so difficult to reach assets moved across national borders?

There is no single answer to that question. First, there is the issue of training and resources: do states have the necessary skills, tools and incentives to locate, freeze assets and obtain confiscation orders? Or do the deficiencies in those areas preclude any success in recovering assets in transnational cases even if the wrongdoer is convicted? If the law enforcement authorities in the jurisdiction where a crime occurs are unwilling, or lack the resources, to attempt to freeze assets or to obtain a confiscation order, the willingness and ability of other states to assist in that process is a moot point.

States also take different views on the legality and efficacy of recovering assets via forfeiture orders obtained as part of a criminal case versus orders obtained in non-conviction-based or 'civil' proceedings. For reasons that I will discuss, a non-conviction-based proceeding will often be the best, or even the only, means of recovering the forfeitable property. For example, it is a particularly effective tool when dealing with a fugitive from justice. But non-conviction-based forfeiture

* Stefan D Cassella served as a federal prosecutor in the United States from 1985 to 2015, specialising in anti-money laundering and asset forfeiture issues. He now works as a consultant to domestic and international law enforcement agencies. His website is www.assetforfeiturelaw.us.

orders are more limited tools when property cannot be traced directly to the underlying crime.

Indeed, tracing requirements, which differ from jurisdiction to jurisdiction, depending in part on whether a forfeiture judgment was obtained in a criminal or non-criminal proceeding, are among the greatest obstacles to recovering assets in transnational cases. The likelihood of recovering assets is greatly diminished if a state will restrain funds and enforce forfeiture orders only if the property is directly traceable to the underlying crime, as opposed to treating the request for pre-trial restraint as a precursor to a personal judgment that may be satisfied out of any of the wrongdoer's assets.

Finally, another obstacle concerns the legal tools that have been put in place to allow courts to register and enforce foreign restraining orders and forfeiture judgments, and the willingness of courts to apply those tools without re-litigating the merits of the underlying order. Many countries still lack the legal means of recognising foreign orders, and in others, including the United States, the courts have shown a visceral distrust of such orders and a general reluctance to use the tools enacted to give them force and effect.

This chapter will attempt to address at least some of these issues. It begins with a discussion of the training and resources necessary even to initiate an attempt to recover forfeitable property. It then discusses the tracing issues that arise in both criminal and non-conviction-based forfeiture cases, and the reasons why, despite the tracing difficulties that may arise, non-conviction-based proceedings are an essential tool in recovering assets, particularly in transnational cases. It then highlights two aspects of US forfeiture law that have proven particularly effective in such cases: the ability to recover money from a foreign bank without requiring the assistance of the government where the bank is located, and the ability to bar fugitives from attempting to contest forfeiture actions without surrendering to face pending criminal charges. Finally, it discusses the American experience giving recognition to foreign forfeiture orders and the difficulty prosecutors in the United States encountered in overcoming judicial resistance to those efforts.

I. Training and Resources

From the American perspective, the prototypical case is one in which someone has committed a crime in the USA but has placed the proceeds overseas. The financial investigation to determine the location of the assets and their connection to the underlying crime is typically done by the same law enforcement agency that is investigating the crime itself. In the USA, that could be any one of a host of federal agencies: the FBI, which has fairly broad jurisdiction over most federal crimes; the Drug Enforcement Administration, which has jurisdiction in drug cases; the Internal Revenue Service, which has jurisdiction in tax and money laundering cases;

Homeland Security Investigations, which has jurisdiction in terrorism, smuggling and immigration cases; and so forth.

Obviously this creates problems of overlapping jurisdiction and battles over turf. Beyond that, there are certain systemic and recurring problems inherent in combining a financial investigation with the investigation of the underlying crime that inhibit full use of the forfeiture remedy.

Many law enforcement agents and criminal prosecutors consider the financial investigation to be a distraction. To obtain a conviction, they must prove beyond a reasonable doubt that a crime was committed and that the defendant is the one who committed the crime; so their focus naturally is on persuading witnesses to cooperate, finding admissible evidence sufficient to prove the case and complying with the rules that require disclosure of evidence to the accused.

Devoting time and resources to finding the defendant's assets necessarily detracts from the time and resources that can be devoted to the primary goal of obtaining a conviction; yet it is obvious that to be effective the financial investigation must be done contemporaneously with the criminal investigation so that the assets can be identified and immobilised at the time that the arrest is made or the indictment is returned.

Moreover, the prosecutor may feel that making a robust effort to recover the defendant's assets may complicate his or her ability to resolve the case in terms of a plea bargain, and thus avoid the uncertainties and the investment of time and resources involved in proceeding to trial. To put it bluntly, many defendants will more readily see the virtues of accepting a plea offer if the government is not insisting on the forfeiture of their assets as part of the package.

Forfeiture law is also viewed as procedurally arcane, and fraught with complications when third parties and competing property rights are involved. Will a court—foreign or domestic—allow the restraint of property in which a spouse or other third party has an interest? Will the third party be allowed to intervene in the case or demand a pre-trial hearing? A prosecutor may say 'I have enough to do without getting into all of that'.

Finally, the agents and prosecutors may feel that the relative improbability of finding recoverable assets in a foreign country and of obtaining that country's assistance in repatriating the property makes the investment of time and effort in navigating the forfeiture labyrinth of questionable value. If it is unlikely that the defendant has retained any forfeitable property, or it is unlikely that it will be found and recovered, the agent or prosecutor may say 'why bother?'

The solutions to these problems are not intuitively obvious, but efforts have been made to overcome them. Training agents to look for assets as they proceed with the criminal investigation and, if possible, assigning additional agents with particular expertise in asset recovery and a prosecutor who specialises in asset recovery as well tend to be essential ingredients. Once the agents and prosecutors are personally invested in the recovery of the property, they are more likely to assign it the priority it requires and less likely to bargain it away when the case is resolved. Moreover, a serious effort has been made to educate agents and prosecutors about the tools available to restrain and recover assets in both domestic and transnational cases, and to make the process less onerous and opaque.

Nevertheless, there are many cases filed in the federal courts in the United States in which less than a full-blooded effort is made to recover the proceeds of the crime. And if that is so in the country that is widely perceived as a world leader in such efforts—with more than $2 billion in criminal proceeds recovered every year—it will come as no surprise that lack of training, resources and institutional commitment hampers asset recovery in most parts of the world. And if no serious effort is made to identify, locate and recover assets in the country where the underlying crime was committed, the willingness of other countries to apply their tools and resources to assist in that effort when the property has moved across a national boundary will not matter.

II. Traceable Assets versus Substitute Assets

Any effort to recover criminal proceeds that have been transferred across national boundaries will involve tracing issues.

In the USA, as in many countries, a criminal forfeiture order can be made in terms of specific assets actually traceable to the offence, or can be a value-based money judgment directed to the wrongdoer personally. If it is an order forfeiting property directly traceable to the offence, there are all manner of tracing issues, which will be discussed below. If it is a value-based money judgment, one can, under US law, name untainted assets of equal value as property that may be used to satisfy the judgment—what are called 'substitute assets'.

But there are problems with forfeiting substitute assets in the international context: some countries have difficulty under their domestic law in enforcing a foreign judgment against property that is not directly traceable to a crime, or they may require a high level of proof that the substitute property, if it is forfeitable at all, actually belongs to the wrongdoer. Criminal defendants, of course, are aware of this, and go to great lengths to conceal and disguise their legal interests not only in the proceeds of their crimes, but in any untainted property that might be used to satisfy a forfeiture judgment—property that seems always to be titled in the name of a corporation or a member of the defendant's extended family.

For these reasons, in most cases it is highly desirable to show that the money in question is actually traceable to the offence of conviction. This is where the tracing issues come in.

There are always tracing issues when it comes to recovering criminal proceeds: money changes form as it goes from the defendant (or his victim) to a corporation, to an investment account, or to a tangible asset that is later sold or mortgaged to generate new funds. And it may be that, after all of the tracing, the existence of a lien, mortgage or other encumbrance has so reduced the equity in the property that it is not worth forfeiting. But the most serious problem involves the commingling of criminal proceeds with untainted assets in a bank account.

Suppose that investigators can show that $100,000 was taken from a victim in the United States and deposited into an account in a European bank on Monday. And suppose that there is still $100,000 in the same account on Friday. Is it the same money?

Suppose the balance fell to zero on Tuesday and another $100,000 from an unknown source was added on Thursday—is the money found in the account on Friday still forfeitable as directly traceable property? Suppose there was already $100,000 in the account on Monday when the tainted deposit was made and the entire $200,000 was withdrawn on Thursday, with half used to buy a yacht and half lost at the blackjack table at a casino. Which $100,000 was used to buy the yacht and which was lost in the casino? Is the yacht traceable to the tainted money or to the untainted money?

To address these problems, will the court allow the government to apply accounting principles such as 'last in/last out' or 'last in/first out'? Is there a 'lowest intermediate balance rule' that says that the money the government is looking for is always in an account until the balance falls below the value of the money it is seeking to recover? Can we simply consider any money found in a bank account to be fungible, so that tracing is not necessary?

Can the government avoid all of these problems by basing its asset recovery theory not on the underlying drug or fraud or human trafficking offence, but on money laundering, which permits the forfeiture of all commingled funds as property 'involved in' the money laundering offence?

Courts in the United States have been struggling with all of these questions for at least two decades and the results are mixed.[1] Some courts will apply accounting principles and some will not, depending on the procedural context.[2] Money

[1] See generally SD Cassella, *Asset Forfeiture Law in the United States*, 2nd edn (Huntington, Juris, 2013) §§ 11-3 and 11-4.

[2] Compare *Luis v United States*, 578 US ___, 136 S Ct 1083, (2016) (approving the use of accounting principles to establish probable cause for the pretrial restraint of property in criminal cases); *United States v Banco Cafetero Panama*, 797 F 2d 1154, 1160 (2d Cir 1986) (to establish that tainted funds remain in a bank account, notwithstanding a fluctuating balance, the government may use a 'last out' rule); *United States v Walsh*, 712 F 3d 119, 124 (2d Cir 2013) (government may rely on *Banco Cafetero*'s accounting principles, such as 'drugs-in, first-out', to establish probable cause to believe restrained property is traceable to the alleged offence, even if it was acquired with commingled funds); *United States v Approximately $620,349.85 Seized from Wachovia Bank Account Numbers Ending *6176 and *6189*, 2015 WL 3604044 (EDNY 5 June 2015) (applying *Banco Cafetero*; the government may use accounting principles to trace tainted funds through several bank accounts, including one held by a third party); and *United States v $88,029.08, More or Less, in US Currency*, 2012 WL 4499084, *5 (SD W Va 28 September 2012) (applying the 'lowest intermediate balance' rule to grant summary judgment as to the forfeitability of drug proceeds in a commingled bank account) with *In re Rothstein, Rosenfeldt, Adler, PA*, 717 F 3d 1205, 1214 (11th Cir 2013) (holding that the government had the burden of tracing the property and refusing to allow it to use accounting principles to do so); *United States v Louthian*, 2013 WL 594232 (WD Va 15 February 2013) (refusing to enter forfeiture order against specific assets purchased with commingled funds; accounting principles approved in *Banco Cafetero* do not satisfy

is considered fungible in some instances but not others.[3] And money laundering is a good alternative, but only if the elements of the offence are satisfied.[4] Otherwise, the government must resort to value-based money judgments and substitute assets, with all of the difficulties that I have already mentioned.

The point is this: if prosecutors in the United States have all of those tracing problems in purely domestic asset recovery cases, one can easily imagine the difficulties that arise when they ask a foreign court to accept their tracing analysis or their money laundering theory. To say the least, if a concept is 'foreign' to a court in the USA, it is very likely to be considered at least equally foreign to a foreign court.

III. Non-conviction Based Forfeiture

All of these problems arise in criminal cases where the money has left the USA and prosecutors are attempting to recover it pursuant to a conviction-based forfeiture or confiscation order. Similar problems, and additional ones, arise if they are trying to enforce a non-conviction-based order.

First, it is important to understand that non-conviction-based forfeiture is absolutely essential to the recovery of assets in the transnational context. In a host of instances, there is simply no other way to recover the assets.[5] For example, if the defendant is a fugitive, he cannot be convicted, and if he cannot be convicted there is no possibility of a conviction-based forfeiture order.[6] In that instance, the

the government's tracing burden of proof by a preponderance of the evidence); *In re One Star Class Sloop Sailboat*, 517 F Supp 2d 546, 553 (D Mass 2007) (*Banco Cafetero* was decided when the burden of proof was on the claimant; it does not apply to cases where the government has the burden of proving forfeitability); and *United States v All Right, Title and Interest (8 Bayview Terrace)*, 2010 WL 143673, *2 (DNJ 4 January 2010) (refusing to apply first-in, first-out to determine which funds in a commingled account are subject to forfeiture; government should not be allowed to use accounting methods to forfeit untainted funds that were deposited into an account that the government intentionally left open after arresting the account holder).

[3] See 18 USC § 984 (providing that the government may regard funds in a bank account to be fungible notwithstanding volatile account activity for one year from the date of the conduct giving rise to the forfeiture); *In re 650 Fifth Ave & Related Props*, 2014 WL 1516328, *29 (SDNY 18 April 2014) (under § 984, if the government shows that the value of the criminal proceeds deposited into a bank account in the past year exceeds the current balance, it is entitled to the forfeiture of the entire balance); *United States v Funds on Deposit at Bank One, Indiana*, 2010 WL 909091, *7–8 (ND Ind 9 March 2010) (under § 984, when $335,000 in drug proceeds was deposited in an account and commingled with other funds, the entire $264,563 remaining in the account within one year of the offence was forfeitable as drug proceeds without having to do any tracing analysis).

[4] See Cassella (n 1) §§ 27-9 and 27–10.

[5] SD Cassella, 'The Case for Civil Forfeiture: Why In Rem Proceedings are an Essential Tool for Recovering the Proceeds of Crime' (2008) 11 *Journal of Money Laundering Control* 8.

[6] See, eg, *United States v $506,069.09 Seized from First Merit Bank*, 2014 WL 7185585 (ND Ohio 16 December 2014) (government files civil forfeiture action against doctor who left fraud proceeds

government needs the capability of obtaining a non-conviction-based order and asking a foreign government to enforce it. The same is true if the defendant has died before a conviction can be obtained or is incompetent to stand trial.[7]

Alternatively, the defendant may be convicted of a crime other than the one giving rise to the forfeiture of the particular asset that the government is seeking to recover. In the USA, the courts have not fully adopted the concept of 'extended confiscation', whereby a conviction for a given offence will give rise to a forfeiture order directed at the proceeds of all other crimes that the same defendant has committed. To the contrary, because criminal forfeiture is regarded as part of the defendant's sentence relating to the commission of a given offence, only property connected to the commission of that offence is subject to criminal forfeiture.[8] In those cases, the government must bring a non-conviction-based forfeiture action to recover any property involved in other offences.

The defendant may also have committed the crime using someone else's property. For example, he may have laundered his money through a third party's business, robbed a bank with a third party's gun or distributed drugs using a third party's aeroplane. Conviction-based forfeiture cannot reach the property of third parties[9]—it would be a violation of the due process rights of third parties to attempt to confiscate their property in a proceeding in which they were not able to participate—but non-conviction-based forfeiture can reach third party property, because in that setting the third party has the right to intervene and defend his property interest by contesting the government's proof on the merits and/or by asserting that he is an innocent owner of the property.[10]

behind in the USA when he fled to Pakistan); *United States v 40 Acres of Real Property*, 629 F Supp 2d 1264, 1268–69 (SD Ala 2009) (government files civil forfeiture against real property held by husband and wife because, although wife pled guilty in criminal case and forfeited her interest, husband was a fugitive).

[7] See, eg, *United States v Real Property at 40 Clark Road*, 52 F Supp 2d 254, 265 (D Mass 1999) (defendant died while criminal forfeiture was pending, making civil forfeiture necessary); *United States v Real Property … 404 W Milton St*, 2014 WL 5808347 (WD Tex 7 November 2014) (husband and wife indicted; wife convicted in criminal case but because husband died before trial, government files civil forfeiture to address his interest in jointly held property).

[8] See *United States v Juluke*, 426 F 3d 323, 328–29 (5th Cir 2005) (the government must prove that the property subject to forfeiture was the proceeds of the drug activity that formed the basis for the defendant's conviction, not of the defendant's drug trafficking generally); *United States v Nava*, 404 F 3d 1119, 1129 no 5 (9th Cir 2005) (even though defendant was engaged in drug dealing as long ago as 1991, government's interest in his property did not vest until 1997 because the only offence for which he was convicted began in that year; there can be no forfeiture based on earlier conduct that was not charged).

[9] See *United States v Nava*, 404 F 3d 1119, 1124 (9th Cir 2005) (explaining the difference between civil and criminal forfeiture; because criminal forfeiture is *in personam*, only the defendant's property can be forfeited; because defendant's daughter was the true owner and not merely a nominee, she was entitled to prevail in the ancillary proceeding); *United States v BCCI Holdings (Luxembourg) SA (Petition of Chawla)*, 46 F 3d 1185, 1190 (DC Cir 1995) ('only the property of the defendant—including property held by a third party pursuant to a voidable transaction—can be confiscated in a RICO proceeding').

[10] See generally Cassella (n 1) ch 12.

In other cases, the perpetrator of the offence giving rise to the forfeiture may simply be unknown. If weapons, flight simulators, contraband electronics or money is intercepted while on the way to a country designated as a supporter of terrorism, but it is unclear who the exporter or recipient of the property might be, there is no one to prosecute and hence no one to convict. But a non-conviction-based order will reach the property and force the property owner to come forward to contest the forfeiture proceeding.

In still other cases, the interests of justice will militate in favour of a non-criminal resolution even if there was a clear violation of a criminal law. For example, suppose a convicted felon persuades his 70-year-old mother to purchase a firearm on his behalf, in a situation where both of them know that it is a violation of federal law for a convicted felon to possess such a weapon. And suppose the mother not only buys the firearm, but lies on the required document when asked if she is buying it for herself or for a third party.

In that case, the mother has clearly violated federal law and would be subject to criminal prosecution. However, faced with the choice between doing nothing (and allowing the felon to retain the weapon) and bringing criminal charges against the aged woman, the government might decide that confiscating the weapon pursuant to a non-conviction-based forfeiture order is the right thing to do.[11]

Finally, returning to cases that arise frequently in the transnational context, suppose the crime was committed outside of the United States, the perpetrator has been convicted in the foreign country, but the property is now in the United States and the foreign country has not (for whatever reason) been able to obtain a confiscation order that the USA is able to enforce. In that instance, either because they lacked jurisdiction over the foreign crime or because there was no reason to prosecute the offender a second time for the same offence, prosecutors in the USA would not be able to obtain a conviction-based forfeiture order against the foreign defendant, but with a non-conviction-based order they could recover the proceeds of the foreign crime and return them to the foreign state. Indeed, cases in which the USA brings civil forfeiture actions to recover the proceeds of foreign crimes—including public corruption—at the behest of the victim country are quite common.[12]

For all of these reasons and many others, prosecutors need to have non-conviction-based forfeiture as part of the arsenal of weapons available to recover assets. Unfortunately, due in large part to media reports linking non-conviction-based forfeiture to currency seizures that occur during traffic stops by local police

[11] See *United States v 6 Firearms, Accessories and Ammunition*, 2015 WL 4660126 (WD Wash 5 August 2015) (guns purchased by 70-year-old woman for her convicted-felon son are subject to forfeiture as property involved in the making of a false statement to a firearms dealer in violation of 18 USC § 922(a)(6)).

[12] See *United States v All Assets Held at Bank Julius Baer & Co*, 2015 WL 4450899 (DDC 20 July 2015) (civil forfeiture action to recover assets of former Ukrainian Prime Minister Pavel Lazarenko).

officers, non-conviction-based forfeiture has become politically controversial in the United States, and there is a danger that Congress will enact changes that will hobble the ability of law enforcement to use this essential tool in a wide variety of contexts that have nothing to do with police officers and traffic stops.

For that reason, it is worth pausing a moment to recall that nothing in non-conviction-based forfeiture procedure threatens individual rights and liberties.[13] It is simply a procedural device for litigating all claims to a particular asset at one time.[14] The government still must prove by a preponderance of the evidence that a crime was committed and that the property was derived from or used to commit that crime; the property owner has the right to trial by jury, to assert an innocent owner defence and to move to suppress evidence illegally seized; the government must comply with strictly-enforced notice requirements and filing deadlines; and all forfeitures are subject to the Excessive Fines Clause of the Eighth Amendment, which proscribes forfeitures that are 'grossly disproportional to the gravity of the offence'. In this regard, the rights of the property owner in a non-conviction-based forfeiture proceeding are no different than the defendant's rights under a panoply of other non-criminal actions that the government may bring to enforce the criminal laws, such as the False Claims Act,[15] which allows the government to seek a civil penalty for making a false claim for payments owed by the USA, and the civil money laundering and RICO statutes,[16] which likewise authorise civil penalties for criminal conduct.

But non-conviction-based forfeiture is no panacea. First, there are the tracing problems we have already discussed. Non-conviction-based forfeiture is limited to property directly traceable to the offence; there is no possibility (at least under US law) of getting a value-based judgment or substitute assets if the property named as the subject of the forfeiture action has been dissipated, lost, transferred outside of the jurisdiction of the court or transferred to a bona fide purchaser for value.[17]

Moreover, the most significant problem in the transnational context is that many, if not most, foreign states either do not recognise non-conviction-based judgments or have not yet enacted non-conviction-based forfeiture statutes that

[13] See generally SD Cassella, 'Civil Asset Recovery: The American Experience' (2013) 3 *Eucrim* 98.

[14] See *United States v Ursery*, 518 US 267, 295–96 (1996) (Kennedy, J concurring) (proceedings *in rem* are simply structures that allow the government to quiet title to criminally tainted property in a single proceeding in which all interested persons are required to file claims contesting the forfeiture at one time); *United States v Real Property Located at 475 Martin Lane*, 545 F 3d 1134, 1144 (9th Cir 2008) ('*in rem* actions are generally considered proceedings against the world' in which 'the court undertakes to determine all claims that anyone has to a thing in question').

[15] 31 USCA § 3730.

[16] 18 USC §§ 1956(b) and 1963(c).

[17] Even so, the USA does have a robust non-conviction-based forfeiture programme. According to statistics provided by the Justice Management Division of the US Department of Justice, of the $8.8 billion forfeited in 2014, $4.3 billion, or 49%, was forfeited in civil/non-conviction-based forfeiture cases.

could be used to assist other states in recovering assets in the circumstances where there is no other way to do so. For that reason, the USA has turned to tools that it may use to recover assets in non-conviction-based forfeiture cases without the assistance of a foreign government when either the property or the wrongdoer, or both, are outside the jurisdiction of the USA.

IV. Fugitive Disentitlement Doctrine

One such tool is called the fugitive disentitlement doctrine.[18] It provides that if a person is a fugitive from justice in a criminal case that is pending in the USA, and there is also a non-conviction-based forfeiture action pending against his property, the fugitive may not intervene in the forfeiture case to defend his property unless he surrenders to face the criminal charges.[19]

Prosecutors in the USA used this most recently in a case called *MegaUpload, Ltd*, in which an individual who called himself Kim Dotcom, and who operated from Hong Kong and New Zealand, used the internet to distribute intellectual property, such as motion pictures, in violation of US intellectual property laws.[20] The crime occurred in the USA, so Mr Dotcom was indicted there, but he and his property were in Hong Kong and New Zealand.

To obtain a forfeiture order without being able to obtain a conviction, the government had to file a non-conviction-based forfeiture action in Virginia and use the fugitive disentitlement doctrine to bar Mr Dotcom from intervening in the case.[21] The prosecutors did that successfully, and obtained a forfeiture order. Whether the countries where the property is located will enforce that judgment remains to be seen, but the point is that the USA was able to obtain the judgment without having to rely on the ability or the willingness of a foreign government to bring either a criminal or a non-conviction-based forfeiture action under its own law.

[18] 28 USC § 2466.

[19] See *Collazos v United States*, 368 F 3d 190, 198 (2d Cir 2004) (§ 2466 has five elements: (1) a warrant or similar process for the claimant's apprehension; (2) knowledge of the warrant; (3) relationship between the criminal and civil cases; (4) claimant must not be confined overseas; and (5) claimant must have deliberately avoided prosecution by leaving or declining to enter or re-enter the United States or otherwise evading the jurisdiction of the court where the criminal case is pending); *United States v $671,160.00 in US Currency*, 730 F 3d 1051, 1055–56 (9th Cir 2013) (same); *United States v $6,976,934.65 Plus Interest*, 554 F 3d 123, 128 (DC Cir 2009) (adopting the five *Collazos* elements, and discussing each in detail); *United States v Salti*, 579 F 3d 656, 663 (6th Cir 2009) (adopting the *Collazos* elements).

[20] *United States v All Assets Listed in Attachment A (MegaUpload, Ltd)*, 89 F Supp3d 813 (ED Va 2015), aff's *United States v Batato*, 833 F.3d 413 (4th cir. 2014).

[21] Under 28 USC § 1355(b), it is sufficient for jurisdictional purposes to show that the acts giving rise to the forfeiture occurred in the district where the non-conviction-based forfeiture action is filed.

V. Section 981(k)

The other, somewhat unusual, aspect of the non-conviction-based forfeiture scheme in the USA involves money deposited into foreign banks that have correspondent accounts in the USA.

Suppose, for example, a person commits a fraud in the USA and deposits the victim's money in a bank account in a foreign country that is not particularly friendly to the USA or that does not provide mutual legal assistance. In such a case, there would be little chance of persuading the foreign government to enforce any forfeiture order that prosecutors in the USA might obtain.

But suppose the bank into which the victim's funds were deposited has an account that it uses to conduct dollar-denominated transactions, in a US bank in New York. Under a statute known as Section 981(k), the United States can seize and commence a non-conviction-based forfeiture action against the funds in the foreign bank's correspondent account, and force the customer to intervene to defend the funds in the US court.[22] If he does not do so, or if his claim fails on the merits, the money will be forfeited from the foreign bank, which in turn may make itself whole by debiting the account of its customer.[23]

For example, in a pending case, an individual called Hikmatullah Shadman allegedly obtained more than $77 million in fraudulent payments from the USA and deposited the money into an account at Afghanistan International Bank (AIB) in Afghanistan. To recover the money, the government filed a civil forfeiture action under Section 981(k) against funds that AIB had on deposit in an interbank account at a bank in New York. In the most recent decision, the court confirmed that the foreign bank lacks standing to contest the forfeiture of the money in its correspondent account as long as there are sufficient funds in the customer's account from which it could make itself whole. It is the bank's customer, in this case Mr Shadman, and not the bank that must come forward to intervene in the forfeiture case.[24]

Whether the government actually prevails on the merits of the case, however, will depend on its ability to obtain admissible evidence of the fraud from Afghanistan—an entirely separate and ever-present obstacle to obtaining and enforcing forfeiture orders in transnational cases.

[22] 18 USC § 981(k).

[23] See *United States v Union Bank for Savings and Investment (Jordan)*, 487 F 3d 8, 17 (1st Cir 2007) (if forfeitable funds are deposited into a foreign bank, and the foreign bank has a correspondent account at a US bank, the forfeitable funds are deemed to be deposited into the correspondent account and may be seized and forfeited); *United States v $70,990,605*, 305 FRD 20 (DDC 2015) (explaining how § 981(k) allows the government to recover funds deposited into a bank in Afghanistan by filing a civil forfeiture action against the Afghan bank's account at a bank in New York).

[24] *United States v $70,990,605*, 305 FRD 20 (DDC 2015).

VI. Enforcement of Foreign Judgments

Finally, we come to the authority to enforce orders or judgments entered by foreign courts. When a court in the USA enters a conviction against a defendant who sent his or her property overseas, the prosecutor may obtain a criminal confiscation order and ask the foreign government to register and enforce it. As I have explained, that does not always work; the foreign government may be willing to help, but may lack the necessary domestic legislation to register and enforce a foreign order, or may run into tracing and ownership issues that might take years to resolve.

One potential way around such problems is to ask the court that entered the criminal conviction and forfeiture judgment to order the defendant to repatriate his property to the United States. A defendant who is capable of repatriating his property but refuses to do so is subject, under US law, to an enhanced sentence;[25] unfortunately, our experience is that defendants would often prefer the extended time in jail to the loss of their criminal proceeds.

An 2015, for example, there was a defendant who perpetrated a fraud scheme in which he induced victims to send him money so that they could claim a sweepstakes prize, and then sent the money to a Swiss bank account. The court ordered him to repatriate the money—which was more than $1 million—but he refused and accepted the increase in his sentence.[26]

The real solution to this problem is to regularise the process by which countries register and enforce each other's confiscation orders without looking behind the order or allowing the defendant to re-litigate the merits. As I have explained before, the problem countries have in attempting to enforce each other's orders is not unlike the problem a traveller has when trying to get his electronic device to work in a foreign country: he needs an adapter to make the plug on his charging unit fit into the electrical socket so that he can run his computer or smart phone, or whatever it is that he needs to work.[27] In the context of the recovery of criminal proceeds, we need an adapter that makes my confiscation order fit into your judicial process so that it can be registered and enforced.

It took 10 years to do so, but the USA finally has an adapter that allows the registration and enforcement of both foreign confiscation orders and the pre-conviction orders that are made to preserve assets pending the entry of a final judgment. There were many false starts, as there was considerable opposition from

[25] 21 USC § 853(e)(4)(B).

[26] *Susi v United States*, 2015 WL 1602074 (WDNC 9 April 2015).

[27] See generally SD Cassella, 'The Recovery of Criminal Proceeds Generated in One Nation and Found in Another' (2008) 9 *Journal of Financial Crime* 268.

the judiciary to the concept of 'blindly' enforcing a foreign order without reopening it to litigation.[28]

For example, in one case called *Tiger Eye Investments*, federal prosecutors attempted to enforce a Brazilian preservation order against the proceeds of a Brazilian fraud scheme that were deposited in investment accounts in the USA. This seemed to be a perfect application of a then relatively new statute allowing US courts to register and enforce foreign forfeiture orders. But the court held that the legislature could not have intended to authorise a procedure that did not allow for judicial review of the merits of the case, the authority of the foreign court to issue the order and the procedure that the foreign court employed.[29]

Ultimately, five years ago, the legislature enacted an amended statute providing expressly for the registration and enforcement of foreign restraining orders and forfeiture judgments.[30]

In the most recent case decided under that statute, which also involved a request from Brazil, a court held that an order restraining $12 million in fraud proceeds could be enforced. Importantly, the court held that the account holders had no right to a hearing at which they could challenge the Brazilian restraining order on the merits; nor could they challenge the order on the ground that the procedures followed by the Brazilian court were different from the procedures that would have been followed by a court in the USA before making the order.[31]

Another court reached the same conclusion with respect to the enforcement of a restraining order made by a court in Curacao in a money laundering investigation. The claimants, who objected to the restraint of their bank accounts in Miami, argued that the Curacao court lacked jurisdiction to make the order, that the Curacao court had reached the wrong conclusion on the merits and that the procedures employed by the Curacao court were incompatible with due process as it is understood in the United States. But the court held that it would not 'pierce the veil of authority' behind the restraining order, that the claimants had no right to re-litigate factual issues already litigated, or that could be litigated in the foreign court, and that minor differences in procedure are no obstacle to the enforcement of a foreign order.

A court in the USA—the court said—'should not lightly sit in judgment of the legal system of a foreign sovereign'.[32] The future of international cooperation in the recovery of assets involved in transnational crime may turn on the ability of all states to enact legislation of this nature, and of the courts in those jurisdictions

[28] For a more detailed discussion of the history of this issue, see, eg, SD Cassella, 'Enforcement of Foreign Restraining Orders' (2013) 16 *Journal of Money Laundering Control* 290.

[29] *In Re Any and All Funds … in the Name of Tiger Eye Investments, Ltd*, 613 F 3d 1122 (DC Cir 2010).

[30] 28 USC § 2467.

[31] *In re Seizure of Approximately $12,116,153.16 and Accrued Interest in US Currency*, 903 F Supp 2d 19 (DDC 2012).

[32] *In re Restraint of All Assets … at UBS Financial Services, Inc*, 860 F Supp 2d 32, 42 (DDC 2012).

to take a similarly benign view of the importance and legality of giving full faith and credit to foreign forfeiture or confiscation orders. Courts in foreign countries have recently expressed a similar willingness to enforce US forfeiture orders. See *Doraville Properties Corp v Her Majesty's Attorney General* [2016] JRC128, Royal Court, Bailiwick of Jersey (July 2016).

Conclusion

Those who have been engaged in the effort to bring the process of recovering assets in transnational cases into the twenty-first century for a decade or more can rightly feel that we have come a long way, but we must readily acknowledge that we still have a long way to go. There are institutional and legal problems that we have yet to overcome.

Some, like the tracing and resource issues, not to mention the obstacles to obtaining admissible evidence from a foreign jurisdiction, are simply inherent in the process of locating the proceeds of crime that are exacerbated in the transnational context. Others, like the reluctance of courts to enforce non-conviction-based forfeiture orders, or any order of a foreign court, without allowing the parties to re-litigate the merits, are problems that we should be able to overcome by enacting twenty-first-century adapters that meld the disparate judicial systems of sovereign nations. But it is only through experience and a coming together of persons with different perspectives and a mutual desire to solve these problems that the problem will in the end finally be solved.

12

The 'Pre-investigative' Role of Financial Intelligence Units in Recovering Assets

MARC PENNA*

Introduction

The commitment to combat money laundering began more than 20 years ago, when a group of industrial countries, including Belgium and Luxembourg, decided to create the Financial Action Task Force (FATF).[1] The FATF is an intergovernmental body established in 1989 which currently comprises 35 member jurisdictions,[2] two regional organisations (the European Commission and the Gulf Co-operation Council) and nine FATF associate members[3] (FATF-Style Regional Bodies, or FSRBs), representing most major financial centres in all parts of the globe.

The mandate of the FATF is to set standards and to promote effective implementation of legal, regulatory and operational measures for combating money laundering (ML), terrorist financing (TF), financing of the proliferation of weapons of mass destruction[4] and other related threats to the integrity of the international financial system.[5]

* Belgian Financial Intelligence Processing Unit (CTIF-CFI).

1 See www.fatf-gafi.org.

2 See www.fatf-gafi.org/pages/aboutus/membersandobservers/.

3 Asia Pacific Group, Caribbean Financial Action Task Force, Council of Europe Committee of Experts on the Evaluation of Anti-Money Laundering Measures and the Financing of Terrorism (Moneyval), Eurasian Group, Eastern and Southern Africa Anti-Money Laundering Group, Financial Action Task Force of Latin America, Inter Governmental Action Group against Money Laundering in West Africa, Middle East and North Africa Financial Action Task Force and Task Force on Money Laundering in Central Africa.

4 This aspect will not be covered in this chapter.

5 See P de Koster and M Penna, 'The Case of Money Laundering. Real Administrative Procedure Used in the Detection of Fraudolent Transactions' in F Galli and A Weyembergh (eds), *Do Labels Still Matter? Blurring Boundaries between Administrative and Criminal Law. The Influence of the EU* (Brussels, IEE, 2014) 69.

In 1990, the FATF adopted a series of 40 Recommendations, which were revised several times (in 1996, 2001, 2003 and 2012)[6] to adapt them to new emerging threats. The FATF 40 Recommendations set out a comprehensive and consistent framework of measures that countries should implement in order to combat ML and TF, as well as financing of the proliferation of weapons of mass destruction. The FATF Recommendations set out the essential measures[7] that countries should have in place to: identify the risks, and develop policies and domestic co-ordination; pursue ML, TF and the financing of proliferation; apply preventive measures for the financial sector and other designated non-financial businesses and professions (DNFBPs);[8] establish powers and responsibilities for the competent authorities (eg investigative, law enforcement and supervisory authorities) and other institutional measures; enhance the transparency and availability of beneficial ownership information of legal persons and arrangements; and facilitate international co-operation.

FATF members and FSRB members committed to implementing this framework of measures. In the European Union, the 40 FATF Recommendations have been translated into EU AML/CFT Directives (in 1991, 2001 and 2005). The latest European Directive (the 4th one), translating the revised 40 FATF Recommendations of February 2012, was adopted by the European Parliament and the Council in May 2015 and published in June 2015.[9] This Directive must be transposed by Member States into national legislation before June 2017 at the latest.

Policy- and lawmakers, the financial sector and the DNFBPs, their supervisory or control authorities, the investigative and law enforcement authorities, and many other services of the state are all involved in some way in the implementation of this framework of measures. The objective of all these measures is to prevent ML and TF activities by increasing the transparency of the financial sector (and the DNFBPs), promoting and ensuring a better and effective detection of the ML/TF financial transactions, and enabling the effective and dissuasive prosecution and sanctioning of ML/TF activities—and, for ML, their related predicate offences.

Amongst the FATF-recommended measures, the ongoing and effective detection by the financial sector and by the DNFBPs of suspicious ML or TF transactions and the co-operation with a central and independent anti-ML and counter-financing of terrorism (AML/CFT) unit, called a Financial Intelligence Unit (FIU), are the cornerstone of the whole AML/CFT regime.

[6] See www.fatf-gafi.org/topics/fatfrecommendations/documents/fatf-recommendations.html.

[7] FATF, *International Standards on Combating Money Laundering and the Financing of Terrorism & Proliferation* (Paris, FATF, 2015) (hereinafter FATF 40 Recommendations).

[8] DNFBPs include: casinos, real estate agents, dealers in precious stones, lawyers, notaries, other independent legal professionals, external accountants and trust and company service providers (general glossary to the FATF 40 Recommendations (ibid) 112).

[9] Directive 2015/849/EU of the European Parliament and of the Council of 20 May 2015 on the prevention of the use of the financial system for the purposes of money laundering or terrorist financing, amending Regulation (EU) No 648/2012 of the European Parliament and of the Council, and repealing Directive 2005/60/EC of the European Parliament and of the Council and Commission Directive 2006/70/EC [2015] OJ L141/73.

This chapter gives an overview of the pre-investigative role of FIUs in recovering criminal assets, with a particular focus on the Belgian experience.

I. What is a Financial Intelligence Unit?

FATF Recommendation number 29 requires that:

Countries should establish a financial intelligence unit (FIU) that serves as a national centre for the receipt and analysis of: (a) suspicious transaction reports; and (b) other information relevant to ML, associated predicate offences and TF, and for the dissemination of the results of that analysis. The FIU should be able to obtain additional information from reporting entities, and should have access on a timely basis to the financial, administrative and law enforcement information that it requires to undertake its functions properly.[10]

Many countries in the world have now set up FIUs and imposed AML/CFT measures to prevent the use of their financial system for ML and TF purposes, and to safeguard the integrity of their financial system.

The main rationale of an FIU is to be a 'buffer' between the financial sector (and, more generally, entities and professionals subject to reporting obligations—DNFBPs) and law enforcement and judicial authorities in charge of financial crime investigations and prosecutions. This national centre could be an administrative one, part of the law enforcement authorities, or of a judicial or prosecutorial type.[11]

A. Administrative-Type FIUs

An administrative FIU is a central national agency, placed under the supervision of a ministry or administration, such as the Ministry of Finance, the Central Bank or a regulatory agency ('autonomous' FIUs), or not placed under such supervision but, rather, independent from law enforcement or judicial authorities ('independent' FIUs).

Administrative-type FIUs are often preferred by the banking sector and by the other reporting entities. Financial institutions and DNFBPs facing a problematic transaction or atypical customer relationship do not have evidence that such a transaction involves ML or criminal activity, or that the customer involved is part of a criminal operation or organisation. They will therefore be reluctant to disclose their suspicions directly to a law enforcement agency. The role of the FIU is to analyse the suspicion, and to send the case for further criminal investigation and prosecution only if the suspicion is substantiated.

[10] See FATF 40 Recommendations (n 7) 24.

[11] See International Monetary Fund and World Bank, *Financial Intelligence Units: An Overview* (Washington DC, 2004).

The powers of administrative-type FIUs are limited to the receipt, analysis and dissemination of information and data related to suspicious ML/TF transactions and other related reports; they do not include investigative or prosecutorial powers.

Employees from administrative-type FIUs are generally civilians, hired by the FIU itself, or officials seconded from various administrative services of the state (customs, tax authorities, etc). Employees from administrative-type FIUs are never in contact with the criminals they investigate regarding ML or TF activities. This means that administrative-type FIUs never intercept, detain or question criminals they suspect of ML or TF activities. Administrative-type FIUs do not have the power to judicially seize criminal money or assets and belongings they suspect to be of criminal origin.

However, countries that have opted for an administrative-type FIU usually also give their FIU the power to postpone the execution of a suspicious financial transaction or the power to block any transactions involving the bank accounts of the criminals or criminal organisation for a short period of time (between two and five days) before the prosecutor's office decides whether to seize the criminal proceeds.

B. Law-Enforcement-Type FIUs

The law-enforcement-type FIU is closer to other law enforcement units, such as a financial crimes unit, and benefits from their expertise and sources of information. In return, information received by the FIU can be accessed more easily by law enforcement agencies and can be used in any investigation. Exchange of information may also be strengthened through the use of existing national and international criminal information exchange networks.[12]

A law-enforcement-type FIU normally has the powers of the law enforcement agency itself (without specific ML/TF legislative authority being required), including the power to freeze transactions and seize assets (with the same degree of judicial supervision applied to other law enforcement powers in the country). This is likely to facilitate the timely exercise of law enforcement powers when this is needed. Therefore, under the control of the prosecutor's office, law-enforcement-type FIUs have the power to seize funds, freeze accounts, conduct interrogations, detain suspects and conduct searches.

C. Judicial or Prosecutorial-Type FIUs

Judicial or prosecutorial-type FIUs are most frequently within the prosecutor's jurisdiction, but, like an administrative FIU, they act independently as a 'buffer'

[12] Such as Europol and Interpol.

between the financial sector, the DNFBPs and the prosecutor in charge of the criminal investigations.

Suspicious financial ML/TF activities are directly reported by the financial sector and the DNFBPs to the designated division of the prosecutor's office.

If the ML or TF suspicions of the financial sector and DNFBPs are confirmed by the first inquiries carried out under its supervision, the prosecutor could immediately decide to start a judicial or criminal investigation, and could request the assistance of an examining magistrate or the law enforcement authorities.

The judicial powers (eg seizing funds, freezing accounts, conducting interrogations, detaining suspects and conducting searches) can then be brought into play without delay. The choice of the prosecutor's office or the law enforcement authorities as the location of an FIU does not exclude the possibility of establishing and positioning the FIU as a department of the prosecutor's office or as a police service with special responsibility for financial investigations.

The principal advantage of this type of arrangement is that disclosed information is passed from the financial sector directly to an agency located in the judiciary.

The circumstances or the context of the country could also justify reporting to an administrative FIU, to the law enforcement authorities or to the prosecutor's office. In countries where the financial sector is reluctant to co-operate directly with the law enforcement or judicial authorities (because of a high bank secrecy, for example), an administrative FIU could be more appropriate.

D. The Belgian Experience

CTIF-CFI[13] is the Belgian FIU and was established by the Law of 11 January 1993 on preventing the use of the financial system for purposes of money laundering or terrorist financing.[14] CTIF-CFI has been operational since 1 December 1993, and is an autonomous public administrative authority, with its own budget (through contributions from the reporting entities).[15] It is supervised by the Minister of Justice and by the Minister of Finance.

The board of CTIF-CFI is composed of eight financial experts, including three magistrates (fully seconded public prosecutors), appointed by the King of Belgium. One of the three magistrates manages the FIU. CTIF-CFI is operationally autonomous: the eight financial experts decide independently and without any constraint if there is any serious indication that the suspicious transactions analysed are related to a potential ML or TF activity. A secretariat of eight people, a team of 30 financial analysts, three strategic analysts, three advisors and a translator assist

[13] Cellule de Traitement des Informations Financières (CTIF)–Cel voor Financiële Informatieverwerking (CFI).

[14] See www.ctif-cfi.be/website/images/FR/law_be/loi937042015.pdf.

[15] Royal Decree of 11 June 1993 on the composition, the organisation, the functioning and the autonomy of the Financial Intelligence Processing Unit.

the eight financial experts. CTIF-CFI acts as a 'buffer' between the financial sector and the DNFBPs, on the one hand, and the law enforcement and judicial and prosecutorial authorities, on the other.

II. What are the FIU's Sources of Information?

Due to their central position in the AML/CFT system, FIUs manage huge databases with mainly two types of information: information issued from 'reports' and information called 'intelligence'.

A. Reports

Reports contain one or more individual suspicious ML/TF transactions. Usually, a report is the starting point of an FIU's financial analysis or administrative investigation. Reports include ML/TF financial transactions collected from suspicious transaction reports (STRs),[16] currency transaction reports (CTRs),[17] cross-border transaction reports (CBTRs)[18] and cross-border cash transactions reports (CBCTRs).[19]

STRs are the result of a subjective but well-documented prior analysis of suspicious transactions by the compliance officers of financial institutions or DNFBPs. The CTRs and CBTRs result from the occurrence of indicators or the exceeding of a defined threshold: CTRs and CBTRs, therefore, are not the result of an actual and substantial analysis.

Depending on the legal system of a country (common or civil law), the country may receive mainly STRs and incidentally threshold-type reports (eg Belgium, France), or mainly CTRs and CBTRs and incidentally STRs (eg United States, Canada). However, all types of FIUs receive copies of CBCTRs or may have access to the CBCTR database.

The STRs, CTRs and CBTRs mainly come from financial institutions (banks, currency exchange offices and payment institutions) and DNFBPs (notaries, real estate agents and accountants). The customs and excise administration is the authority that usually receives and records the CBCTRs, then makes them available to the FIU. Suspicious ML transactions are mostly classified in three categories, according to the different stages of the ML process: injection, layering

[16] STRs: any kind of suspicious transaction reported to the FIU and based on a subjective analysis of the suspicious transactions with regard to the profile of the customer.

[17] CTRs: transactions in cash automatically reported to the FIU when exceeding a given threshold (in general, €/$10,000).

[18] CBTRs: international transactions (wire transfers) automatically reported to the FIU when exceeding a given threshold(in general, €/$10,000).

[19] CBCTRs: declarations made by travellers when they travel with more than €10,000 in cash.

and integration. Each stage corresponds to various types of potential suspicious financial transaction.

In the first stage (injection), the 'criminal' or 'illegal' money is injected in cash into the financial system (eg cash deposit into a bank account, currency exchange in a currency exchange office). It is then wire transferred between multiple bank accounts belonging to the criminal organisation (the layering stage). The objective is to move the funds from one bank account to another (if possible, in different countries) to complicate the paper trail and any criminal investigations. After the first and second stages of ML, the funds can be integrated into high-value goods, such as real estate, securities, gold or diamonds, equity investments in commercial companies. When amounts of cash are injected into the purchase of, for example, real estate, the last stage (integration) is used to classify the suspicious transactions.[20]

B. Preventive Measures Applying to STRs

The effectiveness of the preventive system and adequate detection of suspicious ML/TF transactions depends on the quality of the preventive measures applied by the reporting entities. The preventive measures applicable to the financial sector and DNFBPs mainly include:

- 'know your customer' due diligence measures; measures to identify beneficial owners and beneficial ownership of legal structures;
- constant due diligence measures regarding the (financial) transactions of customers;
- STRing obligations;
- AML/CFT supervision of the financial sector and DNFBPs; and
- vigilance with regard to the nonprofit organisation sector.

The financial sector and the DNFBPs must identify and verify the identity of their customers when establishing a business relationship with a regular customer, in certain types of transactions with occasional customers, in case of doubts about the veracity or adequacy of the identification data regarding an existing customer, and in case of suspicions of ML or TF.

The financial sector and the DNFBPs also have to observe constant due diligence to ensure that the conducted transactions are consistent with the knowledge they have of their customer and of his professional and/or commercial activities.

In large structures, a compliance officer or a compliance department co-ordinates the internal mechanisms designed by the financial institution or the DNFBP to fight ML and TF. In small structures with a limited number of professionals, the compliance officer is one of the professionals.

20 Since 2014, Art 20 of the Law of 11 January 1993 on preventing the use of the financial system for purposes of money laundering or terrorist financing (Law of 11 January 1993), has prohibited any payment in cash for purchasing real estate, even if the amount paid in cash is small.

Compliance officers must closely review any transaction they consider particularly likely, due to its nature, its unusual character in view of the customer's activities, the circumstantial elements or the capacity of the people involved, to be linked to ML or TF. Whenever a financial institution knows or has reason to suspect that a transaction is related to ML or TF, the compliance officer must inform the FIU.

The nature and extent of investigations conducted by the compliance officers on suspicious ML/TF transactions are limited to collecting information available internally (resulting from the implementation of the 'know your customer' due diligence measures and from the analysis of the customers previous transactions profiles) and consulting some specific public commercial databases. Compliance officers do not have access to police, law enforcement, customs or tax authority databases.

Consequently, it is not up to the reporting entities to prove that the suspicious ML/TF transactions detected are ML or TF activities or to identify a potential ML predicate offence. To notify the FIU, financial institutions and DNFBPs only have to suspect transactions of being related to ML or TF activities.

Compliance officers must in good faith assess if there are enough elements to conclude that the suspicious ML/TF transactions could be related to a ML/TF activity and justify an STR to the country's FIU.

The assessment leading to the decision whether or not to notify the FIU must be well reasoned in an internal written report. The assessment (internal written report) made by the compliance officer (ie the reasons why he decided to report (or not report) the suspicious transactions) must be available for review by the supervisory or control authorities. The reporting entities and their representatives are protected from any civil, criminal or disciplinary proceedings if the reporting to the FIU has been made in good faith. Supervisory or control authorities must verify that the reporting entities' internal control mechanisms are adequate and sufficient to meet their legal obligations (including the AML/CFT legal obligations).

C. Measures Applying to CTRs and CBTRs

CTRs and CBTRs never result from a prior subjective analysis by the compliance officer, but they do result from some predefined rules applied automatically to the transactions of customers. The compilation and reporting of the transactions are therefore easier, but require more sophisticated computer software to automatically detect financial transactions and notify the FIU.

FIUs receiving CTRs and CBTRs also have to invest in strong and expansive hardware storage devices, and must invest in adequate computer software to enable them to store and handle all the data received.

The three types of reports (STRs, CTRs and CBTRs) have advantages and disadvantages. STRs present the advantage of resulting from a prior analysis by the compliance officer of the financial institution or DNFBP. Consequently, the suspicious transactions reported are more likely to be ML or TF related.

When the country obliges financial institutions and DNFBPs to complete CTRs and CBTRs, the FIU will receive a large amount of data to store and to handle or analyse. Many CTRs and CBTRs, however, are justified by perfectly legal backgrounds and professional activities, and FIUs may encounter difficulties when trying to extract the illegal or ML/TF transactions from all of the transactions reported (millions are reported each year).

FIUs receiving and handling CTRs and CBTRs depend more on the intelligence coming from a criminal investigation, and they usually initiate an ML/TF investigation after the law enforcement authorities has asked them if they have information about the subjects under investigation.

D. Intelligence

As mentioned earlier, FIUs also collect intelligence. 'Intelligence' is any kind of information (of an ongoing criminal investigation, on suspicions of tax crimes, etc) transmitted spontaneously by a 'non-reporting entity' that the FIU is not authorised to use in order to start an analysis or investigation, but that it can use to understand potential ML or TF activities. Such intelligence may be provided spontaneously by law enforcement authorities, intelligence services, judicial authorities, tax authorities, etc.

Intelligence is not necessarily used immediately; rather, FIUs normally keep the intelligence in their databases for use at a later date, if a suspicious transaction is reported by a financial institution or DNFBP.

E. The Belgian Experience

CTIF-CFI is an administrative FIU that mainly receives STRs from financial institutions and DNFBPs. The financial institutions and DNFBPs have to notify CTIF-CFI before executing a suspicious transaction,[21] and must indicate any deadline for completing the transaction.

If unable to inform CTIF-CFI prior to completion of the transaction because of its very nature (eg exchanges of currencies of relatively small value, money remittance of small amounts, casino operations) or because delaying execution of the transaction is likely to prevent prosecution of the beneficiaries of the suspected ML, the compliance officer of the financial institution or DNFBP must notify CTIF-CFI immediately afterwards, stating the reason(s) for so doing.

CTIF-CFI may receive reports from the financial sector (eg banks, exchange offices, the Belgian Post with regard to their financial services, the Central Bank when doing businesses with natural persons, stockbroking firms, portfolio management and investment advice companies, life insurance companies, payments

[21] Art 23, para 1,of the Law of 11 January 1993.

and electronic money institutions); notaries; real estate agents; external accountants, auditors and external tax advisors; leasing companies; companies issuing or managing credit cards; diamond traders; and lawyers (who address their STRs through the president of their bar association, who verifies their validity).[22] Some reporting entities may (also) report to CTIF-CFI according to thresholds or indicators. For example, casinos, notaries and real estate agents apply indicators or thresholds when reporting financial transactions to the FIU.[23]

Table 1 gives an overview of the number of reports received in 2014 from the main categories of reporting entities.

Table 1: Number of reports received in 2014 from the main categories of reporting entities

Main contributors	Number of reports received	%
Exchange offices and payment institutions (money remittance)	12,504	47.57
Banks	6,955	26.46
Notaries and real estate agents (most of the reports are related to real estate investments)	1,445	5.50
bpost (financial services)	1,392	5.29
Casinos	1,110	4.22
Central Bank	516	1.96
Foreign FIUs	424	1.61
Accountants, tax advisors and auditors	201	0.76
Life insurance companies	138	0.53
Administrative services of the state[a]	1,440	5.48
Supervisors	16	0.06
Others	146	0.56
Total[b]	26,287	100

[a] Includes certificates of tax regularisation received in 2014 for which CTIF-CFI is legally competent to check that the tax regularisation was not used for ML or TF purposes.

[b] Not including the 1,480 cash declarations (CBCTRs) received in 2014 by the Customs and Excise Administration.

[22] In particular, '(a) when they assist their client in the planning or execution of transactions concerning the: buying and selling of real property or business entities; management of his money, securities or other assets; opening or management of bank, savings or securities accounts; organisation of contributions necessary for the creation, operation or management of companies; creation, operation or management of companies, trusts, fiduciaries or similar legal arrangements; (b) or when they act on behalf of and for their client in any financial or real property transaction'.

[23] When reporting to CTIF-CFI, casinos must use the 11 indicators included in the Royal Decree of 6 May 1999 made under Art 26, para 2 of the Law of 11 January 1993. Pursuant to Art 20, para 2 of

When, in the course of their inspections of institutions or persons under their jurisdiction, they identify facts that may be related to ML or TF,[24] the supervisors of the above-mentioned businesses and professions also have to notify CTIF-CFI.

No civil, criminal or disciplinary proceedings can be instituted against and no professional sanction can be imposed upon the institutions or persons referred to above, their employees or representatives, the president of the bar association, or the management or employees of the supervisory authorities, on the grounds of the information they have disclosed in good faith.[25]

It is worth mentioning that since the Law of 11 January 1993 was amended (in 2010 and 2012), CTIF-CFI may also receive STRs from the Federal Public Prosecutor's Office when it is investigating a TF case,[26] and from officials of the state (tax authorities, intelligence services) when they have ML or TF[27] suspicions. Furthermore, according to the Belgian anti-ML law, any request from a counterpart FIU has the same status as an STR, which enables CTIF-CFI to use its investigative powers upon receipt of such foreign request.

In addition to the reports, CTIF-CFI also receives spontaneous intelligence from various administrative services of the state. All this intelligence is maintained in the central database for further use.

III. What is an FIU Investigation (Analysis)?

A. In General

Financial information—including information gathered from STRs, CTRs and CBTRs, as well as from reports on cross-border transportations of cash—has a central role in identifying ML and TF funds, as well as predicate offences.

The recently revised FATF standards now recognise financial investigation and financial intelligence as core elements of the FATF's operational and law enforcement recommendations.[28] In June 2012, the FATF adopted a guidance note, which highlights the importance of financial investigations. This guidance note was intended to help policy makers, public prosecutors and law enforcement

the Law of 11 January 1993, when notaries and real estate agents discover that the provision of Art 20, para 1 has not been respected and that the sales price of a real estate has been paid in cash (even partially) they shall immediately inform the CTIF-CFI in writing or by electronic means.

[24] Art 31 of the Law of 11 January 1993.

[25] Art 32 of the Law of 11 January 1993.

[26] Art 33, para 5 of the Law of 11 January 1993.

[27] Art 33, para 3 of the Law of 11 January 1993.

[28] FATF Recommendation No 30: 'At least in all cases related to major proceeds-generating offences, the designated law enforcement authorities should develop a pro-active parallel financial investigation

authorities to better understand their role[29] in the larger AML/CFT context, specifically addressing the role of financial investigation.

A financial investigation[30] is an enquiry into the financial affairs related to criminal conduct. Its primary goal is to identify and document the movement of money during the course of a criminal activity. The link between the origins of the money, its beneficiaries, when the money is received and where it is stored or deposited can provide information about and proof of criminal activity. Identifying the extent of criminal networks and the scale of crime (and gathering evidence that can be used in criminal proceedings), as well as tracing the proceeds of crime, terrorist funds and other proceeds subject to confiscation, are all part of an overall effective AML/CFT regime. The following can be considered the main objectives of FIU financial investigations:

— identification of all the people and corporate structures involved in ML and criminal activities;
— identification of the beneficial owners of the corporate structures and legal constructions involved;
— tracing of the origin and destination of funds;
— collection of law enforcement information on all the people, corporate structures and legal constructions involved;
— identification of links to people and criminal activities;
— identification of potential predicate offences to the ML transactions;
— identification and disruption of activities of criminals and ML organisations; and
— support of judicial and law enforcement authorities to seize proceeds of crimes.

The FIUs in some countries mainly collect STRs, CTRs, CBTRs, CBCTRs and other relevant data, and make them available on request or on demand of the law enforcement authorities. Other FIUs proactively analyse the STRs, CTRs, CBTRs and CBCTRs to detect potential unknown ML and predicate offence activities.

when pursuing money laundering, associated predicate offences and terrorist financing. This should include cases where the associated predicate offence occurs outside their jurisdictions. Countries should ensure that competent authorities have responsibility for expeditiously identifying, tracing and initiating actions to freeze and seize property that is, or may become, subject to confiscation, or is suspected of being proceeds of crime. Countries should also make use, when necessary, of permanent or temporary multi-disciplinary groups specialized in financial or asset investigations. Countries should ensure that, when necessary, co-operative investigations with appropriate competent authorities in other countries take place.'

[29] The guidance note also applies to those competent authorities which are not law enforcement authorities per se, but which have the responsibility of pursuing financial investigations of predicate offences, to the extent that these competent authorities are exercising functions covered under Recommendation No 30 (anti-corruption enforcement authorities and tax authorities with enforcement powers).

[30] See FATF, 'Operational Issues. Financial Investigations Guidance', available at www.fatf-gafi.org.

To investigate the STRs, most FIUs have the legal power to request (additional) information from various authorities (eg the reporting entity itself, other reporting entities covered by the AML/CFT regime, the law enforcement authorities, the prosecutor's office, the intelligence services, the tax authorities, the social security services).

B. The Belgian Experience

Upon receipt of an STR from one of the above-mentioned reporting entities and/or from a competent authority (federal prosecutor, administrative services of the state), CTIF-CFI is empowered to request and receive any information it deems useful in order to analyse the suspected ML/TF transactions[31] from different authorities, such as the reporting entity itself; all other financial institutions and persons subject to the AML/CFT law; the law enforcement authorities (all police agencies via two liaison officers from the Federal Police); the public prosecutor's office; all administrative services of the state (tax authorities, intelligence services, customs); the supervisory, regulatory or disciplinary authorities of the reporting entities; and the European Commission's Anti-fraud Co-ordination Unit, OLAF. As mentioned above, CTIF-CFI may also receive spontaneous information from these authorities.

The worldwide spread of ML mechanisms, the complexity of arrangements set up by criminal organisations and the extreme mobility of financial transactions make the exchange of information between countries an absolute necessity to combat ML and TF efficiently. CTIF-CFI therefore co-operates with its counterpart FIUs abroad, and actively participates in the work of the Egmont Group of FIUs.[32] CTIF-CFI has signed memoranda of understanding with around 100 other FIUs across the world, but international co-operation may also take place on a case-by-case basis and under conditions of reciprocity. Information is exchanged between FIUs securely through the Egmont Secure Web (a worldwide system) or through the FIU.NET system (between the 28 Member States of the European Union), sponsored by the European Commission.

When identifying serious indications of ML, restricted, however, to one or more of the predicate offences enumerated in the Law of 11 January 1993,[33] or of TF, CTIF-CFI must report the results of its analysis and investigations to the public prosecutor for further investigation and prosecution. CTIF-CFI reports between 1,000 and 1,300 new cases to the public prosecutor's office each year, involving

[31] Art 33, para 1 of the Law of 11 January 1993.

[32] The Egmont Group of Financial Intelligence Units, created in 1995 on the initiative of the Belgian FIU (CTIF-CFI) and the American FIU (FinCEN), currently consists of 151 member FIUs. The main objective of the Egmont Group is to increase and improve international co-operation between FIUs around the world (www.egmontgroup.org/).

[33] Art 5 of the Law of 11 January 1993.

a total amount of between €600 million and €1 billion. CTIF-CFI does not have discretionary power, like magistrates or the public prosecutor's office, to assess whether to prosecute or not. Rather, as soon as CTIF-CFI identifies serious indications of ML or TF, it is obliged to forward the file to the judicial authorities. Most of the time, CTIF-CFI has only 'serious indications' of ML or TF, but no real evidence. Collecting evidence that could be used in court is the task of the judicial and law enforcement authorities.

CTIF-CFI's involvement as a buffer between the reporting entities (and other competent authorities) and the judicial and law enforcement authorities prevents the judicial authorities and police services in charge of criminal investigations from becoming needlessly inundated with irrelevant disclosures and information. At the same time, it allows them to benefit from CTIF-CFI's specific expertise and central role.

It is worth mentioning that the FIU experts, employees, the liaison officers seconded to the FIU and the reporting entities and their representatives may not, under any circumstances, inform the client concerned or third parties that information has been transmitted to the FIU or that an investigation into ML or TF is being carried out. This measure is essential to ensure the efficiency of the preventive system.

IV. FIUs and Asset Recovery

A. In General

Tracing the origin and destination of funds helps the location of criminal proceeds and their seizure. Because law enforcement and judicial or prosecutorial-type FIUs remain in direct contact with the financial sector and DNFBPs (the reporting entities) and receive the STRs directly, they are in a better position to judicially seize the funds before they disappear. However, all types of FIUs (including administrative-type FIUs) can play a significant and important role in asset recovery.

In administrative-type FIUs, reporting entities (financial institutions and DNFBPs) must notify the FIU prior to carrying out a suspicious transaction (especially when the financial transaction involves a large amount of money). The FIU then has the right to request and enforce the postponement of the suspicious transaction within a certain time-frame; such a postponement gives the judicial authorities enough time to judicially seize the funds, in this way counterbalancing the disadvantages of having an intermediary (an administrative-type FIU) between the reporting entities and law enforcement authorities in charge of the criminal investigation.

Administrative-type FIUs now have extensive experience in financial investigations. Furthermore, the legal system and the good relationships between FIUs and financial institutions' and DNFBPs' compliance officers facilitate the access of the FIUs to the financial information held by the financial institutions and DNFBPs.

Most administrative-type FIUs are empowered to obtain from reporting entities all the (financial) information they need within the time-frame they have set. Furthermore, administrative-type FIUs usually obtain this financial information free of charge.

Consequently, the FIU's financial investigation (regardless of the FIU type) is a fundamental resource for the detection of criminal money and criminal assets.

B. The Belgian Experience

When a financial institution reports a suspicious transaction prior to carrying out that transaction, CTIF-CFI will consider the case to be an urgent case requiring immediate attention. The financial institutions generally allow CTIF-CFI a short period (one or two days) to analyse and investigate the reported suspicious transaction.

In order to safeguard the integrity of the related money or property for seizure by the judicial authorities, CTIF-CFI has the power (without having to refer to, or obtain the authorisation of, a court or tribunal) to request the postponement of the reported transaction before the deadline indicated by the reporting institution. This request freezes the transaction for a maximum period of two to five working days. The reporting entity is allowed to inform the customer of CTIF-CFI's postponement only after the first two working days.[34]

In order not to compromise the safety of the financial institutions' and DNFBPs' employees (customers whose money is retained by the bank following a postponement order could become violent), the power to postpone the transaction (for up to five working days) is used with caution and only in a limited number of cases, where there are strong indications of ML or TF, or in cases involving huge amounts of money and highly suspicious financial transactions.

When CTIF-CFI finds, in the course of an investigation, that there are serious indications of ML or TF, the power to postpone the suspicious financial transactions for five days is also used to give judicial and law enforcement authorities more time to examine the ML/TF case and take the most appropriate actions (eg seize the funds, release the funds to avoid disrupting the criminal investigation, request further law enforcement investigation, appoint an examining magistrate). The figures below give an overview of the number of postponements carried out by CTIF-CFI since 2011:

2011 33 postponements, concerning a total amount of €183.59 million
2012 36 postponements, concerning a total amount of €11.81 million

34 Art 23, para 2 of the Law of 11 January 1993.

2013 25 postponements, concerning a total amount of €12.34 million
2014 19 postponements, concerning a total amount of €8.71 million

It is worth highlighting that the number of STRs received prior to the execution of the suspicious transactions remains small (less than 1 per cent). Furthermore, in many ML/TF cases, CTIF-CFI is not in a position to postpone the (suspicious) transactions because further investigations are required to identify serious indications of ML or TF.

However, even though CTIF-CFI has not postponed the financial transactions in many cases, it has been able to trace huge amounts of criminal assets and belongings, and has informed the prosecutor's office that huge amounts of criminal money could be seized in Belgium or abroad. Consequently, one may suggest that there is no relation between the number of postponement actions (and the amounts involved) and the amounts of the seizures and confiscations at the end of the criminal investigations. Indeed, if, during the course of a financial investigation, CTIF-CFI notes—in case of serious indications of ML or TF—that large amounts of money or high-value assets could be seized, the Law of 11 January 1993 obliges CTIF-CFI to notify the public prosecutor's office and also the Central Office for Seizure and Confiscations (COSC).

Each year, CTIF-CFI notifies COSC of about 200 cases in which large amounts of money or high-value assets could be seized. COSC then works together with the public prosecutor's office to seize and manage the criminal proceeds. For example, following notification by CTIF-CFI, €120 million was seized in one case in 2011 and €60 million was seized in three cases in 2014.

Conclusion

The repeatedly revised FATF 40 Recommendations, now implemented in most Western countries, have been very useful in improving the transparency of the financial system and preventing the use of the financial system for ML and TF. The customer due diligence measures imposed on the financial sector and on DNFBPs (identification and verification of the identity of their customers, 'know your customer' measures, ongoing due diligence with respect to the transactions of their customers) have certainly contributed to the improved stability of the financial system.

However, important challenges remain, since the ML/TF techniques and mechanisms evolve constantly and criminals are always finding new channels and new processes to launder the proceeds of their criminal activities. Two of the 40 FATF Recommendations of February 2012 contain important challenges for FATF members. In particular, they recommend that members analyse and evaluate (on a regular basis) the potential ML/TF risks that could affect the country as a whole, the sectors and the individual reporting entities covered by the AML/CFT regime.

Furthermore, they recommend that FATF members take measures to increase the transparency of the legal structures created or established in their country. These include measures to identify the beneficial owners of corporate structures and legal constructions available in the country, and measures to make this information available to the reporting entities, FIUs, law enforcement and the public.

The recently adopted fourth EU AML/CFT Directive[35] requires each Member State to store in a central database information on the beneficial owners of corporate structures and legal constructions created in the country and to keep this database up to date. This is a crucial challenge.

Finally, the use of financial intelligence is an important tool for detecting, tracing and disrupting criminal activities, and confiscating funds and assets from a criminal origin or committed to finance terrorist activities. The recently revised FATF standards now recognise financial investigation and financial intelligence as core elements of the FATF's operational and law enforcement recommendations.

FIUs now have extensive experience in financial investigations. This experience has been used to prevent and prosecute ML (and also TF), but also to trace and ultimately seize and confiscate criminal proceeds. Even if postponement mechanisms are not extensively used, the pre-investigate role of FIUs is becoming more and more important and useful. In Belgium, for example, between 1993 and 2013, in those cases transmitted by CTIF-CFI to the prosecutors, courts and tribunals imposed penalties and confiscations to a total amount of €1.152 billion, representing 5 per cent of the suspicious ML/TF transactions forwarded to the judicial authorities (€22.5 billion) in the same period of time.

It is evident, however, that the effectiveness of the ML/TF investigation and prosecution still needs to be enhanced. The abnormal length of criminal investigations and the exceeding of the acceptable or reasonable time for prosecution are two factors that are increasingly taken into account by courts and tribunals to drop charges. Even if the real percentage of confiscation is probably higher than the United Nations estimate of the proceeds of crime seized worldwide (ie only 1 per cent of the proceeds of crime),[36] one may still conclude that increasing the effectiveness of the fight against ML and TF remains a huge challenge for all policy makers.

[35] Art 30 of Directive 2015/849/EU.

[36] UNODC, 'Estimating Illicit Financial Flows Resulting from Drug Trafficking and Other Transnational Organized Crime', Research Report (Vienna, 2011), available at www.unodc.org.

13

Digital Currencies and the Anti-money Laundering/ Counter-terrorism Financing Regulations in the EU: Imaginary Risk or Real Challenge?

JACEK CZARNECKI*

Introduction

Bitcoin, the decentralised cryptocurrency, is gaining global momentum in the financial world. While Bitcoin and similar digital currencies constitute the most innovative payment solution in recent years, they are often associated with crime and are arguably used by criminals to monetise and transfer assets acquired through criminal activities in an untraceable way.

Digital currencies thus pose a great challenge for domestic and international laws and regulation—as the eight-year-long history of Bitcoin shows all too well. Bitcoin's technical characteristics and its features, such as decentralisation or anonymity, make it difficult to embrace using traditional regulations. However, what is perhaps an even more challenging issue is to regulate Bitcoin and other digital currencies in terms of anti-money laundering and counter-terrorist financing (AML/CTF), and to confiscate proceeds of crime effectively.

The aim of this chapter is to analyse how AML/CTF rules are, and might be, applied to activities associated with cryptocurrencies; define the main challenges for asset recovery rules arising from the use of digital currencies; and describe how the existing EU regulations respond to those challenges and indicate possible future legal developments in this regard.

* Graduate of the University of Warsaw and the University of Oxford. Currently a PhD student at the Warsaw School of Economics.

I. Why Bitcoin Matters for the AML/CTF Regulations

A. Terminological Remarks

Terminology used with regard to digital currencies may cause some confusion. While digital currencies are a broad phenomenon, this name is most often associated with cryptocurrencies, among which Bitcoin is the most prominent example. The term 'virtual currencies', although still sometimes used, is rather being replaced by 'digital currencies'.[1]

This chapter was written with cryptocurrencies in mind, so each time the term 'digital currencies' is used, its meaning should be limited to cryptocurrencies. Bitcoin is frequently referred to, and most conclusions regarding this currency will be similar to or the same as for any other cryptocurrency which is not entirely technologically distinct (such as Litecoin, Ether or other 'crypto-assets', ie units on shared ledgers other than the Bitcoin's blockchain that do not function as currencies but as other types of assets).[2]

B. The Specific Nature of Bitcoin

This chapter does not try to provide a comprehensive description of the technical and economic aspects of Bitcoin or the technology upon which it is built. However, some of the features of Bitcoin (and of cryptocurrencies in general) are important in terms of the application of anti-money laundering laws to various cryptocurrency-related activities. The most significant of them are as follows:

(i) Decentralisation

Bitcoin is built upon a technology called the Blockchain.[3] At the most basic level, it is a permissionless, distributed ledger (database). Data is not stored by a

[1] See definitions in: European Central Bank, *Virtual Currency Schemes* (ECB, 2012), available at www.ecb.europa.eu/pub/pdf/other/virtualcurrencyschemes201210en.pdf (accessed on 5 January 2016); European Central Bank, *Virtual Currency Schemes—A Further Analysis* (ECB, 2015), available at www.ecb.europa.eu/pub/pdf/other/virtualcurrencyschemesen.pdf (accessed on 5 January 2016); Financial Action Task Force (FATF), 'Virtual Currencies: Key Definitions and Potential AML/CFT Risks', available at www.fatf-gafi.org/publications/methodsandtrends/documents/virtual-currency-definitions-aml-cft-risk.html (accessed on 5 January 2016).

[2] See below for further explanation of the concept of 'blockchain'. Cryptocurrency is 'a digital currency in which encryption techniques are used to regulate the generation of units of currency and verify the transfer of funds, operating independently of a central bank', *Oxford Dictionaries*, available at www.oxforddictionaries.com/definition/english/cryptocurrency (accessed on 5 January 2016).

[3] One should differentiate between 'blockchain' and 'the Blockchain'. While the latter is the specific database underlying Bitcoin, the former is used as a more general term for this technology.

central entity but, rather, is distributed among many nodes in the network (and thus decentralised). The innovation behind the blockchain technology (often called more generally distributed ledger or shared ledger technology) is that it allows for identical versions of the database to be maintained by nodes, even though each node is incapable of imposing its own version on the others. This is achieved by using cryptographical solutions, which help consensus among nodes to be achieved regarding which version of the database is valid.

In the case of Bitcoin, which was the first, and so far the most successful, application of this technology,[4] it allows for the issuance of currency without a central issuer (such as a central bank). It also makes possible transactions within the network without a need for intermediaries (such as money remittances or banks). The Blockchain functions as a ledger of all transactions performed in the Bitcoin network and is maintained by a number of nodes dispersed throughout the world. A feature of the Blockchain technology is that no single entity is in charge of maintaining or controlling the Bitcoin network.[5]

(ii) Transnational Nature

As mentioned above, the technology behind Bitcoin practically excludes the possibility of assignment of the control over Bitcoin to any particular entity or even jurisdiction. Bitcoins are generated, sent and traded beyond borders. Although the Bitcoin network is surrounded by a number of businesses facilitating the use of this currency and the laws applicable to them are more or less easily identified, the Bitcoin itself is de facto beyond the control of any public authority.

There is thus no practical difference between sending bitcoins to an address belonging to a person based in the same country or anywhere else. The software for using or 'storing' bitcoins can be downloaded from the internet, so it can be potentially used by anyone, regardless of their location.

(iii) Anonymity

Another feature of the Bitcoin network is anonymity, but only to a certain degree. The Blockchain is publicly available, which means that anyone can browse past transactions and see the addresses of the senders and recipients.[6] In some senses,

[4] Recently blockchain technology has outpaced Bitcoin in terms of the innovative opportunities it brings. It is now a matter of high interest to the financial sector. Moreover, its applications extend beyond financial uses.

[5] Hypothetically, this could happen if one miner or mining pool (mining means adding transactions to the Blockchain by solving complicated mathematical problems and is usually performed by specially designed computer machines with a strong computational power, which also makes the process highly energy-consuming) was able to control more than 50% of the network's hashing power (the so-called '51% attack').

[6] It is a kind of account number, from and to which the bitcoins can be sent. It is not, in fact, an account, because bitcoins are not 'stored' there, but rather an identifier, to which a specific number of bitcoins are assigned in accordance with the ledger (the Blockchain).

Bitcoin's Blockchain is fully transparent, because it contains information on who sent what number of bitcoins to whom and when. However, participants of past transactions can be identified only by their addresses and not, for example, by their personal data, like in the traditional banking system. This is why the term 'pseudonymity' of users is often used.

Therefore, Bitcoin addresses are not easily attributable to specific persons. Moreover, each person can generate practically any number of Bitcoin addresses. There are also websites which offer 'mixing' or 'laundering' of cryptocurrencies. Basically, such activity involves generating numerous transactions between various addresses, which can effectively obliterate any links between the starting and ending addresses.

(iv) Irreversibility of Transaction

By design, cryptocurrency transactions cannot be reversed. When a transaction is sent and processed by miners,[7] there is no possibility for the user to reclaim the amount sent. This is because of the decentralised nature of cryptocurrency (there is no central controller who could reverse the transaction or return its amount in certain circumstances). Irreversibility is also important because transactions are usually processed relatively quickly (in the case of Bitcoin, the network architecture allows for completing a transaction within ten minutes).

In practice, transaction might be reversed only through a so-called "hard fork". Basically, this means that some network members choose to support not the original version of the ledger (blockchain), but another one with a modified history of transactions.

(v) Convertibility

This feature is not built into the Bitcoin protocol, but it nevertheless follows from the economic practice. Bitcoins can be easily converted into another currency (traditional fiat or a digital one) at many exchanges around the world operating online (see below). This means that there is a link between the traditional financial world and the digital currency scheme that allows for bidirectional flow of payments between the systems.

The above features have two important consequences from the AML/CTF point of view. First, they make cryptocurrencies potentially attractive instruments for many kinds of illegal activity, including laundering proceeds of crime. They might also be a useful tool for terrorism financing. As will be shown below, there is some evidence for such use of Bitcoin and other digital currencies. Another consequence is that the use of Bitcoin and other cryptocurrencies for illegal purposes is relatively difficult to combat by public authorities.

[7] See n 5 above.

The decentralised and transnational nature of the Bitcoin network, combined with the far-reaching degree of anonymity of its participants, can thus create certain criminal risks, including AML/CTF risks.

C. Evidence of the Use of Digital Currencies for the Purpose of Money Laundering and/or Terrorist Financing

The use of cryptocurrencies as money laundering or terrorist financing tools has been a subject of interest of many public authorities and organisations, including Interpol and Europol. The latter has described cryptocurrencies as one of the key drivers for change of how serious and organised crime works: 'Virtual currencies increasingly enable individuals to act as freelance criminal entrepreneurs operating on a crime-as-a-service business model without the need for a sophisticated criminal infrastructure to receive and launder money.'[8] Cryptocurrencies have also been called the ideal instrument for money laundering.[9] The claim that digital currencies also pose terrorist financing risks was presented in the FATF report 'Emerging Terrorist Financing Risks', issued in 2015.[10] In the '2015 Internet Organised Crime Threat Assessment',[11] Europol stated that 'Bitcoin is establishing itself as a single common currency for cybercriminals within the EU'[12] and recommended 'harmonised legislative changes at EU level, or the uniform application of existing legal tools such as AML regulations, to address the criminal use of virtual currencies'.[13]

Interpol has even created its own cryptocurrency in order to learn more how to combat crimes that use digital currencies.[14] Interpol and Europol have also formed a partnership 'against the abuse of virtual currencies for criminal transactions and money laundering', which will include 'actions around policy, stimulating operation cooperation and the development and delivery of training to fight the criminal use of virtual currencies, enabling detection, seizure and forfeiture of criminal assets'.[15]

[8] Europol, 'Exploring Tomorrow's Organised Crime' 9, available at www.europol.europa.eu/newsletter/massive-changes-criminal-landscape (accessed on 5 January 2016).

[9] ibid 30.

[10] FATF, 'Emerging Terrorist Financing Risks' (FATF, 2015), available at www.fatf-gafi.org/documents/documents/emerging-terrorist-financing-risks.html (accessed on 5 January 2016).

[11] Europol, '2015 Internet Organised Crime Threat Assessment', available at www.europol.europa.eu/content/internet-organised-crime-threat-assessment-iocta-2015 (accessed on 5 January 2016).

[12] ibid 11.

[13] Europol (n 11) 49.

[14] Interpol, 'Darknet Training Shines Light on Underground Criminal Activities', available at www.interpol.int/News-and-media/News/2015/N2015-108 (accessed on 5 January 2016).

[15] Europol, 'Europol–Interpol Cybercrime Conference Makes the Case for Greater Multisector Cooperation', available at www.europol.europa.eu/latest_news/europol-%E2%80%93-interpol-cybercrime-conference-makes-case-greater-multisector-cooperation (accessed on 5 January 2016).

Nonetheless, it is still not clear whether cryptocurrencies pose excessive AML/CTF risks, especially in comparison with other potential tools, such as traditional fiat currencies (both cash and bank money). In the 'UK National Risk Assessment of Money Laundering and Terrorist Financing', issued by HM Treasury in October 2015,[16] the money laundering risk associated with digital currencies was assessed as low (although with potential to increase along with possibly increasing adoption of digital currencies). It was also stated that there is little evidence to indicate that digital currencies have been used for terrorist financing.

It seems that there is a need for a continuous, evidence-based and in-depth empirical analysis of the use of digital currencies for the purpose of illegal activities. It is vital because new evidence or claims concerning the use of digital currencies for the purpose of money laundering or terrorist financing may soon trigger and accelerate AML/CTF regulatory proposals in the EU.

D. Cryptocurrencies and Confiscation of Proceeds of Crime

The nature of cryptocurrency causes many challenges to effective detection, investigation and confiscation of proceeds of crime, including:[17] (i) a lack of knowledge about digital currencies, their characteristics and technical nature, as well as techniques that could be used to combat crime related to them; (ii) the digital nature of cryptocurrencies, which results in mostly electronic evidence of committed crimes; (iii) very often, the absence of a legislative and regulatory response aimed specifically at recovering proceeds of crime obtained by means of or with the help of digital currencies, as well as supervisory difficulties; and (iv) problems with the coordination of actions undertaken, both nationally and internationally.

Both domestic and international rules on confiscation of proceeds of crime seem to be imperfect in terms of meeting challenges related to digital currencies. There are no established standards of asset recovery at any of the usual steps: tracing, freezing and confiscation of digital currencies. The recently adopted Directive on the freezing and confiscation of instrumentalities and proceeds of crime in the European Union[18] sets forth a framework of the minimum rules required for the detection, tracing and confiscation of proceeds of crime across the EU and is definitely a step in the right direction. However, it remains to be seen whether

[16] HM Treasury, *UK National Risk Assessment of Money Laundering and Terrorist Financing* (HM Treasury, 2015), available at www.gov.uk/government/uploads/system/uploads/attachment_data/file/468210/UK_NRA_October_2015_final_web.pdf (accessed on 5 January 2016).

[17] United Nations Office on Drugs and Crime, 'Basic Manual on the Detection and Investigation of the Laundering of Crime Proceeds Using Virtual Currencies' (UNODC, 2014) available at https://www.imolin.org/pdf/imolin/FULL10-UNODCVirtualCurrencies_final.pdf (accessed on 5 January 2016).

[18] Directive 2014/42/EU of the European Parliament and of the Council of 3 April 2014 on the freezing and confiscation of instrumentalities and proceeds of crime in the European Union [2014] OJ L127/39.

the national implementation laws will be effectively applied to the cases involving Bitcoin or other cryptocurrencies.

E. Bitcoin-Related Businesses

While, in light of the above, it is clear that, like any other currency in the world, Bitcoin (and other digital currencies) can be used for money laundering, terrorist financing or other criminal activities, it is of great importance to understand the ventures that operate in this market. Despite Bitcoin's relatively short history, a number of business models employed by different entities have developed around this currency. Effective prevention of criminal use of digital currencies for money laundering and terrorist financing should be preceded by detailed analysis of what role those entities play in economic reality and what the weak points exploited by criminals may be.

(i) Exchanges

Digital currency exchanges are basically websites on which users can exchange one cryptocurrency for another, or cryptocurrency for traditional fiat currency. The term 'exchange' can be misleading, because there may be both websites whose role is to match traders (buyers and sellers) on the basis of their matching orders (the marketplace model) and also entities that sell or buy cryptocurrencies to or from traders themselves, acting on their own account (the 'exchange office' model).

Exchanges charge fees or commissions for currency exchanges, similarly to traditional bureaux de change or internet currency exchanges. The user can be any person or entity accessing the exchange's website. There is also variation in exchanges' policies regarding registration or identification of their customers.

Digital currency exchanges are specific gateways between traditional financial systems and digital currency schemes. Therefore, they are crucial from the point of view of AML/CTF, because they potentially allow the transfers of funds of unknown origin into the financial system.

(ii) Wallet Providers

Wallets are usually software enabling the cryptocurrency user to 'store' currency units (in fact, wallets store private keys that are associated with public addresses and allow the user to spend cryptocurrency). Wallet providers, although offering a similar user experience, can operate in various ways. The most important division can be made between online and desktop wallets. In principle, in the first case, private keys[19] are stored on the wallet provider's server, and in the second case they are stored on the user's computer. The former type of wallet provider de facto accepts deposits from users (the custodian model).

[19] Numbers assigned to bitcoin addresses, which are required to execute a transaction.

(iii) Payment Processors

Cryptocurrency payment processors (remittances) perform similar functions to their fiat currency counterparts. They provide merchants with the possibility of accepting payments denominated in Bitcoin or other cryptocurrencies.

(iv) Merchants

Merchants are Bitcoin-related businesses in a broad sense. They are entities that accept Bitcoin or other digital currency as a mean of payment for the products or services they offer. Usually they use payment processors' services. Through these, the merchant can receive payment in a fiat currency and does not have to deal with the cryptocurrency paid by the customer.

(v) Other

There are also many other businesses dealing with digital currencies. Some of them perform one or more of the above roles, while at the same time offering other products or services. For example, some entities offer payment cards that make payment at any point of sale possible in digital currency (digital currency units are deducted from the user account and exchanged into a traditional currency that is then transferred to the merchant via an acquirer). Other Bitcoin-related businesses include gambling websites, ATM operators, crowdfunding platforms and peer-to-peer lending platforms.

F. A Broader Picture: Crypto-assets and the Rise of Blockchain Technology

It is important to emphasise that Bitcoin and cryptocurrencies in general do not constitute a separate chapter of financial innovation, but rather have initiated much more far-reaching opportunities in the field. It is often said that Bitcoin was just the first application of the blockchain technology. Subsequent applications go beyond financial applications.

Generally, blockchain technology allows for the creation of different assets ('crypto-assets') that represent value, but exist without any central intermediary. Examples include units in a blockchain that are treated not as a currency, but as shares in a company or other type of right. Moreover, the use of smart contracts (unstoppable and self-executable contracts concluded and executed on a certain blockchain) in some blockchain projects like Ethereum allow for the creation of complicated cooperation structures that operate without any centralised management.[20]

[20] Such structures are often called DAOs (decentralised autonomous organisations). They are based purely on computer code and operate without any person or institution in charge.

There are two main consequences following this state of affairs in terms of AML/CTF regulatory strategies. First, lawmakers and regulators should be aware that currency is just one of many possible applications of blockchain technology. Next generation applications will include other forms of value. These will be based on similar technology, but may have other social applications and economic meanings. Secondly, new developments like DAOs introduce a completely new level of complexity. While cryptocurrencies may well demand an immediate regulatory response, regulators should not lose sight of further blockchain applications.

II. Current EU Policy towards Application of the AML Rules to Bitcoin-Related Businesses

A. International Efforts towards AML and CTF Response to Cryptocurrencies

The topics of money laundering and terrorist financing in connection with cryptocurrencies have aroused the interest of a number of public and private institutions across the world, both national and international. For example, the G7 mentioned the need for an 'appropriate regulation of virtual currencies and other new payment methods' in the context of the fight against terrorism and terrorist financing.[21]

Perhaps the main initiatives that are worth mentioning are two publications issued by the Financial Action Task Force (FATF), an inter-governmental body that is primarily tasked with setting AML/CTF international standards and assisting in their implementation.[22]

In 2014, the FATF published its preliminary assessment of risk arising from what was called the virtual currencies.[23] One year later, another, more in-depth, analysis was published, in the form of a guidance.[24] The aim of the guidance was, inter alia, to 'clarify the application of the relevant FATF Recommendations to convertible virtual currency exchangers'.[25] This objective makes this document

[21] G7 Leaders' Declaration after G7 Summit, 7–8 June 2015, available at www.g7germany.de/Content/EN/_Anlagen/G7/2015-06–08-g7-abschluss-eng_en.pdf?__blob=publicationFile&v=3 (accessed on 5 January 2016).

[22] For a more detailed overview on the AML/CTF measures of the FATF, see M Penna, 'The "Pre-investigative" Role of Financial Intelligence Units in Recovering Assets', this volume, Chapter 12.

[23] FATF (n 1).

[24] FATF, 'Guidance for a Risk-Based Approach to Virtual Currencies' (FATF, 2015), available at www.fatf-gafi.org/documents/documents/guidance-rba-virtual-currencies.html (accessed on 5 January 2016).

[25] ibid 3.

very significant, since FATF Recommendations often play an important role in policies of individual states and organisations (like the EU) towards AML/CTF issues. FATF promotes the idea of the risk-based approach in relation to combating money laundering and terrorist financing. Basically, it means that 'measures to prevent or mitigate money laundering and terrorist financing are commensurate with the risks identified'.[26] FATF upheld this approach in its guidance and underlined that some features of cryptocurrencies, such as anonymity, can increase risk and may require the application of enhanced due diligence measures.

The main practical conclusion of the guidance was that AML/CTF regulations should apply to those Bitcoin-related businesses that are positioned at the intersection of the traditional fiat currency financial system and the cryptocurrency scheme. Such businesses are primarily exchanges, but they also include other entities acting as gatekeepers between the two areas.

B. AML and CTF Framework in the EU and its Application to Digital Currencies

(i) *Third AML Directive*

The so-called Third AML Directive (3AMLD)[27] remains the core AML/CTF legal act in the EU.[28] Definitions of both 'money laundering'[29] and 'terrorist financing'[30] contained in the 3AMLD are broad enough to cover digital currency activities.

Regulations of the 3AMLD apply to certain categories of entities (the so-called 'obliged entities'). These include, inter alia, credit institutions (primarily banks), a wide range of financial market entities (known in EU financial law as 'financial institutions'), entities performing certain professional activities (such as 'managing of client money, securities or other assets' or 'opening or management of bank, savings or securities accounts') and all other natural or legal persons trading in goods, if payments are made in cash in an amount of at least €15,000.[31]

[26] FATF, 'The FATF Recommendations' (FATF, 2012) Recommendation 1, available at www.fatf-gafi.org/media/fatf/documents/recommendations/pdfs/FATF_Recommendations.pdf (accessed on 5 January 2016).

[27] Directive (EU) 2015/849 of the European Parliament and of the Council of 20 May 2015 on the prevention of the use of the financial system for the purposes of money laundering or terrorist financing, amending Regulation (EU) No 648/2012 of the European Parliament and of the Council, and repealing Directive 2005/60/EC of the European Parliament and of the Council and Commission Directive 2006/70/EC [2015] OJ L141/73.

[28] It has been already repealed by the 4th AML Directive (4AMLD), but with effect from 26 June 2017. See below.

[29] Art 1(2) 3AMLD.

[30] Art 1(4) 3AMLD.

[31] Art 1(3)(e) 3AMLD.

The question arises whether Bitcoin-related businesses—in particular, digital currency exchanges—can be assigned to any category of obliged entities. It is clear that they can be included in the category of 'legal persons trading in goods, if payments are made in cash in an amount of at least EUR 15 000'. If digital currency is bought from such an entity for cash in an amount exceeding this sum, there is no doubt that the trader should be deemed an obliged entity. However, most of the digital currency transactions are made online (without using cash), so this provision is perhaps of little practical importance here.

The most important issue is whether any Bitcoin-related businesses can be qualified as 'credit institutions' or 'financial institutions'.

According to the definition currently in force,[32] a credit institution is an undertaking the business of which is to take deposits or other repayable funds from the public and to grant credits for its own account. Although the term 'funds' could be interpreted broadly as covering digital currency, it primarily covers cash and scriptural (bank) money. Moreover, it is unusual for Bitcoin-related businesses to both take deposits (eg by an online wallet provider, though it is debatable whether that should be deemed a deposit) and grant credits in digital currency.

As regards financial institutions, an in-depth explanation of the kinds of entity that comprise this category is beyond the scope of this chapter. However, particular attention should be paid to the following types of financial institution: issuers of electronic money, payment services providers and currency exchange firms. At first glance, payment services and the issuance of e-money are similar to digital currencies. However, currently, the scope of both the E-Money Directive (EMD)[33] and the Payment Services Directive (PSD[34] and the new PSD2)[35] does not cover digital currencies.[36] It also seems that currency exchange should be understood as fiat currency-to-fiat currency exchange and not digital currency-to-fiat currency or digital-to-digital exchange. However, there is some room for different interpretation.[37]

[32] See Art 4(1) of Regulation (EU) No 575/2013 of the European Parliament and of the Council of 26 June 2013 on prudential requirements for credit institutions and investment firms and amending Regulation (EU) No 648/2012 [2013] OJ L176/1.

[33] Directive 2009/110/EC of the European Parliament and of the Council of 16 September 2009 on the taking up, pursuit and prudential supervision of the business of electronic money institutions amending Directives 2005/60/EC and 2006/48/EC and repealing Directive 2000/46/EC [2009] OJ L267/7.

[34] Directive 2007/64/EC of the European Parliament and of the Council of 13 November 2007 on payment services in the internal market, amending Directives 97/7/EC, 2002/65/EC, 2005/60/EC and 2006/48/EC and repealing Directive 97/5/EC [2007] OJ L319/1.

[35] Directive (EU) 2015/2366 of the European Parliament and of the Council of 25 November 2015 on payment services in the internal market, amending Directives 2002/65/EC, 2009/110/EC and 2013/36/EU and Regulation (EU) No 1093/2010 and repealing Directive 2007/64/EC [2015] OJ L337/35.

[36] For more details see N Vandezande, 'Between Bitcoins and Mobile Payments: Will the European Commission's New Proposal Provide More Legal Certainty?' [2014] *International Journal of Law and Information Technology* 1; European Central Bank, *Virtual Currency Schemes* (n 1).

[37] Some Bitcoin-related businesses have already obtained regulatory authorisations based on national implementations of EMD and PSD. Examples include Circle in the UK and Bitstamp in

What follows from the above considerations is that Bitcoin-related businesses do not explicitly fall into any of the categories of the obliged entities listed in the 3AMLD (provided that they do not perform other activities beyond their core business). This is particularly important in the case of digital currency exchanges, which, as mentioned above, are crucial from the point of view of the AML/CTF regulatory framework.

The lack of direct inclusion of exchanges or other Bitcoin-related businesses as obliged entities does not mean that the EU Member States cannot include them in their implementations of the 3AMLD. They can do so because they have maintained a certain degree of discretion with regard to the scope of obliged entities. The 3AMLD allows for an extension of its provisions entirely or partially to professions and categories of undertakings 'which engage in activities which are particularly likely to be used for money laundering or terrorist financing purposes'.

(ii) EU Institutions on the Application of AML and CTF to Digital Currencies

One of the first international attempts to thoroughly analyse digital currencies and public policy towards them was the report issued by the European Central Bank (ECB).[38] The ECB highlighted money laundering risks associated with digital currencies, but did not try to assess whether the EU AML/CTF framework would be an effective response to those risks.

Assessment of involved risks has been made by the European Banking Authority (EBA).[39] In its Opinion, the EBA identified more than 70 risks of digital currencies, including the following risks related to money laundering and terrorist financing (all marked as 'high'): (i) criminals are able to launder proceeds of crime because they can deposit/transfer digital currencies anonymously; (ii) criminals are able to launder proceeds of crime because they can deposit/transfer digital currencies globally, rapidly and irrevocably; (iii) criminals/terrorists use the digital currency remittance systems and accounts for financing purposes; and (iv) criminals/terrorists disguise the origins of criminal proceeds, undermining the ability of enforcement authorities to obtain evidence and recover criminal assets.

One of the main recommendations of the EBA was that market participants at the direct interface between conventional and virtual currencies (eg exchanges) should be deemed 'obliged entities' under the AMLD and thus subject to AML

Luxembourg. There is also some evidence that the European Commission considers broadening the scope of PSD to cover cryptocurrency exchanges. See J Czarnecki, 'This Proposal Could Reshape Europe's Cryptocurrency Policies', *CoinDesk*, 20 February 2016, available at www.coindesk.com/this-overlooked-proposal-could-reshape-europes-cryptocurrency-policies/.

[38] European Central Bank, *Virtual Currency Schemes* (n 1).

[39] European Banking Authority, 'EBA Opinion on "Virtual Currencies"' (EBA, 2014), available at www.eba.europa.eu/documents/10180/657547/EBA-Op-2014-08+Opinion+on+Virtual+Currencies.pdf (accessed on 5 January 2016).

requirements. This recommendation has not, however, been acted upon in the Fourth AML Directive (see below).

(iii) Fourth AML Directive

The Fourth AML Directive (4AMLD) was adopted on 20 May 2015. It should be transposed by Member States into their legal orders by 26 June 2017 (by this date, the 3AMLD will have been finally repealed).

The 4AMLD does not diverge much from the above-mentioned conclusions reached on the basis of the 3AMLD. For example, the scope of cash payments has been extended by lowering the threshold amount from €15,000 to €10,000. But most importantly, Bitcoin-related businesses have not been included in the catalogue of obliged entities. They will thus still remain outside of the scope of the EU AML regulatory framework.[40]

However, there is some evidence that before adoption of the 4AMLD there had been some consideration devoted to whether to include some Bitcoin-related businesses (primarily exchanges) in the list of obliged entities or even to develop new AML regulations specifically for digital currencies. In November 2014, the Commission declared that it was monitoring the development of digital currencies and was participating in studies carried out by both the EBA and the FATF, as well as cooperating with Europol and the Member States. The Commission stated that 'there have been certain discussions to include an approach along the lines of the EBA opinion' (see above) and that 'negotiations are on-going'.[41] The inclusion of digital currency exchanges as 'obliged entities' under the 4AMLD was also mentioned by the UK Commissioner designate Lord Hill in reply to supplementary questions during parliamentary hearings.[42]

However, the final Commission's decision was to not include digital currencies in the 4AMLD in any way. According to the Commission, during the negotiations over the 4AMLD, 'it was considered necessary to leave some time for reflection', due to the very recent introduction of digital currencies.[43]

[40] For more useful information concerning 4AMLD and its provisions for cryptocurrencies, see P Valcke, N Vandezande and N van de Velde, 'The Evolution of Third Party Payment Providers and Cryptocurrencies under the EU's Upcoming PSD2 and AMLD4', SWIFT Institute Working Paper No 2015-001, available at http://www.swiftinstitute.org/wp-content/uploads/2015/09/SIWP-No-2015-001-AML-Risks-of-the-Third-Party-Payment-Providers_FINAL.pdf (accessed on 5 January 2016).

[41] The European Commission's answer to Parliamentary Question No E-006770/2014, available at www.europarl.europa.eu/sides/getAllAnswers.do?reference=E-2014-006770&language=EN (accessed on 5 January 2016).

[42] Reply to supplementary questions addressed by ECON to Commissioner-designate Hill, question 5, available at www.europarl.europa.eu/hearings-2014/resources/library/media/20141006RES73040/20141006RES73040.pdf (accessed on 5 January 2016).

[43] European Commission's answer to Parliamentary Question No E-000685/2015, available at www.europarl.europa.eu/sides/getAllAnswers.do?reference=E-2015-000685&language=EN (accessed on 5 January 2016).

Nevertheless, plans to embrace digital currencies by the AML/CTF regulations were far from abandoned. The Commission revealed some of its plans in the European Agenda on Security and accompanying documents, issued in April 2015.[44] The Commission intended to engage in conducting an assessment of the risks of money laundering and terrorist financing affecting the internal market and relating to cross-border activities,[45] where 'the use of virtual currencies will be subject to particular attention'.[46] The results of this assessment are presented in Section III below.

It might be useful to succinctly present how this type of issue is dealt with internationally. In the USA, the Financial Crimes Enforcement Network (FinCEN) has issued a guidance according to which certain administrators and exchangers of virtual currencies[47] must register as money services businesses (MSBs) and comply with the Bank Secrecy Act.[48] Mere users of virtual currency are not subject to these requirements. Qualification as an MSB effectively brings many Bitcoin-related businesses, in particular digital currency exchanges, under the AML regulations in the USA.

An analysis conducted by the Economics References Committee of the Senate of Australia found that digital currencies such as Bitcoin are not currently covered under the Australia AML/CTF legislation.[49] It was recommended by the statutory review that the AML/CTF regulations should apply to digital currency exchanges.[50]

[44] European Commission, 'The European Agenda on Security', COM (2015) 185 final, available at http://ec.europa.eu/dgs/home-affairs/e-library/documents/basic-documents/docs/eu_agenda_on_security_en.pdf (accessed on 5 January 2016).

[45] Conducting such assessment and preparing a report is a requirement set forth in Art. 6 of the 4AMLD.

[46] European Commission, 'European Agenda on Security—State of Play', press release, 17 November 2015, available at http://europa.eu/rapid/press-release_MEMO-15-6115_en.htm (accessed on 5 January 2016).

[47] FinCEN definition: 'medium of exchange that operates like a currency in some environments, but does not have all the attributes of real currency'. A de-centralised convertible virtual currency is a currency '(1) that has no central repository and no single administrator, and (2) that persons may obtain by their own computing or manufacturing effort'.

[48] FinCEN, 'Guidance on Application of FinCEN's Regulations to Persons Administering, Exchanging, or Using Virtual Currencies', FIN-2013-G001, available at www.fincen.gov/statutes_regs/guidance/html/FIN-2013-G001.html (accessed on 5 January 2016).

[49] Australia's Senate Standing Committees on Economics, *Digital Currency—Game Changer or Bit Player* (P/rliament of Australia, 2015), available at www.aph.gov.au/Parliamentary_Business/Committees/Senate/Economics/Digital_currency/Report (accessed on 5 January 2016).

[50] ibid.

III. Future Regulatory Developments in the EU

A. EU Level

New regulatory developments with regard to digital currencies will very likely follow from tightening the counter-terrorism financing rules in the EU. The terrorist attacks in Paris in January and November 2015, as well as the high risk of further incidents, prompted EU leaders to propose more far-reaching AML/CFT rules than are provided by the current framework. Digital currency has been explicitly named as one of the aspects that should be taken into account.

After the terrorist raid in Paris in January 2015, the members of the European Council called for rapid implementation by the EU Member States of the strengthened rules to prevent money laundering and terrorist financing, and that all competent authorities step up action to trace financial flows and to effectively freeze assets used for financing terrorism.[51] Although digital currencies were not mentioned specifically in this context, it is clear that theymight be covered by such strengthened rules. However, the European Council's appeal has not been reflected by the 4AMLD so far—digital currency-related businesses have not been classified as obligated institutions (see above).

Shortly after the terrorist attacks in Paris in November 2015, the Council of the EU considered how undertaking measures with regard to digital currencies may be a part of combating terrorism. It has previously been reported by the EU Institute for Security Studies that the so-called Islamic State of Iraq and the Levant (ISIL) and its supporters use Bitcoin and other digital currencies to finance terrorist activities while minimising detection risk.[52] In the Conclusions of the Council of the EU and of the Member States meeting within the Council on Counter-Terrorism (20 November 2015),[53] the Council invited the Commission inter alia to undertake actions aimed at 'strengthening controls of non-banking payment methods such as … virtual currencies'.

The much awaited EU stance on the issue is expected to materialise in 2016. In February 2016, the Commission announced the Action Plan for strengthening the

[51] Statement by the members of the European Council after the informal meeting of the Heads of State or Government, Brussels, 12 February 2015, available at www.consilium.europa.eu/en/press/press-releases/2015/02/150212-european-council-statement-fight-against-terrorism/ (accessed on 5 January 2016).

[52] B Berton, 'The Dark Side of the Web: ISIL's One-Stop shop?', ISS Alert No 30, 26 June 2015, available at www.iss.europa.eu/publications/detail/article/the-dark-side-of-the-web-isils-one-stop-shop/ (accessed on 5 January 2016).

[53] Conclusions of the Council of the EU and of the Member States meeting within the Council on Counter-Terrorism on 20 November 2015, available at www.consilium.europa.eu/en/press/press-releases/2015/11/20-jha-conclusions-counter-terrorism/ (accessed on 5 January 2016).

fight against terrorist financing.[54] The proposed measures, aimed at cutting off sources of terrorist financing and improving detection of such funds, follow from the recent terrorist attacks and continuous terrorism threats in different parts of the EU. One of the proposed actions is to bring forward the date for effective transposition and entry into force of the 4AMLD to the end of 2016 at the latest. There is also a list of amendments that are planned to be made to the 4AMLD, including 'bringing anonymous currency exchanges under the control of competent authorities by extending the scope of the 4AMLD to include virtual currency exchange platforms, and have them supervised under AML/CTF financing legislation at national level'. Also, wallet providers will be considered in terms of extending the scope of the 4AMLD. Finally, the Commission mentioned possible amendments to the PSD to apply its 'licensing and supervision' rules to digital currency exchanges.[55]

It thus seems that after the debate about whether AML/CTF rules should be applied to some Bitcoin-related businesses and many appeals from international and EU bodies to do so, there is a political decision by the Commission to recommend such step. Much, however, will depend on the details of the awaited legislative proposal, in particular the subject scope of the future amendment.

B. Member States Level

It follows that, although a systemic change is unlikely in the near future, the EU institutions may sooner or later adopt measures that will effectively enhance AML/CTF control over the use of cryptocurrencies, especially by Bitcoin-related businesses. Moreover, it cannot be ruled out that particular Member States will adopt their own regulations aimed at applying existing AML/CTF rules to new categories of entities.

As mentioned above, both the 3AMLD and the 4AMLD enable Member States to extend their provisions to new categories of entities (other than obliged entities) 'which are particularly likely to be used for the purposes of money laundering or terrorist financing'.[56] Indeed, some Member States have made declarations in that regard. In March 2015, in the UK, HM Treasury issued a response to the call for information regarding digital currencies,[57] in which the UK government provided its regulatory ambitions. Among other proposals, the government intends to apply

[54] See European Commission, 'Communication from the Commission to the European Parliament and The Council on an Action Plan for Strengthening the Fight against Terrorist Financing', COM (2016) 50/2 (2 February 2016).

[55] Details of the Commission plan should be provided in mid-2016.

[56] Art 4(1) of both 3AMLD and 4AMLD.

[57] HM Treasury, *Digital Currencies: Response to the Call for Information* (HM Treasury, 2015), available at www.gov.uk/government/uploads/system/uploads/attachment_data/file/414040/digital_currencies_response_to_call_for_information_final_changes.pdf (accessed on 5 January 2016).

AML regulations to digital currency exchanges.[58] The first step in this direction will be a consultation, by which the UK governments will

> look at how to ensure that law enforcement bodies have effective skills, tools and legislation to identify and prosecute criminal activity relating to digital currencies, including the ability to seize and confiscate digital currency funds where transactions are for criminal purposes.

It is thus possible that some Member States will undertake regulatory response without waiting for EU action. In this case, Member States will have to inform the Commission about their action.[59]

Conclusions

It is important to realise that the innovative technology of cryptocurrency has paramount consequences for the AML/CTF framework, primarily because it facilitates the development of an alternative financial system without applicable regulation and supervision over transactions.[60] While Bitcoin and other cryptocurrencies currently constitute a small fraction of the global financial systems, including payment schemes, they have the potential to grow. Moreover, new applications of the blockchain technology will further complicate the issue for legislators and regulators.

As a consequence, although the money laundering and terrorist financing issues related to digital currencies seem marginal at present, this can eventually change. Any forthcoming decision regarding AML/CTF regulation of digital currencies must take into account such potential developments in the future.

It would seem that Bitcoin-related businesses in the EU, in particular exchanges, should be content with the conclusion that they are not subject to AML requirements. However, the situation is only superficially clear. The implementation of the 3AMLD in Member States differs across the EU; it is also not always entirely clear whether some businesses should comply with the regulations. Some businesses have voluntarily adopted selected AML measures to avoid any doubts of whether they are complying. Moreover, as the example of the USA shows, businesses also face many practical difficulties that can hinder their compliance with regulations.[61]

58 The government also announced that it would contribute to the FATF works on the issue. Conclusions of the FATF report are in line with the government's stance on the application of the AML regulations to digital currency exchanges.

59 Art 4(2).

60 UNODC (n 17).

61 RL Ensign, 'The Morning Risk Report: Virtual Currency Firms Struggle with AML', *The Wall Street Journal*, 7 May 2015, available at http://blogs.wsj.com/riskandcompliance/2015/05/07/the-morning-risk-report-virtual-currency-firms-struggle-with-aml-newsletter-draft/ (accessed on 5 January 2016).

The lack of regulations relating to AML/CTF and digital currencies on the EU level has also resulted in incoherent approaches across Member States. What is more, exchanges sometimes find themselves in particularly difficult situations, as they enable bidirectional flows of funds from the traditional system to the digital currency scheme and vice versa. Financial institutions from which and to which such flows are directed often experience unease related to the fact that they cannot control who is making such transactions (exchanges' customers do not have to be identified by the exchanges), which poses money-laundering and terrorist financing risks for them. This causes conflicts between traditional financial institutions and Bitcoin-related businesses, as happened, for example, in Poland, where the bank accounts of a number of exchanges have been closed due to the alleged occurrence of money laundering.

As the above remarks show, the European Union has not yet decided whether to include digital currencies in its AML/CTF regulations. This procrastination seems to be a result of weighing arguments for and against such measures and, most of all, waiting for future developments that could tip the balance one way or the other. As such, it is a praiseworthy approach as it may lead to systemic changes in the AML/CTF regulations and not just ad hoc amendments to existing laws. Future regulations should reflect the unique characteristics of digital currencies (and other innovative solutions using the blockchain technology). What should be avoided is the adjustment of regulations in accordance with current political and social events. They can (and should) strengthen the debate over the issue, but should not be determining factors when policy-making decisions are being made. The Commission's expected legislative proposal should take all this into account.

This chapter mainly concerns the application of AML/CTF regulations to digital currencies. However, as mentioned above, one has to be aware that cryptocurrencies are just the first category of digital goods (crypto-assets) that pose such issues as the ones outlined above. The opportunities created by the distributed ledger technology are much broader than just Bitcoin and other cryptocurrencies (which, from this perspective, are just the first instance of the application of this technology). The distributed ledger technology allows the decentralised exchange of value, as represented by currency, securities, different kinds of IOUs and other rights. Moreover, the use of smart contracts further expands these possibilities.

One can doubt whether the application of AML/CTF regulations to some aspects of digital currencies will be an adequate regulatory response if more innovative digital goods schemes are coming. It can be argued that any new regulations would be premature, taken into account the rapid progress that the blockchain technology has made in the last months and years. However, lawmakers and regulators have to keep pace with technological developments and react to greater risks. This is why the application of AML/CTF regulations to digital currencies under the EU framework should be supported. Such a step should not be a mere reaction to headlines or tragic events, but a well-balanced action aimed at mitigating systemic AML/CTF risk and avoiding stifling innovation.

14

Asset Sharing as a Tool for a More Efficient Cross-Border Asset Recovery in the EU? The EU Asset Sharing Model and its Implementation in Belgium and the Netherlands

LAURA VANDE REYDE* AND DIRK VAN DAELE**

Introduction

Since the end of the 1980s, international co-operation with regard to confiscation has become a major concern on the criminal justice agenda of international and European organisations and nation states. One of the bottlenecks experienced in this co-operation concerns the absence of concrete and binding legal provisions and agreements with respect to the sharing of confiscated assets between the states involved.[1] Within the European Union (EU), Council Framework Decision 2006/783/JHA of 6 October 2006 on the application of the principle of mutual recognition to confiscation orders[2] tries to remedy this problem by providing a model for the disposal of confiscated assets. As we will see, however, this EU model on the one hand raises new questions and on the other hand does not provide a solution to all potential problems.

This chapter starts with an analysis of the concept and legal basis of international asset sharing. In the second part, we address the aims of this kind of co-operation and the ambiguities surrounding it. Finally, the current asset sharing

* Research assistant at the Leuven Institute of Criminology of the Faculty of Law, KU Leuven.

** Professor at the Institute of Criminal Law and the Leuven Institute of Criminology of the Faculty of Law, KU Leuven.

[1] MJ Borgers and J Moors, 'Targeting the Proceeds of Crime: Bottlenecks in International Cooperation' (2007) 15 *European Journal of Crime, Criminal Law and Criminal Justice* 1, 11–12.

[2] Framework Decision 2006/783/JHA (2006) OJ L328/59.

possibilities in the EU and their strengths and weaknesses are highlighted. It is not be possible to discuss here the implementation of the asset sharing provisions in each Member State; instead, Belgium and the Netherlands are used as examples to illustrate the essential characteristics of the EU asset sharing model. Furthermore, it should be pointed out in advance that, due to the recent implementation of Framework Decision 2006/783/JHA, very few cases in which the model has been applied are known to date. Hence, our analysis concerns merely the detection of possible problems that may be experienced in the future.

I. Concept and Legal Basis of International Asset Sharing

A. International Asset Sharing

International asset sharing can be defined as the sharing of confiscated criminal assets between states in the framework of international judicial co-operation in criminal matters. It concerns the division of criminal monetary and/or property assets between at least two states, following the execution of a confiscation sanction by one of those states. This division of criminal assets should not be taken too literally. Indeed, a partial transfer of criminal assets will not always be possible or desirable, and/or a full transfer of criminal assets can be preferable. In this connection, mention can be made, for instance, of the confiscation of a stolen car the legitimate owner of which is known. Another example is the confiscation of criminal assets from corrupt officials.

What is clear, however, is that the decision of asset sharing concerns a separate enforcement measure, which needs to be distinguished from the recognition and execution of a foreign confiscation decision.[3] Furthermore, international asset sharing should not be confused with asset sharing between different authorities within one state, which is foreseen, for example, in the USA and Switzerland.[4] Finally, the international sharing of criminal assets interpreted in a narrow sense does not refer to questions that concern the allocation of the confiscated criminal assets, eg the donation to specific organised crime funds, the investment in criminal justice projects or the compensation of victims.[5] Such so-called asset

[3] E Francis, 'De uitvoering van de verbeurdverklaring: interne en internationale aspecten' in A Masset and P Traest (eds), *L'exécution des peines—De strafuitvoering* (Bruxelles, La Charte, 2006) 51.

[4] In the USA, the Attorney General or the Secretary of the Treasury is authorised to transfer confiscated criminal assets to other agencies, eg to any state or local law enforcement agency which participated directly in any of the acts which led to the seizure or forfeiture of the property (18 USC §981(e)). In Switzerland, confiscated criminal assets may be shared between the Federal Government and the Swiss cantons (Art 3–10 Bundesgesetz über die Teilung eingezogener Vermögenswerte vom 19. März 2004 (TEVG; SR 312.4)).

[5] *cf* Consideration 16 of the preamble of Framework Decision 2006/783/JHA.

disposal questions may nevertheless influence the international asset sharing decision.

B. International Asset Sharing in International Legal Instruments

Until the late 1980s, a real international legal basis for asset sharing was non-existent. The European Convention on the International Validity of Criminal Judgments of 1970—one of the first legal instruments that provided a legal framework for the international co-operation with regard to confiscation—stipulated in that regard that, in principle, the proceeds of confiscation benefited the requested (ie executing) state.[6] Only one exception to this general rule was provided. Confiscated property that is of special interest for the requesting state—in particular, property of historical or criminological interest[7]—may indeed be remitted to this state if it so requires.[8] However, due to its limited scope and facultative nature, this exception offers no general legal basis for international asset sharing.

More recently, cross-border co-operation regarding confiscation in general and asset recovery in particular has received more international attention. This resulted in several international legal instruments creating the possibility of asset sharing. At the level of the United Nations (UN), asset sharing was explicitly provided for in Article 5, paragraph 5 of the Convention against Illicit Traffic in Narcotic Drugs and Psychotropic Substances 1988;[9] in Article 8, paragraph 3 of the International Convention for the Suppression of the Financing of Terrorism 1999;[10] and in Article 57, paragraphs 2–5 of the Convention against Corruption 2003.[11] The scope of these instruments is respectively limited to drug related criminal activities, the financing of terrorist offences, and corruption. As a result, asset sharing on the basis of these conventions is only possible with regard to assets related to these specific criminal activities. This changed with the entry into force of the United Nations Convention against Transnational Organized Crime of 2000,[12] which applies to a whole range of transnational forms of crime and creates in Article 14, paragraph 3(b) the first more or less general global legal basis for asset sharing.

[6] European Convention on the International Validity of Criminal Judgments (opened for signature 28 May 1970, entered into force 26 July 1974) CETS No 070 (Convention International Validity of Judgments 1970) Art 47, para 1.

[7] Explanatory report to Art 47 of the Convention International Validity of Judgments 1970.

[8] Convention International Validity of Judgments 1970, Art 47, para 2.

[9] United Nations Convention against Illicit Traffic in Narcotic Drugs and Psychotropic Substances (adopted 20 December 1988, entered into force 11 November 1990) 1582 UNTS 95 (UN Drug Trafficking Convention 1988).

[10] International Convention for the Suppression of the Financing of Terrorism (adopted 9 December 1999, entered into force 10 April 2002) 39 ILM 270.

[11] United Nations Convention against Corruption (adopted 31 October 2003, entered into force 14 December 2005) 2349 UNTS 41 (UNCAC 2003).

[12] United Nations Convention against Transnational Organized Crime (adopted 15 November 2000, entered into force 29 September 2003) 2225 UNTS 209 (UNTOC 2000).

Within the Council of Europe, asset sharing became legally anchored in Article 15 of the Anti-Money Laundering Convention of 1990 and in Article 25 of its successor of 2005.[13] Due to the broad scope of these conventions and their high level of ratifications, asset sharing is possible for some forms of crime. However, it should be noted that the explanatory reports to both conventions demonstrate that some members of the Council of Europe have argued for a restrictive interpretation.[14] This applies, for example, to Belgium, which argued that these international legal provisions alone were not sufficient as a basis for asset sharing. According to the Belgian standpoint, a domestic legal basis was deemed necessary for sharing confiscated criminal assets with other states.[15] In that regard, Article 8 of the Belgian Law concerning international co-operation with regard to seizure and confiscation has offered a legal basis for the transfer of confiscated criminal assets to other states since 2006.[16]

With the exception of the United Nations Convention against Corruption,[17] the above-mentioned international legal provisions are quite similar, and stipulate in general that confiscated assets shall be disposed of by the requested party in accordance with its domestic law and administrative procedures, unless the parties involved agree otherwise. This implies that, in the absence of a derogating asset sharing regulation, the confiscated assets accrue to the executing state. The Netherlands, for example, provided a legal basis for asset sharing with the USA in Article 7 of the Bilateral Agreement between the Government of the Kingdom of the Netherlands and the Government of the United States of America Regarding Mutual Cooperation in the Tracing, Freezing, Seizure and Forfeiture of Proceeds and Instrumentalities of Crime and the Sharing of Forfeited Assets.[18] So far, Belgium has concluded only a few asset sharing agreements with other states.[19]

[13] Convention on Laundering, Search, Seizure and Confiscation of the Proceeds from Crime (opened for signature 8 November 1990, entered into force 1 September 1993) CETS No 141 (CoE Anti-Money Laundering Convention 1990); Council of Europe Convention on Laundering, Search, Seizure and Confiscation of the Proceeds from Crime and on the Financing of Terrorism (opened for signature 16 May 2005, entered into force 1 May 2008) CETS No 198 (CoE Anti-Money Laundering Convention 2005).

[14] See Explanatory report to the Anti-Money Laundering Convention 1990, para 55; Explanatory report to the Anti-Money Laundering Convention 2005, paras 192–94.

[15] MvT bij het wetsontwerp diverse bepalingen, *Parl St* Kamer 2005–06, No 51K2518/001, 14–16.

[16] Wet 20 mei 1997 betreffende de internationale samenwerking inzake de tenuitvoerlegging van inbeslagnemingen en verbeurdverklaringen, *BS* 3 July 1997 (Act 20 May 1997).

[17] In the case of corruption offences, as a general rule, all confiscated assets are returned to the requesting state (UNCAC 2003, Art 57, para 3).

[18] Agreement Regarding Mutual Cooperation in the Tracing, Freezing, Seizure and Forfeiture of Proceeds and Instrumentalities of Crime and the Sharing of Forfeited Assets (US–the Netherlands) (adopted 20 November 1992, entered into force 31 July 1994) 2029 UNTS 189.

[19] Financial Action Task Force (FATF), 'Anti-money Laundering and Counter-terrorist Financing Measures. Belgium Mutual Evaluation Report' (FATF, April 2015) 142, available at www.fatf-gafi.org/media/fatf/documents/reports/mer4/Mutual-Evaluation-Report-Belgium-2015.pdf. Given the lack of Belgian statistical data demonstrating the international sharing of confiscated assets, it is not possible to give a detailed overview of all the agreements concluded. Moreover, due to a lack of knowledge of the international rules concerning asset sharing, in practice, criminal assets were shared between Belgium and other states in a more or less informal way. In a previous phase of the international co-operation

Although only the new EU asset sharing rules are discussed in the following sections of this chapter, it should be kept in mind that criminals often hide their criminal proceeds in non-EU Member States. Hence, the older legal asset sharing provisions are still relevant in the co-operation with these countries.

C. The Legal Basis of Asset Sharing in the EU

Almost 20 years ago, the EU action plan of 1997 to combat organised crime recommended that the possibility of the division of confiscated criminal assets between the Member States be examined.[20] A draft decision to this end was presented by the Austrian Republic on 8 November 1999, setting out guidelines on the division of confiscated criminal assets.[21] However, the Council took no action on this initiative. Three years later, the Kingdom of Denmark took the initiative for the adoption of a Council Framework Decision on the execution in the European Union of confiscation orders.[22] In Article 14 of this Draft Framework Decision, the asset sharing between Member States was regulated. After four years of discussion and different changes and amendments to this Draft Framework Decision, including the asset sharing regulation, the final Framework Decision on the application of the principle of mutual recognition to confiscation orders was adopted in 2006.[23] Article 16 of this Framework Decision provides a more or less detailed model for the sharing of confiscated assets between EU Member States. Since the Framework Decision has a broad scope of application, these rules are not limited to specific types of crime. Furthermore, the EU model regulates the international sharing of monetary assets and property assets, as well as the proceeds of the sale of property assets. However, different rules and conditions apply depending on the nature of the confiscated criminal assets.[24]

In the Netherlands, Article 16 of Framework Decision 2006/783/JHA was implemented in 2009[25] in Article 28 of the Dutch general framework legislation

process, often the competent authorities did not make a distinction between seizure aimed at preserving evidence for conviction versus seizure aimed at the preservation of a later confiscation sanction. As a result, following the execution of a request for seizure, the seized criminal assets were often transmitted to the issuing state without a formal request for execution of the confiscation sanction or a formal asset sharing agreement.

[20] Action Plan to Combat Organized Crime [1997] OJ C251/1, recommendation 26 (d).

[21] European Parliament, Report on the initiative of the Kingdom of Denmark with a view to the adoption of a Council Framework Decision on confiscation of crime-related proceeds, instrumentalities and property and a Council Framework Decision on the execution in the European Union of confiscation orders, A5-0383/2002, 7 November 2002, 15–16.

[22] Initiative of the Kingdom of Denmark with a view to the adoption of a Council Framework Decision on the execution in the European Union of confiscation orders [2002] OJ C184/8.

[23] Council Framework Decision 2006/783/JHA on the application of the principle of mutual recognition to confiscation orders [2006] OJ L328/59 (Framework Decision 2006/783/JHA).

[24] See Sections IV.B and IV.C and accompanying notes.

[25] Art 1 (L) van de wet van 5 maart 2009 tot implementatie van het kaderbesluit No 2006/783/JBZ van de Raad van de Europese Unie van 6 oktober 2006 inzake de toepassing van het beginsel van wederzijdse erkenning op beslissingen tot confiscatie, *Stb* 2009, 124.

concerning mutual recognition and enforcement of criminal sanctions of 2007.[26] Almost four years after the implementation deadline, Belgium finally implemented[27] the same EU provision in Article 38 of its general framework legislation concerning the application of the principle of mutual recognition of judicial decisions in criminal matters of 2006.[28] Since the entry into force of these national legal provisions on 1 June 2009 (the Netherlands) and 14 April 2012 (Belgium), confiscated assets between both countries and other EU Member States are shared according to a fixed set of rules, which will be examined more in detail in Section III of this chapter.

II. Aims and Ambiguities

A. Aims of International Asset Sharing

The purposes of international asset sharing can be grouped into two major categories: the stimulation of international co-operation on the one hand and the restoration of damage caused by the criminal act on the other.

With regard to the first objective, it should be kept in mind that confiscated criminal assets traditionally were allocated to the state that executed the confiscation sanction (the executing state), unless an agreement between the states involved stipulated otherwise.[29] Such an approach is not only in accordance with the international principle of sovereignty of states, but can also be justified by the principle of reciprocity. Furthermore, the execution of a foreign confiscation sanction may entail significant costs, which in general are borne by the executing state.[30] In that regard, the obtained criminal assets may (partly) serve as compensation for these costs. Accordingly, granting the confiscated criminal assets to the executing state may encourage it to allocate a part of its limited police and judicial resources to the execution of foreign confiscation sanctions. However, the downside of such

[26] Wet van 27 september 2007 tot implementatie van het kaderbesluit No 2005/214/JBZ van de Raad van de Europese Unie van 24 februari 2005 inzake de toepassing van het beginsel van wederzijdse erkenning op geldelijke sancties, *Stb* 2007, 354 (Act 27 September 2007).

[27] Art 11 wet tot wijziging van de wet van 5 augustus 2006 inzake de toepassing van het beginsel van de wederzijdse erkenning van rechterlijke beslissingen in strafzaken tussen de lidstaten van de Europese Unie, *BS* 4 April 2012.

[28] Wet 5 augustus 2006 inzake de toepassing van het beginsel van de wederzijdse erkenning van rechterlijke beslissingen in strafzaken tussen de lidstaten van de Europese Unie, *BS* 7 September 2006 (Act 5 August 2006).

[29] See Section II.B and accompanying notes.

[30] UN Drug Trafficking Convention 1988, Art 7, para 19; UNCAC 2003, Art 46, para 28; UNTOC 2000, Art 18, para 28; CoE Anti-Money Laundering Convention 1990, Art 34; CoE Anti-Money Laundering Convention 2005, Art 44; Framework Decision 2006/783/JHA, Art 20, para 1.

an approach is that it does not stimulate the state in which a court competent in criminal matters has issued a confiscation decision (the issuing state) to invest in the criminal asset recovery investigation and/or in the enforcement of a confiscation sanction with regard to criminal proceeds located abroad. Criminal (financial) investigations preceding the imposition of a confiscation decision are often complex, costly, time consuming and subject to limited resources, as is the case for the prosecution and investigative measures in the execution phase. In that regard, granting all the confiscated criminal assets to the executing state implies a limited return on investment for the issuing state, which in turn can have a demotivating effect on police officers, magistrates and judges in devoting their limited time and resources to international asset recovery cases.[31] Therefore, the international sharing of confiscated criminal assets may create an incentive for law enforcement authorities from the issuing as well as the executing state to participate in international asset recovery cases.[32]

The second objective of international asset sharing—the restoration of damage—is based on one of the rationales of the confiscation sanction itself, being the restoration of the previously existing situation. This restoration is necessary not only in the executing state, but even more in the issuing state, because the victims of the crime often reside in the latter or this state itself was victimised by the committed crime (eg in the case of tax evasion). Moreover, certain types of crimes affect whole societies, as is the case, for example, with international drug trafficking. As Shelley pointed out: 'Leaving the proceeds of this crime in affluent countries and depositing the money in treasuries of the world's financial centres does nothing to address the root causes of the transnational crime.'[33] By the (partial) transfer of the confiscated criminal assets to the state where the victims are located or to the state which in particular is affected by the crime committed, the damage inflicted on them can at least partly be compensated/restored.[34] However, this is only the case if the receiving state uses the confiscated criminal assets to compensate the victim and/or to rebuild the particular societies affected. In that regard, international asset sharing is interrelated with asset disposal, which concerns questions as to whom and to what the confiscated criminal assets are allocated.

[31] LM Samuel, 'Challenges Facing US Anti- Money Laundering Efforts in Transnational Crime' in UNAFEI (ed), *Resource Material Series No 65* (UNAFEI, March 2005) 54, available at www.unafei.or.jp/english/pdf/RS_No65/No65_08VE_Samuel1.pdf.

[32] Explanatory report to the Anti-Money Laundering Convention 1990, para 55; *Kamerstukken II* 2007/08, 31555, 3, p 18 (MvT) (the Netherlands); LM Joseph, 'Money Laundering Enforcement: Following the Money' (2001) 6(2) *Journal of Economic Perspectives* 11, 14.

[33] L Shelley, 'Transnational Organized Crime and Seized Assets: Moral Dilemmas Concerning the Disposition of the Fruits of Crime' (2000) 7 *Maastricht Journal of European and Comparative Law* 35, 49.

[34] *Kamerstukken II* 2008/09, 31555, 5, 10 (NV II) (the Netherlands); Shelley (ibid) 49–50.

B. Ambiguities

Although the above-mentioned arguments in favour of asset sharing seem very convincing, some counter-arguments can be given as well. This becomes clear if we take into account the diverging national approaches with regard to the legal nature of confiscation. In Belgium, for example, confiscation is defined as a criminal penalty and essentially has a punitive and deterrent character,[35] whereas other countries, for example the Netherlands, conceive the confiscation of criminal proceeds as a measure aimed at the restoration of the previously existing situation.[36] These differences in justification of confiscation may have an influence on the legitimacy of asset sharing. If confiscation is (mainly) regarded as a criminal penalty, it should not make any difference whether the confiscated criminal assets are shared or not. In this view, the only thing that matters is the enforcement of the confiscation sanction. By contrast, asset sharing can play an important role in states where restoration of the previously existing situation is stressed as the main goal of confiscation. It should be admitted, however, that this distinction is merely theoretical. Indeed, most states will justify confiscation at least implicitly both from a punitive and a restorative viewpoint.[37] Furthermore, we have already pointed out that international asset sharing not only seeks to restore the previously existing situation, but also—and even more so—aims to increase the willingness of states to co-operate with each other in international asset recovery cases. In that regard, asset sharing is relevant regardless of the justification of the confiscation sanction.

A more problematic feature of international asset sharing, however, is that it raises the risk that the motivation to co-operate in international criminal cases will be determined by the amount and/or nature of the criminal assets concerned and the extent to which they will be shared.[38] This contrasts with the prevention and reduction of crime as the fundamental objectives of international co-operation in criminal matters, which implies that asset recovery should be

[35] Arts 7 and 7bis Sw; Cass 28 juni 2007, *Arr Cass* 2007, 1501.

[36] *Kamerstukken II* 1989/90, 21504, 3, p 8 (the Netherlands); FW Bleichrodt and PC Vegter, *Sanctierecht* (Deventer, Kluwer, 2013) 309.

[37] See MvT bij het wetsontwerp tot de uitbreiding van de mogelijkheden tot inbeslagneming en verbeurdverklaring in strafzaken, *Parl St* Kamer 2001-02, No 50K1601/001, 6 (Belgium); J. Rozie, *Voordeelsontneming: de wisselwerking tussen de toepassingsvoorwaarden en het rechtskarakter van de verbeurdverklaring van illegale vermogensvoordelen* (Antwerp, Intersentia, 2005); F Verbruggen, 'Hebben en houwen: bezitseffect en afgifteafkeer als inspiratie bij de hervorming van de Belgische verbeurdverklaring' in T Spapens, M Groenhuijsen and T Kooijmans (eds), *Liber Amicorum Cyrille Fijnaut* (Antwerp, Intersentia, 2011) 270 (Belgium); A de Beer, 'Bestraffing of (toch) voordeelontneming?' (2012) 6 *Tijdschrift voor Sanctierecht en Compliance* 196, 200 (the Netherlands).

[38] *Kamerstukken II* 1990/91, 22 083, 3, p 25 (the Netherlands). *cf* DJ Fried, 'Rationalizing Criminal Forfeiture' (1988) 79 *Journal of Criminal Law and Criminology* 328, 365; M Zalman, 'Judges in their Own Case: A Lockean Critique of Law Enforcement Asset Sharing in Drug Forfeiture Law and Practice' (1996) 21 *Criminal Justice Review* 197; K Baicker and M Jacobson, 'Finders Keepers: Forfeiture Laws, Policing Incentives, and Local Budgets' (2007) 91 *Journal of Public Economics* 2113; JH Skolnick, 'Policing Should Not Be for Profit' (2008) 7 *Criminology and Public Policy* 257.

perceived as a common responsibility of (European) states and that co-operation must not depend on the benefits for the states involved. These objectives and values underlying international co-operation are reflected not only in the broad scope of application of the more recent European instruments with regard to asset recovery, but also in the rule that states in principle may not claim from each other the refund of costs relating to the legal assistance offered.

III. The EU Asset Sharing Model

A. Execution of a European Confiscation Order as a Prerequisite for Asset Sharing

Council Framework Decision 2006/783/JHA establishes the rules under which a Member State shall recognise and execute in its territory a confiscation order issued by a court competent in criminal matters of another Member State. Such a confiscation order is defined as a final penalty or measure imposed by a court following proceedings in relation to a criminal offence or offences, resulting in the definitive deprivation of property.[39]

It should be stressed that the asset sharing rules laid down in Article 16 of the Framework Decision are only applicable if confiscated property has been obtained from the execution of a European confiscation order. As a consequence, these rules do not apply to forms of so-called indirect co-operation with regard to confiscation. This kind of co-operation concerns cases where a state gets assistance from another state—for example, by interrogating an important witness or by collecting and transmitting necessary financial information—in order to impose and execute a confiscation decision. In such cases, the enforcement of the confiscation decision is a purely national matter. However, this does not mean that asset sharing is entirely excluded. On the contrary, the international legal instruments discussed earlier in this chapter do not make a distinction between direct and indirect forms of co-operation. Hence, the sharing of criminal assets will be possible if the Member States involved have concluded a specific asset sharing agreement.[40]

B. Disposal of Confiscated Money

Money which has been obtained from the execution of a European confiscation order shall be disposed of by the executing state in accordance with two principles. As a general rule, the executing state shall transfer 50 per cent of the amount which

[39] Art 1, para 1 and Art 2(c) Framework Decision 2006/783/JHA.

[40] eg Agreement Regarding Mutual Cooperation (US—the Netherlands) (n 18) Art 7.

has been obtained to the issuing state.[41] However, this obligation only applies if this amount—which may differ from the amount stipulated in the confiscation order—is at least €10,000 and no derogating agreement between the two states stipulates otherwise. In cases in which less than €10,000 is obtained from the execution of the confiscation order, the old rule of asset sharing still applies. This means that the amount obtained shall accrue to the executing state unless the states involved agree otherwise.[42]

The rationale of this scheme is twofold. On the one hand, for smaller amounts of money, the sharing of criminal assets would not outweigh the costs of processing and transferring them. On the other hand, the amount of €10,000 should at least guarantee that the execution costs—including the procedure of recognition of the confiscation order—are compensated.[43] However, it is not fully clear if this amount refers to the gross proceeds or the net—ie after deducting costs, such as the costs of preserving and managing the assets and the costs of the criminal investigation—proceeds. Taking into account the twofold rationale, in our view it concerns the gross proceeds.

The 50 per cent rule has some practical advantages. First, a fixed percentage prevents time-consuming negotiations in individual cases.[44] Furthermore, it avoids the difficult measurement of the damage caused by the crime, the costs of the criminal investigation and/or the contribution of both states to the international co-operation process. Conversely, a fixed percentage does not take into account the specificities and features of a case—the nature of the crime, concrete victims that are known, a long and difficult criminal investigation, etc. In that regard, a case-related model would be more in accordance with the aims of asset sharing.[45] Hence, Article 14 of the Danish Draft Framework Decision stipulated that 'confiscated assets or proceeds of the sale of confiscated property shall, after deduction of the executing state's costs, be returned to the issuing State unless otherwise agreed between the issuing State and the executing State'. In this approach, the costs of execution were taken into account as well as the damage caused by the crime and the costs of investigation conducted by the issuing state, although it remained unclear how these costs should be measured.

Although this proposal was rejected, another solution was provided. Indeed, the current asset sharing model foresees the possibility for the states involved to derogate from the 50–50 per cent sharing rule.[46] The executing and the issuing state can, for example, agree that only 10 per cent of the obtained assets has to be transmitted, the full amount of money has to be transmitted, nothing has to be

[41] Art 16, para 1(b) Framework Decision 2006/783/JHA; Art 38, para 1(1°) Act 5 August 2006 (Belgium); Art 28, para 1 Act 27 September 2007 (the Netherlands).

[42] Art 16, para 1(a) and para 4 Framework Decision 2006/783/JHA; Art 38, para 1(1°) and para 3 Act 5 August 2006 (Belgium); Art 28, para 1 and 5 Act 27 September 2007 (the Netherlands).

[43] *Kamerstukken II* 2008/09, 31555, 5, p 10 (NV II) (the Netherlands).

[44] ibid, p 10.

[45] See Section III.A and accompanying notes.

[46] Art 16, para 4 Framework Decision 2006/783/JHA; Art 38, para 3 Act 5 August 2006 (Belgium); Art 28, para 5 Act 27 September 2007 (the Netherlands).

transmitted, and so on. Furthermore, states can also agree to share criminal assets in cases in which the minimum amount does not exceed €10,000.

C. Disposal of Property other than Money

If the confiscation order concerns property other than money, the executing state has the choice between selling the property and transferring it to the issuing state.[47] This choice applies to property of any description—corporeal or incorporeal, movable or immovable, legal documents and instruments evidencing title to or interest in such property.[48] If the former option is chosen, the proceeds of the sale shall be disposed of in accordance with the above discussed rules applicable to the disposal of confiscated money.[49]

This basis scheme needs to be nuanced. First of all, it will not always be possible for the executing state to sell the confiscated property or to transfer it to the issuing state. This will be the case if the national law of the executing state stipulates that the confiscated property must be destroyed. Typical examples are the confiscation of drugs and weapons. In such cases, the property may be disposed of in another way in accordance with the law of the executing state.[50]

Secondly, there will be cases where the competent authority of the executing state cannot obtain payment, although the confiscation order concerns an amount of money. In this event, the confiscation order shall be executed on any item of property available for that purpose.[51] However, this property may only be transferred to the issuing state with its consent.[52] In the absence of consent, the executing state has no other option but to sell the property. The proceeds of this sale will be shared according to the rules applicable to the sharing of monetary assets.

Thirdly, the executing state shall not be required to sell or return specific items covered by the confiscation order which constitute cultural objects forming part of its national heritage.[53] Whereas the Netherlands excludes the sale or transfer of cultural objects forming part of their heritage in all cases,[54] Belgium opts for a flexible approach. Hence, according to Belgian law, the sale or transfer of cultural objects forming part of the Belgian heritage is still possible.[55]

[47] Art 16, para 2 Framework Decision 2006/783/JHA; Art 38 para 1(2°) Act 5 August 2006 (Belgium); Art 28, para 2 Act 27 September 2007 (the Netherlands).

[48] Art 2(d) Framework Decision 2006/783/JHA.

[49] Art 16, para 2(a) Framework Decision 2006/783/JHA; Art 38, para 1(2°)(a) Act 5 August 2006 (Belgium); Art 28, para 2(a) Act 27 September 2007 (the Netherlands).

[50] Art 16, para 2(c) Framework Decision 2006/783/JHA; Art 38, para 1(2°)(c) Act 5 August 2006 (Belgium); Art 28, para 2(c) Act 27 September 2007 (the Netherlands).

[51] Art 7, para 3 Framework Decision 2006/783/JHA.

[52] Art 16, para 2(b) Framework Decision 2006/783/JHA; Art 28, para 4 Act 27 September 2007 (the Netherlands). Belgium did not implement this specification.

[53] Art 16, para 3 Framework Decision 2006/783/JHA.

[54] Art 28, para 3 Act 27 September 2007.

[55] Art 38, para 2 Act 5 August 2006.

Finally, in order to take into account the specificities of a case, the issuing and executing states can agree to derogate from the general rules applicable to the sharing of confiscated property.[56] For example, they can agree that the executing state has no choice but to sell the property and to share the proceeds of this sale with the issuing state, they can agree to derogate from the rules applicable to the sharing of the proceeds of the sale or they can agree that no sharing is necessary. However, as is the case for the sharing of monetary assets, no criteria for concluding such a derogating agreement are provided in Framework Decision 2006/783/JHA. That responsibility is left to the Member States. Even though, in practice, it can be preferable to sell confiscated goods and share the proceeds thereof—given the fact that this requires less administrative formalities than the transfer of property[57]—no concrete guidelines thereto exist in Belgium or the Netherlands. Moreover, in certain cases, the transfer of the confiscated property may be preferred, eg if the issuing state benefits more from the property itself than from the proceeds of its sale.[58]

D. Competent Authorities

It is the responsibility of the Member States to designate the authorities competent to decide on asset sharing. In Belgium, this competence is allocated to the public prosecutor of the judicial district where (most of) the confiscated assets are located.[59] At first sight, this seems a rational choice. After all, once the criminal court has declared a foreign confiscation enforceable,[60] it is the public prosecutor who is responsible for the execution of the confiscation.[61] Furthermore, he is aware of the specific features of the case. In the exercise of this executive function, the public prosecutor has to act in accordance with the criminal policy guidelines of the Minister of Justice, including the asset sharing agreements concluded between the latter and the competent authorities of the other Member States.[62] This, in itself, implies an improvement compared to the situation before the implementation of Framework Decision 2006/783/JHA, when the decision about the sharing of criminal assets with other states was taken by the criminal court.[63] This competence of the criminal court—still applicable in cases of asset sharing with non-EU countries—was criticised because the asset sharing decision is an executive

[56] Art 16, para 4 Framework Decision 2006/783/JHA; Art 38, para 3 Act 5 August 2006 (Belgium); Art 28, para 5 Act 27 September 2007 (the Netherlands).

[57] MvT bij het wetsontwerp tot wijziging van de wet van 5 augustus 2006 inzake de toepassing van het beginsel van de wederzijdse erkenning van rechterlijke beslissingen in strafzaken tussen de lidstaten van de Europese Unie, *Parl St* Kamer 2011–12, No 53K1703/001, 22–23 (Belgium).

[58] *Kamerstukken II* 2007/08, 31555, 3, p 19 (MvT) (the Netherlands).

[59] Art 38, para 1 and Art 30, paras 1–2 Act 5 August 2006.

[60] Art 30 Act 5 August 2006.

[61] Art 4, para 2 Act 5 August 2006 and Art 197bis Sv (Belgium).

[62] Art 143 quater Ger. W (Belgium).

[63] Art 8, para 2 Act 20 May 1997.

measure, which does not concern the judiciary.[64] Moreover, as a consequence of the *trias politica* principle, the criminal court decides in full autonomy and is not bound by any instructions of the Minister of Justice.

However, the current Belgian legal framework also has its flaws. Given the fact that the territorial jurisdiction of the Public Prosecution Service depends on the location where (most of) the criminal assets are situated, a centralised build-up of knowledge is not possible. Nonetheless, it is unlikely that every prosecutor has experience with and knowledge of the asset sharing rules, the procedure that has to be followed and the asset sharing agreements that were concluded in similar cases. This raises the risk that sharing of criminal assets with other states is delayed, or even worse, that no asset sharing takes place at all.

The centralisation of the responsibility for the asset sharing decision within one agency may reduce such risks and allows for the development of expertise in asset sharing. In the Netherlands, such a solution was preferred, by making the public prosecutor of Leeuwarden responsible for the execution of foreign confiscation decisions and the sharing of criminal assets.[65] An alternative for such a centralisation would be the creation of a knowledge centre at national level, which offers support to the local public prosecutors. In that regard, the Belgian Central Office for Seizure and Confiscation (COSC) and the Dutch Criminal Assets Deprivation Bureau Public Prosecution Service (CADB) can play a role. Belonging to the Public Prosecution Service, these institutions support national law enforcement authorities in international asset recovery cases, including the international sharing of assets.[66] The Dutch CADB has legal advisors, specialised in international criminal law, who provide general and specific advice on international aspects in confiscation cases. The Bureau is also easily accessible through its five regional offices.[67] The Belgian COSC, in contrast, is mainly concerned with national cases and is contacted only exceptionally with regard to the execution of a confiscation decision. The question therefore remains as to whether the current state of knowledge within the COSC is sufficient to offer support in asset sharing cases.

64 E Francis, 'Enkele bedenkingen bij de nieuwe Belgische regeling inzake "asset sharing"' (2007) 2 *Nullum Crimen* 20, 21. See also the rejected proposed amendment to Art 2 wet 20 juli 2006 houdende diverse bepalingen, *BS* 28 July 2006 (Amendement (T VAN PARYS) op het wetsontwerp houdende diverse bepalingen, *Parl St* Kamer 2005–06, No 51K2518/005, 2–3; Verslag namens de commissie voor de Justitie over het wetsontwerp houdende diverse bepalingen, *Parl St* Kamer 2005–06, No 51K2518/021, 13).

65 Art 28 and Art 4 Act 27 September 2007.

66 Art 3, para 3(8°) wet 26 maart 2003 houdende oprichting van een Centraal Orgaan voor de Inbeslagneming en de Verbeurdverklaring en houdende bepalingen inzake het waardevast beheer van in beslag genomen goederen en de uitvoering van bepaalde vermogenssancties, *BS* 2 May 2003 (Belgium); Art 28 Act 5 August 2006 (Belgium); Art 2 regeling van de directeur-generaal Rechtspleging en Rechtshandhaving van het ministerie van Veiligheid en Justitie van 3 augustus 2012 No 286999, houdende de organisatie van de dienstonderdelen bij het openbaar ministerie, *Stcrt.* 2012, 16568 (the Netherlands); *Kamerstukken II* 2008/09, 31555, 5, p 4–5 (NV II) (the Netherlands).

67 The CADB has a regional office in Leeuwarden, Zwolle, Amsterdam, Rotterdam and Den Bosch.

E. Alternative Arrangements

The rules set out in paragraphs 1–3 of Article 16 of Framework Decision 2006/783/JHA shall apply only insofar as the issuing state and the executing state do not agree otherwise.[68] Member States are thus allowed to make arrangements in which they agree to share the confiscated assets in a different way to that foreseen by the general EU asset sharing rules. In Belgium and the Netherlands, the conclusion of such an agreement is an exclusive competence of the Minister of Justice.[69] In that regard, however, the Belgian Council of State specified that the Minister of Justice has no competence to conclude general asset sharing agreements.[70] According to Belgian law, only specific case-related agreements between Belgium and another Member State are allowed. It can be assumed that the same applies for the Netherlands.

Given the delicate nature of the international relations and the policy aspects inherent to asset sharing, allocating this competence to the Minister of Justice is justified. He indeed has a comprehensive overview of his country's bilateral relations, and the positive and negative experiences and practices in the field of international judicial co-operation.[71] In this way, the risk of jeopardising good international relations is reduced and a consistent asset sharing policy can be developed. Nevertheless, it should be noted that, to date, Belgium has not developed such an asset sharing policy.[72]

Furthermore, it is obvious that alternative arrangements require a clear communication and co-ordination between the different parties involved in the asset sharing process. In that regard, questions arise as to when and how the public prosecutor is informed about the context and content of an asset sharing agreement concluded at ministerial level. Moreover, it does not seem to have been excluded that the Ministers of Justice of Belgium and the Netherlands would conclude an agreement in an early phase of the asset recovery process. This raises such questions as: is such an informal agreement communicated to the public prosecutor? Will the public prosecutor be consulted during the negotiations of such an agreement? How is the final asset sharing decision communicated to the services and institutions which executed the confiscation decision, and where the criminal assets are stored? Are the victims informed, and if so, how?

[68] Art 16, para 4 Framework Decision 2006/783/JHA.

[69] Art 38, para 3 Act 5 August 2006 (Belgium); Art 28, para 5 Act 27 September 2007 (the Netherlands).

[70] Adv RvS 47016/2/V bij het wetsontwerp tot wijziging van de wet van 5 augustus 2006 inzake de toepassing van het beginsel van de wederzijdse erkenning van rechterlijke beslissingen in strafzaken tussen de lidstaten van de Europese Unie, *Parl St* Kamer 2011–12, No 53K1703/001, 119.

[71] See also Francis (n 64) 21.

[72] FATF (n 19) 139.

Conclusion

Given the fact that the costs related to international asset recovery should not be underestimated, the EU asset sharing model containing the obligation to share assets between the Member States involved is certainly an improvement in comparison with the traditional approach, according to which asset sharing is merely a form of voluntary co-operation. This model can without doubt stimulate Member States to increase their co-operation in the field of asset recovery. Obviously this does not mean that international asset sharing is a miracle solution. Indeed, it should be kept in mind that there are a lot of other bottlenecks that hamper international co-operation. In general, these barriers can be divided into three categories: (i) legal barriers (eg limited scope of and/or reservations to international legal instruments, grounds for refusal, late and/or incorrect national transposition of international instruments); (ii) operational barriers (eg not clear who is responsible for sending and executing requests, lack of co-ordination, poor quality of requests, lack of knowledge of international co-operation possibilities and of foreign law, insufficient training); and (iii) policy barriers (eg differences in national criminal policies concerning confiscation, lack of a European criminal policy).[73]

[73] See A Smellie, 'Prosecutorial Challenges in Freezing and Forfeiting Proceeds of Transnational Crime and the Use of International Asset Sharing to Promote International Cooperation' (2004) 8 *Journal of Money Laundering Contro* l 104; MJ Borgers and J Moors, 'Targeting the Proceeds of Crime: Bottlenecks in International Cooperation' (2007) 15 *European Journal of Crime, Criminal Law and Criminal Justice* 1; B Vettori, *Tough on Criminal Wealth: Exploring the Practice of Proceeds from Crime Confiscation in the EU* (Dordrecht, Springer, 2006); K. Stephenson et al, *Barriers to Asset Recovery: An Analysis of the Key Barriers and Recommendations for Action* (Washington DC, The International Bank for Reconstruction and Development, 2011).

15

The Social Reuse of Confiscated Assets in EU Member States: From Current Experiences to an EU Policy for a 'Powered-by-Citizens' Fight Against Crime

BARBARA VETTORI* AND ANDREA DI NICOLA**

Introduction

At the end of any given judicial procedure aimed at removing the proceeds from crime, the issue of what to do with them arises. These issues are dealt with in the disposal phase, which is the phase in which a final confiscation order is enforced and confiscated assets are disposed of. It starts with the final confiscation order and ends with delivery of the assets to designated beneficiaries. Theoretically, different forms of reuse are possible. These range from the traditional transfer of ill-gotten gains into the state budget and its use as any other public money/resources to more innovative forms of disposal, such as the reuse of confiscated assets for social purposes or for 'incentivisation schemes' for law enforcement agencies.[1]

There is currently a lack of knowledge on legislation and practices regarding the disposal of confiscated assets and their reuse in the EU, despite the high relevance of the topic for the effectiveness of the overall asset recovery system: if any problems arise in the last phase of confiscation proceedings, the efforts made by the criminal justice system in tracing, seizing and confiscating criminal assets can be brought

* Barbara Vettori is Assistant Professor of Criminology at the Faculty of Political and Social Sciences, Catholic University of Milan. She is author of the following sections of this chapter: Section II.B, C, D and E, Section III and Conclusion.

** Andrea Di Nicola is Assistant Professor of Criminology at the Faculty of Law of the University of Trento. He is author of the following sections of this chapter: Introduction, Section I and Section II.A.

[1] Under these schemes, which aim at incentivising asset recovery and enabling the involved agencies to recoup some of the costs incurred in confiscation proceedings, the entities that contributed to the seizure and confiscation get back a percentage of the confiscated assets.

to nought. The scant attention paid so far to this key phase explains the current lack of European standards in this area, despite the significant body of EU regulation developed on the investigative and judicial phases of confiscation proceedings. More recently, the EU institutions have provided input into a closer scrutiny of the issue by showing interest in an uncommon form of disposal, which involves giving the criminal proceeds back to the communities affected by (organised) crime and promoting their use in line with communal needs: social reuse.

This chapter aims to add to the current debate on this topic by answering the following questions: which Member States envisage the social reuse of confiscated assets? Could other Member States adopt it and, if so, under which conditions? Based on the lessons learnt from current social reuse experiences, which European standards could be suggested for it? In answering these questions, the chapter presents the results of the EU-funded project RECAST (Reuse of Confiscated Assets for Social Purposes: Towards Common EU Standards).[2]

The chapter is organised as follows: the current state of the art of asset disposal within the European Union is first reviewed (Section I). Attention is then focused on those Member States that envisage social reuse, so as to present and compare existing legislation and practices (Section II), as well as the potential for adoption of this form of disposal by other Member States (Section III). Suggestions for a future EU policy promoting reuse of confiscated assets for social purposes are finally put forward in the concluding section.

I. The Current State of the Art of Asset Disposal in the EU, with Special Attention to Social Reuse

A. Existing Studies

Very few studies have addressed the issue of asset disposal to date. For example, in 2006, one of the authors of this chapter mapped the legislation and practices in the then 15 Member States, focusing on the three key phases of confiscation proceedings, ie the investigative, judicial and disposal phases. One conclusion was that a key problem is the long duration of the disposal phase,

> also as a consequence of the sometimes inadequate resources devoted to it. While the enforcement of confiscation orders generally encounters few problems when the orders

[2] The project was awarded to the Department of European Studies and International Integration at the University of Palermo by the European Commission, DG HOME under the 2010 ISEC Programme. It was carried out in the period November 2011–November 2014 in co-operation with the Center for the Study of Democracy and the FLARE Network, and with the support of Agenzia nazionale per l'amministrazione e la destinazione dei beni sequestrati e confiscati alla criminalità organizzata and UNICRI. Its aim was to promote the development of common European standards on the reuse of confiscated assets for social purposes.

> relate to money ... the enforcement of orders relative to other types of assets like real and personal property is more problematic. In most cases these assets are sold at public auction, where the prices realised are usually very low. It may also happen that criminals are able to buy their assets back. The sale procedure is sometimes overly complex and lengthy, especially when real property is being disposed of. The provisions on the sale of confiscated assets work better than those on their use for social purposes foreseen in a number of countries. The latter provisions are either rarely applied (Belgium and Luxembourg), or when they are applied, the procedure is excessively complex and time-consuming, and the assets are not always in the best condition when given to the recipients.[3]

In 2009, a study commissioned by the European Commission's Directorate-General Justice, Freedom and Security reviewed investigative, judicial and disposal phases of criminal asset recovery in the EU and identified good practices and obstacles. It concluded that

> management and disposal of assets generally suffer from a lack of capability and capacity especially in relation to: real estate; movable high value goods; vehicles of all kinds where depreciation and storage is an issue; and operating companies that are ongoing.[4]

Disposal issues were addressed in 2012 in a study commissioned by the European Commission, Directorate General Home Affairs whose aim was to assist the European Commission by suggesting policy options for EU-level intervention. One of the proposed policy options (No 21) refers to social reuse, and states that 'to promote social reuse in other Member States, the EU could require Member States to establish mechanisms allowing confiscated assets, in appropriate cases, to be returned to deprived and victimised communities through social reuse schemes'.[5] Another 2012 study, carried out by the Basel Institute on Governance for the European Parliament, analysed in-depth the legal framework on asset recovery, both at the EU level and at the level of six selected Member States (Bulgaria, Germany, Italy, France, Spain and the UK), with a view to assessing the feasibility of establishing EU regulation on the use of confiscated assets for civil society and in particular for social purposes. The study also analysed the advantages of social reuse, and concluded that 'there is a clear need for a coherent European approach'.[6]

[3] B Vettori, *Tough on Criminal Wealth. Exploring the Practice of Proceeds from Crime Confiscation in the EU* (Dordrecht, Springer, 2006) 115–16.

[4] Matrix Insight, 'Assessing the Effectiveness of EU Member States' Practices in the Identification, Tracing, Freezing and Confiscation of Criminal Assets—Final Report' (Brussels, European Commission, 2009) 84.

[5] Rand Europe, 'Study for an Impact Assessment on a Proposal for a New Legal Framework on the Confiscation and Recovery of Criminal Assets—Technical Report' (Brussels, European Commission, 2012) 74.

[6] European Parliament, Directorate General For Internal Policies, Policy Department C: Citizens' Rights and Constitutional Affairs, Civil Liberties, Justice and Home Affairs, 'The Need for New EU Legislation Allowing the Assets Confiscated from Criminal Organisations to be Used for Civil Society and in Particular for Social Purposes' (Brussels, European Parliament, 2012) 54.

B. EU Developments

Scant attention has been paid so far to the disposal phase not only by the research community, but also by policy makers. A message in this direction was recently sent by the EU institutions, which, over the past five years, have shown increasing interest towards the reuse of confiscated assets for social purposes. This is highlighted in several documents:

— Directive 2014/42/EU of the European Parliament and of the Council of 3 April 2014 on the freezing and confiscation of proceeds of crime in the European Union[7] invites Member States to 'consider taking measures allowing confiscated property to be used for public interest or social purposes'. It also specifies that such measures may, inter alia, entail earmarking property for law enforcement and crime prevention projects, as well as for other projects of public interest and social utility.

— In the European Parliament Resolution of 25 October 2011 on organised crime in the European Union,[8] the Parliament highlights that

> the re-use of confiscated assets for social purposes fosters a positive attitude to strategies aimed at tackling organised crime, since confiscating an asset is no longer regarded solely as a means of depriving a criminal organisation of resources but is doubly constructive in that it both helps to prevent organised crime and has the effect of boosting economic and social development

and urges the Commission

> to accept and support the urgent need for European legislation on the reuse of crime proceeds for social purposes ... so that the capital of criminal organisations or their associates can be reinjected into legal, clean, transparent and virtuous economic circuits.

— The 2010 Justice and Home Affairs Council Conclusions on confiscation and asset recovery[9] stresse that attention should be focused on all phases of the confiscation procedure and recommend the adoption of measures aimed to ensure the preservation of assets during the confiscation process and their reuse.

— The Communication from the Commission to the European Parliament and the Council of 22 November 2010[10] has announced best practices guidance on the topic. It requests Member States to make by 2014

[7] Directive 2014/42/EU of the European Parliament and of the Council of 3 April 2014 on the freezing and confiscation of instrumentalities and proceeds of crime in the European Union [2014] OJ L127/39.

[8] European Parliament Resolution of 25 October 2011 on organised crime in the European Union (2010/2309(INI)) [2013] OJ C131E/08.

[9] Justice and Home Affairs Council Conclusions on confiscation and asset recovery [2010] 7769/3/10 REV 3.

[10] Commission to the European Parliament and the Council of 22 November 2010, 'The EU Internal Security Strategy in Action: Five Steps Towards a More Secure Europe' (Communication) COM (2010) 673 final.

the necessary institutional arrangements, for example by creating asset management offices, to ensure that frozen assets do not lose their value before they are eventually confiscated. In parallel, the Commission will in 2013 provide best practice guidance on how to prevent criminal groups from reacquiring confiscated assets.

— In the 2010 Stockholm Programme—An open and secure Europe serving and protecting citizens,[11] the European Council calls upon the Member States and the Commission, inter alia, 'to identify assets of criminals more effectively and seize them and, whenever possible, consider re-using them wherever they are found in the EU common space'.
— The Communication from the Commission to the European Parliament and the Council of 20 November 2008[12] recognises that 'different practices exist in the Member States with regard to the destination of the assets confiscated and recovered'. The document adds that 'it is desirable to promote practices which have proven to be effective at national level', including some forms of institutional and social reuse expressly mentioned in the document, such as those existing in the UK and in Italy.

II. Mapping and Comparing Current Social Reuse Experiences in the EU

A. Social Reuse in the EU at a Glance

From a preliminary mapping of national legislation on asset disposal in the Member States, carried out in the context of project RECAST,[13] it emerged that sale is the main disposal option in practically all Member States. An interesting finding, however, was that about two-thirds of Member States envisage, though almost never as first choice, different forms of reuse of the assets/proceeds, via their transfer to state/local institutions ('institutional reuse', via incentivisation schemes) or to society/non-government organisations (NGOs) ('social reuse').

The peculiarity of the reuse of confiscated assets for social purposes is the visibility of confiscated assets among citizens that it promotes. Broadly speaking, even

[11] The Stockholm Programme—An open and secure Europe serving and protecting citizens [2010] OJ C115/01.

[12] Communication from the Commission to the European Parliament and the Council of 20 November 2008, 'Proceeds of Organised Crime: Ensuring that "Crime Does not Pay"' (Communication) COM (2008) 766 final.

[13] The main tool used to gather relevant information was a questionnaire jointly developed by the University of Palermo and the Centre for the Study of Democracy, and administered to one (or more) national expert in each Member State; this information was then complemented with secondary data. All Member States except Latvia replied.

in the context of traditional forms of reuse, assets are used for public purposes (since they become part of the state budget); however, they are mixed up with other public resources, so that citizens cannot link their subsequent public/social reuse to the original nature of their confiscated assets. Social reuse makes this link explicit: what stems from crime is openly given back to society and is used in accordance with community needs. By doing so, it can be seen not only as a social rebalance mechanism (what was previously illicit becomes a benefit to the community), but also as a tool to tangibly spread the message 'crime does not pay'. Citizens who are well aware of this message and who can concretely see how the administration of justice can respond to the needs of their communities will tend to value legality over illegality, be more likely to trust the state, report suspicious activities/behaviours and raise law-abiding children; in short, they will be the most effective barrier to crime. For all these reasons, social reuse can be seen as a disposal mechanism that may incentivise local communities to take a stance against (organised) crime, thus activating a 'social fight' against it.

Looking now at the key social reuse experiences within the EU—which are in Belgium, France, Hungary, Italy, Luxembourg, Scotland (within the UK) and Spain—before analysing them in detail, one can preliminarily note that these experiences fit one of the following two models: the direct reuse of confiscated assets for social purposes, as is the case in Italy, Belgium (Flemish Region) and Hungary (herein referred to as direct social reuse); or the reuse of the proceeds of crime (or from the sale of confiscated assets) via specialised funds that use them either (i) in crime prevention projects, for the immediate benefit of society, or (ii) in incentivisation schemes for entities in charge of crime fighting, so that these entities may have a further incentive to keep on fighting crime, ultimately, even if not directly, in the interests of society. Under this mechanism, therefore, confiscated assets are not straightforwardly passed on to society (rather, the proceeds originating from their sale are) and the proceeds may not always be reused for the immediate, but sometimes mediate (via incentivisation schemes), interests of society. For these reasons, this model, which is in place in France, Spain,[14] Luxembourg and Scotland, is herein referred to as indirect social reuse. These experiences are discussed and compared in more detail below.

B. Key Social Reuse Experiences in the EU

(i) *Belgium: The 'Social Management'* (Sociaal Beheer) *of Real Estate in the Flemish Region*

In Belgium, social reuse for real estate is envisaged in the Flemish Region only. The Decree containing the Flemish Housing Code (Décret contenant le Code

[14] The Spanish model envisages both direct and indirect social reuse. In practice, the second option is predominantly used, and for this reason Spain is herein classified in the related category.

flamand du Logement) of 15 July 1997, at Article 90, provides for the right of the municipalities to temporarily manage unsuitable, uninhabitable or abandoned property of negligent owners on the condition that the property will be restored or renovated and used for social housing for a certain period of time. The owner keeps his rights over the property, but the municipality acquires the right to temporarily manage the buildings for nine years or longer, depending on the time needed to recoup the investments made to improve the real estate and to rent them to people in need. The idea of applying this regime to confiscated real estate came about after the Federal Public Service of Finance had confiscated some derelict properties with illegal occupants and did not know how to handle them. Social management appeared as a win–win option: on the one side, it provided the local authorities with a chance to invest in the properties, recouping their investment via rents while improving the housing problem; and on the other side, the federal government benefited by stopping further deterioration of the real estate and ultimately regaining it renovated and free of illegal occupants, whilst bearing no management costs.

A decision by the Municipal Council starts proceedings for social management. The municipality undertakes the restoration/renovation works and the property is then rented in accordance with social housing rates. The municipality itself does not deal with the renting of the properties—the management is transferred to one of the providers of social housing (ie social housing companies, the Flemish Housing Fund for Large Families, social housing ('tenants') associations, social rental agencies and public centres for social welfare). Although the Decree specifically lists these eligible providers, it does not provide for a specific procedure of selection.

(ii) France: Social Reuse of Proceeds in the Fund Managed by MILDT (Mission interministérielle de lutte contre la drogue et la toxicomanie)

The Interministerial Mission in the Fight against Drugs and Drug Addiction was established in 1982. It reports to the Prime Minister and its mandate is the organisation and co-ordination of national activities regarding the fight against drugs and drug addiction (particularly in three key areas: monitoring, research and prevention of drug use; treatment and reintegration of drug users; and training for those involved in the fight against drugs). MILDT manages the fund (the so-called 'Fonds de concours') established by Decree No 322 of 17 March 1995 to collect the proceeds of confiscated assets in connection with drug trafficking.

The procedure is as follows: a final confiscation order, including a specific statement that certain movable or immovable assets were confiscated in relation to drug crimes, is forwarded to MILDT. AGRASC (Agence de gestion et de recouvrement des avoirs saisis et confisqués)[15] manages the auction sale of the assets and

[15] AGRASC is a public administrative body under the Ministry of Justice and Ministry of Budget, established by Law No 768 of 9 July 2010. It is vested with various tasks designed to improve seizure, management and confiscation; it also plays a key role in the disposal of confiscated assets, since it is tasked with the sale or destruction of all assets that AGRASC previously managed.

the related proceeds are transferred from AGRASC's bank account to MILDT's. MILDT waits until the end of each year for the presentation of the 'Fonds de concours' annual budget. At the same time, the several public institutions involved in the repartition of the proceeds submit their projects. Proceeds are distributed as follows: 60 per cent to the Ministry of Internal Affairs; 20 per cent to the Ministry of Justice; 10 per cent to the Ministry of Economic Affairs and Finances; and 10 per cent to MILDT. MILDT distributes its share to several entities (including the Ministry of Social Affairs, Ministry of Health, Ministry of Agriculture and Ministry of Education), according to their needs and to the projects submitted.

While the quotas assigned to the other ministries can be regarded as an incentivisation scheme, and are largely used to buy equipment to fight drug trafficking, MILDT's 10 per cent quota is used directly for social purposes. A large part of it is forwarded to the Ministry of Social Affairs and the Ministry of Health for the promotion of social and medical campaigns against drug abuse, as well as other forms of addiction. The Ministry of Superior Education and Research and the Ministry of National Education usually use such proceeds for prevention campaigns in universities and schools, and the Ministry of Agriculture uses the proceeds for prevention strategies in the workplace.

MILDT has the exclusive power to select the projects that should be financed by the 'Fonds de concours'.

(iii) Hungary: Offering Personal Assets (Mainly Counterfeited) for Charity Purposes

Confiscated goods may be offered for charity purposes, based on Act XIII of 2000 and on Government Decree No 65/2000. These pieces of legislation have set in place a procedure for offering these goods to charity purposes, referred to as 'use in public interest'. It applies to personal assets only, and cannot cover either vehicles or real estate. In accordance with Article 2 of Act XIII, goods suitable for social reuse must fulfil one of the following purposes: nutrition, clothing, sleeping gear and fixtures, grooming/hygiene, cleaning, washing, education or culture. Also, assets falling into one of the following categories can be socially reused: provisional housing, house maintenance, home equipment, household appliances and tools, kitchen equipment and utensils, communications equipment, toys, leisure sport. In practice, 98 per cent of all goods offered for charity purposes are counterfeit commodities (clothing, shoes or toys). The recipients (end users) of such assets are people in need (individuals only, not public institutions or private organisations), in amounts appropriate to, and not exceeding, their needs. The law also clearly defines the time-frame of the procedure (about two months).

The Charity Council is the body in charge of initiating and co-ordinating these proceedings. The procedure starts either with a final confiscation order issued within criminal proceedings or with a confiscation decision for infringement by the National Tax and Customs Administration within tax and excise proceedings. The goods are transferred to the management offices of the courts territorially competent to take custody of them; these offices assess whether social reuse is possible and, if so, they inform and offer them to the Charity Council. The members of the Charity Council review the offers on a monthly basis and decide whether to accept them against certain criteria, such as if the goods can fulfil any actual needs, as well as feasibility and cost-effectiveness. All members of the Charity Council are highly experienced charity organisations with proven logistics capabilities and a wide network of local offices that collect requests for donations, so at any given time they have good knowledge of local needs. Once the Charity Council accepts an offer, a charity organisation is assigned to take care of the distribution to end users.

As the vast majority of goods offered for social reuse are counterfeit commodities (clothing, shoes, etc), distribution cannot be initiated before the brand owner consents to the procedure. Should the brand owner not consent, the Charity Council could initiate judicial proceedings before the competent court.

(iv) Italy: Social Reuse of Assets Confiscated from Organised Crime

In Italy, Law No 109/1996 was adopted to enable the use for social purposes of assets confiscated from the mafia (in preventative proceedings and in certain criminal proceedings instituted under Article 12-sexies of Law No 356/1992). Relevant regulations are now contained in legislative Decree No 159/2011 (antimafia code), and subsequent amendments.

The key institution involved in the decision-making process is ANBSC (Agenzia nazionale per l'amministrazione e la destinazione dei beni sequestrati e confiscati alla criminalità organizzata),[16] which is competent, from the first degree confiscation order, for asset management and disposal. Notification is made to ANSBC by the court of the final confiscation order. The decision related to the social reuse of assets must be adopted by ANSBC's Executive Committee within 90 days from the notification of the confiscation order (or within 180 days in more complex cases).

Assets suitable for social reuse are immovable assets, movable (and registered) ones and companies. Regarding immovable assets, within six months from the adoption of the final confiscation order, lists of real estate available for social reuse are published by ANBSC on its website, to make potential beneficiaries aware and enable them to put forward applications. Real estate may be: (i) used by the state for justice/public order purposes, or to respond to other governmental or public needs related to the institutional activities carried out by state entities, fiscal entities, universities or cultural institutions; (ii) used for economic purposes by ANBSC, with the approval of the Minister of the Interior; or (iii) transferred for institutional purposes or social reuse to local entities (the municipality where they are located, or the related province/region). The local entities must keep and regularly update the list of assets transferred to them, which shall be made public.

[16] ANBSC was established by Law Decree No 4 of 4 February 2010. It is tasked with, amongst other things, the management and disposal of assets confiscated from organised crime.

They can directly manage the asset or assign it for free to social communities or associations (eg youth centres, charities or therapeutic communities and rehabilitation centres), based on an agreement setting out the duration, modalities of reuse and related monitoring procedures, renewal modalities, etc. Assets that are not allocated may be used by local authorities for profit-making purposes, but the income must be reused for social purposes. If, within one year, the local body has failed to assign an asset, ANSBC shall revoke the transfer and appoint a commissioner with substitutive powers.

Regarding social reuse of companies, these can be rented out by ANBSC to worker co-operatives (for free); alternatively, they can be rented to public or private enterprises (upon payment of a rental fee), sold or liquidated. Movable assets (and also registered ones) can be used by ANBSC in institutional activities or can be assigned to other state bodies, local entities or charities.

Assets are assigned by ANSBC to local entities (and by the local entities to social communities or associations) based on their needs and on the projects of reuse they submit. Even if the assignment decision is largely discretional, equality of treatment must be assured.

(v) Luxembourg: Fonds de lutte contre certaines formes de criminalité

The Law of 17 March 1992 (Article 5) set up the so-called 'Fonds de lutte contre le trafic de stupéfiants' ('Fund to fight against drug trafficking'). Its mission is to foster the development, co-ordination and implementation of instruments to fight drug trafficking, drug addiction, and all their direct and indirect effects. The Fund is made up of all real and personal property, divided and undivided, confiscated under section 8–2 of the Act of 19 February 1973 on the sale of medicinal substances and the fight against drug abuse, as well as under Article 5, paragraph 4 of the 1988 United Nations Convention against Illicit Traffic in Narcotic Drugs and Psychotropic Substances. Following the enactment of the law of 27 October 2010, Article 5 has been modified so as to cover other crimes, such as money laundering and other serious crimes, whose proceeds are therefore attributed to the Fund as well. Due to this amendment, the Fund has been renamed as 'Fonds de lutte contre certaines formes de criminalité' ('Fund to fight against certain forms of criminality').

The Fund is therefore the government institution that receives confiscated proceeds from drug trafficking and money laundering, and it supports programmes in fighting 'certain forms of criminality'. Its beneficiaries include international organisations, national institutions and NGOs. Since it was set up in 1993, the Fund has funded projects worth over €36 million.[17] In 2014, its beneficiaries included, for example: (i) UNODC (for projects in Africa and Asia); (ii) the national public sector, ie the police and justice areas, with projects that supported

[17] See Grand Duche de Luxembourg, Fonds de lutte contre certaines formes de criminalité, 'Rapport d'activité 2014' (Luxembourg, April 2015) 2.

the public prosecutor offices and the Police Grand-Ducale (with training and new equipment to fight drug trafficking), and the health and youth sectors, with, for example, a project with the Health Ministry to build a drug treatment centre and to run a prevention project within schools; (iii) the finance sector, with a training project on money laundering; and (iv) NGOs and other organisations, such as Caritas, with a project for the treatment and rehabilitation of drug addicts in Bangladesh, and the Pompidou Group (Council of Europe), with a project for drug prevention and treatment in the prisons of Moldavia, Ukraine, Romania and the Balkans.[18] The Fund constantly monitors the financed projects and will terminate them in case of anomalies or insufficient results.

(vi) Scotland: Social Reuse via the 'CashBack for Communities' Programme

In Scotland, recovered criminal assets are invested in the 'CashBack for Communities' programme.

The CashBack for Communities programme is a Scottish government programme that takes the ill-gotten gains of crime, recovered through the Proceeds of Crime Act 2002 (POCA), and invests them in community programmes, facilities and activities largely, but not exclusively, for young people at risk of turning to crime and anti-social behaviour as a way of life. Since its launch in 2007, the vast majority of POCA receipts have been allocated by the government to this programme (some funding has been provided to Police Scotland and to the Crown Office for the specific purpose of maximising POCA receipts), subject to a cap on recoveries of £30 million in any one year. Over £74 million recovered from proceeds of crime has so far been invested in sporting, cultural, educational and mentoring activities for young people and their communities.

The programme is intended to be: (i) positive (healthy, fun, active, engaging); (ii) open to all (accessible, well advertised, free of charge, of interest to all, irrespective of age, gender, ethnicity, etc); (iii) developmental (it aims at changing behaviours and attitudes, and at developing skills); and (iv) sustainable.

The procedure is as follows: a confiscation order is placed on an individual or a company by the Scottish Courts Service (SCS); monetary payments of orders are made to the SCS; the SCS transfers monies to the Scottish government; the Scottish government utilises the money to fund partner organisations and associations to deliver programmes of activities or to construct community sports facilities over three-year programme blocks of the CashBack for Communities programme. Payments to partner organisations are made by grant. Applicants for CashBack for Communities funding range from large national associations and organisations to small individual third-sector organisations. All funding applications must deliver activity that aligns to the aims of the programme. Also, they are subject to standard financial and organisational due diligence checking and monitoring. CashBack for Communities can provide additional discretionary

[18] ibid 5–11.

funding to build delivery capacity, if reasonably necessary, within partner organisations.

The current list of successful project partners for the CashBack for Communities programme through to the end of 2016/17 are: Scottish Football Association, Scottish Rugby Union, Scottish Sports Futures, Basketball Scotland, Princes Trust Scotland, Creative Scotland, Youth Scotland, Youth Link Scotland, Glasgow Clyde College, Sportscotland, Street Soccer Scotland, Action for Children, Celtic Foundation and Ocean Youth Trust.

All individual CashBack projects and the overall programme are subject to evaluation for the impact and diverse range of outcomes that are being delivered. Evaluation reports of individual initiatives are on the CashBack website.[19] An independent external evaluation of the programme was published in June 2014:[20] it shows how CashBack is changing individual young people's lives for the better and that significant impact is being made on participation, diversion and progression pathways and engagement outcomes for young people and communities across Scotland. Also, the programme is well advertised and its activities attract comprehensive regional press coverage across Scotland.

(vii) Spain: Fondo de bienes decomisados por tráfico de drogas y otros delitos relacionados

The disposal of proceeds from drug trafficking is laid out by Law No 17 of 29 May 2003. This statute—which further develops rules originally contained in Law No 36 of 1995 (the so-called Ley del Fondo)—has established a fund financed out of the assets confiscated in drug trafficking and related offences, and to be used: (i) to finance programmes for drug addiction prevention, assistance to drug addicts, and their social and occupational rehabilitation; (ii) to promote and improve measures to prevent, investigate, prosecute and repress drug-related crimes; and (iii) to promote international co-operation on such matters. That said, any type of asset confiscated in relation to the above crimes can be disposed of socially: movable and immovable assets, as well as companies.

The fund's beneficiaries are: law enforcement agencies charged with counter-narcotics activities; NGOs and non-profit organisations working in the substance abuse field; regional and local governments and authorities; the Government Delegation for the National Plan on Drugs (Delegación del Gobierno para el Plan Nacional sobre Drogas, DGPNSD); and international organisations and institutions.

DGPNSD—which is a body under the Ministry of Health, Social Services and Equality—is in charge of this social reuse mechanism. When the final confiscation order is adopted, notification is made to DGPNSD, together with a list of

[19] See www.cashbackforcommunities.org/impact.

[20] ODS Consulting, 'National Evaluation of the CashBack for Communities Programme (April 2012–March 2014), Final Report' (ODS, May 2014).

the assets. The key entity within DGPNSD tasked with the management of the fund is the Mesa de Coordinación de Adjudicaciones (Coordinating Bureau for Allocation). Its tasks include the identification of the assets to be allocated to the fund and the adoption of decisions regarding their destination to beneficiaries.[21] Unless the assets have to be abandoned (whether due to deterioration or high management costs) or are definitively assigned to the law enforcement agencies authorised by the court to temporarily use them pending legal proceedings, two key options are foreseen for their social reuse: (i) sale, with the profits from the sale flowing to the fund (indirect social reuse); or (ii) assignment for free to potential beneficiaries (direct social reuse), upon their request. In practice, most assets are sold rather than directly assigned.

In the period 1996–2014, apart from money (about €230 million), the fund gathered 31,945 assets, as follows:[22] 46 per cent of the assets were vehicles (cars, trucks, vans, motorcycles, etc); 2 per cent was real estate (houses, flats, offices, parking, etc); 8 per cent were boats (fishing and sports boats, sailboats, etc); 6 per cent was jewellery (watches, gold ornaments, silver, precious stones etc); and 38 per cent were objects (ie assets not falling under any of the above categories, such as hardware, appliances, clothing, audiovisual equipment, telephones and furniture).

During the same period, 26,394 assets were disposed of, as follows: 53 per cent were abandoned, 7 per cent were finally awarded to law enforcement agencies (mostly vehicles), 16 per cent were sold and 8 per cent were assigned for free.

C. Comparing Social Reuse Experiences in the EU

The above-mentioned social reuse experiences vary significantly in terms of beneficiaries, modalities and asset types involved. Comparing them, one may note that the beneficiaries of social reuse schemes vary widely from country to country. They include: international organisations and institutions (Luxembourg, Spain), national institutions (France, Italy, Luxembourg, Spain), local entities (Belgium, Italy, Spain), charities, civil society organisations, associations and co-operatives (Belgium, Italy, Hungary, Luxembourg, Spain, Scotland).

As regards the procedure for the allocation of assets under the direct reuse model (Italy, Belgium, Hungary), such allocation is decided by the competent authority upon formal request/expression of need by eligible beneficiaries. As regards the procedure for allocation of the proceeds under the indirect reuse model

[21] For more information see www.pnsd.msssi.gob.es/Categoria4/bienes/home.htm.

[22] The statistics presented herein are taken from Delegación del Gobierno para el Plan Nacional sobre Drogas, 'Informe sobre la actividad del fondo procedente de los bienes decomisados por tráfico ilícito de drogas y otros delitos relacionados durante el año 2014, 2015', available at http://www.pnsd.msssi.gob.es/gl/delegacionGobiernoPNSD/fondoBienesDecomisados/InformesFondo/pdf/Memoria__FONDO2014.pdf.

(Luxembourg, France, Spain, Scotland), two approaches can be identified. The first does not envisage any competitive procedure, since the repartitioning of the revenues is ultimately prescribed by law (France). Luxembourg, Scotland and Spain, on the other hand, give more discretionary powers to the bodies managing the funds, and the repartitioning involves a competitive procedure.

The types of confiscated assets suitable for social reuse also differ. In some countries, only movable assets are subject to social reuse (eg Hungary), while in other countries it applies also to companies, lands and real estate (eg Italy, Spain). In some countries, social reuse is possible only in relation to the proceeds from certain offences (typically drug trafficking, such as Spain and France), while other countries (eg Luxembourg, Italy) envisage it in relation to all (serious) crimes. Finally, social reuse typically applies to the entire territory, with the exception of Belgium, where it is envisaged in the Dutch/Flemish Region only.

D. Mapping Practices: Key Problems Affecting Social Reuse of Confiscated Assets in the EU

Looking at existing practices on social reuse, a series of problems have been reported. They can be grouped as follows: (i) problems related to the legal framework; (ii) asset-related problems; (iii) problems related to implementing institutions and procedures; (iv) beneficiary-related problems; and (v) problems in terms of public information and policy evaluation.

(i) Problems Related to the Legal Framework

— Lack of interest in assets available for social reuse by potential beneficiaries: in Belgium, most of the social housing providers are not interested in the social management scheme, as it only allows for temporary management and sub-renting. In Italy, some articles of the antimafia code discourage potential beneficiaries from applying for the assets (eg Article 46, which—should the assets be given back to their owner—requires beneficiaries to pay back a sum of money equivalent to their value).

— Legal limitations in terms of potential beneficiaries: in Hungary, the law allows only for individuals to be recipients of the social reuse regime, thus reducing the eligible target groups (eg schools or hospitals cannot benefit from it).

(ii) Asset-Related Problems

— Third parties' claims in relation to properties under joint ownership and other asset-related obstacles: to provide an example, in Belgium, in 2011, the City of Antwerp took a property under the social management scheme and discovered that a share of it was forfeited to the Federal Public Service of

Finance. One of the landlords claimed that he was still in possession of his share, which resulted in legal disputes between him and the Federal Public Service of Finance, and an appeal against the social management procedure. The same happens in Italy, where assets may also be of too little value, in poor condition, subject to third party claims, including mortgages (which occur with nearly half of all immovable assets), or subject to parallel proceedings; also, there are assets confiscated pro quota, as well as obstacles due to technical and logistical features of the assets (eg difficult access to an estate, unsafe buildings).

— Problems related to the sale of certain assets feeding the indirect social reuse system: in France, AGRASC is in charge of the sale of the assets confiscated in drug-related cases, the proceeds of which pass to the fund managed by MILDT. While movable assets are sold quickly, the sale of immovables is more difficult. In one case, the convicted owner, in reaction to the confiscation, vandalised his property.
— Limitations, in daily practice, to the types of assets suitable for social reuse: in Hungary, the types of confiscated goods suitable for social reuse are defined by law, and also include goods with auxiliary scopes of use (eg provisional housing, house maintenance, home equipment, household appliances and tools). In practice, the offerings to the Charity Council mainly include clothing and shoes, since the other suitable goods are usually of higher value and public sale is preferred.

(iii) Problems Related to Implementing Institutions and Procedures

— Shortage of human resources: Italy and France, where ANBCS and AGRASC were established as the centralised bodies dealing with asset utilisation, report that the agencies are currently suffering from understaffing, which is also due to difficulties in finding competent experts. Hungary also reports a shortage of human resources due to budgetary constraints.
— Uncertainties at the court level on how to ascribe proceeds of crime to dedicated funds: for many years, the fund in France managed by MILDT did not receive all of the confiscated proceeds of crime (only very limited amounts of money were allocated to it) because it was almost unknown to the legal practitioners. The situation has improved since 2008.[23]
— Limited practical application: in Belgium, the procedure has not been widely applied so far. It is, however, expected that the social management procedures regarding forfeited properties will run more smoothly compared to the ones

[23] In order to overcome this problem, for example, a dispatch was circulated on 4 August 2008 asking the courts to establish an annual list of goods confiscated in cases of narcotics and to verify that payments to the fund of competition were correctly made. This initiative contributed to an increase in the fund of more than 400% compared to the previous year.

against private owners, since the Federal Public Service of Finance is a public institution (there should be fewer obstructions against the procedures).

— Overly complex, costly, not always transparent procedures: in Italy, procedures are excessively complex and sometimes lack transparency; a wider direct involvement of associations in the assignment of assets, without the filter of the local authorities, would be advisable.
— Lengthy duration of the social reuse procedure: in Hungary, a clear timetable is set. In practice, however, this timetable is respected only when dealing with original products (2 per cent of all cases), while with counterfeit goods (the remaining 98 per cent) it is hard to keep to the deadlines, and the duration varies depending on the response of the brand owner, the capacity of the contracted de-branding company and the amount of goods. Sometimes brand owners do not respond within the prescribed deadline because there are delays in the authorities' informing them about the current status of the assets.
— Lengthy duration of confiscation proceedings and negative impact on social reuse: in Hungary, judicial proceedings take three years on average, and sometimes up to six years; as a result, some 20 per cent of seized goods are not suitable for social reuse purposes due to deteriorated quality. This precludes the reuse of food as well.
— Intellectual property rights issues and related costs: in Hungary, the removal of brands is expensive and in many cases unfeasible. Most of the brand owners refuse to co-operate, or do not respond within the deadline. This also narrows the range of goods that can be utilised.

(iv) *Beneficiary-Related Problems*

— Lack of economic and technical capacity on the side of beneficiaries: in Italy, beneficiaries are commonly local authorities that seldom have enough economic resources to take on management. Also, most of them lack any dedicated office for managing confiscated assets. As a consequence of this, in many cases local authorities submit reuse projects that are impracticable or not feasible.

(v) *Problems in Terms of Public Information and Policy Evaluation*

— Lack of any systematic publicity about the social reuse scheme: for example, in Hungary, even if some statistics are produced, there is no systematic mechanism in place to inform the general public of them.
— Poor quality of information regarding assets available for social reuse: in Italy, notwithstanding legal provisions, most local entities do not publish the list of assets they have been assigned.
— Lack of any systematic policy evaluation of the outcomes of the social management regime: apart from some evaluation of the direct results of individual

social reuse projects—via some monitoring/reporting activities (Hungary, Italy, Luxembourg)—the overall outputs and outcomes of the social reuse scheme are not systematically assessed, also due to limited experience and recent implementation (Belgium). In most cases, only limited statistics are produced (eg Spain). In France, a purely formal financial, ex post, check of the use of the proceeds is performed.

E. Mapping Best Practices on Social Reuse of Confiscated Assets in the EU

Looking at existing practices on social reuse, these can be grouped as follows: (i) best practices preventing assets' deterioration; (ii) best practices empowering beneficiaries and institutions; (iii) best practices preventing criminals from buying the assets back; and (iv) best practices in terms of public information and policy evaluation.

(i) Best Practices Preventing Assets' Deterioration

— Provisionally assigning seized assets to prevent deterioration and to promptly respond to social needs (Italy): in Italy, the Rome Tribunal provisionally assigns to social reuse seized/provisionally confiscated assets, based on a temporary loan-for-use agreement. This practice has been developed on the basis of regulations making it possible to assign seized movable assets (eg cars) to the police and other public bodies. The Rome Tribunal extended the ratio behind these provisions—which aims at overcoming depreciation, vandalism or management costs—to real estate. This is in order to immediately use the assets, which will eventually be given back (not vandalised or depreciated, etc) to the defendant at the end of the proceeding.

(ii) Best Practices Empowering Beneficiaries and Institutions

— Enhancing beneficiaries' capability to implement social reuse projects (Scotland): in Scotland, the individual partner organisations are provided with assistance from the CashBack for Communities programme on project accountability, output outcomes monitoring and reporting, evaluation and capacity to deliver. This is outsourced to an external delivery partner, which puts in place arrangements to support project partners to provide the core functions (eg management, finance, administration, communications and evaluation) necessary to implement the programme.

— Setting up a mechanism linking institutions and acknowledged charity organisations (Hungary): the strong point of the Hungarian system is the link, via the Charity Council, between government and acknowledged charity organisations. This affirms the credibility of the model, and ensures co-operation from local partners (which provide for better needs assessment and more effective distribution of the goods) and brand owners (that are increasingly consenting to the distribution of counterfeit goods carrying their trademarks without their prior removal).

- External funding to support social reuse: in Hungary, charity organisations must bear all costs related to the utilisation of the goods. However, the Ministry of Human Resources provides financial support through grants amounting to one-third of all costs. The other two-thirds are covered through the organisations' own resources, fundraising, volunteer work, grants or in-kind contributions from local government.

(iii) Best Practices Preventing Criminals from Buying Back the Assets

- Providing for a disposal monitoring, to prevent criminals from buying back their assets (Italy): in Italy, Article 48, paragraph 15 of the Anti-Mafia Code envisages that when, based on reports by citizens or information held at Prefetture (the prefecture), it emerges that confiscated assets have been reacquired by the criminal, then the act that assigned the assets is revoked. An interesting revocation case happened in the Municipality of Formia, where the former mayor, upon having received a confiscated estate, falsely declared that the mobster's wife was indigent, and allowed her to continue living there.
- In relation to confiscated companies, identifying a strict list of prerequisites that applicants must meet (Spain): in Spain, in the so-called *Pazo Bayón* case, a confiscation order was pronounced in 2006 and included the Pazo and other buildings, together with a couple of wine-producing companies. The Award Board, to prevent the former owners from being able to buy the property back, set strict requirements for companies interested in submitting a bid, such as: at least four years in vineyard activities; an average annual turnover not lower than €5 million; agreement to respect all workers' rights, to continue the vineyard activities for at least 15 years and to employ over a 15 year period workers who suffered drug addiction; and to devolve at least 5 per cent of the profits for the first 15 years to programmes oriented towards drug addictions. One Galician company presented the best offer and the whole property was sold for €15 million in July 2008. Since then, the company has met all of the obligations.

(iv) Best Practices in Terms of Public Information and Policy Evaluation

- Setting up mechanisms for the evaluation of the social reuse scheme (Scotland): in Scotland, all individual CashBack projects and the overall programme are subject to self- and independent evaluation for the impact and diverse range of outcomes that are being delivered. All evaluation reports are available online.

III. Exploring the Potential for Adoption of Social Reuse of Confiscated Assets by other Member States

In order to assess the potential for adoption of social reuse of confiscated assets by other Member States, the following topics were analysed: (i) level of knowledge about existing social reuse experiences in the EU and public debate about it; (ii) feasibility of adoption of social reuse by the country, taking into consideration the overall benefits it could bring about, as well as the potential obstacles; and (iii) advisability to develop EU standards on this issue, and key principles for future EU regulation.

Data were gathered via a data collection protocol. Of the 20 EU countries not having any, or not having a well-developed, social reuse system in place (unlike the Member States analysed in depth in this chapter), 12 participated in the survey: Austria, Bulgaria, Cyprus, Estonia, Finland, Ireland, Latvia, Lithuania, Netherlands, Poland, Portugal and Sweden.

Regarding the level of knowledge about social reuse experiences in the EU, the majority of the above countries reported the lack of any debate, either because institutions and other stakeholders were not acquainted with the existing experiences (Cyprus, Lithuania, Poland, Portugal, Sweden) or because the current disposal regime is regarded as efficient enough and there is no need to change it (Finland, Latvia). The only exceptions are Estonia, where there is a debate on the overall effectiveness of the current system for management and disposal at the expert level within responsible institutions, which was provoked by the potential social and economic impact of social reuse; the Netherlands, where the Minister of Security and Justice was recently asked to inform the Parliament about the possibilities of setting up a fund to invest part of the confiscated proceeds in supporting police and public prosecutor activities; Bulgaria, where there is a debate on the overall effectiveness of the current system for management and disposal at the expert level within responsible institutions, provoked by the potential social impact of social reuse; and Ireland, where there is still a debate (though not a very active one) on the introduction of social reuse, mainly in the form of media reports, public discussion in the media and parliamentary debate. It has been provoked by the social aspects of social reuse and by its usefulness especially in relation to drug abuse rehabilitation. What is mainly discussed is the direct social reuse of confiscated assets.

Regarding the potential benefits that social reuse could bring about, the following have been reported by respondents from 11 of the above 12 countries: meeting certain social needs (especially via direct social reuse), also considering that the system may help victims get compensation or social treatment, or help socially vulnerable people; making explicit the willingness of the state to combat crime;

greater awareness of asset seizure and confiscation; more effective communication about confiscation ('crime does not pay') to the wider public; making more visible to the public the activity of law enforcement agencies, prosecution offices and courts, thus raising public interest and support in fighting crime; more efficient disposal of confiscated money, since it may promote a better reuse of certain assets that would otherwise not be used and would be damaged if not reused (eg perishable goods, cars, even real estate, especially when associated with serious organised crime);[24] and positive fiscal effects. One of the respondents could hardly see any real benefits, and expressed a concern, ie the risk that such a system could create an unnecessary administrative burden compared to the current situation.

Regarding potential obstacles to the adoption of this mechanism, both economic factors and political and legal factors have been reported. As regards economic factors, Ireland, for example, has recently experienced an economic crisis; allocating monies on a social reuse basis would not allow the proper reallocation of funds in line with that as set out in government policy. In Bulgaria, confiscated assets are often in poor condition, so the state must use additional budgetary expenses to repair them so that they can become usable; the same applies in Latvia and Lithuania. In Estonia, because of their poor condition, assets are often not usable and extra money from the state budget might be needed for their restoration; this could result in them being more burdensome than beneficial. In Portugal, appropriate logistics and public investment might be needed to enable reuse, especially in relation to some goods (real estate, cars, chips or aircrafts); also, in a significant number of cases, the goods are in very poor condition, potentially making it difficult to socially reuse them.

As regards political and legal factors, in Ireland, for example, choosing certain social or other causes to award assets to could cause difficulties in the selection process by giving preference to one cause/beneficiary over another. In Bulgaria, there are legislative restrictions on the implementation of budgetary resources (legislation on state aids, budget, control, etc). In the Netherlands, the current system is proceeds based, so it is not compatible with certain social reuse regimes; secondly, budgetary rules prescribe that confiscated assets go to the Ministry of Finance. In Cyprus, the confiscation system is proceeds based and confiscated

[24] This was also noted by the Belgian respondent when commenting on the Flemish social reuse experience. In his opinion, social reuse is an option preferable to sale for real estate in unattractive areas: in Belgium, many of the confiscated properties are located in 'problematic', and therefore unattractive, areas. Hence, sale to the general public proves difficult and often results in property going back in the hands of organised crime. In this regard, social management seems to be an alternative that prevents confiscated properties from going back to organised crime via sale while, at the same time, still providing value for money. It also seems to be an option preferable to sale for low-value real estate: in Belgium, much of the confiscated real estate has a very low value, because of its poor condition. Handing such assets over to the local authorities, the Patrimonial Services can reduce the operational costs for their management, and get the real estate back renovated and with a higher value at the end of the procedure. At the same time, municipalities can address the need for more affordable housing.

proceeds go to the state budget or are returned to victims. Regarding Finland, in the current system, fines or confiscated property are not earmarked for any specific purpose, and social reuse could be poorly compatible with the Constitution, according to which the Parliament decides on the state budget.

Regarding the overall feasibility of introducing social reuse in their countries, respondents from seven (Ireland, Netherlands, Latvia, Austria, Sweden, Finland, Poland) out of the 12 countries think that, overall, adoption of this form of disposal is currently not feasible; those from the remaining five (Bulgaria, Cyprus, Lithuania, Portugal, Estonia) countries think the opposite.

All but one of the respondents highlighted that, if one had to make a choice, the social reuse model that would best fit the needs of other countries is the indirect reuse model (reuse of proceeds), rather than the direct reuse of the assets. This is attributed to a variety of reasons: for example, not all assets can be directly reused (eg Rolex watch), and should therefore be sold and the related proceeds used (Ireland); and proceeds are preferable because of flexibility and simplicity of use (Estonia, Poland, Portugal). A confiscated house could in some cases be of little interest; for example, conventional usage might not meet expectations/needs. In most cases, the reuse of proceeds is likely to be simpler, and will better satisfy the diverse and general needs of citizens or institutions. It also overcomes problems typically associated with the reuse of assets. Furthermore, the reuse of the proceeds of confiscated assets through specialised programmes is regarded as more effective and expedient (Lithuania). Finally, it can be more easily incorporated in value-based confiscation systems as well (Cyprus).

The Bulgarian respondent advocated a mixed approach, stating that it is appropriate to apply both models of social reuse simultaneously, together with the possibility of choosing one or the other depending on the specific type, conditions and intended purpose of the asset, as well as in accordance with all the other factors that determine the presence or lack of interest towards its reuse.

Regarding the advisability of having EU standards on the social reuse of confiscated assets, one-third of the respondents (Austria, Finland, Ireland, Netherlands) believe that EU regulation would not be advisable. It was noted, for example, by the Irish respondent that it is questionable if such an approach is in line with thinking on the doctrines of subsidiarity; each country, in his opinion, should rather be allowed to make its own decision on how to deal with confiscated assets. The Dutch expert also thinks that decisions on how to dispose of confiscated assets should stay at the discretion of national governments.

The other two-thirds of the respondents (Bulgaria, Cyprus, Estonia, Latvia, Lithuania, Poland, Portugal, Sweden) believe, instead, that EU regulation would be advisable. This would be a step forward to the common aspiration of the unification of community law and strengthen the message of the social fight against organised crime (Bulgaria). Such regulations would force Member States to act more quickly and unanimously in this way (Lithuania), and would probably be the only way social reuse might be adopted within certain countries (Sweden).

This would also be advisable because it would not conflict directly with the system of law of each Member State (Portugal).

Conclusion: What EU Standards on Social Reuse of Confiscated Assets?

Provided that Member States are guaranteed flexibility—ie they are left free to opt for a direct or indirect social reuse model, or a mixed approach, or for any further standard fitting their national situation—the respondents to the data collection protocol discussed earlier, as well as the experts who took part in the RECAST final working seminar (Palermo, September 2014), agreed on some key principles that could inspire future EU regulations on the social reuse of confiscated assets:

— First, effectiveness, eg by promoting the sale of highly depreciable/not easily reusable seized assets, their immediate reuse after seizure, the production of regular statistics, inter-agency co-operation, the development of NGO networks and their involvement in social reuse, and partnerships at the local level amongst all involved private and public stakeholders.
— Secondly, transparency and accountability, eg by establishing independent committees to prevent political influencing in the identification of priorities for confiscated assets/proceeds allocation; by promoting standardised procedures and adjudication criteria; and by setting up regular monitoring mechanisms following the allocation of the assets/proceeds, with sanctions in case of misuse.
— Thirdly, publicity, eg by making application forms for social reuse easily available on the internet, together with clear guidelines, and by making the list of assets available for social reuse and of awarded social reuse projects publicly available as well.
— Fourthly, equity, eg by envisaging compensation in case of acquittal, as well as safeguards against the misuse of social reuse that might be in direct violation of the rights concerning ownership according to the European Convention on Human Rights.

To conclude, the benefits that social reuse could bring about are widely recognized, but these suggested principles show that there are worries about the possible misuse of social reuse regimes. Reservations related to its legal and, above all, economic implications arise. What is of great concern is how to guarantee fairness in the selection process. Another significant issue relates to the overall economic efficiency of such systems, which seems to be impaired by the bad conditions of confiscated assets in most countries, with the consequence that extra money from the state budget might be needed to restore them. Costs might exceed benefits, in economic terms, in the end. Of course, this shall be weighed against overall benefits of social reuse, including the cultural message that it spreads and the contribution that it could make, in the long run, to the fight against crime. Needless to say, these intangible benefits cannot be measured, but they are still there and should somehow be taken into account.

The social reuse model that seems to best fit the needs of other countries is the indirect reuse model (reuse of proceeds), since it overcomes some key problems associated with the direct reuse of the assets.

EU regulations could encourage a diffusion of social reuse across the EU and help resolve some of the above issues by promoting social reuse systems that are both effective and fair, with transparent procedures for assigning the assets and for monitoring them after assignment, for making all information publicly available, and with procedural safeguards for everyone involved. This could hopefully contribute to finally put a hitherto very much neglected actor, ie the citizen, at the heart of confiscation policies in the EU and, potentially, to a 'powered-by-hundreds-of-millions-of-EU-citizens' fight against crime.

BIBLIOGRAPHY

Abbott, K and Duncan, S, 'Values and Interests: International Legalization in the Fight against Corruption' (2002) 31 *Journal of Legal Studies* 141.

Abrams, N, 'Assessing the Federal Government's "War on White-Collar Crime"' (1980) 53 *Temple Law Review* 984.

Abu-Sada, C (ed), *In the Eyes of Others: How People in Crises Perceive Humanitarian Aid* (Médecins Sans Frontières (MSF)/Humanitarian Outcomes/NYU Center on International Cooperation, 2012), available at www.doctorswithoutborders.org/eyes-others-how-people-crises-perceive-humanitarian-aid.

Adam, R and Zellweger, V, 'The Proposed Swiss Comprehensive Act on Asset Recovery' in G Zinkernagel, C Monteith and G Pereira (eds), *Emerging Trends in Asset Recovery, The Proposed Swiss Comprehensive Act on Asset Recovery* (Bern, Peter Lang, 2013) 173.

Aepli, M, in MA Niggli and S Heimgartner (eds), *Basler Kommentar: Internationales Strafrecht* (Basel, Helbing, 2015).

Alagna, F, 'Non-conviction Based Confiscation: Why the EU Directive is a Missed Opportunity' (2015) 21(4) *European Journal on Criminal Policy and Research* 447.

Albrecht, HJ, 'Countries in Transition: Effects of Political, Social and Economic Change on Crime and Criminal Justice—Sanctions and Their Implementation' (1999) 7 *European Journal of Crime, Criminal Law and Criminal Justice* 353.

Albrecht, HJ and Getoš, AM, 'Researching Terrorism and Organized Crime in Southeast Europe' in W Benedek, C Daase, V Dimitrijević and P Van Duyne (eds), *Transnational Terrorism, Organized Crime and Peace-Building—Human Security in the Western Balkans* (Basingstoke, Palgrave Macmillan, 2010) 117.

Alessandri, A, 'Confisca nel diritto penale' in *Digesto delle discipline penalistiche*, III (Turin, Utet, 1989) 42.

Alldridge, P, 'Money Laundering and Globalization' (2008) 35 *Journal of Law and Society* 437.

Alldridge, P and Mumford, A, 'Tax Evasion and the Proceeds of Crime Act 2002' (2005) 25 *Legal Studies* 353.

Alldridge, P, *Money Laundering Law. Forfeiture, Confiscation, Civil Recovery, Criminal Laundering and Taxation of the proceeds of Crime* (Oxford, Hart Publishing, 2003).

Alldridge, P, *What Went Wrong with Money Laundering Law?* (London, Palgrave, 2016).

Almqvist, G, *Förverkande av egendom* (Uppsala, Iustus förlag, 2013).

Anderson, M, Brown, D and Jean, I, *Time to Listen: Hearing People on the Receiving End of International Aid* (Cambridge, MA, CDA Collaborative Learning Projects, 2012), available at cdacollaborative.org/media/60478/Time-to-Listen-Book.pdf.

Andreas, P, 'Illicit Globalizations: Myths, Misconceptions, and Historical Lessons' (2011) 126 *Political Science Quarterly* 403.

Andreas, P, *Smuggler Nation: How Illicit Trade Made America* (Oxford, Oxford University Press, 2013).

Androulakis, I, *Die Globalisierung der Korruptionsbekämpfung* (Baden-Baden, Nomos, 2007).

Antinucci, M, 'The Principles of Patrimony Due Process of Law: The Punitive Confiscation and the Protection of Third Parties Misrelated to the Crime' [2015] *Iliria International Review* 127.

Anyango Oduor, J, et al, *Left Out of the Bargain: Settlements in the Foreign Bribery Cases and Implications for Asset Recovery* (Washington, DC, International Bank for Reconstruction and Development/World Bank Group, 2014).

Arbour, L, 'Economic and Social Justice for Societies in Transition' (2007) 40 *New York University Journal of International Law and Politics* 1.

Arcifa, G, 'The New EU Directive on Confiscation: A Good (Even if Still Prudent) Starting Point for the Post-Lisbon EU Strategy on Tracking and Confiscating Illicit Money', available at https://free-group.eu/2014/03/25/the-new-eu-directive-on-confiscation-a-good-even-if-still-prudent-starting-point-for-the-post-lisbon-eu-strategy-on-tracking-and-confiscating-illicit-money/.

Arnold, J and Silverman, E, 'Regime Change, State Crime and Transitional Justice: A Criminal Law Retrospective Concentrating on Former Eastern Block Countries' (1998) 6 *European Journal of Crime, Criminal Law and Criminal Justice* 140.

Ashe, M and Reid, P, 'Ireland: The Celtic Tiger Bites—The Attack on the Proceeds of Crime' (2001) 4(3) *Journal of Money Laundering Control* 253.

Ashe, M and Reid, P, *Money Laundering: Risks, Liabilities and Compliance* (Dublin, FirstLaw, 2007).

Ashworth, A, 'Four Threats to the Presumption of Innocence' [2006] *International Journal of Evidence and Proof* 241.

Bacio Terracino, J, *The International Legal Framework against Corruption: States' Obligations to Prevent and Repress Corruption* (Cambridge, Intersentia, 2012).

Baicker, K and Jacobson, M, 'Finders Keepers: Forfeiture Laws, Policing Incentives, and Local Budgets' (2007) 91 *Journal of Public Economics* 2113.

Baker, R, 'Taxation: Potential Destroyer of Crime' (1951) 29 *Chicago-Kent Law Review* 197.

Barak, G, 'Towards an Integrative Study of International Crimes and State-Corporate Criminality: A Reciprocal Approach to Gross Human Rights Violations' in A Smeulers and R Haveman (eds), *Supranational Criminology: Towards a Criminology of International Crimes* (Antwerp, Intersentia, 2014) 51.

Barker, K, 'Private Law: Key Encounters with Public Law' in K Barker and D Jensen (eds), *Private Law: Key Encounters with Public Law* (Cambridge, Cambridge University Press, 2013), 35.

Barnet, T, 'Legal Fiction and Forfeiture: An Historical Analysis of the Civil Asset Forfeiture Reform Act' (2001) 40 *Duquesne Law Review* 77.

Bassiouni, MC, 'Assessing Conflict Outcomes: Accountability and Impunity in the Pursuit of International Criminal Justice, A World Study on Conflicts, Victimization and Post-conflict Justice' in MC Bassiouni (ed), *The Pursuit of International Criminal Justice: a World Study on Conflicts, Victimization, and Post-conflict Justice* (Antwerp, Intersentia, 2010) 3.

Bauer, HP, 'How to Deal with Politically Exposed Persons' in M Pieth (ed), *Recovering Stolen Assets* (Bern, Peter Lang, 2008) 195.

Beccaria, C, *An Essay on Crimes and Punishments Translated from the Italian to Which is Added a Commentary by MD Voltaire* (Philadelphia, Philip H Nicklin, 1819).

Beer, A de, 'Bestraffing of (toch) voordeelontneming?' (2012) 6 *Tijdschrift voor Sanctierecht en Compliance* 196.

Bell, RE, 'The Confiscation, Forfeiture and Disruption of Terrorist Finances' (2003) 7 *Journal of Money Laundering Control* 105.

Benomar, J, 'Justice after Transitions' in N Kritz (ed), *Transitional Justice: How Emerging Democracies Reckon with Former Regimes* (Washington, DC, United States Institute of Peace Press, 1995) 32.

Bergström, M, 'Money Laundering' in V Mitsilegas, M Bergström and T Konstadinides (eds), *Research Handbook on EU Criminal Law* (Cheltenham, Edward Elgar, 2016) 335.

Bernard, D, Dejemeppe, B and Guillaine, C, 'La confiscation pénale: une peine finalmente pas si accessoire' in *Questions spéciales de droit penal* (Brussels, Larcier, 2011) 55.

Berton, B, 'The Dark Side of the Web: ISIL's One-Stop Shop?', ISS Alert No 30, 26 June 2015, available at www.iss.europa.eu/publications/detail/article/the-dark-side-of-the-web-isils-one-stop-shop/.

Beziz-Ayache, A, 'Confiscation' in *Dalloz Répertoire de Droit Pénal et de Procédure Pénale*, II (Paris, Dalloz, 2012).

Bianchi, F and Heimgartner, S, 'Die Rückerstattung von Potentatengeldern' [2012] *Aktuelle Juristische Praxis AJP* 353.

Blanco Cordero, I, *El delito de blanqueo de capitales*, 4th edn (Pamplona, Aranzadi-Thomson Reuters, 2015).

Bleichrodt, FW and Vegter, PC, *Sanctierecht* (Deventer, Kluwer, 2013).

Boer den, M, 'Towards an Accountability Regime for an Emerging European Policing Governance' (2002) 12(4) *Policing and Society* 275.

Boersma, M, *Corruption: A Violation of Human Rights and a Crime under International Law?* (Cambridge, Intersentia, 2012).

Boister, N, '"Transnational Criminal Law"?' (2003) 14 *European Journal of International Law* 953.

Boister, N, 'Human Rights Protections in the Suppression Conventions' (2002) 2 *Human Rights Law Review* 199.

Boister, N, *An Introduction to Transnational Criminal Law* (Oxford, Oxford University Press, 2012).

Boraine, AL, 'Transitional Justice: A Holistic Interpretation' (2006) 60 *Journal of International Affairs* 17.

Borgers, MJ and Moors, J, 'Targeting the Proceeds of Crime: Bottlenecks in International Cooperation' (2007) 15 *European Journal of Crime, Criminal Law and Criminal Justice* 1.

Borgers, MJ, 'Confiscation of the Proceeds of Crime: The European Union Framework' in C King and C Walker (eds), *Dirty Assets. Emerging Issues in the Regulation of Criminal and Terrorist Assets* (Farnham, Ashgate Publishing, 2014) 27.

Boucht, J, 'Civil Asset Forfeiture and the Presumption of Innocence under Article 6(2) ECHR' (2014) 5 *New Journal of European Criminal Law* 221.

Boucht, J, 'European Cooperation in Financial Investigations. An Overview of the Legal Framework and Future Challenges' in Z Durdevic and E Ivicevic Karas (eds), *European Criminal Procedure Law in the Service of the Protection of European Union Financial Interests* (Zagreb, Croatian Association of European Criminal Law, 2016) 117.

Boucht, J, 'Extended Confiscation and the Proposed Directive on freezing and Confiscation of Criminal Proceeds in the EU: On Striking a Balance between Efficiency, Fairness and Legal Certainty' (2013) 21 *European Journal of Crime, Criminal Law and Criminal Justice* 127.

Boucht, J, 'Utvidgat förverkande enligt norska straffeloven § 34a—ökad funktionalitet eller obefogat avsteg från hävdvunna rättssäkerhetskrav?' [2012] *Tidsskrift for strafferett* 410.

Boucht, J, *Limits of Assets Confiscation. A European Perspective on Legitimizing Extended Appropriation of Criminal Proceeds* (Oxford, Hart Publishing, 2017 forthcoming).

Bowling, B and Murphy, C, 'Serious Organised Crime under New Labour' (2007) *Criminal Justice Matters* 32.

Bricola, F, 'Forme di tutela "*ante-delictum*" e profili costituzionali della prevenzione' [1974] *Politica del diritto* 374.

Brown, E and Jonathan, C, 'Neoliberal Reform, Governance, and Corruption in the South: Assessing the International Anti-corruption Crusade' (2004) 36 *Antipode* 272.

Brown, E and Jonathan, C, 'Critical Perspectives on Corruption: An Overview' (2011) 7 *Critical Perspectives International Business* 116.

Brown, E and Jonathan, C, 'Neoliberal Reform, Governance, and Corruption in Central America: Exploring the Nicaraguan Case' (2005) 24 *Political Geography* 601.

Brunhart, R and Gajic, N, 'Policing the Economic Transition in Serbia: Assessment of the Serbian Police Service's Capacities to Fight Economic Crime' (OSCE Mission to Serbia and Montenegro, Belgrade, 2005).

Bruppacher, B, 'Bundesanwalt Lauber krebst zurück' (22 June 2015) *Neue Zürcher Zeitung*, available at www.nzz.ch/schweiz/bundesanwalt-lauber-krebst-zurueck-1.18567077.

Bucy, PH, 'Criminal Tax Fraud: The Downfall of Murderers, Madams and Thieves' (1997) 29 *Arizona State Law Journal* 639.

Bukovansky, M, 'The Hollowness of the Anti-corruption Discourse' (2006) 13 *Review of International Political Economy* 181.

Burgis, T, *The Looting Machine: Warlords, Oligarchs, Corporations, Smuggler and the Theft of Africa's Wealth* (New York, Public Affairs, 2015).

Bynum, TS (ed), *Organized Crime in America: Concepts and Controversies* (New York, Criminal Justice Press, 1987).

Calisse, C, *A History of Italian Law*, vol 1 (Washington, Beardbooks, 1928).

Campbell, L, 'The Recovery of "Criminal" Assets in New Zealand, Ireland and England: Fighting Organised and Serious Crime in the Civil Realm' (2010) 41 *Victoria University of Wellington Law Review* 15.

Campbell, L, 'Organized Crime and National Security: A Dubious Connection?' (2014) 17 *New Criminal Law Review* 220.

Campbell, L, 'Theorising Asset Forfeiture in Ireland' (2007) 71 *Journal of Criminal Law* 441.

Campbell, L, *Organised Crime and the Law: A Comparative Analysis* (Oxford, Hart Publishing, 2013).

Carmichael, HM, *Confiscation and Civil Recovery* (Edinburgh, W Green & Son, 2013).

Carpenter, DM, et al, *Policing for Profit. The Abuse of Civil Asset Forfeiture* (Arlington, VA, Institute for Justice, 2015).

Carr, I and Goldby, M, 'Recovering the Proceeds of Corruption: UNCAC and Anti-money Laundering Standards' (2011) *Journal of Business Law* 170.

Carr, I and Jago, R, 'Corruption, the United Nations Convention against Corruption ("UNCAC") and Asset Recovery' in C King and C Walker (eds), *Dirty Assets: Emerging Issues in the Regulation of Criminal and Terrorist Assets* (Farnham, Ashgate Publishing, 2014).

Carranza, R, 'Plunder and Pain: Should Transitional Justice Engage with Corruption and Economic Crimes?' (2008) 2(3) *International Journal of Transitional Justice* 310.

Carrera, S and Guild, E, *The European Council's Guidelines for the Area of Freedom, Security and Justice 2020: Subverting the 'Lisbonisation' of Justice and Home Affairs?* (CEPS Essays, 14 July 2014).

Cassani, U, 'Les avoirs mal acquis, et après la chute du "potentat"' (2010) 4 *Schweizerische Zeitschrift für internationales und europäisches Recht SZIER/RSDIE* 465.

Cassella, SD, 'Civil Asset Recovery: The American Experience' (2013) 3 *Eucrim* 98.

Cassella, SD, 'Criminal Forfeiture Procedure in 2012: An Annual Survey of Developments in the Case Law' (2012) 48(5) *Criminal Law Bulletin* 863.

Cassella, SD, 'Enforcement of Foreign Restraining Orders' (2013) 16 *Journal of Money Laundering Control* 290.

Cassella, SD, 'The Case for Civil Forfeiture: Why In Rem Proceedings are an Essential Tool for Recovering the Proceeds of Crime' (2008) 11 *Journal of Money Laundering Control* 8.

Cassella, SD, 'The Recovery of Criminal Proceeds Generated in One Nation and Found in Another' (2008) 9 *Journal of Financial Crime* 268.

Cassella, SD, 'The Uniform Innocent Owner Defense to Civil Asset Forfeiture' (2001) 89, 3 *Kentucky Law Journal* 653.

Cassella, SD, 'Third Party Rights in Criminal Forfeiture Cases' (1996) 32(6) *Criminal Law Bulletin* 499.

Cassella, SD, *Asset Forfeiture Law in the United States: A Treatise on Forfeiture Law*, 2nd edn (New York, Juris, 2013).

Cassidy, F, 'Targeting the Proceeds of Crime: An Irish Perspective' in T Greenberg, L Samuel, W Grant and L Gray (eds), *Stolen Asset Recovery: A Good Practices Guide for Non-Conviction Based Asset Forfeiture* (Washington, DC, World Bank, 2009) 153.

Cejp, M and Scheinost, M, 'Organized and Economic Crime: A Common Problem' in A Šelih and A Završnik (eds), *Crime and Transition in Central and East Europe* (London, Springer, 2012) 157.

Cesoni, ML, *Les dispositifs de lutte contre les organisations criminelles* (Gent, Academia Press, 2005).

Chablais, A, 'La nouvelle loi sur les valeurs patrimoniales d'origine illicite', *Jusletter*, 11 January 2016, 1.

Chaiken, D and Sharman, J, *Corruption and Money Laundering: A Symbiotic Relationship*, Palgrave Series on Asian Governance (New York, Palgrave Macmillan, 2009).

Cheh, MM, 'Civil Remedies to Control Crime: Legal Issues and Constitutional Challenges' (1998) 9 *Crime Prevention Studies* 45.

Chhootray, V and Stoker, G, *Governance Theory and Practice: A Cross-Disciplinary Approach* (Basingstoke, Palgrave Macmillan, 2009).

Chin, GJ, 'The New Civil Death: Rethinking Punishment in the Era of Mass Conviction' (2012) 160 *University of Pennsylvania Law Review* 1789.

Claman, D, 'The Promise and Limitations of Asset Recovery under the UNCAC' in M Pieth (ed), *Recovering Stolen Assets* (Bern, Peter Lang, 2008) 333.

Collier, R, 'Intentions, Banks, Politics and the Law: The UK Code of Practice on Taxation for Banks' (2014) *British Tax Review* 478.

Coolidge, J and Ackerman, SR, 'High-Level Rent-Seeking and Corruption in African Regimes: Theory and Cases', World Bank Policy Research Paper No 1780 (1997), 21.

Craig, E, 'The Thickness of a Prison Wall—When Does Tax Avoidance Become a Criminal Offence?' (2011) 17 *New Zealand Business Law Quarterly* 441.

Crow, B, 'Development and Underdevelopment: Definitions' in PA O'Hara (ed), *Encyclopaedia of Political Economy* (London, Routledge, 2001) 206.

Cuervo-Cazurra, A, 'Who Cares about Corruption?' (2006) 37 *Journal of International Business Studies* 807.

Czarnecki, J, 'This Proposal Could Reshape Europe's Cryptocurrency Policies', *CoinDesk*, 20 February 2016, available at www.coindesk.com/this-overlooked-proposal-could-reshape-europes-cryptocurrency-policies/.

Daniel, T and Maton, J, 'Civil Proceedings to Recover Corruptly Acquired Assets of Public Officials' in Pieth, M (ed), *Recovering Stolen Assets* (Bern, Peter Lang, 2008) 243.

Daniel, T and Maton, J, 'Recovering the Proceeds of Corruption: General Sani Abacha—A Nation's Thief' in Pieth, M (ed), *Recovering Stolen Assets* (Bern, Peter Lang, 2008) 63.

Dannacher, M, *Diktatorengelder in der Schweiz* (Basel, Helbing, 2012).

Davide, S, 'La confisca del profitto', Doctoral thesis (Università degli Studi di Milano-Bicocca, 2010).

Davis, K, 'Does the Globalization of Anti-corruption Law Help Developing Countries?' in J Faundez and C Tan (eds), *International Economic Law, Globalisation and Developing Countries* (Cheltenham, Edward Elgar, 2010).

Davis, KE, 'The Effects of Forfeiture on Third Parties' (2003) 48 *McGill Law Journal* 183.

Delaney, P, 'Transitional Corruption: Regulation across Borders' (2006) 47 *Virginia Journal of International Law* 413.

Delegación del Gobierno para el Plan Nacional sobre Drogas (2015) *Informe sobre la actividad del fondo procedente de los bienes decomisados por tráfico ilícito de drogas y otros delitos relacionados durante el año 2014* (Madrid, Delegación del Gobierno para el Plan Nacional sobre Drogas, 2014).

den Boer, M, 'Towards an Accountability Regime for an Emerging European Policing Governance' (2002) 12(4) *Policing and Society* 275.

Department for International Development and The Rt Hon Justine Greening MP, 'New Crime Unit to Investigate Corruption Affecting Developing Countries', press release (9 August 2015), available at www.gov.uk/government/news/new-crime-unit-to-investigate-corruption-affecting-developing-countries.

Department of Justice and Law Reform, *White Paper on Crime. Discussion Document No 3: Organised and White Collar Crime* (October 2010).

Derenčinović, D, 'Criminalization of Illegal Enrichment' (2009) 4 *Freedom from Fear Magazine* 21.

Dershowitz, A, 'The Law of Dangerousness: Some Fictions about Predictions' (1970) 23 *Journal of Legal Education* 24.

Dery, AW, 'Overview of Asset Forfeiture' (2012) *Business Law Today* 1.

Dickson, DJ, 'Towards more Effective Asset Recovery in Member States—The UK Example' (2009) 10 *ERA Forum* 435.

Donatsch, A, Heimgartner S, Meyer F and Simonek M, *Internationale Rechtshilfe unter Einbezug der Amtshilfe im Steuerrecht*, 2nd edn (Zurich, Schulthess, 2015).

Dorn, N, Murji, K and South, N, *Traffickers. Drug Markets and Law Enforcement* (London, Routledge, 1992).

Doyle, C, *Crime and Forfeiture* (Congressional Research Service, 2015).

Drage, G, *The Criminal Code of the German Empire*, 2nd edn (Clark, NJ, Lawbook Exchange, 2007).

Duff, RA, *Answering for Crime. Responsibility and Liability in the Criminal Law* (Oxford, Hart Publishing, 2009).

Dugard, J and Wyngaert van den, C, 'Reconciling Extradition with Human Rights' (1998) 92 *American Journal of International Law* 187.

Đurđević, Z, 'Suvremeni razvoj hrvatskoga kaznenog procesnog prava s posebnim osvrtom na novelu ZKP iz 2011' (2011) 2 *Hrvatski ljetopis za kazneno pravo i praksu* 311.

Eckes, C, *EU Counter-Terrorist Policies and Fundamental Rights* (Oxford, Oxford University Press, 2009).

Engle, SM, *Human Rights and Gender Violence: Translating International Law into Local Justice* (Chicago, IL, University of Chicago Press, 2010).

Ensign, RL, 'The Morning Risk Report: Virtual Currency Firms Struggle With AML', *Wall Street Journal*, 7 May 2015.

Esser, R, 'A Civil Asset Recovery Model. The German Perspective and Human Rights' in JP Rui and U Sieber (eds), *Non-conviction-Based Confiscation in Europe* (Berlin, Duncker & Humblot, 2015) 71.

European Parliament, Directorate General For Internal Policies, Policy Department C: Citizens' Rights and Constitutional Affairs, Civil Liberties, Justice and Home Affairs, *The Need for New EU Legislation Allowing the Assets Confiscated from Criminal Organisations to be Used for Civil Society and in Particular for Social Purposes* (Brussels, European Parliament, 2012).

Faraldo Cabana, P, 'Improving the Recovery of Assets Resulting from Organised Crime' (2014) 22 *European Journal of Crime, Criminal Law and Criminal Justice* 13.

Fazekas, M and Nanopoulos, E, 'The Effectiveness of EU Law: Insight from the EU Legal Framework on Asset Confiscation' (2016) 24 *Journal of Crime, Criminal Law and Criminal Justice* 39.

Federal Department of Foreign Affairs of the Swiss Confederation, 'Illicitly Acquired Assets (PEPs)' (website), available at www.eda.admin.ch/eda/en/fdfa/foreign-policy/financial-centre-economy/illicit-assets-pep.html.

Federal Department of Foreign Affairs of the Swiss Confederation, 'Federal Councillor Calmy-Rey Attends International Conference on the Restitution of Illegal Assets in Paris' (4 June 2010), available at www.eda.admin.ch/eda/en/home/recent/media.html.

Federal Department of Foreign Affairs of the Swiss Confederation, 'Restitution of Illicit Assets in the Context of the Arab Spring: Meeting of Experts in Lausanne', press release (4 January 2012), available at www.news.admin.ch/message/index.html?lang=en&msg-id=43127.

Feldman, D, 'A Survey of English Forfeiture Law' in S Food (ed), *Illicit Drugs and Organized Crime: Issues for a Unified Europe* (Chicago, IL, Office of International Criminal Justice, 1991) 25.

Fellmeth, AX, 'Civil and Criminal Sanctions in the Constitution and Courts' (2005) 94(1) *Georgetown Law Journal* 1.

Fellstrom, C and Peachey, P, 'Ex-Prime Minister of Mauritius under Investigation by UK Anti-corruption Unit' (4 October 2015), available at www.independent.co.uk/news/uk/crime/ex-prime-minister-of-mauritius-under-investigation-by-uk-anti-corruption-unit-a6679111.html.

Ferguson, B, 'The Personal Accountability of Bankers' (2015) 9 *Law and Financial Markets Review* 40.

Fiandaca, G, *Misure di prevenzione (profili sostanziali)*, Digesto delle discipline penalistiche VIII (Turin, Utet, 1994) 116.

Financial Action Task Force (FATF), 'Anti-money Laundering and Counter-terrorist Financing Measures. Belgium Mutual Evaluation Report' (FATF, April 2015).

Financial Services Authority, *Banks' Management of High Money-Laundering Risk Situations* (2011), available at www.fsa.gov.uk/pubs/other/aml_final_report.pdf.

Finkelstein, JJ, 'The Goring Ox: Some Historical Perspectives on Deodands, Forfeitures, Wrongful Death and the Western Notion of Sovereignty' (1973) *Temple Law Quarterly* 46.

Fiolka, G, 'Art 1, 5–7, 11, 19–20a, 32, 39, 40, 67 IRSG, Art 32 GwÜ' in MA Niggli and S Heimgartner (eds), *Basler Kommentar: Internationales Strafrecht* (Basel, Helbing, 2015).

Fisher, J, 'The Anti-money Laundering Disclosure Regime and the Collection of Revenue in the United Kingdom' [2010] *British Tax Review* 235.

Food, S (ed), *Illicit Drugs and Organized Crime: Issues for a Unified Europe* (Chicago, IL, Office of International Criminal Justice, 1991).

Ford, MR, 'Criminal Forfeiture and the Sixth Amendment's Right to Jury Trial Post-Booker' (2007) 101 *Northwestern University Law Review* 1371.

Francis, E, 'De uitvoering van de verbeurdverklaring: interne en internationale aspecten' in A Masset and P Traest (eds), *L'exécution des peines—De strafuitvoering* (Bruxelles, La Charte, 2006) 3.

Francis, E, 'Enkele bedenkingen bij de nieuwe Belgische regeling inzake "asset sharing"' (2007) 2 *Nullum Crimen* 20.

Freiberg, A and Fox, R, 'Evaluating the Effectiveness of Australia's Confiscation Laws' (2000) 33 *Australian and New Zealand Journal of Criminology* 239.

Fried, DJ, 'Rationalizing Criminal Forfeiture' (1988) 79 *Journal of Criminal Law and Criminology* 328.

Gallant, MM, *Money Laundering and the Proceeds of Crime: Economic Crime and Civil Remedies* (Cheltenham, Edward Elgar, 2005).

Gallant, MM, 'Tax and the Proceeds of Crime: A New Approach to Tainted Finance?' (2013) 16 *Journal of Money Laundering Control* 119.

Gallant, MM, 'Money Laundering Consequences: Recovering Wealth, Piercing Secrecy, Disrupting Tax Havens and Distorting International Law' (2014) 17(3) *Journal of Money Laundering Control* 296.

Gallant, MM and King, C, 'The Seizure of Illicit Assets: Patterns of Civil Forfeiture in Canada and Ireland' (2013) 42 *Common Law World Review* 91.

Garland, D, *The Culture of Control: Crime and Social Order in Contemporary Society* (Oxford, Oxford University Press, 2001).

Gray, A, 'Forfeiture Provisions and the Criminal/ Civil Divide' (2012) 15 *New Criminal Law Review* 32.

Garretson, HJ, 'Federal Criminal Forfeiture: A Royal Pain in the Assets' (2008) 18 *Review of Law and Social Justice* 45.

Gathii, JT, 'Defining the Relationship between Human Rights and Corruption' (2009) 31 *University of Pennsylvania Journal of International Law* 161.

Gerber, J and Jensen, EL (eds), *American Style. The Internationalization of Failed Policy and its Alternatives* (Garland Publishing, New York, 2001).

Gie, G, 'Amartya Sen on Elections, Communal Politics and Inequality in India', *Mondiaal Nieuws*, 8 April 2014, available at www.mo.be/en/interview/amartya-sen-elections-communal-politics-and-inequality-india.

Gilbert, G, *Responding to International Crime* (Leiden, Martinus Nijhoff Publishers, 2006).

Global Witness, *Banks and Dirty Money: How the Financial System Enables State Looting at a Devastating Human Cost* (2015), available at www.globalwitness.org/reports/banks-and-dirty-money.

Glynn, P, Kobrin, S and Naim, M, 'The Globalization of Corruption' in K Elliot (ed), *Corruption and the Global Economy* (Washington, DC, Institute for International Economics, 1997).

Goldsmith, M and Linderman, MJ, 'Asset Forfeiture and Third Party Rights: The Need for Further Law Reform' [1989] *Duke Law Journal* 1254.

Gololobov, D, 'The Yukos Tax Case or Ramsay Adventures in Russia' (2008) 7 *FSU Business Review* 165.

Goodwin, M and Rose-Sender, K, 'Linking Corruption and Human Rights: An Unwelcome Addition to the Development Discourse', Tilburg Law School Research Paper (2010) 12, available at http://papers.ssrn.com/sol3/papers.cfm?abstract_id=1623225.

Grand Duche de Luxembourg, Fonds de lutte contre certaines formes de criminalité, *Rapport d'activité 2014* (Luxembourg, Fonds de lutte contre certaines formes de criminalité, 2015).

Grasso, G, 'Commento all' articolo 240' in M Romano, G Grasso and T Padovani (eds), *Commentario sistematico del codice penale*, III (Milan, Giuffré, 2011) 521.

Gray, A, 'The Compatibility of Unexplained Wealth Provisions and "Civil" Forfeiture Regimes with Kable' (2012) 12 *Queensland UT Law and Justice Journal* 18.

Gray, L, et al, *Few and Far: the Hard Facts on Stolen Asset Recovery* (Washington, DC, International Bank for Reconstruction and Development/World Bank and Organisation for Economic Co-operation and Development, 2014).

Greenberg, T, et al, *Politically Exposed Persons: Preventative Measures for the Banking Sector* (Washington, DC, International Bank for Reconstruction and Development/World Bank, 2010), available at http://star.worldbank.org/star/sites/star/files/Politically%20Exposed%20Persons_0.pdf.

Greenberg, TS, Samuel, LM, Grant, W and Gray, L, *Stolen Asset Recovery: A Good Practices Guide for Non-Conviction Based Asset Forfeiture* (Washington, DC, World Bank, 2009).

Groupe de recherche droits de l'homme et logiques juridiques, 'La "matière pénale" au sens de la Convention européenne des droits de l'homme, flou du droit penal' [1987] *Revue de science criminelle et droit pénal comparé* 819.

Gully-Hart, P, 'International Asset Recovery of Corruption-Related Assets: Switzerland' in Pieth, M (ed), *Recovering Stolen Assets* (Bern, Peter Lang, 2008) 165.

Gupta, A, 'Blurred Boundaries: The Discourse of Corruption, the Culture of Politics, and the Imagined State' (1995) 22 *American Ethnologist* 375.

Hall, D, 'Privatisation, Multinationals, and Corruption' (1999) 9 *Development in Practice* 539.

Hallevy, G, *The Right to Be Punished. Modern Doctrinal Sentencing* (Heidelberg, Springer, 2013).

Halliday, T and Shaffer, G, 'Transnational Legal Orders' in T Halliday and G Shaffer (eds), *Transnational Legal Orders* (Cambridge, Cambridge University Press, 2015).

Halliday, T, Levi, M and Reuter, P, *Global Surveillance of Dirty Money* (Champaign, IL, Center on Law and Globalization, 2014).

Hamilton, BA, *Comparative Evaluation of Unexplained Wealth Orders: Prepared for the US Department of Justice, National Institute of Justice* (Washington, DC, 2011).

Harding, C, 'The Interplay of Criminal and Administrative Law in the Context of Market Regulation: The Case of Serious Competition Infringements' in V Mitsilegas, P Alldridge and L Cheliotis (eds), *Globalisation, Criminal Law and Criminal Justice: Theoretical, Comparative and Transnational Perspectives* (Oxford, Hart Publishing, 2015) 199.

Hardy, M, 'Sixth Amendment—Applicability of Right to Counsel of Choice to Forfeiture of Attorneys' Fees' (1990) 80 *Journal of Criminal Law and Criminology* 1154.

Harfield, C, 'SOCA: A Paradigm Shift in British Policing' (2006) 46(4) *British Journal of Criminology* 743.

Harms, B, 'Holding Public Officials Accountable in the International Realm: A New Multi-Layered Strategy to Combat Corruption' (2000) 33 *Cornell International Law Journal* 159.

Harvey, D, *A Brief History of Neoliberalism* (Oxford, Oxford University Press, 2005).

Hawley, S, 'Exporting Corruption: Privatisation, Multinationals & Bribery', The Corner House Briefing No 19 (2000), available at www.thecornerhouse.org.uk/resource/exporting-corruption-0.

Hellman, J, Jones, G and Kaufmann, D 'Seize the State, Seize the Day: State Capture, Corruption and Influence in Transition', World Bank Policy Research Working Papers No 2444 (2002).

Hendry, J and King, C, 'How Far Is Too Far? Theorising Non Conviction Based Asset Forfeiture' (2015) 11(4) *International Journal of Law in Context* 398.

Hesse, C and Post, R, 'Introduction' in C Hesse and R Post (eds), *Human Rights in Political Transitions: Gettysburg to Bosnia* (New York, Zone Books 1999) 20.

HM Treasury and HM Home Office, *UK National Risk Assessment of Money Laundering and Terrorist Financing* (2015), available at www.gov.uk/government/uploads/system/uploads/attachment_data/file/468210/UK_NRA_October_2015_final_web.pdf.

Hodgson, D, *Profits of Crime and their Recovery: The Report of a Committee Chaired by Sir Derek Hodgson* (London, Ashgate Publishing, 1984).

Hollenberg, S, 'The Diverging Approaches of the European Court of Human Rights in the Cases of Nada and Al-Dulimi' (2015) 64 *International and Comparative Law Quarterly* 445.

Holmes, OW Jr, *The Common Law* (Boston, MA, The Law Book Exchange, 1881).

Holzmeyer, C, 'Human Rights in an Era of Neoliberal Globalization: The Alien Tort Claims Act and Grassroots Mobilization in *Doe v Unocal*' (2009) 43 *Law & Society Review* 271.

Hope, B and Wright, T, 'Malaysia Fund 1MDB's Missing Money Problem Grows', *Wall Street Journal*, 18 September 2015, available at www.wsj.com/articles/malaysia-fund-1mdbs-missing-money-problem-grows-1442547656?mod=trending_now_1.

Howse, T, 'England' in K Ligeti (ed), *Toward a Prosecutor for the European Union, Vol 1. A Comparative Analysis* (Oxford, Hart Publishing, 2013) 133.

Hughes, WJ and O'Connell, EH Jr , 'In Personam (Criminal) Forfeiture and Federal Drug Felonies: An Expansion of a Harsh English Tradition into a Modern Era' (1984) 11(4) *Pepperdine Law Review* 613.

Humanitarian Accountability Partnership, 'Humanitarian Accountability Standards 2010', available at www.hapinternational.org/pool/files/2010-hap-standard-in-accountability.pdf.

Interdepartementalen Koordinationsgruppe zur Bekämpfung der Geldwäscherei und der Terrorismusfinanzierung (KGGT), *Schweizerische Eidgenossenschaft, Bericht über die nationale Beurteilung der Geldwäschereiund Terrorismusfinanzierungsrisiken in der Schweiz* (2015), available at www.news.admin.ch/NSBSubscriber/message/attachments/39965.pdf.

International Centre for Asset Recovery (ICAR) at the Basel Institute on Governance, 'Asset Recovery/ICAR' (website), available at www.baselgovernance.org/themes/icar.

International Council on Human Rights Policy and Transparency International, 'Integrating Human Rights in the Anti-corruption Agenda: Challenges, Possibilities and Opportunities' (2010), available at www.ichrp.org/en/projects/131.

Inzelt, E, 'White-Collar Crime during the Political and Economic Transition in Hungary' (2011) 8 *US-China Law Review* 352.

Ivičević, E, *Oduzimanje imovinske koristi stečene kaznenim djelom* (Zagreb, Hrvatsko udruženje za kaznene znanosti i praksu, Ministarstvo unutarnjih poslova RH, 2004).

Ivory, R, *Corruption, Asset Recovery and the Protection of Property in Public International Law, The Human Rights of Bad Guys* (Cambridge, Cambridge University Press, 2014).

Jakobi, A, 'The OECD and Crime: The Fight against Corruption and Money Laundering' in K Martens and A Jakobi (eds), *Mechanisms of OECD Governance: International Incentives for National Policy-Making* (Oxford, Oxford University Press, 2010).

Jakobi, A, *Common Goods and Evils? The Formation of Global Crime Governance* (Oxford, Oxford University Press, 2013).

Jankowski, MA, 'Tempering the Relation-Back Doctrine: A More Reasonable Approach to Civil Forfeiture in Drug Cases' (1990) 76(1) *Virginia Law Review* 165.

Jayawickrama, N, Pope, J and Stolpe, O, 'Legal Provisions to Facilitate the Gathering of Evidence in Corruption Cases: Easing the Burden of Proof' (2002) 2 *Forum on Crime and Society* 23.

Jenkins, R and Newell, P, 'CSR, Tax and Development' (2013) 34 *Third World Quarterly* 378.

Jimu, I, 'Managing the Proceeds of Asset Recovery: The Case of Nigeria, Peru, the Philippines and Kazakhstan', Basel Institute on Governance Working Paper Series No 6 (2009), available at www.baselgovernance.org/fileadmin/docs/publications/working_papers/Managing_Prodceeds_of_AR_Final.pdf.

Johnson, BT, 'Restoring Civility—The Civil Asset Forfeiture Reform Act of 2000: Baby Steps towards a More Civilized Forfeiture Regime' (2001) 35 *Indian Law Review* 1045.

Johnsøn, J, Taxell, N and Zaum, D, 'Mapping Evidence Gaps in Anti-corruption: Assessing the State of the Operationally Relevant Evidence on Donors' Actions and Approaches to Reducing Corruption', U4 Issue 7 (Chr Michelsen Institute, 2012), available at www.u4.no/publications.

Jorgensen, H, 'Hard Graft: The G20 and Anti-corruption' in M Callaghan et al (eds), *G20 Monitor: Tax, Infrastructure, Anti-corruption, Energy and the G20*, available at www.lowyinstitute.org/files/g20_monitor_october_2013.pdf.

Joseph, LM, 'Money Laundering Enforcement: Following the Money' (2001) 6(2) *Journal of Economic Perspectives* 11.

Kälin, W and Künzli, J, *The Law of International Human Rights Protection* (Oxford, Oxford University Press, 2009).

Kaufmann, D and Shang-Jin, W, 'Does "Grease Money" Speed up the Wheels of Commerce?', National Bureau of Economic Research Working Paper No 7093 (1999), available at www.nber.org/papers/w7093.

Kennedy, A, 'Justifying the Civil Recovery of Criminal Proceeds' [2004] *Journal of Financial Crime* 8.

Kilchling, M, 'Finance-Oriented Strategies of Organized Crime Control' in L Paoli (ed), *The Oxford Handbook of Organized Crime* (New York, Oxford University Press, 2014) 655.

Kilchling, M, 'Tracing, Seizing and Confiscating Proceeds from Corruption (and other Illegal Conduct) Within or Outside the Criminal Justice System' (2001) *European Journal of Crime, Criminal Law and Criminal Justice* 264.

Kim, HJ and Sharman, J, 'Accounts and Accountability: Corruption Human Rights, and Individual Accountability Norms' (2014) 68 *International Organization* 417.

King, C, 'Civil Forfeiture and Article 6 of the ECHR: Due Process Implications for England and Wales and Ireland' (2014) 34(3) *Legal Studies* 371.

King, C, 'Follow the Money Trail: "Civil" Forfeiture of "Criminal" Assets in Ireland' in P van Duyne et al (eds), *Human Dimensions in Organised Crime, Money Laundering, and Corruption* (Nijmegen, Wolf Legal, 2013).

King, C, 'Hitting Back at Organised Crime: The Adoption of Civil Forfeiture in Ireland' in C King and C Walker, *Dirty Assets: Emerging Issues in the Regulation of Criminal and Terrorist Assets* (Farnham, Ashgate Publishing, 2014) 141.

King, C, 'Using Civil Processes in Pursuit of Criminal Law Objectives: A Case Study of Non-conviction Based Asset Forfeiture' (2012) 16(4) *International Journal of Evidence and Proof* 337.

King, C and Walker, C, 'Emerging Issues in the Regulation of Criminal and Terrorist Assets' in C King and C Walker (eds), *Dirty Assets: Emerging Issues in the Regulation of Criminal and Terrorist Assets* (Farnham, Ashgate Publishing, 2014).

Kis-Katos, K and Schulze, GG, 'Corruption in Southeast Asia: A Survey of Recent Research' (2013) 27 *Asian-Pacific Economic Literature* 79.

Klip, A, *European Criminal Law*, 3rd edn (Cambridge, Intersentia, 2016).

Kofele-Kale, N, 'Presumed Guilty: Balancing Competing Rights and Interests in Combating Economic Crimes' (2006) 40 *The International Lawyer* 909.

Kofele-Kale, N, *Combating Economic Crimes: Balancing Competing Rights and Interests in Prosecuting the Crime of Illicit Enrichment* (Abingdon, Routledge, 2012).

Kofele-Kale, N, *The International Law of Responsibility for Economic Crimes: Holding State Officials Individually Liable for Acts of Fraudulent Enrichment*, 2nd edn (Aldershot, Ashgate Publishing, 2006).

Krapac, D, *Kazneno procesno pravo Prva Knjiga: Institucije* (Zagreb, Narodne novine, 2015).

Kumar, CR, *Corruption and Human Rights in India: Comparative Perspectives on Transparency and Good Governance* (New Delhi, Oxford University Press, 2011).

Lambourne, W, 'Transitional Justice and Peacebuilding after Mass Violence' (2009) 3(1) *International Journal of Transitional Justice* 28.

Lambsdorff, JG, 'Consequences and Causes of Corruption: What Do We Know from a Cross-Section of Countries?', Passauer Diskussionspapiere: Volkswirtschaftliche Reihe No V-34-05 (2005), available at www.econstor.eu.

Lander, JR, 'Attainder and Forfeiture' (1961) 4(2) *The Historical Journal* 119.

Laplante, LJ, 'On the Indivisibility of Rights: Truth Commissions, Reparations, and the Right to Development' (2004) 10 *Yale Human Rights and Development Journal* 145.

Larionova, M and Kirton, J, 'G7/8 and G20 Accountability' in M Larionova and J Kirton (eds), *The G8–G20 Relationship in Global Governance* (Farnham, Ashgate Publishing, 2015).

Lasky, MR, 'Imposing Indigence: Reclaiming the Qualified Right to Counsel of Choice in Criminal Asset Forfeiture Cases' (2014) 104 *Journal of Criminal Law and Criminology* 165.

Law Reform Commission, *Report on the Confiscation of the Proceeds of Crime* (LRC 35-1991) (Dublin, Law Reform Commission, 1991).

Lea, J, 'Hitting Criminals Where It Hurts: Organised Crime and the Erosion of Due Process' (2004) 35 *Cambria Law Review* 81.

Leburić, A, Matić, R and Quien, M, *Mito i korupcija u hrvatskom društvu* (Redak, 2010).

Lemieux, F, 'Tackling Transnational Drug Trafficking Effectively: Assessing the Outcomes of the Drug Enforcement Administration's International Cooperation Initiatives' in F Lemieux, *International Police Cooperation: Emerging Issues, Theory and Practice* (Cullompton, Willan Publishing, 2010) 260.

Lethaby, H, 'Reflections on Tax and the City' (2014) 1220 *Tax Journal* 10.

Levi, M, 'Combating the Financing of Terrorism: A History and Assessment of the Control of "Threat Finance"' (2010) 50 *British Journal of Criminology* 650.

Levi, M, 'How Well Do Anti-money Laundering Controls Work in Developing Countries?' in Peter Reuter (ed), *Draining Development? Controlling Flows of Illicit Funds from Developing Countries* (Washington, DC, International Bank for Reconstruction and Development/World Bank, 2012).

Levi, M, 'Taking the Profit Out of Crime: The UK Experience' [1997] *European Journal of Crime, Criminal Law and Criminal Justice* 228.

Levi, M, 'Reversal of the Burden of Proof in Confiscation of the Proceeds of Crime: A Council of Europe Best Practice Survey', Best Practice Survey No 2 (Council of Europe, 2000).

Levi, M, 'Following the Criminal and Terrorist Money Trails' in P van Duyne, K von Lampe and JL Newell (eds), *Criminal Finances and Organizing Crime in Europe* (Nijmegen, Wolf Legal Publishers, 2003).

Levi, M and Nelken, D, 'The Corruption of Politics and the Politics of Corruption: An Overview' in M Levi and D Nelken (eds), *The Corruption of Politics and the Politics of Corruption* (Oxford, Blackwell, 1996).

Levi, M and Osofsky, L, *Investigating, Seizing, and Confiscating the Proceeds of Crime*, Crime Detection and Prevention Series No 61 (London, Home Office Police Department, 1995).

Levi, M and Reuter, P, 'Money Laundering' (2006) 24 *Crime and Justice* 289.

Levitsky, M, 'The Dark Side of Globalization' (2003) 5 *International Studies Review* 253.

Levy, LW, *A License to Steal. The Forfeiture of Property* (Chapel Hill, NC, UNC Press, 1996).

Ligeti, K (ed), *Toward a Prosecutor for the European Union*, vol 1 (Oxford, Hart Publishing, 2013).

Linn, CJ, 'Recovering Assets in Investment Fraud Cases' (2009) 45(5) *Criminal Law Bulletin* 744.

Lippke, R, 'Justifying the Proof Structure of Criminal Trials' [2013] *International Journal of Evidence and Proof* 323.

Lord, N, *Regulating Corporate Bribery in International Business: Anti-corruption in the UK and Germany* (Farnham, Ashgate Publishing, 2014).

Lorenzetti, L, Barbot, M and Mocarelli, L (eds), *Property Rights and Their Violations. Expropriations and Confiscations, 16th–20th Centuries* (Bern, Peter Lang, 2012).

Low, L, 'The United Nations Convention against Corruption: The Globalization of Anti-corruption Standards', conference paper (4–5 May 2006), available at www.steptoe.com/assets/attachments/2599.pdf.

Machado, M, 'Similar in Their Differences: Transnational Legal Processes Addressing Money Laundering in Brazil and Argentina' in G Shaffer (ed), *Transnational Legal Ordering and State Change* (Cambridge, Cambridge University Press, 2013).

Manes, V, 'Nullum crimen sine confiscatione' [2015] *Rivista italiana di diritto e procedura penale* 1259.

Mangione, A, *La misura di prevenzione patrimoniale fra dogmatica e politica criminale* (Padova, Cedam, 2001).

Marcelo, SV, 'The Long Road from Zurich to Manila: the Recovery of the Marcos Swiss Dollars Deposit' in M Pieth (ed), *Recovering Stolen Assets* (Bern, Peter Lang, 2008) 89.

Martucci, A, 'Advocating for Asset Forfeiture in the Post-Madoff Era: Why the Government, Not a Bankruptcy Trustee, Should Be Responsible for Recovering and Redistributing Assets from Feedere Funds and Net Winners' (2012) 63 *Case Western Reserve Law Review* 599.

Matrix Insight Ltd, 'Assessing the Effectiveness of EU Member States' Practices in the Identification, Tracing, Freezing and Confiscation of Criminal Assets—Final Report' (Brussels, European Commission, 2009).

Maugeri, A, 'Le Sezioni Unite devono prendere posizione sulla natura della confisca antimafia' [2014] *Diritto penale contemporaneo* (www.penalecontemporaneo.it, 11 May 2014).

Maugeri, A, *Le moderne sanzioni patrimoniali tra funzionalità e garantismo* (Milan, Giuffré, 2001).

Maxeiner, JR, 'Bane of American Forfeiture Law—Banished at Last?' (1977) 62 *Cornell Law Review* 768.

Mazzacuva, F, 'La materia penale e il "doppio binario" della Corte europea: le garanzie al di là delle apparenze' [2013] *Rivista italiana di diritto e procedura penale* 1908.

McBarnet, D, 'It's Not What You Do but the Way that You Do It: Tax Evasion, Tax Avoidance and the Boundaries of Deviance' in D Downes (ed), *Unravelling Criminal Justice* (London, MacMillan, 1992) 247.

McBarnet, D, 'Law, Policy, and Legal Avoidance: Can Law Effectively Implement Egalitarian Policies' (1988) 15 *Journal of Law and Society* 113.

McBarnet, D, 'Legitimate Rackets: Tax Evasion, Tax Avoidance, and the Boundaries of Legality' (1992) 3 *Journal of Human Justice* 56.

McCoy, J and Heckel, H, 'The Emergence of a Global Anti-corruption Norm' (2001) 38 *International Politics* 65.

Meade, J, 'Organised Crime, Moral Panic and Law Reform: The Irish Adoption of Civil Forfeiture' (2000) 10(1) *Irish Criminal Law Journal* 11.

Mégevand, G, *Confiscation et corruption* (Basel, Helbing Lichtenhahn Verlag, 2013).

Meyer, F, '"Reformiert die Rückgewinnungshilfe!"—Denkanstöße für eine Generalüberholung der Vermögensabschöpfung' [2015] *Zeitschrift für die gesamte Strafrechtswissenschaft ZStW* 241.

Meyer, F, 'Auch Potentaten haben Rechte', *Neue Zürcher Zeitung*, 28 June 2015, available at www.nzz.ch/meinung/kommentare/die-rechte-von-potentaten-ld.791.

Meyer, F, 'Herausgabe von Beweismitteln und Vermögenswerten' in K Ambos, P König and P Rackow (eds), *Rechtshilferecht in Strafsachen* (Baden-Baden, Nomos, 2015) 1001.

Michaels, CW, *No Greater Threat: America after September 11 and the Rise of a National Security State*, 2nd edn (New York, Agora Publishing, 2005).

Michaelsen, C, 'The Renaissance of Non-Refoulement? The Othman (Abu Qatada) Decision of the European Court of Human Rights' (2012) 61 *International and Comparative Law Quarterly* 750.

Michalowski, RJ and Kramer, RC (eds), *State-Corporate Crime: Wrongdoing at the Intersection of Business and Government* (New Brunswick, NJ, Rutgers University Press, 2006).

Milanovic, M, 'Norm Conflict in International Law: Whither Human Rights?' (2009) 20 *Duke Journal of Comparative & International Law* 69.

Millington, T and Sutherland Williams, M, *On the Proceeds of Crime*, 3 edn (Oxford, Oxford University Press, 2010).

Mitchell, G, 'Thematic Paper on Organised Crime. Asset Confiscation as an Instrument to Deprive Criminal Organisations of the Proceeds of their Activities' (Special Committee on Organised Crime, Corruption and Money Laundering, September 2012).

Mitsilegas, V, *EU Criminal Law* (Oxford, Hart Publishing, 2009).

Monfrini, E, 'The Abacha Case' in Pieth M (ed), *Recovering Stolen Assets* (Bern, Peter Lang, 2008) 41.

Mongillo, V, 'La confisca del profitto nei confronti dell'ente in cerca d'identità: luci e ombre della recente pronuncia delle Sezioni Unite' [2008] *Rivista italiana di diritto e procedura penale* 1758.

Monteith, C and Gomes Pereira, P, 'Asset Recovery' in N Boister and RJ Currie (eds), *Routledge Handbook of Transnational Criminal Law* (Abingdon, Routledge, 2015) 137.

Monti, A, 'Illegitimate Appropriation or Just Punishment? The Confiscation of Property in *Ancient Régime* Criminal Law and Doctrine' in L Lorenzetti, M Barbot and L Mocarelli (eds), *Property Rights and Their Violations. Expropriations and Confiscations, 16th–20th Centuries* (Bern, Peter Lang, 2012) 4.

Morier, Y, 'Is Autonomous Confiscation the Acme of Asset Recovery?' in M Pieth (ed), *Recovering Stolen Assets* (Bern, Peter Lang, 2008) 267.

Mura, A, 'Towards Greater Cooperation in Freezing and Confiscation of the Proceeds of Crime: A Practitioners Approach', Eurojust Strategic Seminar, The Hague, 11th December 2014.

Muzila, L, Berger, M, Mathias, M and Morales, M, 'Illicit Enrichment: An Emerging Tool in the Asset Recovery Process' in G Zinkernagel, C Monteith and G Pereira (eds), *Emerging Trends in Asset Recovery, The Proposed Swiss Comprehensive Act on Asset Recovery* (Bern, Peter Lang, 2013) 245.

Muzila, L, et al, *On the Take: Criminalizing Illicit Enrichment to Fight Corruption* (Washington, DC, International Bank for Reconstruction and Development/World Bank Group, 2012).

Naim, M, 'The Corruption Eruption' (1995) 2 *The Brown Journal of World Affairs* 245.

Naim, M, *Illicit: How Smugglers, Traffickers and Copycats are Hijacking the Global Economy* (New York, Doubleday, 2005).

Nash, JR, *The Great Pictorial History of World Crime*, vol 2 (Lanham, Rowman & Littlefield, 2004).

Naylor, RT, 'License to Loot? A Critique of Follow-the-Money Methods in Crime Control Policy' (2001) 28 *Social Justice* 121.

Naylor, RT, 'Towards a General Theory of Profit-Driven Crimes' (2003) 43 *British Journal of Criminology* 81.

Naylor, RT, 'Wash-Out: A Critique of Follow-the-Money Methods in Crime Control Policy' [1999] *Crime, Law and Social Change* 1.

Naylor, RT, *Counterfeit Crime Criminal Profits, Terror Dollars, and Nonsense* (Montreal/Kingston, McGill-Queens University Press, 2015).

Nelen, H, 'Hit Them Where It Hurts Most?' (2004) 41(5) *Crime, Law & Social Change* 517.

Nichols, P, 'Are Extraterritorial Restrictions on Bribery a Viable and Desirable International Policy Goal under the Global Conditions of the Late Twentieth Century: Increasing

Global Security by Controlling Transnational Bribery' (1998) 20 *Michigan Journal of International Law* 451.

Nichols, P, '*United States v Lazarenko*: The Trial and Conviction of Two Former Prime Ministers of Ukraine' [2012] *University of Chicago Legal Forum* 41.

Novosel, D, 'Financijske istrage i progon počinitelja gospodarskog kriminaliteta' (2007) 2 *Hrvatski ljetopis za kazneno pravo i praksu* 739.

Novoselec, P, Roksandić Vidlička, S and Maršavelski, A, 'Retroactive Prosecution of Transitional Economic Crimes in Croatia—Testing the Legal Principles and Human Rights' in J Van Erp, W Huisman and G Wande Walle (eds), *The Routledge Handbook of White-Collar and Corporate Crime in Europe* (Oxford, Routledge, 2015) 198.

Nuvolone, P, 'Le misure di prevenzione nel sistema penale italiano' [1974] *Indice penale* 461.

O'Brien, AM, '"Caught in the Crossfire": Protecting the Innocent Owner of Real Property from Civil Forfeiture Under 21 USC § 881(a)(7)' (2012) 65 *St John's Law Review* 521.

O'Donnell, I and O'Sullivan, E, 'The Politics of Intolerance—Irish Style' (2003) 43(1) *British Journal of Criminology* 41.

O'Higgins, M, 'The Proceeds of Crime Act 1996' [1996] *Bar Review* 12.

Ochnio, AH, 'Implementation of the New EU Directive on Confiscation in Poland: The Challenge of Overcoming the Negative Historical Experiences of Confiscation Orders' (2016) 24 *European Journal of Crime, Criminal Law and Criminal Justice* 19.

ODS Consulting, 'National Evaluation of the CashBack for Communities Programme (April 2012–March 2014), Final Report' (Glasgow, ODS Consulting, 2014).

Olaniyan, K, *Corruption and Human Rights Law in Africa* (Oxford, Hart Publishing, 2014).

Omejec, J, 'Kontrola ustavnosti ustavnih normi (ustavnih amandmana i ustavnih zakona)' (2010) 1 *Godišnjak Akademije pravnih znanosti Hrvatske* 1.

Oxfam, 'Rich Countries Provide a Poor Outcome at Addis Financing for Development Conference: Oxfam', press release (15 July 2015), available at http://oxf.am/ZPkE.

Panović-Đurić, S (ed), *Impact Study on Civil Forfeiture* (Belgrade, Council of Europe, 2013).

Panzavolta, M and Flor, R, 'A Necessary Evil? The Italian "Non-Criminal System" of Asset Forfeiture' in JP Rui and U Sieber (eds), *Non-Conviction-Based Confiscation in Europe* (Berlin, Duncker & Humblot, 2015) 111.

Paoli, L and Fijnaut, C (eds), *Organized Crime in Europe. Concepts, Patterns and Control Policies in the European Union and Beyond* (Dordrecht, Springer, 2004).

Perković, M and Puljiz, V, 'Ratne štete, izdaci za branitelje, žrtve i stradalnike rata u Republici Hrvatskoj' (2001) 8 *Revija za socijalnu politiku* 235.

Peters, A, 'Korruption und Menchschenrechten' (2015) *Juristen-Zeitung*, available at http://ssrn.com/abstract=2635443.

Petrini, D, *La prevenzione inutile* (Napoli, Jovene, 1996).

Pieth, M, 'Collective Action and Corruption' in M Pieth (ed), *Collective Action: Innovative Strategies to Prevent Corruption* (Zurich, Dike, 2012).

Pieth, M, 'Financing of Terrorism: Following the Money' in M Pieth (ed), *Financing Terrorism* (Dordrecht, Kluwer Academic Publishers, 2012) 115.

Pieth, M, 'International Standards against Money Laundering' in M Pieth and G Aiolfi (eds), *A Comparative Guide to Anti-money Laundering: A Critical Analysis of Systems in Singapore, Switzerland, the UK and the USA* (Cheltenham, Edward Elgar, 2004).

Pieth, M, 'Introduction' in M Pieth, L Low and N Bonucci (eds), *The OECD Convention on Bribery: A Commentary*, 2nd edn (Cambridge, Cambridge University Press, 2014).

Pieth, M, 'Preface: Are We Recovering Any Assets Yet?' in G Fenner-Zinkernagel, C Montieth and P Gomes Pereira (eds), *Emerging Trends in Asset Recovery* (Bern, Peter Lang, 2013).

Pimentel, D, 'Forfeiture Revisited: Bringing Principle to Practice in Federal Court' (2010) 13 *Nevada Law Journal* 1.

Plucknett, TFT, *A Concise History of the Common Law* (Indianapolis, Liberty Fund, 2010).

Polzer, T, 'Corruption: Deconstructing the World Bank Discourse', DESTIN Development Studies Institute Working Paper No 1 (2001), available at www.lse.ac.uk/internationalDevelopment/pdf/WP/WP18.pdf.

Posadas, A, 'Combating Corruption under International Law' (2000) 10 *Duke Journal of Comparative and International Law* 345.

Prime Minister's Office, 10 Downing Street and The Rt Hon David Cameron MP (UK), 'G8 Action Plan Principles to Prevent the Misuse of Companies and Legal Arrangements', policy paper (18 June 2013), available at https://www.gov.uk/government/publications/g8-action-plan-principles-to-prevent-the-misuse-of-companies-and-legal-arrangements.

Pujas, V, 'Immunity and Extradition: Obstacles to Justice' in R Hodess et al, *Transparency International: Global Corruption Report 2004* (London, Pluto Press, 2004).

Rand Europe, 'Study for an Impact Assessment on a Proposal for a New Legal Framework on the Confiscation and Recovery of Criminal Assets—Technical Report' (Brussels, European Commission, 2012).

Reuter, P, 'Introduction' in P Reuter (ed), *Draining Development? Controlling Flows of Illicit Funds from Developing Countries* (Washington, DC, International Bank for Reconstruction and Development/World Bank, 2012).

Reuter, P and Truman, EM, *Chasing Dirty Money. The Fight against Money Laundering* (Washington, DC, Institute for International Economics, 2004).

Rhodes, R and Bosworth-Davies, R, '*Regina v Charlton, Cunningham, Kitchen and Wheeler* [1995]' (1999) 2 *Journal of Money Laundering Control* 197.

Richter, D, 'Potentatengelder in der Schweiz: Rechtshilfe im Spannungsfeld der Menschenrechte von Tätern und Opfern' [1998] *Zeitschrift für ausländisches öffentliches Recht und Völkerrecht ZaöRV* 541.

Ridadu, N, 'Challenges and Opportunities of Asset Recovery in a Developing Economy' in M Pieth (ed), *Recovering Stolen Assets* (Bern, Peter Lang, 2008).

Robinson, M, 'Corruption and Human Rights' in R Hodess et al (eds), *Transparency International: Global Corruption Report 2004* (London, Pluto Press, 2004).

Robinson, P, 'Punishing Dangerousness: Cloaking Preventive Detention as Criminal Justice' (2001) 114(5) *Harvard Law Review* 1429.

Roksandić Vidlička, S, 'Possible Future Challenge for the ECtHR?: Importance of the Act on Exemption and the Sanader Case for Transitional Justice Jurisprudence and the Development of Transitional Justice Policies' (2014) 64(5–6) *Zbornik Pravnog Fakulteta u Zagrebu*.

Room, R, 'Legalizing a Market for Cannabis for Pleasure: Colorado, Washington, Uruguay and Beyond' (2014) 109 *Addiction* 345.

Roth-Arriaza, N and Mariezcurrena, J (eds), *Transitional Justice in the Twenty-First Century: Beyond Truth Versus Justice* (Cambridge, Cambridge University Press, 2006).

Rozie, J, *Voordeelsontneming: de wisselwerking tussen de toepassingsvoorwaarden en het rechtskarakter van de verbeurdverklaring van illegale vermogensvoordelen* (Antwerp, Intersentia, 2005).

Rui, JP, 'Introduction' in JP Rui and U Sieber (eds), *Non-conviction-Based Confiscation in Europe* (Berlin, Duncker & Humblot, 2015) 1.

Rui, JP and Sieber, U, 'NCBC in Europe: Bringing the Picture Together' in JP Rui and U Sieber (eds), *Non-conviction-Based Confiscation in Europe* (Berlin, Duncker & Humblot, 2015) 263.

Ryder, N, 'To Confiscate or Not To Confiscate? A Comparative Analysis of the Confiscation of the Proceeds of Crime Legislation in the United States of America and the United Kingdom' (2013) 8 *Journal of Business Law* 767.

Salacuse, J, 'From Developing Countries to Emerging Markets: A Changing Role for Law in the Third World' [1999] *The International Lawyer* 875.

Salomon, M, 'From NIEO to Now and the Unfinishable Story of Economic Justice' (2013) 62 *International and Comparative Law Quarterly* 31.

Samuel, LM, 'Challenges Facing US Anti-money Laundering Efforts in Transnational Crime', Resource Material Series No 65 (UNAFEI, March 2005).

Savona, E, 'The Businesses of Italian Mafias' (2015) 21(2) *European Journal on Criminal Policy and Research* 217.

Schabas, WA, 'Introduction' in WA Schabas and S Darcy (eds), *Truth Commissions and the Court, the Tension between Criminal Justice and the Search for Truth* (Dordrecht, Kluwer, 2004) 1.

Schmid, E and Nolan A, '"Do No Harm"? Exploring the Scope of Economic and Social Rights in Transitional Justice' (2014) 8(3) *International Journal of Transitional Justice* 1.

Schödler, S, *Dritte im Beschlagnahme-und Einziehungsverfahren* (Zurich, Schulthess, 2012).

Schomburg, W, et al, 'Einleitung' in W Schomburg et al (eds), *Internationale Rechtshilfe in Strafsachen* [*International Cooperation in Criminal Matters*], 5th edn (Munich, Verlag CH Beck, 2012).

Schönke, A and Schröder, H, *Strafgesetzbuch. Kommentar*, 27 aufl (Munich, Verlag CH Beck, 2006).

Selvaggi, N, 'On Instruments Adopted in the Area of Freezing and Confiscation' [2015] *Diritto penale contemporaneo* (www.penalecontemporaneo.it, 31 July 2015).

Shaffer, G, 'Transnational Legal Ordering and State Change' in G Shaffer (ed), *Transnational Legal Ordering and State Change* (Cambridge, Cambridge University Press, 2013).

Sharman, JC, *Chasing Kleptocrats' Loot: The International Campaign against Grand Corruption* (Ithaca, NY, Cornell University Press, 2016 forthcoming).

Sharp, DN, 'Introduction: Addressing Economic Violence in Times of Transition' in DN Sharp (ed), *Justice and Economic Violence in Transition* (New York, Springer Science+Business Media, 2014) 1.

Shelley, L, 'Transnational Organized Crime and Seized Assets: Moral Dilemmas Concerning the Disposition of the Fruits of Crime' (2000) 7 *Maastricht Journal of European and Comparative Law* 35.

Shelton, D, 'International Law and "Relative Normativity"' in M Evans (ed), *International Law*, 4th edn (Oxford, Oxford University Press, 2014).

Siems, M, *Comparative Law (Law in Context)* (Cambridge, Cambridge University Press, 2015).

Simon, J, *Governing Through Crime: How the War on Crime Transformed American Democracy and Created a Culture of Fear* (New York, Oxford University Press, 2007).

Simonato, M, 'Directive 2014/42/EU and Non-conviction Based Confiscation: A Step Forward on Asset Recovery?' (2015) 6(2) *New Journal of European Criminal Law* 213.

Simonato, M, 'Extended Confiscation of Criminal Assets: Limits and Pitfalls of Minimum Harmonisation in the EU' (2016) 41(5) *European Law Review* (723).

Simonato, M and Lassalle, M, 'A Fragmented Approach on Asset Recovery and Financial Investigations: A Threat to Effective International Judicial Cooperation?' in Z Durdevic and E Ivicevic Karas (eds), *European Criminal Procedure Law in Service of Protection of European Union Financial Interests: State of Play and Challenges* (Zagreb, Croatian Association of European Criminal Law, 2016) 132.

Simser, J, 'Perspectives on Civil Forfeiture' in S Young, *Civil Forfeiture of Criminal Property: Legal Measures for Targeting the Proceeds of Crime* (Cheltenham, Edward Elgar, 2009) 13.

Skolnick, JH, 'Policing Should Not Be for Profit' (2008) 7 *Criminology and Public Policy* 257.

Skorup, B, 'Ensuring Eight Amendment Protection from Excessive Fines in Civil Asset Forfeiture Cases' (2012) 22 *Civil Rights Law Journal* 427.

Smellie, A, 'Prosecutorial Challenges in Freezing and Forfeiting Proceeds of Transnational Crime and the Use of International Asset Sharing to Promote International Cooperation' (2004) 8 *Journal of Money Laundering Control* 104.

Smith, I, 'Civil Asset Recovery—The English Experience' in JP Rui and U Sieber (eds), *Non-conviction-Based Confiscation in Europe* (Berlin, Duncker, 2015) 31.

Smith, I, Owen, T and Bodnar, A, *Asset Recovery: Criminal Confiscation and Civil Recovery* (Oxford, Looseleaf, 2014).

Solomon, PH Jr, 'Criminalisation, Decriminalization and Post-communist Transition: The Case of the Russian Federation in Building Justice' in K Goodall, M Malloch and B Munro (eds), *Post-transitional Europe? Processes of Criminalization within Central and Eastern European Societies* (Oxford, Routledge, 2013) 95.

Spalding, AB, 'Corruption, Corporations, and the New Human Right' (2013) 91 *Washington University Law Review* 1365.

Stephenson, K, et al, *Barriers to Asset Recovery: An Analysis of the Key Barriers and Recommendations for Action* (Washington, DC, International Bank for Reconstruction and Development/World Bank Group, 2011).

Stephenson, K, Gray, L, Power, R, Brun, JP, Dunker, G and Panjer, M, *Barriers to Asset Recovery: An Analysis of the Key Barriers and Recommendations for Action* (Washington, DC, International Bank for Reconstruction and Development, 2011).

Stessens, G, *Money Laundering. A New International Enforcement Model* (Cambridge, Cambridge University Press, 2000).

Suarez-Martinez, A, *Closing Down the Safe Havens: Ending Impunity for Corrupt Individuals by Seizing and Recovering their Assets in the UK* (Transparency International UK, 2013), available at www.transparency.org.uk/publications/15-publications/809-closing-down-the-safe-havens/809-closing-down-the-safe-havens.

Sweeney, J, 'Freedom of Religion and Democratic Transition' in A Buyse and M Hamilton (eds), *Transitional Jurisprudence and the ECHR: Justice, Politics and Rights* (Cambridge, Cambridge University Press, 2011) 103.

Tadros, V, 'Criminalization and Regulation' in A Duff, L Farmer, SE Marshall, M Renzo and V Tadros (eds), *The Boundaries of the Criminal Law* (Oxford, Oxford University Press, 2010) 163.

Teitel, RG, 'Transitional Justice Genealogy' (2003) 16 *Harvard Human Rights Journal* 69.

Templeman, L, 'Tax and the Taxpayer' (2001) 117 *Law Quarterly Review* 575.

Theobold, R, *Corruption, Development and Underdevelopment* (Durham, Duke University Press, 1990).

Transparency International, 'Putrajaya Declaration: Zero Tolerance for Impunity' (4 September 2015), available at www.transparency.org/news/feature/the_putrajaya_declaration.

Transparency International, 'The Anti-corruption Plain Language Guide' (2009), available at www.transparency.org/whatwedo/pub/the_anti_corruption_plain_language_guide.

Träskman, PO, 'Omvänt eller bakvänt. Om konststycket att lägga bevisbördan i brottmål på den tilltalade, utan att det kommer bak på människorättigheterna' [1998] *Nordisk Tidsskrift for Kriminalvidenskab* 363.

Trechsel, S, *Human Rights in Criminal Proceedings* (Oxford, Oxford University Press, 2006).

Treisman, D, 'What Have We Learned about the Causes of Corruption from Ten Years of Cross-National Empirical Research?' (2007) 10 *Annual Review of Political Science* 211.

Tröndle, H and Fischer, T, *Strafgesetzbuch und Nebengesetze*, 51 aufl (Munich, Verlag CH Beck, 2003).

Tsingou, E, 'Global Financial Governance and the Developing Anti-money Laundering Regime: What Lessons for International Political Economy?' (2010) 47 *International Politics* 617.

Tuori, K, 'Transnational Law: On Legal Hybrids and Perspectivism' in M Maduro, K Tuori and S Sankari (eds), *Transnational Law: Rethinking European Law and Legal Thinking* (Cambridge, Cambridge University Press, 2014).

Turone, G, 'Legal Frameworks and Investigative Tools for Combating Organized Transnational Crime in the Italian Experience' [2007] *UNAFEI 134th International Training Course Visiting Experts' Papers* 48.

Tyler, T and Jackson, J, 'Popular Legitimacy and the Exercise of Legal Authority: Motivating Compliance, Cooperation, and Engagement' (2014) 20 *Psychology, Public Policy and Law* 78.

Unger, B, Ferwerda, J, van den Broek, M and Deleanu, I, *The Economic and Legal Effectiveness of the European Union's Anti-money Laundering Policy* (Cheltenham, Edward Elgar, 2014).

United Nations Office on Drugs and Crime Division for Treaty Affairs, *Legislative Guide for the Implementation of the United Nations Convention against Corruption* (2006), available at https://www.unodc.org/pdf/corruption/CoC_LegislativeGuide.pdf.

United States Senate, Permanent Subcommittee on Investigations, Committee on Homeland Security and Governmental Affairs, *Keeping Foreign Corruption out of the United States: Four Case Histories* (2010), available at www.hsgac.senate.gov/download/report-psi-staff-report-keeping-foreign-corruption-out-of-the-united-states-four-case-histories.

US Department of Justice, 'Attorney General Holder at the African Union Summit, Kampala Uganda, Sunday, July 25, 2010', press release, available at www.justice.gov/opa/speech/attorney-general-holder-african-union-summit.

Valcke, P, Vandezande, N and van de Velde, N, 'The Evolution of Third Party Payment Providers and Cryptocurrencies under the EU's Upcoming PSD2 and AMLD4', SWIFT Institute Working Paper No 2015-001, available at www.swiftinstitute.org/wp-content/uploads/2015/09/SIWP-No-2015-001-AML-Risks-of-the-Third-Party-Payment-Providers_FINAL.pdf.

Van den Berg, M, 'Proposing a Transactional Approach to Civil Forfeiture Reform' (2015) 163 *University of Pennsylvania Law Review* 867.

van den Broek, M and Addink, H, 'Prevention of Money Laundering and Terrorist Financing from a Good Governance Perspective' in B Unger and D van der Linde, *Research Handbook on Money Laundering* (Cheltenham, Edward Elgar, 2013) 368.

Van der Willebois, E and Brun, P, 'Using Civil Remedies in Corruption and Asset Recovery Cases' [2013] *Case Western Reserve Journal of International Law* 615.

Van Duyne, PC, Groenhuijsen, MS and Schudelaro, AAP, 'Balancing Financial Threats and Legal Interests in Money-Laundering Policy' (2005) 43 *Crime, Law & Social Change* 117.

Van Hoek, A and Luchtman, M, 'Transnational Cooperation in Criminal Matters and the Safeguarding of Human Rights' (2005) 1 *Utrecht Law Review* 1.

Vandezande, N, 'Between Bitcoins and Mobile Payments: Will the European Commission's New Proposal Provide More Legal Certainty?' (2014) 22 *International Journal of Law and Information Technology* 295.

Veglio, P, Siegenthaler, P, 'Monitoring the Restitution of Looted State Assets: The Role of Multilateral Development Banks (MDBs)' in M Pieth (ed), *Recovering Stolen Assets* (Bern, Peter Lang, 2008) 315.

Verbruggen, F, 'Hebben en houwen: bezitseffect en afgifteafkeer als inspiratie bij de hervorming van de Belgische verbeurdverklaring' in T Spapens, M Groenhuijsen and T Kooijmans (eds), *Liber Amicorum Cyrille Fijnaut* (Antwerp, Intersentia, 2011) 263.

Verbruggen, F, 'Proceeds-Oriented Criminal Justice in Belgium: Backbone or Wishbone of a Modern Approach to Organised Crime?' (1997) 5(3) *European Journal of Crime, Criminal Law and Criminal Justice* 314.

Verhage, A, *The Anti Money Laundering Complex and the Compliance Industry* (London, Taylor & Francis, 2011).

Verstraeten, R and Verbruggen, F, *Strafrecht en Strafprocesrecht* (Antwerp, Maklu, 2014).

Vervaele, JAE, 'Economic Crimes and Money Laundering: A New Paradigm for the Criminal Justice System?' in B Unger and D van der Linde (eds), *Research Handbook on Money Laundering* (Cheltenham, Edward Elgar, 2013) 379.

Vervaele, JAE, 'La saisie et la confiscation à la suite d'atteintes punissables au droit aux Etats-Unis' (1998) 78 *Revue de Droit Pénal et de Criminologie* 974.

Vettori, B, *Tough on Criminal Wealth: Exploring the Practice of Proceeds from Crime Confiscation in the EU* (Dordrecht, Springer, 2006).

Viljanen, P, *Konfiskaatio rikosoikeudellisena seuraamuksena* (Helsinki, Edita Publishing, 2007).

Virgo, G, *The Principles of the Law of Restitution*, 2nd edn (Oxford, Oxford University Press, 2006).

Vogel, J, 'The Legal Construction That Property Can Do Harm' in JP Rui and U Sieber (eds), *Non-conviction-Based Confiscation in Europe* (Berlin, Duncker & Humblot, 2015) 225.

Vujosević, M, Zeković, S and Marić, T, 'Post-socialist Transition in Serbia and Its Unsustainable Path' (2012) 20 *European Planning Studies* 1707.

Walton, G, 'The Limitations of Neoliberal Logic in the Anti-corruption Industry: Lessons from Papua New Guinea' (2013) 60 *Crime, Law and Social Change* 147.

Wang, H and Rosenau, J, 'Transparency International and Corruption as an Issue of Global Governance' (2001) 7 *Global Governance* 25.

Watson, A, *Legal Transplants: An Approach to Comparative Law* (Edinburgh, Scottish Academic Press, 1974).

Weyembergh, A, 'Introduction' in F Galli and A Weyembergh (eds), *Do Labels Still Matter? Blurring Boundaries between Administrative and Criminal Law* (Brussels, IEE, 2014) 9.

Weyembergh, A, 'The Functions of Approximation of Penal Legislation within the European Union' (2005) 12 *Maastricht Journal of European and Comparative Law* 149.

Weyembergh, A and Joncheray, N, 'Punitive Administrative Sanctions and Procedural Safeguards: A Blurred Picture that Needs to be Addressed' (2016) 7(2) *New Journal of European Criminal Law* 190.

Whitman, J, 'What is Wrong with Inflicting Shame Sanctions?' (1998) 107(4) *Yale Law Journal* 1055.

Whitman, J, *Harsh Justice* (Oxford, Oxford University Press, 2005).

Williams, M, Holcomb, J, Kovandzic, T and Bullock, S, *Policing for Profit. The Abuse of Civil Asset Forfeiture* (Arlington, VA, Institute for Justice, 2010).

World Bank and UN Office on Drugs and Crime (UNODC), 'Our Work' (website), available at http://star.worldbank.org/star/about-us/our-work.

World Bank and UN Office on Drugs and Crime (UNODC), 'Partnership Charter', 7 November 2008, available at http://star.worldbank.org/star/sites/star/files/StAR_Partnership_Charter_1_0.pdf.

World Bank Group, *Helping Countries Combat Corruption: Poverty Reduction and Economic Management* (1997), available at www1.worldbank.org/publicsector/anticorrupt/corruptn/coridx.htm.

Wouters, J, Ryngaert, C and Cloots, AS, 'The International Legal Framework against Corruption: Achievements and Challenges' (2013) 14 *Melbourne Journal of International Law* 205.

Zalman, M, 'Judges in Their Own Case: A Lockean Critique of Law Enforcement Asset Sharing in Drug Forfeiture Law and Practice' (1996) 21 *Criminal Justice Review* 197.

Zaloznaya, M, 'Beyond Anti-corruptionism: Sociological Imagination and Comparative Study of Corruption' (2013) 12 *Comparative Sociology* 1.

Zaloznaya, M, 'Social Psychology of Corruption: Why It Does Not Exist and Why It Should' (2014) 8 *Sociology Compass* 187.

Zimmermann, R, *La coopération judiciaire internationale en matière pénale*, 4th edn (Bern, Stämpfli, 2014).

Zinkernagel, F and Attisso, K, *Returning Stolen Assets—Learning from Past Practice: Selected Case Studies* (Bern, Basel Institute on Governance, 2013).

INDEX

www.ingramcontent.com/pod-product-compliance
Lightning Source LLC
LaVergne TN
LVHW011835200926
848484LV00002B/357